MW00614467

NATURE AND EMPIRE IN OTTOMAN EGYPT

In one of the first environmental histories of the Ottoman Empire, Alan Mikhail examines relations between the empire and its most lucrative province of Egypt. Based on both the local records of various towns and villages in rural Egypt and the imperial orders of the Ottoman state, this book charts how changes in the control of natural resources fundamentally altered the nature of Ottoman imperial sovereignty in Egypt and throughout the empire. In revealing how Egyptian peasants were able to use their knowledge and experience of local environments to force the hand of the imperial state, *Nature and Empire in Ottoman Egypt* tells a story of the connections of empire stretching from canals in the Egyptian countryside to the palace in Istanbul, from Anatolian forests to the shores of the Red Sea, and from a plague flea's bite to the fortunes of one of the most powerful states of the early modern world.

Alan Mikhail is Assistant Professor in the Department of History at Yale University.

Studies in Environment and History

Editors
Donald Worster, University of Kansas
J. R. McNeill, Georgetown University

Editor Emeritus
Alfred W. Crosby, University of Texas at Austin

Other Books in the Series

Donald Worster *Nature's Economy: A History of Ecological Ideas, Second Edition*
Kenneth F. Kiple *The Caribbean Slave: A Biological History*
Alfred W. Crosby *Ecological Imperialism: The Biological Expansion of Europe, 900–1900, Second Edition*
Arthur F. McEvoy *The Fisherman's Problem: Ecology and Law in the California Fisheries, 1850–1980*
Robert Harms *Games Against Nature: An Eco-Cultural History of the Nunu of Equatorial Africa*
Warren Dean *Brazil and the Struggle for Rubber: A Study in Environmental History*
Samuel P. Hays *Beauty, Health, and Permanence: Environmental Politics in the United States, 1955–1985*
Donald Worster *The Ends of the Earth: Perspectives on Modern Environmental History*
Michael Williams *Americans and Their Forests: A Historical Geography*
Timothy Silver *A New Face on the Countryside: Indians, Colonists, and Slaves in the South Atlantic Forests, 1500–1800*
Theodore Steinberg *Nature Incorporated: Industrialization and the Waters of New England*
J. R. McNeill *The Mountains of the Mediterranean World: An Environmental History*
Elinor G. K. Melville *A Plague of Sheep: Environmental Consequences of the Conquest of Mexico*
Richard H. Grove *Green Imperialism: Colonial Expansion, Tropical Island Edens and the Origins of Environmentalism, 1600–1860*
Mark Elvin and Tsui'jung Liu *Sediments of Time: Environment and Society in Chinese History*
Robert B. Marks *Tigers, Rice, Silk, and Silt: Environment and Economy in Late Imperial South China*
Thomas Dunlap *Nature and the English Diaspora*
Andrew C. Isenberg *The Destruction of the Bison: An Environmental History*
Edmund Russell *War and Nature: Fighting Humans and Insects with Chemicals from World War I to Silent Spring*
Judith Shapiro *Mao's War Against Nature: Politics and the Environment in Revolutionary China*

(*continued after Index*)

NATURE AND EMPIRE IN OTTOMAN EGYPT

AN ENVIRONMENTAL HISTORY

Alan Mikhail
Yale University

CAMBRIDGE
UNIVERSITY PRESS

CAMBRIDGE
UNIVERSITY PRESS

32 Avenue of the Americas, New York NY 10013-2473, USA

Cambridge University Press is part of the University of Cambridge.

It furthers the University's mission by disseminating knowledge in the pursuit of education, learning, and research at the highest international levels of excellence.

www.cambridge.org
Information on this title: www.cambridge.org/9781107640184

© Alan Mikhail 2011

This publication is in copyright. Subject to statutory exception and to the provisions of relevant collective licensing agreements, no reproduction of any part may take place without the written permission of Cambridge University Press.

First published 2011
Reprinted 2011 (twice), 2012
First paperback edition 2013
Reprinted 2013

A catalog record for this publication is available from the British Library.

Library of Congress Cataloging in Publication data
Mikhail, Alan,
Nature and empire in Ottoman Egypt : an environmental history / Alan Mikhail.
p. cm. – (Studies in environment and history)
Includes bibliographical references and index.
ISBN 978-1-107-00876-2 (hardback)
1. Human ecology – Egypt. 2. Human beings – Effect of environment on – Egypt. 3. Irrigation – Social aspects – Egypt. 4. Egypt – History – 1517–1882. 5. Technology and civilization. I. Title. II. Series.
GF711.M55 2011
304.20962 – dc22 2010047013

ISBN 978-1-107-00876-2 Hardback
ISBN 978-1-107-64018-4 Paperback

Cambridge University Press has no responsibility for the persistence or accuracy of URLs for external or third-party Internet Web sites referred to in this publication, and does not guarantee that any content on such Web sites is, or will remain, accurate or appropriate.

To my parents, Adib and Nadia

CONTENTS

MAPS

FIGURES

TABLES

NOTE ON TRANSLITERATION AND DATES

In transliterating Ottoman Turkish and Arabic source materials, I have used the system of the *International Journal of Middle East Studies.* Because of the high degree of overlap between Ottoman Turkish and Arabic in the early modern period and because writers often used an amalgam of the two, one can face many difficulties when choosing how to transliterate a particular text. In general, I have transliterated according to the language of the original source. Words of Arabic origin used in texts that are otherwise Ottoman Turkish are transliterated as Turkish, and likewise words of Turkish origin found in Arabic texts are rendered with their Arabic transliteration. This is true of place-names and titles as well. When I use terms and titles in a general sense apart from a particular text, I have rendered the word on the basis of its language of origin. Ottoman Turkish words commonly found in modern Turkish are given with their modern Turkish spelling. In cases where I have thought it useful, I have given both Arabic and Turkish transliterations. Ottoman Turkish and Arabic words that have made their way into English are given with their standard English spelling.

Common Era dates are used throughout the text. In citing archival documents, I give the full *hijrī* date followed by the Common Era date.

ABBREVIATIONS

AHR	*American Historical Review*
AI	*Annales Islamologiques*
AO	*Archivum Ottomanicum*
BOA	Başbakanlık Osmanlı Arşivi
DKM	Dār al-Kutub al-Miṣriyya
DWQ	Dār al-Wathā'iq al-Qawmiyya
EHR	*Egyptian Historical Review*
EI	*Encyclopaedia of Islam.* 2nd ed. Leiden: E.J. Brill, 2006.
HAT	Hatt-ı Hümayun
IJMES	*International Journal of Middle East Studies*
IJTS	*International Journal of Turkish Studies*
JESHO	*Journal of the Economic and Social History of the Orient*
JTS	*Journal of Turkish Studies*
MM	Mühimme-i Mısır
NPT	*New Perspectives on Turkey*
OA	*Osmanlı Araştırmaları*
PHR	*Pacific Historical Review*
QJBM	Ramzī, Muḥammad. *al-Qāmūs al-Jughrāfī lil-Bilād al-Miṣriyya min 'Ahd Qudamā' al-Miṣriyyīn ilā Sanat 1945.* 6 vols. in 2 pts. Cairo: al-Hay'a al-Miṣriyya al-'Āmma lil-Kitāb, 1994.
SK	Süleymaniye Kütüphanesi
TSMA	Topkapı Sarayı Müzesi Arşivi
TSMK	Topkapı Sarayı Müzesi Kütüphanesi

Ottoman Turkish Islamic Month Abbreviations (Arabic in parentheses)

M	Muharrem (Muḥarram)
S	Safer (Ṣafar)

Ra	Rebiülevvel (Rabīʿ al-Awwal)
R	Rebiülahir (Rabīʿ al-Thānī)
Ca	Cemazilevvel (Jumādā al-Ūlā)
C	Cemaziyel'ahır (Jumādā al-Ākhira)
B	Receb (Rajab)
Ş	Şaʿban (Shaʿbān)
N	Ramazan (Ramaḍān)
L	Şevval (Shawwāl)
Za	Zilkade (Dhū al-Qaʿda)
Z	Zilhicce (Dhū al-Ḥijja)

ACKNOWLEDGMENTS

The seeds of this book were first put down in the fertile soils of Berkeley; immensely rich and overwhelming archival silt in Istanbul and Cairo covered the planted seeds and provided the nutrients needed for this book's first sprouts; the life-giving waters of Stanford University nurtured its young life and helped it grow; the sun and energy of Yale University brought out its full fruit. Thankfully, the road from seed to fruit is usually much shorter than the one taken by this book. Over this work's long gestation period, I have received much generosity and have therefore accrued many debts. I hope the final product is worthy testament to all it has been given.

The Department of History at the University of California, Berkeley, was the ideal place for me to be a graduate student. More than anyone else, Beshara Doumani and Leslie Peirce (now at New York University) taught me how to think about and understand the early modern Middle East. I thank Beshara Doumani for his constant support of me and my work and for the example of his commitments to the past and the present of the Middle East. Leslie Peirce's boundless energy and knowledge and love of the early modern Ottoman Empire are clear to all who know her. I thank her for imparting some of this knowledge and love to me. Khaled Fahmy accepted me as a student when he did not have to and continues to astound me with his generosity and immense knowledge of Egypt's past. The opportunity to watch Thomas W. Laqueur in action as a historian was one of the most important and instructive parts of my life as a graduate student. His insatiable appetite for ideas is nothing short of inspiring, and I thank him for his continued interest in my work. Paul Rabinow provided the perfect model of the productive scholar, writer, and teacher. I thank him for making me a part of his conversations.

In Berkeley, I was fortunate enough to have many other teachers as well. Maria Mavroudi never ceases to amaze with her abilities to scale intellectual walls and to make the seemingly unrelated deeply intertwined. I thank her for always giving of her time and wisdom. Other members of the Department of History at the University of California, Berkeley, provided me with support, advice, and encouragement. It gives me great pleasure to thank Eugene Irschick, Kerwin Lee Klein, James Vernon, and Carla Hesse. Outside of Dwinelle Hall, many other teachers, colleagues, and friends in Berkeley supported me and this work. I thank Charles Hirschkind, Hamid Algar, Samera Esmeir, Nezar AlSayyad, Saba Mahmood, Preeti Chopra, Murat Dağlı, Hasan Karataş, Malissa Taylor, Penny Ismay, Alyse Han, Heather Ferguson, Corrie Decker, Ayla Algar, Nell Gabiam, Angie Heo, and Nadia Samii.

My years of archival research in Cairo and Istanbul were some of the most pleasant of my life. In Cairo, I thank first and foremost the staff of the Egyptian National Archives. Nadia Mustafa and her assistants tirelessly provided me with register after register, and for this, I cannot begin to express my gratitude. The relationships I developed with a group of gifted and generous historians connected to the archives influenced my thinking about this book in ways too numerous to account for here. I especially thank Magdi Guirguis for being a teacher, friend, and sounding board. He generously shared his immense knowledge of Egyptian history with me and continues to give of his expertise. Imad Abu Ghazi helped me think about my research in new ways and provided many keys for opening doors throughout Egypt. Emad Hilal knows the archives perhaps better than anyone else, and his guidance was and is unmatched. His indefatigable work ethic and ability seemingly to never sleep is something I envy. Shauqi Hasan Shaʿban spent many hours with me on the Nile reading and talking. Our sunny afternoons on the river were always happy and productive moments. I also thank the staffs of the Egyptian National Library and the Arab League Manuscripts Collection for opening their doors to me and for helping me throughout my research in Cairo.

I was lucky enough to share my time in Cairo with many Egyptian and foreign scholars. All of them helped with ideas in this book and provided friendship and support. Each deserves a paragraph of acknowledgment, and thus I apologize for only giving a list of names: Lisa Pollard, Mara Naaman, John Meloy, Jennifer Derr, Nasir Ibrahim, Jessica Barnes, Nelly Hanna, Husam Abdul Muʿti, Will Hanley, Zeinab Abul-Magd, Muhammad ʿAfifi, James Baldwin, Mirvit al-Sayyid, Nasir ʿUthman, Nasra ʿAbd al-Mutagalli, Muhammad Hakim, Jennifer Pruitt, Humphrey Davies, Raja Adal, Pascale Ghazaleh, Samer Shehata, and Riem El-Zoghbi.

Istanbul provided the other archival leg on which this book stands. The amazingly rich archival and manuscript collections in the city provided some of the most fantastic and humbling research moments of my life. I thank the staffs of Prime Ministry's Ottoman Archive (Başbakanlık Osmanlı Arşivi); the Topkapı Palace Museum Archive and Library; the

Süleymaniye Library; the Istanbul University Library; the American Research Institute in Turkey; the İslâm Araştırmaları Merkezi (İSAM); and the Research Centre for Islamic History, Art, and Culture (IRCICA). I especially want to thank Ülkü Altındağ of the Topkapı Palace Museum Archive for facilitating my research there. Merve Çakır helped with my research in Turkey more than anyone else. I thank her immensely for offering her expertise and for her support of this book. For their help, advice, and direction in Istanbul, I also want to thank Murat Dağlı, Zeynep Türkyılmaz, Antony Greenwood, and Selim Kuru.

I cannot express how thankful I am for the two years I enjoyed as a member of the Andrew W. Mellon Fellowship of Scholars in the Humanities at Stanford University. I thank Seth Lerer, J. P. Daughton, Lanier Anderson, and the Department of History at Stanford, as well as Laura Engelstein and the Department of History at Yale, for making this possible. The time and resources afforded by this program helped to make this book a reality. The scholars and friends that surrounded me at Stanford were unparalleled in their brilliance and generosity of spirit and intellect. Getting to know Edith Sheffer (and the entire Sheffer clan) was one of the best parts of my two years at Stanford. One wonders how we never met during seven years together as graduate students at Berkeley. As a friend, critic of my work, and co-teacher, Edith has taught me a great deal about how to write, how to teach, and how to recognize all manner of ponzi scheme. Bradley Naranch was also a dear friend and colleague at Stanford, and I am grateful for all I learned through our many conversations. As a historian and friend, Tom Mullaney is an inspiration, and I feel lucky to know him. J. P. Daughton, Joel Beinin, Bob Crews, Paula Findlen, Aron Rodrigue, Priya Satia, Caroline Winterer, Allyson Hobbs, Will Shearin, Alex Cook, Shahzad Bashir, and Sean Hanretta were all very generous in their support of and interest in this work. I thank each of them for making Palo Alto a welcoming place to be a scholar.

My time as a member of the Yale University Department of History has been the most exhilarating period of my intellectual life. My colleagues have done the utmost to welcome me to New Haven and the Department and have humbled me with their brilliance, commitment to intellectual inquiry, and immensely deep understandings of the past. Abbas Amanat has supported me and my work since our very first meeting. His intellectual generosity and commitment to the history of the Middle East are a model I can only hope to emulate. Francesca Trivellato has always given generously of her time and intellect and has been a very supportive colleague. In thinking about early modern history, she sets the bar very high. Laura Engelstein, Paul Freedman, Joseph G. Manning, Charles Walton,

Peter C. Perdue, Steve Pincus, Ivan Marcus, Mary Lui, Adel Allouche, Frank Griffel, Frank Snowden, Fabian Drixler, Paul Sabin, Kishwar Rizvi, and Robert Nelson have all been wonderfully gracious and supportive colleagues. I thank them all for their advice and interests in my research. As a young scholar, I am honored and humbled to be surrounded by such an accomplished and committed group of historians.

I must also mention numerous other scholars, colleagues, and friends that made this book possible. Ussama Makdisi first taught me how to think about the Middle East as an undergraduate. He has moved from being my teacher to now my friend and mentor. I thank him for everything. Suraiya Faroqhi and Jane Hathaway have read my work on numerous occasions and given me very valuable and useful advice. I thank Mona Russell, Arash Khazeni, Diana K. Davis, Amy Singer, and Dana Sajdi for being very supportive and generous colleagues. Jeff Joseph has been my friend longer than anyone else, and for that I am most thankful. Mona Iskander and her family are the kind of people everyone should know. I thank Mrinalini Rajagopalan for opening a door in Berkeley and another in Boston.

The research and writing of this book were generously supported by the Fulbright-Hays Commission; the American Research Center in Egypt; the Council of American Overseas Research Centers; the Institute of Turkish Studies; the Center for Middle Eastern Studies at the University of California, Berkeley; the Center for Arabic Study Abroad; the Departments of History at Yale University and the University of California, Berkeley; and the Andrew W. Mellon Fellowship of Scholars in the Humanities at Stanford University. I acknowledge and thank each of these institutions.

Earlier versions of parts of this book were presented at meetings of the American Historical Association, the Middle East Studies Association, the American Society for Environmental History, the Agricultural History Society, the International Water History Association, and the American Institute for Maghrib Studies. I received valuable feedback in these venues and from audiences at Yale University; Stanford University; Harvard University; the University of California, Berkeley; New York University; Georgetown University; the University of North Carolina at Chapel Hill; the University of Bath; the University of Iowa; Swarthmore College; Florida State University; the University of Pittsburgh; Vanderbilt University; Queens College; the University of South Carolina; Virginia Tech; the University of Montana; Iowa State University; the American University in Cairo; L'Institut français d'archéologie orientale du Caire; Cairo University; Le Centre d'études et de documentation économiques, juridiques et sociales in Cairo; the Egyptian Association for Historical

Studies; the American Research Center in Egypt; and the Egyptian High Council of Culture. I thank everyone who thought about this work and offered their advice, critiques, and suggestions.

John R. McNeill, Donald Worster, Abbas Amanat, Francesca Trivellato, Joel Beinin, Sam White, Fred Lawson, Yuen-Gen Liang, Edith Sheffer, and two anonymous reviewers each read full drafts of this book and helped to shape it in important ways. I especially want to thank John R. McNeill and Donald Worster for including this book in the series Studies in Environment and History. I am humbled by this honor. John R. McNeill has the distinction of being the person who has read more versions of this book than anyone else. Words alone cannot express how grateful I am for all his support of this book, for reading it closer than anyone else, and for always giving of his time and expertise. I thank Donald Worster as well for reading drafts of this book, for offering his perspective and suggestions as one of the fathers of the field of environmental history, and for his constant support of this project. Over the past few years, Sam White has been my teammate in Middle East environmental history. I thank him for his advice and support through the panels, articles, and now books.

Eric Crahan at Cambridge University Press has been the model editor. At Cambridge, I also thank Frank Smith and Jason Przybylski for making this book happen. Shana Meyer and her entire production team deserve special recognition for putting up with my many requests and questions and for their consummate professionalism in producing this book. For permission to reproduce materials from their collections, I thank the Prime Ministry's Ottoman Archive in Istanbul, the Egyptian National Archives in Cairo, the Süleymaniye Library in Istanbul, and the Istanbul University Library.

My extended family in Egypt, the United States, Canada, Saudi Arabia, Bahrain, England, Australia, and New Zealand has always supported me and this book. My family in Egypt constantly fed me, housed me, encouraged me, protected me, and helped me as I carried out the research and writing of this book. My aunts were my mothers in Cairo and my cousins my brothers and sisters. I cannot imagine life there without them, and I cannot thank them enough for everything they did and continue to do for me.

The love and generosity of my mother and father know no bounds. They have always supported me, put up with long absences, and loved me in ways too numerous and deep for me even to begin to comprehend. As much as I might like it to be otherwise, nothing I can say or do can ever return to them what they have always given me. I thank them, respect them, and love them.

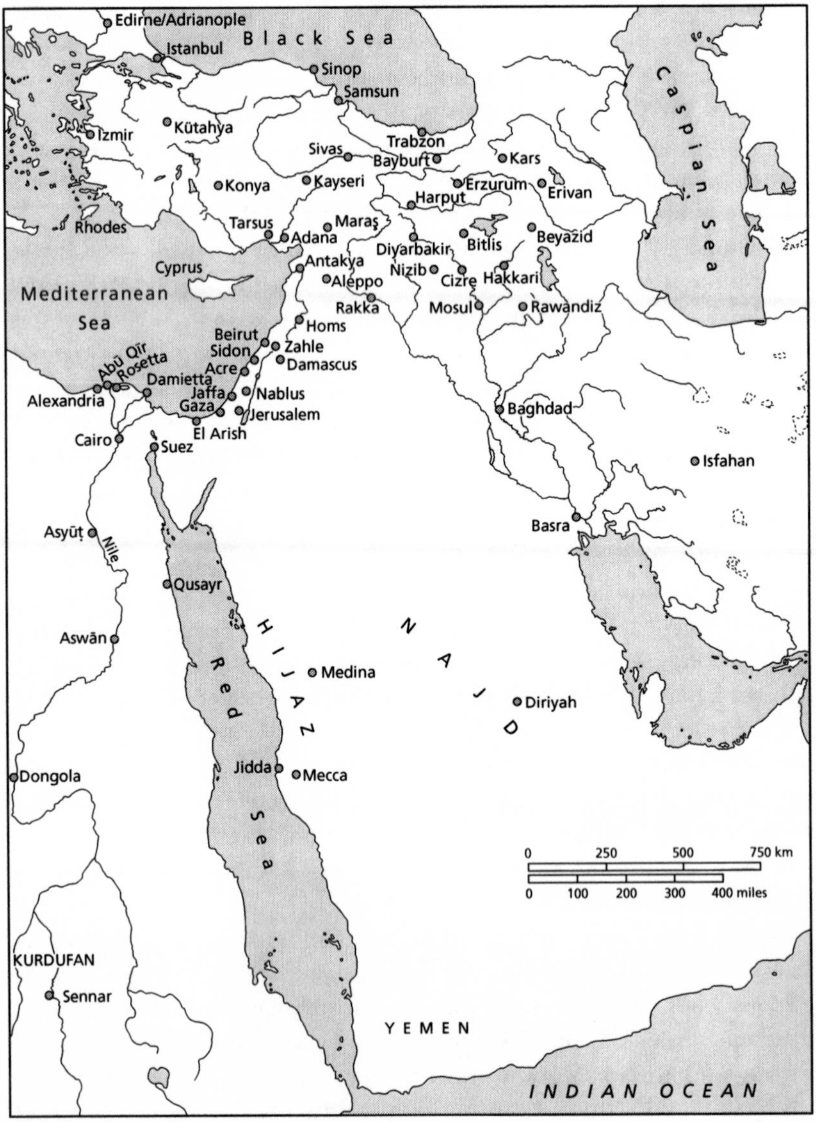

Map 1. Egypt and the Ottoman Empire

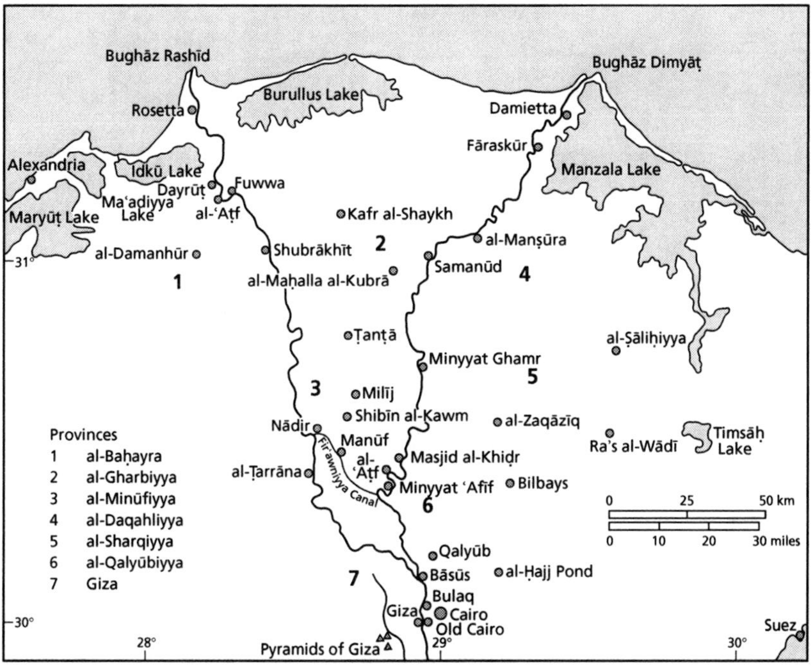

Map 2. Lower Egypt (Nile Delta)

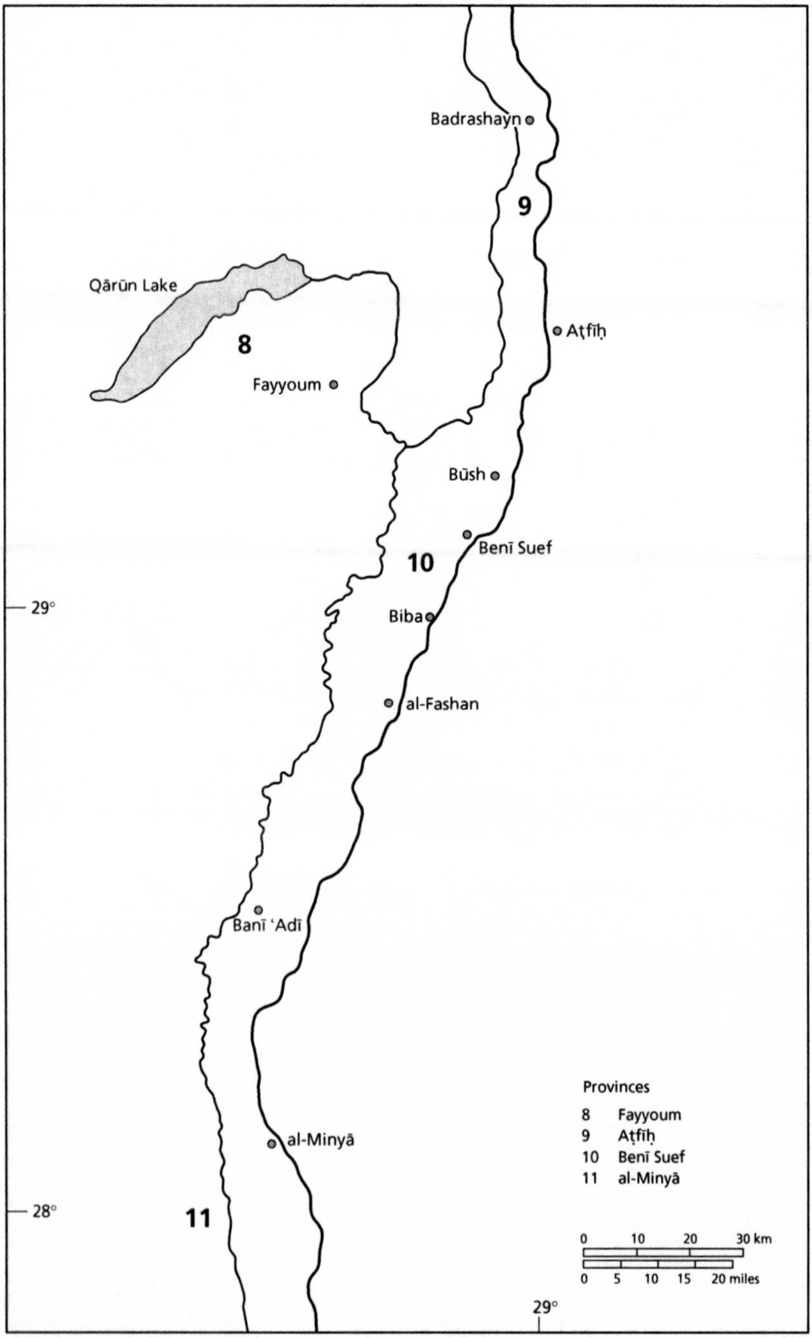

Map 3. Middle Egypt

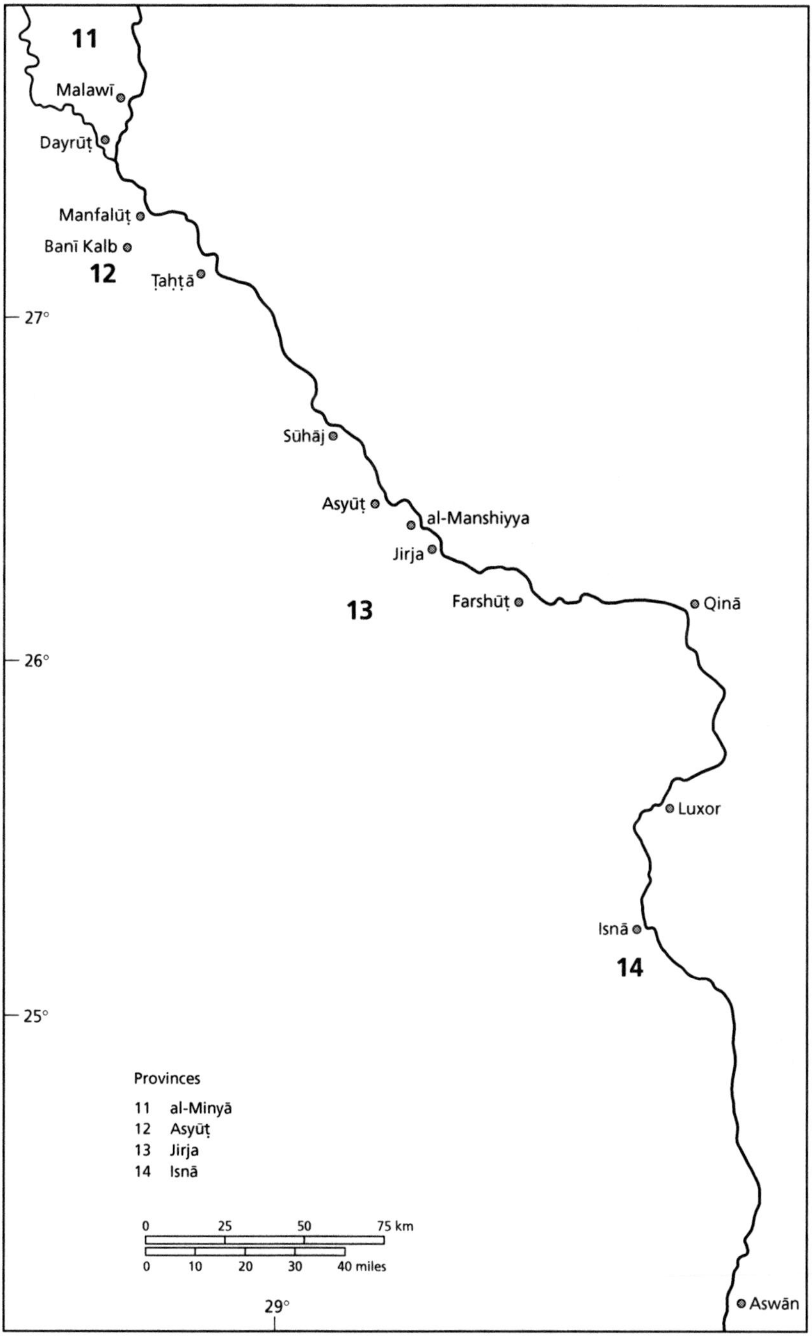

Map 4. Upper Egypt

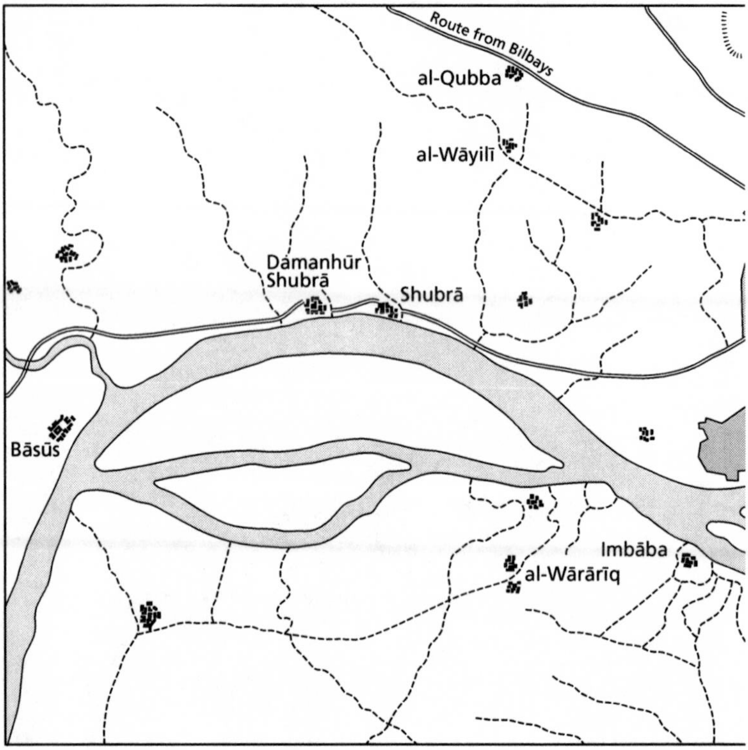

Map 5. Cairo and Surroundings, 1801

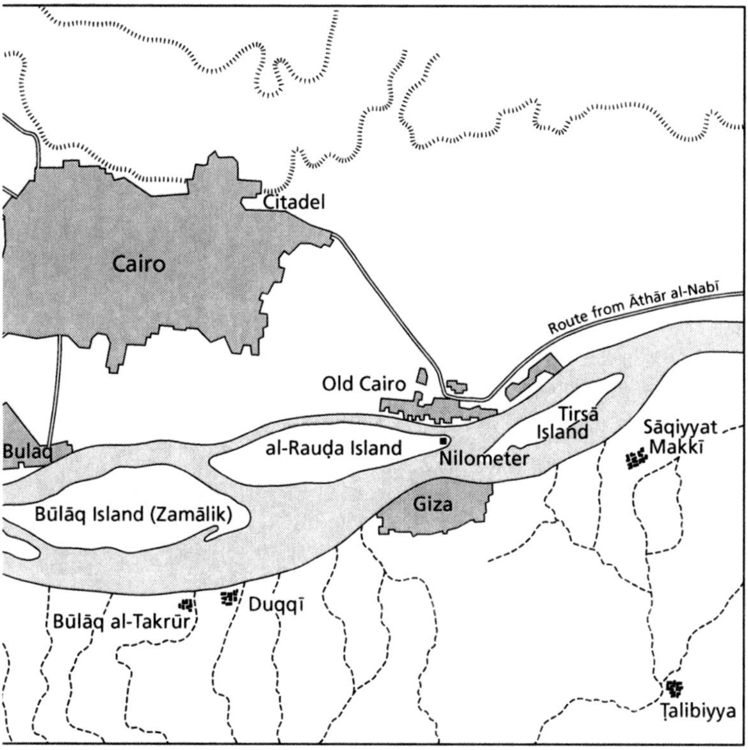
Citadel
Cairo
Route from Āthār al-Nabī
Old Cairo
Tirsā
Island
Sāqiyyat
Makkī
Bulaq
al-Rauḍa Island
Nilometer
Būlāq Island (Zamālik)
Giza
Būlāq al-Takrūr
Duqqī
Ṭalibiyya

INTRODUCTION

EMPIRE BY NATURE

Water lends itself to cliché – its beauty, its power, its abundance or absence, its transformative capabilities. Long before and after Herodotus observed Egypt to be "the gift of the Nile," others have offered clichés about the role of the Nile's waters in Egypt's history.[1] This book avoids those and other clichés altogether in favor of a social and environmental history of water usage and irrigation in the Egyptian countryside in the long eighteenth century (1675 to 1820).[2] Water, however, is only one part of this environmental story of Egypt. Timber, plague, animals, wind, grain, and microbes all have their roles to play as well in this account of struggle and community, of want and excess, of import and export, and ultimately of literal life and death.[3]

[1] For Herodotus's comments on Egypt and the Nile, see: Herodotus, *The History*, trans. David Grene (Chicago: University of Chicago Press, 1987), 2.5.

[2] Social and environmental histories of water that have informed this study include the following: André E. Guillerme, *The Age of Water: The Urban Environment in the North of France, A.D. 300–1800* (College Station: Texas A&M University Press, 1988); Norris Hundley Jr., *The Great Thirst: Californians and Water, A History* (Berkeley: University of California Press, 2001); Jean-Pierre Goubert, *The Conquest of Water: The Advent of Health in the Industrial Age*, trans. Andrew Wilson (Princeton, NJ: Princeton University Press, 1989); Paolo Squatriti, *Water and Society in Early Medieval Italy, AD 400–1000* (Cambridge: Cambridge University Press, 1998); Roberta J. Magnusson, *Water Technology in the Middle Ages: Cities, Monasteries, and Waterworks after the Roman Empire* (Baltimore: Johns Hopkins University Press, 2001); Thomas F. Glick, *Irrigation and Hydraulic Technology: Medieval Spain and Its Legacy* (Brookfield, VT: Variorum, 1996); Glick, *Irrigation and Society in Medieval Valencia* (Cambridge, MA: Harvard University Press, 1970); David Blackbourn, *The Conquest of Nature: Water, Landscape, and the Making of Modern Germany* (New York: W. W. Norton, 2006). See also the following ambitious volumes on the history of water: Terje Tvedt and Eva Jakobsson, eds., *Water Control and River Biographies*, vol. 1 of *A History of Water* (London: I. B. Tauris, 2006); Terje Tvedt and Richard Coopey, eds., *The Political Economy of Water*, vol. 2 of *A History of Water* (London: I. B. Tauris, 2006); Terje Tvedt and Terje Oestigaard, eds., *The World of Water*, vol. 3 of *A History of Water* (London: I. B. Tauris, 2006).

[3] Notions of life and death abound in descriptions of land and water in the archival and literary record of Ottoman Egypt. Unirrigated – and hence barren – land was often

In the chapters that follow, I first detail an Ottoman imperial system of natural resource allocation and balance that served to move grains – the products of irrigation – out of Egypt and wood supplies – vital material needed for Egypt's rural irrigation infrastructure – into this most lucrative of the Empire's provinces.[4] Water bound Egyptian peasants in even the

referred to with the adjective *dead* or *lifeless* (*mawāt* in Arabic, *mevat* in Turkish). See, e.g.: DWQ, al-Jusūr al-Sulṭāniyya 786, pp. 113v–114r, no case no. (18 Z 1117/2 Apr. 1706). Moreover, the word often used to describe the irrigation of land was *iḥyā'*, meaning "enlivening," "revitalization," "revival," and the like. For examples of the use of this word in this context, see: DWQ, Maḥkamat al-Manṣūra 19, p. 374, no case no. (9 M 1124/16 Feb. 1712); BOA, MM, 6:238 (Evasıt Ca 1158/12–21 Jun. 1745). Thus, images of life and death were intimately connected to the ability of water to make possible or to preclude the productivity of land. Consider the following Quranic verse in this regard: "We send down pure water from the sky, so that We may give life to a dead land and quench the thirst of countless beasts and men We have created" (Quran, 25:48–49). We are also reminded of the Quranic verse very often found on communal fountains and other water structures throughout the Muslim world: "We made every living thing from water" (*wa ja'alnā min al-mā' kulla shai'in ḥayyin*) (Quran, 21:30). Generally on water in the Muslim world, see: *EI*, s.v. "Mā'" (T. Fahd et al.); *Encyclopaedia Iranica*, s.v. "Āb ii. Water in Muslim Iranian Culture" (I. K. Poonawala).

4 The political, economic, and administrative histories of Ottoman Egypt that have proved most useful for my analysis are the following: Stanford J. Shaw, *The Financial and Administrative Organization and Development of Ottoman Egypt, 1517–1798* (Princeton, NJ: Princeton University Press, 1962); Laylā 'Abd al-Laṭīf Aḥmad, *al-Idāra fī Miṣr fī al-'Aṣr al-'Uthmānī* (Cairo: Maṭba'at Jāmi'at 'Ayn Shams, 1978); Aḥmad, *al-Mujtama' al-Miṣrī fī al-'Aṣr al-'Uthmānī* (Cairo: Dār al-Kitāb al-Jāmi'ī, 1987); Aḥmad, *Tārīkh wa Mu'arrikhī Miṣr wa al-Shām ibbāna al-'Aṣr al-'Uthmānī* (Cairo: Maktabat al-Khānjī, 1980); Michael Winter, *Egyptian Society under Ottoman Rule, 1517–1798* (London: Routledge, 1992); Peter Gran, *Islamic Roots of Capitalism: Egypt, 1760–1840* (Austin: University of Texas Press, 1979); the relevant sections of P. M. Holt, *Egypt and the Fertile Crescent, 1516–1922: A Political History* (London: Longmans Green, 1966); the relevant contributions to P. M. Holt, ed., *Political and Social Change in Modern Egypt: Historical Studies from the Ottoman Conquest to the United Arab Republic* (London: Oxford University Press, 1968); the relevant contributions to M. W. Daly, ed., *Modern Egypt, from 1517 to the End of the Twentieth Century*, vol. 2 of *The Cambridge History of Egypt* (Cambridge: Cambridge University Press, 1998); Ibrahım el-Mouelhy, *Organisation et fonctionnement des institutions ottomanes en Egypte (1517–1917): étude documentaire, d'après les sources archivistiques égyptiennes* (Ankara [?]: Imprimerie de la Société turque d'histoire, 1989); Daniel Crecelius, *The Roots of Modern Egypt: A Study of the Regimes of 'Ali Bey al-Kabir and Muhammad Bey Abu al-Dhahab, 1760–1775* (Minneapolis: Bibliotheca Islamica, 1981); Jane Hathaway, *A Tale of Two Factions: Myth, Memory, and Identity in Ottoman Egypt and Yemen* (Albany: State University of New York Press, 2003); 'Abd al-Raḥīm 'Abd al-Raḥman 'Abd al-Raḥīm, *al-Rīf al-Miṣrī fī al-Qarn al-Thāmin 'Ashar* (Cairo: Maktabat Madbūlī, 1986); Stanford J. Shaw, ed. and trans., *Ottoman Egypt in the Eighteenth Century: The Nizâmnâme-i Mısır of Cezzâr Aḥmed Pasha* (Cambridge, MA: Center for Middle Eastern Studies of Harvard University, 1964); Galal H. El-Nahal, *The Judicial Administration of Ottoman Egypt in the Seventeenth Century* (Minneapolis: Bibliotheca Islamica, 1979); Kammāl Ḥāmid Mughayth, *Miṣr fī al-'Aṣr al-'Uthmānī 1517–1798: al-Mujtama' ... wa al-Ta'līm* (Cairo: Markaz al-Dirāsāt wa al-Ma'lūmāt al-Qānūniyya li-Ḥuqūq al-Insān, 1997); 'Irāqī Yūsuf Muḥammad, *al-Wujūd*

most rural locations to the center of the Empire in Istanbul because the status of a dam or canal in Egypt held wide imperial consequences.[5] The disrepair of irrigation works and the destruction of agricultural land that would surely ensue meant less food and less money for this early modern land-based, agrarian polity.[6] This arrangement ensured that Egyptian peasants held near-absolute authority over the function and repair of irrigation works because they were the ones with the most specialized and longest experience of those irrigation features and of the environments they served.

At the end of the eighteenth century and the beginning of the nineteenth, however, this system of balance, transport, and extreme localism with respect to the elements of Egypt's irrigation infrastructure was replaced by a much more centralized and authoritarian regime of environmental resource management in Egypt. To show this change, I follow the stories of labor and plague over the course of the long eighteenth century to document how governance in Egypt by the beginning of the nineteenth century resulted in the forced labor of more than three hundred thousand peasants – more than the population of Cairo at that time – and the death of a third of those workers in the reconstruction of the Maḥmūdiyya Canal between the Nile and Alexandria.

The driving force behind this change in the nature of political rule over peoples and environments in Egypt over the course of the long eighteenth century (again, 1675 to 1820) was the province's move away from its position as the most important territory in the Ottoman Empire toward a form of independent Cairo-based sovereignty in the early nineteenth century. Beginning a few decades earlier at the end of the eighteenth century, various Ottoman governors of Egypt attempted to break away from the Empire to seize autonomous control of the province's revenues for themselves. As part of this process of challenging the central administration of the Empire, Egypt developed strong institutions of its own

al-ʿUthmānī fī Miṣr fī al-Qarnayn al-Sādis ʿAshar wa al-Sābiʿ ʿAshar (Dirāsa Wathāʾiqiyya), vol. 1 (Cairo: Markaz Kliyūbātrā lil-Kumbiyūtar, 1996); Muḥammad, *al-Wujūd al-ʿUthmānī al-Mamlūkī fī Miṣr fī al-Qarn al-Thāmin ʿAshar wa Awāʾil al-Qarn al-Tāsiʿ ʿAshar* (Cairo: Dār al-Maʿārif, 1985).

5 For two of the few studies of irrigation in the early modern Ottoman Empire, see: Rhoads Murphey, "The Ottoman Centuries in Iraq: Legacy or Aftermath? A Survey Study of Mesopotamian Hydrology and Ottoman Irrigation Projects," *JTS* 11 (1987): 17–29; *EI*, s.v. "Māʾ. 8. Irrigation in the Ottoman Empire" (Halil İnalcık).

6 Indeed, on this point, Rhoads Murphey writes of Ottoman Iraq that "water, more than land itself, was the basis of agriculture in the Middle East." Murphey, "Mesopotamian Hydrology and Ottoman Irrigation Projects," 21.

(schools, military forces, and eventually ministries) and independent sources of capital accumulation (new forms of taxation, peasant laboring classes, and a mint). All of this required an extremely strong and vast centralized bureaucracy.

Egyptian peasants' experience of this transition from an Ottoman imperial system of natural resource management to a centralized Egyptian bureaucracy was a difficult one. Because this change in political rule meant that Egypt could no longer benefit from its historical links to other areas of the Empire – links that provided it with wood and the means to fix irrigation works – the province had to seek out its own lumber supplies, grain markets, sources of cash, laboring power, and other necessities. The demands for those and other items and the pressures they caused drove the Egyptian bureaucracy of the early nineteenth century to ask much more of the Egyptian peasantry and of the land they tilled – to produce more, to work more, and to give up more. Egyptian peasants were thus robbed of autonomy over their fields and labor, of their generations of rootedness in local environments, and eventually of many of their lives as well. Over the course of the long eighteenth century, they went from having quite a bit of room to maneuver in an Ottoman imperial system to essentially having none in an Egyptian one. As they came to suffer more and more under this new political system, so, too, did the Egyptian rural environment.

My ultimate claim is, thus, that the very moment Egypt purposefully bypassed the Ottoman system of natural resource balance documented in the first three chapters of this book – a moment of supposed modernity and independence – was one in which water, labor, environmental resources, local control over rural irrigation, and ultimately Egyptian peasants' biological lives were taken over as never before by a despotic form of bureaucratic government.

A Very Short Introduction to the Ottoman Empire

Before examining transformations in the long eighteenth century in detail, I offer a very quick (and largely political) overview of the arc of the history of the Ottoman Empire as a whole to orientate those readers unfamiliar with the Empire and Egypt's place in it.[7] The Ottoman Empire

[7] For a very useful and accessible synthetic treatment of the entirety of Ottoman history, see: Caroline Finkel, *Osman's Dream: The History of the Ottoman Empire, 1300–1923* (New York: Basic Books, 2006).

was the longest-lasting and geographically largest empire to rule in the Mediterranean basin since antiquity. Its rule for more than six hundred years across the Middle East, North Africa, and southeastern Europe both continued and created precedents for nearly all modern states in these regions. The Empire first emerged around the turn of the fourteenth century in the context of centuries of steady migrations by nomadic Turkic peoples through Central Asia, the Mongol invasions of Anatolia, and internal crises in the Byzantine Empire. Through a series of military victories, Osman, the leader of one of the many Turkish tribal groups that came to settle in what was then still Byzantine northwestern Anatolia, was able to carve out for himself an area of autonomy from which to extend his power. Osman's son Orhan captured the city of Bursa from the Byzantines in 1326, making it the first capital of the rising polity that would come to be known as the Ottoman Empire.

Ottoman military conquests in western Anatolia and around the Sea of Marmara continued throughout the rest of the fourteenth century and the beginning of the fifteenth. The final blow to waning Byzantine power in Anatolia and southeastern Europe and the greatest conquest of the early Ottoman state was the capture of Constantinople in 1453. With this new strategic and symbolic capital – Istanbul – the Empire was fully in place to strengthen and extend its rule throughout the second half of the fifteenth century in the Morea, the southern Black Sea coast, the Crimea, and areas further south and west. Süleyman "the Magnificent" was the first major sultan of the Empire in the sixteenth century. His reign, traditionally referred to as the Ottoman "Golden Age," saw the Empire gain Egypt and most of the Arab world from the Mamlūks, including the religious centers of Mecca and Medina. In what one scholar has called "a sixteenth-century world war," Süleyman's military forces fought not only the Mamlūks in the Arab world and the Safavids in Iran on their eastern frontiers but also the Spanish and the Habsburgs in the western Mediterranean; the Portuguese in the Indian Ocean; the Hungarians, Serbs, and Bulgarians in the Balkans; and the Venetians and Genoese in the central Mediterranean and the Aegean.[8]

These sixteenth-century military successes came in addition to and themselves necessitated new modes of imperial rule (some of which I discuss shortly) in these vast, newly acquired territories. Numerous law codes were promulgated during the period; the functions of various kinds of

[8] Donald Quataert, *The Ottoman Empire, 1700–1922* (Cambridge: Cambridge University Press, 2000), 21.

legal courts and other venues were adapted to changing circumstances throughout the Empire; new forms of administrative practices, taxation regimes, and means of revenue collection were instituted and refined; commercial relations were further strengthened and extended. As the central imperial bureaucracy expanded in the sixteenth century, the day-to-day administration of the Empire slowly moved away from the person of the sultan to his surrounding retinue in the palace – to the mothers and wives of sultans, to the Empire's grand viziers (chief administrators), and to others in the dynasty's ruling elite. Political power thus became decentralized and more diffuse from the end of the sixteenth century through the seventeenth as new power brokers emerged. Chief among these were the large households of viziers and other elites throughout the Empire that, even as they challenged central imperial authority, came to mirror the internal workings of the royal family in their hierarchies, their abilities to accumulate wealth and followers, and eventually also in their power in various urban and rural locales.

The Ottoman eighteenth century has usually been noted for the Empire's military defeats, territorial losses, internal urban and rural rebellions, and increasing inability to compete economically with Europe on both global and local scales. Because most of this book is about the eighteenth-century Empire, I leave it to the reader to decide whether the eighteenth century should be deemed a period of "decline," as has traditionally been the case in Ottoman historiography. I have more to say on the specific issue of decline later in this introduction.

The Empire's territorial losses continued into the nineteenth century, now under the guise of what was referred to in European capitals as the Eastern question – namely, how were European powers to deal geopolitically and strategically with the Empire's continual losses of territory? For the Russians, the British, and the French (and eventually the Germans as well), the answer was to keep a weakened Empire limping along so as to check the encroachment of any one power over Ottoman lands. This was, however, mostly only a European conversation.

For their part, the Ottomans responded to nineteenth-century ideas and political reforms like most other states in the period. Their governmental bureaucracy greatly expanded with the establishment of new ministries, schools, and legislative bodies. New industries, military units, medical institutions, and social clubs were either founded or greatly expanded during the period. As with most other polities in the world, the Ottomans also had to deal with the specter of various rising nationalisms during the nineteenth century. Given the multiethnic, multiconfessional, and multilinguistic makeup of the Empire's populations, there were all sorts of competing and overlapping nationalisms, interests, and desires at work as the century wore on. Sometimes encouraged by outside forces interested in weakening or ending the Ottoman Empire altogether, Arab, Turkish, Balkan, and other nationalists pushed their claims against the Ottoman state. The crucible of World War I brought these conflicting passions and political agendas to a violent climax that saw the eventual dismemberment of the Ottoman Empire after more than six centuries of rule and its replacement by various states. As with the establishment of all borders, some won in this affair and many more lost.

Land and Water in Ottoman Egypt

After its conquest by Ottoman armies in 1517, Egypt immediately became the most important province of the Empire. It was the Empire's largest producer of agricultural goods, it generated more revenue for the state than any other province, and its capital was the second-largest city in the Empire after Istanbul. It was the gateway to the Red Sea and Indian Ocean and to North and sub-Saharan Africa, and it was a crucial hub for the management of the pilgrimage sites of Mecca and Medina. The basis for Egypt's wealth, population, and power was its land and water.[9] To understand its history, we must therefore begin here – in Egypt's mud.

As outlined in the Kanunname (Ottoman law code) of Egypt, almost all of the province's land from the sixteenth to the eighteenth centuries was legally owned by the Ottoman state.[10] For administrative purposes, all

9 For particularly useful treatments of the status of land, agriculture, and landholding in the Ottoman Empire, see: Çağlar Keyder and Faruk Tabak, eds., *Landholding and Commercial Agriculture in the Middle East* (Albany: State University of New York Press, 1991); Huri İslamoğlu-İnan, *State and Peasant in the Ottoman Empire: Agrarian Power Relations and Regional Economic Development in Ottoman Anatolia during the Sixteenth Century* (Leiden: E. J. Brill, 1994); Huri İslamoğlu-İnan, ed., *The Ottoman Empire and the World-Economy* (Cambridge: Cambridge University Press, 1987).

10 I consulted the following versions of the Kanunname-i Mısır: *Ḳānūn-nāme-i Mıṣr*, TSMK 1845 (E.H. 2063); Aḥmad Fu'ād Mutawallī, trans. and intro., *Qānūn Nāmah Miṣr, alladhī Aṣdarahu al-Sulṭān al-Qānūnī li-Ḥukm Miṣr* (Cairo: Maktabat al-Anjlū al-Miṣriyya, 1986); Ömer Lûtfi Barkan, *Kanunlar*, vol. 1 of *XV ve XVIinci asırlarda Osmanlı İmparatorluğunda Ziraî Ekonominin Hukukî ve Malî Esasları*, İstanbul Üniversitesi Yayınlarından 256 (Istanbul: Bürhaneddin Matbaası, 1943), 355–87. Mutawallī's Arabic translation contains a copy of Barkan's Turkish text. For discussions of the status of land under the Kanunname, see: Kenneth M. Cuno, *The Pasha's Peasants: Land, Society, and Economy in Lower Egypt, 1740–1858* (Cambridge: Cambridge University Press, 1992), 25–27; Stanford J.

rural land was divided into plots known as *muqāṭaʿāt* (singular *muqāṭaʿa*) that were further divided into twenty-four parts (known as *qīrāṭ*, with one *qīrāṭ* roughly equaling 175 square meters). A *muqāṭaʿa* generally consisted of a principal village, its surrounding villages and towns, and their cultivated areas. By the early seventeenth century, rights to the products of most *muqāṭaʿāt* in Egypt were bought from the Ottoman administration by rural Egyptian peasant leaders as tax farms (*iltizāms*).[11] These *multazims* (those who held *iltizāms*) were responsible for paying the state treasury a basic yearly tax and for maintaining irrigation works and agricultural fields in areas under their control.[12] The incentive for a *multazim* to take on this responsibility of delivering to the state a set amount of revenue every year was the right to raise additional amounts of profit for himself (*fāʾiḍ* in Arabic, *faiz* in Turkish). Thus, the Ottoman state devolved authority over the day-to-day maintenance of agriculture to these local leaders, who, in turn, guaranteed the state's revenues and were also able to make a profit for themselves.[13] The ultimate cash remittance paid out by the vali (provincial governor) of Egypt to the Ottoman state

Shaw, "Landholding and Land-Tax Revenues in Ottoman Egypt," in *Political and Social Change in Modern Egypt: Historical Studies from the Ottoman Conquest to the United Arab Republic*, ed. P. M. Holt (London: Oxford University Press, 1968), 91–103. See also: G. Frantz-Murphy, "Parallel Cyclical Patterns in Pre-Ottoman and Ottoman Land Tenure in Egypt," *AO* 9 (1988): 17–24.

[11] On these shifts in taxation and the legal status of land, see: Baber Johansen, *The Islamic Law on Land Tax and Rent: The Peasants' Loss of Property Rights as Interpreted in the Hanafite Legal Literature of the Mamluk and Ottoman Periods* (London: Croom Helm, 1988), 85–97. For general discussions of *iltizāms* in the Ottoman Empire, see: Joseph E. Matuz, "Contributions to the Ottoman Institution of the *Iltizâm*," *OA* 11 (1991): 237–49. On *iltizāms* in Ottoman Egypt, see: Umniyya ʿĀmir, "Niẓām al-Iltizām: al-Taḥawwul min al-Milkiyya al-Ḥukūmiyya ilā al-Milkiyya al-Khāṣṣa," *al-Rūznāma: al-Ḥauliyya al-Miṣriyya lil-Wathāʾiq* 1 (2003): 267–85. On the *iltizām* system in Egypt during the French occupation, see: Nāṣir Ibrāhīm, "al-Firinsiyūn wa Niẓām al-Iltizām," *AI* 37 (2003): 31–54.

[12] For a clear statement of these dual responsibilities of *multazims*, see: DWQ, Rūznāma 4557 – Daftar Irtifāʿ al-Miyāh bi-Baḥr Sayyidnā Yūsuf lihi al-Ṣalāh wa al-Salām ʿan al-Qabḍa al-Yūsufiyya Tābiʿ Wilāyat al-Fayyūm (Raqam al-Ḥifẓ al-Nauʿī 1, ʿAyn 59, Makhzin Turkī 1, Musalsal 4557), p. 22, no case no. (28 R 1127/2 May 1715). These duties of *multazims* in Ottoman Egypt were quite similar to those of Han gentry landlords in early modern China. See: John F. Richards, *The Unending Frontier: An Environmental History of the Early Modern World* (Berkeley: University of California Press, 2003), 118–22.

[13] In Stanford J. Shaw's judgment, "The tax-farm system was ideal for Ottoman Egypt, given the conditions of the time. It assured the [imperial] Treasury of a continued flow of revenues with a minimum of administrative cost to itself. It gave the tax-farmers a permanent and continued interest in the fertility of the land, so that they would not over-exploit it and drive the peasants away. It subjected the cultivators to regular taxes, and protected them against arbitrary illegal impositions." Shaw, "Landholding," 102.

was known as the *irsāliyye-i ḫazīne.*[14] The profit garnered by the Empire from this payment – more than that from any other single province – was the ultimate reason for the Ottoman state's control and maintenance of irrigation, land, and agriculture in Egypt.[15]

The annual cycle of agricultural cultivation in Egypt was, of course, timed to the Nile's flood.[16] Summer rains in the Ethiopian highlands

[14] For references to the preparation and sending of the Egyptian *irsāliyye-i ḫazīne*, see: TSMA, E. 664/4 (n.d.); TSMA, E. 664/64 (1 C 1059/12 Jun. 1649); TSMA, E. 5207/57 (Evail B 1056/12–21 Aug. 1646); TSMA, E. 5207/58 (Evasıt B 1056/22–31 Aug. 1646); TSMA, E. 7016/95 (n.d.); TSMA, E. 5207/49 (Evahir Ca 1056/5–14 Jul. 1646). The following case concerns problems with the delivery of this annual remittance: TSMA, E. 664/66 (n.d.). For an example of the accounting of the *irsāliyye-i ḫazīne* from the year 1649/1650, see: TSMA, E. 4675/2 (20 N 1061/6 Sep. 1651). The following case concerns the sending of two thousand *guruş* from the villages of Egypt as part of the *irsāliyye-i ḫazīne*: TSMA, E. 3522 (24 Ş 1148/8 Jan. 1736). For a detailed discussion of the *irsāliyye-i ḫazīne*, see: Shaw, *Financial and Administrative Organization and Development*, 283–312 and 399–401.

[15] Jane Hathaway, *The Politics of Households in Ottoman Egypt: The Rise of the Qazdağlıs* (Cambridge: Cambridge University Press, 1997), 6. Michael Winter claims that the Empire was content with any amount of autonomy or independence of its functionaries in Egypt as long as the *irsāliyye-i ḫazīne* was paid to the Ottoman state and Egypt formally recognized the sultan's authority and contributed soldiers to imperial campaigns. Winter, *Egyptian Society under Ottoman Rule*, 20. For a detailed accounting of each component of the annual *irsāliyye-i ḫazīne* of 1596 to 1597, see: Stanford J. Shaw, *The Budget of Ottoman Egypt, 1005–1006/1596–1597* (The Hague: Mouton, 1968).

[16] The only direct archival evidence of the annual flood in the long eighteenth century is a series of two registers from the high divan (al-Dīwān al-ʿĀlī) of Egypt in Cairo: DWQ, al-Dīwān al-ʿĀlī 1; DWQ, al-Dīwān al-ʿĀlī 2. For a study of these two registers, see: Jīhān Aḥmad ʿUmrān, "Dirāsa Diblūmātiyya li-Wathāʾiq Wafāʾ al-Nīl bi-Sijillāt al-Dīwān al-ʿĀlī maʿ Nashr Namādhij minhā," *Waqāʾiʿ Tārīkhiyya: Dauriyya ʿIlmiyya Muḥakkama* (2004): 347–81. As part of its assigned responsibilities, the Ottoman high divan served to certify the official height of the flood, as read by the Nilometer on the island of al-Rauḍa in Cairo, with an entry in its registers. The twenty-seven entries we have of this sort in the two surviving registers of al-Dīwān al-ʿĀlī are spread over the period from 1741 to 1804. The magic number of sixteen cubits for the height of the annual flood represented the minimum flood level required to be able to assess taxes on the *iltizāms* of Egypt. Not surprisingly, none of the entries of this "official" level of the flood was less than sixteen cubits. The flood's height was recorded in each of these cases either on the very same day of the flood or on the day after – an indication of the importance of registering an official record of the Nile's height as soon as possible. For a study of the increase in the Nile's maximum flood level over the course of the fifteenth century, see: Stuart J. Borsch, "Nile Floods and the Irrigation System in Fifteenth-Century Egypt," *Mamlūk Studies Review* 4 (2000): 131–45. For a spectral study of long-term trends in the river's flood levels, see: D. Kondrashov, Y. Feliks, and M. Ghil, "Oscillatory Modes of Extended Nile River Records (A.D. 622–1922)," *Geophysical Research Letters* 32 (2005), L10702.

For a detailed history of the Nilometer compiled from various historical sources, see: Amīn Sāmī, *Taqwīm al-Nīl*, 5 vols. in 3 pts. (Cairo: Dār al-Kutub wa al-Wathāʾiq al-Qawmiyya, 2003), pt. 1, 65–95. In this regard, see also: William Popper, *The Cairo*

swelled the river, causing it to rise in Aswan in Upper Egypt by June and in Cairo by early July. Water continued to rise through the summer, until its peak in Cairo in late August or early September. From then, it began to fall steadily, reaching half of its flood height by the middle of November and its minimum by May before the cycle began anew. The onset of the flood in the late summer was designated as the start of the agricultural year in Egypt. Lands in Upper and Lower Egypt watered at the beginning of the agricultural year in September or October produced the major annual harvest, consisting of wheat, barley, lentils, clover, flax, chickpeas, onions, and garlic. This was known as the winter crop (*al-shitwī*). Lands were also planted and harvested from January through May with stored water from basins and canals, thus producing a second major yield for the agricultural year known as the summer crop (*al-ṣayfī*), consisting mainly of wheat, barley, cotton, melons, sugarcane, and sesame. There was, of course, wide regional variation in the kinds and amounts of crops grown. Rice cultivation, for example, was concentrated in northern Lower Egypt, tobacco and sugarcane in Upper Egypt, cotton in Middle and Lower Egypt, and flax in the interior of the Delta and in the Fayyoum oasis. Wheat was grown almost everywhere.

The legal status of the water of Ottoman Egypt that grew foodstuffs and other crops was far more nebulous than the status of land. No single entity "owned" the waters of the Nile or a canal. At the same time, however, the equitable use of water was a priority maintained by the Ottoman administration at all costs.[17] Thus, although water was owned by no

Nilometer: Studies in Ibn Taghrî Birdî's Chronicles of Egypt, I (Berkeley: University of California Press, 1951); Nicholas Warner, *The True Description of Cairo: A Sixteenth-Century Venetian View*, 3 vols. (Oxford: Arcadian Library, in association with Oxford University Press, 2006), 2:123–25. On the identity of one of the Nilometer's earliest engineers, see: Ihāb Aḥmad Ibrāhīm, "Muhandis Miqyās al-Nīl: Maʿlūmāt Jadīda fī Ḍau' al-Nuqūsh al-Kitābiyya lil-Miqyās," *AI* 39 (2005): 1–8. Muṣṭafā ʿĀlī, who visited Egypt at the end of the sixteenth century, describes the Nilometer as "indeed one of the rare creations of the world and of the curious works resembling magical devices." Andreas Tietze, *Muṣṭafā ʿĀlī's Description of Cairo of 1599: Text, Transliteration, Translation, Notes* (Vienna: Verlag Der Österreichischen Akademie Der Wissenschaften, 1975), 30.

For a detailed fifteenth-century account of the island of al-Rauḍa, see: Jalāl al-Dīn al-Sayūṭī, *Kawkab al-Rauḍa*, ed. Muḥammad al-Shashtāwī (Cairo: Dār al-Āfāq al-ʿArabiyya, 2002).

17 For a discussion of the management of water resources and irrigation during the Mamlūk period, see: Sato Tsugitaka, *State and Rural Society in Medieval Islam: Sultans, Muqtaʿs and Fallahun* (Leiden: E. J. Brill, 1997), 220–33. For a very general geohydrologic history of water and irrigation in Egypt from the Pharaohs to the late twentieth century, see: Wizārat al-Ashghāl al-ʿĀmma wa al-Mawād al-Māʾiyya, *al-Nīl wa Tārīkh al-Riyy fī Miṣr* (Cairo: al-Lajna al-Ahliyya al-Miṣriyya lil-Riyy wa al-Ṣarf, n.d.). Similarly, see the relevant sections of the following: Akādīmiyyat al-Baḥth al-ʿIlmī wa al-Tiknūlūjiyā, *Tārīkh al-ʿUlūm*

one, it was in many ways owned by all the users of a particular water source or conduit. In the Kanunname-i Mısır, we find a clear statement of the interests of the Ottoman Empire in maintaining Egypt's irrigation network. This law code was promulgated by the Grand Vizier Ibrahim Paşa in 1525, less than a decade after the Ottoman conquest of Egypt in 1517. The very first duty enumerated by the document as incumbent on each subprovincial *kāshif* (district or village leader) in Egypt was "the proper and timely repair of canals and the work of dredging them."[18] Likewise, the law code also stipulated that village elders and the peasantry of Egypt were to maintain canals that ran through their villages on a regular basis so that no land in the province fell *sharāqī.*[19] Similarly – the Kanunname continues – in the season of the flood, peasants were required to plant irrigated land so that no land with access to water was left uncultivated. If watered land was not cultivated, ultimately it was the *kāshif* of that area that was to be held responsible for any problems that arose with agriculture or the collection of taxes.[20] The punishment for leaving watered land uncultivated could be execution.[21]

wa al-Tiknūlūjiyā al-Handasiyya fī Miṣr fī al-Qarnayn al-Tāsiʿ ʿAshar wa al-ʿAshrīn, 2 vols. (Cairo: Akādīmiyyat al-Baḥth al-ʿIlmī wa al-Tiknūlūjiyā, 1993); Majdī ʿAbd al-Ḥamīd Muḥammad al-Sirsī, "al-Riyy wa Mushkilāt al-Zirāʿa fī Daltā al-Nīl: Dirāsa Jughrāfiyya" (Ph.D. diss., ʿAyn Shams University, 1985). For an account of the nineteenth-century divan of public works, see: Nihād Muḥammad Kamāl al-Dīn Fu'ād, "Sijillāt Dīwān al-Ashghāl al-ʿUmūmiyya fī al-Fatra min 1277 ilā 1297 (1860–1880): Dirāsa Arshīfiyya wa Wathā'iqiyya wa Tārīkhiyya" (Ph.D. diss., Cairo University, 1993).

18 Mutawallī, *Qānūn Nāmah Miṣr*, 29–30; Barkan, *Kanunlar*, 360.

19 The Egyptian Arabic word *sharāqī* is one we will encounter a great deal. It refers to land that is not reached by water and is hence parched and dry. In contrast to *būr* land, which is uncultivable wasteland, *sharāqī* earth has the potential for cultivation given the proper amount of water. The classical Arabic dictionary *Lisān al-ʿArab* does not give a definition for *sharāqī.* See: *Lisān al-ʿArab*, 4 vols. (Beirut: Dār Lisān al-ʿArab, 1970), s.v. *sharaqa.* Edward Lane does suggest, however, that the word derives from the Arabic verb *sharraqa*, meaning to turn toward the east. Hence, the notion is that the strength of the eastern sun parched the earth. Edward William Lane, *An Arabic-English Lexicon*, 8 vols. (Beirut: Librairie du Liban, 1968), s.v. *sharaqa.* However, there is also possibly a Turkish derivation from the word *çürük* meaning "putrid," "rotten," "decayed," "unsound," or "useless." See: Aḥmad Fu'ād Mutawallī, *al-Alfāẓ al-Turkiyya fī al-Lahjāt al-ʿArabiyya wa fī Lughat al-Kitāba* (Cairo: Dār al-Zahrā' lil-Nashr, 1991), 55. Others have claimed a possible Coptic origin for the word. See: El-Said Badawi and Martin Hinds, *A Dictionary of Egyptian Arabic* (Beirut: Librairie du Liban, 1986), s.v. *shīn, rā', qāf.* For a discussion of *sharāqī* land and nineteenth-century Egypt's irrigation network, see: Ghislaine Alleaume, "Les systemes hydrauliques de l'Égypte pré-moderne: Essai d'histoire du paysage," in *Itinéraires d'Égypte: Mélanges offerts au père Maurice Martin S.J.*, ed. Christian Décobert (Cairo: Institut français d'archéologie orientale, 1992), 315–20.

20 Later, the Kanunname outlines similar responsibilities for Bedouin shaykhs. Mutawallī, *Qānūn Nāmah Miṣr*, 37; Barkan, *Kanunlar*, 363.

21 Mutawallī, *Qānūn Nāmah Miṣr*, 30–31; Barkan, *Kanunlar*, 360–61.

Much of the Kanunname, and especially those sections dealing with irrigation in Egypt, was based on earlier laws and precedents. Throughout the text of the law code, we find references to what was done during the reign of Qaitbay, the Mamlūk ruler of Egypt at the end of the fifteenth century, only decades before the Ottoman conquest.[22] One of the precedents established during his reign and referenced in the Kanunname was the following. If during the time of the flood a village's canal embankments were overwhelmed or otherwise destroyed and that village's tax revenues were not enough to cover the repair of the canal, then the peasants of that village were to pay for the repairs themselves. If the peasants' funds were insufficient, then – and only then – was money to be supplemented from the *irsāliyye-i ḫazīne.*

Though not unexpected, the inclusion of irrigation in this foundational document of Ottoman rule in Egypt goes a long way in illustrating just how vital irrigation was to the entire project of the Ottoman Empire in what would prove its richest province. Canals and the water they carried were given as much attention as the various military cadres of Egypt, religious institutions, tax revenues, and trade.[23] Again, irrigation was of the utmost concern not only to those peasants who lived along canals in the countryside but also to the sultan in Istanbul. The point is clear in this document: water made everything else possible in Ottoman Egypt.

Laws of Nature

Much of this book is about how the extreme localism of rural Egypt affected the imperial regime of the Ottoman Empire. As I argue in Chapter 1, for instance, centuries of peasant experience with and knowledge of particular canals directed the Ottoman bureaucracy of Egypt how to manage the irrigation works. To get at this intersection of the local

[22] For reference to Qaitbay's irrigation policies serving as precedent for the Ottoman Kanunname-i Mısır, see: Mutawallī, *Qānūn Nāmah Miṣr,* 32–33; Barkan, *Kanunlar,* 360–62.

[23] With the onset of Ottoman rule in Egypt came a new military regime in the province consisting of seven regiments: the ʿAzeban, Çavuşan, Çerakise, Gönüllüyan, Mustahfızan (Janissaries), Müteferrika, and Tüfenkciyan. Each of these names of a military cadre has its Arabicized equivalent. On these military ranks, see: Mutawallī, *Qānūn Nāmah Miṣr,* 9–28; Barkan, *Kanunlar,* 355–59; Shaw, *Financial and Administrative Organization and Development,* 189–210; Winter, *Egyptian Society under Ottoman Rule,* 37–43; ʿAbd al-Raḥīm, *al-Rīf al-Miṣrī,* 71–81; Hathaway, *Politics of Households,* 5–16. For more on the military and administrative organization of Ottoman Egypt, see also: *Niẓām-nāme-i Mıṣr,* TSMK 1846 (B. 288).

and the imperial, I have relied heavily on the records of various rural Islamic law courts (*al-maḥākim al-sharʿiyya*) throughout Ottoman Egypt, which controlled the function of much in the province through the appointment of judges and the promulgation of law codes and imperial decrees.[24] The hundreds of these courts spread throughout the domain of the Ottoman Empire were unique institutions that kept copious records, thus affording the social and environmental historian of the Ottoman Empire a wealth of empirical and ecological data.

Because these institutions were the most immediate and most visible presence of the Ottoman state in rural areas of the Empire, the court was the means by which the majority of Ottoman subjects in Egypt and elsewhere "saw" the Empire most often.[25] It was here that rural Egyptians came to register marriages and divorces, to document property transactions, and to deal with the estates of deceased relatives. Less often – but most important for our purposes – Egyptian peasants also used the court to adjudicate disputes concerning irrigation works, water usage issues, and the cultivation of foodstuffs. What comes through in the records is a complicated picture of a rural world in constant flux. Canal embankments broke often, upstream villages regularly cut into canals and siphoned off more water than was their due, and large repairs needed laborers. As noted by many historians, a further strength of court records is their ability to capture local voices, some of which we hear in the pages that follow.[26]

[24] On the legal system of Ottoman Egypt, see: El-Nahal, *Judicial Administration of Ottoman Egypt*; Aḥmad, *al-Idāra fī Miṣr*, 241–93. For a recent, very suggestive study of the function of courts and law in an Ottoman provincial setting, see: Boğaç A. Ergene, *Local Court, Provincial Society and Justice in the Ottoman Empire: Legal Practice and Dispute Resolution in Çankırı and Kastamonu (1652–1744)* (Leiden: E. J. Brill, 2003).

[25] We have no reliable statistics for the population of Egypt during most of the Ottoman period (1517 to 1882). We do know that in 1800 the population of the entire province was 4.5 million and that the population of Cairo was 260,000. André Raymond estimates that the population of Cairo averaged two hundred thousand during the more than three centuries of Ottoman rule in Egypt, with various periods of increase and decrease. André Raymond, "La population du Caire et de l'Égypte à l'époque ottomane et sous Muḥammad ʿAlî," in *Mémorial Ömer Lûtfi Barkan* (Paris: Librairie d'Amérique et d'Orient Adrien Maisonneuve, 1980), 169–78.

[26] See, e.g.: Leslie Peirce, *Morality Tales: Law and Gender in the Ottoman Court of Aintab* (Berkeley: University of California Press, 2003), 8–9; Peirce, "'She is trouble . . . and I will divorce her': Orality, Honor, and Representation in the Ottoman Court of Aintab," in *Women in the Medieval Islamic World: Power, Patronage, Piety*, ed. Gavin R. G. Hambly (New York: St. Martin's Press, 1998), 267–300. For a critical stance on "voice" in Ottoman court records, see: Ergene, *Local Court, Provincial Society and Justice*, 133–38.

We should note at the outset that we really have no reliable way of knowing what percentage of disputes over water or irrigation works were handled outside the courts either by the parties themselves or through some other form of mediation. Clearly, what we see in the court records of Ottoman Egypt represents only a very tiny fraction of water disputes during the Ottoman period. We do, nevertheless, sometimes get a glimpse of independently negotiated legal settlements in the records of the courts of rural Egypt.[27]

As Ottoman legal institutions with long documentary histories, provincial courts help us understand the various meanings and different castings of the practice of law and of juridical power in Ottoman Egypt during the long eighteenth century. The law technically governing the legal operations and rulings of these courts was the *sharīʿa* – Islamic religious law codified in the writings of religious jurists throughout Islamic history. Tellingly, though, as I discuss in more detail later, what comes to be the dominant form of law cited in the workings of these courts is not *sharīʿa* but customary practice, or *qānūn*. *Qānūn* is not cited as an "official" body of legal writing but is rather invoked by parties at court and by judges themselves as precedent. In none of the thousands of cases that make up the backbone of the empirical base of this study was *sharīʿa* ever cited in the adjudication of a case. Rather, we most often find phrases such as *min qadīm al-zamān* (Arabic) or *kadim ül-eyyamdan* (Ottoman Turkish) and the like, which all roughly mean "from times of old." Precedent, in other

[27] For example, in a case from the southern city of Manfalūṭ, two brothers, Ḥasan and ʿAbd al-Jawād, came to the court over a dispute concerning a canal they shared in a district of the city known as al-Shaykh ʿAlī al-Armanī. DWQ, Maḥkamat Manfalūṭ 3, p. 38, case 72 (n.d.). According to this case, ʿAbd al-Jawād suddenly seized the entire canal from his brother and took over its operation and maintenance. For his part, Ḥasan conceded to his brother any rights he had over the canal, its usage, and its water. This case was clearly settled outside of the court. And though it appears in the archival record of Ottoman Egypt as documentary evidence to which parties in the case could refer should the need arise, the only reason this dispute came to court at all was likely the desire of one or both men to lend the agreement a further degree of legitimacy. This practice is known as "anticipation of consequences" and was a common use of the Ottoman court system as a "community registry." I borrow the term *community registry* from the following: Peirce, *Morality Tales*, 89. For further examples of this use of the court, see: ibid. and the citations therein. Also on this point, Beshara Doumani instructively writes that the Nablus Islamic Court "functioned as a public-records office." Doumani, *Rediscovering Palestine: Merchants and Peasants in Jabal Nablus, 1700–1900* (Berkeley: University of California Press, 1995), 10. For a very useful discussion of some of the strategic uses of documents by litigants in Ottoman courts, see: Boğaç Ergene, "Document Use in Ottoman Courts of Law: Observations from the *Sicils* of Çankırı and Kastamonu," *Turcica* 37 (2005): 83–111.

words, and not theoretical *sharīʿa* law as delineated in the law books of Ottoman jurists and others, was the driving logic behind the function of rural courts in eighteenth-century Ottoman Egypt.

Despite this lack of evidence of *sharīʿa*'s influence on the adjudication of disputes over irrigation and water usage in rural Egypt, this body of legal ideas was nevertheless intimately connected to water.[28] Indeed, the earliest meanings of the word *sharīʿa* had more to do with water than they did with law. The word's original meaning was "a watering place" or "a resort of drinkers."[29] It referred to a water source that was "permanent, and apparent to the eye, like the water of rivers, not water from which one draws with the well-rope."[30] The word *sharīʿa* thus referred to a wellspring – a font that gave forth the life-giving substance of water that sustained a community. These latent meanings persist in the usage of the word in the context of law. *Sharīʿa* as law was meant to be the governing basis of the Muslim community.[31] Knowledge sprung forth from this body of law to quench the desires and meet the needs of the community. This example of the etymology of *sharīʿa* again shows us both how water was conceived to be and how it actually did serve as a constitutional and transformative element of Muslim societies in Egypt and elsewhere.

Toward an Environmental History of the Ottoman Empire

Unlike most studies of the early modern Ottoman Empire or of Egypt, the arguments and descriptions of this book very much take their cues from and are largely grounded in the relatively young field of environmental history. Beginning in the 1970s, this field took shape first and foremost

[28] The common institution of the *sabīl-kuttāb* was another instance of this connection between water and knowledge in Ottoman Egypt. These often very ornate structures not only provided water but also served as schools and community gathering points.

[29] *Lisān al-ʿArab*, s.v. *sharaʿa*. Lane, *An Arabic-English Lexicon*, s.v. *sharīʿa*. For a longer discussion of the meanings of *sharīʿa* in various historical periods, see Frank Griffel's introduction to the following: Abbas Amanat and Frank Griffel, eds., *Shari'a: Islamic Law in the Contemporary Context* (Stanford: Stanford University Press, 2007), 1–19.

[30] Lane, *An Arabic-English Lexicon*, s.v *sharīʿa*. The Jordan River, for example, is called *nahr al-sharīʿa*. See also: *Lisān al-ʿArab*, s.v. *sharaʿa*.

[31] For more on the relationships between *sharīʿa* and water, see: Chibli Mallat, "The Quest for Water Use Principles: Reflections on *Sharīʿa* and Custom in the Middle East," in *Water in the Middle East: Legal, Political and Commercial Implications*, ed. J. A. Allan and Chibli Mallat, with Shai Wade and Jonathan Wild (London: I. B. Tauris Academic Studies, 1995), 127–37; William Lancaster and Fidelity Lancaster, *People, Land and Water in the Arab Middle East: Environments and Landscapes in the Bilâd ash-Shâm* (Amsterdam: Harwood Academic Publishers, 1999), 129–30.

in the United States and more specifically in the western United States. In the 1980s and even more so in the 1990s, the field came to include most regions of the world and most historical periods.[32] As J. R. McNeill observes, however, environmental history has yet to have a significant impact on the writing of Middle Eastern history. In an article published in 2003, McNeill writes, "In Arab and Ottoman historiography, almost all researchers remain indifferent to the possibilities of environmental history, although not for reasons of political ideology. Arab and Iranian historiography has its share of works on agriculture and irrigation, but few of them take the further step of considering these subjects in the contexts of environmental change generally."[33] More recently, Edmund Burke III similarly maintains that "the environment is rarely mentioned in most histories of the modern [we could add as well Ottoman] Middle East. It tends to hover on the margins of discussions of other, presumably more important topics, such as the onset of imperialism and nationalism and the region's political and economic transformation. Indeed, most histories of the modern [and again Ottoman] Middle East regard the environment as a source of backwardness, which only the application of modern science and technology can overcome."[34]

In the case of Egypt, many Egyptian historians frame their analyses with some statement about the role of the Nile and the flood in Egypt.[35] As valuable as those studies are, they do not, however, take their central unit of analysis to be the ecological or the environmental; nor does environmental change figure prominently in their arguments.[36] Thus,

32 For brief historiographical accounts of the emergence and development of environmental history as a discipline, see: Richard White, "Environmental History: The Development of a New Historical Field," *PHR* 54 (1985): 297–335; J. R. McNeill, "Observations on the Nature and Culture of Environmental History," *History and Theory* 42 (2003): 5–43; Donald Worster, "History as Natural History: An Essay on Theory and Method," *PHR* 53 (1984): 1–19; Worster, "World without Borders: The Internationalizing of Environmental History," *Environmental Review* 6 (1982): 8–13; Alfred W. Crosby, "The Past and Present of Environmental History," *AHR* 100 (1995): 1177–89.

33 McNeill, "Nature and Culture of Environmental History," 30.

34 Edmund Burke III, "The Transformation of the Middle Eastern Environment, 1500 B.C.E.–2000 C.E.," in *The Environment and World History*, ed. Edmund Burke III and Kenneth Pomeranz (Berkeley: University of California Press, 2009), 81.

35 See, e.g.: Cuno, *The Pasha's Peasants*, 17–18. For a description of the role of the Nile in Egyptian popular culture, see: Rushdī Ṣāliḥ, *Miṣr wa al-Fallāḥ wa al-Nīl* (Cairo: al-Hayʾa al-Miṣriyya al-ʿĀmma lil-Kitāb, 1975).

36 Two works are perhaps most noteworthy in this regard. First is the most sustained work of Egyptian history to center the Nile in its analysis: Amīn Sāmī's multivolume compendia of statistics and historical narratives about the river, its flood, agriculture, and more

we have precious few historical accounts of how Egyptian peasants and others actually lived with and used water. Likewise, most histories of Ottoman Egypt in English are of Cairo, the "second city of the Ottoman Empire."[37] Though very important and useful, these works clearly represent only a small fraction of the historical experience of most Egyptians during the centuries of Ottoman rule in Egypt, as the majority of Egyptians did not (and do not) live in Cairo. Most lived in small towns and villages spread throughout Egypt. Although, of course, one could (and should) write an environmental history of Cairo and other Middle Eastern cities, the environmental issues I focus on in this book get us outside of the city to the countryside, where most Egyptians lived.[38] My focus on the *rural* environmental history of Ottoman Egypt

general topics first published in 1928. Even this work, though, does not analyze the history of Egypt from an environmental perspective. Given, as outlined earlier, the relatively recent emergence of environmental history as a field of study, however, this should not be too surprising. See: Amīn Sāmī, *Taqwīm al-Nīl*.

The other multivolume work that must be mentioned here is Jamāl Ḥamdān's *Shakhṣiyyat Miṣr: Dirāsa fī ʿAbqariyyat al-Makān*, which advances a kind of nationalist environmental determinism in which the geography of the Nile Valley is the primary protagonist endowing Egypt with the potential for a sophisticated civilization and history. As Ḥamdān's subtitle clearly states, it is the genius (*al-ʿabqariyya*) of the physical space (*al-makān*) of Egypt – its geography, ecology, geology, and climate – that he sees as determining its history. See: Jamāl Ḥamdān, *Shakhṣiyyat Miṣr: Dirāsa fī ʿAbqariyyat al-Makān*, 4 vols. (Cairo: ʿĀlam al-Kutub, 1981–1984).

37 Suraiya Faroqhi, "Crisis and Change, 1590–1699," in *An Economic and Social History of the Ottoman Empire: Volume 2, 1600–1914*, ed. Halil İnalcık, with Donald Quataert (Cambridge: Cambridge University Press, 1994), 440. For histories of Ottoman Cairo, see, e.g.: Nelly Hanna, *Making Big Money in 1600: The Life and Times of Ismaʿil Abu Taqiyya, Egyptian Merchant* (Syracuse, NY: Syracuse University Press, 1998); Hanna, *In Praise of Books: A Cultural History of Cairo's Middle Class, Sixteenth to the Eighteenth Century* (Syracuse, NY: Syracuse University Press, 2003); Doris Behrens-Abouseif, *Egypt's Adjustment to Ottoman Rule: Institutions, Waqf, and Architecture in Cairo, 16th and 17th Centuries* (Leiden: E. J. Brill, 1994).

38 For a case concerning the cleaning and dredging of Cairo's major canal (known as *al-Khalīj*), see: Maḥkamat Miṣr al-Qadīma 90, pp. 386–87, case 1932 (13 Z 969/14 Aug. 1562). My thanks to Magdi Guirguis for bringing this case to my attention. On the course and general history of this canal, see: André Raymond, *Cairo: City of History*, trans. Willard Wood (Cairo: American University in Cairo Press, 2001), 123–27 and 221–24; Suʿād Māhir, "Majrī Miyāh Famm al-Khalīj," *EHR* 7 (1958): 134–57. The mouth of this canal was the site of the major annual festival commemorating the coming of the flood. On this and other festivals connected to the Nile, see: Huda Lutfi, "Coptic Festivals of the Nile: Aberrations of the Past?" in *The Mamluks in Egyptian Politics and Society*, ed. Thomas Philipp and Ulrich Haarmann (Cambridge: Cambridge University Press, 1998), 254–82; Paula Sanders, *Ritual, Politics, and the City in Fatimid Cairo* (Albany: State University of New York Press, 1994), 99–119; *ʿAwāʾid al-Miṣriyyīn ʿAnd Izdiyād al-Nīl*, DKM, Zakiyya 584.

is thus meant to be a corrective to the historiographical emphasis on Ottoman Cairo and on Ottoman cities more generally.

One of my goals is, then, to argue for an environmental perspective in the study of Egypt and the Ottoman Empire specifically, but also in the study of the Middle East as a whole. Whether in cities or towns, in forests or on mountains, in families or in courts of law, the natural world was and is everywhere. In a place such as the Middle East – a region, like most, in which the vast majority of people until quite recently lived very close to the land – a study of the environment, natural resources, or ecology is of particular usefulness. This book thus represents an effort to bridge the gap between the fields of Middle Eastern history and environmental history, two scholarly fields that have for the most part ignored each other.

In the field of environmental history, the Middle East is one of the few regions yet to receive serious scholarly attention. Global environmental histories and environmental histories of the Mediterranean have tended for the most part to sidestep the Middle East altogether. Without the requisite linguistic tools and historiographical background, most global environmental historians are not able to conduct primary research in the historical sources of the region. Such work is vital, however, if we are to complete our picture of the world's environmental past. The Middle East and North Africa have historically been a crucial zone of connection between, on the one hand, Europe and the Mediterranean world and, on the other hand, South Asia, the Indian Ocean, and sub-Saharan Africa. From various ice ages to the Cold War, global trends in trade, climate, and disease both affected and were affected by what was happening in the Middle East's many environments.

Moreover, the Middle East's millennia of documented history prove crucial to advancing our knowledge of environmental change. Unlike most regions of the globe, the Middle East offers environmental historians both the empirical depth and detail necessary to track changes to environments and landscapes over the *longue durée*. In the case of Egypt, we have a vast corpus of source material from the ancient period to the present, replete with ecological data and stories of environmental change. In this book, I use only a small part of this massive source base – the records of the Ottoman bureaucracy in Egypt during the long eighteenth century. These sources offer environmental historians enormous opportunities to examine, refine, and rethink climate change, water usage in arid climates, and numerous other environmental processes.

By the same token, despite some fleeting references, the environment nevertheless remains outside the analytical purview of most histories of the Ottoman Empire and of the Middle East more generally.[39] I offer

[39] More than a decade ago, Suraiya Faroqhi noted the reticence of Ottoman historians to take an environmental perspective toward the Empire. With reference to climatic change during the Little Ice Age, she writes, "Where Ottoman history is concerned, historians on both the left and the right of the political spectrum are reluctant for different reasons to consider the possibility of 'extra-social' factors impinging on society." Faroqhi, "Crisis and Change," 468. In this regard, see also: Suraiya Faroqhi, "Ottoman Peasants and Rural Life: The Historiography of the Twentieth Century," *AO* 18 (2000): 154–58. For some works on Ottoman environmental history, see: Wolf-Dieter Hütteroth, "Ecology of the Ottoman Lands," in *The Cambridge History of Turkey, Volume 3: The Later Ottoman Empire, 1603–1839*, ed. Suraiya N. Faroqhi (Cambridge: Cambridge University Press, 2006), 18–43; Alan Mikhail, "The Nature of Plague in Late Eighteenth-Century Egypt," *Bulletin of the History of Medicine* 82 (2008): 249–75; Ronald C. Jennings, "The Locust Problem in Cyprus," in *Studies on Ottoman Social History in the Sixteenth and Seventeenth Centuries: Women, Zimmis and Sharia Courts in Kayseri, Cyprus and Trabzon* (Istanbul: Isis Press, 1999), 471–516; Sam White, "Ecology, Climate, and Crisis in the Ottoman Near East" (Ph.D. diss., Columbia University, 2008); William Griswold, "Climatic Change: A Possible Factor in the Social Unrest of Seventeenth Century Anatolia" in *Humanist and Scholar: Essays in Honor of Andreas Tietze*, ed. Heath W. Lowry and Donald Quataert (Istanbul: Isis Press, 1993), 37–57; Bekir Koç, "Tanzimat Sonrası Hukuk Metinlerinde Çevre Bilincinin Arka-planı Olarak 'Av Yasak ve Sınırlılıkları' Üzerine Bazı Düşünceler," *Ankara Üniversitesi Osmanlı Tarihi Araştırma ve Uygulama Merkezi Dergisi*, no. 19 (2006): 271–81; Elizabeth Zachariadou, ed., *Natural Disasters in the Ottoman Empire* (Rethymnon: Crete University Press, 1999). On the environmental history of the wider Middle East, see, e.g.: Jeff Albert, Magnus Bernhardsson, and Roger Kenna, eds., *Transformations of Middle Eastern Natural Environments: Legacies and Lessons* (New Haven, CT: Yale School of Forestry and Environmental Sciences, 1998); Sharif Elmusa, ed., *Culture and the Natural Environment: Ancient and Modern Middle Eastern Texts* (Cairo: American University in Cairo Press, 2005); Richard W. Bulliet, *The Camel and the Wheel* (New York: Columbia University Press, 1990); Bulliet, *Cotton, Climate, and Camels in Early Islamic Iran: A Moment in World History* (New York: Columbia University Press, 2009); Faruk Tabak, *The Waning of the Mediterranean, 1550–1870: A Geohistorical Approach* (Baltimore: Johns Hopkins University Press, 2008); Peter Christensen, *The Decline of Iranshahr: Irrigation and Environments in the History of the Middle East, 500 B.C. to A.D. 1500* (Copenhagen: Museum Tusculanum Press, 1993); Diana K. Davis, *Resurrecting the Granary of Rome: Environmental History and French Colonial Expansion in North Africa* (Athens: Ohio University Press, 2007); Burke, "The Transformation of the Middle Eastern Environment"; J. M. Wagstaff, *The Evolution of Middle Eastern Landscapes: An Outline to A.D. 1840* (London: Croon Helm, 1985); William C. Brice, ed., *The Environmental History of the Near and Middle East Since the Last Ice Age* (London: Academic Press, 1978); Robert McC. Adams, *Land behind Baghdad: A History of Settlement on the Diyala Plains* (Chicago: University of Chicago Press, 1965). For studies of the environmental history of the Mediterranean that sometimes include considerations of the Ottoman Empire or the Middle East, see: J. R. McNeill, *The Mountains of the Mediterranean World: An Environmental History* (Cambridge: Cambridge University Press, 1992); J. V. Thirgood, *Man and the Mediterranean Forest: A History of Resource Depletion* (London: Academic Press, 1981); A. T. Grove and Oliver Rackham, *The Nature of Mediterranean Europe: An Ecological History* (New Haven, CT: Yale University

just three examples of the utility of an environmental perspective in the study of the Middle East – of the reasons why it deserves to be considered a category of analysis alongside gender, class, and culture.

First, the practice of environmental history is necessarily transterritorial. Water currents, disease vectors, and migratory animals do not recognize and are not (until perhaps very recently) controlled by politico-territorial demarcations of geographic space. The implication, then, is that to study such a topic, one must not take the space of the imperial province or the nation-state as a bounded and sealed unit of analysis. Although clearly the artificiality of these distinctions has long been recognized, environmental history as a method centers the crossing of borders and the transterritoriality of movement as foundational rather than innovative. There is really no way of getting around the fact that, for example, the Nile River flows through most of the countries of East Africa or that the Little Ice Age affected all of the Ottoman Empire (let alone much of the world) and not simply one or another province. Thus, to do a proper analysis of the ecology of the Nile or of the effects of climate change on the early modern Ottoman Empire, one would have to consider the impact of the river and of temperature in a multitude of places with all of their political, cultural, and geographic nuance and difference. Moreover, as I show with the examples of food and wood, one of the most productive ways of employing environmental history to get us past any static notion of territory or movement is to follow the trail of a particular set of natural resources. By making the history of a material object or a natural resource the focus of our inquiries, we can bypass many of the assumptions and preconditions already embedded in much historical work that accepts the territorial unity of the imperial province or the nation-state as a given.

Second, environmental history widens the lens of what is considered an acceptable historical actor. As we shall soon see, the story of irrigation and natural resource management in the early modern Ottoman Empire included peasants, water buffaloes, fleas, dirt, salt, microbes, trees, and various other agents that have traditionally escaped the consideration of historians of the Middle East. Of all those actors, peasants have clearly received the most attention.[40] A generation of scholars using

Press, 2001); J. Donald Hughes, *The Mediterranean: An Environmental History* (Santa Barbara, CA: ABC-CLIO, 2005); Robert Sallares, *The Ecology of the Ancient Greek World* (Ithaca, NY: Cornell University Press, 1991).

40 For general historiographical discussions of peasants in Ottoman studies, see: Suraiya Faroqhi, "Agriculture and Rural Life in the Ottoman Empire (ca 1500–1878) (A Report

court records from various locations throughout the Ottoman Middle East has given us a quite detailed picture of how peasants interacted and dealt with various state polities under whom they lived.[41] The bulk of these studies have attempted to insert peasants into larger frameworks – imperial systems of governance, global commercial networks, and wider religious or cultural communities. Building on those analyses, the environmental perspective I offer here shows how peasants were not merely participants in these larger webs of power but also often those actually pulling the reins of power. When it came to understanding the intimate details of a village's environment or of irrigation in rural Ottoman Egypt, only Egyptian peasants, who had lived on that land for generations and who knew its topographies and idiosyncrasies, could direct the management and usage of that land. They were the ecological experts on whom the Ottoman state had to rely.

Animals were clearly also key historical actors in the early modern agrarian economy of the Ottoman Empire. Water buffaloes, camels, oxen, donkeys, and various other domesticated ungulates transported heavy loads across vast distances, turned waterwheels, and dredged canals. Beyond the simple fact that until quite recently most of the world's population interacted with animals on an almost-daily basis, animals in eighteenth-century Ottoman Egypt were not only laborers but also significant forms of property, sources of food and heat, stores of economic value, hedges against crop failure, and symbols of status.

Much of the work of environmental history has gone toward arguing for the role of nature as a historical actor. In this book's story, this means that the water flowing through Egypt's canals, the dirt that clogged those waterways, and the salt that saturated much of the Egyptian delta's soil all have significant roles to play. They affected the history of Ottoman Egypt in ways as important as – and often more important than – imperial bureaucrats, Egyptian peasants, war, or the global price of commodities.

on Scholarly Literature Published between 1970 and 1985)" *NPT* 1 (1987): 3–34; Faroqhi, "Ottoman Peasants and Rural Life," 153–82. For further studies of Ottoman peasants during the early modern period, see: Faroqhi, "The Peasants of Saideli in the Late Sixteenth Century," *AO* 8 (1983): 215–50; Faroqhi, "Rural Society in Anatolia and the Balkans During the Sixteenth Century, I," *Turcica* 9 (1977): 161–95; Faroqhi, "Rural Society in Anatolia and the Balkans During the Sixteenth Century, II," *Turcica* 11 (1979): 103–53.

41 See, e.g.: Doumani, *Rediscovering Palestine*; Peirce, *Morality Tales*; Dror Ze'evi, *An Ottoman Century: The District of Jerusalem in the 1600s* (Albany: State University of New York Press, 1996).

Figure I.1. Water buffalo pulling waterwheel, late eighteenth century. Commission des Sciences et Arts d'Egypte, *État moderne II*, vol. 9 of *Description de l'Égypte, ou, recueil de observations et des recherches qui ont été faites en Égypte pendant l'éxpédition de l'armée française, publié par les ordres de Sa Majesté l'empereur Napoléon le Grand* (Paris: Imprimerie impériale, 1809–1828), 50 (plate 3).

Indeed, it would not be an overexaggeration to say that rainfall in the Ethiopian highlands that created the annual flood had more of an impact on Egypt's history than any political entity that controlled the territory over its millennia of documented history.

Finally, like other analytical frameworks, environmental history affords us the opportunity to revisit and reinterpret various historical events and phenomena. Perhaps the best-known example of this kind of environmental reinterpretation in Ottoman history is William Griswold's assertion that the Celâlî revolts at the end of the sixteenth and the beginning of the seventeenth centuries were largely the result of ecological pressures brought about by the period of global cooling known as the Little Ice Age.[42] The manifestations of this climatic change in central

[42] Griswold, "Climatic Change," 37–57; Griswold, *The Great Anatolian Rebellion, 1000–1020/1591–1611* (Berlin: Klaus Schwarz Verlag, 1983). For a recent sustained study of the effects of the Little Ice Age on the early modern Ottoman Empire, see: White, "Ecology, Climate, and Crisis." For White's discussion of the Little Ice Age and the Celâlî revolts, see: ibid., 231–67. On the potentials, problems, and methodologies of studying the effects of climatic change, see: Robert I. Rotberg and Theodore K. Rabb, eds., *Climate and History: Studies in Interdisciplinary History* (Princeton, NJ: Princeton University Press,

Anatolia – drought, famine, plagues of livestock and people, and ultimately increasing rates of mortality among Ottoman peasants – led to the violence and banditry that eventually coalesced into an organized rebellion against the Ottoman state. Thus, the causes of the Celâlî revolts are not simply to be found in the realms of the economic or the political; rather, we must also account for the crucial role of climate change in these historical events.

Why Irrigation?

Egypt is a desert with a river running through it. Any environmental history of rural Egypt must thus give water management priority of place. But what can a history of irrigation in Ottoman Egypt offer Ottoman and Egyptian historians? An initial answer to this question is that an environmental history of irrigation, water usage, timber, food cultivation, and plague in Ottoman Egypt allows us to write a fuller history of the Ottoman state as a whole. Indeed, irrigation is a particularly good lens through which to view relations between the peasants of the Empire's provinces and the Ottoman imperial bureaucracy. Irrigation was a process grounded in the very local environments of thousands of villages throughout Egypt and, at the same time, a process with wide imperial implications. The destruction of one village's dam had the potential to lead to food shortages for the people of Istanbul, Mecca, and elsewhere. Because Egypt was the largest food-producing province of the Empire, the Ottoman state paid particular attention to irrigation in its countryside.

The study of irrigation and of environment more generally thus pushes us past two other clichés. In Ottoman studies, the paradigm of center and periphery and the continuing fascination with debates over the supposed decline of the Empire linger as kinds of historiographical shadows over much of the scholarship produced on the early modern period.

Briefly put, the model of center and periphery in the Ottoman Empire asserts that the imperial capital of Istanbul drew to itself grains, cash, conscripts, and raw materials from the rest of the Empire.[43] In this

1981); T. M. L. Wigley, M. J. Ingram, and G. Farmer, *Climate and History: Studies in Past Climates and Their Impact on Man* (Cambridge: Cambridge University Press, 1981); Emmanuel Le Roy Ladurie, *Times of Feast, Times of Famine: A History of Climate since the Year 1000*, trans. Barbara Bray (Garden City, NY: Doubleday, 1971).

43 For classical accounts of this model, see: Halil İnalcık, "Centralization and Decentralization in Ottoman Administration," in *Studies in Eighteenth Century Islamic History*,

model, the various provinces of the Empire are seen as a kind of collective hinterland serving the center. In a recent study, Karen Barkey uses a hub-and-spoke metaphor to describe this representation of the Ottoman Empire, in which "the central state negotiates and maintains more or less distinct compacts between itself and the various segments of this polity."[44] According to the traditional narrative, the Empire was not interested in inculcating anything akin to "an Ottoman identity" or culture in its many territories.[45] They were sources of food and labor and nothing more. In the same regard, various nationalist traditions of formerly Ottoman provinces paint the period of Ottoman rule as one of political and economic stagnation, of foreign colonial rule, and of general imperial despotism.[46] Thus, for example, many nationalist writers claim that the essential kernel of Egyptian or Tunisian or Bulgarian culture and society was untouched by centuries of imperial Ottoman rule, because the Ottomans only took natural and economic resources from these areas without contributing anything cultural or material of their own. We have very few studies, therefore, that examine relationships either between various "peripheries" or between other "centers" in the Empire apart from Istanbul.

As this book shows, by contrast, any notion of a set of spokes radiating out from Istanbul with no mutual interaction of their own is an incorrect characterization of the Ottoman Empire. There were rather

ed. Thomas Naff and Roger Owen (Carbondale: Southern Illinois University Press, 1977), 27–52; Şerif Mardin, "Center-Periphery Relations: A Key to Turkish Politics," *Daedalus* 102 (1973): 169–91; Albert Howe Lybyer, *The Government of the Ottoman Empire in the Time of Suleiman the Magnificent* (Cambridge, MA: Harvard University Press, 1913). For some recent critiques of this model, see: Dina Rizk Khoury, *State and Provincial Society in the Ottoman Empire: Mosul, 1540–1834* (Cambridge: Cambridge University Press, 1997); Peirce, *Morality Tales.* See also the following very useful historiographical essay: Dina Rizk Khoury, "The Ottoman Centre versus Provincial Power-Holders: An Analysis of the Historiography," in *The Cambridge History of Turkey, Volume 3: The Later Ottoman Empire, 1603–1839*, ed. Suraiya N. Faroqhi (Cambridge: Cambridge University Press, 2006), 135–56.

44 Karen Barkey, *Empire of Difference: The Ottomans in Comparative Perspective* (Cambridge: Cambridge University Press, 2008), 9.

45 For a study that refutes this thesis through a thorough examination of Ottoman cultural influence and politics in nineteenth-century Egypt, see: Ekmeleddin İhsanoğlu, *Mısır'da Türkler ve Kültürel Mirasları: Mehmed Ali Paşa'dan Günümüze Basılı Türk Kültürü Bibliyografyası ve Bir Değerlendirme* (Istanbul: İslam Tarih, Sanat, ve Kültür Araştırma Merkezi, 2006).

46 For the Egyptian case, see: ʿAbd al-Raḥīm, *al-Rīf al-Miṣrī*; ʿAbd al-Raḥman al-Rāfʿī, *ʿAṣr Muḥammad ʿAlī* (Cairo: Dār al-Maʿārif, 1989).

multiple "centers" and multiple "peripheries" in the Ottoman Empire. Indeed, Egypt itself functioned contemporaneously as both a center and a periphery. It moved food to the Hijaz for the annual pilgrimage, was part of commercial networks stretching across North Africa and the Red Sea that operated largely independent of Istanbul, and served to direct the Ottoman capital about the management of irrigation works in the Egyptian countryside. At the same time, Egypt was the Empire's most lucrative province. It sent food and money to Istanbul, was politically under the suzerainty of the Ottoman state, and operated in the context of an early modern Ottoman imperial system of natural resource balance. Beyond the realm of the environmental, Egypt was also, to take the example of just one region, greatly influenced intellectually and commercially by its relations with North Africa.[47] By tracing the connections created across the Ottoman world by Egypt's capacity to produce food, its shortages of wood, and its complex irrigation network, we come to see the Ottoman Empire as a polity in which threads of power, influence, and the sharing of resources stretched from the smallest villages to the largest cities, from North Africa to Europe, and from rural peasants to those in the halls of the imperial palace.[48]

[47] On the various impacts of North Africans in Ottoman Egypt, see: ʿAbd al-Raḥīm ʿAbd al-Raḥman ʿAbd al-Raḥīm, *Wathāʾiq al-Maḥākim al-Sharʿiyya al-Miṣriyya ʿan al-Jāliya al-Maghāribiyya ibbāna al-ʿAṣr al-ʿUthmānī*, ed. and intro. ʿAbd al-Jalīl al-Tamīmī (Zaghwān, Tunisia: Markaz al-Dirāsāt wa al-Buḥūth al-ʿUthmāniyya wa al-Mūrīskiyya wa al-Tawthīq wa al-Maʿlūmāt, 1992); ʿAbd al-Raḥīm, *al-Maghāriba fī Miṣr fī al-ʿAṣr al-ʿUthmānī (1517–1798): Dirāsa fī Taʾthīr al-Jāliya al-Maghāribiyya min Khilāl Wathāʾiq al-Maḥākim al-Sharʿiyya al-Miṣriyya* (Tunis: al-Majalla al-Tārīkhiyya al-Maghribiyya, 1982); Ḥusām Muḥammad ʿAbd al-Muʿṭī, "al-Buyūt al-Tijāriyya al-Maghribiyya fī Miṣr fī al-ʿAṣr al-ʿUthmānī" (Ph.D. diss., Manṣūra University, 2002); ʿAbd al-Muʿṭī, "Riwāq al-Maghāriba fī al-Jāmiʿ al-Azhar fī al-ʿAṣr al-ʿUthmānī," *al-Rūznāma: al-Ḥauliyya al-Miṣriyya lil-Wathāʾiq* 3 (2005): 165–204; Husam Muhammad Abdul Muʿti, "The Fez Merchants in Eighteenth-Century Cairo," trans. Sawsan al-Baqli, in *Society and Economy in Egypt and the Eastern Mediterranean, 1600–1900: Essays in Honor of André Raymond*, ed. Nelly Hanna and Raouf Abbas (Cairo: American University in Cairo Press, 2005), 117–41; Khaled el-Rouayheb, "Was There a Revival of Logical Studies in Eighteenth-Century Egypt?" *Die Welt des Islams* 45 (2005): 1–19. See also: ʿAbd Allāh Muḥammad ʿAzabāwī, "al-ʿAlāqāt al-ʿUthmāniyya-al-Maghribiyya fī ʿAhd Kullin min Maulāya Muḥammad (1757–1790) wa Ibnihi Yazīd (1790–1792)," *EHR* 30–31 (1983–1984): 379–413.

[48] This is part of an effort to bring Ottoman historiography more in line with that of other early modern and modern empires, in which simple center-periphery models no longer maintain much traction. It would be impossible, for instance, to tell the story of modern Britain or early modern Spain without recognizing the complex and mutually determinative relationships between component parts of the British and Spanish empires.

The second major historiographical debate in early modern Ottoman studies has been that over decline versus decentralization.[49] The traditional narrative of Ottoman history is that the Empire reached its peak of geographical expanse, legal and cultural production, and military prowess in the fifteenth and sixteenth centuries.[50] After a series of military defeats – this narrative continues – the Empire turned in on itself beginning in the seventeenth century, becoming increasingly insular and oppressive and suffering at the hands of a growing world economy. As the Empire declined over the course of the eighteenth century, it found itself vulnerable to European colonial ventures in the nineteenth century.

I argue that this debate over the supposed decline of the Empire is largely a historiographical red herring. Beyond the fact that the decline of the Empire, beginning with the death of Süleyman in 1566, took nearly 350 years to bring the Empire to its final end, the back and forth between advocates and opponents of the decline thesis has operated until now at a sort of metadiscursive level, with little specific historical analysis of the period of supposed decline, particularly the seventeenth and eighteenth centuries. What falls between the cracks of decline versus antidecline – and indeed between center and periphery as well – is any sense of what is going on, on the ground, in the eighteenth century. This book is thus a modest attempt to fill in some of this empty historical space by examining how Egyptian peasants and Ottoman bureaucrats stationed in Egypt dealt with the problems of irrigation, food production, disease, timber, and other environmental phenomena. By attempting to see what the Ottoman Empire looked like from the perspective of peasants in the Empire's most lucrative province, we can break free from

49 Decentralization has alternatively been termed devolution of power or – more broadly and nondescriptly – antidecline.

50 The classical accounts of Ottoman decline are the following: Bernard Lewis, *The Emergence of Modern Turkey* (London: Oxford University Press, 1962); Lewis, "Some Reflections on the Decline of the Ottoman Empire," *Studia Islamica* 9 (1958): 111–27; İnalcık, "Centralization and Decentralization." The critiques are many. One of the earliest and still best is the following: Mehmed Genç, "Osmanlı Maliyesinde Malikane Sistemi," in *Türkiye İktisat Tarihi Semineri Metinler/Tartışmalar*, ed. Osman Okyar (Ankara: Hacıtepe Üniversitesi Yayınları, 1975), 231–96. See also: Cemal Kafadar, "The Question of Ottoman Decline," *Harvard Middle Eastern and Islamic Review* 4 (1997–98): 30–75. For recent critiques and reviews of the literature of decline, see: Donald Quataert, "Ottoman History Writing and Changing Attitudes towards the Notion of 'Decline,'" *History Compass* 1 (2003): 1–9; Dana Sajdi, "Decline, Its Discontents and Ottoman Cultural History: By Way of Introduction," in *Ottoman Tulips, Ottoman Coffee: Leisure and Lifestyle in the Eighteenth Century*, ed. Dana Sajdi (London: Tauris Academic Studies, 2007), 1–40.

vague and ungrounded debates over essentialist and overarching historical processes like "decline."

This view of the Ottoman Empire through the eyes of Egyptian peasants, however, allows us to see different kinds of declines at play in the long eighteenth century. There are two interrelated declines I trace in this book. The first is a decline in the lives and well-being of Egyptian peasants. As Egypt moved from its position in an early modern Ottoman imperial system of natural resource management to a more independently run Egyptian bureaucracy centered in Cairo – in short, a move from the Ottoman Empire to an Egyptian state – peasants became more and more disconnected from their lands, canals, and crops and were increasingly treated as laboring units to be managed and manipulated by the state. As a result of this process – and this is the second decline I follow in this book – there was also a steady erosion in the sustainable uses of the Egyptian rural environment over the same period. Like peasants, crops and natural resources came to be seen as commodities to be harnessed and maximized by a "productive" early-nineteenth-century state administration. The capitalist impulse driving such transitions in the use of peoples and natural resources is a familiar one to environmental historians, who have come to identify it as part of the declensionist narrative of environmental history. In an early casting of this formulation, William Cronon writes that "capitalism and environmental degradation went hand in hand.... The transition to capitalism [and in the case of Ottoman Egypt, we could add "the transition to a centralized Egyptian bureaucracy"] alienated the products of the land as much as the products of human labor, and so transformed natural communities as profoundly as it did human ones."[51] Thus, in the case of rural Ottoman Egypt, as elsewhere, when peasants were no longer the primary stewards of the land, both they and the rural environments they called home saw a downturn in their fortunes.

[51] William Cronon, *Changes in the Land: Indians, Colonists, and the Ecology of New England*, rev. ed. (New York: Hill and Wang, 2003), 161 and 170. For a very useful sustained treatment of the declensionist narrative in environmental history, see also: Cronon, "A Place for Stories: Nature, History, and Narrative," *Journal of American History* 78 (1992): 1347–76. On the subject of the transition to a capitalist economy in Egypt, see: Gran, *Islamic Roots of Capitalism*; Gran, "Late-Eighteenth – Early-Nineteenth-Century Egypt: Merchant Capitalism or Modern Capitalism?" in *The Ottoman Empire and the World-Economy*, ed. Huri İslamoğlu-İnan, 27–41; E. R. J. Owen, *Cotton and the Egyptian Economy, 1820–1914* (Oxford, UK: Clarendon Press, 1969); Cuno, *The Pasha's Peasants*; Alan R. Richards, "Primitive Accumulation in Egypt, 1798–1882," in *The Ottoman Empire and the World-Economy*, ed. Huri İslamoğlu-İnan, 203–43.

Sources

My efforts to use an environmental approach to challenge and rework debates over center and periphery relations, decline versus antidecline, and other such historiographical questions in the early modern Ottoman Empire demand an imaginative and rigorous use of sources. Again, because irrigation was both a highly local process grounded in the Egyptian countryside and one with wide imperial implications, it proves a particularly good lens through which to view relations between Egypt and the rest of the Ottoman Empire. Thus, the Arabic and Ottoman Turkish sources used in this study reflect both the local and the imperial registers of irrigation in the Ottoman Empire's most lucrative province. The vast majority of the sources are archival documents from both the Egyptian National Archives in Cairo (Dār al-Wathāʾiq al-Qawmiyya), a storehouse of documentation about Egypt from roughly the thirteenth to the twentieth centuries, and from the Prime Ministry's Ottoman Archive in Istanbul (Başbakanlık Osmanlı Arşivi), the primary repository for the documents of the central Ottoman bureaucracy from the fifteenth to the twentieth centuries.[52]

[52] On the use of both these archives for the history of Ottoman Egypt, see: Stanford J. Shaw, "Cairo's Archives and the History of Ottoman Egypt," *Middle East Institute Report on Current Research* (1956): 59–72; Shaw, "The Ottoman Archives as a Source for Egyptian History," *Journal of the American Oriental Society* 83 (1962): 447–52.

I have done my best to cite these archival documents in such a way as to give the maximum amount of information in as efficient a manner as possible. The driving force behind my citation method is to allow the reader to be able to find and reaccess the materials I have used. That said, there are certain difficulties one faces when citing many of the archival documents used in this study. In the case of court records and other documents from the Egyptian National Archives, I have given the name of the archival unit, followed by the number of the register used from that unit, the page and case numbers (if available), and the date (again, if available). In many cases, the pages of registers are not numbered at all or are numbered twice using different systems. The same holds for individual cases. Often consecutive cases and pages have the same number. Bound registers often contain groups of pages that – on the basis of the hand or the dates of the documents – clearly did not belong to the same original register. Dates are often incomplete. In a word, a great many problems of archival labeling and classification are met when using and referencing the documentary wealth of this archive.

In the case of the Prime Ministry's Ottoman Archive, the most common problem is one of dating. Often the date of a document provided in the catalog (a luxury usually not available in the Egyptian National Archives) does not match the date on the document itself, or the document does not contain a date at all. In the former case, I give precedence to the date cited in the document itself. In the latter case, I note in my citation the date given in the catalog with a parenthetical statement alerting the reader

In the former archive, I used mostly the records of various Islamic courts spread throughout the Egyptian countryside.[53] I chose rural courts from different geographic and demographic regions in Egypt – chiefly from the Delta and Upper Egypt – to produce a representative sampling of the kinds of environmental issues surrounding irrigation faced by Egyptian peasants and Ottoman bureaucrats in the long eighteenth century.[54] The court was the most immediate representative of the Ottoman state in rural Egypt. It was here that Egyptians came to register marriages, divorces, and inheritances; where property was bought and sold; and where disputes came to be adjudicated. The bulk of the registers are filled with Arabic court cases about these and various other issues. They also contain copies of imperial orders and firmans sent from the Ottoman bureaucracy of Egypt in Cairo and Istanbul to the courts. The orders are written in Ottoman Turkish and are usually found at the back of registers. They represent responses to petitions sent by local Egyptians to the Ottoman state about various issues of imperial implication. Irrigation was a common subject of these orders. And one often finds in them comments that petitions or firmans were translated from Ottoman Turkish or Arabic into the other language.[55] Imperial bureaucrats, state institutions, and indeed many Egyptian imperial subjects moved quite fluidly between Arabic and some form of Ottoman Turkish.[56]

that there is no internal evidence in the document itself for this date (it is not clear in these cases how the date of the document was determined). For documents from the Topkapı Palace Museum Archive, if no date is given in my citation, the reader should assume that there is no internal reference in the document to a date. More generally, I have cited dates of documents as completely as possible given the information available in the document itself. Again, my goal in all these citations is to provide as much information as possible to allow researchers to return to the documents.

53 On the utility of these court records for the history of Ottoman Egypt, see: ʿAbd al-Wudūd Yūsuf, "Sijillāt al-Maḥākim al-Sharʿiyya ka-Maṣdar Asāsī li-Tārīkh al-ʿArab fī al-ʿAṣr al-ʿUthmānī," *EHR* 19 (1972): 325–35.

54 Though rarely covering the eighteenth century, see the following studies of the geography, cultural ecology, and political economy of regions of Egypt not covered in this book: Nawāl Fuʾād Ḥāmid, "Muḥāfaẓat al-Sharqiyya: Dirāsa fī Jughrāfiyyat al-Rīf" (Ph.D. diss., Zaqāzīq University, 1987); Mājida Muḥammad Aḥmad Jumʿa, "Madīnat al-Aqṣur: Dirāsa Jughrāfiyya" (M.A. thesis, ʿAyn Shams University, 1983); Rasmī Dummar Muḥammad Dunyā, "Madīnat Ṭanṭā: Dirāsa fī Jughrāfiyyat al-Mudun" (Ph.D. diss., ʿAyn Shams University, 1982); ʿĪsā ʿAlī Ibrāhīm, "Muḥāfaẓat Aswān: Dirāsa fī Jughrāfiyyat al-Tanmiyya al-Iqtiṣādiyya" (Ph.D. diss., Alexandria University, 1984).

55 For a seventeenth-century Ottoman perspective on Arabic and other languages, see: Robert Dankoff, "The Languages of the World According to Evliya Çelebi," *JTS* 13 (1989): 23–32.

56 For a discussion of Ottoman Turkish, Arabic, and language usage more generally in the Arab provinces of the Ottoman Empire, see: Jane Hathaway, with contributions by

The original versions of these imperial orders recorded in the courts of Ottoman Egypt are to be found in the central Ottoman archive in Istanbul. In fortunate instances, one finds a copy of the original petition of an Egyptian peasant registered in a rural court and now housed in the Egyptian National Archives, the answer to this petition recorded in an archival unit known as Mühimme-i Mısır housed in Istanbul, and the copy of this Ottoman response recorded in the back of the register of the original court of petition in Egypt. The archival unit Mühimme-i Mısır contains records of thousands of orders sent to Egypt from Istanbul from the end of the seventeenth century to the middle of the nineteenth. These records prove a treasure trove for the historian wanting to trace connections between Egypt and the rest of the Ottoman Empire. Egypt is the only province of the Empire with its own separate collection of *mühimmeler* – further commentary on the centrality and significance of Egypt in the function of the entire imperial bureaucracy. I also use various other documents from the Prime Ministry's Ottoman Archive in various other archival units and from the Topkapı Palace Museum Archive (Topkapı Sarayı Müzesi Arşivi) that deal with similar issues about Egypt and other provinces.

The vast majority of histories of Egypt during the Ottoman period use only one or the other of these two archives. My deliberate use of both source bases is thus meant to be a methodological contribution to how the history of Ottoman Egypt – and indeed that of other Ottoman provinces as well – is researched and written. The Egyptian National Archives – and specifically the court records it houses – offer the social and environmental historian a wealth of information about Egyptian society, culture, and ecology.[57] Use of only these records, however, and of only the Arabic cases they contain, paints just one part of the story of Egypt in this period. Too often these histories give a picture of Egypt with little or no context of a wider Ottoman and early modern world. One gets the sense when reading such works that Egypt was an independent protonationalist entity set apart from any larger imperial Ottoman world. This would be akin to writing the history of colonial America from local sources as if London or the British Empire did not exist.

Karl K. Barbir, *The Arab Lands under Ottoman Rule, 1516–1800* (Harlow, UK: Pearson Education, 2008), 231–32.

57 Studies based on this archive include the following: André Raymond, *Artisans et commerçants au Caire au XVIIIe siècle*, 2 vols. (Damascus: Institut français de Damas, 1973); Khaled Fahmy, *All the Pasha's Men: Mehmed Ali, His Army and the Making of Modern Egypt* (Cambridge: Cambridge University Press, 1997); ʿAbd al-Raḥīm, *al-Rīf al-Miṣrī*; Behrens-Abouseif, *Egypt's Adjustment to Ottoman Rule.*

By the same token, histories of Ottoman Egypt based solely on the records of the central Ottoman bureaucracy give us only the other side of the story. Usually ascribing to the paradigm of center and periphery described earlier, these histories posit Egypt as one in a list of imperial provinces that provided Istanbul with grains and cash. Goods, people, and knowledge in these works move in one direction, from Egypt to Istanbul. Again, only by integrating these two archival bodies do the relationships and connections between Egypt and the rest of the Empire come to the fore.

Moreover, my use of both Ottoman imperial records and those of local institutions like the court in Egypt is part of the effort to imagine the Empire beyond current national borders and beyond the parameters of center and periphery. This more holistic view of early modern empire in the Muslim world takes into account the multiple actors, territories, and forces that made the Ottoman Empire function. Rather than seeing the Empire as a series of piecemeal provinces with little mutual interaction (as peripheries around one center), I show how irrigation, food production, disease, and a lack of domestic timber supplies intimately connected Egypt not only to Istanbul but also to the Hijaz, Greater Syria, Anatolia, and North Africa. Moreover, the mass of empirical data that forms the core of my analysis shows that any simplistic notion of Ottoman decline or antidecline lacks the explanatory force necessary to capture the complexities of the early modern period.

Beyond Wittfogel

In the following pages, I analyze how the presence of a diffuse and elaborate irrigation system in Egypt did indeed demand a large amount of administrative involvement on the part of the Ottoman state in the province. It did not, however, entail despotism along the lines of the thesis advanced some years ago by Karl Wittfogel.[58] Wittfogel's notion of Oriental despotism has been met by the most stringent of critiques.[59] The

[58] Wittfogel's seminal work is the following: Karl A. Wittfogel, *Oriental Despotism: A Comparative Study of Total Power* (New Haven, CT: Yale University Press, 1957). For a more abbreviated form of his main arguments, see: Wittfogel, "The Hydraulic Civilizations," in *Man's Role in Changing the Face of the Earth*, ed. William L. Thomas Jr. (Chicago: University of Chicago Press, 1956), 152–64.

[59] For some of the many critiques of Wittfogel's work, see: Arthur Maass and Raymond L. Anderson, *... And the Desert Shall Rejoice: Conflict, Growth, and Justice in Arid Environments* (Cambridge: Massachusetts Institute of Technology Press, 1978); Rene Millon, Clara Hall, and May Diaz, "Conflict in the Modern Teotihuacan Irrigation System," *Comparative Studies in Society and History* 4 (1962): 494–524; Robert C. Hunt and Eva Hunt, "Canal

counterexamples to and omissions in his work are many, and, what is more, empirically the historical data simply do not bear out his arguments.[60] Arnold Toynbee, for instance, begins his review of Wittfogel's magnum opus with the relatively favorable description of it as "a queer book by a fine scholar" and ends his review with the rather more direct statement that the book is "something of an aberration and still more of a menace."[61] As with many other things, highly complex and coordinated systems of irrigation *can* lead to authoritarian forms of government, but this – as I show in this book – is by no means a foregone conclusion.

Through his study of irrigation in the American West, Donald Worster has done more than any other single environmental historian to salvage some form of Wittfogelian analysis.[62] Mindful of its shortcomings and excesses, Worster is nevertheless keen to identify in Wittfogel's work the

Irrigation and Local Social Organization," *Current Anthropology* 17 (1976): 389–98; Susan H. Lees, "On Irrigation and the Conflict Myth," *Current Anthropology* 30 (1989): 343–44. For critiques focused on China, one of Wittfogel's key case studies, see: Mark Elvin, *The Retreat of the Elephants: An Environmental History of China* (New Haven, CT: Yale University Press, 2004), 106 and 117–18; Peter C. Perdue, *China Marches West: The Qing Conquest of Central Eurasia* (Cambridge, MA: Harvard University Press, 2005), 15; Lillian M. Li, *Fighting Famine in North China: State, Market, and Environmental Decline, 1690s–1990s* (Stanford, CA: Stanford University Press, 2007), 40–41. For the specific case of Egypt, one of the most recent critiques is the following: Stuart J. Borsch, *The Black Death in Egypt and England: A Comparative Study* (Austin: University of Texas Press, 2005), 13–23.

60 National socialist Germany, California, and czarist and communist Russia are European and American examples of hydraulic societies that are absent from Wittfogel's analysis – this despite the fact that, as a German émigré to the western United States, Wittfogel knew the former two quite intimately. On the German and Russian examples as instances of hydraulic societies and Wittfogel's choice to ignore them, see: Arnold Toynbee, "Review of *Oriental Despotism: A Comparative Study of Total Power* by Karl A. Wittfogel," *American Political Science Review* 52 (1958): 195–98. On the applicability of Wittfogel's thesis to California, see: Donald Worster, "Hydraulic Society in California: An Ecological Interpretation," *Agricultural History* 56 (1982): 503–15. About California, Worster writes, "Irrigation would do little to promote democracy . . . [;] instead it was capable of creating Leviathan in the desert" (ibid., 507).

61 Toynbee, "Review of *Oriental Despotism*," 195 and 198. Apart from this review of Wittfogel's book, Arnold Toynbee intersects with this book in a very different way. He was the master's supervisor at London University of the so-called father of modern historical scholarship in Egypt, Shafīq Ghurbāl. For more on Toynbee's influence on Ghurbāl's school of Egyptian historiography, see: Yoav Di-Capua, "The Thought and Practice of Modern Egyptian Historiography, 1890–1970" (Ph.D. diss., Princeton University, 2004), 156–86. For an account of Toynbee's visit to Egypt after Ghurbāl's death, see: Muḥammad Anīs, "Ziyārat al-Mu'arrikh Arnūld Tawīnbī lil-Jumhūriyya al-ʿArabiyya al-Muttaḥida," *EHR* 9–10 (1960–1962): 267–68.

62 Donald Worster, *Rivers of Empire: Water, Aridity, and the Growth of the American West* (Oxford: Oxford University Press, 1992).

"ecological question... that will place human society firmly in, rather than beyond or above, nature."[63] In Wittfogel's "link between water and power," Worster sees the most profound of questions facing the environmental historian: "how, in the remaking of nature, do we remake ourselves?"[64] These connections between the natural and the social are what interest me in Wittfogel's writings and what drive my study of irrigation and environment in Ottoman Egypt. To use the words of another American environmental historian, Richard White, "We cannot understand human history without natural history and we cannot understand natural history without human history."[65]

Contrary to Wittfogel's model, I show here how the complex system of irrigation in Ottoman Egypt that, among other things, brought wood from Anatolia to grow and move food to Mecca and Istanbul was characterized above all by a sort of coordinated localism. That is, the local experience and knowledge of Egyptian peasants came to inform the Ottoman bureaucracy's management of water resources in rural Egypt. Thus, through a variety of mechanisms connecting the smallest and most remote Egyptian villages to the imperial capital and to areas all over the Empire, Egyptian peasants were able to shape Ottoman rule in Egypt and elsewhere. This peasant involvement in empire was an integral aspect of the function of the Ottoman Empire in Egypt and of other early modern empires elsewhere.

In upholding peasant knowledge and expertise as the gold standard in dealing with the environment, I do not mean either to uncritically admire peasants, the local, the rural, and the customary or to naively and even dangerously romanticize the relationship between Egyptian peasants and the Ottoman Empire. I am, in other words, not arguing for either the superiority of local customary knowledge and practice or the primacy of imperial power in the early modern Ottoman system of natural resource management. Rather – and in contrast to what followed

63 Worster, "History as Natural History," 6.

64 Worster, *Rivers of Empire*, 29–30. For very useful anthropological treatments of water and power in India, see: Akhil Gupta, *Postcolonial Developments: Agriculture in the Making of Modern India* (Durham, NC: Duke University Press, 1998), 204–10 and 265–85; Anand Sankar Pandian, "Landscapes of Redemption: Cultivating Heart and Soil in South India" (Ph.D. diss., University of California, Berkeley, 2004), 309–81.

65 Richard White, *The Organic Machine: The Remaking of the Columbia River* (New York: Hill and Wang, 1995), ix. Similarly, William Cronon writes, "Our project must be to locate a nature which is within rather than without history, for only by so doing can we find human communities which are inside rather than outside nature." Cronon, *Changes in the Land*, 15.

in the nineteenth century – I see Egyptian peasants and representatives of the early modern Ottoman Empire participating in and constituting a unified system of natural resource use and management. Peasant understandings of rural environments thus did not reflect some primitive, idyllic state of nature. They were in Ottoman Egypt, as in all contexts, infused materially and ethically with the economic and political demands, needs, and desires of the polity and society around them. At the same time, however, the imperial history of the Ottoman Empire in Egypt and throughout its realms cannot be understood without some accounting for the influence of local practice and knowledge in the function of the state. In James C. Scott's formulation, "formal schemes of order are untenable without some elements of practical knowledge that they tend to dismiss."[66] Thus, before Egypt began to pull away from the Ottoman Empire to become a kind of empire in its own right, the province was integral to an Ottoman system that cultivated and instrumentalized peasant knowledge, experience, and expertise.

In the first three chapters of this book, I sketch in some detail the workings of this early modern system of Ottoman natural resource management. In that system, Egyptian peasants operated and indeed used the Ottoman bureaucracy to irrigate soil to grow food that fed thousands across the Empire. Because water was the connection tying Egyptian peasants to the Empire, I show in Chapter 1 how peasants and Ottoman bureaucrats in Egypt negotiated over and managed Egypt's water resources and how water was the principal engine of environmental change in Ottoman Egypt. Chapters 2 and 3 examine two sides of the Ottoman imperial system of natural resource management, coordination, use, and transport in Egypt. Connections that moved food out of Egypt to Mecca, Istanbul, and other parts of the Empire (Chapter 2) also served to bring much-needed wood supplies to Egypt (Chapter 3). My main argument in the first three chapters is that Egyptian peasants' knowledge of and experience with local environments determined that they – and not imperial Ottoman bureaucrats – were the main protagonists in the management of water resources, food cultivation, and timber in the Egyptian countryside.

In the final three chapters, I examine how this system of coordinated localism in imperial natural resource balance, management, and movement eroded toward the end of the eighteenth century as the growing

[66] James C. Scott, *Seeing Like a State: How Certain Schemes to Improve the Human Condition Have Failed* (New Haven, CT: Yale University Press, 1998), 7.

Egyptian bureaucracy undertook larger and larger irrigation repair jobs and other public works projects that resulted in more sophisticated bureaucratic methods and tighter means of social control. Whereas earlier in the eighteenth century, dozens of Egyptian peasants worked for a few days to repair irrigation works that fed water directly to their own fields, at the end of this period, they were forcibly moved from their villages by the hundreds to work on larger and more central irrigation works. Likewise, plague in the same period transformed from a known and constructive social and environmental phenomenon to an external and destructive force to be quarantined. Thus, changes in labor (Chapter 4) and the management of plague (Chapter 5) revamped Egyptians' interactions with their environments, with water, and with the Ottoman Empire. The power of the local was thus colonized by a growing Ottoman-Egyptian centralizing state, peasant laborers were forcibly removed from their local communities, and the sick were taken from their families. In the final chapter, I focus on the reconstruction of the Maḥmūdiyya Canal between the Nile and Alexandria in the first quarter of the nineteenth century. Requiring more than three hundred thousand peasant laborers, the canal was the end both of local control over irrigation works and of the eighteenth-century imperial system of natural resource management I detail in the first half of the book. All of this was replaced by the autocratic regime of Mehmet ʿAli, which represented the culmination of the forces of authoritarianism and growing state power embodied in the stories of labor and plague.

The transition from an empire to a state in Egypt was thus a very violent one. Most nationalist histories of this change in political power in various parts of the Ottoman Empire and elsewhere see this transformation as resulting in an improvement in the lives of the new states' subjects. If we are being generous, we could say that in Egypt (and I would argue elsewhere as well), these "certain schemes to improve the human condition" did most certainly fail to improve the lives of those affected.[67] If we are less charitable, but perhaps more historically accurate, then we might say that Mehmet ʿAli's government in the early nineteenth century had no intention at all to "improve the human condition"; rather, his interests were in independence from the Ottoman Empire, hereditary rule for his family, independent sources of wealth, and – ultimately – political power.

[67] I am again borrowing this phrase from James C. Scott's by now classic study *Seeing Like a State*.

Indeed, the only instance of Wittfogelian Oriental despotism in the story this book tells is Mehmet ʿAli's reconstruction of the Maḥmūdiyya Canal. I go to great lengths in the first three chapters to show how a complex system of irrigation does *not* have to be managed despotically. Nevertheless, in the first quarter of the nineteenth century, at the very moment, according to an Egyptian nationalist narrative, that Egypt gained its independence and entered upon modernity, the management of irrigation in Egypt did indeed become despotic. The bitter irony in this is the fact that the Ottoman imperial system of the long eighteenth century afforded Egyptian peasants the autonomy and space in which to manage their lives, lands, crops, and water largely as they pleased. This kind of freedom, though, was taken from them by the Egyptian state itself in the nineteenth century as it came to control the management of nature, disease, and irrigation. Nationalist history, in Egypt as elsewhere, thus sails into troubled waters when one takes fuller account of human affairs by recognizing the roles of water, soil, animals, timber, and microbes in rural life and in the fortunes of empires.

There were therefore multiple ways in which the Ottoman Empire was an empire by nature in Egypt over the course of the long eighteenth century. In the earlier period, Ottoman imperial rule in Egypt and throughout the Empire was predicated on the successful and sustainable harnessing, organization, preservation, and management of natural resources in its realm. Irrigation, agricultural cultivation, forest management, peasant knowledge and experience, and the understanding of how diseases functioned in rural Egypt were key to the sustenance and longevity of the Ottoman Empire for more than half a millennium.[68] It was thus through, by, and with nature that the Ottoman Empire affected its rule, durability, and authority.

By contrast, the nature of political rule in Egypt in the early nineteenth century constituted a very different kind of empire by nature, in which the provincial government created an imperative to rule from the top down. Thus, again in contradiction to much conventional historiographical thinking, imperial government came to Egypt in the early nineteenth century with the falling away of the kind of Ottoman order I sketch out for the beginning of the long eighteenth century. Egypt, in other words, came to be governed imperially *only* when it moved toward a modicum of independent rule under Mehmet ʿAli. It is crucial to understand that

[68] This was, of course, also the case for many other early modern empires. Richards, *Unending Frontier.*

there was nothing "natural" about this imperial character of Egyptian government that began in the early nineteenth century. Choices made to centralize, to bureaucratize, to regularize, and to order the countryside and the Egyptian peasantry set into motion actions and chains of events that have endowed Egypt with a form of government that has seemed since the early nineteenth century and that continues to seem even until today hopelessly ("naturally") imperial. As this book shows, however, the fact that Egypt now functions as an empire by nature is a completely human-made and historical phenomenon that began in the first decades of the nineteenth century.

1

WATERING THE EARTH

No land ever depended on water management more than Egypt. Its irrigation system is among the world's oldest. When the Ottomans conquered Egypt in 1517, they inherited a complex system, the result of millennia of careful trial and error, accumulated knowledge, and hard labor. Their prior experience in Anatolia and the Balkans, although it included irrigation, did not suffice to allow them to grasp the Egyptian situation fully. They thus needed expert help with the management of water in Egypt, and they got it from Egyptian peasants.

In the Ottoman imperial system of natural resource balance and extraction, irrigation in Egypt created sets of connections, tensions, and relationships that tied the province to the rest of the Empire. Egypt could function as the most agriculturally and financially productive area of the Empire only if its fields had adequate supplies of water. Thus, throughout the long eighteenth century, Egyptian peasants came to the network of Islamic courts maintained throughout Egypt by the Ottoman administration of the province to stake claims to water usage in the countryside.[1] Using only a necessarily tiny fraction of the vast wealth of archival materials related to irrigation in eighteenth-century rural Egypt, this chapter charts the history of Egyptian peasants' and Ottoman bureaucrats' efforts to organize water usage and the repair and maintenance of irrigation works.[2]

I make three main arguments in this chapter. The first is that water usage created community. Using both the irrigation survey conducted by the Ottomans shortly after their conquest of Egypt in 1517 and court

[1] On the legal system of Ottoman Egypt, see: El-Nahal, *Judicial Administration of Ottoman Egypt*; Shaw, *Financial and Administrative Organization and Development*, 58–60; Hanna, *Making Big Money*, xv–xxvi.

[2] For a critical reading of the use of these sources, see: Majdī Jirjis, "Manhaj al-Dirāsāt al-Wathā'iqiyya wa Wāqiʿ al-Baḥth fī Miṣr," *al-Rūznāma: al-Ḥauliyya al-Miṣriyya lil-Wathā'iq* 2 (2004): 237–87.

cases initiated by Egyptian peasants, I show how the shared use of a canal, dam, or other irrigation work tied together the fates of peasant communities and the Empire as a whole into a cooperative relationship of mutual reliance and influence. Without properly maintained irrigation, and hence access to water, no food could be grown in Egypt. Thus, what I term *communities of water*, with specific social and ecological ethics including the sharing of natural resources and the collective maintenance of irrigation works, developed all over Egypt.

Second, I argue that, in these communities of water, the Ottoman state purposefully devolved authority over the day-to-day management of irrigation and water to Egyptian peasants, whose understanding of precedent and experience and knowledge in individual rural ecosystems influenced and often even controlled the Ottoman management of water resources. This was a practical solution to the complexities and continual change of the rural Egyptian environment. Indeed, even the smallest changes on a single irrigation feature in one part of the Egyptian countryside could have enormous effects on the food supplies of Cairo, Istanbul, Mecca, and other areas of the Empire.[3] Thus, to manage this system most effectively, the Ottoman administration of Egypt relied on the very local and intimate knowledge of Egyptian peasants who understood the countryside and how best to use its water.

Finally, I argue that water and its irrigation were principal engines of change in Ottoman Egypt. Because irrigation in Egypt was really about the cultivation and collection of food and revenues for the Empire (as the following chapter discusses in more detail), this chapter ends by considering some of the ways in which water defined the ecological and social spaces of productive agriculture in Ottoman Egypt – reclamation projects, village abandonment, and relations between sedentary peasant communities and Bedouin. Reclamation through the addition of water to barren land or its drainage from canals or sections of the Nile was a primary determining factor in forging the constantly changing shape of the Egyptian countryside. At the same time, Egyptian peasants and the Bedouin who understood the power of water to define community leveraged this knowledge to their advantage. These very conscious efforts on the parts of the Ottoman administration of Egypt, Egyptian peasants, and the Bedouin to create new agricultural land and ecological environments

[3] On this and other principles of irrigation, see: Paul Trawick, "The Moral Economy of Water: Equity and Antiquity in the Andean Commons," *American Anthropologist* 103 (2001): 361–79.

had very visible and durable impacts on the physical spaces of the Egyptian countryside and on the cultivation of foodstuffs and resources for the Ottoman Empire.

Ottoman Hydro-Logics

Soon after its conquest of Egypt in 1517, the Ottoman Empire undertook a detailed survey of irrigation in its new province. Although such surveys of the resources of new territories were routine, conducting a special one solely concerned with irrigation was not, and thus reflected the particular condition of Egypt as a land reliant on the harnessing of the Nile's waters. The results of the survey are preserved in a group of five registers known collectively as al-Jusūr al-Sulṭāniyya.[4] As best we know from internal and paleographic evidence, the registers were first compiled by the Ottomans in 1539 or 1540 and were still in use in the seventeenth and eighteenth centuries.[5]

[4] For a somewhat incomplete sketch of this archival unit (only the first three registers of the five are addressed), see: Nicolas Michel, "Les Dafātir al-ǧusūr, source pour l'histoire du réseau hydraulique de l'Égypte ottomane," *AI* 29 (1995): 151–68. The five registers under the archival heading of al-Jusūr al-Sulṭāniyya are numbered 784, 785, 786, 787, and 788 and are classified under the larger archival heading of al-Rūznāma. The last two registers (787 and 788) are accounting books related to matters of irrigation, whereas the first three consist of records of individual canals, organized by subprovince and then by village.

[5] What we know about the date of the compilation of the registers comes mainly from the section dealing with the subprovince of al-Minūfiyya, northwest of Cairo. One of the cases in this section references the year 1539 or 1540 (946), but there is no date given for the actual recording of this case in the register. From other internal evidence in the register and from the scribal hand, it is clear, however, that the case was written into the registers of al-Jusūr al-Sulṭāniyya at some point in the seventeenth or eighteenth century. Thus, the descriptions of canals and the procedures for managing them described in the registers were still of relevance in the seventeenth and eighteenth centuries, even if they were copied from sources compiled centuries earlier. The registers, thus, functioned as a point of reference for the contemporary moment. They were earlier descriptions of canals still in existence and of others that were no longer functioning. They served, in other words, as a kind of bureaucratic updating of previous information about Egypt's irrigation network – a sort of workbook that was constantly changed and updated so as to be as useful and accurate in the present moment as possible. To manage Egypt's irrigation network effectively and properly, the state clearly needed the most current and the most exact information about the present state of canals and other irrigation works, and the registers reflect the desire to ascertain that information. Cases similar to this one about irrigation in al-Minūfiyya were sent to various other subprovincial courts in Egypt to help with the organization of the survey in those areas as well. For the entry of this case in the register of the subprovince of al-Qalūbiyya, see: DWQ, al-Jusūr al-Sulṭāniyya 786, p. 158v, no case no. (n.d.). On this register, see: Michel, "Les Dafātir al-ǧusūr," 152–56. For Fayyoum, see: DWQ, al-Jusūr al-Sulṭāniyya 785, p. 2v, no case no. (17 Z 956/5 Jan. 1550). On register number 785, see: Michel, "Les Dafātir al-ǧusūr,"

The imperial goal of the survey of irrigation in Egypt was to delineate and map the many communities that water and irrigation created in the Egyptian countryside. By determining which villages used which waterways, Ottoman state would have a record of how communities were connected to one another through water and, perhaps more important, of who was collectively responsible for maintaining irrigation works, as those who shared water also shared the responsibility for maintaining the irrigation works carrying that water.[6] This collection of information could then be put toward the state's ultimate desires that the villages and agricultural lands of Egypt be agriculturally productive and that the province enjoy a state of full and total irrigation (*ḥuṣūl al-riyy al-kāmil al-shāmil*).[7]

To achieve the Empire's goals of mapping the irrigation network of rural Egypt, of determining responsibility for the upkeep of irrigation works, and of maintaining the agricultural productivity of Egypt, the survey sought answers to the following questions. Did a particular canal serve the common interests and needs of a large group of peasants, their lands, or a *waqf* (property endowed in perpetuity for a particular purpose

160–63. For Benī Suef (al-Bahnasāwiyya), see: DWQ, al-Jusūr al-Sulṭāniyya 785, p. 4v, no case no. (Evahir Za 996/12–21 Oct. 1588). The circulation of this text was meant to ensure that the Ottoman administration of Egypt's survey of rural irrigation features was as complete as possible, and the bureaucracy used its already-existing network of rural Islamic courts to distribute instructions to its functionaries throughout the Egyptian countryside. Thus, the Ottoman Empire's rural courts not only served to adjudicate disputes, manage estates, register marriages, and the like but also functioned as kinds of Ottoman imperial embassies in the rural environs of Egypt through which the Ottoman state could administer, rule, and provide for its subjects. On this point, Leslie Peirce describes the court "as the provincial nexus of empire-wide administrative networks." Peirce, *Morality Tales*, 90.

6 This was also the case in various other places besides Egypt. By way of comparison, see the Andean example in Paul B. Trawick, "Successfully Governing the Commons: Principles of Social Organization in an Andean Irrigation System," *Human Ecology* 29 (2001): 1–25; the Western Indian example in Arjun Appadurai, "Wells in Western India: Irrigation and Cooperation in an Agricultural Society," *Expedition* 26 (1984): 3–14; and the Balinese example in Clifford Geertz, "The Wet and the Dry: Traditional Irrigation in Bali and Morocco," *Human Ecology* 1 (1972), 26–31. Cases involving the sharing of a canal among various communities provide good examples of how the use of water also entailed the responsibility for the upkeep of irrigation works. These cases also document the disputes this sharing of responsibility often produced. See, e.g.: DWQ, Maḥkamat al-Manṣūra 12, p. 446, no case no. (15 Ca 1104/22 Jan. 1693); DWQ, Maḥkamat al-Baḥayra 10, p. 220, case 523 (3 C 1191/8 Jul. 1777); DWQ, Maḥkamat al-Manṣūra 19, p. 374, no case no. (9 M 1124/16 Feb. 1712); DWQ, Maḥkamat al-Manṣūra 19, p. 368, no case no. (A) (13 M 1125/9 Feb. 1713); DWQ, Maḥkamat al-Manṣūra 19, p. 379, no case no. (23 M 1123/13 Mar. 1711); DWQ, Maḥkamat al-Manṣūra 12, p. 425, no case no. (2 Za 1102/28 Jul. 1691); DWQ, Maḥkamat al-Manṣūra 24, p. 288, case 628 (28 N 1136/20 Jun. 1724).

7 DWQ, al-Jusūr al-Sulṭāniyya 784, pp. 182–83, no case no. (13 Ş).

or group), or conversely, did the canal serve only the narrower interests of a particular set of people? Did the repair of a canal lead to equality among peasants and serve the common good (*al-maṣlaḥa al-ʿāmma*)? Answers to these and other similar questions informed one of the most basic defining characteristics of canals in rural Egypt – the distinction between *sulṭānī* and *baladī* canals and the differences in the sorts of communities these waterways created.[8] If a canal served a large group of peasants rather than the interests of a small privileged few, contributed to the common good, or aided in the achievement of equality among peasants, then it was considered a *sulṭānī* canal, the responsibilities for which fell on the Ottoman state in Egypt. *Baladī* canals, by contrast, were those that served the irrigation needs of one particular community and no one else. These were to be maintained by local leaders. Although both *sulṭānī* and *baladī* canals ultimately remained the property of the state, their upkeep often fell on the shoulders of Egyptian peasants who lived near them, as they were the ones who most directly relied on the waterways.[9] By walking along the banks of every canal in Egypt, those Ottoman state employees charged with compiling the survey were to determine the length, width, and height of the *sulṭānī* and *baladī* canals; to decide which needed dredging, cleaning, and general maintenance (*al-jarāfa*); and to specify how the canals served as borders of property and dividers of rural space.

Their reports were furthermore meant to ascertain which canals had been abandoned and were no longer maintained in any regular way. These were canals that had dried up, become filled in with earth, or were no longer clearly visible on the ground. Surveyors were to determine why the canals had been abandoned and for how long. Moreover, given the history of the canals, if resources were put toward their repair, would they ever again return to being fully useful? Was there some inherent ecological problem with the earth, geography, or topography of a particular area of a canal or with a canal's water flow? In short, was it better to accept the environmental reality of the canal and to leave it abandoned or to

[8] On the difference between *sulṭānī* and *baladī* canals, and for useful schematic drawings of irrigation communities in the Egyptian countryside, see: Stuart J. Borsch, "Environment and Population: The Collapse of Large Irrigation Systems Reconsidered," *Comparative Studies in Society and History* 46 (2004): 458–60. For citations to relevant medieval texts on the difference between *sulṭānī* and *baladī* canals and dikes, see: Sato, *State and Rural Society*, 225–27.

[9] In the following case, the Ottoman bureaucracy asserted its ultimate authority over rural irrigation works by preventing the *multazim* of Minyyat Gharb from repairing a canal in his village: DWQ, Maḥkamat al-Manṣūra 18, p. 245 or p. 246, no case no. (B) (24 S 1122/24 Apr. 1710).

attempt to revitalize it? And who was responsible for the reconstruction of an abandoned canal? Was it the charge of the ruling Ottoman divan, the holders of *waqfs*, or those who used the canal to irrigate their lands? Likewise, what were the costs of previous repairs to a particular irrigation work? Above all, did human technical knowledge and experience allow for the construction and maintenance of such a canal despite the limitations of the natural environment?

To answer these questions and to aid in the Ottoman state's attempt to match lands to canals and people – and agricultural areas to sources of water – the survey accounted for how all waterways and bodies of water served as sources of irrigation in the Egyptian countryside. Thus, it had to establish which villages were irrigated from waterways and which were irrigated from lakes or other water sources. It also determined which waterways were free from obstruction and which were clogged. Moreover, was it beneficial to open the clogged waterways, or was it better to leave them closed?

These were questions with obvious imperial motives behind them, but they were also questions that suggested an understanding that humans could not conquer the natural environments around them. They could not – at least not easily – irrigate a patch of land if there was some ecological imperative preventing the ground from properly receiving water. Likewise, it behooved the Ottoman state to maintain certain established social and environmental practices of irrigation in Egypt. If a canal had historically served a certain community or had been clogged for centuries, from the perspective of an administration seeking efficacy and stability, it was probably best to preserve the status quo. The Ottoman bureaucracy in Egypt recognized these and other features of the rural Egyptian world and did not want to put resources toward something that either was impossible to accomplish or would cause undue conflict with local communities.

To answer the foregoing questions and to record the current irrigation situation of the entire province of Egypt, an enormous amount of detail and minutiae was marshaled by the Ottoman bureaucracy in the survey. From an accounting of the centuries of usage of a particular irrigation work down to the details of an individual waterwheel or sluice gate, the survey represented a vast undertaking by an early modern state attempting to determine the wealth of natural and economic resources newly under its control. The records of this survey in the registers of al-Jusūr al-Sulṭāniyya are thus a storehouse of useful information about the history of irrigation in Ottoman Egypt.

The survey and the registers of al-Jusūr al-Sulṭāniyya are organized first by subprovince and then by village. Under each subprovincial section heading, a typical entry or case begins with the name of a village and then gives the name or names of the shaykhs of that village and the size of the village (in the unit of the *ḥiṣṣa*). This numerical rendering of an amount of property is then further divided into various kinds of property – the most common being *waqf* and state land (*al-dīwān al-sharīf*).[10] After designating the kinds of land found in a village, the irrigation features are mentioned. Canals are designated as being either *sulṭānī* or *baladī*, and their starting and ending points and dimensions are also given.[11] Waterwheels, aqueducts, bridges, and other kinds of irrigation features are also commonly mentioned in these cases.[12] Typical entries of this sort tell us who was responsible for the irrigation work in question and offer us a small history of the repair work undertaken on the canal, waterwheel, or sluice gate.[13] For example, in a village named Ziftā Jawād in the subprovince of al-Gharbiyya, directly to the north of Cairo, several waterwheels and a bridge were badly in need of repair.[14]

[10] For example, the size of a village named Disūq in the subprobvince of al-Gharbiyya was twelve *ḥiṣṣas*; five of these belonged to the state and the other seven were *waqf* lands. DWQ, al-Jusūr al-Sulṭāniyya 784, p. 89, case 146 (n.d.). On Disūq, see: *QJBM*, pt. 2, 2:47. When available, I have referenced Muḥammad Ramzī's *QJBM* on the various villages mentioned in this book and have also observed his spelling conventions. If no reference is given for a particular village, the reader should assume it was not found in the *QJBM*.

[11] For example, in a typical entry in the section of the registers concerning the subprovince of al-Minūfiyya, northwest of Cairo, we read that a waterway known as the canal of Ashmūn Jirīsan that began and ended in the village of Ashmūn was a *baladī* canal with three distinct parts (*thalātha qiṭaʿ*). Because it was a *baladī* canal, its maintenance, protection, and repair were the responsibilities of the peasants who used its waters, and the entry goes on to list the villages that relied on the canal's waters. DWQ, al-Jusūr al-Sulṭāniyya 784, p. 188, no case no. (n.d.). On Ashmūn, see: *QJBM*, pt. 2, 2:157.

[12] For a general discussion of waterwheels in Ottoman Egypt, see: ʿAbd al-Raḥīm, *al-Rīf al-Miṣrī*, 199–200. See also: Cuno, *The Pasha's Peasants*, 142, 185, 187, 191–92. For court cases in which waterwheels are used as defining markers of property and buildings, see: DWQ, Maḥkamat Manfalūṭ 2, pp. 93–94, case 326 (29 S 1180/5 Aug. 1766); DWQ, Maḥkamat al-Baḥayra 6, p. 9, case 17 (10 Za 1169/7 Aug. 1756); DWQ, Maḥkamat al-Baḥayra 15, p. 152, case 346 (30 R 1199/12 Mar. 1785); DWQ, Maḥkamat al-Baḥayra 15, p. 4, case 8 (29 S 1199/5 Aug. 1766); DWQ, Maḥkamat al-Baḥayra 15, pp. 38–39, case 92 (11 Ra 1199/22 Jan. 1785).

[13] For cases of repairs to waterwheels in various locations throughout Egypt, see: DWQ, Maḥkamat Asyūṭ 8, p. 35, case 72 (4 B 1209/25 Jan. 1795); DWQ, Maḥkamat al-Baḥayra 16, p. 87, case 150 (8 L 1200/3 Aug. 1786); DWQ, Maḥkamat Manfalūṭ 2, p. 91, case 317 (11 S 1180/18 Jul. 1766); DWQ, Maḥkamat al-Baḥayra 16, p. 268, case 465 (7 C 1201/27 Mar. 1787); DWQ, Maḥkamat al-Baḥayra 16, p. 282, case 488 (9 B 1201/27 Apr. 1787).

[14] DWQ, al-Jusūr al-Sulṭāniyya 784, p. 170, case 318 (n.d.). On Ziftā Jawād, see: *QJBM*, pt. 2, 2:57.

The bridge had been repaired many times before, and the entry in the survey makes clear that it was to be the responsibility of the *multazim* of the village to oversee the repairs and to provide the oxen and the food the workers required.[15] After discussing the irrigation features present in a particular village, the entries in al-Jusūr al-Sulṭāniyya typically then tell of the source of the irrigated water of these villages – the Nile, a particular branch of the river, or a canal – and the final section of the cases gives the four borders of the village.

Clearly, the more the Ottoman administration knew about the irrigation situation on the ground in rural Egypt – village by village and canal by canal (*baladan baladan wa jisran jisran*) as stated in this survey – the better it would be able to manage water and to maximize its productivity and, hence, its profitability.[16] Creating a bureaucratic map of the thousands of communities of water in the Egyptian countryside demanded and deserved this kind of work, because, at its base, this was an exercise meant to improve management and administrative techniques through the collection of what the Ottoman state deemed useful information. As a preface to organizational mechanisms of rule we will discuss in later chapters, this project represented an early attempt to detail the minutiae of a complex network of thousands of canals over a vast geographical area. This enormous administrative undertaking required thousands of Ottoman imperial functionaries and Egyptian peasants, specialized tools, a great amount of paper, easy communication channels, and – in particular – a very organized and efficient bureaucracy to manage all of this. Moreover, the histories of irrigation elucidated by the survey served to situate the newly arrived Ottoman administration of Egypt in a long sequence of actors who had attempted to repair and maintain irrigation works in Egypt.[17]

The registers of al-Jusūr al-Sulṭāniyya thus allowed the state to "see" the countryside in a very abstract and organized way; they allowed it

[15] In another case, we are given a much clearer picture of the human labor to be used in repair work. This case concerns a dam (*ḥibs al-faiḍ*) in the subprovince of al-Minūfiyya known as the dam of Awlād Abū al-Rajīlāt, which was built near the *baladī* canal of Ṭanb. Both this dam and the canal were under the supervision of the *khawlī* and the peasants of this area. Moreover, because this was a *baladī* canal, its maintenance was the responsibility of local peasants – not the state. As such, the case goes on to list the villages from which peasant workers were to be collected for the maintenance of the canal and its dam. DWQ, al-Jusūr al-Sulṭāniyya 784, p. 185, no case no. (n.d.).

[16] DWQ, al-Jusūr al-Sulṭāniyya 784, pp. 182–83, no case no. (13 Ş).

[17] The survey was perhaps also a kind of reflexive moment for the Ottoman state to think about its position in Egypt vis-à-vis previous regimes and local populations through the lens of the management of irrigation works.

to collate data and to compare villages with one another very easily.[18] Though perhaps cumbersome and tedious to compile, once recorded, the Ottoman administration could use the information in the registers in an efficient, fast, and orderly manner. As a map, the survey was a tool used to achieve a certain end – here the administrative control of rural Egypt and its water resources. By its very nature, this information was of a very local and specific variety. It dealt with the subtleties and variations of thousands of villages all over Egypt. In this compendium of the various communities water created, we find individuals' names and very specific information about local canals, plots of land, and other features of the village environment. Al-Jusūr al-Sulṭāniyya was thus both exhaustive in its coverage of rural Egypt and exacting in its detail. Each of the communities listed was only one part of a vast, complex system of irrigation in rural Egypt, and thus the registers of al-Jusūr al-Sulṭāniyya represent an attempt to weave these communities of water together into the larger tapestry of Egypt's irrigation network. The data in the registers represent a mass of very small details meant to evoke the "reality" of the whole of Ottoman Egypt.[19]

Communities of Water

Despite its detail, breadth, and the fact that it was updated at various points over the centuries of Ottoman rule in Egypt, the Empire's survey of rural irrigation resources was in many ways always incomplete. This necessarily had to be the case, because environmental change in the Egyptian countryside was both regular and rapid. Water levels in the Nile and in canals constantly fluctuated, waterways silted, embankments and dams broke, and fields flooded. To understand the constant negotiation, contestation, and conflict that this environmental change precipitated for Egyptian peasants and Ottoman bureaucrats stationed in Egypt, we must turn our attention to the copious records of the network of Islamic courts spread throughout rural Egypt.[20] These court cases provide us

[18] The analogy of sight is borrowed here again from James C. Scott's *Seeing Like a State.*

[19] In an admittedly very different context, Thomas W. Laqueur identifies "detail as the sign of truth." He writes, "Unprecedented quantities of fact, of minute observations... become the building blocks of the 'reality effect'... through which the experiences of others are represented as real." Thomas W. Laqueur, "Bodies, Details, and the Humanitarian Narrative," in *The New Cultural History*, ed. Lynn Hunt (Berkeley: University of California Press, 1989), 177.

[20] For an example of a case that was stricken from the legal record of the court of al-Baḥayra because of changed environmental conditions, see: DWQ, Maḥkamat al-Baḥayra 39,

with a nearly daily accounting of disputes over water; irrigation repairs; and myriad other social, familial, and economic issues that arose in the countryside.

What comes through most strongly from a consideration of court records is that Egyptian peasant communities were governed by sets of conventions and traditions that stemmed from the shared usage of water and that were based on the physical properties of the liquid's movement, viscosity, and flow rate.[21] One of these we have already seen outlined in the records of al-Jusūr al-Sulṭāniyya: peasants who benefited from the waters of a canal also had to maintain it.[22] Another overriding principle of water usage in the countryside was the notion that the welfare of the whole always trumped the interests and desires of the few.[23] This ideal of cooperative and collective responsibility arose from the fact that, throughout the countryside, scores of villages relied on the function of a single set of irrigation features for their entire supply of water – some combination of a canal, a dam, a section of the Nile, a waterwheel, a sluice gate, and other irrigation works.[24] In these hundreds of ecosystems organized around the shared usage of water and irrigation features, the actions of a few directly affected the welfare of the whole community.[25]

p. 397, no case no. (28 B 1245/24 Jan. 1830). The case was "removed" from the records of the court by a series of closely spaced vertical lines that ran the entire length of the page over the text of the case. The date of the drawing of the lines is later than that of the latest case in the register, which suggests that the crossed out case was referenced and then found to be no longer relevant to the current changed ecological circumstances.

21 For comparative examples of different communities of water, see: Geertz, "The Wet and the Dry," 23–39.

22 This was also the case in the early modern Netherlands, where "dike maintenance was an obligation divided among the villages that benefitted from it; they, in turn, divided their stretch of dike among the land users who were each made responsible for a specific segment." Jan de Vries, *The Dutch Rural Economy in the Golden Age, 1500–1700* (New Haven, CT: Yale University Press, 1974), 197. The Dutch rural problem was, of course, the opposite of the Egyptian case – one of drainage rather than of irrigation.

23 For comparative instances of this notion of community water management, see: Trawick, "Moral Economy of Water," 361–79.

24 For examples of the ideal workings of irrigation and the maintenance of irrigation works in Ottoman Egypt, see the following cases about the repair and upkeep of the major canal known as Baḥr al-Manzala or Baḥr al-Ṣaghīr in the subprovince of al-Daqahliyya in the eastern Nile Delta: DWQ, Maḥkamat al-Manṣūra 14, p. 100, case 219 (12 L 1110/13 Apr. 1699); DWQ, Maḥkamat al-Manṣūra 1, p. 232, no case no. (Z 1058/Dec. 1648 and Jan. 1649); DWQ, Maḥkamat al-Manṣūra 18, p. 244 or p. 245, no case no. (14 S 1122/14 Apr. 1710); DWQ, Maḥkamat al-Manṣūra 19, p. 373, no case no. (8 R 1124/14 May 1712).

25 For examples of how seemingly minor changes in one part of Egypt's irrigation network had far-reaching effects, see: DWQ, Maḥkamat al-Manṣūra 16, p. 119, case 224 (11 S

The necessary regulation of water in Egypt was not the result of the Ottoman conquests. Indeed, water, water usage, and irrigation had been regulated in Egypt since Pharaonic times.[26] Perhaps more than most peoples, therefore, Egyptians understood the necessity of rules governing water access, even if those rules were often broken and constantly challenged out of self-interest.[27] From the Ottoman state's perspective, the question of how to distribute and administer a finite amount of water in Egypt's multiple ecosystems was determined primarily by the Empire's economic interests in the province. At the same time, the Empire continuously had to weigh its economic interests against both the ecological realities of the countryside and the principle of channeling water to those agricultural regions that would benefit the greatest number of people, not just in Egypt but throughout the Empire. Because the Ottoman bureaucracy sought to irrigate land both to feed populations in Egypt and elsewhere and, perhaps more important, to increase the state's economic resources, it viewed water as a commodity to be put toward those ends – a raw material subject to the pressures and demands of a state with diverse and enormous responsibilities, interests, and challenges. The Empire could neither invent nor create water. It could only find ways to manage effectively what it already had. How was the Ottoman bureaucracy to meet its imperial and human demands in the face of this

1110/17 Aug. 1698); DWQ, Maḥkamat al-Manṣūra 12, p. 447, no case no. (A) (10 L 1103/25 Jun. 1692); DWQ, Maḥkamat al-Manṣūra 12, p. 450, no case no. (27 C 1104/5 Mar. 1693).

26 For an account of the history of water regulation in Egypt, see: Worster, *Rivers of Empire*, 42–44. For a sustained study of irrigation in the ancient period, see: Karl W. Butzer, *Early Hydraulic Civilization in Egypt: A Study in Cultural Ecology* (Chicago: University of Chicago Press, 1976).

27 It should be noted that Egypt is thus a perfect example of a highly regulated commons, in distinction to Garrett Hardin's somewhat-infamous thesis of the "tragedy" of unregulated commons like fisheries and pastures. Hardin posits that human societies cannot agree on sustainable ways to productively share common-property resources and are thus destined to conflict and the degradation of environmental resources. Garrett Hardin, "The Tragedy of the Commons," *Science* 162 (1968): 1243–48. Irrigation has proved a very fruitful terrain from which to challenge and disprove this notion. See, e.g.: Maass and Anderson, *Desert Shall Rejoice*; Robert Y. Siy Jr., *Community Resource Management: Lessons from the Zanjera* (Quezon City: University of the Philippines Press, 1982); Robert Wade, *Village Republics: Economic Conditions for Collective Action in South India* (Cambridge: Cambridge University Press, 1988); Elinor Ostrom, *Governing the Commons: The Evolution of Institutions for Collective Action* (Cambridge: Cambridge University Press, 1990); Elinor Ostrom and Roy Gardner, "Coping with Asymmetries in the Commons: Self-Governing Irrigation Systems Can Work," *Journal of Economic Perspectives* 7 (1993): 93–112; Trawick, "Successfully Governing the Commons"; Trawick, "Moral Economy of Water," 361–79; Appadurai, "Wells in Western India."

natural limit? This was the challenge of irrigation in Egypt – a challenge to administer and to harness both natural resources and the people who used them and were connected by them.

The subprovince of al-Daqahliyya in the eastern Nile Delta was irrigated by a canal known as Baḥr al-Manzala or al-Baḥr al-Ṣaghīr.[28] One area in al-Daqahliyya supported by the canal was a community of water consisting of thirty-one villages, thousands of peasants, and hundreds of hectares of fields.[29] Itself a tributary, the canal relied on its own water from the Nile and from other canals, and, thus, to understand the history of these thirty-one villages, we have to account for their relationships to one another; to this single source of the al-Manzala canal; and to the many worlds – in Egypt and throughout the Ottoman Empire – to which they were connected through other waterways, through the export of food, and through the Ottoman bureaucracy.[30] Because all these actors in Egypt and beyond were in some capacity consumers of this single canal's water, they were all implicated in managing the ecological reality that there was simply not enough water to irrigate fully all the villages in and around the canal of al-Manzala.

Given the limited water supply and the great demands placed on it, tributary canals from the main canal of al-Manzala to villages like Manzala, Bizrārī, and Ikhṭāb were regularly dammed so as to allow more water to flow downstream through the main artery.[31] This damming of upstream canals came in response to the petitions of downstream villagers who complained that their planted fields were not receiving enough water to cultivate food. Indeed, in 1703, many of these peasants assembled in the court to state that their villages had been forgotten (*köylerimiz mensiyye*), clearly indicating that their water needs were not being adequately met. These peasants further intimated that the Ottoman state had to take some sort of action further upstream to divert

28 For a detailed study of the subprovince of al-Daqahliyya during the Ottoman period based largely on the records of the court of al-Manṣūra, see: Nāṣira ʿAbd al-Mutajallī Ibrāhīm ʿAlī, "al-Daqahliyya fī al-ʿAṣr al-ʿUthmānī" (M.A. thesis, ʿAyn Shams University, 2005).

29 For a statement that the villages formed a single unit of administration and irrigation, see: DWQ, Maḥkamat al-Manṣūra 16, p. 402, no case no. (C) (25 M 1116/29 May 1704). For another case that makes the point that this set of villages functioned as a single community, see: DWQ, Maḥkamat al-Manṣūra 16, p. 403, no case no. (A) (30 Ca 1115/12 Oct. 1703).

30 For a comparative discussion of similar issues of rights to water usage in the modern Middle East, see: Lancaster and Lancaster, *People, Land and Water*, 150–51.

31 DWQ, Maḥkamat al-Manṣūra 16, p. 403, no case no. (B) (n.d.).

water to their thirty-one downstream villages. The Ottoman bureaucracy in this case took the downstream villagers' petition seriously and ordered upstream canals closed. As we see in this case, and in many others like it, downstream villagers often came to rural Egyptian courts with complaints against upstream villages that either were taking too much water or were not properly irrigating their fields and, thus, adversely affecting peasants below them.[32]

In addition to the opening and closing of canals, the Ottoman bureaucracy of Egypt sought to make the entire cooperative system of the thirty-one villages – and, indeed, of irrigation in Egypt as whole – more efficient by alleviating water pressure on the largest possible number of peasants through the removal of dirt and debris from the beds of canals.[33] Thus, in our present case about the canal of al-Manzala, we are told that two stamped orders (*temessük*) were sent in the same year as the previous decree to an official named ʿUthmān Bey to dredge, reinforce, and clear the main canal to allow water to flow freely through this waterway to the lands and fields of al-Daqahliyya. Thus, the Ottoman administration of rural Egypt sought to deal with the many problems of a finite supply of water in this particular community by increasing the overall amount of water the area received at the expense of other villages.[34] In the hierarchy of water allotment in Egypt, these thirty-one villages were therefore deemed more deserving of water at this particular moment than they had been previously.

In a case eight months later, however, we learn that many of the same thirty-one villages, and those upstream villages whose canals were previously sealed off, remained unirrigated.[35] Thus, in an order that was the exact opposite of the previous one, an official named ʿAlī Jāwīsh (Çavuş in Turkish) was appointed to reopen the mouths of the canals running to the villages of al-Manzala, Bizrārī, and Ikhṭāb.[36] Like the

[32] For another example of this kind of case, see: DWQ, Maḥkamat al-Manṣūra 17, p. 388, no case no. (17 Z 1118/22 Mar. 1707).

[33] For a comparable case, see: DWQ, Maḥkamat al-Manṣūra 7, p. 310, case 767 (19 S 1093/27 Feb. 1682).

[34] As part of these efforts, inspections of these villages and of their supporting canals were regularly ordered. See, e.g.: DWQ, Maḥkamat al-Manṣūra 17, pp. 28–29, case 58 (11 Z 1117/26 Mar. 1706).

[35] DWQ, Maḥkamat al-Manṣūra 16, p. 402, no case no. (A) (25 M 1116/29 May 1704).

[36] For other orders to open canals (some initiated by peasants and others not), see: DWQ, Maḥkamat al-Manṣūra 17, p. 389, no case no. (12 Ca 1118/21 Aug. 1706); DWQ, Maḥkamat al-Manṣūra 17, p. 393, no case no. (28 Z 1117/12 Apr. 1706); DWQ, Maḥkamat al-Manṣūra 17, p. 389, no case no. (12 Ca 1118/21 Aug. 1706).

main canal of al-Manzala, these smaller waterways branching off of it were also to be cleaned and dredged to allow for a greater amount of water to flow through them more easily. Indeed, the order was sent in May to ensure that when the canal mouths were cut open during the season of the flood, the waterways would be ready to receive the largest amount of water possible for the greatest number of villages in the area. In summary, then, this set of canals in a particular irrigation community around the main artery of al-Manzala was ordered closed and then reopened in the span of eight or nine months as the Ottoman administration of Egypt adapted to changing demands for water and shifting environmental conditions in the area.

The constant closing and opening of canals to divert the flow of the Nile's waters was one of the most effective means for both Ottoman administrators and Egyptian peasants to manage the allocation of the river's resources in communities of water.[37] The kind of balancing act we see in this case – and throughout the eighteenth-century legal record – was akin to opening and closing valves in a long and complex series of intertwined pipes. It reflected a recognition that nearly the entire irrigation network of Egypt was tied together in one system of cooperation

[37] For a comparative example of the regulation of the opening and closing of canals in Balinese irrigation schemes, see: Geertz, "The Wet and the Dry," 29. Opening too many canals on a central artery of water, thus draining the main channel to the point that it was rendered unusable for irrigation, was a rather common problem in the Egyptian countryside. See, e.g.: DWQ, Maḥkamat al-Manṣūra 18, p. 249 or p. 250, no case no. (B) (23 Ş 1121/27 Oct. 1709); DWQ, Maḥkamat al-Manṣūra 19, p. 386, no case no. (1 Ş 1122/24 Sep. 1710); DWQ, Maḥkamat al-Manṣūra 19, p. 371, no case no. (9 Ş 1124/11 Sep. 1712). For a case in which peasants themselves pushed the state to close canals that were siphoning water out of a main waterway, see: DWQ, Maḥkamat al-Manṣūra 14, p. 206, case 482 (17 Za 1111/7 May 1700). In another case about the irrigation of the village of al-Manzala from the year 1652, an Ottoman *buyuruldu* (literally, "it has been ordered") instructed that all canals feeding off al-Baḥr al-Ṣaghīr were to remain sealed until the amount of water in the main waterway was sufficiently large enough to constitute a sea (*deniz*). DWQ, Maḥkamat al-Manṣūra 2, p. 273 or p. 293, no case no. (5 Ca 1062/14 Apr. 1652). On al-Manzala, see: *QJBM*, pt. 2, 1:203–4. Of note here is the use of the word *deniz* to describe the shape and enormity of the water resources needed to irrigate al-Manzala. The choice of this word suggests that the sea was conceptualized as the largest body of water possible. For peasants or others resident in the Egyptian countryside who had likely never seen the sea in their lifetimes, the idea of this great body of water represented to them the superlative of what was imaginable as a mass of water; it was, in other words, the ultimate amount of water for Egyptian peasants, capable of meeting all their irrigation needs and demands. As with Ottoman Turkish, a similar usage occurs in Arabic, where the word *baḥr* (sea) – as in al-Baḥr al-Ṣaghīr – is often used to refer to both large canals and to other bodies of water to express the idea of their enormity and importance to a local community.

and collective usage. The breaking, destruction, or deliberate opening of canals or dams in one section of the countryside affected the amount of water available to other areas throughout Egypt, their levels of agricultural production, and the overall health and well-being of Egypt's rural population and of others elsewhere in the Ottoman Empire.

The case of the canal of al-Manzala also expresses a recognition not only that water and irrigation created communities of interaction around the sharing of a limited resource but also that there were different dynamics of power and influence among different villages in those communities – usually on the basis of which was further upstream and which had historically been responsible for maintaining irrigation works. Villages, in other words, were able to lobby the Ottoman state for water. Communities in good stead with the imperial bureaucracy would obviously stand to benefit the most from this arrangement.[38] This form of imperial rule over society and the natural resources on which it depended could function only if the state understood the details of local geography and the environment in each and every village. After its survey of irrigation in Egypt, the only other way the Ottoman state could attain this sort of information was by relying on the very local knowledge of Egyptian peasants, who lived in various communities of water and who understood their environmental specificities. We therefore turn now to what peasants knew about water and irrigation and to how both they and the Ottoman state used this information.

The Viscosity of Precedent

Much of what Egyptian peasants knew of water usage and irrigation and of what they actually practiced on the ground was the result of precedent – centuries of accumulated experience and knowledge of local practices connected to a specific geography and environment. Precedent was so powerful a force in the management of water in rural Egypt that the Ottoman imperial bureaucracy more often than not deferred to it in its legal courts. Thus, in the thousands of cases concerning water and irrigation in the archival record of Ottoman Egypt – cases produced in courts ostensibly based on *sharīʿa* – how things had been done from times

[38] For the petition of a group of peasants from the village of Minyyat al-Dimna who were adversely affected by the state's denial of water to them through the closing of their canals, see: DWQ, Maḥkamat al-Manṣūra 19, p. 372, no case no. (17 R 1124/23 May 1712).

of old (the operative phrase being *min qadīm al-zamān*) was almost always cited as the legal justification for the adjudication of disputes. Precedent was law in Ottoman Egypt.

There was good reason for this. First and foremost, it was easy. Beyond simply not fixing what was not broken, the Ottoman state in Egypt in the seventeenth and eighteenth centuries had little interest in improving the efficiency or productive levels of agriculture in Egypt. Things already worked well enough, and the state understood that changing local practices was much more difficult than upholding and appropriating them. Moreover, by maintaining and, indeed, sanctioning local practice, the Ottoman administration was able to prevent disaffection among local populations in the Egyptian countryside. Thus, even if precedent did not necessarily always represent the most efficient means of governing irrigation and water (as we will see in the following example), it proved in many ways the least troublesome and, hence, most effective means of natural resource management for the Empire.[39]

The village of Daqdūqa in the subprovince of al-Baḥayra in the western Nile Delta was surrounded by water. The village nevertheless found itself unable to irrigate its own fields from the small canals that formed its borders.[40] Instead of using the water closest to them for irrigation – water

39 As an example of the bureaucratic inefficiency involved in the establishment of precedent, see the following case about the drafting of a firman to repair one of the Cairo Citadel's aqueducts: BOA, MM, 10:311 (Evail Ca 1202/9–18 Feb. 1788). The drafters of this decree in Istanbul could not find in the *başmuhasebe* any reports of previous repairs to the aqueducts. They also searched in the records of the Divan-i Hümayun, in other places of inquiry (*sair cüstucu olunan mahallar*), and in collections of letters and reports sent from Egypt. Unable to find any citable precedent for the repairs, officials in Istanbul deemed it impossible (*mümkün olmayıp*) to determine the financial needs of the repairs and were thus unable (or perhaps unwilling) to issue an order for the waterway's repair. On the usefulness of the records of the *başmuhasebe* for the historian of the eighteenth century, see: Suraiya Faroqhi, *Approaching Ottoman History: An Introduction to the Sources* (Cambridge: Cambridge University Press, 1999), 50.

40 For additional examples of cases in which canals and other irrigation works were used to demarcate and define rural space in the Egyptian countryside, see: DWQ, Maḥkamat Manfalūṭ 3, p. 118, case 229 (17 Z 1209/4 Jul. 1795); DWQ, Maḥkamat Rashīd 122, pp. 49–50, case 83 (8 Ca 1131/29 Mar. 1719); DWQ, Maḥkamat Isnā 5, p. 8, case 21 (13 Ra 1173/3 Nov. 1759); DWQ, Maḥkamat Rashīd 130, pp. 132–34, case 187 (8 Ca 1136/4 Feb. 1724); DWQ, Maḥkamat Asyūṭ 6, p. 74, case 169 (20 Ca 1201/10 Mar. 1787); DWQ, Maḥkamat al-Baḥayra 5, p. 215, case 390 (1 Ca 1165/17 Mar. 1752); DWQ, Maḥkamat Manfalūṭ 1, p. 98, case 215 (19 L 1210/27 Apr. 1796); DWQ, Maḥkamat Asyūṭ 5, p. 45, case 100 (2 Ş 1188/8 Oct. 1774); DWQ, Maḥkamat Asyūṭ 6, p. 416, case 885 (24 Ca 1207/7 Jan. 1793); DWQ, Maḥkamat Asyūṭ 6, p. 431, case 920 (7 N 1207/18 Apr. 1793); DWQ, Maḥkamat Manfalūṭ 3, p. 181, case 375 (7 Ca 1264/11 Apr. 1248); DWQ, Maḥkamat Manfalūṭ 1, p. 30, case 58 (5 R 1212/26 Sep. 1797);

that could have easily been siphoned out of these bordering canals – the peasants of Daqdūqa had since time immemorial (*min qadīm al-zamān*) resorted to a larger canal further away. The irrigation of their village relied on water trapped by a dam in the large canal of Baḥr al-Aḥkām in the village of Ramsīs and on a smaller waterway stretching from Baḥr al-Aḥkām directly to their village.[41] As precedent further dictated, water in the canals bordering Daqdūqa belonged to other villages. Although it might have been easier, more expedient, and cheaper for the villagers of Daqdūqa simply to cut into the canals around their lands, they chose not to do so because of the legal power of precedent. Thus, for example, in 1787 two *multazims* and a group of villagers from Daqdūqa petitioned the Ottoman state in their local court complaining about the flow of water to their fields.[42] In response, an imperial firman was issued commanding that the canal feeding water from Baḥr al-Aḥkām to Daqdūqa be widened and dredged to improve the flow of water to the village's fields. No mention was made of using the water in the canals that surrounded the village. The imperial order also stipulated that anyone resisting the implementation of these orders would be dealt with summarily, and a case recorded in the same court a month later (which in fine bureaucratic form cited the present case) reiterated the need for the construction of a better waterway from Baḥr al-Aḥkām to the village of Daqdūqa and again warned against any resistance to this order.[43]

Although it might seem initially counterintuitive that the peasants of Daqdūqa would draw their water from a canal much further away than those canals forming their village's borders, there were practical social, economic, and ecological reasons for the establishment and maintenance of this precedent, and though unstated in this case, we can nevertheless easily surmise what those were. First, taking water from a canal that ran

DWQ, Maḥkamat al-Manṣūra 22, p. 237, no case no. (22 R 1152/28 Jul. 1739); DWQ, al-Rizaq al-Iḥbāsī 5, p. 239, no case no. (16 L 967/10 Jul. 1560); DWQ, al-Rizaq al-Iḥbāsī 24, p. 2, no case no. (27 S). For an empirical study of the archival unit known as al-Rizaq al-Iḥbāsī, see: Nicolas Michel, "Les rizaq iḥbāsiyya, terres agricoles en mainmorte dans l'Égypte mamelouke et ottoman. Étude sur les Dafātir al-Aḥbās ottomans," *AI* 30 (1996): 105–98. On the symbolism of crossing borders of water in the Ottoman world, see: Palmira Brummett, "The River Crossing: Breaking Points (Metaphorical and 'Real') in Ottoman Mutiny," in *Mutiny and Rebellion in the Ottoman Empire*, ed. Jane Hathaway (Madison: University of Wisconsin Press, 2002), 45–60.

41 On Ramsīs, see: *QJBM*, pt. 2, 2:249.

42 DWQ, Maḥkamat al-Baḥayra 16, p. 327, case 554 (22 Ca 1201/12 Mar. 1787). To corroborate their description of irrigation in their village, the peasants in this case included with their petition a report (*kashf*) from al-Dīwān al-ʿĀlī in Cairo about the village. On Daqdūqa, see: *QJBM*, pt. 2, 2:249.

43 DWQ, Maḥkamat al-Baḥayra 16, p. 329, case 558 (22 C 1201/11 Apr. 1787).

between two or more villages was one of the most common causes of disputes between peasants.[44] Thus, by drawing water from a canal much further away, Daqdūqa could avoid conflict with its neighboring villages.[45]

44 For an example of this kind of case, see: DWQ, Maḥkamat al-Manṣūra 2, p. 17, case 22 (19 L 1060/15 Oct. 1650).

45 As an example of the range of conflicts that broke out between neighboring villages, consider the following case of the cultivation of rice by the *multazim* of the village of al-Bidmāṣ in al-Daqahliyya, a man named al-Amīr Shaʿbān: DWQ, Maḥkamat al-Manṣūra 3, p. 328, case 986 (27 Za 1066/16 Sep. 1656). Peasants from a neighboring village directly to the east of al-Bidmāṣ came to court to complain about the planting of rice because of the crop's water demands. Rice is a water-intensive foodstuff that must be planted and grown in standing water for the majority of its maturation. Moreover, the large amount of water used in its cultivation creates a great deal of runoff as fields are drained. Thus, in addition to the large amount of water consumed by the rice fields of al-Bidmāṣ, the main problem cited by the peasants in this case was that the runoff of the fields in the canal between the two villages was muddy and dirty from the debris of rice and other items that collected in the water as it stood for a long period of time. In addition, the *multazim* of al-Bidmāṣ also burnt excess rice leaves after the cultivation of his fields. The burning of those materials let off a noxious odor that infiltrated all the villages around al-Bidmāṣ. Unable to tolerate the smell and the lack of clean water, al-Bidmāṣ's neighboring peasants came to the court of al-Manṣūra to ask the judge to intervene in the situation.

In response, the court sent its representatives to the area of the two villages to inspect the location and the claims of the villagers. As stated in the report of the court officials, the canal between the two villages was indeed completed filled with brackish runoff from the rice fields (*al-miyāh al-qadīma al-nāzila min ghayṭ al-aruz*) of al-Bidmāṣ. They reported as well that the people of the neighboring village had dammed the mouth of the canal that fed their own fields to protect their lands from the dirty water. The case further stated that the *multazim* of al-Bidmāṣ had never before planted rice on his fields – and thus went against the dictates of established practice – and that that action was the direct cause of the ruin of the adjacent village's fields. Although not stated explicitly in the text of the case, it seems likely, especially given the break with established precedent, that the court found in favor of the plaintiffs.

For general discussions of riziculture and its various elements, see: D. H. Grist, *Rice*, 5th ed. (London: Longman, 1975); Lucien M. Hanks, *Rice and Man: Agricultural Ecology in Southeast Asia* (Chicago: Aldine Atherton, 1972), 16–68. On the early history of rice in the Islamic world, see: Andrew M. Watson, *Agricultural Innovation in the Early Islamic World: The Diffusion of Crops and Farming Techniques, 700–1100* (Cambridge: Cambridge University Press, 1983), 15–19. On the history of rice cultivation in the Ottoman Empire, see: Halil İnalcık, "Rice Cultivation and the Çeltükci-Reʿâyâ System in the Ottoman Empire," *Turcica* 14 (1982): 69–141; M. L. Venzke, "Rice Cultivation in the Plain of Antioch in the 16th Century: The Ottoman Fiscal Practice," *AO* 12 (1987–1992): 175–276; N. Beldiceanu and Irène Beldiceanu-Steinherr, "Riziculture dans l'Empire ottoman (XIVe-XVe siècle)," *Turcica* 9:2–10 (1978): 9–28. On the financial implications of the cultivation of rice in Ottoman Egypt (especially in the Delta), see: Shaw, *Financial and Administrative Organization and Development*, 52, 125–26, 274; Cuno, *The Pasha's Peasants*, 55–60 and 135–37; Helen Anne B. Rivlin, *The Agricultural Policy of Muḥammad ʿAlī in Egypt* (Cambridge, MA: Harvard University Press 1961), 144–46 and 258–62. On the cultural role of rice cultivation in Balinese irrigation, see: Geertz, "The Wet and the Dry," 30.

Second, because the canals that formed the borders of Daqdūqa with other villages were much smaller than the one from Baḥr al-Aḥkām, they likely did not hold sufficient amounts of water to feed multiple villages at the same time. Thus, if the village of Daqdūqa could secure for itself a direct and exclusive source of water from the larger canal of Baḥr al-Aḥkām, this would clearly be a steadier, more abundant, and more reliable source of water – despite its distance from the village – than the canals surrounding it. These practices of irrigation embodied in the actions of the peasants of Daqdūqa and legalized through the sanction of the Ottoman court of al-Baḥayra had been tested over time and proved the most effective – even if perhaps not the most efficient – means of bringing water to their village.

In addition to justifying the maintenance of certain practices, precedent was also used as evidence in the adjudication of disputes stemming from environmental change in local communities. One of the most common forms of environmental change in rural Egypt was the silting of the Nile and other waterways, which resulted in the emergence of new areas of land and otherwise changed the geography of the countryside. In 1680, a case was filed in the court of al-Manṣūra in the Nile Delta involving three villages on the banks of a branch of the Nile that ran through that city, an island, and three waterwheels on the island.[46] Two of the three villages, Bashshār Naqqāsh and Minyyat ʿAntar, were in the subprovince al-Gharbiyya, and the other, al-Khayyāriyya, was in the subprovince of al-Daqahliyya.[47] The canal in which the island was found ran between the three villages and served as the border of the two subprovinces. The peasants of the two villages in al-Gharbiyya, Bashshār Naqqāsh and Minyyat ʿAntar, asserted in court that the island in question was theirs, owing to the facts that they had built three waterwheels on the island and had been constantly farming its land for many years.

Recently, however, the riverbed underneath the section of the canal that separated the island from the village of al-Khayyāriyya in al-Daqahliyya (on the opposite side of the island from the plaintiffs' villages) had silted up to the point that earth was now showing from underneath the water.[48] This section of the river had, in other words, become so

46 DWQ, Maḥkamat al-Manṣūra 7, p. 90, case 240 (3 Ca 1091/31 May 1680).

47 On al-Khiyāriyya, see: *QJBM*, pt. 2, 1:214.

48 This and other similar cases beg the following question. What was the legal status of land beneath water? As we have already seen, the cleaning and dredging of the beds of canals were the responsibilities of communities that used the water from those canals. This

shallow that it now all but connected the island to the mainland in al-Daqahliyya, thereby allowing the villagers of al-Khayyāriyya to walk easily back and forth between the mainland and the island. Thus, according to the testimony of peasants from the two villages in al-Gharbiyya, the people of al-Khayyāriyya had taken advantage of the new land bridge to commence the planting and farming of the island. Because the villagers of Bashshār Naqqāsh and Minyyat ʿAntar claimed the island as their own, they asserted that the cultivation of the island by the peasants of al-Khayyāriyya was illegal and, thus, had to be stopped by the court.

The individual plaintiff in this case, a case filed in the court of al-Manṣūra, was the *multazim* of the two villages in al-Gharbiyya, a man named al-Amīr Darwīsh Aghā. The fact that a *multazim* from al-Gharbiyya filed a case in the court of al-Manṣūra shows that claimants not resident in a particular subprovince still had the right to bring cases to that subprovince's court.[49] Indeed, we are told in this case that Darwīsh Aghā brought his complaints to the courts of both al-Manṣūra and al-Gharbiyya because the case involved peasants in both subprovinces. He implored the judge of each court to appoint his own dependable men to inspect the current situation of the island. The two courts complied and sent their own officials to the area.[50] After their investigations, the men returned to their respective courts to report their findings. They verified the *multazim*'s claims. Water between the island and the mainland in al-Daqahliyya was indeed very shallow, whereas water on the al-Gharbiyya side of the island remained deep enough to allow large cargo ships (*al-sufun al-mawsūqa*) to easily pass through that section of the river.

In the interests of establishing precedent, other witnesses were also brought to court to verify the plaintiff's claims that the island was the

suggests that being underwater did not significantly change the legal status of land. That all land – whether underwater or not – was considered of the same legal status is further hinted at by the fact that underwater buildups of sand and mud in riverbeds were also often termed *islands* in the archival record of Ottoman Egypt. For example, a series of cases from the court of al-Manṣūra from early in the eighteenth century concern the cleaning and dredging of a series of islands and steps (*cezireler ve atebeler*) in the canal of al-Baḥr al-Ṣaghīr, which was estimated to cost more than fifty thousand *para*. DWQ, Maḥkamat al-Manṣūra 16, p. 397, no case no. (A) (6 Za 1115/12 Mar. 1704); DWQ, Maḥkamat al-Manṣūra 16, p. 397, no case no. (B) (6 Za 1115/12 Mar. 1704).

49 For a discussion of urban merchants' uses of courts in multiple cities other than their own, see: Hanna, *Making Big Money*, 51–53.

50 For other examples of court-ordered inspections of irrigation works, see: DWQ, Maḥkamat Asyūṭ 1, p. 201, case 583 (12 Za 1067/22 Aug. 1657); DWQ, Maḥkamat Asyūṭ 1, p. 287, case 844 (18 Za 1068/18 Aug. 1658); DWQ, Maḥkamat al-Manṣūra 22, p. 236, no case no. (13 S 1152/21 May 1739).

rightful possession of the people of Bashshār Naqqāsh and Minyyat ʿAntar. The carpenters and other builders who constructed the three waterwheels on the island testified that they had built the irrigation works many years earlier to serve the people of the two villages in al-Gharbiyya. Peasants from other nearby villages were also brought to court to verify that it was the villagers of Bashshār Naqqāsh and Minyyat ʿAntar, and not those of al-Khayyāriyya, who had been farming the island for many years.

Customary practice, the continuous cultivation of a piece of land, and the presence of physical structures connected to a certain group of peasants (facts on the ground) were all used in this case as evidence of the precedent of use rights in the adjudication of a dispute initiated to deal with the changing landscape of rural Egypt. Because of the constant movement of water, its converse lack of movement that allowed sediment to settle, its flow power, and its ability to forge the contours of land, Egyptian peasants' environments were constantly changing shape. As seen here, islands that temporarily attached to land created all sorts of challenges to social, legal, communitarian, familial, and agricultural structures, institutions, and traditions.[51] For the Ottoman state and for Egyptian peasants, one of the primary ways to maintain a sustainable social order in the face of changing natural and social environments was to rely on the instructive power of precedent and past experience.

An Ottoman Solution

So far in this chapter we have discussed the Ottoman imperial vision for irrigation in rural Egypt delineated in the pages of al-Jusūr al-Sulṭāniyya, the actual practice of the Empire's management of irrigation works and communities of water, and the ideals of shared usage and precedent that governed the upkeep and maintenance of irrigation features in the Egyptian countryside. In this framework of imperial rule, Egyptian peasants were invested with a great deal of responsibility to oversee the day-to-day function of irrigation works, and they were able to use this power – stemming from their vast knowledge of the countryside – to get what they wanted from the Ottoman bureaucracy. Indeed, because irrigation was both a highly local process that could be understood only

[51] For other examples of disputes arising from the changing shape of islands, see: DWQ, Maḍābiṭ al-Daqahliyya 34, pp. 93–94, case 198 (21 S 1211/25 Aug. 1796); DWQ, Maḥkamat al-Baḥayra 21, p. 152, case 298 (12 Ş 1206/4 Apr. 1792); DWQ, Maḥkamat al-Baḥayra 21, p. 480, case 943 (25 B 1206/19 Mar. 1792).

through an intimate knowledge of the rural Egyptian environment, and at the same time a process with wide imperial implications, Egyptian peasants were uniquely positioned in the administration of irrigation to affect the Ottoman governance of their province in very real ways.

As an example of this process, consider a firman sent to the court of al-Baḥayra in the northwestern Delta from the divan of Egypt in the spring of 1786.[52] The firman – recorded in the registers of the court in Arabic – came to al-Baḥayra in response to a petition sent to the divan by the *multazims* of the villages of Kunayyiset al-Ghayt and Qarṭasā in al-Baḥayra.[53] The *multazims*' petition to the high divan of Egypt informed that body that a bridge over the major canal of the city of al-Damanhūr – the subprovincial seat of al-Baḥayra – had badly deteriorated. The wood and stones that made up the bridge had fallen and piled up in the canal, thus causing the structure to function more like a dam than a bridge, thereby preventing precious water from reaching people and fields in and around al-Damanhūr.

In their petition to the divan, the *multazims* of Kunayyiset al-Ghayt and Qarṭasā entreated this highest of Ottoman administrative bodies in Egypt to allow them to begin constructing a new bridge over the canal in the village of Abū al-Rīsh to the east of the current dilapidated structure.[54] The new bridge would allow water to flow freely through the canal so as to irrigate land and would also allow people to cross over the waterway during the flood. Once the new bridge was finished, the debris of the old one currently hindering the flow of the canal could be removed. In its answer to this petition, the divan gave permission to begin the reconstruction of the new bridge and further instructed the *multazims*

[52] DWQ, Maḥkamat al-Baḥayra 16, p. 259, case 449 (23 C 1200/22 Apr. 1786).

[53] The original petition in this case sent by *multazims* in al-Baḥayra to the divan was translated into Arabic (*yuʿarriba maḍmūnaha*) presumably from Ottoman Turkish – an important indication that *multazims* in rural Egypt were able to communicate in Ottoman Turkish. That the resulting firman was written in Arabic suggests, however, that although the bureaucracy of Ottoman Egypt functioned predominantly in Ottoman Turkish, Arabic was also widely used throughout. Moreover, that the divan of Egypt wrote this firman in Arabic most likely means that the case was to be addressed to and read by (or to) those Egyptian peasants who originally brought the case to court. Like other cases in the vast sea of paper that made up the Ottoman bureaucracy of Egypt, the instructions in this case were meant to serve as a record in the registers of the court to be referenced later when and if the need arose. To be most useful to the community of Egyptian peasants who used the Ottoman court of al-Baḥayra most often, the language of this record had to be Arabic. On Kunayyiset al-Ghayt, see: *QJBM*, pt. 1, 391. On Qarṭasā, see: *QJBM*, pt. 2, 2:290.

[54] On Abū al-Rīsh, see: *QJBM*, pt. 2, 2:288–89.

to pay for all the materials and costs of the work from their own money, which would be repaid to them later. In this regard, the imperial firman ends by directing that the subprovincial leaders addressed in this decree (the *qāḍī*, *kāshif*, *qāʾim-maqām*, *khawlī*, and the heads of the seven military blocs stationed there) were to oversee this work, to help in any way possible with the construction, and to repay the *multazims* once construction was completed.[55]

This case serves as telling evidence of how two *multazims* were able to harness the authority and resources of the Ottoman administration of Egypt to affect change in their local community of water. What made the reconstruction of a broken bridge possible was both the reality that its disrepair hindered the flow of a major canal – and, hence, adversely affected dozens of villages, hundreds of peasants, and overall levels of food production in the Empire – and the realization on the part of the *multazims* of Kunayyiset al-Ghayt and Qarṭasā that the proper function of this irrigation work connected their villages' well-being to that of the Empire as a whole. In other words, this structure was crucial not only to the financial interests, agricultural production capacities, and lives of peasants in the two villages in al-Baḥayra, but its disrepair also had wider imperial implications; without it, the region would produce less food – and, in turn, less money – for the Empire. Because the dual destinies of the imperial state and Egyptian peasants depended on the proper function of a bridge, the latter were able to force the hand of the Ottoman bureaucracy to give them the means and resources to improve their local and personal situations.

Hundreds of other similar cases not only illustrate how Egyptian peasants were able to make the state work for them but also help elucidate what exactly the Ottoman state was on the ground in rural Egypt. In this case, as in many others, the imperial polity comes across as a logistical and financial mechanism through which rural Egyptian leaders were able, as in this example, to facilitate the building and maintenance of a new bridge.[56] Moreover, the Ottoman bureaucrats present in al-Damanhūr

[55] In particularly flowery language, the firman commands these men "to let go of idle talk and to follow the truth in secret" (*tark al-qīl wa al-qāl wa itbāʿ al-ḥaqq fī al-sirr*).

[56] On the various means through which the Ottoman administration of Egypt financed irrigation repair works to both the benefit and detriment of affected peasants, see: DWQ, Maḥkamat al-Manṣūra 12, p. 422, no case no. (29 Ş 1102/28 May 1691); DWQ, Maḥkamat al-Manṣūra 12, p. 424, no case no. (5 L 1102/1 Jul. 1691); DWQ, Maḥkamat al-Manṣūra 12, p. 423, no case no. (25 L 1102/21 Jul. 1691); BOA, MM, 1:310 (1 M 1126/18 Jan. 1724); BOA, MM, 5:46 (Evail Ca 1146/9–18 Oct. 1733); DWQ, Maḥkamat

in this case were instructed by the Ottoman divan of Egypt to obey the petitioning Egyptian peasant *multazims*, not to contradict them, to reimburse them for their expenses, and generally to assist them in every way possible. Thus, it was the *multazims* – not the provincial *kāshif* or the court of al-Baḥayra – who were the real decision makers in the management and execution of the new bridge's reconstruction.[57]

This is not too surprising given that practicality and financial stability were, as I have been arguing, the ultimate underpinnings of the logic of the Ottoman bureaucracy in Egypt.[58] Because the bureaucracy understood that a lack of irrigation in villages around a major Egyptian city like al-Damanhūr was potentially devastating for its imperial rule in Egypt and elsewhere, it sought the quickest and most efficient way to fix a broken bridge that was hurting the agricultural production potential of Egypt: to allow local *multazims* and others with intimate knowledge of and experience in the area to manage the repair themselves. For the Ottomans, rural Egypt was the goose that laid golden eggs, and they thus treated it accordingly.

Cases like the previous one in which local Egyptian peasants seemingly used the Ottoman state for their own ends were not the anomalous result of the machinations of exceptionally savvy leaders who were able to work the system. Rather, the process of devolving authority over irrigation works to local leaders and peasants was a constitutive, deliberate, and integral facet of Ottoman administration in rural Egypt. That is, the Ottoman bureaucracy in Egypt understood that those who knew the most about the function and history of irrigation works in the local

al-Manṣūra 12, p. 445, no case no. (B) (4 Ca 1104/11 Jan. 1693); DWQ, Maḥkamat al-Manṣūra 18, p. 249 or p. 250, no case no. (A) (1 Ş 1121/5 Oct. 1709); DWQ, Maḥkamat al-Manṣūra 19, no page no., no case no. (9 Ra 1122/8 May 1710); DWQ, Maḥkamat al-Manṣūra 15, p. 205, no case no. (20 L 1113/19 Mar. 1702); BOA, MM, 8:337 (Evahir Z 1178/10–19 Jun. 1765); BOA, MM, 6:558 (Evahir N 1162/4–13 Sep. 1749); BOA, MM, 5:189 (Evasıt Ş 1147/6–15 Jan. 1735); DWQ, Rūznāma 4557 – Daftar Irtifā' al-Miyāh bi-Baḥr Sayyidnā Yūsuf lihi al-Ṣalāh wa al-Salām 'an al-Qabḍa al-Yūsufiyya Tābi' Wilāyat al-Fayyūm (Raqam al-Ḥifẓ al-Nau'ī 1, 'Ayn 59, Makhzin Turkī 1, Musalsal 4557), p. 22, no case no. (28 R 1127/2 May 1715). For instances of the theft of funds made available for irrigation repairs, see: DWQ, Maḥkamat al-Manṣūra 51, p. 159, case 297 (Ca 1203/Jan. and Feb. 1789); DWQ, Maḥkamat al-Manṣūra 19, p. 368, no case no. (B) (2 M 1125/29 Jan. 1713).

57 For a similar case involving the repair of a dike, in which the local experience and knowledge of Egyptian peasants was privileged over that of the *ḥākim* of the subprovince of al-Daqahliyya – the highest subprovincial authority – see: DWQ, Maḥkamat al-Manṣūra 24, p. 146, case 333 (3 M 1136/3 Oct. 1723).

58 In this vein, Michael Winter describes the regime in Egypt as "the realistic Ottomans." Winter, *Egyptian Society under Ottoman Rule*, 20.

environments of rural Egypt were the very Egyptian peasants who used them most often, who benefited from them, and whose lives and livelihoods most directly depended on them.

Thus, in contrast to descriptions of eighteenth-century rural Egypt that stress the oppressive nature of Ottoman rule in the countryside, I therefore argue here that it was really Egyptian peasants who controlled Ottoman bureaucrats – not the other way around – in the determination and execution of repairs to irrigation works in the countryside.[59] The imperially coordinated localism characterized by the investment of local peasant actors with the freedom and wherewithal to initiate and control repairs to Egypt's irrigation network from beginning to end was, therefore, what I call an Ottoman solution to the problem of flood and agriculture in the countryside of the Empire's most lucrative province. Lest I be misunderstood, allow me to state explicitly here that my objective is not to argue for some sort of notion of Ottoman benevolence toward Egyptian peasants.[60] Above all else, the motivations of the Ottoman administration of Egypt were practicality.

Central to the function of this imperial system in Egypt and elsewhere was the institution of the court. A case from the court of al-Manṣūra from the middle of the eighteenth century further illustrates the processes by which Egyptian peasants were able to use the Ottoman court to ameliorate the common environmental problem of the restriction of water flow due to the silting of canals.[61] Recorded in the registers of the court of al-Manṣūra, this case was a firman sent from the divan of Egypt – the

59 For works that stress the oppressiveness of Ottoman rule in rural Egypt, see: ʿAbd al-Raḥīm, *al-Rīf al-Miṣrī*; al-Rāfʿī, *ʿAṣr Muḥammad ʿAlī*.

60 For a very useful treatment of peasants in the Ottoman Empire, see: Karen Barkey, *Bandits and Bureaucrats: The Ottoman Route to State Centralization* (Ithaca, NY: Cornell University Press, 1994), 85–140. Studies of peasants in various locations throughout the Empire abound. My thinking on the subject has been most shaped by the following: Doumani, *Rediscovering Palestine*; Amy Singer, *Palestinian Peasants and Ottoman Officials: Rural Administration around Sixteenth-Century Jerusalem* (Cambridge: Cambridge University Press, 1994); Khoury, *State and Provincial Society*.

61 In the following case, after a very formulaic general restatement of the imperial Ottoman principle that the state was to protect the overall well-being of the people (*reʿaya*) under its care, we find a very succinct statement that the responsibilities of the imperial bureaucracy in Egypt were to preserve a steady flow of revenue to the state's coffers and a steady flow of water in the province's canals: DWQ, Maḥkamat al-Manṣūra 12, p. 461, no case no. (20 Z 1104/22 Aug. 1693). Effective irrigation was meant to ensure both that peasants would have water for the cultivation of food and, in turn, that the state would have a consistent base of taxation. As conduits of both water and good imperial governance, canals and irrigation thus sat at the crossroads of the economic maintenance of the state and the caloric sustenance of the Empire's peoples.

highest official representative of the Ottoman state in Egypt – to the *ḥākim* and *qāḍī* of the subprovince of al-Daqahliyya as well as to other officials in the area.[62] The firman begins by recounting how the divan of Egypt received from the leaders (*al-ḥukkām*) of al-Manzala – a village in the subprovince discussed earlier – a petition stating that a group of peasants, village elders, and the poor came to the court to report that certain sections of the canal of al-Baḥr al-Ṣaghīr had silted up with dirt, sand, and debris, thus restricting the waterway's flow and preventing irrigation water from reaching their villages.[63] Moreover, the presence of many ditches along the length of the canal drew water out of this main conduit, adversely affecting the strength of its overall flow downstream.

The Egyptian peasants who came to the court thus reported that areas of buildup in the canal needed to be dredged and that many of the ditches and small canals along the length of this waterway had to be dammed or otherwise sealed to improve the overall flow of the main waterway of al-Baḥr al-Ṣaghīr.[64] The peasants also reasserted that each village along the length of the canal should be held responsible for cleaning and dredging the section of the waterway nearest its own village and also for the reinforcement of the canal's embankments in each of those areas. This series of actions would improve access to water resources for all the villages along the length of the canal and those elsewhere that relied on the canal for their supplies of water. Citing the many advantages of the peasants' suggestions, officials in al-Manzala sent their petition to the divan of Egypt requesting that the local court be allowed to sanction the peasants' requests. The firman sent back to the court from the divan thus represented official imperial permission to sanction and begin executing the peasants' plans.

Following the bureaucratic trail traced in this case suggests how the Ottoman bureaucracy of irrigation in Egypt and the province's peasants used one another – each to its own benefit – in the management of the complicated and ever-changing rural environment of the Egyptian countryside. Set into motion by a group of peasants and villagers in their local Ottoman court in the subprovincial city of al-Manṣūra, the

62 DWQ, Maḥkamat al-Manṣūra 22, p. 228, case 497 (25 Za 1184/12 Mar. 1771).

63 For a similar case of a silted over canal, see: DWQ, Rūznāma 4557 – Daftar Irtifāʿ al-Miyāh bi-Baḥr Sayyidnā Yūsuf lihi al-Ṣalāh wa al-Salām ʿan al-Qabḍa al-Yūsufiyya Tābiʿ Wilāyat al-Fayyūm (Raqam al-Ḥifẓ al-Nauʿī 1, ʿAyn 59, Makhzin Turkī 1, Musalsal 4557), p. 14, no case no. (3 C 1200/2 Apr. 1786).

64 For an example of Egyptian peasants petitioning the Ottoman state to open canals, see: DWQ, Maḥkamat al-Manṣūra 12, p. 426, no case no. (15 Za 1102/10 Aug. 1691).

bureaucratic flow of this case took the peasants' petition from the court to the divan of Egypt in Cairo for approval and instruction, and the divan then responded to the request with a firman sent back to the local court.[65] Bureaucratically, this was an extremely unproblematic case because all seemed to agree that the peasants' ideas were practical and worthwhile. The divan of Egypt's function was thus merely to approve the peasants' requests and to issue a firman to the local court of al-Manṣūra in this regard – underscoring that this rural court could not approve the requests on its own and had to defer to the divan of Cairo as the highest imperial administrative body in Egypt. As part of the Ottoman solution to the complexities of the administration of irrigation and environment in rural Egypt, we see here (as elsewhere) that it was Egyptian peasants themselves who suggested the most efficient and expedient means of managing the water resources and maintenance of the canal of al-Baḥr al-Ṣaghīr.[66] They lived on it and understood that if peasants in each of the villages on the canal managed the small portion of the canal that passed by or through their village, then the entire length of this main artery and all those who relied on Egypt's imperially consequential irrigation infrastructure would be best served.[67]

The Ottoman solution to irrigation in rural Egypt was not only the result of clever Ottoman governance or savviness on the part of Egyptian peasants. It was also a function of the ecological realities of the speed of water and of the collection of sand and dirt on canal beds. The churning of the Ottoman bureaucracy of Egypt could in no way move quickly enough to keep up with the flow of water in Egypt's canals.[68] As an

65 The text of this case from the registers of the court of al-Manṣūra does not give any indication that the divan of Egypt sent this request all the way to Istanbul for direction. In many cases, of course, petitions of this sort and other requests and disputes were sent from Cairo to Istanbul for resolution. Because no major dispute or point of contention existed in this case though, there was really no reason to send it all the way to Istanbul.

66 For additional examples of similar peasant initiatives, see the following cases from the court of al-Manṣūra: DWQ, Maḥkamat al-Manṣūra 4, p. 108, case 281 (1 M 1075/24 Jul. 1664); DWQ, Maḥkamat al-Manṣūra 12, p. 448 no case no. (11 C 1104/17 Feb. 1693); DWQ, Maḥkamat al-Manṣūra 16, p. 402, no case no. (B) (30 Za 1115/5 Apr. 1704).

67 For additional cases illustrating the effective authority of local peasant communities over irrigation works in their villages, see: DWQ, Maḥkamat al-Manṣūra 16, p. 47, case 86 (13 B 1115/23 Nov. 1703); DWQ, Maḥkamat al-Manṣūra 19, p. 33, case 88 (11 C 1122/7 Aug. 1710); DWQ, Maḥkamat al-Manṣūra 18, p. 245 or p. 246, no case no. (A) (15 Z 1122/3 Feb. 1711).

68 In the following cases, the Ottoman administration of Egypt sought to move quickly enough to repair a broken canal embankment before all the canal's waters wastefully spilled onto the land around the canal: DWQ, Maḥkamat al-Manṣūra 18, p. 266, no case no. (A and D) (21 C 1121/27 Aug. 1709); DWQ, Maḥkamat al-Manṣūra 18, p. 266, no case no. (C) (6 B 1121/10 Sep. 1709).

early modern polity based on the management of the natural worlds of agriculture and irrigation, the Ottoman Empire was clearly subservient to the courses and flows of the environments under its suzerainty.[69] This was a further reason for the central involvement of local populations in the management of irrigation works in rural Egypt.[70] Although the Empire could of course never fully control the environmental forces in its realm, by having local Egyptian peasants on the ground effectively watching over rural irrigation features and informing the state of their status, the Ottoman bureaucracy could much more efficiently rule over Egypt's irrigated ecosystems. At the same time, Egyptian peasants could not repair irrigation works in their communities without the resources of the Ottoman state – resources of course based fundamentally on the agricultural labor of Egyptian peasants themselves. Thus, alone, neither peasants nor the Ottoman administration of Egypt could repair irrigation works in the Egyptian countryside; it was only cooperatively that this work could be achieved.

This reality was an effect of, on the one hand, the constant demands of a changing natural environment that regularly overwhelmed local communities and that affected the resources on which they relied and, on the other hand, an Ottoman imperial system that privileged local expertise and historical specificity over any notion of empirewide homogeneity or cultural or social uniformity. The relationship between the Ottoman capital in Istanbul and peasants in rural Egypt was thus one predicated on mutual political, infrastructural, and economic benefit. The Ottoman state pooled the revenues generated by Egyptian peasants and used some of them to finance the maintenance of the irrigation system. In this way, it functioned very much like a bank – the mobilization of capital for

69 For an example of the Ottoman bureaucracy's flexibility in responding effectively to environmental changes in the agricultural productivity levels of land in Egypt, see: DWQ, Maḥkamat al-Baḥayra 14, p. 390, case 612 (23 L 1200/18 Aug. 1786).

70 For examples of peasant petitions for greater allotments of water from Egypt's rural irrigation network, see: DWQ, Rūznāma 4557 – Daftar Irtifāʿ al-Miyāh bi-Baḥr Sayyidnā Yūsuf lihi al-Ṣalāh wa al-Salām ʿan al-Qabḍa al-Yūsufiyya Tābiʿ Wilāyat al-Fayyūm (Raqam al-Ḥifẓ al-Nauʿī 1, ʿAyn 59, Makhzin Turkī 1, Musalsal 4557), p. 11, no case no. (21 Ra 1192/19 Apr. 1778); DWQ, Rūznāma 4557 – Daftar Irtifāʿ al-Miyāh bi-Baḥr Sayyidnā Yūsuf lihi al-Ṣalāh wa al-Salām ʿan al-Qabḍa al-Yūsufiyya Tābiʿ Wilāyat al-Fayyūm (Raqam al-Ḥifẓ al-Nauʿī 1, ʿAyn 59, Makhzin Turkī 1, Musalsal 4557), p. 12, no case no. (21 Ra 1195/17 Mar. 1781); DWQ, Rūznāma 4557 – Daftar Irtifāʿ al-Miyāh bi-Baḥr Sayyidnā Yūsuf lihi al-Ṣalāh wa al-Salām ʿan al-Qabḍa al-Yūsufiyya Tābiʿ Wilāyat al-Fayyūm (Raqam al-Ḥifẓ al-Nauʿī 1, ʿAyn 59, Makhzin Turkī 1, Musalsal 4557), p. 13, no case no. (9 S 1197/13 Jan. 1783); DWQ, Maḥkamat Asyūṭ 2, p. 235, case 558 (22 Z 1107/22 Jul. 1696).

investment in infrastructure – while at the same time ensuring its own future revenues.

In the archival record of this relationship between the imperial Ottoman bureaucracy of Egypt and Egyptian peasants, certain actors appear over and over again as pivotal informants for the Empire on the ground in rural Egypt. These were a group of men known as *erbab-ı vukuf* or *erbab-ı hibre* in Ottoman Turkish or *ahl al-wuqūf* or *ahl al-khibra* in Arabic. These local men of knowledge, expertise, and experience were regularly used by the system of Ottoman imperial courts in rural Egypt to carry out periodic checks and inspections of canals and other irrigation works in the countryside.[71] Furthermore, these local leaders assured the court that peasants – as those who most directly benefited from the waters of canals – would take full responsibility for the protection and maintenance of the canals.

Again, it was the testimony of local Egyptian peasants who understood the specific history, topography, and needs of irrigation works and of users of those works in particular environments that convinced the Ottoman state that a canal was in full working condition. Without the very local knowledge and input of Egyptian men of knowledge, the Ottoman bureaucracy of Egypt would not have been able to control the irrigation infrastructure under its suzerainty. This massive bureaucracy thus had to subsume within itself the experience, expertise, and knowledge of local peasant men to be able to ascertain the extremely complex and constantly changing details it needed to manage irrigation in Egypt.

Water Making Dirt

Through the upholding of precedent and its reliance on the local knowledge and experience of peasants, the Ottoman state in Egypt maintained

[71] For cases involving these local early modern experts, see: BOA, Cevdet Nafia, 120 (Evasıt Ca 1125/5–14 Jun. 1713); BOA, MM, 8:469 (Evasıt L 1180/12–21 Mar. 1767); DWQ, Maḥkamat al-Manṣūra 18, p. 266, no case no. (B) (6 B 1121/10 Sep. 1709); BOA, MM, 9:424 (Evail C 1194/4–13 Jun. 1780); DWQ, Maḥkamat Asyūṭ 4, p. 206, case 645 (11 C 1156/2 Aug. 1743); DWQ, Maḥkamat Asyūṭ 2, p. 238, case 566 (13 M 1108/11 Aug. 1696); DWQ, Maḥkamat Asyūṭ 5, p. 179, case 343 (20 C 1189/17 Aug. 1775); DWQ, Maḥkamat Asyūṭ 8, p. 260, case 563 (14 S 1211/18 Aug. 1796); DWQ, Maḍābiṭ al-Daqahliyya 19, p. 299, case 878 (1185/1771 and 1772); DWQ, Maḍābiṭ al-Daqahliyya 19, p. 299, case 875 (1185/1771 and 1772); DWQ, Maḍābiṭ al-Daqahliyya 19, p. 299, case 874 (1185/1771 and 1772); DWQ, Maḍābiṭ al-Daqahliyya 19, p. 299, case 876 (1185/1771 and 1772); DWQ, Maḍābiṭ al-Daqahliyya 19, p. 299, case 877 (1185/1771 and 1772); DWQ, Maḍābiṭ al-Daqahliyya 19, p. 299, case 872 (1185/1771 and 1772); DWQ, Maḍābiṭ al-Daqahliyya 19, p. 299, case 873 (1185/1771 and 1772); DWQ, Maḍābiṭ al-Daqahliyya 19, p. 300, case 880 (1185/1771 and 1772).

a productive social, economic, and environmental order based on the shared usage of water and the cultivation of foodstuffs. In the earlier discussion of a dispute over the cultivation of an island, we saw how water and its movement literally changed the shape of agricultural land in Egypt. In this section, I focus on how the addition and removal of water made agricultural land and, hence, made money for the Ottoman state in Egypt. Both the reclaiming of desert and the reclamation of land from the Nile resulted in the forging of new agricultural, economic, and ecological environments in Egypt – thus creating new fields; building new canals; attracting peasants to live on and to work the lands and maintain the canals; and constructing new areas of cultivation and of human, animal, and plant life.[72] The very deliberate action on the part of the Ottoman state to create new life worlds through the manipulation of water access permanently changed both the physical realities of Egyptian peasants and the economic potentialities of the province of Egypt as a whole.

In a case from the southern city of Asyūṭ in the year 1657, we see how water and the proper function of irrigation works were used in the reclamation of agricultural lands. A group of diggers and reinforcers (*al-ḥufrāʾ wa al-mudamasīn*) who regularly worked on a series of three canals in Asyūṭ came to the court to testify that they had cleaned, dredged, and reinforced them as required and that they – along with the people of the fifteen villages along the canals who were represented at court by the elders (*mashāʾikh*) of each village – remained responsible for the upkeep of the waterways.[73] The elders of the fifteen villages also reported to the court that, by actively maintaining the three canals, they had been able to increase the overall area of agricultural land in their villages. Whereas previously there had been only 25 *ardabbs* of arable land, now these peasants had 37.5 *ardabbs* on which to plant and harvest. This case was followed by a nearly identical one the following year in which the same workers were identified as working on the same canals with the same results: an increase in the amount of land under cultivation

72 For a discussion and analysis of other cases about water and the shifting topography of rural Ottoman Egypt, see: Alan Mikhail, "Piles of History: The Nile, Dirt, and Humans in Ottoman Egypt," forthcoming in *Environmental Imaginaries of the Middle East: History, Policy, Power, and Practice*, ed. Diana K. Davis and Edmund Burke III (Athens: Ohio University Press).

73 DWQ, Maḥkamat Asyūṭ 1, p. 201, case 583 (12 Za 1067/22 Aug. 1657). All three canals were near the city of Asyūṭ. One stretched from the Nile to the village of al-Muṭīʿa, another began in the village of Safḥ al-Mayl al-Gharbī and ended in the village of Kafr al-Muṭīʿa, and the third began in this latter village and ended at the major intersection (*al-maqṭaʿ al-kabīr*) near the village. On al-Muṭīʿa, see: *QJBM*, pt. 2, 4:27.

and improvements in the irrigation system that fed water to the lands.[74] These cases not only exemplify, yet again, the influential role of local knowledge in the management of irrigation works in rural Egypt but also clearly show how irrigation created new environments, new worlds, new ecologies, new fields, new planting and work opportunities, new crops, and new physical and natural spaces.[75] Improvements to the irrigation network in this area led to a 50 percent increase in the area of agricultural land made available to the peasants of fifteen villages.

In another effort to self-consciously shape the ecology of the Egyptian countryside by reclaiming land through water, the *qāʾim-maqām* of Egypt, the amir Ismāʿīl Bey, sent a *buyuruldu* to the judge of the court of al-Damanhūr in the subprovince of al-Baḥayra about a piece of land in the village of al-Shūka located next to the property of one Abū Ḥammād.[76] The earth in al-Shūka was said to be barren and uncultivated (*mawāt*). The high Ottoman divan in Cairo intervened in the fate of this land by putting it under the control of a man named al-Shaykh Shams al-Dīn Muḥammad al-Shāhīnī, who was afforded installments of cash from the imperial council (*taqsīṭ dīwānī*) under the auspices of the *qāʾim-maqām* Ismāʿīl Bey to care for the land and to make it fertile once again. Clearly hoping to gain from this investment in the agricultural potential of a particular piece of land, the divan required that the property return two hundred *niṣf fiḍḍa* (or *para*) to the state on an annual basis.[77] The most crucial factor in the fertilization and reclamation of this land from its barrenness was the maintenance of its only major source of water, a small creek known as Baṭn al-Dīb that flowed into the canal of al-Khashiyya and that served both as the property's southern border and as part of its western border. The high divan's use of cash installments is a unique feature of this case.[78] As mentioned earlier, the payments represented

74 DWQ, Maḥkamat Asyūṭ 1, p. 287, case 844 (18 Za 1068/18 Aug. 1658).

75 For another example of the deliberate use of irrigation to turn barren earth into productive agricultural land, see the following rather complicated cases about the village of Damanhūr in the subprovince of Manfalūṭ: DWQ, Maḥkamat Manfalūṭ 3, p. 18, case 30 (1227/1812 and 1813); DWQ, Maḥkamat Manfalūṭ 3, p. 8, case 8 (11 Ca 1228/12 May 1813).

76 DWQ, al-Jusūr al-Sulṭāniyya 786, pp. 113v–114r, no case no. (18 Z 1117/2 Apr. 1706). The judge's name was Muṣṭafā Ibn Aḥmad Effendi al-Ḥanafī. On the village of al-Shūka, see: *QJBM*, pt. 2, 2:283.

77 According to Shaw, "the silver coin in common use during Mamlûk and Ottoman times in Egypt was called *nısf fıḍḍe* colloquially and *para* officially." Shaw, *Financial and Administrative Organization and Development*, 65n169.

78 One clue as to why the state paid out installments in this case and not in others is the identity of the recipient of the funds, al-Shaykh Shams al-Dīn Muḥammad al-Shāhīnī.

a bold kind of early modern Ottoman venture capitalism – with all its accrued risks and rewards – aimed at reclaiming agricultural land for cultivation and at collecting high revenues for the state. This is another example of the banking function served by the Ottoman bureaucracy of Egypt. It put forth modest sums of money to invest in making barren land fertile and productive and, hence, capable of generating large returns.[79]

Various other kinds of deliberate action to change the physical and natural environments of the Egyptian countryside through water were also undertaken in the eighteenth century. Many of these involved reviving land that had once been fertile but had fallen into disuse or had become barren. An example of this kind of reclamation of land from barrenness is a case from the court of al-Baḥayra in the northwestern Nile Delta from the year 1782 concerning a section of earth measuring eight feddans and bordered on three of its four sides by water.[80] Its northern border was a canal; to its east lay a ditch that divided it from the village of al-Qūja; and its western border was a basin known as Ḥawḍ al-Sharrawi separating it from the village of Ṭāmūs.[81] Because of the state of disrepair and deterioration that had gripped each of the irrigation features, the land in question had not properly received water for some time and was no longer suitable for cultivation.

In an effort to restore the land to its once-fertile status, the court ordered an inspection of the area and of its agricultural fields. Five

Not only was he a shaykh; he was also – as we are told in this case – the son of a respected scholar at al-Azhar in Cairo. He was, in other words, from a known, respected, trusted, and – importantly – connected family of high social and religious standing. The Ottoman administration of Egypt thus took a calculated risk that it could trust him with its money and safely expect the financial returns it sought. On the social role of al-Azhar in Egyptian history, see: Muṣṭafā Muḥammad Ramaḍān, *Dawr al-Azhar fī al-Ḥayah al-Miṣriyya ibbāna al-Ḥamlah al-Faransiyya wa Maṭlaʿ al-Qarn al-Tāsiʿ ʿAshar* (Cairo: Maṭbaʿat al-Jabalāwī, 1986); Bayard Dodge, *Al-Azhar: A Millennium of Muslim Learning* (Washington, D.C.: Middle East Institute, 1961).

79 Another case from the court of al-Baḥayra in 1820 clearly indicates the economic logic underlying the Ottoman bureaucracy's projects to reclaim land from the desert for agricultural uses. Seeking to increase the amount of taxable agricultural land in Egypt, the Ottoman state in this case instructed that a certain amount of formerly desolate (*būr*) land was to be fully irrigated and planted. Most important for our purposes is the fact that the state specified exactly how much new land was needed to meet its monetary goals of taxation on the lands of this particular subprovince. This very deliberate action on the part of the Ottoman state to create new land in rural Egypt permanently changed both the physical realities of Egyptian peasants and the economic potentialities of the province of Egypt as a whole. DWQ, Maḥkamat al-Baḥayra 38, p. 300, case 707 (26 Za 1235/4 Sep. 1820).

80 DWQ, Maḥkamat al-Baḥayra 12, p. 158, no case no. (12 Za 1196/19 Oct. 1782).

81 On Ṭāmūs, see: *QJBM*, pt. 2, 2:288–89.

men – one of whom was the *khawlī* of the region – went to inspect the land and found it and the waterways that formed its borders to be collectively filled with dirt and garbage (*al-atriba wa al-qumāmāt*).[82] As such, the men asked the court for a removal mechanism (*jihāz izāla*) to clean the land and the waterways around it to make the fields once again suitable for planting and cultivation.[83] After hearing the men's testimony,

[82] The personality of the *khawlī* was often employed by the state to inspect irrigation works in rural Egypt and, more generally, to oversee matters concerning irrigation and the upkeep of canals, waterwheels, basins, and other such waterworks. On the position of the *khawlī*, see: ʿAbd al-Raḥīm, *al-Rīf al-Miṣrī*, 46–50. In this section, ʿAbd al-Raḥīm cites the opening section of a register of the archival unit of al-Jusūr al-Sulṭāniyya, which makes explicit mention of the fact that the *khawlī* was the official responsible for the upkeep and proper function of canals. He writes that this register (no. 784) covers the subprovince of al-Gharbiyya, al-Sharqiyya, and al-Minūfiyya, but he is slightly mistaken in this regard, because the register covers only the subprovinces of al-Gharbiyya and al-Minūfiyya. He makes special note of the fact that he put forth a concerted effort to locate other registers of this archival unit but was unable to do so. By the time I and other scholars like Nicholas Michel consulted this archival unit, there were five registers in total made available to researchers.

Cuno defines the *khawlī* as a "village functionary." Cuno, *The Pasha's Peasants*, 269. See also: Yāsir ʿAbd al-Minʿam Maḥārīq, *al-Minūfiyya fī al-Qarn al-Thāmin ʿAshar* (Cairo: al-Hayʾa al-Miṣriyya al-ʿĀmma lil-Kitāb, 2000), 138–39 and 156–57; Sato, *State and Rural Society*, 186; DWQ, Maḥkamat al-Bāb al-ʿĀlī 120, p. 45, case 89 (Evahir M 1049/24 May–2 Jun. 1639). It should be noted that this register is incorrectly labeled as belonging to the court of al-Bāb al-ʿĀlī. The cases inside make clear that they are from the court of al-Bahnasāwiyya (Benī Suef), a court whose records are otherwise unavailable to researchers.

The post of the *khawlī* was often hereditary. For example, the *khawlī* of Asyūṭ in 1723 was a Christian man named Jirjis who had inherited the position from his father. DWQ, Maḥkamat Asyūṭ 3, p. 780, case 2127 (24 L 1135/27 Jul. 1723). In some cases, *khawlī*s functioned as kinds of judges. For example, a *khawlī* arbitrated a bitter dispute between a widow named Fāṭin Bint Sirāj al-Dīn al-Ṣāwī and her recently deceased husband's other male heirs over the inheritance of his estate. DWQ, Maḍābiṭ al-Daqahliyya 19, p. 152, case 452 (28 S 1186/31 May 1772). Elsewhere we read that *khawlī*s were responsible for the collection of the jizya. DWQ, Maḥkamat Asyūṭ 8, p. 95, case 195 (2 Ra 1051/11 Jun. 1641). In the following case, the members of a *khawlī*'s family were held hostage until he properly completed his charge: DWQ, Maḥkamat al-Bāb al-ʿĀlī 120, pp. 96–97, case 187 (22 Ca 1049/20 Sep. 1639).

[83] Compare this case to the following, in which the *kāshif* of Manfalūṭ was ordered to prepare a series of irrigation tools (*alât-ı carâfa*) to be used in the repair of a group of *sulṭānī* canals in the southern city: DWQ, Maḥkamat Manfalūṭ 2, p. 183, case 619 (16 Ca 1179/31 Oct. 1765). There is no specification in either case of what exactly the tools or instruments were, but they were likely items such as shovels, pickaxes, baskets, and the like. Although we often read of the building materials – brick, mud, plaster, and so on – used in repair projects, these are some of the few cases in the archival record of eighteenth-century Ottoman Egypt to mention directly the use of tools in the repair of canals and other irrigation works. These and other cases serve as important reminders of the need to think critically about the role of technology – in the form of

the court decided that the cleaning and restoration of the land was an issue deserving of its attention.

As we see once again in this case, the fate of agricultural land in Egypt was tied to water. Given the vicissitudes of the availability of this precious commodity, agricultural lands regularly experienced phases of use and disuse, fertility and barrenness, neglect and attention. In this case, the collection of dirt and garbage in its surrounding waterways made land agriculturally moribund. Thus, both the shape and status of land in rural Egypt were constantly changing. Peasants moved; deserts were made fertile; rich soils were sometimes abandoned; and fields went through constant cycles of cultivation, fallow, and neglect. Water was almost always at play because it was the vital substance whose presence made land fertile and whose absence kept it barren.

In these examples, the reclamation of land to increase the overall area of agricultural production in Egypt was achieved by bringing water to formerly unirrigated earth. Another means of reclaiming land in Egypt was the opposite process – the removal of water from areas of the Nile or other waterways to recover land from beneath water. Because of the vagaries of the annual flood, certain fields were occasionally covered over with water, whereas others emerged when water receded. For example, in May 1812, the Nile in Cairo dried up to such an extent that it was almost possible to traverse the entire width of the river from Bulaq to Imbaba on the opposite shore by walking on the many "sand hills" that emerged from underneath the receded water.[84]

This situation, one that "was unparalleled in this age," lasted only a few months, however, until the floodwaters of late summer covered the riverbed once again. The outline of the Nile's shores was also in constant flux. Properties in both Upper and Lower Egypt were continually becoming larger and smaller as water ebbed and flowed through thousands of channels throughout the countryside.[85]

shovels, waterwheels, dams, various modes of transport, and even the selective breeding of crops – in rural Egypt for the cultivation of food, irrigation, and much more.

84 ʿAbd al-Raḥman al-Jabartī, *ʿAbd al-Raḥman al-Jabartī's History of Egpyt: ʿAjāʾib al-Āthār fī al-Tarājim wa al-Akhbār*, ed. Thomas Philipp and Moshe Perlmann, 4 vols. (Stuttgart: Franz Steiner Verlag, 1994), 4:213. Given the centrality of al-Jabartī's text to the period under study, I have chosen to aid the reader by referencing the foregoing English translation of the text. I have used my own translations only where indicated relying on the following Arabic version of the text: ʿAbd al-Raḥman Ibn Ḥasan al-Jabartī, *ʿAjāʾib al-Āthār fī al-Tarājim wa al-Akhbār*, ed. ʿAbd al-Raḥīm ʿAbd al-Raḥman ʿAbd al-Raḥīm, 4 vols. (Cairo: Maṭbaʿat Dār al-Kutub al-Miṣriyya, 1998).

85 Ibid., 4:293.

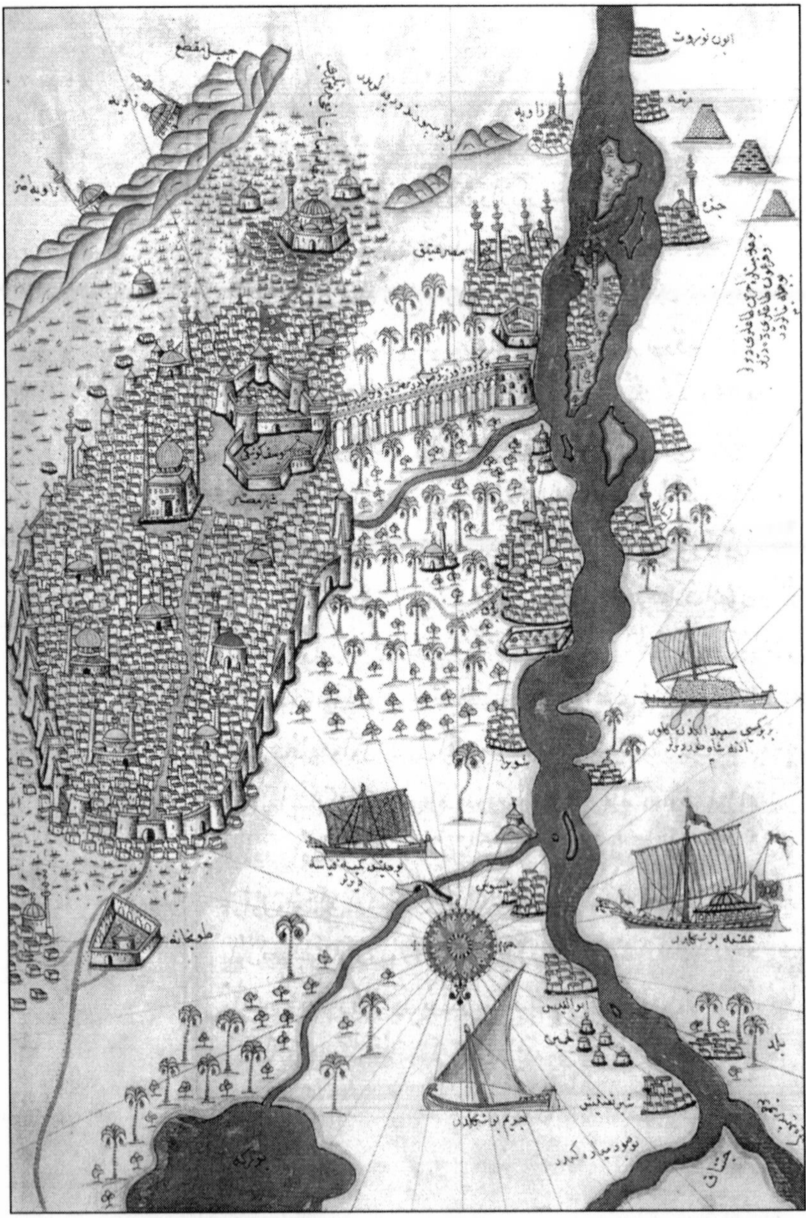

Figure 1.1. A sixteenth-century rendition of the Nile in Cairo. Piri Reis, *Kitâb-ı Bahriye*, İstanbul Üniversitesi Kütüphanesi, Nadir Eserler, TY. 6605, 302r. Used by permission of the Istanbul University Library.

These natural changes to the course and size of the Nile were common enough and understood by Egyptians to be part of the ecology of their natural environment. In addition to these phenomena, however, there were also very deliberate human attempts to shape shorelines and properties by reclaiming land from beneath the Nile's waters. One of the most striking examples of such a project was an effort by ʿAlī Bey al-Kabīr in 1771 and 1772 to recraft a section of the Nile shore in Cairo. The unintended consequences of this project are a telling example of how the human manipulation of the Egyptian environment affected Egyptians' interactions with the Nile and the natural world around them. According to al-Jabartī:

> ʿAlī Bey erected also the huge complex on the Nile bank in Būlāq, at the timber-yards, at the foot of al-Khurnūb Tenement. It is a huge covered market, with two gates leading from north to south or vice versa. He also built an extensive khan, surmounted on either side by residential buildings, while outside of it was a grain depot and shops along the Nile, together with a medium-sized mosque. The foundation of the entire complex was dug until water was reached; then curbs like minarets were constructed of stone, rubble, and other material. These were sunk into the trench, until the construction was on solid ground. Then the trench containing the curbs was filled with stone, rubble, and so forth, and over it they erected solidly constructed buildings of hewn stones, with vaults, columns, and solid beams of wood....
>
> It was a most unfortunate project. For the Nile was deflected by it from the Būlāq shore, its current was halted and pushed toward Imbāba, so that the land rose and alluvial deposits continually increased from the corner of that construction down to the grain depot, rising steadily from year to year, until finally the water reached it only in years of high inundation. It went from bad to worse. People built houses and coffeehouses north of the construction, continually pushing westward to the water, and dumping the earth from the excavations. The professional excavators and others followed suit, with no one to put a halt to the practice. The water receded more and more, the current weakened, and the ground swelled up and rose and increased until the area was full of mounds that were hideous to behold and that filled the breath with dust, especially in the midday heat. Yet this used to be a delightful pleasure spot. Beforehand, we saw the Nile current flowing into the area from Būlāq al-Takrūr, passing with full force at the foot of the walls of the southern houses and commercial buildings, the grain depots, the spice-trade center, the onion market, al-Sinānīya Mosque, and al-Khurnūb Tenement, down to the Jīʿānīya. It would swing to al-Ḥillī Palace and Shaykh Faraj in summer and winter unimpeded, and nobody dared throw any dirt on the Nile Bank....

> As a result of this construction, the ground rose by four times the human height. We used to count over 20 steps from the grain merchants' *wakāla* to the river, when we lived there before the construction; there were a similar number of steps on the staircase that led down to the river from the house of Shaykh ʿAbdallāh al-Qamarī. But all the steps have disappeared, covered by soil.[86]

Although this "most unfortunate project" did succeed in expanding the commercial spaces of Cairo on the banks of the Nile and in increasing the geographical area of the city more generally, its results were extremely detrimental for those Cairenes who had become accustomed to a certain regular interaction with the river. Indeed, silting and the dirtying of the river's waters and of the atmosphere transformed this once "delightful" area into one big mound of dirt. One of the environmental impacts of this sort of reclamation was thus to cover areas of Cairo with all sorts of dirt and sand that changed the ways Egyptians came to relate to the river. No longer were they able to walk down to the river as before or to rely on its waters for drinking, bathing, cleaning, or otherwise.[87] In summary, then, whereas more soil and dirt in the Egyptian countryside were assets to the rural economy and were hence supported through state and local reclamation efforts, an excess of dirt and earth in the city, though it created opportunities for more commercial property, was often a polluting nuisance and an irritant with various negative consequences.

Irrigation as Protest

Water made agricultural land in Ottoman Egypt. Peasants, though, made agricultural land productive. Without their knowledge of local village environments, labor in maintaining irrigation works, and contributions to the generating of revenues and food for the Empire, ample supplies of water were not enough for growing food in the fields of Egypt. As we saw earlier, because irrigation in Egypt had wide economic consequences for the Empire as a whole, Egyptian peasants were able to use the Ottoman provincial bureaucracy to improve their lot through the dredging of canals, the reinforcement of embankments, and the strengthening of dams. In many instances, however, Egyptian peasants could not get their way by working within the imperial system; rather, they made their

86 Ibid., 1:640–41.

87 The home of al-Jabartī's father's paternal grandmother, for example, used to lie directly on the banks of the Nile in the Khurnūb district of Cairo. After ʿAlī Bey's reclamation projects and the consequent rising of the city's shoreline, however, the home became landlocked, a fact lamented by al-Jabartī. See ibid., 1:653.

concerns and discontent known to the Ottoman state through avenues other than the court, provincial bureaucrats, or petitions. One of the most dramatic and effective means by which peasants forced the hand of the imperial bureaucracy was through the wholesale abandonment of villages – a phenomenon that powerfully changed the physical and demographic history of the rural Ottoman Egyptian environment.[88]

By completely abandoning a village and leaving its fields unirrigated and untended, Egyptian peasants were able to affect with great impact the well-being both of the Egyptian countryside and of the Ottoman bureaucracy managing it.[89] In the face of dire and desperate situations, peasants readily undertook such wrenchingly disruptive transformations in their own lives and in the demography of the countryside because they understood that the threat and act of abandonment was highly effective in achieving their goals. A village without peasants to plant and harvest fields and to maintain irrigation works could not survive and could not generate revenues.

In a court case from 1688, we see that the collective abandonment of a village on the part of a group of peasants was able to reverse a situation in favor of the peasants' interests. In that year, a group of *multazims* and other notable representatives of the seven military blocs of Egypt stationed in the subprovince of al-Daqahliyya came to the court of al-Manṣūra in the northeastern Nile Delta to investigate the transfer of the village of Famm Ẓāfir to the *iltizām* of an amir named Aḥmad Jalabī Ibn al-Marḥūm al-Amīr Muṣṭafā Bey.[90] Located on the banks of the major canal of al-Baḥr al-Ṣaghīr, Famm Ẓāfir had been administered by the village of al-Kashūfiyya from time immemorial (*min qadīm al-zamān*) and had generally enjoyed

[88] Peasant flight, village abandonment, and other similar actions are collectively referred to by Michael Adas as avoidance protest. For his useful analysis of those forms of peasant resistance, see: Adas, "From Avoidance to Confrontation: Peasant Protest in Precolonial and Colonial Southeast Asia," *Comparative Studies in Society and History* 23 (1981): 217–47.

[89] On the subject of village abandonment by Egyptian peasants during the Ottoman period, see: Nicolas Michel, "Migrations de paysans dans le Delta du Nil au début de l'époque ottoman," *AI* 35 (2001): 241–90; Michel, "Villages désertés, terres en friche et reconstruction rurale en Égypte au début de l'époque ottoman," *AI* 36 (2002): 197–251; Zayn al-ʿĀbidīn Shams al-Dīn Najm, "Tasaḥḥub al-Fallāḥīn fī ʿAṣr Muḥammad ʿAlī, Asbābuhu wa Natā'ijuhu," *EHR* 36 (1989): 259–316; Naṣra ʿAbd al-Mutajallī, "al-Muqāwama bil-Tasaḥḥub fī Rīf Miṣr al-ʿUthmāniyya," in *al-Rafḍ wa al-Iḥtijāj fī al-Mujtamaʿ al-Miṣrī fī al-ʿAṣr al-ʿUthmānī*, ed. Nāṣir Ibrāhīm and Ra'ūf ʿAbbās (Cairo: Markaz al-Buḥūth wa al-Dirāsāt al-Ijtimāʿiyya, 2004), 127–36. For a comparative example of village abandonment on the part of peasants in Ottoman Palestine, see: Amy Singer, "Peasant Migration: Law and Practice in Early Ottoman Palestine," *NPT* 8 (1992): 49–65.

[90] DWQ, Maḥkamat al-Manṣūra 9, p. 36, case 83 (20 B 1099/20 May 1688). *Jalabī* is the Arabicized form of the Turkish title *Çelebi*.

prosperity, proper irrigation, and ample cultivation. When control of the village was given over to Aḥmad Jalabī, however, things quickly began to change for the worse. Fighting and all other kinds of evils (*shurūr*) took hold of the village, thereby visiting great harm, disrepair, and hardship on the social, economic, familial, and public works structures of the rural community. Irrigation, sowing, and planting in the village stopped as did the payment of taxes to the state. Things came to a head in the year this case was brought to court as a huge deadly fight broke out in the village between some of its peasants. During the course of this battle, numerous fields in the village were destroyed and could not be planted, and, as such, many peasants decided to leave Famm Ẓāfir for good out of fear that its problems would never be solved.

This upheaval in Famm Ẓāfir further resulted in the people of that village failing to dredge the imperial canal that ran through their village, a waterway known as Jisr al-Ẓafar, which meant that little or no water reached many of the villages downstream from Famm Ẓāfir.[91] Moreover, because the canal had not been properly dredged, water collected behind silted up areas of the waterway, overflowing its banks, and flooding parts of villages like al-Manzala. Thus, problems of administration in Famm Ẓāfir and its peasants' dissatisfied reactions to those problems resulted in a lack of proper irrigation both in Famm Ẓāfir and in other nearby areas. From an imperial Ottoman perspective, the great destruction wrought in this village and its effects on communities around it meant great losses to the state's budget and created a pressing situation.

The report of these notables in the court of al-Manṣūra in 1688 was only the beginning of Famm Ẓāfir's troubles. As agreed in the court, the *multazim* of the village of Tahākān, a village neighboring Famm Ẓāfir, was sent with a letter of peace for the people of Famm Ẓāfir to investigate further the situation in the village.[92] He asked those still living there why the community had fallen into ruin and destruction and why so many peasants had left their lands. The peasants informed him that, since time immemorial (*min qadīm al-zamān*), their village had fallen under the administration of the village of al-Kashūfiyya and, moreover, that no individual – not the *kāshifs*, the amirs, or the heads of the seven military blocs – had the right to take the village away from al-Kashūfiyya for his

[91] As the name of this village suggests, Famm Ẓāfir was strategically situated at the mouth of the canal of Jisr al-Ẓafar and could thus very much control the supply of water to villages further downstream.

[92] This *multazim* was the amir Riḍwān Ibn al-Marḥūm al-Amīr Jaʿfar.

own personal gain. The peasants went on to say that when control of the village was taken over by Aḥmad Jalabī, he caused all sorts of civil strife and infighting to break out amongst the villagers. The remaining peasants threatened to abandon the village as well and never again to maintain its canal or cultivate its fields as long as it remained under the control of Aḥmad Jalabī. As if this were not strong enough of a statement, the villagers also vowed to prevent any other peasants – those loyal to Aḥmad Jalabī or those from other villages – from planting the fields of Famm Ẓāfir. The entire village of Famm Ẓāfir was, in other words, to be left deserted forever unless it was returned to the control of the village of al-Kashūfiyya.

If all were restored to its former state, though, the peasants of Famm Ẓāfir promised to return to their village to plant its fields, to restore its built structures, and to uphold the maintenance and protection (*ḥifẓ wa ḥarāsa*) of its canal in accordance with previous laws.[93] Understanding the seriousness of the peasants' threats and their own inabilities to do anything in the face of them, all the *multazims* and other imperial officials in the court acquiesced to the peasants' demands and recommended that Famm Ẓāfir be reattached to the administration of al-Kashūfiyya. Thus, the peasants of Famm Ẓāfir successfully leveraged their powers as cultivators and sources of revenue to expel an unjust and corrupt ruler and to return their village to the administrative control of al-Kashūfiyya. By abandoning their village and preventing it from functioning as a productive agricultural unit (by essentially breaking the factory's machines), peasants were able to force the hand of *multazims* and of the Ottoman administration of Egypt itself to agree to their demands to remove Aḥmad Jalabī.

The role of irrigation works was central to this case, because their failure to function properly was the reason the peasants of Famm Ẓāfir were able to win the support of the leaders of nearby villages. Indeed, because the peasants of Famm Ẓāfir purposefully allowed the canal in their village to fall into disrepair, numerous other villages were not able to irrigate their fields and were thereby also made victims of the hardships visited upon the peasants of Famm Ẓāfir by Aḥmad Jalabī. The canal and the waters it carried were thus strategically used to great effect by

93 Tellingly, the phrase *ḥifẓ wa ḥarāsa* (*hıfz ü hiraset* in Turkish) was used in reference to the upkeep and protection not only of Egyptian irrigation works but also of the Ottoman state's finances and well-being. For examples of the latter uses of the phrase, see: TSMA, E. 664/52 (n.d.); TSMA, E. 664/63 (Evail Ra 1159/24 Mar.–2 Apr. 1746).

the peasants of Famm Ẓāfir. Not only does this case (and numerous others) prove that Egyptian peasants indeed had agency and voice in the eighteenth-century countryside; it also exemplifies how peasants were able to affect Ottoman rule in Egypt by altering the material conditions of their rural world through changing the course of a canal and, in turn, the course of their own history.

Irrigation's Others

As a final example of how irrigation created rural communities in Ottoman Egypt and of how those communities were sites of continual contestation and conflict affecting ecologies and state revenues, I consider how the Bedouin fit into the bureaucracy of irrigation described in this chapter.[94] As we saw earlier, the overarching logic governing the interactions of Egyptian peasants and the Ottoman imperial administration over water resources was that communities had shared interests in the upkeep of irrigation works because they served collective rather than individual welfare. The Bedouin, however, in many ways stood outside of these cooperative arrangements, seeking to acquire for themselves the advantages and resources of communities established around the shared use of irrigation works without actually entering into the cooperative formations that maintained those communities.[95]

From the perspective of the Ottoman state and of Egyptian peasants, the Bedouin embodied the very antithesis of the kinds of communities of water described in this chapter. They were transitory, did not "belong" to any one place, stole, often employed physical violence, usually inhabited outlying areas away from the Nile, and were unpredictable and indefinable through established normative Egyptian social forms and rules.[96] Perceived of as a kind of anticommunal force on the outskirts of sedentary Egyptian society, the Bedouin and their actions helped define the contours and limits of communities of water throughout Egypt. From a Bedouin perspective, by contrast, irrigation was most assuredly more of

94 On the Bedouin in Ottoman Egypt, see: ʿAbd al-Raḥīm, *al-Rīf al-Miṣrī*, 169–87.

95 For a comparative example of Bedouin notions of water and land in twentieth-century Jordan, see: Miriam R. Lowi, *Water and Power: The Politics of a Scarce Resource in the Jordan River Basin* (Cambridge: Cambridge University Press, 1993), 52–53.

96 For an instructive treatment of the relationship among movement, migration, and sovereignty in the Ottoman Empire, see: Reşat Kasaba, *A Moveable Empire: Ottoman Nomads, Migrants, and Refugees* (Seattle: University of Washington Press, 2009). For the case of nineteenth-century Iran, see: Arash Khazeni, *Tribes and Empire on the Margins of Nineteenth-Century Iran* (Seattle: University of Washington Press, 2010).

a nuisance than an asset. It destroyed good forage land for animals and created borders that hindered movement. Given their understanding that the communal use of water was one of the most important facets of sedentary social forms that came to dominate most of Egyptian society in this period, the Bedouin thus often targeted irrigation works during their raids knowing full well that breaking a canal's embankments or destroying a waterwheel was a very effective means of crippling the rural economy and of disrupting Egyptian peasants' lives.

Thus, an Ottoman firman recorded in the court of al-Baḥayra in the year 1751, for example, aimed specifically at protecting the subprovince's *sulṭānī* canals from what it referred to as the corruption and wretchedness of the Bedouin.[97] The order instructed officials in al-Baḥayra in the northwestern Nile Delta to capture Bedouin raiders whenever possible and to punish (*te'dib*) them most harshly.[98] Fearing that the state's imperial funds would also be targeted by the Bedouin, this order further directed officials in al-Baḥayra to send all state monies to the divan of Egypt as quickly as possible.

Irrigation, location, and relative degrees of settlement in communities were always factors at play in various incidents involving Bedouin raids throughout the eighteenth century. These raids most often aimed at securing supplies of food, water, money, and other necessities, and although the Ottoman administration of Egypt was largely unable to

97 DWQ, Maḥkamat al-Baḥayra 5, p. 213, case 387 (7 L 1164/28 Aug. 1751).

98 It is not clear from the text of this case how exactly the punishment was to be administered. Were the local officials of al-Baḥayra to exact the punishment themselves, or were they to send these Bedouin to Cairo upon their capture? There were police and local prisons in cities like al-Baḥayra and other subprovincial areas during the Ottoman period, so perhaps the Bedouin were to be sent to those facilities by the police. On police in Ottoman Egypt, see: Mirfat Aḥmad al-Sayyid, "Idārat al-Shurṭa fī Miṣr fī al-ʿAṣr al-ʿUthmānī," *AI* 40 (2006): 51–70. On the police in nineteenth-century Egypt, see: Khaled Fahmy, "The Police and the People in Nineteenth-Century Egypt," *Die Welt des Islams* 39 (1999): 340–77. For a more general account of police in twentieth-century Egypt, see: ʿAbd al-Wahhāb Bakr, *al-Būlīs al-Miṣri, 1922–1952* (Cairo: Maktabat Madbūlī, 1988). On prisons in nineteenth-century Ottoman Egypt, see: Khaled Fahmy, "Medical Conditions in Egyptian Prisons in the Nineteenth Century," in *Marginal Voices in Literature and Society: Individual and Society in the Mediterranean Muslim World*, ed. Robin Ostle (Strasbourg: European Science Foundation, in collaboration with Maison méditerranéenne des sciences de l'homme d'Aix-en-Provence, 2000), 135–55; Rudolph Peters, "Controlled Suffering: Mortality and Living Conditions in 19th-Century Egyptian Prisons," *IJMES* 36 (2004): 387–407; Peters, "Egypt and the Age of the Triumphant Prison: Legal Punishment in Nineteenth Century Egypt," *AI* 36 (2002): 253–85; Peters, "Prisons and Marginalisation in Nineteenth-century Egypt," in *Outside In: On the Margins of the Modern Middle East*, ed. Eugene Rogan (London: I. B. Tauris, 2002), 31–52.

prevent such incursions on rural Egyptian villages, it did take steps to protect those areas considered most vulnerable to Bedouin attack.[99] One of the most common ways of dealing with raids was to move entire villages away from areas thought susceptible to Bedouin attacks. The role of water in this was paramount, as the villages most often attacked by Bedouins were those geographically distant from areas of densely irrigated lands and, hence, with high population concentrations. Thus, by moving villages closer to centers of irrigation, cultivation, and population, the Ottoman government of Egypt sought to protect them from Bedouin raiders who took advantage of the relative isolation of villages on the outskirts of major irrigation and population communities.

As an example of this kind of thinking on the part of the imperial Ottoman administration of Egypt, consider the case of a firman sent from the high divan of Egypt in 1793 to the court of al-Baḥayra in response to the petition of a *multazim* in the village of Minyyat Saʿīd, a man named ʿUthmān Bey.[100] In his original petition, which we are told was written in Turkish and later translated into Arabic at the divan, ʿUthmān Bey wrote that all of the structures and homes of peasants in Minyyat Saʿīd were located at some distance from the banks of the Nile and that only a small part of the village's agricultural lands were close to the river. The remoteness of most of the homes, storage areas, and people of the village from the Nile and from other villages made them susceptible to Bedouin raids. Indeed, the *multazim* ʿUthmān Bey reported that peasants had suffered great distress and hardship as a result of rebel Bedouin who had destroyed portions of the village's properties and lands, making it impossible for the village to pay the monies it owed to the state in a complete and timely fashion. To rectify the situation described in ʿUthmān Bey's petition, the high divan issued the firman. It ordered that all the structures and homes of this village be moved to an area of the village next to the Nile itself, so as to protect the village's peasants, their resources and homes, and the monies they owed the state from Bedouin attack.

As these few cases involving Bedouin raids again show, water represented life, community, and security in rural Ottoman Egypt. Not only did it irrigate fields that grew food that would then feed thousands across

[99] For an example of Ottoman attempts to protect Egypt from Bedouin raids, see also the following case appointing a special imperial functionary to oversee the protection of pilgrims during the pilgrimage season: TSMA, E. 664/6 (n.d.).

[100] DWQ, Maḥkamat al-Baḥayra 23, p. 6, case 6 (3 M 1208/10 Aug. 1793). On the village of Minyyat Saʿīd, see: *QJBM*, pt. 2, 2:276.

the Ottoman Empire; it was also a substance around which communities formed and which offered mutual protection to those living in these collectives. It determined the literal shape of the Ottoman state in Egypt. Water was thus geographically and figuratively at the center of rural Egyptian life. Indeed, villages on the outskirts of the Nile or other canal-centered environments exposed themselves to the dangers of those who preyed on communities that could not adequately protect themselves. Tellingly, the solution offered to protect communities from Bedouin raids was to bring them into closer proximity to settled communities constructed around irrigation works. Once in the center of a rural population, peasants who were formerly on the outside of the rural Egyptian world and who were therefore vulnerable to Bedouin raids would be able to protect themselves and to take comfort in the fact that they were surrounded by other villages and peasants, all of whom had a stake in the mutual protection, upkeep, productivity, and general well-being of their collective community of water.[101]

As outlined in this chapter, the communities that water created in rural Egypt, described by the Ottomans in their survey of irrigation in the sixteenth century, were governed by a set of collective rules that, above all, privileged the welfare of the whole over the interests of a few. This was a system in which precedent and peasant knowledge and experience came to inform imperial control and management of rural irrigation works and of water usage. For the Ottomans in Egypt, controlling how water met earth was ultimately about producing as much food as possible in the most effective, economical, and sustainable way. Indeed, the only reason Egyptians, Ottomans, and others ever sought to irrigate Egypt in the first place was to take advantage of its rich soils. Irrigation was, as always, more about the potential of dirt to grow food than it was about water. We now turn to the fruits of this meeting of water and earth – the cultivation of foodstuffs for Egypt and the rest of the Ottoman Empire.

[101] It should be noted that we have no indication in the archival record of Ottoman Egypt of the frictions that surely occurred between receiving communities and peasants who relocated to these new communities either to avoid Bedouin attack or in the cases of village abandonment discussed previously.

2

THE FOOD CHAIN

The cultivation and movement of food – grown in earth irrigated through the social, ecological, and infrastructural mechanisms discussed in the previous chapter – was central to the Ottoman administration of Egypt in the long eighteenth century.[1] Egypt was the breadbasket of the Ottoman Empire, producing more foodstuffs than any other single province in the Empire. The fertile soils of rural Egypt renewed every year by the sediment-rich waters of the Nile flood provided a steady supply of nutrients for the cultivation of all sorts of grains and vegetables in the Egyptian countryside. Rains in the Ethiopian highlands collected nutrients from the volcanic rock of the mountains on which they fell and from the Sudd swamps in the Sudan through which the floodwaters eventually traveled every year to Egypt. Once those waters covered the soil in Egypt, seemingly endless supplies of sunshine for photosynthesis produced vast quantities of chemical energy stored in the calories of food grown throughout southern Egypt and the Delta. As I discuss in detail in Chapter 4, a large peasant and animal population throughout the province provided the

[1] For studies of food production, transport, and provisioning in the early modern Ottoman Empire, see: Faruk Tabak, *The Waning of the Mediterranean, 1550–1870: A Geohistorical Approach* (Baltimore: Johns Hopkins University Press, 2008); Margaret L. Venzke, "The Question of Declining Cereals' Production in the Sixteenth Century: A Sounding on the Problem-Solving Capacity of the Ottoman Cadastres," *JTS* 8 (1984): 251–64; A. Makovsky, "Sixteenth-Century Agricultural Production in the Liwā of Jerusalem: Insights from the *Tapu Defters* and an Attempt at Quantification," *AO* 9 (1984): 91–127; B. McGowan, "Food Supply and Taxation on the Middle Danube (1568–1579)," *AO* 1 (1969): 139–96; Virginia H. Aksan, "Feeding the Ottoman Troops on the Danube, 1768–1774," *War and Society* 13 (1995): 1–14; Margaret L. Venzke, "The Ottoman Tahrir Defterleri and Agricultural Productivity: The Case for Northern Syria," *OA* 17 (1997): 1–61; Stefka Parveva, "Agrarian Land and Harvest in South-West Peloponnese in the Early 18th Century," *Études Balkaniques* 1 (2003): 83–123; Evangelia Balta, "The Bread in Greek Lands during the Ottoman Rule," *Tarih Araştırmaları Dergisi* 16 (1992–1994): 199–226; Kate Fleet, "Grain Exports from Western Anatolia at the End of the Fourteenth Century," *JESHO* 40 (1997): 283–93.

labor needed to harvest, pack, and move this food, which would eventually make its way to other parts of Egypt, to Istanbul, to the cities of Mecca and Medina, and to many other areas of the Empire. Egypt's surplus energy thus provided the caloric power necessary to maintain the political power of the Ottoman Empire.

As I discuss in this chapter, the Ottoman administration of Egypt and the province's peasant and urban populations created, maintained, and harnessed an established web of storage facilities, labor, and shipping networks that provided the infrastructure necessary for the movement, trade, and consumption of massive quantities of Egyptian foodstuffs and goods throughout the Empire. The story of food in Ottoman Egypt is thus really a story of imperial connections and relationships stretching across the geographical expanse of the Empire – a story of early modern natural resource management. The need to move food out of Egypt created and relied on a complex and shifting constellation of linkages maintained by both the Ottoman bureaucracy of Egypt's massive expenditures of resources and by peasant energies put toward the cultivation of foodstuffs in rural Egypt. Thus, both the Ottoman state and Egyptian peasants worked in tandem not only to irrigate Egypt but also to grow and move food from the province to the rest of the Empire.

As important nodes in this imperial system, grain storage facilities (*wakālas*) in cities like Cairo, Rashīd, Alexandria, and Suez housed large amounts of grain and, perhaps more important, provided the commercial environments in which these foodstuffs could be bought and sold. The strategic location of each of these major cities was meant to serve a specific area of the Ottoman Empire: grains in Suez were destined for the Hijaz, whereas food in Rashīd and Alexandria served Istanbul and other cities in North Africa, the Levant, and Anatolia. Linking all these places and providing the means to transport this food was a network of shipping and trade that served as the vital strings connecting various locales to one another. Moving the proper amount of food from areas of excess like Egypt to other areas of need in the Ottoman Empire was a fundamental interest of the imperial state as it sought to balance various natural resources around the Ottoman Empire. Food served as a vital commodity for trade and commerce, and it sustained urban and rural populations throughout the Empire. Egyptian food moreover also sustained the Ottoman army on campaign and was thus a strategic good.

To plow the fields that would grow these grains, farmers used large wooden tools pulled by animals. Thus, wood, animals, humans, and the labor of the latter two came together to cultivate food. This production of food and its movement and trade brought the countryside, urban hinterlands, and cities throughout Egypt much closer together as peasants took their goods to towns and then to cities so that these products of the land could then be transported even further away from their original points of growth and harvest. Lentils, wheat, maize, and, above all, rice were the primary foodstuffs grown and shipped from Egypt.[2] Each of the organisms that produced these consumable goods required a specialized amount of knowledge and a specific kind and amount of labor to turn its products into commodities that could then be moved and traded. In the genetic and physical makeup of each of these organic structures was a specific history of human interaction with the natural world. The improvement of each of these organisms through the human technology of selective breeding ensured that the history of these grains; the lives of the animals who helped cultivate them; and the lives of humans who harvested them, moved them, and consumed them would remain forever intertwined. The patchwork of fields in which this biota grew dictated the natural and built environment of much of rural Egypt. The countryside was a quilt of different colors and hues as rice fields bordered those of wheat, corn, and various other foodstuffs. Fences and concerns over property were largely tied up in the need to maximize food production for a demanding market. In short, the push to grow grains in the Egyptian countryside was perhaps the largest factor dictating the lives and futures of Egyptian peasants and their relationships to urban centers, the natural world, and the Ottoman administration of Egypt.

That both Egyptian peasants and Ottoman bureaucrats charged with the administration of the province expended so much caloric energy, time, and resources on the maintenance, repair, and improvement of Egypt's irrigation infrastructure is proof enough of the importance of food cultivation and production in Ottoman Egypt. After all, "food supply was the Achilles heel of the early modern state."[3] Indeed, food and grain were the very reasons the Ottoman administration of Egypt and Egyptian peasants cared so deeply about the irrigation system of the province. Without water, the fields of Egypt would not have been able to supply the quantities and kinds of grains needed for the trade and transport that was so central to the longevity and durability of the Ottoman Empire. As we

[2] Maize, for example, was known as Egyptian grain (*mısır*) among the Turks of Istanbul and Anatolia. And, suggesting the itinerary of its transmission throughout the Old World (from Egypt to Anatolia to Europe), it was known as Turkish grain in the Balkans and Italy (*granturco* in Italian). McNeill, *Mountains of the Mediterranean*, 89.

[3] Scott, *Seeing Like a State*, 29.

have already seen, irrigation and its maintenance demanded much from both the Ottoman administration of Egypt and those peasants under its administration. Indeed, the Nile's flood and the management of its waters were central to the production of food and to the general well-being of Egypt – a theme that runs throughout much of the correspondence between Egypt and Istanbul.

The Road from Earth to Stomach

Despite numerous instances of famine, drought, and massive flooding over the course of the long eighteenth century, when food was properly grown and harvested in the Egyptian countryside, it immediately entered a network of shipping and transport that allowed grain and other foodstuffs to move from villages to towns, to cities, and then to capitals.[4] This network relied on peasant and animal labor, a web of roads and canals, proper storage facilities, money, credit, and shipping to ensure that Egyptian crops arrived in Mecca, Medina, Dubrovnik, Istanbul, Tunis, Rhodes, and various other locales throughout the Ottoman Empire. Once foodstuffs were cultivated in villages, they moved to a number of large regional cities – places like Asyūṭ, Jirja, al-Damanhūr, al-Manṣūra, and Manfalūṭ. Such medium-size cities were usually the centers of subprovinces in Ottoman Egypt, the seats of major Islamic courts, and hubs of commerce. In terms of the transport of grains throughout the Empire, they were important regional nodes in a vast imperial network of commerce, as it was to these cities that grains and other foodstuffs from Egypt's thousands of villages first went after harvest.

Some of this grain was bought and sold in the markets of each city to be used by local merchants and others. The bulk of it, however, was shipped from the cities via the Nile to usually either Cairo, Alexandria, or Rashīd. Cairo was, of course, the largest single marketplace in eighteenth-century Ottoman Egypt and had a thriving commercial life. Ships carrying Egypt's grains and other foodstuffs left from Alexandria, Rashīd, and Suez for locations throughout the Empire. In each of those three Egyptian port cities, there were storage facilities for grain, sleeping quarters for merchants coming from all over the Ottoman Empire and from elsewhere,

4 Although focused more on passenger transportation than on commercial shipping, the following has proved especially useful to me in thinking about waterborne movement and transport in the early modern period: Jan de Vries, *Barges and Capitalism: Passenger Transportation in the Dutch Economy, 1632–1839* (Utrecht: HES Publishers, 1981).

market weighers and overseers, and an entire infrastructure of commerce. In this general schema of commerce and transport, the central means of getting grains from the villages of Egypt to subprovincial cities were roads. Dirt roads, waterways, and seas were the primary conduits of goods, people, animals, and bureaucrats that connected all parts of the Ottoman world. The city of Manfalūṭ in southern Egypt, for example, was a central point from which emanated dozens of roads leading to smaller villages in its hinterland. Many of the smaller villages then served as nodes from which roads led to other villages. For its part, Manfalūṭ was then connected by roads to other large cities. Thus, cities like Manfalūṭ served as both destinations and points of origin for grain shipments moving on dendritic networks of roads and waterways throughout Egypt and between it and the other regions of the Empire.

There were two main kinds of road in Ottoman Egypt. The first was known as *al-shāriʿ al-maslūk* and was a commonly accessible road of general use in the countryside.[5] These roads were the most common in the Egyptian countryside and were the equivalent of public roads.[6] The maintenance and upkeep of these roads were the responsibilities of the villages and peasants who used them. The second kind of road was known

[5] Some of the many cases involving *al-shāriʿ al-maslūk* include the following: DWQ, Maḥkamat al-Baḥayra 6, p. 33, case 63 (25 L 1169/23 Jul. 1756); DWQ, Maḥkamat al-Baḥayra 8, p. 45, case 67 (15 R 1176/2 Nov. 1762); DWQ, Maḥkamat al-Baḥayra 11, p. 131, case 285 (20 Za 1197/17 Oct. 1783); DWQ, Maḥkamat al-Baḥayra 15, pp. 166–67, case 367 (15 Ca 1199/26 Mar. 1785); DWQ, Maḥkamat al-Baḥayra 22, p. 349, case 735 (23 Z 1207/1 Aug. 1793); DWQ, Maḥkamat al-Baḥayra 31, p. 9, case 9 (10 M 1222/20 Mar. 1807); DWQ, Maḥkamat al-Baḥayra 32, p. 133, case 194 (20 Ca 1223/14 Jul. 1808); DWQ, Maḥkamat Rashīd 132, pp. 134–35, case 207 (7 L 1137/18 Jun. 1725); DWQ, Maḥkamat Rashīd 134, pp. 257–58, case 335 (16 Ca 1140/29 Dec. 1727); DWQ, Maḥkamat Rashīd 137, pp. 112–13, case 196 (1 Za 1144/26 Apr. 1732); DWQ, Maḥkamat Rashīd 139, pp. 96–98, case 154 (8 S 1146/20 Jul. 1733); DWQ, Maḥkamat Rashīd 142, pp. 255–64, case 226 (1 Ra 1149/10 Jul. 1736); DWQ, Maḥkamat Rashīd 145, pp. 267–69, case 241 (1 S 1153/27 Apr. 1740); DWQ, Maḥkamat Rashīd 146, p. 225, case 212 (22 L 1153/10 Jan. 1741); DWQ, Maḥkamat Rashīd 148, p. 151, case 182 (8 Za 1154/15 Jan. 1742); DWQ, Maḥkamat Rashīd 151, p. 195, case 216 (19 S 1159/12 Mar. 1746); DWQ, Maḥkamat Rashīd 154, pp. 281–85, case 314 (15 R 1163/24 Mar. 1750); DWQ, Maḥkamat Rashīd 155, pp. 46–47, case 55 (1 Za 1163/2 Oct. 1750); DWQ, Maḥkamat Rashīd 156, p. 210, case 161 (8 Ra 1164/5 Feb. 1751); DWQ, Maḥkamat Rashīd 157, p. 322, case 312 (13 R 1166/17 Feb. 1753); DWQ, Maḥkamat Rashīd 158, p. 253, case 223 (30 L 1166/30 Aug. 1753); DWQ, Maḥkamat Rashīd 159, p. 156, case 104 (30 R 1167/23 Feb. 1754).

[6] *Al-shāriʿ al-maslūk* was sometimes referred to as *al-ṭarīq al-maslūk*. See, e.g.: DWQ, Maḥkamat Rashīd 137, p. 8, case 15 (1 Z 1143/6 Jun. 1731).

as *al-shāri' al-sulṭānī*.[7] These roads were the property and responsibility of the Ottoman state. Although they were usually longer and wider than *al-shāri' al-maslūk* and were maintained by government representatives, peasants and others were allowed to use the roads with the understanding that they could be held liable for any problems that arose as a result of their usage.[8] Moreover, the Ottoman administration of Egypt could seize these roads at anytime for its exclusive use. Given the vast number of references to both kinds of roads in the records of subprovincial courts, it is clear that the Egyptian countryside in the eighteenth century supported and was crisscrossed by a large and complex network of roads connecting even the smallest villages to towns, cities, and eventually to the entire expanse of the Ottoman Empire.[9]

The network of roads that was so central to bringing grains from villages to towns and then to cities was dwarfed in scale and importance by Egypt's ultimate road – the Nile itself. As seen in the previous chapter, and indeed throughout the entire archival record of Ottoman Egypt, the presence of the Nile and its many branches linked extremely distant areas of Egypt together into one system of collective responsibility, commerce, and transport. It was akin to a massive highway running the entire length of Egypt that connected top to bottom and sea to village.[10] This colossal thoroughfare, along with a vast network of canals branching off of the

7 For some of the many cases involving *al-shāri' al-sulṭānī*, see: DWQ, Maḥkamat Asyūṭ 6, p. 361, case 763 (22 Ş 1206/14 Apr. 1792); DWQ, Maḥkamat Asyūṭ 7, p. 53, case 116 (6 Ca 1212/26 Oct. 1797); DWQ, Maḥkamat Asyūṭ 8, p. 188, case 411 (10 N 1210/20 Mar. 1796); DWQ, Maḥkamat Asyūṭ 9, p. 10, case 26 (17 Za 1217/11 Mar. 1803); DWQ, Maḥkamat al-Baḥayra 11, p. 19, case 37 (20 C 1195/13 Jun. 1781); DWQ, Maḥkamat al-Baḥayra 32, p. 136, case 198 (23 Ca 1223/17 Jul. 1808); DWQ, Maḥkamat Rashīd 146, pp. 230–31, case 220 (1 N 1153/21 Nov. 1740). In the latter three cases, *al-shāri' al-sulṭānī* is referred to as *al-ṭarīq al-sulṭānī*.

8 DWQ, Maḥkamat Rashīd 130, pp. 132–34, case 187 (8 Ca 1136/4 Feb. 1724); DWQ, Maḥkamat Rashīd 134, p. 105, case 129 (24 M 1140/10 Sep. 1727).

9 The most common reason these two kinds of roads are referenced in the court records of Ottoman Egypt is to define the borders of property. For cases involving *al-shāri' al-maslūk* as a border of property see: DWQ, Maḥkamat Rashīd 132, pp. 56–57, case 80 (26 B 1137/10 Apr. 1725); DWQ, Maḥkamat Rashīd 137, pp. 102–3, case 177 (7 L 1144/3 Apr. 1732); DWQ, Maḥkamat Rashīd 154, pp. 198–99, case 223 (1 C 1162/18 May 1749). For examples of cases in which *al-shāri' al-sulṭānī* constitutes the border of property, see: DWQ, Maḥkamat Asyūṭ 9, p. 34, case 98 (16 B 1218/1 Nov. 1803); DWQ, Maḥkamat Asyūṭ 9, p. 88, case 202 (20 Ş 1219/23 Nov. 1804); DWQ, Maḥkamat Asyūṭ 9, p. 249, case 504 (24 L 1220/14 Jan. 1806).

10 On shipping and commerce on the Nile during the Ottoman period, see: 'Abd al-Ḥamīd Ḥāmid Sulaymān, *al-Milāḥa al-Nīliyya fī Miṣr al-'Uthmāniyya (1517–1798)* (Cairo: al-Hay'a al-Miṣriyya al-'Āmma lil-Kitāb, 2000).

river and roads connecting villages and cities, ensured that food was in constant motion within Egypt and that foodstuffs were able to move quickly and efficiently from Egypt's hundreds of villages to its major port cities and on from there.

Caloric Connections

Cities like al-Damanhūr, Asyūṭ, Manfalūṭ, Jirja, al-Manṣūra, and Isnā – medium-size towns that were smaller than Rashīd, Suez, Alexandria, and Cairo but significantly larger than most villages – served as collection points for grains and other foodstuffs destined for Cairo, Egypt's ports, and other cities across the Ottoman Empire.[11] These sources of caloric energy were transported by animals and people on the many roads of rural Egypt from the hundreds of villages that formed the hinterlands of these middling cities. In the southern Egyptian city of Asyūṭ, for example, there was a thriving state market (*sūq sulṭānī*) in which one could buy and sell grains and other goods from villages all over the Asyūṭ hinterland.[12] Peasants, Ottoman officials, merchants, weighers, people serving tea and coffee, and many others jostled their way through the crowded marketplace in one of Egypt's subprovincial centers to sample the wares on display and to acquire the food and provisions necessary to sustain their lives and livelihoods. In cities like Asyūṭ, the Ottoman administration of Egypt demanded that set amounts of money and grain (*mal ve gılâl-ı mirî*) be paid to the state every year.[13] This fixed amount was to be acquired from the harvests and taxes of all the villages in the orbit of Asyūṭ – in other words, those villages in the hinterland of the city that would use

[11] For an extremely lucid and provocative analysis of the influence of urban Egypt over the countryside in the first half of the nineteenth century, see: Muḥammad Ḥākim Jād Jahāwī, "al-Ta'thīrāt al-Tabāduliyya bayn al-Qarya wa al-Madīna: Taḥlīl Sūsiyūlūjī li-Namaṭ al-Taḥaḍḍur fī Miṣr fī al-Qarn al-Tāsiʿ ʿAshar" (M.A. thesis, Cairo University, 1995). See also in this regard: Kenneth M. Cuno, "Commercial Relations between Town and Village in Eighteenth and Early Nineteenth-Century Egypt," *AI* 24 (1988): 111–35.

[12] DWQ, Maḥkamat Asyūṭ 7, p. 20, case 42 (1 S 1208/7 Sep. 1793); DWQ, Maḥkamat Asyūṭ 7, p. 34, case 73 (28 R 1208/2 Dec. 1793); DWQ, Maḥkamat Asyūṭ 9, p. 85, case 196 (9 B 1219/13 Oct. 1804); DWQ, Maḥkamat Asyūṭ 9, p. 88, case 202 (20 Ş 1219/23 Nov. 1804); DWQ, Maḥkamat Asyūṭ 9, p. 178, case 402 (25 Ca 1219/31 Aug. 1804). For a description of the villages in Asyūṭ's hinterland, see: *QJBM*, pt. 2, 4:1–85.

[13] In 1596, for instance, Asyūṭ paid the Ottoman treasury 1,542,166 *para* of the total amount of 66,080,476 *para* due from Egypt that year. Shaw, *Budget of Ottoman Egypt*, 21 and 92. For an example of an Ottoman firman ordering the transfer of money and grain from Asyūṭ to the state, see: DWQ, Maḥkamat Asyūṭ 3, p. 338, case 1001 (17 Za 1135/18 Aug. 1723).

its markets, courts, and other resources. Each village was to contribute a part to this overall amount.[14]

An Ottoman firman from 1717 to the *kāshif* of the southern city of Asyūṭ makes clear the system by which state grain and money were to be acquired.[15] According to this decree, at the beginning of the Coptic month of Tūt (the first month of the Egyptian agricultural year), the *kāshif* ʿUthmān arrived in Asyūṭ (the subprovince fell under the sovereignty of Jirja).[16] As was customary in years past, the *kāshif* ʿUthmān was to make sure that each of the villages surrounding Asyūṭ sent its required annual share of grain to the city. Once all the grain was collected and inspected in Asyūṭ, it was then put onto ships in the port of Asyūṭ and sent to the royal granaries (*enbar-i âmire*) of Cairo. This decree ends with a warning against any mistakes in this charge and with an entreaty to defend the ships carrying the state's grain to Cairo against Bedouin attack. The firman thus illustrates how grain moved from link to link on the Empire's food chain – from villages outside Asyūṭ to the city itself and on to Cairo before it was either sold there or sent further away to somewhere else in the Empire. In a similar Ottoman firman, we read of an excess of grain in Asyūṭ.[17] The amount of grain collected in

[14] For example, in 1743, the village of Benī Muḥammad provided four hundred *ardabbs* of grain toward the overall amount to be given to the state from Asyūṭ that year. DWQ, Maḥkamat Asyūṭ 4, p. 235, case 702 (1 Ş 1156/19 Sep. 1743). The value of an *ardabb* varied greatly over the course of the long eighteenth century, from a minimum of 75 liters (L) in 1665 to 184 L in 1798. Raymond, *Artisans et commerçants*, 1:lvii; Walther Hinz, *Islamische Masse und Gewichte umgerechnet ins metrische System* (Leiden: E. J. Brill, 1955), 39–40. For another case addressing similar payments, see: DWQ, Maḥkamat Asyūṭ 4, p. 232, case 698 (Ş 1156/Sep. and Oct. 1743).

[15] DWQ, Maḥkamat Asyūṭ 2, p. 484, case 1213 (23 Ca 1129/5 May 1717).

[16] On the Coptic month of Tūt as the first month of the Egyptian agricultural calendar, see: Midhat Sertoğlu, *Osmanlı Tarih Lûgatı* (Istanbul: Enderun Kitabevi, 1986), 347; Sato, *State and Rural Society*, 189–91. For a case that makes clear the importance of the first of Tūt to the Ottoman administrative calendar, see: BOA, Cevdet Maliye, 27049 (Evahir S 1148/12–21 Jul. 1735). The following case directed toward the cities of both Asyūṭ and Jirja testifies to the fact that the two cities were considered part of the same administrative unit: DWQ, Maḥkamat Asyūṭ 9, p. 378, case 756 (28 S 1219/7 Jun. 1804). Other cases offer further evidence of this bureaucratic designation. Unfortunately, the court records of the city of Jirja are not available to researchers. On Ottoman Jirja, see: Laylā ʿAbd al-Laṭīf Aḥmad, *al-Ṣaʿīd fī ʿAhd Shaykh al-ʿArab Hammām* (Cairo: al-Hayʾa al-Miṣriyya al-ʿĀmma lil-Kitāb, 1987); Muḥammad Ibn Muḥammad Ḥāmid al-Marāghī al-Jirjāwī, *Tārīkh Wilāyat al-Ṣaʿīd fī al-ʿAṣrayn al-Mamlūkī wa al-ʿUthmānī: al-Musammā bi-"Nūr al-ʿUyūn fī Dhikr Jirjā min ʿAhd Thalāthat Qurūn,"* ed. Aḥmad Ḥusayn al-Namakī (Cairo: Maktabat al-Nahḍa al-Miṣriyya, 1998); Hamza ʿAbd al-ʿAziz Badr and Daniel Crecelius, "The Waqf of the Zawiyya of the Amir ʿIsa Agha Çerkis: A Circassian Legacy in XVIIth Century Jirje," *AI* 32 (1998): 65–85 and 239–47.

[17] DWQ, Maḥkamat Asyūṭ 3, p. 507, case 1446 (17 B 1096/20 Jun. 1685).

the city in the year 1685 was much greater than expected, and there were not enough ships to transport that quantity of grain from Asyūṭ to Cairo. To avoid a lapse or loss to the state's income, the sultan thus instructed his representative to do immediately whatever he could to acquire more empty ships to move the grain.

In other medium-size cities throughout Egypt there was a similar administration in place to move grains and other foodstuffs from villages to cities and on to Cairo, Alexandria, and elsewhere. Various cases from the court of al-Baḥayra in the northwestern Nile Delta, for example, sketch out a very robust trade in large quantities of wheat grown in the hinterland of large cities like al-Damanhūr to be shipped elsewhere in Egypt and the Ottoman Empire more generally.[18] As was Asyūṭ, the city of al-Damanhūr (the seat of the court of al-Baḥayra) was an important regional center of trade and commerce. An Ottoman decree from 1771 about the dispatch of ships to al-Damanhūr confirms the importance of the city's markets to trade in and beyond Egypt.[19] On this point, we read in another Ottoman decree from 1777 about the buying and selling of cotton in al-Damanhūr that was destined to be shipped to Alexandria and from there to other cities in the Empire.[20]

To ensure the proper transport of grains from smaller Egyptian cities like Asyūṭ or al-Damanhūr to the large Mediterranean port cities of Alexandria and Rashīd or to Cairo, the Ottoman state often appointed a grain official (*gılâl ağası*) to oversee the collection, inspection, and transport of grains from smaller cities to larger ones.[21] In Manfalūṭ, for example, a man named Habahancı Başı was appointed as the official

[18] On the wheat trade in al-Baḥayra, see, e.g.: DWQ, Maḥkamat al-Baḥayra 30, p. 27, case 50 (Evail L 1219/2–11 Jan. 1805); DWQ, Maḥkamat al-Baḥayra 30, p. 34, case 60 (8 Za 1219/8 Feb. 1805). On the hinterland of al-Damanhūr, see: *QJBM*, pt. 2, 2:282–97.

[19] DWQ, Maḥkamat al-Baḥayra 9, p. 206, no case no. (19 N 1185/26 Dec. 1771).

[20] DWQ, Maḥkamat al-Baḥayra, 10, p. 316, case 733 (13 S 1191/23 Mar. 1777). Likewise, the following series of Ottoman *buyuruldus* sent to the court of Manfalūṭ in 1782 aimed at preparing a group of ships to carry barley and other items from that city to Cairo: DWQ, Maḥkamat Manfalūṭ 1, p. 316, case 788 (28 L 1196/6 Oct. 1782); DWQ, Maḥkamat Manfalūṭ 1, p. 316, case 789 (28 L 1196/6 Oct. 1782). For a similar case about the transport of *miri* goods, see: DWQ, Maḥkamat Manfalūṭ 1, p. 317, case 794 (12 L 1196/20 Sep. 1782). On cotton cultivation in Egypt, see: Owen, *Cotton and the Egyptian Economy*.

[21] For an example of a dispute over the pricing of grain between investors in the same piece of land in Manfalūṭ, see: DWQ, Maḥkamat Manfalūṭ 3, p. 34, case 61 (n.d.). For an extremely useful discussion of the enormous economic impact on grain markets of even the smallest changes in pricing, see: William Cronon, *Nature's Metropolis: Chicago and the Great West* (New York: W. W. Norton, 1991), 97–147.

grain overseer for the years between 1765 and 1767.[22] Part of the newly appointed official's duties was to put an end to the rebelliousness of a group of sailors resident in Manfalūṭ. From time immemorial (*öteden beri*), ships on the Nile docking in Manfalūṭ's port were assessed a duty of eight *riyāl*.[23] In 1766, however, a group of greedy men (*tama hâmiller*, literally, "greed bearers") led by one Shaykh Ḥalīm Anbābī refused to pay the tariff. Egyptians were – not surprisingly – quick to resist when confronted with regulations they deemed unjust, and given the Ottoman administration's desire to maximize its income from a province like Egypt, there were many impetuses for the kind of resistance undertaken by Shaykh Ḥalīm Anbābī and his men.[24] However, citing the great potential harm failing to pay tariffs would cause to the income and morale of the state, this Ottoman decree instructed the *gılâl ağası* along with the *qāḍī* and *kāshif* of Manfalūṭ to force payment from the sailors.

Similar to Manfalūṭ or al-Damanhūr, the northeastern city of al-Manṣūra was also the center of an extremely rich agricultural area, and the Ottoman administration of Egypt was likewise keen to ensure the most expedient means possible to transport grain and other foodstuffs from this city to other areas of the Empire. As such, much of the grain sent from al-Manṣūra bypassed the larger coastal cities of Rashīd and Alexandria altogether on its way to Istanbul and elsewhere.[25] This direct link between al-Manṣūra and the Ottoman capital of Istanbul is evidenced by numerous *buyuruldu*s sent to the court of al-Manṣūra about the preparation of ships to transport this grain and about the appointment of an imperial functionary to oversee this work.[26] It was also common for

22 DWQ, Maḥkamat Manfalūṭ 2, p. 184, case 620 (1 R 1179/17 Sep. 1765). The following is the Ottoman firman instructing that this same man's tenure as *gılâl ağası* be renewed: DWQ, Maḥkamat Manfalūṭ 2, p. 184, case 621 (8 R 1180/13 Sep. 1766).

23 DWQ, Maḥkamat Manfalūṭ 2, p. 187, case 627 (24 Ca 1180/28 Oct. 1766).

24 For another example of peasant defiance of Ottoman rule, see: DWQ, Maḥkamat al-Baḥayra 10, p. 314, case 731 (15 Ca 1190/2 Jul. 1776). In this case, villagers take the repair of certain buildings and irrigation works into their own hands because the Ottoman administration of the village had left those places in ruin for more than fifteen years, which resulted in great hardship for the peasants of that area.

25 The ships charged with transporting this grain from al-Manṣūra docked in and left from the branch of the Nile that ran through the city known as al-Baḥr al-Ṣaghīr (Bahr-i Sagir in Ottoman Turkish). DWQ, Maḥkamat al-Manṣūra 12, p. 455, no case no. (9 B 1104/16 Mar. 1693).

26 Cases of this sort include the following: DWQ, Maḥkamat al-Manṣūra 12, p. 439, no case no. (14 L 1103/29 Jun. 1692); DWQ, Maḥkamat al-Manṣūra 12, p. 454, no case no. (18 B 1104/25 Mar. 1693); DWQ, Maḥkamat al-Manṣūra 17, p. 381, no case no. (18 R 1119/18 Jul. 1707). The following case is a *buyuruldu* dated 1709 about preparing

the Ottoman administration – in al-Manṣūra and elsewhere – to keep and store excess grains and foodstuffs in the possession of Egyptian merchants and notables.[27] Shipments of grain from al-Manṣūra and from other Egyptian cities were, moreover, under a nearly constant threat of attack from bandits and Bedouin, and numerous Ottoman decrees directed great caution to fend off such raids.[28]

The transport of grain from smaller cities like al-Manṣūra, Manfalūṭ, and Jirja to Cairo, Rashīd, Istanbul, or Alexandria was not always organized and carried out by the Ottoman state itself. Indeed, the imperial bureaucracy transported only those grains and foodstuffs that would eventually make it into its own coffers. Alongside this imperial system of grain transportation, many wealthy individual merchants thus financed their own shipments of grain and other items from smaller to larger cities. One such individual – a Cairene merchant named al-Shaykh Humām Yūsuf – hired two brothers, Ḥusayn and Shāwīsh, who owned their own boat, to acquire for him 249 *ardabbs* of wheat.[29] Al-Shaykh Humām Yūsuf did not specify from where the wheat was to be obtained, but he promised to pay the brothers one *ardabb* of wheat for every hundred *ardabbs* they brought him. The two brother sailors recorded in the court of Isnā

nineteen ships filled with *miri* grain to be sent to Istanbul from the village of Ṭalkhā: DWQ, Maḥkamat al-Manṣūra 18, p. 264 or 265, no case no. (10 Ca 1121/18 Jul. 1709). This decree stipulates that a man named Mustafa Ağa was to be appointed to oversee the work and to ensure that the grains were sent as quickly as possible and without mistake. For examples of other cases of direct shipments from al-Manṣūra to Istanbul, see: DWQ, Maḥkamat al-Manṣūra 3, p. 255 or 258, case 794 (20 R 1065/27 Feb. 1655); DWQ, Maḥkamat al-Manṣūra 18, p. 244 or 245, no case no. (27 S 1122/27 Apr. 1710). In the first case, large and small (*büyük ve küçük*) ships were ordered to transport thirty *ardabbs* of grain from al-Manṣūra to Istanbul, and in the second case, twenty *ardabbs* were required. In the following case, two men from the Mustahfızan bloc were appointed to oversee the shipment of twenty additional *ardabbs* of grain from al-Manṣūra to Istanbul: DWQ, Maḥkamat al-Manṣūra 17, p. 384, no case no. (21 M 1119/24 Apr. 1707).

27 For example, according to a *buyuruldu* recorded in the court of al-Manṣūra in 1691, the amīr Dhū al-Faqqār Çavuş, one ʿAbd Allah al-Jindī, his brother Hicazî Bishāra, and a man named Ghānim Ibn Ismail (all in the village of Ṣāfūr) were charged by the state with storing 300 *ardabbs* of grain, 100.5 *ardabbs* of wheat, 180 *ardabbs* of barley, 17 *ardabbs* of Egyptian clover, and 6 *ardabbs* of lentils. The decree also served to appoint a state functionary to oversee the recollection of these goods in al-Manṣūra and their shipment to Istanbul. DWQ, Maḥkamat al-Manṣūra 12, p. 419, no case no. (20 Ca 1102/19 Feb. 1691). On the village of Ṣāfūr, see: *QJBM*, pt. 2, 1:191.

28 See, e.g.: DWQ, Maḥkamat al-Manṣūra 12, p. 441, no case no. (15 L 1103/30 Jun. 1692); DWQ, Maḥkamat al-Manṣūra 17, p. 379, no case no. (29 R 1119/29 Jul. 1707).

29 DWQ, Maḥkamat Isnā 7, p. 36, case 67 (16 B 1173/4 Mar. 1760). For another example of an Egyptian merchant renting a transport ship for a short period of time, see: DWQ, Maḥkamat Rashīd 125, p. 147, case 257 (27 Z 1132/29 Oct. 1720).

(situated at an impressive distance of more than 724 kilometers south of Cairo) that they were able to get the 249 *ardabbs* requested by the merchant from two different sources in Isnā (150 *ardabbs* from one unnamed source and 99 from another) before returning with it to Cairo.[30]

This case is particularly striking because of the long distance traversed by Ḥusayn and Shāwīsh in delivering wheat to Cairo. We are unfortunately lacking several important pieces of information about the case. Did the brothers solicit the work in Cairo and then sail up and down the Nile looking for the best and cheapest source of wheat? Did they know that wheat was much more easily obtained in Isnā than anywhere else? Did they calculate that the better price of wheat in Isnā was worth the long trip? Was there perhaps a shortage of wheat in Egypt at the time, thereby forcing the two brothers to sail very far away (again, more than 724 kilometers) from Cairo to find it? Or were they perhaps already in Isnā when commissioned for the job? If so, how did they communicate with al-Shaykh Humām Yūsuf? Despite the lack of clear answers to these and other questions, what is clear from this case is that merchants and those they charged to acquire and transport their goods were part of a huge network that stretched far beyond major cities like Cairo and that included peasants, sailors, merchants, government officials, animals, shipbuilders, lifters, and many others.

The large amount of wheat moved in this case is but one example of the fact that enormous quantities of agricultural products were everywhere in eighteenth-century Egypt and, more important, that they were probably the most common living organisms with which human Egyptians interacted. The lives of most Egyptian peasants were dictated by the responsibilities of growing and sustaining the organisms that would bring them bodily and economic sustenance. They lived in fields and among their crops and interweaved their own histories into the lives of the plants. Through selective breeding and crop rotations, humans changed the course of Egyptian plants' histories at the same time that the dictates of agricultural and economic life determined much of the course of Egyptian peasants' own histories.

As evidence of this, probate records testify to the fact that food often formed very large portions of people's inheritable estates.[31] This was

30 For another case involving shipping to and from Isnā, see: DWQ, Maḥkamat Isnā 7, p. 6, case 7 (Ca 1173/Dec. 1759 and Jan. 1760).

31 See, e.g.: DWQ, Maḥkamat Manfalūṭ 1, pp. 50–51, case 100 (22 Z 1215/6 May 1801). In this case, grain constituted almost a third (32 percent) of the value of the inheritable

especially true of a commodity like coffee, which was an important form of capital for many individuals.[32] Moreover, because the variety and amount of food an individual consumed (and served) was a sign of status and wealth in Ottoman Egypt, it was quite common for those endowing *waqfs* to make provisions in their endowment deeds for the gifting of food and water.[33] Food was also sometimes used to pay the salaries of those

estate. For more on the relative prices and values of different kinds of foodstuffs, see: DWQ, Maḥkamat Rashīd 137, p. 299, case 446 (8 Ra 1144/10 Sep. 1731); DWQ, Maḥkamat Asyūṭ 2, p. 235, case 559 (17 M 1108/15 Aug. 1696).

[32] For an example of an instance in which rice formed the bulk of an individual's personal wealth, see: DWQ, Maḥkamat Rashīd 132, p. 63, case 89 (1 Ş 1137/14 Apr. 1725).

[33] For examples, see: DWQ, Maḥkamat al-Manṣūra 51, p. 125, case 237 (n.d.); DWQ, Maḥkamat Isnā 3, pp. 15–16, case 29 (8 L 1171/14 Jun. 1758); DWQ, Maḥkamat Rashīd 137, pp. 196–98, case 296 (20 L 1146/26 Mar. 1734); DWQ, Maḥkamat Asyūṭ 1, p. 418, case 1160 (19 L 1069/9 Jul. 1659); DWQ, Maḥkamat Asyūṭ 3, p. 330, case 890 (23 L 1135/26 Jul. 1723); DWQ, Maḥkamat Manfalūṭ 2, p. 189, case 631 (24 Ca 1179/8 Nov. 1765); DWQ, Maḥkamat Manfalūṭ 2, p. 190, case 632 (20 C 1179/4 Dec. 1765); DWQ, Maḥkamat Manfalūṭ 2, p. 190, case 633 (3 Z 1180/2 May 1767); DWQ, Maḥkamat Asyūṭ 2, p. 235, no case no. (23 Z 1107/23 Jul. 1696); BOA, MM, 6:603 (Evahir Ca 1162/8–17 May 1749).

For general discussions of *waqf* in Ottoman Egypt, see: Muḥammad ʿAfīfī, *al-Awqāf wa al-Ḥayāh al-Iqtiṣādiyya fī Miṣr fī al-ʿAṣr al-ʿUthmānī* (Cairo: al-Hayʾa al-Miṣriyya al-ʿĀmma lil-Kitāb, 1991); ʿAfīfī, "Asālīb al-Intifāʿ al-Iqtiṣādī bil-Awqāf fī Miṣr fī al-ʿAṣr al-ʿUthmānī," *AI* 24 (1988): 103–38; Shaw, *Financial and Administrative Organization and Development*, 41–47 and 269–71; Cuno, *The Pasha's Peasants*, 21–22; Daniel Crecelius, "The Organization of *Waqf* Documents in Cairo," *IJMES* 2 (1971): 266–77; Crecelius, "The Waqf of Muhammad Bey Abu al-Dhahab in Historical Perspective," *IJMES* 23 (1991): 57–81; Crecelius, "Incidences of *Waqf* Cases in Three Cairo Courts: 1640–1802," *JESHO* 29 (1986): 176–89; Dānyāl Krīsaliyūs, ed., *Fihris Waqfiyyāt al-ʿAṣr al-ʿUthmānī al-Maḥfūẓa bi-Wizārat al-Awqāf wa Dār al-Wathāʾiq al-Tārīkhiyya al-Qawmiyya bil-Qāhira* (Cairo: Dār al-Nahḍa al-ʿArabiyya, 1992). For an architectural take on *waqf* in Ottoman Egypt, see: Behrens-Abouseif, *Egypt's Adjustment to Ottoman Rule*; Aymān Muḥammad Abū Salīm, "Wathāʾiq Waqf al-Wazīr Muḥammad Bāshā al-Silaḥdār fī Miṣr: Dirāsa wa Taḥqīq wa Nashr" (M.A. thesis, Cairo University, 1987).

On the important role of *waqf* in establishing the authority of families, see: Beshara Doumani, "Endowing Family: *Waqf*, Property Devolution, and Gender in Greater Syria, 1800 to 1860," *Comparative Studies in Society and History* 40 (1998): 3–41. For a detailed study of the capital accumulation – through *waqf* and various other means – of various families in Ottoman Cairo, see: Marie-Pascale Gazalé, "Généalogies patrimoniales. La constitution des fortunes urbaines: Le Caire, 1780–1830" (Ph.D. diss., École des hautes études en sciences sociales, 2004).

For a rare example of a *waqf* on a canal, see: DWQ, Taqārīr al-Naẓar 10, p. 21, case 133 (14 Ca 1177/20 Nov. 1763). My thanks to Magdi Guirguis for bringing this case to my attention. This *waqf* was a deed for a canal in the city of al-Maḥalla al-Kubrā in the subprovince of al-Gharbiyya that ran past the villages of Ṣandafā and Shubrā Damsīs. In addition to the canal, the *waqf* also included two bridges and a mosque. For a more common but still noteworthy example of a *waqf* on a group of islands near the coastal city of Rashīd, see: DWQ, Rūznāmja 92 – Daftar Furūkh Muqāṭaʿāt (Raqam

in the employ of the Ottoman state.[34] Food is, of course, at the core of human society. In Donald Worster's words, "every group of people in history has had to identify such resources [foodstuffs] and create a mode of production to get them from the earth and into their bellies."[35] In Egypt, this centrality of food to society was seen in part by the presence of various markets for different consumable foods.[36] Cities large and small had very robust marketplaces that were usually at the geographic and economic centers of cities.[37] As a hub of export, for example, the city of Rashīd contained many kinds of markets, one of the most important being its thriving rice market.[38] Not surprisingly, Rashīd also had a fish market.[39] There were also markets for pigeons, though both pigeons and fish were considered luxury items, which most Egyptians could not afford to eat save on very special occasions.[40]

al-Ḥifẓ al-Nauʿī 325, ʿAyn 5, Makhzin Turkī 1, Musalsal ʿUmūmī 325), no page no., case 842 (25 Ra 1129/9 Mar. 1717). This is the first written case in the entire register. It is written in Ottoman Turkish and represents one of the few written cases in this register, a register made up almost entirely of daily accounting calculations. In another case involving water, we find that Beshir Aghā, a former member of the Istanbul imperial elite, endowed his own *waqf* in Cairo, complete with a *sabīl* and a school. TSMA, E. 5419/16 (n.d.).

34 For example, a group of surgeons (*cerrahīn*) in the Ottoman navy received ten double loaves of bread (*on çift nan*), four portions of mutton (*dört kıtʿ lâhm-i ganem*), and ten rations of barley (*on yem şair*) on a daily basis as payment for their services. BOA, Cevdet Sihhiye, 518 (14–25 Ş 1215/31 Dec. 1800–11 Jan. 1801). On the kinds and prices of meat products in eighteenth-century Egypt, see: al-Jabartī, *ʿAjāʾib al-Āthār*, 1:168–69, 332; 2:219, 225, 292; 3:319, 459, 531. For a very useful analysis of the provisioning of meat to Istanbul, see: Antony Greenwood, "Istanbul's Meat Provisioning: A Study of the *Celepkeşan* System" (Ph.D. diss., University of Chicago, 1988).

35 Donald Worster, "Transformations of the Earth: Toward an Agroecological Perspective in History," *Journal of American History* 76 (1990), 1091–92. For a recent take on the role of food in environmental history, see the four essays in the following forum: Nicolaas Mink, Robert N. Chester III, Jane Dusselier, and Nancy Shoemaker, "Having Our Cake and Eating It Too: Food's Place in Environmental History, a Forum," *Environmental History* 14 (2009): 309–44.

36 On the markets of Cairo, see: Raymond, *Artisans et commerçants*, 1:307–72.

37 For an Ottoman *buyuruldu* about the important market of al-Manṣūra and the need to protect it from bandit raids, see: DWQ, Maḥkamat al-Manṣūra 12, p. 441, no case no. (5 M 1104/16 Sep. 1692). On the market of al-Damanhūr, see: DWQ, Maḥkamat al-Baḥayra 9, p. 206, no case no. (19 N 1185/26 Dec. 1771).

38 DWQ, Maḥkamat Rashīd 125, pp. 323–24, case 530 (12 M 1133/13 Nov. 1720); DWQ, Maḥkamat Rashīd 132, p. 198, case 305 (13 B 1137/28 Mar. 1725); DWQ, Maḥkamat Rashīd 132, p. 206, case 323 (5 M 1138/12 Sep. 1725).

39 DWQ, Maḥkamat Rashīd 134, p. 332, case 443 (30 B 1140/11 Mar. 1728).

40 This was not from a lack of fish or pigeons in the Delta; rather, rights to fishing and hunting were held as a state monopoly used to generate revenue. Shaw, *Ottoman Egypt*

Shipping the Breadbasket

Although Egypt's network of roads connecting villages to towns and towns to cities ensured a constant circulation of foodstuffs within the province, trading relationships that stretched beyond Egypt to other parts of the Ottoman Empire proved much more significant to the harvesting of grains in rural Egypt than did the domestic Egyptian market. Thus, the external demands and pressures produced by Egypt's and its countryside's intimate connections with other areas of the Ottoman Empire very much shaped the contours and histories of rural Egypt. Indeed, as the largest single area of agricultural production anywhere in the Ottoman Empire, Egypt was the breadbasket of the Empire that fed peoples very far away from its borders. Countless Ottoman orders were sent to various Egyptian cities over the course of the long eighteenth century to direct the shipment of food to places like Tunis,[41] Yemen,[42] Aleppo,[43] Morocco,[44] Izmir,[45] western Tripoli,[46] eastern Tripoli,[47] Crete,[48] Salonica,[49]

in the Eighteenth Century, 19 and 47. On the keeping of pigeons, see: DWQ, Maḥkamat al-Baḥayra 8, p. 24, case 37 (19 S 1176/8 Sep. 1762).

41 DWQ, Maḥkamat Rashīd 125, p. 328, case 540 (8 Za 1132/11 Sep. 1720); DWQ, Maḥkamat Rashīd 132, p. 196, case 298 (25 R 1137/10 Jan. 1725).

42 DWQ, Maḥkamat Rashīd 125, p. 333, case 548 (23 L 1132/28 Aug. 1720).

43 DWQ, Maḥkamat Rashīd 125, p. 287, case 452 (13 Ca 1132/22 Mar. 1720).

44 DWQ, Maḥkamat Rashīd 125, pp. 323–24, case 530 (12 M 1133/13 Nov. 1720).

45 DWQ, Maḥkamat Rashīd 125, p. 319, case 517 (28 Ra 1133/27 Jan. 1721); DWQ, Maḥkamat Rashīd 154, p. 3, case 5 (6 C 1159/25 Jun. 1746); DWQ, Maḥkamat Rashīd 154, p. 4, case 8 (12 M 1162/2 Jan. 1749); DWQ, Maḥkamat Rashīd 154, p. 5, case 10 (23 M 1162/13 Jan. 1749); DWQ, Maḥkamat Rashīd 154, p. 5, case 11 (20 Ra 1162/10 Mar. 1749); DWQ, Maḥkamat Rashīd 154, p. 5, case 12 (12 M 1162/2 Jan. 1749); DWQ, Maḥkamat Rashīd 154, p. 10, no case no. (A) (29 S 1161/29 Feb. 1748); DWQ, Maḥkamat Rashīd 154, p. 10, no case no. (B) (29 S 1161/29 Feb. 1748); DWQ, Maḥkamat Rashīd 154, p. 10, no case no. (26 C 1160/5 Jul. 1747); DWQ, Maḥkamat Rashīd 154, p. 12, no case no. (4 Ca 1160/14 May 1747); DWQ, Maḥkamat Rashīd 154, p. 149, no case no. (3 Ra 1162/21 Feb. 1749); DWQ, Maḥkamat Rashīd 154, p. 341, no case no. (8 S 1163/17 Jan. 1750); DWQ, Maḥkamat Rashīd 154, p. 341, no case no. (6 R 1163/15 Mar. 1750).

46 DWQ, Maḥkamat Rashīd 125, p. 147, case 257 (27 Z 1132/29 Oct. 1720).

47 DWQ, Maḥkamat Rashīd 125, p. 287, case 452 (13 Ca 1132/22 Mar. 1720).

48 DWQ, Maḥkamat Rashīd 154, p. 341, no case no. (22 M 1163/1 Jan. 1750). For cases involving the transport of provisions and military supplies from Egypt to Crete, see: TSMA, E. 5207/62 (Evail M 1057/6–15 Feb. 1647); TSMA, E. 664/55 (n.d.).

49 DWQ, Maḥkamat Rashīd 125, p. 319, case 517 (28 Ra 1133/27 Jan. 1721); DWQ, Maḥkamat Rashīd 154, p. 3, case 6 (8 R 1162/27 Mar. 1749); DWQ, Maḥkamat Rashīd 154, p. 2, no case no. (15 R 1162/3 Apr. 1749); DWQ, Maḥkamat Rashīd 154, p. 3, case 4 (12 M 1162/2 Jan. 1749); DWQ, Maḥkamat Rashīd 154, p. 4, no case no. (25 S 1162/13 Feb. 1749); DWQ, Maḥkamat Rashīd 154, p. 4, case 7 (12 M 1162/2 Jan.

Algeria,[50] Istanbul,[51] and the Ḥaramayn (Mecca and Medina).[52] Shipping food to the latter two places (Istanbul and the Ḥaramayn) was the subject of much correspondence between Istanbul and Egypt and shall receive special attention later.[53]

Ships were the key vehicles by which vast quantities of food emanated out from Egypt and by which Egyptians and Ottoman bureaucrats alike linked the economically, environmentally, and politically vital province of Egypt to the rest of the Ottoman world.[54] If roads and canals from

1749); DWQ, Maḥkamat Rashīd 154, p. 8, no case no. (12 M 1162/2 Jan. 1749); DWQ, Maḥkamat Rashīd 154, p. 10, no case no. (25 Ca 1161/23 May 1748); DWQ, Maḥkamat Rashīd 154, p. 12, no case no. (19 Ca 1160/29 May 1747); DWQ, Maḥkamat Rashīd 154, p. 341, no case no. (4 Ra 1163/11 Feb. 1750).

50 DWQ, Maḥkamat Rashīd 154, p. 10, no case no. (21 S 1161/21 Feb. 1748).

51 For a very small sampling of the thousands of cases involving shipments of grain from Egypt to Istanbul, see: DWQ, Maḥkamat Rashīd 122, p. 67, case 113 (21 Ca 1131/11 Apr. 1719); DWQ, Maḥkamat Rashīd 123, p. 142, case 241 (25 B 1131/14 Jun. 1719); DWQ, Maḥkamat Rashīd 124, p. 253, case 352 (1 Ca 1132/10 Mar. 1720); DWQ, Maḥkamat Rashīd 125, p. 318, case 516 (26 Ra 1133/25 Jan. 1721); DWQ, Maḥkamat Rashīd 125, p. 319, case 517 (28 Ra 1133/27 Jan. 1721); DWQ, Maḥkamat Rashīd 125, p. 337, no case no. (12 Ş 1133/7 Jun. 1721); DWQ, Maḥkamat Rashīd 130, p. 404, no case no. (3 Ş 1136/27 Apr. 1724); DWQ, Maḥkamat Rashīd 132, p. 199, case 310 (2 C 1137/15 Feb. 1725); DWQ, Maḥkamat Rashīd 134, p. 344, case 462 (28 Ş 1140/8 Apr. 1728); DWQ, Maḥkamat Rashīd 137, p. 6, case 13 (19 Za 1143/26 May 1731); DWQ, Maḥkamat Rashīd 139, p. 60, case 95 (23 M 1146/5 Jul. 1733); DWQ, Maḥkamat Rashīd 142, p. 51, case 45 (1 B 1149/4 Nov. 1736); DWQ, Maḥkamat Rashīd 146, p. 139, case 116 (1 C 1153/24 Aug. 1740); DWQ, Maḥkamat Rashīd 148, p. 176, case 219 (21 Z 1154/27 Feb. 1742); DWQ, Maḥkamat Rashīd 151, p. 315, case 357 (12 M 1160/23 Jan. 1747); DWQ, Maḥkamat Rashīd 154, p. 182, case 203 (25 Z 1162/6 Dec. 1749); DWQ, Maḥkamat Rashīd 157, p. 324, case 319 (15 R 1166/19 Feb. 1753).

52 DWQ, Maḥkamat Manfalūṭ 2, p. 189, case 631 (24 Ca 1179/8 Nov. 1765); DWQ, Maḥkamat Manfalūṭ 2, p. 190, case 632 (20 C 1179/4 Dec. 1765); DWQ, Maḥkamat Manfalūṭ 2, p. 190, case 633 (3 Z 1180/2 May 1767); DWQ, Maḥkamat Asyūṭ 2, p. 235, no case no. (23 Z 1107/23 Jul. 1696). More complex cases dealing with the shipment of grains from Egypt to the Ḥaramayn are dealt with in a later section.

53 I should also note that there were instances of famine in Egypt during which food was moved from elsewhere in the Empire to the province. In the following case, for example, shortages of rice in Egypt were met by shipments from Crete: TSMA, E. 2444/107 (n.d.).

54 On ships, ship transport, and Ottoman naval power generally, see: Palmira Brummett, *Ottoman Seapower and Levantine Diplomacy in the Age of Discovery* (Albany: State University of New York Press, 1994); İdris Bostan, *Osmanlı Bahriye Teşkilâtı: XVII. Yüzyılda Tersâne-i Âmire* (Ankara: Türk Tarih Kurumu Basımevi, 1992); Bostan, *Kürekli ve Yelkenli Osmanlı Gemileri* (Istanbul: Bilge, 2005); İsmail Hakkı Uzunçarşılı, *Osmanlı Devletinin Merkez ve Bahriye Teşkilâtı* (Ankara: Türk Tarih Kurumu Basımevi, 1948); Rhoads Murphey, *Ottoman Warfare, 1500–1700* (New Brunswick, NJ: Rutgers University Press, 1999), 16–25; Andrew Hess, "The Evolution of the Ottoman Seaborne Empire in the Age of Oceanic Discoveries, 1453–1525," *AHR* 75 (1970): 1892–1919; Colin H. Imber, "The Navy of Süleiman the Magnificent," *AO* 6 (1980): 211–82; Imber, "The Costs of Naval

Egyptian villages to town and cities linked the rural world to the urban, ships linked towns and cities to each other and to places far beyond the distance a peasant or donkey could walk. Roads were likely used only to traverse distances of sixteen kilometers (ten miles) or less.[55] Beyond that, the energy expenditure of a donkey would cancel out too much of the energy value of the food it was carrying, thereby rendering the venture an overall net loss of energy. Thus, water was used to cover distances of more than sixteen kilometers because wind and water currents were free sources of energy. Without ships, Egypt would never have been conquered by the Ottomans and would have remained too distant a territory for their administration from Istanbul. Likewise, without ships, Egyptian merchants could not have benefited from opportunities to trade with a network much larger than Egypt itself. Egypt's robust and extensive Mediterranean and Red Sea shipping networks were the primary reason Egypt's major urban centers – with the important exception of Cairo, of course – were all port cities. Of these, Alexandria, Rashīd, and Suez proved the most important for shipping and transport during the long eighteenth century.[56]

We have already seen how Egyptian merchants used ships to collect and transport grains from various parts of Egypt to other areas of the province. The goal of linking all the major and medium-size cities of

Warfare, The Account of Hayreddin Barbarossa's Herceg Novi Campaign in 1539," *AO* 4 (1972): 203–16; Svat Soucek, "Certain Types of Ships in Ottoman-Turkish Terminology," *Turcica* 7 (1975): 233–49; Giancarlo L. Casale, "The Ottoman Age of Exploration: Spices, Maps and Conquest in the Sixteenth-Century Indian Ocean" (Ph.D. diss., Harvard University, 2004).

55 In reference to England and Wales, Fernand Braudel similarly observes that in 1600 grain was not transported overland for distances of sixteen kilometers (ten miles) or more and that most often overland trips were less than eight kilometers (five miles). Fernand Braudel, *The Wheels of Commerce*, vol. 2 of *Civilization and Capitalism, 15th–18th Century*, trans. Siân Reynolds (London: Collins, 1982), 43.

56 For two cases dealing with the high volume of commerce that passed through the port of Rashīd, see: DWQ, Maḥkamat Rashīd 125, p. 91, case 158 (12 L 1132/17 Aug. 1720); DWQ, Maḥkamat Rashīd 130, no page no., no case no. (A) (6 Ca 1136/2 Feb. 1724). A case about Alexandria from 1720 estimates that the daily income of the city from shipping and commerce was the impressive figure of 198 copper coins (*bakır*) and 482 *akçe*. DWQ, Maḥkamat Rashīd 125, p. 341, no case no. (16 L 1132/21 Aug. 1720). The volume of commerce passing through Alexandria and Rashīd was so high, in fact, that under the new financial system instituted by Selim III's *nizam-ı cedid*, known as the *irade-i cedid hazinesi*, there was an official specifically appointed to oversee the highly lucrative tariffs assessed on the vast quantities of wheat and rice traded in those cities. BOA, MM, 11:498 (Evahir N 1219/24 Dec. 1804–2 Jan. 1805). For an account of Selim III's reign, see: Stanford J. Shaw, *Between Old and New: The Ottoman Empire under Sultan Selim III, 1789–1807* (Cambridge, MA: Harvard University Press, 1971).

Egypt by waterway so as to facilitate the movement of grains and other foodstuffs was one that continued well into the nineteenth century. Indeed, the multiple attempts to link Alexandria and Cairo by canal that I discuss in Chapter 6 were aimed at ensuring that the city of Alexandria was fed by a constant supply of food and water and that goods could be easily shipped from Cairo to other areas of the Mediterranean littoral and beyond.[57]

The construction of ships was very costly and difficult in the eighteenth century for several reasons. First, wood (as I show in the following chapter) was a very expensive building material that did not grow in large quantities in Egypt. Second, the labor needed to bring wood to Egypt and to construct ships was also very costly. In most cases, ships were commissioned by the Ottoman government of Egypt to facilitate the shipping of grains and other foodstuffs from Egypt primarily, but by no means exclusively, to Istanbul. Although the cost of buying a ship was prohibitively expensive for most Egyptians, some wealthy individual merchants and entrepreneurs (like the previous two brother sailors who transported wheat from Isnā to Cairo) did own their own ships.[58]

Because of the high price of materials and construction costs, shipbuilding was most often undertaken by the Ottoman administration of Egypt itself. Numerous cases recorded in the courts of Ottoman Egypt evidence the large sums paid by the Ottoman state for the construction of ships in Egypt.[59] There were also great efforts to maintain and service

57 For more on the problem of food shortages in Alexandria and on nineteenth-century attempts to construct a canal between Cairo and Alexandria, see: BOA, HAT, 131/5411 (29 Z 1232/9 Nov. 1817); BOA, HAT, 342/19546 (17 C 1233/23 Apr. 1818).

58 The case involving the two brothers is: DWQ, Maḥkamat Isnā 7, p. 36, case 67 (16 B 1173/4 Mar. 1760). Estate inventories also give us information about the private ownership of ships. A very successful merchant in Manfalūṭ, for example, left as the most expensive part of his estate a small ship valued at 407 *riyāl* (36,630 *para*). DWQ, Maḥkamat Manfalūṭ 1, pp. 50–51, case 100 (22 Z 1215/6 May 1801). As stated in the text of this case, 1 *riyāl* equaled 90 *niṣf faḍḍa* (or *para*). Another example of the high price of ships in Egypt was the case of a purchase made by the governing council of the city of Rashīd in 1731 from the income collected from the city's tariffs. As part of this expenditure, the divan purchased a series of corvettes (*naqā'ir*) and other boats to aid in the transport of food to the city. The total cost of the boats was 47,400 *riyāl* (4,266,000 *para*), which represented more than 67 percent of the total cost of this purchase and included in it the price of mules to transport food from the ships when they arrived in port and the price of food to sustain the mules. DWQ, Maḥkamat Rashīd 137, p. 59, case 107 (1 Za 1143/8 May 1731).

59 In the following case, 91,500 *para* were put toward the construction of forty ships in the port of Rashīd: DWQ, Maḥkamat Rashīd 123, p. 147, case 251 (16 Ş 1131/4 Jul. 1719). In another case, the sultan appointed an official to oversee the rapid construction of

ships after their construction. In the winter of 1775, for instance, a firman was sent to the head of the Ottoman navy ordering him to prepare twelve ships to be ready to set sail on the Mediterranean the following spring.[60] Any necessary repairs were to be carried out immediately, and the ships were to be painted, caulked, and greased as soon as possible.

An important series of Ottoman firmans sent to the court of Rashīd over the course of a few months in 1725 exemplified the necessity of shipbuilding to the maintenance of Ottoman networks of trade and transport and to the delivery of food to sustain populations in various parts of the Empire. The firmans concern the construction of three galleons in the port of Suez on the Red Sea to be used to transport grains from Egypt to the people of the Ḥaramayn. The timber needed to build the ships did not grow in Egypt, however, so wood was acquired from the royal dockyards of Istanbul. The wood was shipped first from Istanbul to Alexandria aboard state and merchant galleons and was then inspected and recorded once it arrived in Alexandria.[61] In Alexandria, the lumber was moved to a different set of smaller boats known as *al-jarīm* (*cerîm* in Ottoman Turkish), which were more suited to sailing on the Nile.[62] The wood then moved by ship to Rashīd; entered the western branch of the Nile; and continued on to Bulaq, north of Cairo, where the entire load was transferred yet again onto the backs of camels, which carried the lumber from Bulaq through the eastern desert of Egypt to Suez (a distance of approximately 125 kilometers).[63]

Having arrived in Suez, this wood that had originated in the forests of Anatolia (and in other instances Thrace) was finally used to construct ships to transport grains from Egypt to Mecca and Medina.[64] This instance of ship construction exemplifies the empirewide connections and networks of shipping and material consumption that were involved in ensuring that people in various parts of the Empire had adequate amounts of food. The need to feed, in other words, required the cutting of trees in Anatolia and their movement from forests to Istanbul; then

twelve ships, also in Rashīd, that would cost a total of 10,500 *para*. DWQ, Maḥkamat Rashīd 123, p. 146, case 250 (16 Ş 1131/4 Jul. 1719). For another case involving the building of ships in Rashīd, see: DWQ, Maḥkamat Rashīd 123, p. 130, case 217 (30 L 1131/15 Sep. 1719).

60 BOA, Cevdet Bahriye, 7333 (8 Za 1189/31 Dec. 1775).

61 DWQ, Maḥkamat Rashīd 132, p. 199, case 308 (16 Ş 1137/29 Apr. 1725); DWQ, Maḥkamat Rashīd 132, p. 199, case 309 (17 Ş 1137/30 Apr. 1725).

62 DWQ, Maḥkamat Rashīd 132, p. 88, case 140 (17 Ş 1137/30 Apr. 1725).

63 DWQ, Maḥkamat Rashīd 132, pp. 200–1, case 311 (3 N 1137/16 May 1725).

64 DWQ, Maḥkamat Rashīd 132, p. 201, no case no. (15 N 1137/28 May 1725).

across the Mediterranean to Alexandria, Rashīd, and Bulaq; and finally overland to Suez. The staggering amount of effort, money, coordination, energy, labor, and organization marshaled in various areas of the Empire to construct these three ships all stemmed from the need to move grain across the Red Sea from Egypt to the Ḥaramayn.

Moreover, once ships like these were built, there was an equally impressive amount of labor and organization put toward the actual movement of food from Egypt to other parts of the Empire. In most cases, the Ottoman administration of Egypt appointed one of its functionaries in a port city to oversee the management and shipment of foodstuffs.[65] In cases either when ships could not be built in a timely fashion or when the Ottoman government did not want to incur the costs, one of the main responsibilities of the Ottoman bureaucrat charged with overseeing this work was to organize merchant ships and sailors to transport the needed grains and foodstuffs.[66] Thus, in addition to the cases of irrigation discussed in the previous chapter, this reliance on the ships and labor of local Egyptians to carry out the work of the Ottoman state is another example of how the Ottoman Empire relied on local expertise and experience to perform some of its most vital functions.[67] Alternatively, the Ottoman government of Egypt also sometimes enlisted Egyptian soldiers to undertake the work of transporting food. In 1724, for example, the Ottomans ordered that three thousand men from the ranks of the Egyptian military were to be used to ship provisions and food from Rashīd to Istanbul.[68]

Biscuits of Empire

The use of ships in the transport and movement of biscuits (*beksemad* or *beksemat* in Ottoman Turkish and *peksimet* in modern Turkish) between Egypt and the rest of the Ottoman Empire for the benefit of both the

65 See, e.g.: DWQ, Maḥkamat Rashīd 123, p. 137, case 230 (23 N 1131/10 Aug. 1719).

66 DWQ, Maḥkamat Rashīd 125, p. 320, case 520 (S 1133/Dec. 1720); DWQ, Maḥkamat Rashīd 132, p. 196, case 299 (26 S 1137/17 Nov. 1724). In the first case, Egyptian merchants were commissioned to ship coffee and rice to Istanbul. In the second case, the load consisted of five hundred *ardabbs* of rice.

67 The cases cited here give no indication as to whether the laborers were actually paid for their work; it seems likely, however, that they were compensated in some way for their labor, as it was a common practice to rent merchant vessels for shipping. For an example of a case involving the Ottoman administration of Egypt renting merchant ships in Rashīd, see: DWQ, Maḥkamat Rashīd 132, p. 67, case 99 (22 M 1137/10 Oct. 1724).

68 DWQ, Maḥkamat Rashīd 130, no page no., no case no. (B) (9 Ca 1136/5 Feb. 1724).

imperial navy and construction workers is a particularly good example of how imperial connections of transportation and shipping functioned in the Empire.[69] Because the hard, dry biscuits rarely spoiled, they were ideally suited for movement across long distances. They were light and had enough calories to provide sufficient amounts of energy to groups of soldiers, sailors, or workers. In an imperial order to the *mutasarrıf* of the *sancak* of Rhodes, for example, we read that a letter had recently arrived to Istanbul from the captain of the royal navy, Ghazi Hasan Paşa, requesting additional supplies of food for sailors who were to remain on their ships for the duration of the winter in the ports of Alexandria, Damietta, Suez, and Rashīd.[70] Acting on this request, the sultan ordered the *mutasarrıf* of Rhodes to make ready 13,200 *qinṭār* (585,156 kilograms) of biscuits to send to the sailors in Egypt's ports.[71] Employing numerous officials, sailors, and workers in many distant places, this typical kind of decree from Istanbul about the transport of biscuits shows us how huge amounts of food were moved from Rhodes to the Egyptian port cities of Rashīd, Alexandria, Damietta, and Suez.[72]

In a similar case, the governing divan of the city of Rashīd made a significant purchase of biscuits for the city's storage facilities and for sailors stationed in the port.[73] The divan also made funds available for ships and for mules to be used in the transport of this food to the city.

69 These biscuits are also a good example of the cultural influence of the Ottoman Empire on Egypt, as both the food and its name entered Egyptian culture during the Ottoman period. The name was Arabicized to *buqsumāṭ*, and the biscuits are still eaten widely in Egypt today. For the history of the entrance of this originally Greek and then Turkish word into Egyptian Arabic, see: Mutawallī, *al-Alfāẓ al-Turkiyya fī al-ʿArabiyya*, 31.

70 BOA, Cevdet Bahriye, 769 (11 C 1216/19 Oct. 1801).

71 Of this amount, five thousand *qinṭār* (221,650 kilograms) were to be sent immediately because the soldiers were in dire need of additional food supplies. I am using here the conversion cited by Raymond as the most standard for Ottoman Egypt: one *qinṭār* = 44.33 kilograms. Raymond, *Artisans et commerçants*, 1:lvii. Note, however, that conversions for the *qinṭār* range from 44.33 kilograms to 120 kilograms, depending on the commodity in question, the place, and the historical period. Hinz, *Islamische Masse und Gewichte*, 24–25. See also: Halil İnalcık, "Introduction to Ottoman Metrology," *Turcica* 15 (1983): 311–48.

72 For a similar case about the sending of biscuits to men stationed on Ottoman naval ships for the winter in the Mediterranean ports of Egypt, see: BOA, Cevdet Bahriye, 6306 (18 Ra 1218/8 Jul. 1803). This order is a kind of correction to a previous decree to send biscuits to twenty-eight ships stationed in Egypt. Initially, 3,500 *qinṭār* were to be sent to the soldiers, but according to the corrections outlined in this document, only 1,521 *qinṭār* were actually sent.

73 DWQ, Maḥkamat Rashīd 137, p. 59, case 107 (1 Za 1143/8 May 1731). The divan purchased two kinds of biscuits: one costing 190 *nisf fadda* (or *para*) and another

In another case, a firman was sent to the defterdar to make available biscuits for an engineer, his men, and many laborers who were on their way to Alexandria to work on the construction of the Ashrafiyya Canal between the Nile and Alexandria.[74] To ensure that the one hundred men had enough food to last them the entire course of their journey to Alexandria, they were to be provided with eighty *qinṭār* of biscuits. Thirty *qinṭār* of the total amount were to come from the supplies of the head of the biscuit makers in Istanbul, and the remaining fifty *qinṭār* were to be taken from the biscuit storehouses of Bulgarians resident in Gallipoli. As in the previous case, this movement of food was a complex venture involving many people in multiple locations. And like the shipment of grains from Egypt to other distant destinations in the Ottoman Empire, the flow of biscuits between various locations throughout the Empire was contingent on the construction and utilization of ships.

Feeding Istanbul

The two most frequent destinations for Egyptian grain were first Istanbul and then the Ḥaramayn of Mecca and Medina. Istanbul was by far the most common destination of the two over the course of the long eighteenth century.[75] It was the Empire's capital and largest city and, thus, demanded an enormous quantity of calories to feed its residents.[76]

costing 120 *para*. The combined cost of the biscuits was 18,600 *para* of a total of 70,550 *para* spent on the transport of the biscuits to Rashīd.

74 BOA, Cevdet Nafia, 1605 A (13 L 1216/16 Feb. 1802). Although not stated explicitly in this case, a subsequent document about the same order makes clear that the men were sent to Alexandria to work on the repair of a dam and waterway (*sedd ve ruh-i ab*). The work was carried out under the supervision of Muḥammad Ṣāliḥ, an Ottoman representative sent by Istanbul to oversee construction work in and around Alexandria. See: BOA, Cevdet Nafia, 1605B (14 L 1216/17 Feb. 1802).

75 On the general provisioning of Istanbul, see: Rhoads Murphey, "Provisioning Istanbul: The State and Subsistence in the Early Modern Middle East," *Food and Foodways* 2 (1988): 217–63.

76 The first census in Istanbul was carried out in the 1820s and 1840s and determined that the city's population was approximately 375,000. Charles Issawi, *The Economic History of Turkey, 1800–1914* (Chicago: University of Chicago Press, 1980), 34–35. On the basis of a comparison of the available published evidence, Daniel Panzac cites the city's population in the 1830s as 427,984. Panzac, *La peste dans l'Empire Ottoman, 1700–1850* (Louvain: Association pour le développement des études turques, 1985), 276. Stanford J. Shaw reports the population of the city's males in 1844 to be 213,992. Shaw, "The Population of Istanbul in the Nineteenth Century," *IJMES* 10 (1979): 266. Despite the variance in these data, it is probably safe to assume that the city's population was approximately 350,000 in the second half of the eighteenth century.

Table 2.1. *Number of Ottoman Decrees Sent to Rashīd for the Shipment of Grains to Istanbul*

Year	Number
1718–1719	11
1727–1728	4
1740–1741	8
1741–1742	7
1747–1748	5
1748–1749	31
1749–1750	41
1750–1751	125
1751–1752	20
1752–1753	23
1753–1754	5

Note: For citations to the cases referenced here, please see the Appendix.

As Table 2.1 shows, there were literally hundreds of decrees sent from Istanbul to its various courts throughout Egypt ordering the transport of grain from Egypt to Istanbul.[77] From a sampling of years from the middle of the eighteenth century, I outline in Table 2.1 the number of cases sent to the court of Rashīd about the transport of grain from that city to Istanbul. Similar charts could be made for other Egyptian cities, although they would probably not express as high a volume of grain as we find here, because Rashīd and Alexandria were the largest Egyptian ports of export.[78]

The vast majority of these decrees concerned the shipment of coffee, rice, lentils, sugar, and flax to Istanbul in usually quite large amounts.

[77] For additional imperial decrees ordering the shipment of food and other supplies from Egypt to Istanbul, see: TSMA, E. 664/33 (n.d.); TSMA, E. 664/59 (n.d.); TSMA, E. 510 (7 B 1056/18 Aug. 1646); BOA, MM, 12:18 (28 Ca 1220/24 Aug. 1805). In the following case, shortages and scarcity of provisions (*zahirenin kıllet ve müzayakası*) in Istanbul were cited as the reasons for the immediate need for food supplies from Egypt: TSMA, 2380/25 (n.d.).

[78] Michael J. Reimer correctly writes that "the Ottoman period was the heyday of Rashīd." Reimer, "Ottoman Alexandria: The Paradox of Decline and the Reconfiguration of Power in Eighteenth-Century Arab Provinces," *JESHO* 37 (1994): 114. For an important example of commercial transactions in Rashīd, see: DWQ, Maḥkamat Rashīd 8, p. 12, case 46 (Evahir N 983/24 Dec. 1575–2 Jan. 1576). On Ottoman Rashīd, see also: Ṣalāḥ Aḥmad Harīdī ʿAlī, "al-Ḥayāh al-Iqtiṣādiyya wa al-Ijtimāʿiyya fī Madīnat Rashīd fī al-ʿAṣr al-ʿUthmānī, Dirāsa Wathāʾiqiyya," *EHR* 30–31 (1983–1984): 327–78; Nāṣir ʿUthmān, "Maḥkamat Rashīd ka-Maṣdar li-Dirāsat Tijārat al-Nasīj fī Madīnat al-Iskandariyya fī al-ʿAṣr al-ʿUthmānī," *al-Rūznāma: al-Ḥauliyya al-Miṣriyya lil-Wathāʾiq* 3 (2005): 355–85.

For example, Table 2.2 details the quantities of rice requested in the eleven orders sent to Rashīd in 1719.

Table 2.2. *Rice Shipments from Rashīd to Istanbul, 1719 (1131)*

Date of Order	Quantity of Rice (*ardabb*)
11 Apr. 1719 (21 Ca 1131)	276
14 Jun. 1719 (25 B 1131)	242
28 Jun. 1719 (10 Ş 1131)	400
28 Jun. 1719 (10 Ş 1131)	400
28 Jun. 1719 (10 Ş 1131)	400
28 Jun. 1719 (10 Ş 1131)	400
28 Jun. 1719 (10 Ş 1131)	594
26 Jul. 1719 (8 N 1131)	400
4 Aug. 1719 (17 N 1131)[a]	800
22 Aug. 1719 (6 L 1131)	292
23 Aug. 1719 (7 L 1131)	300
Total	**4,504**

Note: The citations for these cases are in the Appendix.
[a] In this case, 370 *ardabb* of lentils were also ordered to be sent with the 800 *ardabb* of rice.

Another example of the kinds and quantities of food sent from Rashīd to Istanbul is shown in Table 2.3, which outlines food shipments from the year 1741–1742 (1154).

Table 2.3. *Food Shipments from Rashīd to Istanbul, 1741–1742 (1154)*

Date of Order	Kind and Quantity
23 Oct. 1741 (13 Ş 1154)	Rice (amount unspecified)
27 Feb. 1742 (21 Z 1154)	Rice (120 *ardabb*)
27 Feb. 1742 (21 Z 1154)	Sugar (25 *ardabb*)
27 Feb. 1742 (21 Z 1154)	Rice (14 *ardabb*)
27 Feb. 1742 (21 Z 1154)	Sugar (25 *ardabb*)
27 Feb. 1742 (21 Z 1154)	Lentils (167 *ardabb*)
27 Feb. 1742 (21 Z 1154)	Lentils (150 *ardabb*)

Note: The citations for these cases are in the Appendix.

Likewise, Table 2.4 summarizes the massive quantities of food and flax ordered by Istanbul to be sent from Rashīd in the year 1750–1751 (1164).

Table 2.4. *Food and Flax Shipment Totals from Rashīd, 1750–1751 (1164)*

Commodity	Total Amount Ordered
White rice	41,969 *ardabb*
Coffee	9,880 *firda*[a]
Flax	455 *ardabb*
Sugar	142 *ardabb*

Note: The citations for these cases are in the Appendix. Of the 125 cases, 102 were written in Ottoman Turkish and the remaining 23 were written in Arabic. That the vast majority of the cases were written in Ottoman Turkish suggests their origins in the central administration of the Ottoman state in Istanbul.

[a] The value of a *firda* ranged between 3 and 3.5 *qinṭār*. Raymond, *Artisans et commerçants*, 1:lvii.

Even from this small sampling, it is clear that enormous amounts of food were moved from Egypt to Istanbul throughout the eighteenth century. How should we understand this consistent and massive movement of huge quantities of food from the province to the imperial capital? Clearly, as the Empire's largest city, the imperial seat, and the home of the sultan and his ruling elites, Istanbul acquired for itself the most and best the Empire had to offer. This need and demand for calories, however, was met by a relative dearth of vast quantities of agricultural land in the immediate hinterland around Istanbul. The closest expansive areas of agricultural land near Istanbul were in the Balkans and central Anatolia, both long and arduous overland journeys from the imperial capital. As such, it was much more expedient and easier for the Ottoman capital to bring food from a place like Egypt – despite its greater distance from Istanbul – because the majority of the journey could be carried out by ship.[79] In addition to the relative ease of sea travel they enjoyed because of copious amounts of free energy from wind and water currents, boats allowed for greater amounts of food to be shipped than could be achieved by any form of overland transport. Because food imports from Egypt were more common, more plentiful, and more important than shipments from anywhere else in the Empire, it is thus no surprise that the docking area for boats carrying food from across the Empire to the capital city came to be known as the Egyptian Bazaar

[79] A similar argument could be made about grain shipments from various parts of the western coast of the Black Sea to Istanbul.

(Mısır Çarşısı).[80] Egypt was, in other words, renowned in Istanbul and in other parts of the Ottoman Empire for being the Empire's most important source of food and trade commodities. Shipments included not only food from Egypt but also coffee and other commodities from Yemen and spices from India that came to Istanbul via Egypt. Egypt was thus the largest and most vital conduit of food to Istanbul and, indeed, to the Empire as a whole.[81]

A case from the early nineteenth century addresses in exact detail just how much food and other supplies were to be sent from Egypt to Istanbul for various uses.[82] This case concerns rope and other materials needed for the imperial dockyards (*tersâne-i âmire*), grains and other foodstuffs required by the royal storage facilities (*kilâr-i maʿmure*), and food for the sultanic kitchen (*matbah-ı âmire*). In each year, it was customary that 42,680 *okka* (52,445 kilograms) of sugar, 50,000 *kile* (1,283,000 kilograms) of rice, 4,000 *okka* (4,915 kilograms) of coffee, and 2,500 *kile* (64,150 kilograms) of lentils be shipped from Egypt to the sultanic kitchen; in addition, 2,000 *qinṭār* (88,660 kilograms) of raw oakum (*üstüpü-ü ham*), 100 *qinṭār* (4,433 kilograms) of spun twine (*rişte-i ıspavlî*), and 50 *qinṭār* (2,216.5 kilograms) of Egyptian twine (*fitil Mısrî*) were also sent to Istanbul from Egypt on an annual basis.[83] All of these foodstuffs and supplies were transported from Egypt to Istanbul aboard ships of the imperial navy. Whether the ships left from Rashīd or Alexandria, before making their way to Istanbul, they had to pass through the office of the Egyptian customs official, where their cargo was entered into the registers of the customs authority.[84] The foregoing numbers are taken from correspondence between Cairo and Istanbul and represent rough estimates of how much of each good was actually sent from Egypt to Istanbul. Although we do not have the written registers of the customs authority of Alexandria, from various other documents we can establish how much

[80] Sertoğlu, *Osmanlı Tarih Lûgatı*, 225. Following the rebuilding of the market after the great fire of 1689, it became known as the Yeni Çarşı.

[81] For a discussion of Istanbul's guilds and of Evliya Çelebi's lively account of a dispute between Istanbul butchers and Egyptian rice, hemp, sugar, and coffee merchants in the city in the seventeenth century, see: Bernard Lewis, *Istanbul and the Civilization of the Ottoman Empire* (Norman: University of Oklahoma Press, 1963), 117–20.

[82] BOA, Cevdet Bahriye, 1568 (23 L 1216/26 Feb. 1802).

[83] Following from Gábor Ágoston, I take 1 *okka* to equal 1.2288 kilograms and 1 *kile* to equal 25.66 kilograms. For a discussion of the difficulties involved in establishing these measurements and for their wide variance, see: Ágoston, *Guns for the Sultan: Military Power and the Weapons Industry in the Ottoman Empire* (Cambridge: Cambridge University Press, 2005), 244–45; Hinz, *Islamische Masse und Gewichte*, 41–42.

[84] On the customs houses of Egypt, see: Shaw, *Financial and Administrative Organization and Development*, 101–17.

food was actually sent from Egypt for certain years. For instance, Table 2.5 shows the amounts of food that were sent to Istanbul in 1795–1796 and 1797–1798.

Table 2.5. *Food Shipments from Egypt to the Sultanic Kitchens, 1795–1796 (1210) and 1797–1798 (1212)*

Year	Sugar (*okka*)	Rice (*kile*)	Coffee (*okka*)	Lentils (*kile*)
1795–1796 (1210)	50,000 (61,400 kg)	60,000 (1,539,600 kg)	3,160 (3,883 kg)	1,500 (38,490 kg)
1797–1798 (1212)	42,860 (52,666.4 kg)	16,210 (415,948.6 kg)	4,000 (4,915.2 kg)	7,817 (200,584.2 kg)

As the numbers in Table 2.5 show, Egypt was clearly a significant source of food and supplies for the imperial palace, for other government institutions, and for the markets of Istanbul more generally.

In the same regard, consider an accounts register of food shipments from Egypt to the Sultan's imperial palace in Istanbul – the physical seat of power in the Ottoman Empire.[85] The register summarizes shipments of food from Egypt to the palace around the year 1748 and focuses mainly on shipments of sugar and coffee from the province to the capital.[86] A firman included in the register ordered a sufficient amount of money to be paid to men named Hacı Hasan and Hacı Ibrahim to cover the costs of the shipments of various foods from Cairo to Istanbul. The food items and other related costs are given in Table 2.6.[87]

As we can clearly see in the expenses of this single year, meeting the food demands of the Ottoman imperial palace was a rather costly undertaking. Coffee, sugar, and rice were quite desirable items in the palace and the source of much business for Egyptian merchants involved in trade with Istanbul.[88]

85 For more on the provisioning of the palace, see: Tülay Artan, "Aspects of the Ottoman Elite's Food Consumption: Looking for 'Staples,' 'Luxuries,' and 'Delicacies' in a Changing Century," in *Consumption Studies and the History of the Ottoman Empire, 1550–1922: An Introduction*, ed. Donald Quataert (Albany: State University of New York Press, 2000), 107–200.

86 TSMA, D. 2886 (22 N 1161/15 Sep. 1748). This is the date given on the cover of the register, which is titled simply "this is the register of Cairo, Egypt" (*Mısır-ı Kahire-i Defterindir*).

87 TSMA, D. 2886, p. 5v (1 Z 1161/22 Nov. 1748).

88 This register also tells us that the total costs of shipments of coffee and sugar from Egypt consumed in the female quarters of the palace (*Enderun-i Hümayun*) from September 1748 to September 1749 and from September 1749 to September 1750 were 12,099 *akçe* and 11,204 *akçe*, respectively. In each of these 24 months, the impressive figure of 350 *qinṭār* (15,516 kilograms) of coffee was shipped from Egypt to the imperial harem. TSMA, D. 2886, p. 8r (22 L 1161/15 Oct. 1748); TSMA, D. 2886, p. 8r (1 L 1162/13 Sep. 1749). The most complete history of the palace harem remains: Leslie P. Peirce, *The*

Table 2.6. *Expenses of Food to Be Sent from Cairo to the Topkapı Palace, 22 November 1748 (1 Zilhicce 1161)*

Expense	Price (*akçe*)
Coffee and sugar	4,358
Sugar	1,000
Shipping of sugar	1,345
Rice	2,000
Shipping of rice	357.5
Promissory note (*poliça*)	100
Money handler fee (*defaʿ-i sarraf*)	2,000
Money handler fee	1,120
Coffee	2,000
Coffee	2,000
Sugar	390
Coffee	2,133
Coffee	423.5
Coffee	3,279.5
Coffee	1,287
Money handler fee	830
Sugar	375
Sugar	61
Total	**25,059.5**

As evidenced in these and other cases, Egypt was the main supplier of most of the Empire's coffee, and it thus played a very important role in the trade and diffusion of this increasingly coveted good in the Ottoman Empire.[89] Though most of the Empire's coffee was grown in Yemen and

Imperial Harem: Women and Sovereignty in the Ottoman Empire (Oxford: Oxford University Press, 1993).

89 On the coffee trade between Egypt and the rest of the Empire, see: Suraiya Faroqhi, "Coffee and Spices: Official Ottoman Reactions to Egyptian Trade in the Later Sixteenth Century," *Wiener Zeitschrift für die Kunde des Morgenlandes* 76 (1986): 87–93; Michel Tuchscherer, "Commerce et production du café en mer Rouge au XVIe siècle," in *Le commerce du café avant l'ère des plantations coloniales: espaces, réseaux, sociétés (XVe-XIXe siècle)*, ed. Michel Tuchscherer (Cairo: Institut français d'archéologie orientale, 2001), 69–90; Muhammad Husām al-Din Ismāʿil, "Le café dans la ville de Rosette à l'époque ottomane XVIe-XVIIe siècle," in *Le commerce du café*, 103–9; André Raymond, "Une famille de grands négociants en café au Caire dans la première moitié du XVIIIe siècle: les Sharāybī," in *Le commerce du café*, 111–24; Mehmet Genç, "Contrôle et taxation du commerce du café dans l'Empire ottoman fin XVIIe – Première moitié du XVIIIe siècle," in *Le commerce du café*, 161–79; Hathaway, *Politics of Households*.

Ethiopia and not in Egypt, Egypt controlled the trade of this commodity as the fulcrum of commercial networks between the Red and Mediterranean seas. As did the rest of Ottoman society, the palace took to consuming this beverage, and by the eighteenth century, coffee was a staple in the Ottoman world.[90] Most other goods – grains, animals, and many kinds of foodstuffs – could be acquired from various other places in the Empire, but coffee beans grown in Yemen and Ethiopia were imported almost exclusively from Egypt during the long eighteenth century. Moreover, as these cases show, coffee was big business in the eighteenth-century Ottoman Empire, and Egyptian merchants were constantly vying for a piece of the highly lucrative trade. Providing the imperial palace with even a modest portion of the quantities of coffee outlined here could be a very significant source of income for Egyptian merchants. Istanbul's thirst for coffee, in other words, drove the economic success of many Egyptian coffee merchants.

The case of coffee in the Ottoman imperial palace also gives us some sense of the value of the commodity in this period. Of the three main goods dealt with in the previous case – sugar, coffee, and rice – only coffee's price saw significant fluctuations, a function of the higher revenues to be gained from its trade and the greater fluidity of the coffee market in Ottoman Egypt. Merchants were constantly aware of and sensitive to price fluctuations, harvest yields, and other statistical indicators of the coffee trade. Because of the enormous volume of coffee commerce in Egypt, even a small change in any one of these factors could greatly affect revenues. The sensitivity and volume of the coffee market are also evidenced by the mention in these cases of money handlers, promissory notes, storage facilities, and the like. Money had to move quickly, and ships had to be fast and big enough to transport coffee at a suitable rate to keep up with demand. Local representatives and others were key actors in the trade as well. Another entry in this register helps show the enormity of the trade, the capital it required, and the many people it involved. We find that fifty thousand *akçe* were paid out in promissory notes to Egyptian coffee merchants and that another twenty thousand *akçe* were paid in promissory notes to a *çuhadar* (a lackey) in Egypt.[91]

[90] On the general history of coffee in the Ottoman Empire, see: Ralph Hattox, *Coffee and Coffeehouses: The Origins of a Social Beverage in the Medieval Near East* (Seattle: University of Washington Press, 1985); Alan Mikhail, "The Heart's Desire: Gender, Urban Space and the Ottoman Coffee House," in *Ottoman Tulips, Ottoman Coffee: Leisure and Lifestyle in the Eighteenth Century*, ed. Dana Sajdi (London: I. B. Tauris, 2007), 133–70; Cengiz Kırlı, "The Struggle over Space: Coffeehouses of Ottoman Istanbul, 1780–1845" (Ph.D. diss., State University of New York, Binghamton, 2000).

[91] TSMA, D. 2886, p. 7r (13 N 1162/27 Aug. 1749).

Because so much capital was in constant motion across vast distances between Egypt, Istanbul, and elsewhere, there were ample opportunities for problems to arise on the seas between those areas. One of the most common problems on these journeys was piracy.[92] Instances of piracy are useful in showing us how the protection offered and facilitated by the Ottoman imperial system allowed grains to be shipped from Egypt to Istanbul on merchant ships in relative safety from regular attack and plunder. Moreover, piracy evidences the fact that the ships of Christian and Muslim empires were in constant contact in the ports and shipping channels of the Mediterranean during the early modern period. Although the instances of positive, indifferent, or neutral interactions among sailors far outweighed instances of attack, conflicts over commerce, authority, and booty – most usually not religion – did sometimes occur.[93]

Food moving from Egypt to Istanbul encountered various other kinds of challenges apart from piracy. One of the most common was the theft of merchandise by those charged with its care. A firman sent in 1750 from the sultan to the vali of Egypt, Ahmet Paşa; to the province's defterdar; and to the captains of *miri* (imperial) ships in both Alexandria and Damietta highlighted this very problem.[94] In the letter, the sultan expresses his anger and frustration at recent shipments of grain provisions for the royal storehouses and of rope for the royal shipyards that were brought to Istanbul from Egypt aboard merchant ships originating in the ports of Alexandria and Damietta.[95] According to the sultan, because of the dishonesty and treachery (*irtikâp ve hıyanet*) of the captains and crews of the ships, the merchandise arrived in very poor condition. The bags of grain were not pure (*pak*) and seemed to have been mixed with some

92 On piracy and corsairs in the Ottoman Empire, see: Brummett, *Ottoman Seapower and Levantine Diplomacy*, 94–102 and 135–36; Bostan, *Osmanlı Gemileri*, 372 and 376; Molly Greene, "The Ottomans in the Mediterranean," in *The Early Modern Ottomans: Remapping the Empire*, ed. Virginia Aksan and Daniel Goffman (Cambridge: Cambridge University Press, 2007), 113–16.

93 In this regard, see: Molly Greene, *A Shared World: Christians and Muslims in the Early Modern Mediterranean* (Princeton, NJ: Princeton University Press, 2000). In the following case, a fleet of Christian ships attacked Egyptian vessels carrying grains from Egypt to Istanbul in the Aegean between Rhodes and İstanköy (the modern-day Greek island of Kos): TSMA, E. 7008/12 (n.d.).

94 BOA, MM, 6:601 (Evahir Ca 1163/28 Apr.–7 May 1750).

95 The rope was of three kinds: oakum (*üstüpü*), nautical twine (*ıspavlî*), and wick twine (*fitil*). On the movement of French ships between the Egyptian city of Damietta and other Ottoman port cities in the eighteenth century, see: Daniel Crecelius and Hamza 'Abd al-'Aziz Badr, "French Ships and Their Cargoes Sailing between Damiette and Ottoman Ports 1777–1781," *JESHO* 37 (1994): 251–86.

sort of dirt or lesser-quality grain, and the shipments of both grains and ropes were largely incomplete.

Previously noting the extremely poor condition of goods transported by merchant ships to Istanbul, the sultan had issued an *amr* in this regard demanding that foodstuffs and other commodities sent from Egypt be carried by ships of the royal navy that frequented Egyptian ports rather than by Egyptian merchant ships.[96] In his letter of frustration, the sultan makes the point yet again that the shipping of grain from Egypt to Istanbul was no simple matter. As seen here, this kind of transport presented many opportunities for personal gain because it was indeed quite simple for peasants and merchants involved in the shipping of grains from Egypt to Istanbul to cheat the state out of large amounts of whatever commodity was being moved and to keep it for themselves. When dumped into a bag that would soon be tied, grains of varying qualities and various other materials that were not grains at all were nearly indistinguishable. Thus, if a peasant charged with contributing an amount of his grains to a shipment destined for Istanbul replaced a small amount of grain with one of lesser quality, with dirt, or with some other cheap item, it would be very difficult to detect.[97] Likewise, it was very difficult to know if and when small amounts of grain were stolen from the large quantities regularly sent to Istanbul. It would be even more difficult to determine who was responsible for such theft. In a system involving thousands of individuals (some of whom spoke the same language and some of whom did not) spread across a huge geographic area, attempts to determine the identity

96 To make sure that his orders were carried out in this regard, the sultan instructed that this decree in 1750 be delivered by one of the state's deaf functionaries. The man's name was Hasan, and he is described as the tongueless leader of the men of beckonings and signs (*kıdvet erbab ül-ima ve ül-işaret bizeban Hasan*). It was quite common in the Ottoman bureaucracy to employ the deaf for very important imperial functions (indeed, they were some of the most favored servants in the sultan's palace) because they were considered more trustworthy and to possess greater intuitive skills of perception (*firaset*) than other hearing state officials. For discussions of deafness in the early modern Ottoman Empire, see: M. Miles, "Signing in the Seraglio: Mutes, Dwarfs and Jestures at the Ottoman Court 1500–1700," *Disability and Society* 15 (2000): 115–34; Sara Scalenghe, "The Deaf in Ottoman Syria, 16th–18th Centuries," *Arab Studies Journal* 12–13 (2004–5): 10–25; Nicholas Mirzoeff, "Framed: The Deaf in the Harem," in *Deviant Bodies: Critical Perspectives on Difference in Science and Popular Culture*, ed. Jennifer Terry and Jacqueline Urla (Bloomington: Indiana University Press, 1995), 49–77; Sara Scalenghe, "Being Different: Intersexuality, Blindness, Deafness, and Madness in Ottoman Syria" (Ph.D. diss., Georgetown University, 2006), 152–91.

97 For an instructive comparative example of this phenomenon, see: Cronon, *Nature's Metropolis*, 109–19.

of individuals who stole a minuscule amount from a vast sea of grain would be tantamount to finding the proverbial needle in a haystack.

The complexity and vastness of the Ottoman bureaucracy allowed it to control huge areas of territory and to shift goods and resources from one region to another.[98] Those, however, were the very same attributes that allowed merchants and peasants to cheat the system so easily. That the preceding order to use state ships rather than Egyptian merchant ships was sent several times suggests that those Ottoman functionaries charged with enforcing royal decrees benefited themselves greatly by *not* enforcing them. As with peasants, merchants, and sailors, state officials could also siphon off of Istanbul's grain shipments to keep some of the commodity for their own consumption or to sell it for personal profit. At great physical distance from the Mediterranean coast of Egypt and from the machinations of his own subjects and bureaucrats, the sultan could do little more than issue decree after decree in an attempt to stop the seemingly endemic theft of grain.

Provisioning the Pilgrimage

Just as Egypt served the Ottoman capital city of Istanbul to its north, it was also a major supplier of food to the Ḥaramayn of Mecca and Medina to its southeast. Indeed, this was the second most common destination for Egyptian grains over the course of the long eighteenth century.[99] As the location of al-Masjid al-Ḥaram, the holiest site in Sunni Islam, Mecca was one of the most important symbolic and spiritual cities in the Ottoman Empire. It and Medina – home of the mosque of the Prophet, where Muḥammad, Abū Bakr, and ʿUmar are buried – were the site of the annual pilgrimage (*ḥajj*), the last of the five pillars of Sunni Islam. Surely the largest annual single gathering of people anywhere in the early modern

98 On the role of Egyptian provisions and resources in Ottoman warfare, see: TSMA, E. 1173/75 (26 N 1215/10 Feb. 1801); Murphey, *Ottoman Warfare*, 50–51 and 58–63.

99 On the general provisioning of Mecca and Medina from Egypt, see: BOA, MM, 3:210 (Evail Ş 1133/27 May-5 Jun. 1721); BOA, HAT 29/1358 (29 Z 1197/24 Nov. 1783); BOA, HAT 28/1354 (7 Za 1198/22 Sep. 1784); BOA, HAT 26/1256 (10 Za 1200/3 Sep. 1786). There is no internal evidence for the date of this final case. The date given is the one assigned by the BOA. TSMA, E. 3218 (n.d.); TSMA, E. 5657 (13 Ra 1204/1 Dec. 1789); TSMA, E. 664/40 (n.d.); TSMA, E. 5225/12 (Evahir S 1194/27 Feb.–7 Mar. 1780); TSMA, E. 664/51 (n.d.); TSMA, E. 2229/3 (n.d.). For a detailed study of Egyptian relations with the Hijaz during the Ottoman period, see: Ḥusām Muḥammad ʿAbd al-Muʿṭī, *al-ʿAlāqāt al-Miṣriyya al-Ḥijāziyya fī al-Qarn al-Thāmin ʿAshar* (Cairo: al-Hayʾa al-Miṣriyya al-ʿĀmma lil-Kitāb, 1999).

world, the preparations for and the organization of the *ḥajj* were a major responsibility of those in charge of the wider Hijaz region in which were located Mecca and Medina, and in the eighteenth century, the Ottoman Empire was the responsible polity.[100] There were two main caravan routes in the Empire that carried pilgrims to the Ḥaramayn – one through Damascus and the other through Cairo.[101] The former brought pilgrims from Istanbul, Anatolia, Greater Syria, Iran, and regions of Central Asia to the Ḥaramayn, whereas the latter was the point from which pilgrims from Egypt, North Africa, and other parts of Africa traveled toward the Hijaz.

The organization of the annual Egyptian pilgrimage caravan that left from Cairo was a huge economic and bureaucratic affair. Animals, food, supplies, and protection were just some of the expenses incurred by the state in its organization of the caravan.[102] Despite (or perhaps

[100] On the Ottoman management of the yearly pilgrimage, see: Suraiya Faroqhi, *Pilgrims and Sultans: The Hajj under the Ottomans* (London: I. B. Tauris, 1994); Shaw, *Financial and Administrative Organization and Development*, 239–71.

[101] On the Damascus route, see: Menderes Coşkun, "Stations of the Pilgrimage Route from Istanbul to Mecca via Damascus on the Basis of the *Menazilü'l-Tarik İla Beyti'llahi'l-ʿAtik* by Kadri (17th Century)," *OA* 21 (2001): 307–22. On the sources of water available along the Damascus pilgrimage route, see: Hishām Ibn Muḥammad ʿAlī ʿAjīmī, "al-Qilāʿ wa Manāhil al-Miyāh fī Ṭarīq al-Ḥājj al-Shāmī min Khilāl Wathīqa ʿUthmāniyya," *al-Rūznāma: al-Ḥauliyya al-Miṣriyya lil-Wathāʾiq* 3 (2005): 545–82. On the portion of the route from Istanbul to the Ḥaramayn by sea, see: ʿĀiḍ bin Khazzām al-Rūqī, "Juhūd al-Dawla al-ʿUthmāniyya fī Taʾmīn al-Ṭarīq al-Baḥrī min ʿĀṣimat al-Dawla ilā al-Ḥaramayn al-Sharīfayn," *EHR* 42 (2004–2005): 541–72.

[102] Take the following as an example of some of the financial complexities involved in the organization of the yearly pilgrimage. According to an imperial Ottoman *buyuruldu*, the amount normally spent by Mustafa Bey during his tenure as Emir ül-Hac (head of the pilgrimage) was 696 *kise akçe* (17,400,000 *para*). In 1776–1777 (1190), however, Mustafa Bey spent 1556 *kise akçe* (38,900,000 *para*), a full 860 *kise akçe* (21,500,000 *para*) more than the customary amount. Mustafa Bey made a request that the state cover the extra 860 *kise akçe* (21,500,000 *para*) needed for the *ḥajj*, because much of the revenue of *khawāṣ* lands earmarked for the pilgrimage did not meet their obligations that year.

In his response to this request, the sultan refused Mustafa Bey the desired money. He then proceeded to review the multiple forms of revenue the state had made available for the Egyptian pilgrimage caravan in recent years. In 1744–1745 (1157), it was determined that Mustafa Bey's predecessors had made it their custom to take an extra 150 *kise akçe* (3,750,000 *para*) from the *irsāliyye-i ḫazīne* each year to put toward the expenses of the pilgrimage. Though doing so was technically illegal, the sultan was willing to grant the *emir ül-hac* these funds for the pilgrimage. Moreover, all coffee merchants passing through Suez were required to pay a tax of one gold coin (*fındık altunı*) on every bale of coffee in their possession to help offset expenses related to the pilgrimage. In 1761–1762 (1175), it was also agreed that, in addition to the normal amount of 100 *kise akçe* (2,500,000 *para*) collected from each *muqāṭaʿa* in Egypt, an extra 150 *kise akçe* (3,750,000 *para*) would be assessed on each piece of land to be put

because of) the enormous costs, Egypt nevertheless always remained central to the organization and execution of the yearly *ḥajj*.[103] The most important role Egypt played in the history of the *ḥajj* was ensuring that pilgrims going to the holy cities had sufficient amounts of food to sustain them while in the Hijaz. Egypt was the main supplier of food for the two cities of Mecca and Medina during the pilgrimage season and, indeed, throughout the remainder of the year as well.[104] As noted previously, boats from Egypt left for the Hijaz from the Egyptian Red Sea port city of Suez, and the construction of ships in the port was of central importance to the Ottoman administration of food transport from Egypt to the Ḥaramayn.[105] Any delay in the shipment of Egyptian grains to Mecca and Medina would cause the people of those cities great hardship and suffering, and thus the complete and proper transport of grains was of the utmost importance to the Ottoman state.[106]

toward the pilgrimage caravan. A Hatt-ı Hümayun was issued on the matter to clarify which funds were earmarked for the pilgrimage, and a later *emr-i şerif* in June or July 1766 made explicit that no further funds were to be spent from the *irsāliyye-i ḫazīne* of Egypt for the sake of the *ḥajj*. Thus, having reviewed all that information, the sultan's denial of Mustafa Bey's requests for extra funds also included a reprimand of him for spending beyond his authorized limits. BOA, Cevdet Maliye, 15566 (15 C 1191/20 Jul. 1777). For another example of the great financial and bureaucratic costs associated with the organization of the Egyptian pilgrimage caravan, see: BOA, HAT, 177/4744 (12 Ra 1206/9 Nov. 1791).

103 On the sending of gold from Egypt for the financing of the *ḥajj*, see: TSMA, E. 5581 (Evahir B 1056/1–10 Sep. 1646).

104 On Egypt's provisioning of food to Mecca and Medina, see: BOA, HAT 29/1364 (28 N 1198/15 Aug. 1784).

105 For a series of Ottoman firmans about the construction of ships in the port of Suez, see: DWQ, Maḥkamat Rashīd 132, p. 88, case 140 (17 Ş 1137/30 Apr. 1725); DWQ, Maḥkamat Rashīd 132, p. 199, case 308 (16 Ş 1137/29 Apr. 1725); DWQ, Maḥkamat Rashīd 132, p. 199, case 309 (17 Ş 1137/30 Apr. 1725); DWQ, Maḥkamat Rashīd 132, pp. 200–1, case 311 (3 N 1137/16 May 1725); DWQ, Maḥkamat Rashīd 132, p. 201, no case no. (15 N 1137/28 May 1725). Both the complete dependence of the Ḥaramayn on food shipments from Egypt and the importance of this food to the preservation of the cities and the people who lived and traveled there are outlined in the following firman from the Ottoman sultan to Vali Muḥammad Paşa in 1732: BOA, MM, 4:426 (Evasıt B 1144/9–18 Jan. 1732). The document explicitly states that the daily sustenance and food (*kuvvet ve maʿishet*) of the people of Mecca and Medina was limited exclusively to those grains that were customarily sent from Egypt.

106 These are points made consistently throughout the archival record of grain shipments from Egypt to the Hijaz. For a case that adamantly makes the point that there must be continuous supplies of grain sent from Egypt to the Ḥaramayn with no breaks in the flow of food, see: TSMA, E. 5225/9 (Evahir Ca 1191/27 Jun.–6 Jul. 1777).

Because of the great imperial interest in the movement of grain from Egypt to the Hijaz and to ensure that it was completed correctly and expediently, the state, for example, sent one of its most trusted and dependable functionaries – a man named Süleyman – to Egypt in 1732 to assist Vali Muḥammad Paşa in overseeing this work. The necessary grains were to be obtained as quickly as possible from the appropriate sources in Egypt and then to be sent to Suez to be loaded onto state ships (*mîrî sefineleri*) as soon as possible. If, however, these ships were not enough to transport the entire load, then private vessels (*mülki sefineleri*) were to be obtained as well to ship the remaining amount. The order in this case also states that if any grain was missing from last year's shipment, it should be compensated by adding extra grain to this year's shipment. The firman then warns against any amount of laziness, delay, or ignorance in the matter, as even an iota's worth (*mikdar-ı zerre*) of delay or mistake would lead to great harm for the people of the Ḥaramayn, because they had no sources of food other than those grains coming from Egypt. The spoils and fortunes of the Nile flood and the ability of Egypt's irrigation system and of the peasants who worked on it to deal with the yearly inundation thus affected the lives of thousands of people in the Ḥaramayn and elsewhere far beyond the Nile Valley.

That the presence and proper function of ships was vital to the delivery of grains to Mecca and Medina is a point made over and over again in the archival record of Ottoman Egypt.[107] An especially telling example of

[107] For general discussions of Ottoman commerce in the Red Sea and between Egypt and the Hijaz, see: Suraiya Faroqhi, "Trade Controls, Provisioning Policies, and Donations: The Egypt-Hijaz Connection during the Second Half of the Sixteenth Century," in *Süleymân the Second and His Time*, ed. Halil İnalcık and Cemal Kafadar (Istanbul: Isis Press, 1993), 131–43; Faroqhi, "Red Sea Trade and Communications as Observed by Evliya Çelebi (1671–72)," *NPT* 5–6 (1991): 87–105; Daniel Panzac, "International and Domestic Maritime Trade in the Ottoman Empire during the 18th Century," *IJMES* 24 (1992): 194–95; Tuchscherer, "Commerce et production du café en mer Rouge au XVIe siècle," in *Le commerce du café*, 69–90; Hathaway, *Politics of Households*; C. G. Brouwer, "Non-Western Shipping Movements in the Red Sea and Gulf of Aden during the 2nd and 3rd Decades of the 17th Century, According to the Records of the Dutch East India Company, Part 1," *Die Welt des Islams* 31 (1991): 105–67; Brouwer, "Non-Western Shipping Movements in the Red Sea and Gulf of Aden during the 2nd and 3rd Decades of the 17th Century, According to the Records of the Dutch East India Company, Part 2," *Die Welt des Islams* 32 (1992): 6–40; Colin Heywood, "A Red Sea Shipping Register of the 1670s for the Supply of Foodstuffs from Egyptian *Wakf* Sources to Mecca and Medina (Turkish Documents from the Archive of 'Abdurrahman ''Abdi' Pasha of Buda, I)," *Anatolia Moderna* 6 (1996): 111–74; André Raymond, "A Divided Sea: The Cairo Coffee Trade in the Red Sea Area during the Seventeenth and Eighteenth Centuries," in *Modernity and Culture: From the Mediterranean to the Indian*

this point is a firman that was sent to the vali of Egypt in 1732 about the improper use of boats meant to transport grains to the Ḥaramayn.[108] The most common kind of ship employed by the Ottoman state to make the very frequent and important trip between Suez and Jidda was the *galleta* (*kalite*).[109] Many of those ships, though, had recently fallen into disrepair and in the spring of 1732 were thus grounded in Suez. Because the ships were used not only to move grains but also to escort other larger transport ships and to protect them from pirate attack, their return to the route between Suez and Jidda was judged to be of the utmost consequence, and their repair was thus ordered in this decree.

The order further stipulated that six frigates (*firkata*) were to be constructed to protect grain ships and to aid in the movement of goods from Egypt to the Ḥaramayn.[110] Previously, frigates, ships of three sails that were smaller than the Ottoman *kalite* and outfitted with cannons and artillery, were grounded in Suez because certain state officials had used them for their personal gain in shipping goods and merchandise from Egypt for sale in Mecca and Medina.[111] The decree instructed that the six new frigates slated for construction in Suez were to be used only to protect grain ships from pirate and Bedouin raids, as that was their original purpose.[112] Any other use of the ships would therefore be considered

Ocean, ed. Leila Tarazi Fawaz and C. A. Bayly (New York: Columbia University Press, 2002), 46–57.

108 BOA, MM, 4:478 (Evasıt N 1144/8–17 Mar. 1732).

109 On the use of Alexandria's customs duties in Jidda, see: BOA, HAT 26/1256B (10 Za 1200/3 Sep. 1786).

110 On the Ottoman *firkata*, see: Sertoğlu, *Osmanlı Tarih Lûgatı*, 114; Bostan, *Tersâne-i Âmire*, 22–27 and 98–101; Bostan, *Osmanlı Gemileri*, 228–33.

111 On the *kalite*, see: Sertoğlu, *Osmanlı Tarih Lûgatı*, 168–69; Bostan, *Tersâne-i Âmire*, 124–27 and 130–35; Bostan, *Osmanlı Gemileri*, 224–28.

112 As with Mediterranean shipping, another challenge facing the transport of grains and people between Egypt and the Ḥaramayn was the constant danger of pirate or Bedouin attack. For examples of piracy in the Red Sea, see: Brouwer, "Non-Western Shipping, Part 2," 14 and 32. In addition to using *galletas* and frigates to protect Egypt's links to Mecca and Medina, the Ottoman administration of Egypt also employed a group of Bedouin horsemen known as *jerde* to escort the Egyptian pilgrimage caravan on its journeys between Cairo and Mecca and Medina. Having co-opted groups of Bedouin horsemen to work in the Ottoman fold, the Ottoman government of Egypt used these men to fight against other would-be Bedouin raiders. For example, in 1777, a group of Bedouin attacked a pilgrimage caravan led by Emir ül-Hac Mustafa Bey on its return from Mecca. After five hours of intense fighting, the pilgrims and the *jerde* battling alongside them had seemingly gained the upper hand on their Bedouin attackers. Soon, though, word arrived in Cairo that the Bedouin had regrouped, had managed to turn the tide against the *jerde*, and had them confused and distraught (*perişan*). Having received this ominous news, the Egyptian amirs Laşin Bey, Murat Bey, and Halil

an act against the interests of the state. The use of ships for purposes other than those officially sanctioned or for the illegal transport of items was a phenomenon found all over Egypt and one not confined merely to shipping routes between Suez and the Hijaz.[113] Trade in forbidden goods was thus an important aspect of the story of the transportation of goods out of and within Egypt.[114]

In addition to providing the people of Mecca and Medina with grain and other foodstuffs and to ensuring the safe passage of this food and of people between Egypt and the Ḥaramayn, the Ottoman bureaucracy of Egypt was also charged with the maintenance of the Hijaz's water supply, especially that of the city of Mecca.[115] Given Egypt's vast wealth, proximity to the Ḥaramayn, and history of irrigation and water resource management, it is not surprising that the province was partly responsible for the supply of water in Mecca and Medina.[116] This fact also proves significant, as it serves to highlight once again the ways in which the Ottoman state rotated resources, experience, and knowledge around the Empire.[117] Where there was want, the Ottoman state sought to address the deficiency by moving excess from elsewhere. In this case, Egypt's

Bey along with the heads of the seven military blocs organized a supply of emergency provisions and assembled a cavalry force of 1,500 to aid the pilgrims (together the expenses totaled 300 *kise akçe* or 7,500,000 *para*). The supplies and men proved more than sufficient to defeat the Bedouin raiders, and the pilgrimage caravan arrived safely in Cairo shortly thereafter. BOA, Cevdet Maliye, 15566 (15 C 1191/20 Jul. 1777).

113 In the court of Rashīd, for instance, there were numerous cases entreating Ottoman officials to prevent ships without the proper license (*ruhsat*) from transporting coffee, rice, and other goods. See, e.g.: DWQ, Maḥkamat Rashīd 130, no page no., case 416 (11 C 1136/7 Mar. 1724). In the language of the Ottoman state, these illegal acts were the result of nothing but pure greed (*tama-i ham sebebi ile*) and hurt the overall well-being of the Empire. DWQ, Maḥkamat Rashīd 132, p. 199, case 310 (2 C 1137/15 Feb. 1725).

114 For other examples of this illegal trade, see: DWQ, Maḥkamat Rashīd 124, p. 253, case 353 (n.d.); DWQ, Maḥkamat Rashīd 125, p. 337, no case no. (A) (27 B 1133/24 May 1721).

115 For examples of orders enlisting the Ottoman administration of Egypt in the repair of waterways (*su mecraları*) in Mecca, see: BOA, HAT 266/15433 (29 Z 1204/9 Sep. 1790); BOA, HAT 547/26996 (29 Z 1232/9 Nov. 1817). There is no internal evidence for the date of either case. The dates given are those assigned by the BOA.

116 In the following cases, tools and materials were to be sent from Egypt for the repair of waterways in Medina, see: BOA, HAT 228/12681 (29 Z 1205/29 Aug. 1791); BOA, HAT 1301/50670 (29 Z 1215/13 May 1801). There is no internal evidence for the date of either case. The dates given are those assigned by the BOA. See also: TSMA, E. 5204/11 (Evasıt B 1024/6–15 Aug. 1615).

117 For examples of the use of the Egyptian *irsāliyye-i ḫazīne* to fund repairs of general infrastructure in Mecca and Medina and to address other matters in the Hijaz, see: BOA, HAT 95/3856A (27 Z 1215/11 May 1801); BOA, HAT 16/716A (29 Z 1189/19

surplus resources were the solution to the problem of Mecca's want of food and water. This kind of balancing of natural resources and knowledge around the Empire was – as I have been arguing – a hallmark of Ottoman imperial rule in the early modern period.

To get an idea of the ways in which Egypt came to participate in the management of Mecca's water resources, consider the following example.[118] A firman from 1733 takes as its subject both the deteriorated state of Mecca's waterways (*suyun yolları*), fed by water from Lake Nuʿmān, and the similarly dismal state of several lakes that drew their water from the well of ʿArafāt (ʿAyn ʿArafāt).[119] The lakes and waterways were constantly in need of repair and were most recently attended to during a period of work from December 1731 or January 1732 to May or June 1733.[120] On every day of that seventeen-month period, more than four hundred workers were used for the repair job. Once the work was completed, the sherif of Mecca along with other notables in the city, the muftis of the four schools of Islamic jurisprudence, a large number of Meccans, and several engineers of prudent judgment (*mühendisīn sahih ül-tahmin*) visited the repair sites to inspect the dimensions and quality of the repairs and to compile a *defter* detailing the expenses incurred during the work. They determined that the total cost of labor was 155 *kise akçe* and 100 *guruş* (3,878,500 *para*).[121]

Most significant for our purposes here in establishing the connection between Egypt and public works repairs in Mecca is the fact that the funds for such work very often came from the Egyptian *irsāliyye-i ẖazīne*.[122] Egypt was thus uniquely situated at the financial and bureaucratic center of Ottoman repair works in Mecca. In the bureaucratic web of the Ottoman

Feb. 1776). There is no internal evidence for the date of this last case. The date given is the one assigned by the BOA. See as well: TSMA, E. 664/10 (n.d.).

118 As further evidence of Egypt's discursive, financial, and bureaucratic connections to the supply of water in Mecca, note that there was a lake in the city named Lake Egypt (*Mısır Birkesi*). For further information on repairs carried out on irrigation works related to this and other lakes in Mecca, see: BOA, Cevdet Belediye, 4804 (13 B 1207/24 Feb. 1793).

119 BOA, MM, 5:33 (Evail R 1146/10–19 Sep. 1733).

120 For another case involving the upkeep of ʿAyn ʿArafāt and the repair of waterways in Mecca, see: TSMA, E. 4070 (n.d.). For an order to repair aqueducts (*su kemerleri*) and waterways in Jidda and Mecca before the time of the approaching pilgrimage season, see: TSMA, E. 7019/251 (n.d.).

121 According to Raymond, the value of one *guruş* ranged between thirty and forty *para*. Raymond, *Artisans et commerçants*, 1:39. I take one *guruş* to equal thirty-five *para*.

122 For another example of the use of funds from the Egyptian *irsāliyye-i ẖazīne* for infrastructural repairs in Mecca, see: TSMA, E. 4830 (17 C 1194/20 Jun. 1780).

Empire, Egypt served to make water and food flow to the people of Mecca and to the thousands of pilgrims who came to the city every year. And as the primary supplier both of water and food and of expertise in irrigation repairs, Egypt therefore functioned as a veritable lifeline to thousands of Ottoman subjects outside the Nile Valley.

As briefly mentioned earlier, an important aspect of connections between Egypt and the Hijaz were the numerous *waqf*s endowed in Egypt devoted to the interests and well-being of the people of the Hijaz.[123] Part of the function and purpose of one such *waqf* – the *waqf* of Sulṭān Murād Khān in Cairo – was to produce grains earmarked for the Ḥaramayn.[124] The grains were sent overland from Cairo to Suez to be boarded onto ships destined for the Hijaz. Because the *waqf*'s grains gradually (*ceste ceste*) came to Suez, it was necessary to build a new *wakāla* in the city to store all the grains safely and securely until the full amount was ready to ship to the Hijaz. The arrival of the grains in the Hijaz was, however, not a foregone conclusion once placed aboard ships in Suez. As a sea that is unusually deep relative to its slender width, the Red Sea's unique ecology presented many dangers for the transport of food from Egypt to the Hijaz. Corals are an enormous risk in the Red Sea, with many of them reaching very close to the water's surface and being largely invisible from the deck of a ship. Various other large underwater rock formations also made shipwreck a common danger in the Red Sea. Thus, in 1765, for example, a ship named *God's Bounty* (*Feyz-i Rabbi*) carrying grains from the aforementioned *waqf* of Sulṭān Murād Khān shipwrecked on its way from Suez to the Hijaz.[125] To replace the *waqf*'s lost vessel, a firman was

[123] See, e.g.: BOA, Evkaf, D. 5401 (6 S 1178/4 Aug. 1764); TSMA, E. 2445/124 (n.d.); TSMA, E. 1605/114 (n.d.). The following case is about problems with the delivery of grains to the Ḥaramayn from a *waqf* in Egypt earmarked for that purpose: TSMA, E. 5211/22 (Evasıt Za 1110/11–20 May 1699). On the general Ottoman administration and maintenance of various kinds of *waqf*s in Egypt, see: TSMA, E. 5419/16 (n.d.); TSMA, E. 7544/2 (n.d.). For an example of the imperial administration's overseeing of the complicated repairs of a mosque outside of a *waqf* complex in Egypt, see: TSMA, E. 11901 (n.d.). On the establishment of a *waqf* through the will of one particular *ḥajj* pilgrim from Crete at the end of the eighteenth century, see: Antonis Anastasopoulos, "In Preparation for the Hajj: The Will of a *Serdengeçti* from Crete (1782)," *AO* 23 (2005/06): 79–92.

[124] BOA, Cevdet Bahriye, 698 (17 N 1178/9 Mar. 1765).

[125] On the shipwreck of Ottoman vessels in the Red Sea generally and on one shipwreck in particular, see: Cheryl Ward, "The Sadana Island Shipwreck: An Eighteenth-Century AD Merchantman off the Red Sea Coast of Egypt," *World Archaeology* 32 (2001): 368–82; Ward, "The Sadana Island Shipwreck: A Mideighteenth-Century Treasure Trove," in *A Historical Archaeology of the Ottoman Empire: Breaking New Ground*, ed. Uzi Baram

issued to build a new ship.[126] Built from Indian teak, the new ship was said to be as beautiful as an Indian boat (*sefine-i Hindîyeye muadil bir keşti ziban*) and was loaded with materials and several emergency rescue ships in case of further troubles at sea.[127]

In the cases of both the Red Sea and the Mediterranean Sea, the technology of the ship was used in an effort to harness the power of wind and water current for the needs of human caloric consumption.[128] The *waqf* of Sulṭān Murād Khān in Cairo and the entire Ottoman system of food transport outlined in this chapter relied on an ability to use natural power to fuel the movement of materials and foodstuffs across the Empire. Cases of shipwreck highlight how this system of human technology was often overcome by the very same ecological sources of energy it sought to harness, and the examples here thus represent limit cases of the human exploitation of nature's energy on the Red Sea in the eighteenth century.

Moreover, the use of Indian teak in the construction of the new boat in this case points to the fact that Egypt's Red Sea coast operated as just one part of a much wider system of trade that connected Egypt to the Horn of Africa, the southern Arabian Peninsula, Iran, and South and Southeast Asia.[129] Indeed, the fact that lumber harvested from trees in India was

and Lynda Carroll (New York: Kluwer Academic and Plenum, 2000), 185–202; Cheryl Ward and Uzi Baram, "Global Markets, Local Practice: Ottoman-Period Clay Pipes and Smoking Paraphernalia from the Red Sea Shipwreck at Sadana Island, Egypt," *International Journal of Historical Archaeology* 10 (2006): 135–58.

126 This new replacement ship measured forty-five *zirā*ʿ (29.5 m) and was built with the help of local men of knowledge and experience (*ehl-i vukuf*), which clearly indicates that their experience with ship construction in Suez informed the Ottoman state of how best to handle the treacheries of the Red Sea. Because the citation of this length comes as part of the building of a ship, I use the equivalent of the engineering *zirā*ʿ, where 1 *zirā*ʿ *al-handasa* equals 0.656 meters. Hinz, *Islamische Masse und Gewichte*, 58.

127 The total cost of this new ship's construction was 92 *kise akçe* and 21,410 *para* (2,321,410 *para*).

128 On the imperative that environmental history examine "the various ways people have tried to make nature over into a system that produces resources for their consumption," see: Worster, "Transformations of the Earth," 1090.

129 On the role of Cairo "as something of a second capital" in administering Ottoman rule in the Red Sea and Indian Ocean, see: Giancarlo Casale, "An Ottoman Intelligence Report from the Mid Sixteenth-Century Indian Ocean," *JTS* 31 (2007): 186–87. On the Ottomans in the Indian Ocean more generally, see: Patricia Risso, "Cross-Cultural Perceptions of Piracy: Maritime Violence in the Western Indian Ocean and Persian Gulf Region during a Long Eighteenth Century," *Journal of World History* 12 (2001): 293–319; Risso, "Muslim Identity in Maritime Trade: General Observations and Some Evidence from the 18th Century Persian Gulf/Indian Ocean Region," *IJMES* 21 (1989): 381–92; Casale, "The Ottoman Age of Exploration"; Panzac, "International and Domestic

present in the port of Suez suggests a vibrant circuit of trade in natural goods in this Indian Ocean network. As I discuss in the next chapter, the reality of a lack of wood in Egypt meant that this essential material had to be acquired from elsewhere. Here we see how wood often came to Egypt from India, and in the next chapter we see how wood more often came from Anatolia and the Black Sea coast.

Furthermore, this example of the use of Indian wood in Egypt suggests to us yet again how extremely vital ships were to the early modern Ottoman economy. Although Suez was certainly geographically closer to Anatolia than to India, it was not on the Mediterranean coast. And as we have seen, Anatolian wood destined for Suez had to be transported overland from Egypt's Mediterranean coast to the Red Sea. Clearly, it was much easier to transport wood directly to Suez via ship, even from as far away as India, than to move it nearly 125 kilometers overland from Cairo. Finally, this case also confirms that Indian teak – a famously durable ship timber – was a desirable building material in Ottoman Egypt and that Indian ship design was considered worthy of emulation.

As we see in this case, and as I address more thoroughly in the following chapter, wood was the key component in the construction of ships to move food from Egypt to other areas of the Empire. The movement of these two commodities – food and wood – exemplified the various ways in which the Ottoman bureaucracy sought to balance natural resources across the Empire – excess goods in one locale were moved through established shipping and trading networks to other areas of the Empire that needed those goods. Thus, because Egypt produced a vast quantity of grain, the foodstuffs were sent to other provinces that were not as naturally endowed as Egypt with fine soils, supplies of water, and vast stocks of peasant and animal labor. By the same token, Egypt's lack of extensive forested land meant that wood had to be brought from elsewhere to the province. Thus, connections established and maintained by the Ottoman bureaucracy of Egypt created possibilities for the movement of food and

Maritime Trade," 190–91. For a general discussion of the Ottoman Red Sea fleet, see: Michel Tuchscherer, "La flotte impériale de Suez de 1694 à 1719," *Turcica* 29 (1997): 47–69. For a very interesting account of Ottoman-Portuguese rivalry in the Persian Gulf, see: Salih Özbaran, "Bahrain in 1559: A Narrative of Turco-Portuguese Conflict in the Gulf," *OA* 3 (1982): 91–104. For a discussion of general attitudes toward the sea in eleventh-century Egypt and North Africa, see: Abraham L. Udovitch, "An Eleventh Century Islamic Treatise on the Law of the Sea," *AI* 27 (1993): 37–54.

wood to achieve a more balanced distribution of natural resources across the Empire.

As an early modern land-based agrarian society, the Ottoman Empire was a polity in which the greatest portion of its own revenues came from the cultivation and taxation of foodstuffs. Thus, as we have seen throughout this chapter, the Ottoman Empire regularly undertook massively complex operations to move grains between Egypt and other areas of the Empire to get food into the stomachs of people and animals across the Ottoman world. Achieving caloric parity across the Empire was thus largely an exercise by the Ottoman administration of Egypt in natural resource management that necessitated the organization of ships, traders, warehouses, and farmers. It was also, importantly, a bureaucratic arrangement not characterized by the kind of authoritarianism described by Karl Wittfogel. To the contrary, this massively elaborate system, which existed to irrigate Egyptian earth to grow food for the entire Ottoman Empire, was based primarily on an extreme form of Egyptian localism in which peasant knowledge and experience shaped how the imperial bureaucracy functioned on the ground in Egypt.

Because of nutrients from Ethiopian volcanic rocks and the swamps of the Sudan's Sudd, because of the reliable flood that brought those nutrients downstream to Egypt, and because of endless supplies of sunshine for photosynthesis, Egypt produced a huge surplus of chemical energy in the form of food. Its energy surplus powered the Ottoman Empire, supplying calories to Istanbul, to the Hijaz, to pious pilgrims, to farmers, and to the Ottoman military. Egypt was thus the caloric engine of the Empire. Its surplus energy supplies fueled the political authority and function of the Ottoman state – powering the brain of the palace and the capital, the religious heart of the Hijaz, and the Empire's military muscle. As we have seen in this chapter, to move the calories of Egypt's surplus energy, wind and boats were needed. The wind was free; the boats were not. To understand how Egypt secured the wood for boats, for irrigation infrastructural projects, and for fuel, we now turn to the history of wood usage and import in Ottoman Egypt.

3

THE FRAMEWORK OF EMPIRE

Despite being everywhere in the province, wood was a very scarce natural resource in Egypt. It came from elsewhere to be shaped into chests and decorations, to be used in constructing homes and mosques, to build Egypt's rural irrigation network, and to make ships to move Egypt's food supplies. Wood was strong; relatively easy to work; and – because of these factors and its relative dearth in Egypt – eventually very expensive.[1] As with the case of food in the previous chapter, the story of wood in eighteenth-century Ottoman Egypt is really the story of a system of Ottoman imperial connections that – as we will see in this chapter – functioned to bring wood to Egypt. Because Egypt did not have large indigenous forests, it relied on the wider Empire of which it was an integral part to supply the province with the wood it needed.[2] Thus, the natural resource management problem facing Egypt and the Ottoman imperial system with which it was inextricably linked was how to balance a dearth of wood and massive amounts of grains in such a way that there were sufficient amounts of both goods in Egypt and across the Empire.

This linking of grain and wood followed the principle of comparative advantage. Egypt was an overly productive source of grain; sections of Anatolia and the Levant had large supplies of timber. For the Ottoman Empire, this was a perfectly acceptable and sustainable situation because it could benefit from the presence of both natural resources in its realms.

[1] The high price of certain woods because of the relative paucity of trees in Egypt was a problem throughout its history. Roger S. Bagnall, *Egypt in Late Antiquity* (Princeton, NJ: Princeton University Press, 1993), 41. On wood in ancient Egypt, see: Russell Meiggs, *Trees and Timber in the Ancient Mediterranean World* (Oxford, UK: Clarendon Press, 1982), 57–68; John Perlin, *A Forest Journey: The Story of Wood and Civilization* (Woodstock, VT: Countryman Press, 2005), 131–34.

[2] For a very useful comparative example of how early modern Venice dealt with a scarcity of wood, see: Karl Appuhn, *A Forest on the Sea: Environmental Expertise in Renaissance Venice* (Baltimore: Johns Hopkins University Press, 2009).

The key to maintaining this system of resource use was therefore an efficient network of transport and movement. Challenges to the Ottoman Empire's political power – like Mehmet ʿAli's, which I discuss at the end of this chapter – thus not only broke apart this system of imperial natural resource balance and movement but also demanded a completely new commercial and political configuration to maintain the productive system of ecological comparative advantage created and sustained by the Empire's unity.

Before examining the intersections of wood with the Ottoman system in detail, I first briefly outline the ecological, historical, and geographic factors underlying the lack of indigenous wood supplies in Egypt. I then turn to the social and economic roles of wood in Ottoman Egypt. At the end of this chapter, I examine how the Ottoman bureaucracy of Egypt in the early nineteenth century under Mehmet ʿAli attempted to seize for itself timber stocks in Egypt and elsewhere in a direct affront to the existing Ottoman imperial system of balancing natural resources around the Empire developed over the course of the long eighteenth century that I have been discussing so far.

Trees, Soil, and Salt

The most significant reason for a historical lack of native forests in Egypt was, of course, its location in the dry desert of the Sahara. Since the collection of such statistics began, average rainfall in Egypt has been measured at less than one centimeter a year.[3] Most of the rain falls along the Mediterranean littoral and decreases precipitously as one moves south into the rest of Egypt.[4] The Nile fed water to Egypt's land and people, and because the water was needed primarily for food production, clearly none of it could be spared to irrigate forests. Aridity in Egypt thus made the maintenance of native forests nearly impossible.

Still, some evidence suggests that Egypt did in fact have trees and some woodland areas as late as the thirteenth century. Indeed, some of the

[3] On the climate, topography, and geomorphology of Egypt, see: Rushdi Said, *The Geology of Egypt* (New York: Elsevier, 1962), 8–17.

[4] For a historical account of annual rainfall in eighteenth-century Egypt, see: John Antes, *Observations on the Manners and Customs of the Egyptians, the Overflowing of the Nile and its Effects; with Remarks on the Plague and Other Subjects. Written During a Residence of Twelve Years in Cairo and Its Vicinity* (London: Printed for J. Stockdale, 1800), 99–100 and 105–06. See also: Sāmī, *Taqwīm al-Nīl*, pt. 1, 107–16.

oldest wood carvings in the world, dating to 2700 BCE, come from the doors of tombs in Egypt.[5] The doors were made from a single piece of wood and were drawn from native timber stocks. Such grand wooden structures, though, were the exceptional products of native Egyptian wood supplies. Most of the wood in Egypt was acacia, tamarisk, sycamore fig, date palm, doom palm, sidder, some varieties of persea, and willow. These tree varieties offered only the smallest amounts of usable wood, suitable mostly for decorative purposes and some fuel needs.[6] Indeed, because the trees did not provide supplies of heavy timbers, they were most often used and reused by fastening them together with ropes, pegs, and dowels to create larger and more functional pieces of wood. Visiting Egypt in the fifth century BCE, Herodotus described Egyptian boat makers stacking and gluing small pieces of wood "together like bricks" to create larger structures.[7]

In the eleventh and twelfth centuries, Egypt seems to have had quite extensive forested lands in the subprovinces of Benī Suef, Minyā, and Qūṣ and a highly complex administration in place to deal with wood supplies from those areas[8] Between Jirja and Aswan, there was reported to be a forest of some 8,094 hectares (twenty thousand acres). Wood was controlled through government monopoly, with most of the best wood supplies being put toward the construction of ships. These forests were depleted beginning at the end of the Ayyubid period in the thirteenth century. Trees were cut illegally as peasants took to selling them for profit. Some estimates cite that more than 5,059 hectares (12,500 acres) of forest were destroyed during the period and that, for example, in forests in and around al-Qalyūbiyya alone more than four thousand trees were cut. Egypt's small acreage of naturally forested land was thus steadily depleted over millennia until the beginning of the Ottoman period.

In addition to the human consumption of native timber stocks, much of Egypt's topsoil, especially in the Delta, contained a high percentage of salt that adversely affected the growth of trees. John Antes, an American

5 J. V. Thirgood, *Man and the Mediterranean Forest: A History of Resource Depletion* (London: Academic Press, 1981), 87–94.

6 Meiggs, *Trees and Timber*, 59–61.

7 Herodotus, *History*, 2.96.

8 The main source on this forest and its administration is the following medieval chronicle: al-Asʿad Ibn Muhadhdhab Ibn Mammātī, *Kitāb Qawānīn al-Dawāwīn*, ed. Aziz Suryal Atiya (Cairo: Royal Agricultural Society, 1943). For a general account of Egyptian forestry based on this chronicle, see: Perlin, *A Forest Journey*, 140–42.

resident in Egypt at the end of the eighteenth century, had this to say about the saline nature of soil in the Delta:

> The salt-pits are all near the sea shore, and mostly about Rosetta, and but very little elevated from the surface of the sea. All the ground in their vicinity is entirely impregnated with salt, which is every-where discernible in summer, in the fields and gardens, so that even the river, when it is lowest, becomes a little brackish several miles up the country, though there is not the least tide observable from the sea. Here they have salt-pits, where they let the water of the Nile in when high, by which the salt is drawn out of the ground, and found in great quantities after the water is dried up by the heat of the sun: it is of very good quality.[9]

The problems of saline soil and the mixing of salt and fresh water caused many disputes in the Ottoman court of Rashīd throughout the long eighteenth century. These cases usually involved accusations that peasants in a particular community of water had allowed salt and fresh water to mix because they had not properly maintained an irrigation work.[10] Although salinity was indeed one of the great obstacles to farming in and around Rashīd, most peasants were able to overcome it through the careful use of irrigation canals, dams, cisterns, and waterwheels.[11] For example, although its western border was a salt marsh, an estate of dates and lemon trees in Rashīd was able to keep its fields under cultivation by using a set of cisterns as a source of fresh water.[12] This example notwithstanding, Egyptian peasants living near the Mediterranean coast were locked in a constant struggle to prevent the infiltration of salt into their freshwater supplies and into their fields.

Irrigation in arid climates always leads to problems of salinization. Standing water dissolves salts in the root zone of plants, thereby elevating salt into the very fresh water meant to grow crops. Much of the accumulated salt can be flushed away with the replenishing waters of each year's flood, but a place like Rashīd – one of the final downstream points

9 Antes, *Observations*, 80. For more on salt in Egypt's soils, see: ibid., 103.

10 In one such case, a group of peasants came to the court of Rashīd to accuse one of their fellow peasants of mixing salt water with fresh Nile water brought to their fields – fields we are told that were rich in date trees and vineyards – by a wooden waterwheel. This introduction of salt water immediately caused all the trees near their lands to weaken (*aḍʿafa*) and delayed their scheduled time of planting for that season, both of which caused them great agricultural and financial losses. DWQ, Maḥkamat Rashīd 6, p. 50, case 238 (10 Ca 981/7 Sep. 1573).

11 For another example of the problems caused by the salinity of soil in Rashīd, see: DWQ, Maḥkamat Rashīd 155, pp. 8–9, case 9 (24 Ş 1163/28 Jul. 1750).

12 DWQ, Maḥkamat Rashīd 146, pp. 240–42, case 232 (30 L 1153/18 Jan. 1741).

on the entire Nile system – had to deal with the steady accumulation of salt along the entire length of the world's longest river. The peasants of Rashīd were, in Donald Worster's words, "the last man on the last ditch [who] might as well be dipping from the ocean."[13]

A related problem contributing to the extremely saline character of soil in the Delta was the fact that much of the land had been reclaimed over centuries from the Mediterranean itself.[14] The massive amounts of sand and soil that eventually collected to form the Nile Delta had thus been soaked in a combination of salt and fresh water for millennia, thus endowing the land with a high salt content. At the end of the eighteenth century, John Antes observed the following: "The large quantities of muscle and oyster beds, with other productions of the sea, which are to be found under ground in various places, even not far from Grand Cairo, made me sometimes think, that most probably the whole Delta was originally nothing but a shallow bay of the sea, of unequal depth."[15] He continues: "as a further proof of the Delta being thus produced, it might also be added, that no monuments of very great antiquity are to be found in these low places, but only on some few elevated spots, and even these few do not seem to be so old as those found in the upper parts of the country."[16] Thus reclaimed from the Mediterranean, the Delta was a region of relatively recent geological formation, as a result of which its soils – especially those in close proximity to the coast – were extremely saline.[17] Salt in the Delta's soil inhibited tree growth and further added to the imperative that Egypt's least saline soils were to be used for food production.

Using Wood in Ottoman Egypt

Despite natural hindrances to the growth and sustenance of forests in Egypt, wood and its byproducts were commonly found throughout

[13] Worster, *Rivers of Empire*, 320.

[14] For a geological explanation of this event, see: J. C. Harms and J. L. Wray, "Nile Delta," in *The Geology of Egypt*, ed. Rushdi Said (Rotterdam: A. A. Balkema, 1990), 329–43. See also: John R. McNeill, *Something New under the Sun: An Environmental History of the Twentieth-Century World* (New York: W. W. Norton, 2000), 171.

[15] Antes, *Observations*, 64.

[16] Ibid., 75.

[17] According to John R. McNeill, the Delta was "born" 7,500 years ago and even as recently as the nineteenth century grew by as much as five to eight kilometers in some areas over the course of that century. McNeill, *Something New under the Sun*, 171.

Ottoman Egypt as a building material, form of capital, and luxury good.[18] This wood was either harvested from Egypt's tiny amount of native supplies or, as I discuss in more detail later in this chapter, imported from other regions of the Mediterranean or even from as far away as the Indian subcontinent.[19] Wood's ubiquity in Egypt ensured that it was enmeshed in all sorts of economic and social relations, in military conflicts, in estate inventories, and in public works projects. For instance, wooden objects like chests and tables were often given as part of a bride's dowry.[20] Those who could afford it used wood to construct all sorts of ornate and practical structures.[21] For example, in 1748, when the Coptic patriarch of Egypt visited Jerusalem, he and his entourage built and decorated a series of wooden platforms to be placed on top of camels to make their ride more comfortable.[22]

The rich and powerful in Ottoman Egypt favored using wood as a building material for its strength and durability.[23] In 1720, for example, the notable Salīm Ḥabīb built a grand complex of houses and guest quarters in the subprovince of al-Qalyūbiyya.[24] Wood allowed people like Salīm Ḥabīb to build larger and more complex structures more

[18] Wood was also used in the preparation and storage of medicines. Al-Jabartī, *ʿAjāʾib al-Āthār*, 1:558.

[19] On the importation of wood to Egypt in the ancient period, see: Meiggs, *Trees and Timber*, 63–68.

[20] DWQ, Maḥkamat Rashīd 132, p. 169, case 255 (15 Za 1137/25 Jul. 1725).

[21] As part of the festivities associated with a lavish wedding celebration, ʿAli Bey Bulut Kapan built a woooden stage over the surface of al-Fīl pond in Cairo so that revelers and performers could gather and walk over the surface of the pond. Al-Jabartī, *ʿAjāʾib al-Āthār*, 1:417. Wood was also used to build a series of forty waterproof containers filled with boiled Nile water for drinking that were taken to the Hijaz by Mehmet ʿAli in September 1813 as he went to perform the pilgrimage and to establish control over his newly conquered territory. The forty containers were made waterproof by lining their insides with tin covered with wax and gum. Ibid., 4:249.

[22] Aḥmad al-Damurdāshī Katkhudā ʿAzabān, *Kitāb al-Durra al-Muṣāna fī Akhbār al-Kināna*, ed. ʿAbd al-Raḥīm ʿAbd al-Raḥman ʿAbd al-Raḥīm (Cairo: Institut français d'archéologie orientale, 1989), 247. For an English translation of this text, see: Daniel Crecelius and ʿAbd al-Wahhab Bakr, trans., *al-Damurdashi's Chronicle of Egypt, 1688–1755: al-Durra al-Musana fi Akhbar al-Kinana* (Leiden: E. J. Brill, 1991). Unless otherwise noted, I have used the Arabic text throughout.

[23] DWQ, Maḥkamat Manfalūṭ 1, p. 218, case 541 (5 Ş 1218/20 Nov. 1803); DWQ, Maḥkamat Rashīd 132, pp. 128–29, case 198 (15 L 1137/26 Jun. 1725); DWQ, Maḥkamat Rashīd 139, pp. 183–85, case 272 (3 C 1146/10 Nov. 1733); al-Jabartī, *ʿAjāʾib al-Āthār*, 3:370 and 4:103, 124, 287, 331, 381, 396. In the following case, an individual purchased one hundred *niṣf fiḍḍa* (*para*) worth of wood for his construction project: DWQ, Maḥkamat Rashīd 134, p. 326, case 438 (5 Ş 1146/11 Jan. 1734).

[24] Al-Damurdāshī, *al-Durra al-Muṣāna*, 135. On al-Qalyūbiyya, see: *QJBM*, pt. 2, 1:11–61.

easily than could have been constructed with brick and limestone.[25] A storehouse built by a wealthy Rashīdī merchant in 1724 near the city's customs house exemplifies this use of wood to build enormous structures of imposing stature meant to display an individual's personal wealth. In addition to features of stone and brick and storage tanks for water, the storehouse had two large wooden doors, a row of long wooden benches (*masāṭib*), five large wooden columns, wooden roof supports, and wooden stairs.[26] As in this example, and as we saw previously as well, it was especially common to build doors out of wood because of the material's strong rigidity relative to its light weight.[27] Indeed, wood was the material preferred to fix the door of the banquet hall of a structure of no less import than the Citadel of Cairo itself.[28] The most sought after doors were those hewn from a single piece of wood.[29]

Moreover, because the wood trade in Ottoman Egypt was so lucrative, lumber was often one of the most prized forms of booty in battles throughout the long eighteenth century.[30] In 1714, for example, Ismāʿīl Bey ʿAwaḍ and his troops attacked the encampment of a leader

[25] In the following case, for instance, a large hall or room (*qāʿa*) consisting of four different kinds of wood was just one of the features included in a new building. DWQ, Maḥkamat Rashīd 157, pp. 317–18, case 308 (21 R 1166/25 Feb. 1753).

[26] DWQ, Maḥkamat Rashīd 130, pp. 193–94, case 272 (12 C 1136/8 Mar. 1724).

[27] DWQ, Maḥkamat Rashīd 125, pp. 199–200, case 338 (11 Ra 1133/10 Jan. 1721); DWQ, Maḥkamat Manfalūṭ 3, p. 240, case 513 (15 Ca 1223/9 Jul. 1808); DWQ, Maḥkamat Rashīd 145, p. 126, case 101 (30 Z 1151/9 Apr. 1739); al-Jabartī, *ʿAjāʾib al-Āthār*, 4:315.

[28] BOA, MM, 4:562 (Evasıt C 1145/29 Nov.–9 Dec. 1732). On the history of the Cairo Citadel, see: Nasser O. Rabbat, *The Citadel of Cairo: A New Interpretation of Royal Mamluk Architecture* (Leiden: E. J. Brill, 1995); Paul Casanova, *Two Studies on the History and Topography of Cairo* (Frankfurt: Institute for the History of Arabic-Islamic Science at the Johann Wolfgang Goethe University, 1992); Philipp Speiser, "The Remodeling of the Cairo Citadel from the 16th to the 20th Century," *AI* 38 (2004): 79–93. For a study of a document related to the aqueducts and waterwheels feeding water to the Citadel, see: Jīhān ʿUmrān, "Wathīqat Kashf ʿalā al-Sawāqī wa al-Majrā al-Sulṭānī (Dirāsa Wathāʾiqiyya)," *AI* 40 (2006): 1–23.

[29] In the following, those wishing to enter a house with a locked wooden door attempted to burn it down with firewood on the outside: al-Jabartī, *ʿAjāʾib al-Āthār*, 1:281. In the city of al-Manṣūra in 1796, one individual spent 63,020 *nisf fiḍḍa* (*para*) on just the wood for the doors to his new home. DWQ, Maḍābiṭ al-Daqahliyya 34, p. 64, case 137 (16 Z 1210/22 Jun. 1796). As with doors, wood was also the preferred material for constructing staircases. See, e.g.: DWQ, Maḥkamat Rashīd 139, pp. 96–98, case 154 (8 S 1146/20 Jul. 1733); DWQ, Maḥkamat Rashīd 130, pp. 193–94, case 272 (12 C 1136/8 Mar. 1724); DWQ, Maḥkamat Rashīd 137, p. 86, case 146 (27 Z 1144/20 Jun. 1732).

[30] For other instances of the seizure of wood during battle, see: al-Jabartī, *ʿAjāʾib al-Āthār*, 1:166; 4:145.

named Ḥabīb in the village of Dijwā.[31] When Ismāʿīl Bey ʿAwaḍ's forces opened fire on Ḥabīb's location with their muskets, the besieged leader fled with his troops to the province of al-Sharqiyya. Thereby having free reign in Ḥabīb's abandoned villages, Ismāʿīl Bey ʿAwaḍ and his troops looted them, broke down all the structures in Ḥabīb's encampments, and loaded the buildings' wood onto their ships. There was so much wood that they were able to fill three ships to capacity. They then shipped the enormous stockpile of wood to the markets of Bulaq and sold it for a hefty sum.[32] The attacking soldiers in this case knew that wood was a valuable commodity and thus took advantage of their seizure of an enemy's encampment to make extra money from the sale of the wood they captured.[33] Similarly, in times of acute scarcity or war, certain valis and amirs also took advantage of their political and military power to seize wood from merchants and individuals.[34] Moreover, nonelite Egyptians also often demolished buildings to sell the wood as a raw material or to use it for their own construction or fuel needs.[35]

For their part, Napoleon's French troops also suffered from a lack of wood while stationed in Egypt during their colonial expedition from 1798 to 1801.[36] When building fortifications in and around Cairo in late 1798, they resorted to destroying a number of structures – including a number of mosques – in the city so as to use the buildings' materials to construct their barracks, supply houses, and so on.[37] The French also cut down whatever trees and date palms they could find in and around Cairo to use in building their encampment.[38] Finding it noteworthy, al-Jabartī reports that they only cut wood in "an engineering fashion in right angles and straight lines."[39] As in the foregoing cases of battles involving Bedouins, Egyptians likewise seized their opportunities during the French occupation to take wood from buildings that the French had

[31] Al-Damurdāshī, *al-Durra al-Muṣāna*, 120. On Dijwā, see: *QJBM*, pt. 2, 1:45.

[32] The timber yards of Bulaq were at the base of al-Khurnub Tenement near a huge market complex built from stone and wood. Al-Jabartī, *ʿAjā'ib al-Āthār*, 1:640.

[33] For an account of a similar raid against the encampment of Ḥabīb's Bedouin forces at Dijwā, see: ibid., 1:579.

[34] Ibid., 3:261.

[35] Ibid., 4:88.

[36] For general historical accounts of the French occupation of Egypt, see: Juan Cole, *Napoleon's Egypt: Invading the Middle East* (New York: Palgrave Macmillan, 2007); André Raymond, *Égyptiens et français au Caire (1798–1801)* (Cairo: Institut français d'archéologie orientale, 2004).

[37] Al-Jabartī, *ʿAjā'ib al-Āthār*, 3:46. For later examples, see also: ibid., 3:216, 251, 254.

[38] Ibid., 3:46, 52–53, 254.

[39] Ibid., 3:53.

either abandoned or destroyed during fighting.[40] And on reclaiming Cairo from the French, Egyptian and Ottoman forces secured wood supplies by destroying buildings, trenches, and canal embankments built by the French.[41]

Estate inventories from various Egyptian cities also testify to the presence of wood in one form or another throughout the Nile Valley during the long eighteenth century, and the records give a clear sense of the relative values of wood and its products. Although the sources only give us a snapshot of the wealth of an individual at the time of his death and do not trace capital over the course of a lifetime, they do give us an indication of the ways in which wealth was distributed and stored in Ottoman Egypt. Many of the items found in these records, things like coffee and soap, were used on a regular basis and – except when held in extremely large quantities – did not represent significant investments in capital.[42] Wood, in contrast, tied up a lot of capital and was usually one of the more costly items in an estate.

Wood generally appeared in probate records in one of two forms. Most commonly, wood was owned as a finished luxury good like a trunk, wall decoration, or table.[43] Similar to other major items found in estate inventories like jewelry, animals, or textiles, wooden objects were items of high value in most homes.[44] The second way in which wood appeared in estate inventories was as a raw building material to be used in later

40 Ibid., 3:142.

41 Ibid., 3:289–90.

42 For probates that included soap and coffee, see: DWQ, Maḥkamat Rashīd 120, no page no., case 44 (9 C 1129/20 May 1717); DWQ, Maḥkamat Rashīd 154, p. 240, case 264 (3 Z 1162/14 Nov. 1749); DWQ, Maḥkamat Rashīd 132, p. 278, case 419 (10 Ra 1138/15 Nov. 1725); DWQ, Maḥkamat Rashīd 120, p. 209, case 334 (23 C 1130/24 May 1718).

43 For example, along with three wooden chests that were each finished with a strip of marble, the estate of one Muḥammad ʿAzabān Ibn ʿAbd al-Karīm contained a rug, soap, a full set of twenty-one Chinese coffee cups, a red shawl, some textiles, a silver chain, and many other items. The most expensive items in his estate were the three wooden chests totaling 152 *nisf faḍḍa* (*para*); the shawl, which cost 101 *para*; the silver chain, which was priced at 160 *para*; and the soap, which totaled 171 *para*. DWQ, Maḥkamat Rashīd 120, p. 209, case 334 (23 C 1130/24 May 1718). For a probate that contained wall decorations, see: DWQ, Maḥkamat Rashīd 154, p. 240, case 264 (3 Z 1162/14 Nov. 1749). For an example of a case involving wooden barrels and the coal inside them, see: DWQ, Maḥkamat Rashīd 148, pp. 51–53, case 63 (30 C 1154/11 Sep. 1741).

44 For probates involving animals, see: DWQ, Maḥkamat Rashīd 132, p. 278, case 419 (10 Ra 1138/15 Nov. 1725); DWQ, Maḥkamat Rashīd 144, pp. 493–95, case 525 (25 Ra 1152/2 Jul. 1739). For some examples involving jewelry, see: DWQ, Maḥkamat Rashīd 120, no page no., case 44 (9 C 1129/20 May 1717); DWQ, Maḥkamat Rashīd 120, p. 209, case 334 (23 C 1130/24 May 1718).

projects or to be sold.[45] In those cases, wood was an asset stored like money in a bank to be spent when required or sold when an individual needed cash. The point here is that wood – either in the form of a finished product or as a raw material – represented a significant portion of the wealth of numerous individuals throughout Ottoman Egypt.[46]

45 For example, in the estate of the deceased Muḥammad Ibn al-Ḥājj ʿAbd al-Karīm, wood was second only to rice as the largest share of his bequeathed capital. In contrast to previous cases, a large quantity of the wood was left in raw form rather than finished into various products. DWQ, Maḥkamat Rashīd 144, pp. 493–95, case 525 (25 Ra 1152/2 Jul. 1729). For a similar example of wood as a raw material in an estate inventory, see: DWQ, Maḥkamat Rashīd 132, p. 278, case 419 (10 Ra 1138/15 Nov. 1725). Unfinished wood was primarily sought out for use in fires or as fuel. See, e.g.: al-Jabartī, *ʿAjāʾib al-Āthār*, 3:415; 4:212–13, 361, 434. For a discussion of the procurement and use of firewood in Istanbul, see: Çevre ve Orman Bakanlığı, *Osmanlı Ormancılığı ile İlgili Belgeler*, 3 vols. (Ankara: Çevre ve Orman Bakanlığı, 1999–2003), 1:xiv. On the lack of woodworking in late-antique Egypt as a function of wood's scarcity, see: Bagnall, *Egypt in Late Antiquity*, 85.

46 Given the high value of wood, it is thus no surprise that is was at the center of numerous inheritance disputes and various other kinds of conflicts throughout Ottoman Egypt. For example, a case from the court of Manfalūṭ from the end of the seventeenth century documents a heated argument between two brothers over the allotment of their father's sizable wealth held in large amounts of unfinished wood, animals, and fields. DWQ, Maḥkamat Manfalūṭ 1, p. 296, case 738 (12 Z 1098/19 Oct. 1687). In another case from the year 1719, the court of Rashīd adjudicated a fight between two men, one of whom was from the Muteferrika military bloc, involving the use of wood as a weapon. The plaintiff in the case asserted that the argument in question began on the banks of the Nile near the Rashīd rice market and quickly escalated to the point that the defendant hit the plaintiff with a piece of wood. It was reported to be an incredible strike (*ḍarba muhawwila*) that split open the plaintiff's head, removing large sections of skin and leading to massive amounts of bleeding. When asked to respond to the plaintiff's charges, the defendant in this case denied hitting him with the piece of wood. However, a subsequent medical examination by the chief surgeon in Rashīd confirmed the nature of the plaintiff's charges. DWQ, Maḥkamat Rashīd 122, p. 59, case 100 (11 Ca 1131/1 Apr. 1719). The most common use of wood for the sake of weaponry was the construction of bows and arrows. For a discussion of this work and of various kinds of bows, see: al-Jabartī, *ʿAjāʾib al-Āthār*, 2:356–57. For a more general treatment of the use of wood in warfare, see: ibid., 3:145; 4:15.

Merchants also cheated in the marketplace in their dealings in wood. For example, an Ottoman firman from Istanbul was sent to Rashīd ordering the punishment of a market measurer (*qabbānī*) who was cheating in his measurements of wood. As part of his punishment, this cheating merchant was ordered to pay for any losses to state funds resulting from his illegitimate weighing. DWQ, Maḥkamat Rashīd 125, p. 288, case 454 (13 Z 1132/15 Oct. 1720). In a similar case five years later, another Ottoman firman was sent to the court of Rashīd in response to a petition from the people of that city complaining of the hardship (*zulm ve taaddi*) such dishonest weighing was having on them and on those in the subprovince of al-Baḥayra as a whole. The firman ordered the court to ensure that the corrupt weighing was stopped and that established law (*kanun-ı kadim*) was reconstituted in Rashīd. DWQ, Maḥkamat Rashīd 132, p. 198, case 304

The natural dearth of forests in the Nile Valley meant that this vast quantity of wood present in Egypt had to come from elsewhere via land or sea. This necessity of import ensured not only that wood was very expensive and valuable in Egypt but also that its business was potentially very lucrative for those who could successfully navigate the large amounts of overhead (ships, labor, animals, rope, and so on) needed to transport lumber to Egypt. Private merchants who did not have their own ships or other suitable means of transport had to come up with other solutions to move a commodity as large as lumber. Without its own ships, a group of merchants in Manfalūṭ, for instance, rented one-third of a ship to move wood and iron between Manfalūṭ and other parts of Egypt.[47] For those lucky enough to succeed in the business of wood, the returns were high.

Here as well, numerous estate inventories document the large wood holdings of merchants in cities as varied as Cairo, Asyūṭ, and Rashīd. In the latter city especially, many merchants made their fortunes by importing wood from outside Egypt to sell in the Egyptian market.[48] Moreover, we have evidence of thriving and lucrative markets in wood and lumber in a place like early-nineteenth-century Asyūṭ, a city that was not a major center of capital in the period.[49]

Wood also played a major role in the repair of large communal structures like *wakālas*, mosques, *ḥammāms*, and *waqf* complexes. Because they served a wide need and a vital economic and social function, these structures' repairs received very detailed treatments in the courts of Ottoman Egypt. There were, for instance, major repairs involving wood carried out on *wakālas* in Rashīd in 1720, 1727, and 1747.[50] In the case of the

(29 C 1137/14 Mar. 1725). On the general cheating of market weighers (*qabbānīs*) and measurers (*kayyāls*), see: Raymond, *Artisans et commerçants*, 1:275–76.

47 DWQ, Maḥkamat Manfalūṭ 3, p. 15, case 21 (11 C 1228/10 Jun. 1813). For another case involving the transport of wood in Egypt, see: DWQ, Maḥkamat Isnā 7, p. 6, case 7 (Ca 1173/Dec. 1759 and Jan. 1760).

48 See, e.g.: DWQ, Maḥkamat Rashīd 154, p. 74, case 87 (15 B 1162/30 Jun. 1749); DWQ, Maḥkamat Rashīd 120, no page no., case 44 (9 C 1129/20 May 1717). In the following case from 1732, two wealthy wood merchants came to the court of Rashīd in a dispute over an amount of capital (*ra's māl*) owned by the plaintiff: DWQ, Maḥkamat Rashīd 137, pp. 61–62, case 111 (15 Za 1144/10 May 1732). That the merchants came to court at all to register and settle their disagreement is evidence of the large amount of money at stake in this dispute.

49 DWQ, Maḥkamat Asyūṭ 9, p. 192, case 422 (20 Za 1219/20 Feb. 1805).

50 DWQ, Maḥkamat Rashīd 125, pp. 92–93, case 159 (11 L 1132/16 Aug. 1720); DWQ, Maḥkamat Rashīd 134, p. 167, case 204 (29 S 1140/15 Oct. 1727); DWQ, Maḥkamat Rashīd 151, pp. 366–69, case 413 (15 Ra 1160/17 Mar. 1747).

latter year, an entire section of the repair's report was devoted solely to the fourteen different types of wood used in the project.[51] A similar list of six varieties of wood is found in a case about the repair of a small mosque (*zāwiya*) inside another Rashīd *wakāla* in 1746.[52] As institutions of common interest and use, *ḥammāms* – whether or not in *waqf* complexes – were also subject to intricate repairs involving wood.[53] As we saw in Chapter 1 with respect to rural irrigation works, the Ottoman administration of Egypt was quick to repair and maintain institutions and areas of common usage that bound large swaths of the Egyptian population into communities of sharing. *Ḥammāms* were subject to a similar kind of dynamic, and the use of wood in their repair and upkeep further suggests the centrality of this material to the overall edifice of rule in Ottoman Egypt.[54]

When ownership over a home or other structure was transferred, established, or otherwise recorded in the court, rights over the material and immaterial parts of the building were often expressed using a set phrase meant to establish and declare a kind of totalizing possession of the structure. In the most literal sense, the phrase asserts that the new possessor of a property overtook the rights (*al-ḥuqūq*), the borders (*al-ḥudūd*), the

51 DWQ, Maḥkamat Rashīd 151, p. 366, case 413 (15 Ra 1160/17 Mar. 1747). Unfortunately, the section of the register's page listing the total amount spent on this collection of wood is missing.

52 DWQ, Maḥkamat Rashīd 151, pp. 38–39, case 49 (28 Z 1158/20 Jan. 1746). The six kinds of wood used in this case totaled 2,956 *niṣf faḍḍa*. Similarly, in the middle of the eighteenth century, ʿAbd al-Raḥman Katkhuda undertook the repair of the roof of the hall of the al-Azhar mosque, rebuilding it with a variety of precious woods. Al-Jabartī, *ʿAjāʾib al-Āthār*, 2:6. Repairs involving multiple kinds of wood were also carried out on the mosque of ʿAmr Ibn al-ʿĀṣ in 1798. Ibid., 3:263–64.

53 For repairs to a *ḥammām* in Rashīd, see: DWQ, Maḥkamat Rashīd 145, p. 126, case 101 (30 Z 1151/9 Apr. 1739). For a case involving repair work on the roofs, *ḥammām*, and waterwheel of a *waqf*, see: DWQ, Maḥkamat Rashīd 125, p. 179, case 300 (30 M 1133/1 Dec. 1720). On wood for public baths more generally, see: Çevre ve Orman Bakanlığı, *Osmanlı Ormancılığı*, 1:128–29.

54 On Cairo's *ḥammāms*, see: André Raymond, "Les bains publics au Caire à la fin du XVIIIe siècle," *AI* 8 (1969): 129–50; Raymond, "La localization des bains publics du Cairo au quinzième siècle d'aprés les Hitat de Makrizi," *Bulletin d'Études Orientales* 30 (1978): 347–60; Nicholas Warner, "Taking the Plunge: The Development and Use of the Cairene Bathhouse," in *Historians in Cairo: Essays in Honor of George Scanlon*, ed. Jill Edwards (Cairo: American University in Cairo Press, 2002), 49–79. On related issues of water and public hygiene in late-nineteenth-century Cairo, see: Ghislaine Alleaume, "Hygiène publique et travaux publics: Les ingénieurs et l'assainissement du Caire (1882–1907)," *AI* 20 (1984): 151–82; Khaled Fahmy, "An Olfactory Tale of Two Cities: Cairo in the Nineteenth Century," in *Historians in Cairo: Essays in Honor of George Scanlon*, ed. Jill Edwards (Cairo: American University in Cairo Press, 2002), 155–87.

particularities (*al-maʿālim*), the marks (*al-rusūm*), the doors (*al-abwāb*), the timbers (*al-akhshāb*), the doorsteps (*al-aʿtāb*), and the bricks (*al-aṭwāb*) of the recently acquired structure.[55] Though a set phrase, taken together, this list of items constituted a declaration of total authority and ownership over a piece of property. It expressed the important notion that ownership involved complete possession not just of the physicality of a building – which was here generally conceptualized to include wood – but also of the rights and specific history accrued to the structure.[56]

Wood and Water

Though certainly important for the construction of homes and other structures in urban areas of Egypt, wood was perhaps most crucial in the countryside, where, because of its strength and durability, it was used in all sorts of infrastructural repair and construction projects. Because wood was the preferred material for the construction and maintenance of dams, canal embankments, and bridges, it was in the repair of irrigation works that its scarcity was most acutely felt. The Ottoman administration of Egypt thus expended much bureaucratic energy in ensuring that its own officials and Egyptian peasants had adequate supplies of wood.

[55] As a part of formal legal procedure, there are literally thousands of examples of the usage of this phrase in the courts of Ottoman Egypt. For some of the many instances, see: DWQ, Maḥkamat al-Baḥayra 6, p. 37, case 67 (30 Z 1169/25 Sep. 1756); DWQ, Maḥkamat al-Baḥayra 7, p. 112, case 211 (3 N 1171/11 May 1758); DWQ, Maḥkamat Asyūṭ 9, p. 178, case 402 (25 Ca 1219/31 Aug. 1804); DWQ, Maḥkamat al-Baḥayra 8, p. 37, case 56 (21 Ra 1176/9 Oct. 1762); DWQ, Maḥkamat al-Baḥayra 9, pp. 229–30, case 485 (7 Z 1185/12 Mar. 1772); DWQ, Maḥkamat al-Baḥayra 10, p. 247, case 585 (13 Ş 1191/15 Sep. 1777); DWQ, Maḥkamat al-Baḥayra 11, p. 150, case 331 (18 Z 1197/13 Nov. 1783); DWQ, Maḥkamat al-Baḥayra 12, p. 143, case 334 (12 S 1196/26 Jan. 1782); DWQ, Maḥkamat al-Baḥayra 15, p. 58, case 141 (21 Ra 1199/1 Feb. 1785); DWQ, Maḥkamat al-Baḥayra 16, p. 205, case 360 (10 R 1201/30 Jan. 1787). When the building in question contained stone, the word *al-aḥjār* (the stones) was also added to the list of objects and rights. See, e.g.: DWQ, Maḥkamat al-Baḥayra 5, p. 153, case 265 (18 C 1165/3 May 1752).

[56] A comparable set phrase was also often used to express the ownership of all wood products involved in certain property transactions. As a typical example of this kind of case, consider a piece of property sold in al-Baḥayra in 1809 described as having within it the wood of waterwheels, trees, and date palms (*akhshāb al-sawāqī wa al-ashjār wa al-nakhīl*). DWQ, Maḥkamat al-Baḥayra 32, p. 237, case 375 (20 R 1224/4 Jun. 1809). For a similar case, see: DWQ, Maḥkamat al-Baḥayra 32, p. 300, case 465 (2 B 1224/14 Aug. 1809). Not only do these formulaic statements suggest the widespread use of wood – for how else would it come to constitute a part of oft-repeated phrases? – but they also point toward the notion that the materiality of a structure or piece of property was as important to its ownership as an abstract notion of rights or authority.

Without wood, the irrigation infrastructure of Egypt – a system that harnessed water to grow food for the entire Ottoman Empire – would have had to rely on brick, mud, and stone. Although stone was surely stronger than wood, it was too heavy to move easily and too difficult to shape and mold. It required a large expenditure in labor and transportation costs, especially given that most of Egypt's stone reserves were located at some distance from the fertile lands of the countryside, where the material was most needed for irrigation works.

As one of the crucial materials for the maintenance of Egypt's irrigation network, wood in the Egyptian countryside was a key component in the construction of various forms of second nature throughout this rural built environment. Dams, embankments, dikes, waterwheels, and canals were all attempts to harness, control, and variously affect the course of the Nile and its flood. Wood allowed irrigation works to function more reliably and more effectively, thus allowing Egyptians to regulate their interactions with the Nile more closely and affording the Ottoman government of Egypt the opportunity to ensure the maintenance of tax revenue. The difference between a dam holding and a dam breaking was often the difference between a season of plenty and a season of want, between food and starvation, between life and death. Because directing and determining the course of the Nile's water was largely the work of a commodity as scarce as wood, the pressure and desire to acquire wood – not to mention its cost – were constantly increasing.

To illustrate this phenomenon further, consider the example of a dam on the canal of Abū al-Minjā in the subprovince of al-Qalyūbiyya that was destroyed by the very rapidly rising Nile of the summer of 1785.[57] The river did not rise at all that summer until July 5, but once it arrived in al-Qalyūbiyya, its waters reached their full flood levels in only nine days. In the first day alone, the river rose three cubits. This huge surge of water in such a short period of time was too much for the dam of Abū al-Minjā to handle, and it was soon swept away entirely. An unnamed amir was charged with rebuilding the dam and was dispatched from Cairo with a supply of wood to meet the shaykh of Qalyūb, a man named Ibn Abī Shawārib. Together the men assembled a group of peasants to work on the reconstruction of the dam.[58] Once the repair work had begun, it soon became clear that much more wood was quickly needed for this project. Thus, to secure additional supplies, the men dismantled five ships in the

57 Al-Jabartī, *ʿAjāʾib al-Āthār*, 2:158.

58 For a comparable case of the repair of a dam on the Firʿawniyya Canal, see: ibid., 4:171.

canal of Abū al-Minjā. Unfortunately, after a few more days of work, it soon became clear that the men would still not be able to restore the dam to its previous state. The men in this case thus attempted to meet the extreme need for the scarce commodity of wood to repair a dam by destroying five boats, but even that amount of wood proved insufficient to defend against the powerful surges of the Nile.[59]

In another case from the year 1723, Sulaymān Jāwīsh, the *multazim* of the village of Badawāy in al-Manṣūra, took responsibility for the repair of an embankment.[60] This embankment was broken in two places and, as in the previous case, required a large expenditure of supplies and labor.[61] Wood, hay, nails, rope, men, brick, animals, and various other items were all enlisted in the repair of the embankment. The repairs were especially important because the broken embankment was threatening the water supplies of the villages beneath it. As we saw in Chapter 1, if such an embankment remained broken and water continued to spill out of the canal, villages below Badawāy would not be able to cultivate their fields properly and would suffer greatly. After a thorough inspection of the proposed repair site, wood, hay, mud, brick, and earth were used to close and reinforce the broken areas of the embankment.[62]

In the foregoing examples, we see how local Egyptian peasants valued and used wood in the repair of Egypt's rural irrigation infrastructure. There was little direct involvement of Ottoman authorities in such cases. Indeed, it seems that the Ottoman state in Egypt left repairs of this sort largely to the expertise and oversight of local Egyptians, who understood the needs and demands of the areas being served by the irrigation repairs. As we saw in Chapter 1, local actors were akin to rural points of reference for the Ottoman bureaucracy in Egypt – the eyes and ears of the Empire in the province.

59 Taking wood from boats for the reconstruction of dams in rural Egypt and even the sinking of whole ships to serve as blockages to water flow was a common occurrence throughout the eighteenth century. For another example, see: ibid., 2:177. In this case, iron archers and firewood were sunk along with a number of ships in an attempt to dam part of the Pharaonic Canal. All of the items were taken from their owners without any sort of compensation.

60 On the village of Badawāy, see: *QJBM*, pt. 2, 1:217.

61 DWQ, Maḥkamat al-Manṣūra 24, p. 154, case 346 (15 M 1136/15 Oct. 1723).

62 DWQ, Maḥkamat al-Manṣūra 24, p. 154, case 347 (15 M 1136/15 Oct. 1723). Not only does this short case reveal peasants' understandings of the fact that their interactions with the Nile and attempts to change its flow and course had very important effects on other villagers relying on the resources of the river; it also exemplifies the high costs of wood and the ways in which this material commodity came to affect the built environment – the second nature – of irrigation works in the Egyptian countryside.

Although we know a great deal about the intimate involvement of peasants in the repair of irrigation features in the Egyptian countryside, what remains less clear is how this construction work was financed.[63] Were the needed funds subtracted from the annual *irsāliyye-i ḫazīne* sent by the *multazim* to Istanbul, or was the *multazim* charged with paying for the repairs from the funds he earned from his *iltizām* as a kind of incentive to keep costs low and to fix damaged areas correctly and quickly? The specific manner in which *multazims* organized the labor of peasants in their charge is also not clear.[64]

In numerous other cases involving the use of wood in the repair of irrigation works, the direct involvement of the Ottoman bureaucracy is much clearer. The Ottoman government of Egypt was well aware of the difficulties caused by a lack of natural wood reserves in Egypt, and it

[63] In the following example, rural peasant leaders came to the court of al-Manṣūra seeking legal and bureaucratic recognition of their efforts to use wood in an irrigation repair job: DWQ, Maḥkamat al-Manṣūra 11, p. 8, case 16 (3 Ra 1113/8 Aug. 1701). An amir named Aḥmad, *multazim* of Kafr al-Madmāṣ, went to the court in 1701 to record the work he had done the year before in reinforcing a wooden embankment in his village. The particular embankment had been broken earlier in 1700, and the *multazim* spent 16,118 *niṣf fiḍḍa* (*para*) to repair it. Of the total amount, 9,040 *niṣf fiḍḍa* (more than 56 percent) were spent on the wood needed for the repair work, and another 500 *niṣf fiḍḍa* were paid to transport the wood and other needed supplies to the village. Although not stated explicitly, the wood was most likely acquired in the city of al-Manṣūra itself, as that was the nearest major urban center to the village and the home of a thriving wood market. On the village of Kafr al-Madmāṣ, see: *QJBM*, pt. 2, 1:222–23.

Indeed, it was customary for the *qāḍī* of al-Manṣūra, in consultation with the city's lumber merchants, to record in his court the kinds, amounts, and prices of wood coming into the city's lumber market. In 1774, for instance, there were nine separate varieties of wood available in al-Manṣūra's wood market. DWQ, Maḍābiṭ al-Daqahliyya 20, p. 189, no case no. (30 Ş 1188/5 Nov. 1774). In most cases, we do not know whether *multazims* like Aḥmad, who were in need of wood to repair an embankment or dam, went themselves to al-Manṣūra to inspect the materials and to secure their transport, sent someone else to do it, or communicated with merchants with whom they already had established connections. What is clear, though, is that there was a network of communications and transport for requesting and moving goods and materials from medium-size rural cities to their hinterlands. Thus, the foregoing *multazim*, the amir Aḥmad, was prepared to spend a large sum to buy and transport wood from al-Manṣūra to his village because he knew that the repair of a broken embankment was crucial to the success of future agricultural seasons. His recording of this transaction in the court of al-Manṣūra is testament enough to its importance and enormous size.

[64] Although we know a great deal about interactions between *multazims* and the Ottoman bureaucracy, we have yet to understand fully the relationships between *multazims* and peasants in their *iltizāms*. This was one of the most crucial relationships in the entire Ottoman Empire, as the most direct interaction of peasants – the overwhelming majority of imperial subjects – with the Empire was through the *multazims* above them.

expended a great amount of resources and effort attempting to ameliorate the problem. In an Ottoman firman from January or February 1768 addressed to the vali of Egypt, Muḥammad Paşa, the amirs of Egypt, the *qāḍī* of Alexandria, and other important officials and notables, the sultan expressed his frustrations at the high costs of wood used to repair the dam of Alexandria (an irrigation feature I discuss in detail in the final chapter).[65] To make his point even clearer, the sultan – having checked the records of the *başmuhasebe* – enumerated in detail the various repairs carried out on the dam over the previous few decades along with the costs of wood and other attendant expenses the government paid out for the work.[66]

Although undoubtedly some of the high costs of the dam's repairs accrued from the theft and dishonesty the sultan sternly complained about in the firman, the largest expense associated with this work was lumber. The wood used in the project came from trees harvested in Anatolia. The labor and transport costs involved in moving the trees from Anatolia to Egypt were enormous. More important, the dam of Alexandria was a very complex repair project demanding careful and constant oversight and ample supplies of wood. Built to protect hundreds of villages in the agricultural hinterland south of Alexandria from the salty waters of the Mediterranean, this dam and others near it were some of the most difficult irrigation works to maintain in all of Egypt because of the strength and constant pounding of the sea's waves against them.

As seen in this case, the sultan was so taken aback by the costs of wood used in the repair of the Alexandria Dam that he went to the trouble of listing major repairs to the dam involving wood over a period of nearly seventy years before this case in 1768. In one of those years, 1745, there was an important correspondence between Istanbul and the Egyptian Vali Raghab Muḥammad Paşa in Cairo about the repair of the Alexandria

65 BOA, Cevdet Nafia, 337 (Evasıt N 1181/31 Jan.–9 Feb. 1768).

66 The total spent on the repairs of this dam between 1701 and 1763 was the impressive sum of 29,475,000 *akçe* and 14,987,500 *para*. The breakdown of this total is as follows: In 1701–1702, more than 40 *kise akçe* (1,000,000 *para*) were spent on wood for the dam; in 1715–1716, the cost of wood was 50 *kise akçe* (1,250,000 *para*); in 1719–1720, it cost 15 *kise akçe* (375,000 *para*); in 1727–1728, it was 7 *kise akçe* (175,000 *para*); in 1741–1742, it was 58 *kise akçe* (1,450,000 *para*); in 1745–1746, 41 *kise akçe* (1,025,000 *para*) were spent; from 1746 to 1748, after the appointment of a new official to oversee the repairs, more than 295 *kise akçe* (7,375,000 *para*) were spent on wood; in 1748–1749, wood cost 93.5 *kise akçe* (2,337,500 *para*); from 1753 to 1755, more than 196.5 *Rumi kise akçe* (9,775,000 *akçe*) were spent on wood; and in 1762–1763, more than 394 *Rumi kise akçe* (19,700,000 *akçe*) were spent on wood for the repair of the dam of Alexandria.

Dam in which the high cost of moving wood was the central concern.[67] The sultan expressed consternation at the fact that his officials in Cairo were giving him mixed messages about the urgency of the dam's repair. Initially, they reported to Istanbul that both the dam of Alexandria and the Nāṣiriyya Canal (the forerunner to the Ashrafiyya Canal, which I discuss in Chapter 6) needed repair. After further examination, though, it was determined that if the embankments of the Nāṣiriyya Canal were repaired in a very sturdy manner, then the state could wait to repair the Alexandria Dam.

During the period of this correspondence, arrangements were already being made for the expensive transportation of various kinds of wood from unspecified remote locations throughout the Empire (most likely southwestern Anatolia, the Levant, or areas around the Black Sea littoral). If, as suggested by secondary inspections of damage to the irrigation works, it were at all possible to delay or forgo altogether the shipment of wood, then doing so would save the state a great amount of money. If, however, the repairs and the shipments of wood they required were determined to be absolutely unavoidable, then supporting funds were to be taken from the *irsāliyye-i ḫazīne* of 1741–1742, which was the customary source of payment for such expenses. Moreover, should that money prove insufficient for the work and for the purchase of the wood it required, additional funds were to be secured from the Ruznamçe. The most important point to take away from this case is that it was the very high cost of wood that determined both the sultan's extreme concern for properly understanding the necessity of repairing the Alexandria Dam and his attempts to avoid unneeded expenditures.

The danger posed by the breaking of the Alexandria Dam was dramatically illustrated in the spring of 1743 when the waters of the Mediterranean completely overwhelmed the wooden structure. The dam had recently been reinforced with a series of *sandıks*, large pieces of very strong wood regularly used in fortifications or coffers.[68] These were usually installed behind dams on the side opposite the sea and were sunk underground beneath the water as deep as possible. Between the series of vertical supports was also installed a new face for the dam consisting of a fresh set of long, straight, horizontal wooden board planks (*lauḥas*). As stated in this case, the planks were usually installed either on top of the old boards or in place of those most badly damaged. For added

67 BOA, MM, 6:197 (Evahir S 1158/25 Mar.–3 Apr. 1745).
68 BOA, MM, 6:37 (Evasıt Ra 1156/6–15 May 1743).

protection, a large ditch was also built near the dam under the direction of a man named ʿAbdallah Corbaci to help in siphoning off the large amounts of water that regularly collected behind it.[69]

All those measures, however, were not enough to keep the powerful waters of the Mediterranean at bay that spring. The unremitting smashing of the sea's waves coupled with very strong winds destroyed most of the dam's new wooden sections. All the dam's new timbers and *lauḥas* were thus swept away in a rush of salt water along with the dam's old pieces of wood and its weakened supports (*sandıks*) that had survived from past floods. The sea burst through the dam like a strait (*boğaz*) flooding the entire area behind it and covering the villages of al-Baḥayra directly beneath the dam like a great sea (*derya-i azîme*).[70] The main road from Alexandria to its sister city Rashīd that normally took fifteen hours to trek was rendered fully impassable by the huge deluge. In addition to the flooding of the road and many villages in al-Baḥayra, rushing salt water reached all the way to the Nāṣiriyya Canal. If the sweet waters of that canal were compromised by the relentless, salty onrush of the Mediterranean, the results would be especially dangerous for the city of Alexandria, whose people relied on the canal for the bulk of their drinking water. The sultan specifically warned that it would be a great disaster should the canal and its dikes break, as that would lead directly to a lack of water and, hence, to great suffering for the people of Alexandria.[71]

This dismal situation was made all the worse by the ravages wrought earlier that year by the Nile's rushing flood waters on another wooden irrigation work – the dam of al-Gharaq in Fayyoum.[72] In the previous year,

69 BOA, MM, 6:2 (Evahir S 1156/16–25 Apr. 1743).

70 Ibid.

71 Ibid.

72 On the politics of the dam of al-Gharaq and other irrigation works in Ottoman Fayyoum, see: Alan Mikhail, "An Irrigated Empire: The View from Ottoman Fayyum," *IJMES* 42 (2010): 569–90. More generally on Fayyoum's geography and irrigation works, see: R. Neil Hewison, *The Fayoum: A Practical Guide* (Cairo: American University in Cairo Press, 1984), 1–17; W. Willcocks and J. I. Craig, *Egyptian Irrigation*, 2 vols. (London: E. & F. N. Spon, 1913), 1:441–47; Sato, *State and Rural Society*, 221–25. Most helpful in this regard is the following volume including a reprint of the thirteenth-century Arabic account of Fayyoum by Abū ʿUthmān al-Nābulusī and a collection of essays on this text and on Fayyoum more generally: Fuat Sezgin, Mazen Amawi, Carl Ehrig-Eggert, and Eckhard Neubauer, eds., *Studies of the Faiyūm Together with* Tārīḫ al-Faiyūm wa-Bilādihī *by Abū ʿUṯmān an-Nābulusī (d. 1261)*, vol. 54 of *Islamic Geography* (Frankfurt: Institute for the History of Arabic-Islamic Science at the Johann Wolfgang Goethe University, 1992). I also consulted the following manuscript versions of this text: Fakhr al-Dīn ʿUthmān al-Nābulusī, *Iẓhār Ṣanʿat al-Ḥayy al-Fayyūm fī Tartīb Bilād al-Fayyūm*, SK, Ayasofya 2960; Abī ʿUthmān al-Nābulusī al-Ṣafadī, *Tārīkh al-Fayyūm wa Bilādihi*, DKM, Tārīkh 1594. On the history of Fayyoum more generally, see also: *EI*, s.v. "al-Fayyūm" (P. M. Holt). On the

a construction project to reinforce the Fayyoum dam was not completed before the time of the annual flood and was left to be finished the following year. With the full force of the flood pushing against it, however, the partially repaired dam could not withstand the pressure of the river's floodwaters and completely collapsed. Because of a natural depression that extends from the region of Fayyoum north toward Alexandria, the Ottoman administration of Egypt expressed profound fear in this case that the salty waters rushing into al-Baḥayra from the Mediterranean and the fresh water that had overwhelmed the Fayyoum dam would meet in a deadly rendezvous, flooding a huge portion of Egypt and thereby drowning hundreds of villages.[73]

Although imperial fears of a deadly whirlpool (*girdap*) were perhaps a bit overstated, it was indeed quite possible for massive flooding simultaneously to overwhelm many villages in both al-Baḥayra and Fayyoum. The sultan ordered his officials to inspect the embankments of the Nāṣiriyya Canal and the integrity of dams in Alexandria and Fayyoum to determine whether the damaged structures could withstand the combined forces of the Nile flood and the encroaching sea. The officials reported that the wood and labor needed to repair the canal and various dams along the Mediterranean coast would be very costly.[74] Despite the high costs, however, the sultan ordered his men to complete the repairs as quickly as possible, because to ignore the situation much longer would cost even more later in both human suffering and state money.[75] This case thus clearly shows how wood and its scarcity served to shape the course of irrigation in Ottoman Egypt.

lake of Birkat Qarun in Fayyoum, see: Butzer, *Early Hydraulic Civilization*, 36–38, 92–93, 108; Ali Shafei Bey, "Fayoum Irrigation as Described by Nabulsi in 1245 A.D. with a Description of the Present System of Irrigation and a Note on Lake Moeris," in *Studies of the Faiyūm*, ed. Fuat Sezgin, Mazen Amawi, Carl Ehrig-Eggert, and Eckhard Neubauer, 308–9. On the canal of Baḥr Yūsuf, see: Shafei Bey, "Fayoum Irrigation," 298–99; Rivlin, *Agricultural Policy of Muḥammad ʿAlī*, 238–39; Willcocks and Craig, *Egyptian Irrigation*, 1:441–44; Butzer, *Early Hydraulic Civilization*, 16, 36–38, 53. For examples of additional repairs carried out on the dam of al-Gharaq, see: BOA, Cevdet Nafia, 2570 (Evahir Ş 1174/28 Mar.–6 Apr. 1761); BOA, Cevdet Nafia, 458 (9 Ra 1158/12 Apr. 1745). For technical details and drawings of drainage and discharge in Fayyoum, see: Willcocks and Craig, *Egyptian Irrigation*, 1:442–47; Shafei Bey, "Fayoum Irrigation," 286–309. On some of the particularities of agricultural cultivation in Fayyoum, see: Watson, *Agricultural Innovation*, 17, 28, 40.

73 BOA, MM, 6:2 (Evahir S 1156/16–25 Apr. 1743).

74 The canal would cost more than 50 *kise akçe* (1,250,000 *para*) to repair, whereas reconstructing the Mediterranean dams would require nearly 175 *kise akçe* (4,375,000 *para*).

75 BOA, MM, 6:2 (Evahir S 1156/16-25 Apr. 1743); BOA, MM, 6:37 (Evasıt Ra 1156/6–15 May 1743).

Wood as Commodity

Natural flooding events like this one in 1743 greatly affected the Egyptian peasantry, the landscape of Egypt, and the income of the imperial capital in Istanbul.[76] The Ottoman provincial bureaucracy and the Egyptian peasantry, therefore, had a common interest in protecting not only their lands but also their own bodies from the torrents of water that visited Egypt on at least a yearly basis. To that end, wood and the irrigation system it helped construct became the primary means of protecting humans, crops, animals, and income from water. Shielding Egypt's rich agricultural land from the sea's salty waters and the Nile's unpredictable flood meant a massive expenditure in lumber, money, and labor. The latter two (money and labor) were easily acquired in Ottoman Egypt. The Ottoman administration in Egypt and Istanbul had huge cash reserves that could, if necessary, be put toward large public works repair projects, and Egyptian peasants were very regularly treated as a nearly endless labor pool by almost all governments that ever ruled Egypt.[77] The single object most sorely needed in Egypt for purposes of irrigation was wood. Without lumber, there could have been no dams, no waterwheels, no rigid reinforcement of canal embankments, and no channeling of water to protect the Empire's most lucrative province from massive losses of human and agricultural capital. Thus, the main problem facing the Ottoman bureaucracy of Egypt was how to get wood to the province.

The solution to this problem for the Ottoman administration of Egypt was the commodification of nature – turning trees into lumber.[78] If – as we saw in the previous chapter – Egypt was the main producer and storehouse of grain for various areas of the Ottoman Empire, then

[76] On the history and historiography of natural disasters (mostly earthquakes) in the Ottoman Empire, see: Zachariadou, *Natural Disasters in the Ottoman Empire*. For a more general treatment of earthquakes in the Ottoman Empire, see also: N. N. Ambraseys and C. F. Finkel, *The Seismicity of Turkey and Adjacent Areas: A Historical Review, 1500–1800* (Istanbul: Eren, 1995).

[77] For a very useful discussion of various national and colonial attitudes toward Egyptian peasants, see: Timothy Mitchell, *Rule of Experts: Egypt, Techno-Politics, Modernity* (Berkeley: University of California Press, 2002), 123–205.

[78] On Ottoman forestry, see: Selçuk Dursun, "Forest and the State: History of Forestry and Forest Administration in the Ottoman Empire" (Ph.D. diss., Sabancı University, 2007). See also the following very general history of Turkish forestry: Yücel Çağlar, *Türkiye Ormanları ve Ormancılık* (Istanbul: İletişim Yayınları, 1992). For useful collections of documents on Ottoman forestry, see: Halil Kutluk, ed., *Türkiye Ormancılığı ile İlgili Tarihi Vesikalar, 893–1339 (1487–1923)* (Istanbul: Osmanbey Matbaası, 1948); Çevre ve Orman Bakanlığı, *Osmanlı Ormancılığı*.

Anatolia was the primary forest serving the Empire's lumber needs.[79] The only major mesic forests in the Ottoman Empire were in areas around the Black and Caspian seas.[80] There were additionally some regions of open forest and tall maquis around the Mediterranean in southern Anatolia and on the Levantine coast. The vast majority of those forests had *miri* status, and, thus, cutting their trees, grazing, building, or hunting in them was strictly forbidden without the proper permissions.[81] The Ottoman imperial bureaucracy successfully monopolized Anatolian timber stocks to serve as a steady source of income for the Empire in the sixteenth century. Indeed, before their conquest of Egypt, the Ottomans used their monopoly over Anatolian wood to trade with the Mamlūks of Egypt for pepper and other spices.[82]

Some of Anatolia's *miri* forests were designated as Cibâl-i Mübâha, which meant that the state allocated the forests to be used freely by the *reaya* for timber, construction, and firewood. The management of these forests fell to the administrative unit of the Ottoman Imperial Dockyards (Tersâne-i Âmire), reflecting the fact that most lumber supplies in Anatolia were harvested to build ships for the Ottoman navy.[83] Thus, the fate of Anatolia's forests rested largely on the successes and failures of the Ottoman navy. The Imperial Dockyards were also in charge of the management of Ottoman forests because of the proximity of most forests to port cities and the fact that seafaring ships were the preferred means of transporting wood.[84]

79 On the trade in Taurus lumber, see: McNeill, *Mountains of the Mediterranean*, 93–94.

80 On the forests of the Middle East, see: Carlos E. Cordova, *Millennial Landscape Change in Jordan: Geoarchaeology and Cultural Ecology* (Tucson: University of Arizona Press, 2007), 3–4.

81 My discussion of Ottoman imperial forest management policies comes from the following: Çevre ve Orman Bakanlığı, *Osmanlı Ormancılığı*, 1:xi–xvi; Dursun, "Forest and the State." For examples of imperial orders preventing imperial subjects from using forests, see: Çevre ve Orman Bakanlığı, *Osmanlı Ormancılığı*, 1:2–3, 6–7, 18–19, 22–23, 24–25, 26–27, 38–39, 104–5, 106–7, 110–11, 114–15, 120–21, 124–25, 150–51, 172–73; 2:2–3, 42–43, 46–47, 48–49; 3:4–5, 6–7, 8–9, 16–17, 18–19.

82 Brummett, *Ottoman Seapower and Levantine Diplomacy*, 144.

83 Other major consumers of these forests included the Imperial Arsenal of Ordnance and Artillery (Tophâne-i Âmire), the Imperial Barn (Istabl-ı Âmire), and the city of Istanbul. Cases concerning the use of wood by the Imperial Arsenal of Ordnance and Artillery include the following: Çevre ve Orman Bakanlığı, *Osmanlı Ormancılığı*, 1:90–91, 118–19, 136–37. For cases about the transport of wood for the Imperial Barn, see: ibid., 1:72–73, 116–17. For cases involving the provisioning of Istanbul with firewood and other wood products, see: ibid., 1:62–63, 64–65, 68–69, 80–81, 130–31, 132–33. On the Tersâne-i Âmire, see: Bostan, *Tersâne-i Âmire*.

84 On the Ottoman preference to build ships in coastal cities near large timber stocks, see: Brummett, *Ottoman Seapower and Levantine Diplomacy*, 96. See also: Imber, "The Navy of Süleiman the Magnificent."

Turning the trees of Anatolia into lumber was a massively difficult and complicated process that required labor and capital of its own. The office of the *kereste emîni* (timber superintendent) was under that of the Imperial Dockyards superintendent and was the body directly responsible for organizing the harvesting of timber in Anatolia.[85] The *kereste emîni* managed a veritable army of laborers (*amele*) in the work of cutting and moving trees.[86] Various military cadres (*yaya, müsellem, yörük, canbaz*) and specialized craftsmen (*neccar, teksinarcılar, kalafatçı*) worked to turn trees into wood products.[87]

Once harvested, the movement of lumber from Anatolia to other parts of the Empire, moreover, relied on networks of shipping and transport that, as we have seen, were already in place to move grain and other foodstuffs, people, and information among Istanbul, Anatolia, Egypt, and the rest of the Empire.[88] Unlike grain, though, which most often moved out of Egypt to Istanbul, Mecca, or Tunis, lumber went in the opposite direction – that is, *into* Egypt. These multiple and opposing directions of consumption challenge the picture of the Ottoman Empire as a central administration in Istanbul sucking in resources from its various territories. Though perhaps not at the same scale as Istanbul, Egypt certainly consumed goods and materials from across the Empire. If Egypt was the grain hinterland of Istanbul, then it is fair to say that parts of Anatolia were the lumber hinterland of relatively small Egyptian cities like Rashīd or al-Manṣūra.

More generally in the Empire, there were all kinds of overlapping hinterlands in which one region's source of natural goods was another's consumer of them. The Empire was, therefore, not a series of ever-larger concentric circles of influence and consumption emanating out from the center in Istanbul.[89] This model of center and periphery is far too simplistic a schema to be useful. Instead, the image should be

85 On the office of the *kereste emîni*, see: Çevre ve Orman Bakanlığı, *Osmanlı Ormancılığı*, 1:94–95. For a discussion of Ottoman guilds related to forestry in the context of the wider early modern Mediterranean world, see: Hughes, *The Mediterranean*, 97–99.

86 For cases involving the organization of laborers in the harvesting of lumber from Anatolian forests, see: Çevre ve Orman Bakanlığı, *Osmanlı Ormancılığı*, 1:8–9, 46–47, 48–49, 56–57, 60–61.

87 For more on these and other positions related to the harvesting of timber, see: ibid., 1:xiii.

88 On the movement of goods between Istanbul and Egypt, see: TSMA, E. 840 (n.d.).

89 For a description and critique of the German Johann Heinrich von Thünen's model of the isolated state, based on the notion of a series of imbedded concentric circles of agricultural production, see: Cronon, *Nature's Metropolis*, 48–52.

one in which overlapping circles of interests, advantages, desires, and needs came together to a form a series of connections and networks meant to achieve the optimal balance of all these forces. To strike this balance, the Ottoman Empire thus sought to meet one region's wants with the excesses of another by moving natural resources around the Empire.

Much of this system of management rested on the utilization of existing networks of trade to move goods. The Ottoman bureaucracy understood, for example, that trees in the form of lumber were a valuable commodity that it could ship using existing networks to locations lacking wood. A firman on this subject from 1802 stated as much when it commanded that lumber be shipped from Anatolia to Alexandria.[90] Wood was needed in Egypt to repair parts of the Alexandria Canal that linked the coastal city to the Nile. The firman begins by stating that the most important item needed for the repair work was wood, which was not in existence anywhere in ʿArabistan – the general term used for the Arab provinces of the Empire. Offering a solution to the problem, the decree states that, given the large reserves of lumber in the *sancaks* of Tekke and Alâiye and in the mountains around Menteşe, and given that the ports of those areas were so close to the forests, wood from the Anatolian regions should be sent to Alexandria without delay.

Citing precedent, this case further states that all wood used in ʿArabistan had always come from these areas because ʿArabistan had none of its own. The remainder of the decree directs how the wood should be transported and instructs those involved to keep close records of all the steps taken in bringing the wood from Anatolia to Egypt. The *mutasarrıf* of Rhodes, who was the authority responsible for those areas of southwestern Anatolia, was instructed to rent the necessary merchant vessels for the shipment and to record the date, port of embarkation, and amount of inventory. On arrival in Egypt, similar information was to be recorded, after which time all the documentation was to be sent to Istanbul to serve as verification of the lumber's proper transfer.

Mention of the act of cutting down trees in Anatolia for their use in Egypt is also found in a request made to use excess wood for the repair of a mosque and a school in an unnamed location in the province.[91] The wood cut from trees on the southern Black Sea coast was originally

90 BOA, Cevdet Nafia, 302 (23 Za 1216/28 Mar. 1802).
91 BOA, Cevdet Bahriye, 5701 (n.d.).

to be used for the building of bridges over certain areas of the Nile.[92] However, before the lumber left Istanbul's Imperial Dockyards for Egypt, it was determined that the province already had sufficient amounts of wood for the construction of the bridges and that the wood could thus be put toward other uses in Egypt. This request therefore asked the sultan to allow the lumber to be transported from the Istanbul dockyards to Egypt anyway to be used in the repair of a mosque and a school. In this case, apart from a passing reference to the fact that trees were cut from mountain ranges in Anatolia, the lumber was transferred to Egypt, traded, and thought of not as a natural resource but as a commodity like any other.[93]

As we have seen throughout this chapter so far, wood was used to build dams that stored water, to construct embankments that channeled water, and to make waterwheels that lifted water. There were, however, many other ways in which the histories of wood and water in Ottoman Egypt intersected. For example, in a letter sent to Istanbul in 1799 from the head of the Ottoman navy, we read of how wood was used to store water aboard Ottoman ships stationed in Alexandria for the spring.[94] Similar to previous cases, one of the most central concerns expressed in this letter was a desire to ensure the proper movement of wood to build various wooden water storage tanks (*su mancanaları*) on the ships. Indeed, the entire project of building the storage casks on the ships in Alexandria depended on the availability of adequate amounts of wood, and, thus, the most important objective of this case was to ensure that appropriate supplies of wood were available in Alexandria.

92 On Ottoman rule in the Black Sea, see: Halil İnalcık, *Sources and Studies on the Ottoman Black Sea* (Cambridge, MA: Harvard University Press, 1996); Victor Ostapchuk, "Five Documents from the Topkapı Palace Archive on the Ottoman Defense of the Black Sea against the Cossacks (1639)," *JTS* 11 (1987): 49–104; Charles King, *The Black Sea: A History* (Oxford: Oxford University Press, 2004), 111–36; Nagy Pienaru, "The Black Sea and the Ottomans: The Pontic Policy of Bayezid the Thunderbolt," *IJTS* 9 (2003): 33–57; Alan Fisher, "Sources and Perspectives for the Study of Ottoman-Russian Relations in the Black Sea Region," *IJTS* 1 (1980): 77–84.

93 Wood was similarly conceived of as a commodity moving from Anatolia to Egypt in a letter from the *emin ül-bina* (the overseer of construction) about the repair of the Alexandria Dam in 1776. In the letter, the *emin ül-bina*, a man named Mustafa, confirmed that he received wood from harvested trees to be used for the repair of the Alexandria Dam. Specifically, he received in Alexandria 8,513 individual pieces of wood as well as 273 *qinṭār* (12,102 kilograms) of raw iron. This and the previous order are some of the few instances in which the actual act of cutting trees is specifically mentioned, thus reconnecting the objectified lifeless commodity of lumber to the living organism of the tree. BOA, Cevdet Nafia, 644 (28 R 1190/15 Jun. 1776).

94 BOA, Cevdet Bahriye, 1513 (17 Ca 1214/17 Oct. 1799).

The wood was to be collected from as far away (*taşradan*) as was necessary, and a firman was previously issued in that regard for the purchase of requisite supplies. Moreover, the work of moving this wood to Egypt and of building the casks was to be undertaken with the knowledge of the head of the Imperial Dockyards, the overseer of customs, and the head of lumber customs in Galata. The signature of the sultan at the top of the order instructed that the wood materials were to be attained immediately and that construction of the casks was to commence as soon as there was enough wood, as sufficient supplies of drinking water were clearly essential for the sustenance of sailors aboard Ottoman naval ships. In other words, Alexandria could not provide Ottoman naval ships and their sailors with the wood needed to make possible the human consumption of water. This case, then, like others we have seen, was an attempt to address the problem of a lack of adequate lumber supplies in Egypt and the problem of how wood could be used as a commodity to store, control, and otherwise manipulate water.

Moving the Forest

As I have already suggested, human interaction with wood in Ottoman Egypt was primarily a relationship of consumption rather than production. Forests were cut, logs were stripped and shaped, and lumber used in dams and embankments was eventually destroyed by the rushing waters of the Mediterranean or of the Nile. At no point in the process of bringing wood from somewhere like Anatolia to Egypt or in eventually destroying it and allowing it to be swept away did human labor improve the natural properties of wood to make a better product. Unlike a commodity like coffee that had to be roasted, ground, and cooked before attaining its full value, wood's full value was achieved by cutting it, stripping it, shaping it, burning it, and eventually destroying it.

Thus, wood was expensive because it was useful, strong, and big, not because human hands cut and moved it from Anatolia to Egypt. Wood's economic value derived not from human hands but from the sun's thermal wealth and from nutrients in the soil that had accumulated in forests for millennia. Without supplies of trees in the forests of Anatolia, the Ottoman Empire would have had to import lumber from outside the Empire at extremely high costs. The presence and abundance of forests in Anatolia allowed a place like Egypt to benefit from the use of lumber in the construction of dams, embankment walls, and all sorts of other objects. And it was the unity of Ottoman governance, its established bureaucratic links, and its commercial networks of trade that allowed Egypt to harness that natural abundance.

A very telling series of Ottoman firmans sent to the court of Rashīd in 1725 about the transport of wood from Anatolia to the Red Sea port of Suez for the construction of three galleys serves to flesh out the process of bringing wood to Egypt.[95] The ships to be built were needed both for the transport of grain and other foodstuffs from Suez to Mecca and Medina and for the movement of pilgrims between the areas during the season of the annual pilgrimage. As discussed in the previous chapter, this was the normal course of food and people moving between Egypt and the Hijaz. The wood for the construction of the three ships was to be sent from the Imperial Dockyards in Istanbul to Alexandria in Egypt, where it was to be met by an unnamed customs official in that city.[96] One of the functions of the Dockyards was to act as a repository of wood cut from forests in Anatolia and regions of the Black Sea. From Istanbul, the wood was then distributed to various areas of the Empire where and when it was needed most.

When it was determined that there existed a need to construct ships in Suez, wood in Istanbul was readied to be shipped to Alexandria. To move the enormous load, the Ottoman bureaucracy used its own imperial vessels and rented a group of merchant galleys.[97] Depending on the availability of state ships and the season, it was quite common for the Empire to rent merchant vessels to aid in the transport of goods and peoples.[98] This leg of the journey from Istanbul to Egypt was the wood's longest from its point of origin in the forests of southwestern Anatolia or the southern Black Sea to its eventual ending point in Jidda. Not only was

95 There was an attempt at a comparable transport of lumber in 1510. In that year, eleven galleons were dispatched from the Egyptian port of Damietta to secure wood supplies from the coastal city of Ayas, at the very northeastern corner of the Mediterranean in Anatolia, for the construction of ships in Suez. Suspicious that this movement of ships to Ayas was part of an Ottoman-Mamlūk plot against Rhodes, the leaders of Rhodes attacked and destroyed the convoy of ships from Egypt. Brummett, *Ottoman Seapower and Levantine Diplomacy*, 115–16. For another example of the transport of wood from Anatolia to build ships on the Red Sea, see: ibid., 174. On the use of wood for the construction of ships in the royal dockyards, see: Bostan, *Tersâne-i Âmire*, 102–18.

96 DWQ, Maḥkamat Rashīd 132, p. 199, case 308 (16 Ş 1137/29 Apr. 1725).

97 DWQ, Maḥkamat Rashīd 132, p. 199, case 309 (17 Ş 1137/30 Apr. 1725).

98 The Ottoman state also sometimes leased out its own ships to merchants and others to transport lumber from Anatolia to Alexandria. Brummett, *Ottoman Seapower and Levantine Diplomacy*, 144.

it the longest single distance traveled by the wood, but it was also perhaps the most dangerous part of the trip, because of the Mediterranean's rough waters, the threat of piracy, and the possibility of damage to the ship's cargo.

When the ships arrived safely in Alexandria, their cargo was entered into the customs registers of the city – a requirement of all cargo entering Egypt via the Mediterranean – and assessed the appropriate customs duties.[99] Only after the proper payments were made could the wood continue its journey. The next leg of this wood's trip required that it pass through Cairo. There were, however, several problems with moving the wood from Alexandria to Cairo. The first was one posed by Egypt's geography. For most of its history, Alexandria – Egypt's second city – was not connected to the Nile Valley via waterway or canal (hence the importance of the building of the Maḥmūdiyya Canal, which I discuss in the final chapter). As such, to access the Nile from Alexandria, ships loaded with wood or other goods had to sail east along the Mediterranean coast to enter the mouth of the Rashīd branch of the Nile so that they could continue on to Cairo. The mouth of the Rashīd branch was historically a very difficult entry point into the Nile. For much of the year, prevailing winds blew out to sea over the port city, thus making it extremely tricky and complicated for ships to enter this branch of the Nile. Also, the mouth of the Rashīd branch was a point where salt and fresh water met, and, as such, the water there churned a great deal, especially given the force of the river's current pushing out to sea.

Another major obstacle in getting the wood from Alexandria to Cairo was the very fact of the type of ship used to bring it from Istanbul to Alexandria. The galleys that brought wood to Egypt were especially good at navigating the rough waters of the Mediterranean. The enormous ships were, however, not made to sail on smaller, narrower waterways like the Nile, and thus their entire loads had to be moved to a new set of ships. These more compact and nimbler ships were known in Arabic as *al-jarīm* (*cerîm* in Ottoman Turkish) and were commonly used throughout the Ottoman period to navigate the Nile.[100]

99 DWQ, Maḥkamat Rashīd 132, p. 88, case 140 (17 Ş 1137/30 Apr. 1725).

100 On *al-jarīm* ships, see: Bostan, *Osmanlı Gemileri*, 253–59. For a case about the imperial hiring of sailors of *al-jarīm* ships, see: BOA, Cevdet Bahriye, 208 (14 Ra 1204/2 Dec. 1789).

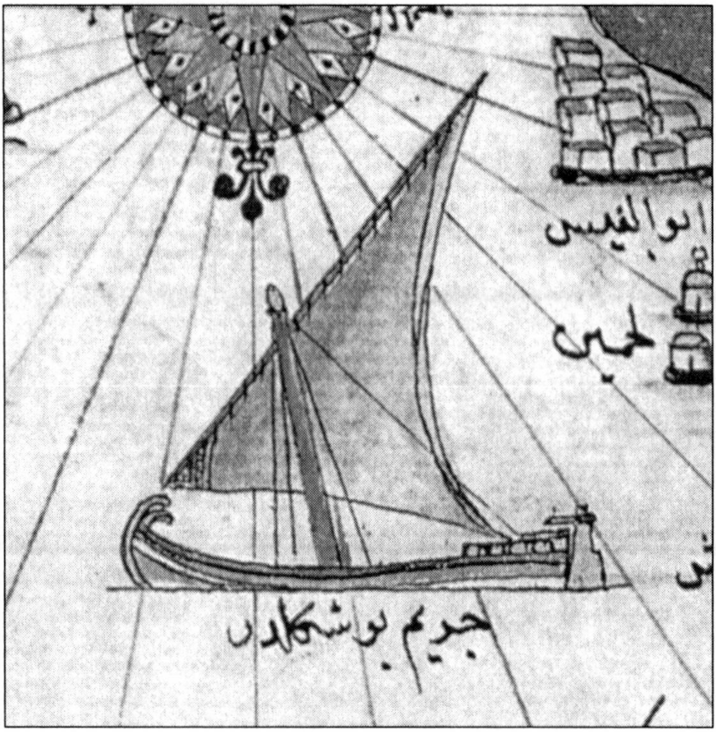

Figure 3.1. *Al-Jarīm* (*Cerîm*). Piri Reis, *Kitâb-ı Bahriye*, İstanbul Üniversitesi Kütüphanesi, Nadir Eserler, TY. 6605, 302r. Used by permission of the Istanbul University Library.

The transfer of this massive amount of very heavy cargo from ship to ship was no small task; it required a great deal of labor, patience, and care so as to protect the wood against damage and theft. Once the wood was placed on the smaller vessels, it could then continue its journey to Suez via Rashīd and Cairo.[101]

When it arrived in Bulaq, the commercial trading center of Cairo just to the north of the city, the load was readied for yet another transfer. Bulaq was the place where ships coming to Cairo unloaded their goods; where merchants bought, sold, and negotiated; and where goods were distributed to various locations throughout Egypt.[102] It was also the point

[101] DWQ, Maḥkamat Rashīd 132, p. 88, case 140 (17 Ş 1137/30 Apr. 1725); DWQ, Maḥkamat Rashīd 132, pp. 200–1, case 311 (3 N 1137/16 May 1725).

[102] On Ottoman Bulaq, see: Nelly Hanna, *An Urban History of Bulaq in the Mamluk and Ottoman Periods* (Cairo: Institut français d'archéologie orientale, 1983).

where goods bought in Cairo were sent down the Nile to the Mediterranean and off to areas all over the world.

For almost the entire journey until this point (from forests in southwestern Anatolia or the Black Sea coast, to Istanbul, to Alexandria, to Rashīd, and then to Bulaq), the wood in this case moved by water. Indeed, the chosen route was meant to maximize the proportion of the trip traversed on water, as this was clearly the fastest, cheapest, and easiest way to move the timbers. From Cairo to Suez, though, there was no waterway – only desert. Thus, in Cairo, the entire load of wood was placed on the backs of camels to move it overland to Suez. This was the trickiest, most complex, and most expensive part of the entire trip. Though perhaps unwieldy as a labor force, camels were clearly one of the few means to move this enormous load over the 125 kilometers between Cairo and Suez.[103]

One of the Ottoman firmans in this case allotted a suitable amount to pay for the use of the camels and to cover the costs of paying those who loaded and unloaded the wood onto and off of the camels.[104] Camels did not come cheap in Ottoman Egypt. In a list of forty-six expenses related to the pilgrimage of the year 1696 (the closest year to 1725 for which we have such figures), we find that the total expenditure on animal labor was more than the impressive sum of 1 million *para* – nearly 10 percent of the total expended from the treasury of Egypt on that year's pilgrimage.[105] This massive investment in and reliance on animal labor to move goods like lumber across the desert goes a long way in showing us the importance of animals to the early modern Ottoman economy, as the power and stamina provided by camels, water buffaloes, and other beasts could not be found anywhere else in this agrarian economy.[106]

[103] Donald Quataert estimates that camels in the Ottoman Empire could carry a quarter ton of weight for at least twenty-five kilometers a day, 20 percent more than horses and mules and more than three times the distance donkeys could carry the equivalent load. Quataert, *The Ottoman Empire*, 119.

[104] DWQ, Maḥkamat Rashīd 132, pp. 200–1, case 311 (3 N 1137/16 May 1725).

[105] Shaw, *Financial and Administrative Organization and Development*, 264–67.

[106] On the importance of camels for Ottoman transportation and military ventures, see: Halil İnalcık, "'Arab' Camel Drivers in Western Anatolia in the Fifteenth Century," *Revue d'Histoire Maghrebine* 10 (1983): 256–270; İnalcık, "The Ottoman State: Economy and Society, 1300–1600," in *An Economic and Social History of the Ottoman Empire: Volume I, 1300–1600*, ed. Halil İnalcık, with Donald Quataert (Cambridge: Cambridge University Press, 1994), 38–39 and 62–63; Suraiya Faroqhi, "Camels, Wagons, and the Ottoman State in the Sixteenth and Seventeenth Centuries," *IJMES* 14 (1982): 523–39. In 1399, for example, Bayezid the Thunderbolt (1389–1402) took ten thousand camels as booty from his conquest of the region of Antalya. İnalcık, "'Arab' Camel Drivers," 265.

Once the lumber finally made it to Suez, it was unloaded from the camels, and the work of actually building the ships in the port city began at last.[107] The journey of the wood from southwestern Anatolia or the Black Sea coast; to Istanbul; through Alexandria, Rashīd, and Cairo; and finally to Suez was long, inefficient, and difficult for numerous reasons. If the construction of the ships were an urgent matter, then the itinerary of moving wood to Suez was cause for much concern indeed. It would surely take, as in this case, at least several weeks (or perhaps longer) before the materials for construction even arrived to their final destination, and once in Suez, one still had to wait for the construction itself to be completed.

Another problem with this transport was the fact that it required multiple transfers. Wood was packed from the Imperial Dockyards onto ships in Istanbul, sailed to Alexandria, transferred to another kind of ship, sailed to Cairo via Rashīd, packed onto the backs of camels, and only then finally unloaded in Suez to be used for its ultimate purpose of ship construction. All these transfers, and especially the overland leg, made the lumber susceptible to damage, theft, and exposure. The wood could have been dropped, lost, chipped, stolen, or damaged in any number of ways. This work was furthermore undertaken in late spring, and although it was not yet the peak of summer, the desert between Bulaq and Suez was surely not a hospitable place at that time of year. And, of course, the transport involved great financial expense: the price of ships and sailors, customs, camels and camel drivers, food for sailors, and so on. Despite these difficulties and costs, however, the Ottoman imperial bureaucracy had few alternatives.[108] If the goal was the construction of ships in Suez, then wood was needed, and because Egypt had no wood, it had to be brought from elsewhere. Those were the realities and costs of the absence of forests in Egypt.

Another series of correspondence from early in the eighteenth century shows once again how the harvesting and movement of wood connected disparate parts of the Empire into a working whole and how merchants and others traveled great distances to secure supplies of lumber. The correspondence in question began with a petition to the sultan from one Hacı Halil Reis, who was the captain of a fleet of Egyptian merchant

[107] For a similar example of the movement of wood for the construction of ships in Suez, see: al-Jabartī, *ʿAjāʾib al-Āthār*, 4:146.

[108] It was this lack of alternatives that drove numerous governments throughout Egypt's history to contemplate the construction of a waterway connecting the Mediterranean and Red seas. The Ottomans entertained and then scrapped plans for such a project in the late 1560s. Colin Imber, *The Ottoman Empire, 1300–1650: The Structure of Power* (New York: Palgrave Macmillan, 2002), 62.

ships then stationed in the Black Sea.[109] In the letter, Halil Reis wrote to the sultan to inform him that the *şayka* ships (vessels of Hungarian origin used throughout the Black Sea) under his command were in a bad state of disrepair and were no longer functional. Halil Reis wrote his petition from the Black Sea port city of Sinop, where he was stationed with his fleet. The petitioner continued on to inform the sultan that he was willing to use his own money to finance the construction of forty-two new galleys to replace the aging fleet of Egyptian merchant vessels. Despite his willingness to personally commission and pay for the construction project, however, the ship captain could not independently secure adequate supplies of wood for the work. Thus, he asked the sultan to issue a firman to the *qāḍīs* of Sinop and the nearby town of Çâir Ağza ordering them to appoint someone to oversee the cutting of trees in the region to supply the lumber needed to build the ships.

In his response, the sultan was swift to give Halil Reis exactly what he wanted, ordering that trees be cut and sent to the port of Sinop to build the forty-two boats. Moreover, the sultan took the opportunity of this firman to reiterate that nothing was to be done to obstruct the free movement and trading of Egyptian merchants in either the Black Sea or the Mediterranean. To make this point even more explicit, he added a separate marginal note (*derkenar*) to his response to the petition, making clear his desire for the free movement of the ships around the entirety of the Ottoman Empire.

This marginal note penned by the sultan about the free movement of Egyptian ships in the Black and Mediterranean seas made clear the centrality of Egyptian merchants to imperial commerce not only in Egypt itself but indeed throughout the entire Empire. That these traders were key to the movement of goods and people was evidenced by the fact that the sultan issued this separate order specifically with their interests in mind. The ships in the Black Sea could have been carrying goods to or from Egypt or could have been rented by the imperial bureaucracy or by entrepreneurial merchants to transport goods from one area of the Empire to another. Whatever the case, the important point is that Egyptian merchants were involved in trade far beyond the shores of Egypt itself; indeed, Sinop, on the southern coast of the Black Sea, was a great distance (approximately 1,025 nautical miles, or 1,900 kilometers) from the ports of Alexandria or Rashīd. Moreover, the fleet was no small convoy. Although the exact number of Egyptian *şayka* ships in Sinop was

[109] BOA, Cevdet Bahriye, 1413 (Evasıt R 1120/30 Jun.–9 Jul. 1708 and 20 Za 1124/19 Dec. 1712).

not specified in this case, the fact that forty-two new ships were to be built suggests that they were replacing quite a large fleet.[110]

As we saw previously, the southern Black Sea coast was one of the most important regions of lumber production in the Empire. In the foregoing case of the Egyptian fleet in Sinop, the sultan ordered wood from five different locations on the Black Sea coast (İznikmid, Sinop, Çâir Ağza, Kemer, and Bîğa) to meet what was no doubt a large demand for wood to build the forty-two vessels. The wood needed in this case could be managed, traded, and moved only through the coordination, resources, and bureaucracy of the Ottoman state. Indeed, Halil Reis recognized that, although he was able to finance the labor and material costs associated with the building of the ships, he could not meet the exorbitant costs of acquiring and moving the large amounts of wood demanded by the construction. Thus, Halil Reis's petition was written precisely to ask the sultan for the wood needed in this project, as without the state's resources, there would have been no way for Halil Reis to get wood from areas around Sinop to the port.

As we saw in our discussion of irrigation repair projects in Chapter 1, Egyptian peasants and others often harnessed the power and resources of the Ottoman state to meet their own needs. In this case, Halil Reis needed wood and was able to convince the sultan to get it for him. No doubt this project also served the interests of the Ottoman state, as the captain's fleet helped facilitate trade throughout the Empire. The repair and construction of these ships is thus most usefully seen as a kind of joint venture between Halil Reis and the Ottoman administration – between an entrepreneurial imperial subject and the Ottoman bureaucracy. Halil Reis oversaw repairs and managed the overall well-being of the fleet, and the state provided the capital and resources to secure and move the timber needed for the work. As with the Ottoman solution to irrigation discussed in Chapter 1, both parties in this arrangement contributed to the task at hand and both benefited.

The movement of trees in the form of lumber from Anatolia and the Black Sea to Egypt and elsewhere shows how the consumption of natural goods in the Ottoman Empire followed the networks, movements, and

110 Other examples of Egyptian connections to and involvement in shipping and commerce throughout the Empire abound in the records of the Ottoman state. One such example of these connections was an order sent by the vali of Egypt, ʿAli Paşa, in 1706 to the high commander of the Mediterranean battle fleet, Canim Hoca. In the order, the Egyptian vali instructed Canim Hoca on matters related to the shipping of goods to Egypt. Here, as in other cases, it is the Egyptian vali – not the sultan or other high imperial figures – that commanded state officials on matters extraterritorial to Egypt. BOA, Cevdet Bahriye, 1334 (11 C 1118/19 Sep. 1706).

demands of market forces controlled and manipulated by the Empire itself. That the story of wood and grain in the early modern Ottoman Empire is simply one of the human consumption of nature is – though of course true – too vague and vacuous an observation to be analytically useful. Rather, as we have been discussing in this and the previous chapter, although Egypt was an abundant producer of grain and so exported it to areas of the Empire that were in want of foodstuffs, it had no usable supply of lumber and thus had to rely on shipments of wood from elsewhere in the Empire. In short, the Ottoman Empire was able to balance its relative wants and excesses of material resources by shifting them around until each want was filled by suitable excess from elsewhere. From the perspective of both imperial subjects and the dynastic elite, no one – except perhaps God or his shadow on Earth, the sultan – owned nature in the way that a human owned a building or a sack of coffee. Plants, trees, and other natural resources – though often commodified, moved, and transferred – were not simple commodities like any other. These living things were, in some senses, everyone's and at the same time no one's.

Moreover, there was another way in which lumber products did not follow the rules of other commodities. According to the labor theory of value, the value of most goods reflects the work of humans, whose sweat and toil produces objects for the market. Although human labor and energy went into the cutting, transport, and readying of wood for use in a dam more than 1,600 kilometers away, much (or perhaps most) of the utility and value of the wood came from nature itself. It was the first nature of the sun's thermal energy, of nutrients in the soil, and of rain that made trees in Anatolia tall and strong and suitable and desirable for use in Egypt. Without those natural forces, no amount of second nature in the form of human labor or tools could "produce" lumber suitable for use in Egypt. As William Cronon writes with reference to the American West, "the fertility of the prairie soils and the abundance of the northern forests had far less to do with human labor than with autonomous ecological processes that people exploited on behalf of the human realm – a realm less of *production* than of *consumption*."[111] Indeed, the fact that wood was a commodity whose value came not from the amount of labor put into it but from its natural properties of strength and size is clear when one considers wood in relation to other building materials used throughout Ottoman Egypt.[112]

[111] Cronon, *Nature's Metropolis*, 149. Emphasis in original.

[112] In 1732, for example, a series of repairs were undertaken in and around the Citadel of Cairo. There were three main areas of the structure that needed to be rebuilt: sections

Although the process of converting Anatolian trees into bridges, dams, waterwheels, and ships in the Egyptian countryside was primarily one of consuming natural wealth, it did, in the end, produce a new kind of nature – the second nature of peasant life in Egypt. As we have seen in this chapter, wood was everywhere in rural Egypt, and without it, peasants could not have functioned as they had for centuries. Wood came to be so "natural" a part of the countryside's environment that it would be hard to imagine Egyptian villages without dams, canals, waterwheels, embankments, and other wooden structures and equally as hard to imagine Egypt without ships to move grain across the Empire. This overlay of human construction in and onto the natural landscape of the Egyptian countryside came to be part of the second nature of peasant life that took these built objects as "natural" and inseparable elements of the rural world. Indeed, without those objects, Egyptian peasants could not irrigate otherwise uncultivable land, and they could not protect themselves against the ravages of the flood. In short, given their millennia of interactions with wood and their dependence on it, peasants could not live without the material and what they made of it.

As discussed in Chapter 1, the construction of second-nature irrigation in Egypt served to connect Egyptian peasants to ecosystems and peoples at great geographical distances from their own communities. With the story of wood in Ottoman Egypt, we see that it was the demand for and use of lumber by both Egyptian peasants and the imperial bureaucracy of the province that led to the removal of large portions of forest in Anatolia.[113] Put differently, Egyptian peasants – who had never seen

of the walls of the Citadel itself, parts of the stable walls that were adjacent to the aqueduct that fed the Citadel from Old Cairo, and portions of the roof of the main state storage facilities in Old Cairo. Lumber was needed to repair both the Citadel wall and the roof of the state storehouse. For the wall, two hundred trees and one hundred boards (*taht*) were requested. Each tree cost fifty *para* and each board, forty *para*. The total cost of repairing the roof of the storage facilities was an additional 3,700 *para*. Although the high price of lumber is telling in and of itself, what is more significant is the fact that the hefty cost was only for the material itself. The labor of moving and trimming the trees to make them into smaller, more usable pieces, in other words, did not figure into the costs of the wood. Although this fact may seem trivial, it stands in stark contrast to the mud, brick, and stone used in the same repair project. For each of these other materials, we read of the intensity and cost of the labor that went into cleaning, shaping, and moving those physical objects. None of this is mentioned in reference to the lumber. BOA, MM, 4:562 (Evasıt C 1145/29 Nov.–8 Dec. 1732).

113 For more examples of the import of wood from Anatolia to Egypt, see: al-Jabartī, *ʿAjāʾib al-Āthār*, 4:212, 219, 221, 361.

Anatolia and likely never heard of the place – affected its history in massively important ways. As forests were cut, ecosystems were altered or destroyed, soil fertilities depleted, and animal habitats changed. What do these connections between Egyptian peasants and Anatolian forests mean for our understanding of the environmental history of the Ottoman Empire?

First, they suggest that the imperial calculus of the Ottoman state deemed certain natural environments more important than others. Egypt, a place of great agricultural potential, was clearly, from both an Ottoman and a local Egyptian perspective, worth the alteration and consumption of other natural landscapes to provide the Nile Valley with the materials needed to take advantage of its rich soils, plentiful waters, and large laboring population. Knowingly or not – most likely not – Egyptian peasants participated in the consumption of large sections of the first nature of Anatolia to construct for themselves an infrastructure of second nature meant to allow them to harness more effectively the first nature of their own immediate surroundings. These two histories of Anatolian forests and of the Egyptian countryside must therefore be taken together as two parts of one process of the consumption and use of nature.

Furthermore, from the imperial perspective of the Ottoman government in Istanbul and Cairo, connecting Anatolia to Egypt made perfect sense. It allowed the Empire to shift a resource of excess in a certain region to a place where that excess could fill a vital need that would eventually allow Egypt to grow food to feed people in yet other places. One can easily conceive of a process, then, whereby the Ottoman bureaucracy surveyed the Empire moving different pieces around to achieve the optimal configuration of rule: Anatolian lumber to Egypt to irrigate land to cultivate grains and other crops that were sent to Istanbul, Mecca, and other population centers in the Empire. As I have been arguing, this chain of movement in which Egypt and Anatolia exchanged grain for wood followed the principle of comparative advantage. By concentrating the labor, skill, and expertise found in certain areas of the Empire on the production of natural resource commodities like lumber or grain, the Ottoman Empire was able to increase its overall levels of productivity. For this system to work most efficiently, transportation networks – as we have seen – had to move goods quickly and with a minimal amount of energy loss. This system of comparative advantage was not governed by a free market but rather through imperial initiative and an extremely coordinated system of local autonomy.

First nature was consumed to construct second nature to make possible the human necessity of caloric food consumption. Egypt was in some senses, then, a kind of grain factory for the Ottoman Empire that required certain basic materials unavailable locally – foremost among them wood – to keep its operations in motion. This factory, like its later industrial counterparts, was a teeming universe of organic life and physical objects. Its millions of living and nonliving parts moved together in regular and unique ways specific to that collective; it was a machine that worked efficiently but that sometimes broke down; it swayed and belched along at its own rhythm. At its heart lay the powerful force of the river – a power that fueled the various parts of the machine to thrust in tandem. Of equal importance was the raw material of wood that helped create the structures, housings, channels, and vessels that harnessed, obstructed, moved, and in general attempted to turn this substance of water into a productive force.

Seizing the Forest

The final chapter in the story of wood in Ottoman Egypt over the course of the long eighteenth century ends in the fourth decade of the nineteenth century during the rule of the Ottoman governor Mehmet ʿAli. Described by some as the founder of modern Egypt and by others as simply an Ottoman imperial official out to secure personal wealth and hereditary rule for his family, Mehmet ʿAli has emerged as quite a controversial figure in the past few decades of Egyptian and Ottoman historiography alike.[114] For my purposes here, I stress his continual role as Ottoman governor of the Empire's most lucrative province, his maintenance of connections with the Ottoman capital in Istanbul, and his strident identity as an Ottoman first (he, for example, spoke Ottoman Turkish throughout his life, never bothering to learn Arabic during the forty-three years of his reign in Egypt). I also view his invasion of Ottoman territories outside of Egypt as an internal struggle for power within the Empire rather than a clash between two diametrically opposed independent political forces. Although Mehmet ʿAli was an Ottoman governor who challenged the Empire on numerous occasions, his governance of Egypt remained both legally and bureaucratically very much within an

[114] For accounts outlining the former view, see: al-Rāfʿī, *ʿAṣr Muḥammad ʿAlī*; Henry Dodwell, *The Founder of Modern Egypt: A Study of Muhammad ʿAli* (Cambridge: The University Press, 1931). For the latter perspective, see: Fahmy, *All the Pasha's Men*; Fahmy, *Mehmed Ali: From Ottoman Governor to Ruler of Egypt* (Oxford, UK: Oneworld, 2009).

Ottoman framework of rule. Nevertheless, because he sought nominal independence from the Ottoman Empire, he had to replace the early modern Ottoman system of natural resource management I have been describing with another more autonomous and Egypt-centered means of acquiring wood, cash, and markets for grain.

After his massacre of Mamlūk forces in 1811, Mehmet ʿAli solidified his power to the point of being able to concentrate on ever-larger and grander projects of rule and conquest. His ambitions to challenge the Ottoman state and to establish himself and his line as the hereditary rulers of Egypt clearly necessitated a large amount of wood – naval timbers and other wood supplies for public works and architectural and other infrastructural projects. Whereas previous imperial governors in Egypt who worked in the Ottoman imperial system could consistently rely on receiving wood supplies from Anatolia, Mehmet ʿAli's desires for nominal independence meant that he had to find independent sources of timber. The lack of timber supplies for an Egypt outside the Ottoman fold was a potentially crippling strategic liability for Mehmet ʿAli and put him in a much weaker position than previous Ottoman provincial governors. As I discuss shortly, wood was thus a key factor in his invasions of Syria and Anatolia.[115] More than a decade before these campaigns, however, we see efforts on the part of Mehmet ʿAli's Ottoman bureaucracy in Egypt to secure adequate, independent, and reliable supplies of wood.

In 1813, Mehmet ʿAli was in need of large amounts of wood both for the remodeling of his palace and for a few small public works projects.[116] Thus, he ordered all the mulberry trees and Christ's thorns throughout Upper and Lower Egypt to be cut down. He dispatched his functionaries to carry out the work, and they succeeded in felling as many trees as they could find, sparing only those whose owners were able to bribe state officials. These local timber stocks were added to a small amount of wood imported from Anatolia. Al-Jabartī writes that "those who saw it [the wood] were astonished by the enormous amount." Clearly, attempting to cut down most of Egypt's indigenous trees was a very shortsighted, unsustainable, and disastrous undertaking that would eventually result in the further depletion of the province's already-minimal supplies of wood.[117]

115 On these points, see: McNeill, *Mountains of the Mediterranean*, 246–47.

116 Al-Jabartī, *ʿAjāʾib al-Āthār*, 4:219.

117 For a very general discussion of the lack of responsible forest harvesting in the pre-Tanzimat Ottoman Empire, see: Çevre ve Orman Bakanlığı, *Osmanlı Ormancılığı*, 1:xiv.

Thus, in a series of cases that are quite rare in the archival record of the Ottoman state in Egypt, the bureaucracy actually ordered the planting of trees in rural Egypt – most likely in an attempt to replace those it had just systematically cut down. On April 24, 1817, a firman was recorded in the registers of the court of al-Baḥayra ordering the planting of trees along the canals, waterways, and roads of the subprovince.[118] The ostensible reasons given in this decree for the planting were to ensure "that no land in the subprovince be left without benefit, that goodness (*al-khayr*) be visited upon the poor and peasants, and that all those coming and going be safe and at peace." The case goes on to give three more specific reasons for the directed planting of trees in al-Baḥayra. First, the trees would be of benefit to owners of the land on which they were planted. Second, they would help with strengthening the embankments of canals in the subprovince. Third, the trees were to provide – presumably because of the shade they offered – comfort on the roads for those who came and went (*al-wāridīn wa al-mutaraddadīn*).

No matter whether one was a peasant or a village elder (*fallāḥ aw shaykh*), he was required to plant these trees on his land. This case goes on to specify the varieties to be planted: *Acacia nilotica* (*sanṭ*) and *Zizyphus spina-christi* (*nabq*). Both trees may or may not give fruit depending on the season and growth conditions, and both *Acacia nilotica* and *Zizyphus spina-christi* are known for their strength and for their use as lumber in construction works. In addition to its natural strength, *Acacia nilotica* is also resistant to termites, twice as hard as teak, and extremely shock resistant. Likewise, *Zizyphus spina-christi* also yields a termite resistant wood, which is red or dark brown and very hard and heavy. In other words, the wood of both of the trees ordered by the Ottoman administration to be planted in al-Baḥayra was strong, durable, hard, and termite resistant.

The wood was thus perfectly suited for use in the construction and repair of various kinds of irrigation works in rural Egypt. Indeed, of the three justifications given in this case for planting the trees, only the second – that their wood was to be used to strengthen the subprovince's embankments – specifically mentioned the direct use of the trees.[119] The first – that they would benefit the owners of the land on which they were planted – did not really spell out how the trees would help

[118] DWQ, Maḥkamat al-Baḥayra 37, p. 204, case 425 (7 C 1232/24 Apr. 1817).

[119] By way of comparison, in 1816, a dike was constructed from the Bulaq Road to Shubra. Here, as well, it was ordered that mulberry trees be planted along either side of the dike, because – as stated in this case – it was customary to do so. Al-Jabartī, *ʿAjāʾib al-Āthār*, 4:362.

landholders. Presumably, if they grew flowers or fruit, that would have been of some benefit to peasants. More to the point, *Acacia nilotica* is known as one of the most effective plants in rehabilitating degraded soils, so it was likely favored to enrich and sustain the soils of al-Baḥayra. As with the first reason, the third reason given for planting the trees – that they would benefit those on the roads of the subprovince – was also not delineated further. Shade was the obvious reason the trees would be useful for those using al-Baḥayra's roads, although, again, this was not stated directly. Given the order's direct statement about the utility of trees in the reinforcement of irrigation works and the vagueness of this order's other directives, it seems likely that the decree to plant trees in al-Baḥayra was promulgated primarily in the interests of the subprovince's rural irrigation network.

Moreover, we can go a step further here and suggest that the firman was issued in an effort to cultivate a usable domestic supply of wood for the repair of the Ashrafiyya Canal, which I discuss in detail in Chapter 6. Suffice it to say here, though, that in the spring of 1817, the Ottoman vali of Egypt, Mehmet ʿAli, first started to draft serious plans for the canal's repair. Thus, it was likely with an eye toward securing a ready supply of wood near this work site – most of the length of the Ashrafiyya Canal ran through the subprovince of al-Baḥayra – that Mehmet ʿAli ordered the planting of the trees. His attempts to cultivate a domestic wood supply went along with his efforts to make Egypt as independent as possible from other areas of the Ottoman Empire. By planting trees along the canals and waterways of al-Baḥayra, Egypt could reduce its reliance on imported wood. Thus, even if the wood in this case were not destined for use in the repair of the Ashrafiyya Canal, it was clearly planted in al-Baḥayra to increase the supply of local wood in Egypt that could be put toward the building and repair of irrigation works in the countryside. Mehmet ʿAli's efforts, in other words, were an attempt to secure ecological self-sufficiency.

This was an issue of the gravest concern for Vali Mehmet ʿAli and his Ottoman bureaucracy in Egypt. In a subsequent firman on the subject of these trees sent from the divan of Egypt in Cairo to the shaykhs and planters (*al-muzāriʿīn*) of the villages of al-Baḥayra on September 4, 1817, the anxiousness and urgency of the Ottoman bureaucracy's need for native wood supplies came through clearly.[120] As in the previous case, this firman opened with a statement outlining the purpose behind this order: to cultivate "benefits for the state and for the peasants [literally,

[120] DWQ, Maḥkamat al-Baḥayra 37, p. 202, case 422 (22 L 1232/4 Sep. 1817).

'for us and for you (pl.)'] and to ensure that everything of the earth is of benefit." These ends could be achieved, according to this case, only by the planting of trees along the banks of all the subprovince's ditches and canals and along the main thoroughfares of al-Baḥayra. Should those charged with the task not fulfill it to the state's liking, they were to be physically punished.

Furthermore, this case instructs that the planting of the trees was to occur before the waters of that year's flood receded from al-Baḥayra so that the new trees could receive the full benefit of the flood's rich sediment. Thirty days after the date of the order, state officials were to be sent to al-Baḥayra to inspect the subprovince. If they found that any individual had not planted trees along a canal, ditch, or road that ran through his property, they were to punish that person.[121] On the threat of physical violence, the people of al-Baḥayra thus had to work very quickly to plant the trees in the thirty days before the state's inspectors came to the countryside. Wood was so vital to the sustenance of the Mehmet ʿAli's bureaucracy in 1817 that the state threatened the very lives of Egyptian peasants to meet its demands for local and reliable supplies of this raw material. This exemplifies how the move away from the Ottoman imperial system to a more centralized Egyptian bureaucracy took autonomy over the rural environment away from Egyptian peasants and added to their physical suffering.

Despite these attempts to grow trees in Egypt and the threats of violence that accompanied them, Mehmet ʿAli soon came to realize what governments in Egypt had understood since the time of the Pharaohs: the most reliable sources of wood for Egypt were not found domestically but secured elsewhere. As we saw earlier, over the course of the long eighteenth century, the Ottoman bureaucracy regularly supplied Egypt with wood from trees harvested in various Anatolian forests. Regions of the Sudan also contained forests, but those supplies were difficult to transport from the south to Egypt.[122] An overland route was too costly and arduous, and the Nile was too narrow in certain points and too curvy in others to make feasible the large-scale importation of wood via the river. After his conquest of the Sudan in 1820, Mehmet ʿAli nevertheless attempted to make possible the importation of wood from the south.[123]

[121] In this section of the firman, the order eloquently states in rhyme (*sajʿ*) that "repentance after inaction is useless" (*lā yanfaʿa al-nadam baʿda al-ʿadam*).

[122] There is evidence for the importation of wood from Ethiopia to Egypt in the ancient period. Meiggs, *Trees and Timber*, 61.

[123] Asad J. Rustom, *The Royal Archives of Egypt and the Origins of the Egyptian Expedition to Syria, 1831–1841* (Beirut: American Press, 1936), 63–64.

He commissioned a corps of engineers to explore the possibilities of widening and straightening sections of the Nile near Aswan and elsewhere to make them more navigable for large quantities of wood. The scale and complexity of the project, however, soon rendered it impossible. Indeed, despite being at a greater distance from Egypt than the Sudan, Anatolia was still the most easily accessible source of wood for Egypt precisely because its forests were along the Black and Mediterranean seas and, thus, quickly and efficiently transportable by ship to Egypt. The importation of wood to Egypt was so important to Mehmet ʿAli and his administration that he personally oversaw all affairs related to the commerce of wood in Egypt.[124]

Of all the possible sources of wood for Egypt over its history, Greater Syria (including sections of south-central and southeastern Anatolia) remained the most accessible and the most used. Indeed, from the ancient period through late antiquity and the medieval period, Egypt resorted most often to the forests of Greater Syria for its wood.[125] Undergrowth and larger trees covered parts of the Galilee and the western approaches to ʿAjlun and Gilead east of the Jordan River.[126] The hills around Beirut were covered with oak and pine, and other sections of Lebanon abounded in the iconic mulberry and cedar.[127] Mulberry and sycamore were also found in the forests of Syria and Cilicia. Larch, oak, fir, and juniper grew in great quantities in and around Adana and in forests throughout Greater Syria.[128] Given the wealth of forests in Greater Syria and the difficulties he faced in the cultivation of trees in Egypt, Mehmet ʿAli in 1831 moved his armies north into Palestine, motivated in large part by his desire to acquire some of its vast supply of wood.[129]

The Egyptian invasion of Greater Syria lasted from 1831 to 1841 and saw Egyptian armies reach deep into Anatolia, almost within striking

124 Al-Jabartī, *ʿAjāʾib al-Āthār*, 4:361.

125 Bagnall, *Egypt in Late Antiquity*, 41; Meiggs, *Trees and Timber*, 63–68; Rustom, *Egyptian Expedition to Syria*, 64.

126 On the locations of forests of various varieties of trees, see: Rustom, *Egyptian Expedition to Syria*, 64–66.

127 On the forests of Lebanon in the ancient period, see: Meiggs, *Trees and Timber*, 49–87.

128 For some information on forest degradation in Greater Syria, see: Norman N. Lewis, "Malaria, Irrigation and Soil Erosion in Central Syria," *Geographical Review* 39 (1949): 289–90.

129 The most immediate temporal precedents for Mehmet ʿAli's invasion of Greater Syria in 1831 were those military campaigns undertaken by ʿAlī Bey al-Kabīr and Muḥammad Bey Abū al-Dhahab in the 1770s and the invasions of ʿAcca and other areas of Palestine by French forces stationed in Egypt at the end of the eighteenth century. On the Beys' military maneuvers in the 1770s, see: Crecelius, *Roots of Modern Egypt*, 79–91 and 159–68.

distance of Istanbul itself. The settlement of this act of aggression directed against the Ottoman state by one of its own provincial governors involved several European powers and resulted in the investiture of hereditary rule on Mehmet ʿAli and his progeny.[130] The centrality of wood to the military campaign was made clear in negotiations between the Ottoman state and Mehmet ʿAli's government in early 1833. On January 21, 1833, Ottoman representatives named Halil Rıfat Paşa and Âmedci Reşid Bey arrived in Alexandria to negotiate an end to hostilities with Mehmet ʿAli.[131] They were instructed to confirm him as governor of Egypt, Crete, Jidda, Sayda, eastern Tripoli, Jerusalem, and Nablus and to bestow on him the sultan's full pardon for military actions taken against the Ottoman state. Should Mehmet ʿAli – as it was suspected he might – also demand the governorships of Damascus and Aleppo and rights to the timber of Adana, the sultan's representatives were instructed to refuse him the governorships of Damascus and Aleppo outright. Although Mehmet ʿAli's desire for wood from Adana was clearly motivated by his plans to rebuild his fleet of warships, the sultan directed his representatives that negotiations were not to breakdown over the issue of wood in Adana.

While the discussions were still under way, Ibrahim Paşa – Mehmet ʿAli's son and chief military officer in the Syrian invasion – sent a letter to his father on February 3, 1833, from his post in Kütahya.[132] In the letter, Ibrahim Paşa pushed his father to demand as many concessions as possible from the Ottoman state. Foremost among those was complete independence from the Ottoman Empire. He also pressed his father to insist on the governorships of Antalya, Alaiye (Alanya), Cilicia,

[130] The imperial decree conferring this right on Mehmet ʿAli and his descendents is the following: BOA, MM, 15, pp. 11–12 (Evahir Z 1256/13–22 Feb. 1841). A facsimile of this document can be found in Muhammad H. Kutluoğlu, *The Egyptian Question (1831–1841): The Expansionist Policy of Memed Ali Paşa in Syria and Asia Minor and the Reaction of the Sublime Porte* (Istanbul: Eren, 1998), 205–6. Kutluoğlu also includes an English translation of the document in the following: Kutluoğlu, *The Egyptian Question*, 195–97. For more on the Egyptian invasion of Greater Syria and its diplomatic settlement, see: Şinasi Altundağ, *Kavalalı Mehmet Ali Paşa Isyanı: Mısır Meselesi, 1831–1841* (Ankara: Türk Tarih Kurumu, 1988); Mālik Muḥammad Aḥmad Rashwān, "al-Shām Taḥt Ḥukm Muḥammad ʿAlī (1247–57)" (Ph.D. diss., al-Azhar University, 1984). For a detailed archival account of the Egyptian military during the period of the Syrian campaign, see: Fahmy, *All the Pasha's Men*.

[131] Kutluoğlu, *The Egyptian Question*, 90.

[132] DWQ, ʿAbdin 253, doc. 85 (13 N 1248/3 Feb. 1833). Facsimiles of this document are given in both of the following: Rustom, *Egyptian Expedition to Syria*, before p. 57; Kutluoğlu, *The Egyptian Question*, 209. Each author also provides a slightly different translation of the document: Rustom, *Egyptian Expedition to Syria*, 57–59; Kutluoğlu, *The Egyptian Question*, 200.

Cyprus, Tunis, and western Tripoli. Of those places, it was most important that Egypt acquire sovereignty over Antalya, Alaiye (Alanya), Cilicia, and Cyprus because of their vast timber resources and Egypt's need to build naval vessels. As Ibrahim Paşa wrote to his father, a country (*memleket*) without wood cannot maintain a navy. He continued: "England is a poorly wooded country, and when it sought to obtain timber from the Austrian, the latter rejected the request and . . . the difficulty of Egypt in this respect was confirmed by the instructions I have previously received from you [Mehmet ʿAli] in which you said[,] 'My son give as much care to the matter of timber as you would to crippling the army of İstanbul.'"[133]

Seeing as he was clearly more intransigent than his father, imperial Ottoman representatives arrived in Kütahya on April 5, 1833, to negotiate directly with Ibrahim Paşa.[134] Refusing to budge on his demands, Mehmet ʿAli's son eventually forced the Ottoman state's representatives to grant him both Aleppo and Damascus and to agree that he would be allowed to take trees from Adana, despite being denied total control over the province. In the end, however, an agreement was finally reached whereby Ibrahim Paşa and his armies gave up claims to Alaiye (Alanya) and Cilicia in exchange for total control over the province of Adana. Ibrahim Paşa ensured, however, that he would still be allowed to take timber from Alaiye (Alanya) and Cilicia. Access to forests and to wood was clearly foremost in the minds of Ibrahim Paşa and Mehmet ʿAli as they negotiated with the Ottoman state. Indeed, in the period between 1831 and 1833, Mehmet ʿAli insisted on receiving daily reports on the progress of timber harvesting in Greater Syria.[135] The two main purposes of this wood brought to Egypt were the construction of naval ships and the burning of firewood to feed industries such as foundries, the mint, the armory, and so on. Without this vital fuel, Mehmet ʿAli's imperial and domestic projects would clearly not have been possible.

Lumbering toward the Nineteenth Century

Mehmet ʿAli's ten-year incursion into Syria and Anatolia was largely driven by his desire to acquire usable wood supplies for his province. This imperial move was not only a threat to the geographical and

[133] This translation is from the following: Kutluoğlu, *The Egyptian Question*, 200.

[134] Ibid., 99–100.

[135] DWQ, ʿAbdin 240, doc. 135; DWQ, ʿAbdin 241, doc. 4, 34, 70, 102, 119, cited in Rustom, *Egyptian Expedition to Syria*, 67.

political integrity of the Ottoman state but also an affront to an entire Ottoman system of connections, networks, and balances that developed over the course of the previous centuries to move natural goods from areas of excess to those of need in the Empire. Thus, instead of working through the frustratingly slow and cumbersome bureaucratic channels of the Empire of which he remained a part, Mehmet ʿAli sought to bypass the system altogether by annexing for himself areas of heavy timber. Instead of a province centered on the Nile, Mehmet ʿAli wanted to make Egypt into an imperial territory that included the Hijaz, Greater Syria, Crete, and parts of Anatolia. In so doing, he wanted nothing less than to change what Egypt was altogether. The impetus behind these ambitions was, to a large extent, Mehmet ʿAli's desire to overcome what Asad Rustom identifies as "the insufficiency of the Nile Valley."[136]

Egypt needed wood. To get it, the government of Mehmet ʿAli's Egypt – having attempted and failed to grow trees in a place like al-Baḥayra – looked outside of Egypt, like so many governments had before it, for its needed wood supplies. Whereas in the eighteenth century, the government controlling this process of wood importation was centered in Istanbul, by the second and third decades of the nineteenth century, that government was Mehmet ʿAli's in Cairo. In the earlier imperial system, the Ottoman Empire had plenty of timber supplies of its own in Anatolia and elsewhere and did not really mind that Egypt had none, as wood could easily be transferred there when the need arose. By contrast, Mehmet ʿAli's semiautonomous Egypt had no wood of its own, and given his desire to assemble a navy and to undertake large public works projects, timber was a strategic good for him that had to be acquired from elsewhere. It was, in the end, the very nature of Ottoman Egypt's lack of forests – whether in 1620 or 1820 – that dictated the need for the importation or later the seizure of wood from elsewhere.

Significantly, Mehmet ʿAli's invasion of Greater Syria represented one facet of the increasingly authoritarian and even colonial nature of the nascent Egyptian state in the early nineteenth century.[137] As I discuss in the remaining chapters, the Ottoman bureaucracy of Egypt became progressively more repressive and violent at the end of the long eighteenth

[136] Rustom, *Egyptian Expedition to Syria*, 15.

[137] For a critical study of Egypt's military conquests and expansion in the early nineteenth century, see: Fred H. Lawson, *The Social Origins of Egyptian Expansionism during the Muhammad ʿAli Period* (New York: Columbia University Press, 1992).

century. Instead of operating in an imperial framework of Ottoman rule that – as we have seen with the twin examples of grain and wood – balanced natural resources between Egypt and the rest of the Empire, this province under both Mehmet ʿAli's rule and that of several other previous Ottoman imperial governors sought to disconnect itself from the whole of the Ottoman Empire at the end of the eighteenth century and the beginning of the nineteenth. In this light, the invasions of Greater Syria by ʿAlī Bey al-Kabīr and Muḥammad Bey Abū al-Dhahab in the 1770s serve as important examples of Egypt's increasingly imperial ambitions over the course of the long eighteenth century.[138] Each effort to centralize and monopolize political power in Egypt at the expense of the Ottoman administration resulted in huge demands being placed on the Egyptian peasantry. Not only were they forcibly conscripted to serve in the Egyptian army; they were also pressed to grow more trees and more food and to irrigate more land.[139] As I explain in the following chapter, Egyptian peasants' labor was thus no longer their own and soon came to be managed by the centralizing provincial bureaucracy.

Egypt's momentary, and ultimately unsuccessful, attempts at colonial invasion and rule were thus in many ways results of processes set into motion much earlier in the eighteenth century. It is to those processes that we now turn. As I address in the coming chapters, transformations in the Ottoman bureaucracy of Egypt's use of peasant and animal labor (Chapter 4), treatment of disease (Chapter 5), and implementation of large public works projects (Chapter 6) all presaged the kind of colonial character the nascent Egyptian state enacted in the Syrian invasion of the 1830s.

[138] On this period in Egypt generally, see: Crecelius, *Roots of Modern Egypt*. And on the Beys' invasions of Greater Syria in particular, see: ibid., 79–91 and 159–68.

[139] On forced conscription in the Egyptian army, see: Fahmy, *All the Pasha's Men*.

4

IN WORKING ORDER

The foregoing chapters sketch a system of natural resource balance, management, and movement across the Ottoman Empire that emphasizes the centrality of grains and wood. This was a massively complex system built around irrigation and coordinated through the extreme localism of Egyptian peasant knowledge and experience as filtered through the administration of an Ottoman imperial system of rule. The motor force that powered the entire system was the caloric energy output of human and animal labor. For the Ottoman bureaucracy of Egypt, labor was the answer to the question of how best to maximize and marshal the cultivation potentials of the Egyptian countryside. As I argue in this chapter, shifts in labor on irrigation works and other construction projects over the course of the long eighteenth century ushered in new conceptions of the Ottoman state, of the Egyptian social body, and of the relationship between the two. The single most important factor affecting this transition in the forms and practices of labor over the period was an increase in the relative size of repair projects to irrigation works and other structures at the beginning of the nineteenth century as compared to the end of the seventeenth. Irrigation works became larger over the course of the long eighteenth century to keep up with increases in the demand for irrigated land and agricultural production necessitated by Egypt's move toward a centralized bureaucracy disconnected from the rest of the Ottoman imperial system.

This chapter first shows how at the beginning of the long eighteenth century repairs of irrigation features in rural Egypt were small and local affairs. Groups of ten to several dozen peasants worked to repair dams and embankments in the immediate vicinity of their villages. The irrigation works fed water directly to these peasants' fields and families, and peasants thus had a vested interest in their proper function. Although the vast majority of these early repair jobs were of a very intimate and local nature, their consequences were clearly imperial. As we saw in

Chapter 1, the proper function of irrigation works even in the remotest areas of rural Egypt was of imperial Ottoman concern, as the food their water grew fed people all over the Empire. Thus, the labor of a very small number of Egyptian peasants and animals on minor dikes or canals in the Egyptian countryside connected them to peoples and locales at great distance from themselves. Their labor was, in other words, part of an Ottoman imperial economy spread across the Middle East, southeastern Europe, and North Africa.

At the end of the eighteenth century and the beginning of the nineteenth, however, as repair projects became ever larger to meet the demands of the growing Egyptian state bureaucracy, the opposite phenomenon occurred. Egyptian peasants were brought from all over rural Egypt to locations at some distance from their home villages to work on large-scale irrigation repair projects that affected only the province of Egypt in specific rather than the Ottoman imperial community as a whole. Thus, perhaps paradoxically, the smaller projects of the earlier period were of larger imperial consequence than the massive projects at the end of the long eighteenth century. The labor of Egyptian peasants at the beginning of the nineteenth century, in other words, did not connect them to populations in Anatolia or Istanbul; rather, their efforts were expended with the goal of improving Egypt's own economy, irrigation network, and agricultural sector as it drove toward greater independent control. Thus, in the second part of this chapter, I show how labor was conceptualized in such larger infrastructural projects at the end of the long eighteenth century. Workers, animals, natural resources, and material goods were enumerated by the thousands in highly regularized and ordered labor charts that undergirded new ideas of Egyptian society and environment.

I argue further that shifts in labor were part of a new more authoritarian imagination of what Egypt was and of how its population could and should be managed and used instrumentally by political power. The precise moment of this reimagination of Egyptian labor is also the point at which – according to the nationalist narrative of Egyptian history – modernity supposedly came to Egypt as it further separated from the Ottoman Empire. This was not mere coincidence, I argue, but rather a constitutive and integral part of the Egyptian state's growing bureaucracy at the end of the eighteenth century and the beginning of the nineteenth. In the same way the increasingly autonomous Egyptian provincial state served to commodify trees into lumber or grains into units of caloric energy – living organisms into lifeless raw materials – it also made peasants into hollow lifeless castings of men, laboring machines to be used to carry out a task. As James C. Scott puts it: "If one could reshape nature to design a more suitable forest, why not reshape society to create a more suitable population?"[1] Indeed, as we will see in this chapter, the organization and enumeration of labor on massive irrigation repair projects at the beginning of the nineteenth century contributed to the crystallization of new conceptions of population and society in Egypt.

These new notions of population were largely based on a bureaucratic logic of enumeration, statistics, charts, and counting that had fully developed by the beginning of the nineteenth century. As we have already seen, this logic was not without its precedents. Ömer Lütfi Barkan, for example, has documented the intense organization and the abstract recording of numbers of workers and their hours, building materials, and so on undertaken by Ottoman authorities during the building of the Süleymaniye Mosque complex in Istanbul from 1550 to 1557.[2] More specifically for our purposes, from the very onset of Ottoman rule in Egypt and throughout the long eighteenth century, various kinds of projects were undertaken in the Egyptian countryside to count and organize lengths, objects, villages, finances, and so on. The most relevant examples of this bureaucratic concern with counting were the various surveys of canals and irrigation works ordered by the Ottoman administration of Egypt during the period of its rule. Clearly, such surveys of canals, dikes, dams, waterwheels, quays, and the like were necessary first steps in organizing the labor needed to carry out the maintenance and repair of these irrigation features.[3] Indeed, in 1539 or 1540 – a few short decades after the Ottoman conquest of Egypt in 1517 – the survey of the province's rural irrigation network known as al-Jusūr al-Sulṭāniyya, discussed in Chapter 1, was ordered to delineate the contours of the rural landscape.[4]

With respect to our present topic of labor, the records of al-Jusūr al-Sulṭāniyya make very clear that repairs to irrigation works were to be organized locally throughout the Egyptian countryside. They were organized according to subprovince and then – in each subprovincial section – by individual village. A typical entry for a village included its location – defined by the roads, villages, and other important landmarks

[1] Scott, *Seeing Like a State*, 92.

[2] Ömer Lütfi Barkan, *Süleymaniye Cami ve İmareti İnşaatı (1550–1557)*, 2 vols. (Ankara: Türk Tarih Kurumu Basımevi, 1972–1979).

[3] On quays, see: DWQ, Maḥkamat al-Manṣūra 16, p. 289 or p. 290, case 599 (17 S 1117/9 Jun. 1705); DWQ, Maḥkamat al-Manṣūra 16, p. 257, case 527 (18 Z 1116/12 Apr. 1705).

[4] DWQ, al-Jusūr al-Sulṭāniyya 784, pp. 182–83, no case no. (13 Ş).

that surrounded it – a list of local village elders and notables, and information related to the irrigation situation of that village. Where is the village? What are its borders? Is it fully irrigated? From where does it get its water? What are the relevant features of the history of irrigation in this village? What irrigation works are presently in need of repair? And, above all, who is responsible for the repairs, and who will carry them out?

Likewise, at the very end of the long eighteenth century from 1805 to 1811, the Ottoman government of Egypt undertook another large-scale surveying project to determine what percentage of land in every village was under cultivation and what amount was *sharāqī*.[5] In both the earlier survey and this later one, imperial surveyors were to walk along the banks of every canal in the countryside to calculate its length, width, and height in an effort to measure and map the entire irrigation network of Egypt. Ottoman imperial canal surveyors were also to determine how much had previously been spent on the repair of each canal and to chart which agricultural areas and villages were irrigated by which canal or waterway. These highly complex and tedious bureaucratic exercises were meant to serve as initial baseline studies of the countryside, which would help in determining which canals needed dredging, cleaning, and general maintenance in the future.

From the middle of the sixteenth century to the early nineteenth century, the Ottoman bureaucracy of Egypt thus took great care in its management of irrigation features to determine the size, length, and location of canals, waterwheels, basins, and the like.[6] And more important

5 This survey was organized by subprovince, and its results are recorded in the following registers. For the subprovince of al-Sharqiyya, see: DWQ, Taḥrīr Aṭyān al-Sharāqī wa al-Riyy 3019 (1220/1805 and 1806). For al-Minūfiyya, see: DWQ, Taḥrīr Aṭyān al-Sharāqī wa al-Riyy 3020 (1220/1805 and 1806) and 3027 (1226/1811 and 1812). For al-Qalyūbiyya, see: DWQ, Taḥrīr Aṭyān al-Sharāqī wa al-Riyy 3021 (1222/1807 and 1808), 3024 (1225/1810 and 1811), and 3025 (1226/1811 and 1812). For al-Baḥayra, see: DWQ, Taḥrīr Aṭyān al-Sharāqī wa al-Riyy 3022 (1222/1807 and 1808). For al-Manṣūra, see: DWQ, Taḥrīr Aṭyān al-Sharāqī wa al-Riyy 3023 (1222/1807 and 1808) and 3028 (1226/1811 and 1812). For al-Gharbiyya, see: DWQ, Taḥrīr Aṭyān al-Sharāqī wa al-Riyy 3026 (1226/1811 and 1812).

6 For example in 1783 or 1784, an order was sent to the court of al-Baḥayra to measure the length of an important canal known as the al-Shūla Canal that ran through the villages of Qarṭasā and Kunayyiset al-Ghayt. When they received the order to measure the canal, officials from the court along with the imperial *khawlī* of al-Baḥayra, a representative of the *multazims* of the area, and other important local personalities set out to begin their work. After a period of thorough group investigation (*uqyisit baṭnan wa ẓahran bil-ʿaṣaba*), the men reported back to the court that the total length of the canal was 26.3 feddan (31.5 kilometers, with each feddan equaling 300 *qaṣaba*) and that the canal extended from its southern-most end at a bridge in an area of Bedouin fields to a series of embankments in the north known as al-Khashabī. DWQ, Maḥkamat al-Baḥayra 13,

for the purposes of this chapter, throughout the eighteenth century, this emphasis on precise measure increasingly came to inform the management of the rural irrigation network and the use and organization of labor on this network. Indeed, as labor in Ottoman Egypt morphed from a quite local affair to one that was highly regulated, regimented, and bureaucratized, enumeration, numbers, and counting became the primary tools for ordering Egyptian peasant laborers.[7]

Forms of Peasant Labor

Both human and animal labor helped shape the physical environment of the eighteenth-century Egyptian countryside and the function of irrigation works in that world.[8] Peasant labor measured fields and worked to separate them from one another; it built dams, bridges, storage tanks,

p. 113 or p. 115, case 234 (n.d.). On Kunayyiset al-Ghayt, see: *QJBM*, pt. 1, 391. On Qarṭasā, see: *QJBM*, pt. 2, 2:290. I have converted lengths taking one *qaṣaba* to be 3.99 meters, which is the conversion given in the established standard text on Islamic measurements: Hinz, *Islamische Masse und Gewichte*, 63. In her discussion of the Maḥmūdiyya Canal, Rivlin takes one *qaṣaba* to equal 3.64 meters. Rivlin, *Agricultural Policy of Muḥammad ʿAlī*, 218. Elsewhere, however, she writes that the *qaṣaba* ranged between 3.75 meters and 3.99 meters. Ibid., 125. Unless otherwise noted, I use 3.99 meters as my conversion for one *qaṣaba*.

7 On these subjects, see the following very useful essay: Ian Hacking, "Biopower and the Avalanche of Printed Numbers," *Humanities in Society* 5 (1982): 279–95.

8 For a useful comparative discussion of labor in the management of water resources in early modern Bursa, see: Süreyya Faroqhi, "Water, Work and Money-Grabbing: Mobilizing Funds and Rural Labour in the Bursa Region around 1600," *AO* 23 (2005–2006): 143–54. Of all irrigation works in the Egyptian countryside, the waterwheel was the one that most often used the strength and stamina of large agricultural animals. Without the vital energy provided by domesticated ungulates, most of Egypt's waterwheels – irrigation works that brought water to canals and fields – could not have functioned. In a case from the court of al-Baḥayra from the year 1792, a man named al-Ḥājj Muṣṭafā Ibn al-Marḥūm al-Ḥājj Darwīsh ʿIzzat Ibn ʿUbayd from the city of al-Damanhūr bought an ox from al-Shāb ʿAlī Ibn Sīdī Aḥmad al-Muzayyin for the price of thirty-five *riyāl* (3,150 *para*) to be used specifically to turn the waterwheel on his land. Unfortunately for al-Ḥājj Muṣṭafā, the ox died the very night he brought it home. DWQ, Maḥkamat al-Baḥayra 21, p. 177, case 343 (24 N 1206/16 May 1792). Thus, as evidenced by other cases like this one and numerous estate inventories from rural Egyptian courts, part of the reason animals like oxen and *jāmūsas* (buffalo cows) were very expensive was their ability to move waterwheels. For more on the relative prices of these and other animals, see the following estate inventories and other court cases: DWQ, Maḥkamat Isnā 6, pp. 1–3, case 1 (23 Ca 1172/23 Jan. 1759); DWQ, Maḥkamat Isnā 6, pp. 73–79, case 131 (12 L 1172/8 Jun. 1759); DWQ, Maḥkamat Isnā 8, pp. 111–12, case 177 (23 Ra 1173/14 Nov. 1759); DWQ, Maḥkamat al-Baḥayra 10, p. 101, case 229 (1 Ra 1190/20 Apr. 1776); DWQ, Maḥkamat al-Baḥayra 25, p. 17, case 30 (26 Z 1211/22 Jun. 1797); DWQ, Maḥkamat al-Baḥayra 26, pp. 28–29, case 52 (28 S 1212/21 Aug. 1797).

and embankments throughout the Egyptian countryside to create an irrigation infrastructure to water fields; it constructed institutions like homes, mosques, and *waqf* complexes in which Egyptians created and enacted the social, cultural, economic, and political structures and practices of their society; and it also cleared roads maintained to connect peoples and goods. Rural labor was thus a vital component of the cycle of irrigation, construction, flood, and food cultivation that structured and defined the lives of Egyptian peasants in the early modern period. Peasants reaped, sowed, built dams, dredged canals, reinforced embankments, and hauled dirt to make the production of food possible. The calories provided by that food were then converted into energy through metabolic processes and were further expended in the performance of the many necessary rural labor functions. Thus, labor built an irrigated rural world that brought water to fields that grew food, which allowed peasants to work, and so on and so forth, in a cyclical process of irrigation, cultivation, consumption, and energy expenditure. Each part of the cycle made the others possible.

Human laborers performed many different tasks in rural Ottoman Egypt. Although multiple kinds of labor were used on various categories of repair and maintenance projects, the men who made up the ranks of the workers were most often *ahālī al-nāḥiya* (the people of the village) or *man yastaʿīnūnuhu bihi* [those who benefit from its (in our case, a particular irrigation feature's) use]. This particular way of specifying laborers directs us to one of the most salient features of human labor in the first half of the eighteenth century – its extremely local and small-scale character. Workers in these cases rarely ever received any monetary or financial compensation for their work. Their incentive to work, and hence "payment," if you like, was the fact that their repairs of irrigation works and other structures directly benefited themselves, their families, and their agricultural lands.[9] Indeed, this was the very reason these men were put to work on repair projects in the first place – their vested interests in the proper function of irrigation features. There were other cases, though, as we will soon see, in which workers were indeed paid in cash or kind for their labor.

Perhaps the most common category of laborer on irrigation projects in Egypt was *al-hufrāʾ* (ditchdiggers).[10] These men cleared excess mud, dirt,

9 For a comparative example of this phenomenon, see: Appadurai, "Wells in Western India."

10 On the involvement of these workers in irrigation projects in Ottoman Iraq, see: Murphey, "Mesopotamian Hydrology and Ottoman Irrigation Projects," 23 and 27.

branches, and leaves that often collected in canals and along embankments. They were also charged with clearing some of the mud and silt that collected along the shallow bottoms of canals, which was then often put toward reinforcing embankments or fertilizing fields. Other kinds of workers were those known as *al-mudamasīn*. As were *al-ḥufrā'*, these workers were also responsible for digging and for making sure dirt was properly used in the reinforcement of embankments. Repair and construction projects moreover also needed bodies to carry all sorts of items: building materials from the market to the work site and dirt and garbage from the work area. These lifters or carriers were most usually referred to as *al-shayyālīn* or *al-ḥammālīn* and could be either men or animals.[11]

It was also quite common for those known as *aṣḥāb al-idrāk* (literally, "possessors of discernment" or those of knowledge and experience), whom we met in Chapter 1, to be used in irrigation

[11] Lifters and carriers are used in many of the cases cited in this chapter. For a case involving men charged with carrying lumber, see: DWQ, Maḥkamat Rashīd 132, pp. 200–1, case 311 (3 N 1137/16 May 1725). See also: DWQ, Maḥkamat al-Baḥayra 5, p. 314, case 389 (10 Ş 1165/22 Jun. 1752); DWQ, Maḥkamat Rashīd 145, p.126, case 101 (30 Z 1151/9 Apr. 1739). In this latter case, several donkeys were hired to remove dirt from the area in which repairs were being done to a *ḥammām*. They cost more to hire for this project than the weigher (*qabbānī*), for instance, but the human workers brought to labor on this construction were collectively more expensive than the donkeys. Because the relative numbers of animals and humans are not given in this case, it is impossible to determine the actual cost of a single donkey as compared to that of an individual human. For evidence of a donkey market in Cairo in the latter half of the seventeenth century, see: Ibrāhīm Ibn Abī Bakr al-Ṣawāliḥī al-ʿUfī al-Ḥanbalī, *Tarājim al-Ṣawāʿiq fī Wāqiʿat al-Ṣanājiq*, ed. ʿAbd al-Raḥīm ʿAbd al-Raḥman ʿAbd al-Raḥīm (Cairo: Institut français d'archéologie orientale, 1986), 54.

Human and animal labor was often conflated in Ottoman Egypt. For example, the repair of two waterwheels (the waterwheel of Bāb al-Naṣr and another known as al-Kitāniyya) in al-Damanhūr in the subprovince al-Baḥayra shows us how both animals and humans came to be conceptualized by the Ottoman administration of Egypt as the same unit of expense – laborer. DWQ, Maḥkamat al-Baḥayra 24, p. 56, case 102 (1 Ra 1209/26 Sep. 1794). This case lists expenses incurred during the five years required for the repair of the two waterwheels from the beginning of 1790 to the end of 1794. The majority of the more than thirty-seven *niṣf faḍḍa* spent on this work went toward the price of the necessary bricks, wood, and lime. Human and animal workers, though, also each received an entry in this expense list: workers and builders were needed to move and arrange materials, and donkeys were used to haul mud to and from the work site. The fact that human and animal laborers were listed in almost the same breath as part of the same analytical category of laborer suggests to us that their work was considered of the same importance and ilk. This bureaucratic conflation of human and animal labor is a point to which I return at the end of this chapter. For a more sustained discussion of animal labor and its role in constituting the high value of animals in the rural Egyptian economy, see: Alan Mikhail, "Animals as Property in Early Modern Ottoman Egypt," *JESHO* 53 (2010): 621–52.

projects.[12] These were likely older men who did not do a great deal of menial labor per se but served a more advisory and directive role in the projects. They understood the specific topography and geography of the place in question and knew what areas needed the most work. Thus, as discussed previously, these men's experience endowed them with a certain amount of local knowledge about the irrigation works of a particular area that made them important sources of local expertise for the Ottoman state. All laborers, whatever their title or role in maintenance and repairs, were to work day and night (*laylan wa nahāran*) until irrigation was fully achieved (*ilā ḥīn tamām al-riyy*).[13]

Thus, in a case about the opening of canals that fed off of the "sea" (*derya*) formed by the waters of the canal of al-Baḥr al-Ṣaghīr, the *kāshif* of al-Manṣūra – in accordance with custom (*muʿtad olan*) – was ordered to acquire men to work on the project from the villages of that area.[14] Likewise, in another case from 1707 about the reinforcement of the embankments of the same canal of al-Baḥr al-Ṣaghīr, we find instructions to extract (*ihrac*) from villages near the canal beasts of burden, peasants, and those with experience in the maintenance of canals to help with the waterway's cleaning and upkeep.[15] As part of established customs of repair, the use of local forms of labor was thought to be the most effective and expedient means of preserving and protecting the canal and other like irrigation works. Employing those who would directly benefit from the repair of certain irrigation works to actually carry out the repairs was the surest means of guaranteeing that repairs were undertaken swiftly and correctly. That the maintenance and repair of irrigation works were

[12] DWQ, Maḥkamat al-Manṣūra 3, p. 285 or p. 282, case 876 (18 N 1066/11 Jul. 1656).

[13] DWQ, Maḥkamat al-Manṣūra 3, p. 285 or p. 282, case 876 (18 N 1066/11 Jul. 1656); DWQ, Maḥkamat al-Manṣūra 3, p. 51, case 168 (5 B 1063/1 Jun. 1653).

[14] DWQ, Maḥkamat al-Manṣūra 2, p. 292 or p. 272, no case no. (1 Ca 1062/10 Apr. 1652).

[15] DWQ, Maḥkamat al-Manṣūra 17, p. 383, no case no. (11 M 1119/14 Apr. 1707). Animals were key actors in the digging and dredging of canals and in the reinforcement of canal embankments. In a case from 1774, for instance, camels, donkeys, and horses were used in the redigging and redredging of a series of canals in the province of al-Daqahliyya that ran to the villages of Minyyat Ṭalkhā and Minyyat Ḥaḍr from al-Baḥr al-Ṣaghīr. DWQ, Maḍābiṭ al-Daqahliyya 20, pp. 110–11, no case no. (7 C 1188/15 Aug. 1774). Camels were also often used to clear wells of debris and mud that hindered their proper function. Al-Damurdāshī, *al-Durra al-Muṣāna*, 131. In another case, a group of buffalo cows was used in the maintenance of a canal's embankments in a village near Sandūb in al-Daqahliyya. DWQ, Maḥkamat al-Manṣūra 3, p. 10, case 31 (19 S 1063/19 Jan. 1653). In this case, the canal in question was a *sulṭānī* canal, and the expenses incurred in its repair were thus requested to be reimbursed to the local peasants who actually cared out the work. The largest expense the villagers reported was that of renting the buffalo cows for the heavy labor needed during the repair work.

the responsibilities of those who lived near them, used them, and relied on them to irrigate their fields was, therefore, a principle underlining the repair of these structures throughout the first half of the long eighteenth century.

Early Modern Measures of the Locality of Labor

The process whereby the local peasant character of irrigation repairs changed into an altogether different system of forced labor; time charts; and the large-scale movement of earth, resources, and people occurred subtly, slowly, and nonlinearly over the course of the long eighteenth century. Whereas in the first half of the period, repair jobs employed perhaps a dozen or two dozen men who worked for a few days to repair a canal that fed water directly to their own fields and families, later in the period, projects undertaken by the centralizing Ottoman bureaucracy of Egypt grew to the point of requiring hundreds and then thousands of peasants.[16] And yet even as this bureaucracy moved toward an ordered and enumerated spatialization of peasant labor, its foundation of "expertise," especially in the early part of the period, remained largely based on extremely local and intimate peasant knowledge of irrigation works and local geographies that were understood best by those rural people who lived near irrigation works.

Thus, early in the long eighteenth century, village heads were required to secure for any particular repair job a labor force consisting of the necessary numbers of men and animals, as determined by precedent and through consultation with local authorities. And, importantly, both kinds of beasts of burden – for that is how the state viewed both men and animals – were usually given some sort of compensation for their work.[17]

[16] Curiously, in many cases where labor would certainly have been required to complete major repair works, labor or expenses related to workers were not listed. See, e.g., the following two cases involving the repair of the same broken embankment: DWQ, Maḥkamat al-Manṣūra 24, p. 154, case 346 (15 M 1136/15 Oct. 1723); DWQ, Maḥkamat al-Manṣūra 24, p. 154, case 347 (15 M 1136/15 Oct. 1723).

[17] We notice a similar conflation of human and animal labor in the case of repair work done to a dam in the village of Shūbar in the subprovince of al-Gharbiyya. The repairs outlined in this case called for both human and animal labor to haul and position straw and dirt in the dam: one hundred men (*rajul*) and sixty-two oxen (*thaur*). Provisions of beans (*fūl*) were made for the human and animal laborers to sustain them as they worked. The casting of the laborers on the pages of this register, the fact that food was not delineated as going only to peasants or only to oxen, and the fact that the two kinds of workers were treated as a single unit of labor suggest to us that in the realm of work on irrigation features in the Egyptian countryside, the Ottoman bureaucracy

A typical example of this kind of labor was the repair of a state (*sulṭānī*) dike in the village of Mīt ʿĀfiyya in the subprovince of al-Gharbiyya.[18] This village's head was required to conscript nine men for the repair of the dam and was also instructed to provide each of them with provisions and shelter for one night during the period of their work. The Ottoman state in this case enlisted a very small amount of local labor to repair a part of the state's rural irrigation infrastructure; nine men from the same village who likely knew one another quite well were given food and shelter for a night while they worked in their own village to repair a dam that trapped water for the people of their community. In a similar case from the village of Birkat al-Sabʿa, also in the province of al-Gharbiyya, we see again that twelve men charged with dredging 1,150 *qaṣaba* (4.6 kilometers) of a state canal were to be provided food and shelter for the several nights they worked.[19]

Whereas the vast majority of repairs to irrigation works in the first part of the long eighteenth century were very similar to the two previous cases involving about a dozen men each, there were also many much larger repair cases requiring the labor of several dozen, a hundred, or a few hundred men. These medium-size irrigation repair projects served the water needs of groups of villages – rather than just one – and usually lasted for several weeks or longer. For example, ninety-six men from more than ten villages served by a major canal known as al-Baḥr al-Bandarānī in the subprovince of al-Gharbiyya were needed to repair the mouth of this waterway.[20] The names of the villages on the canal were given in this case, along with the number of men (from three to twenty) to be secured from each. How were the men chosen? How did the state know how many men were needed for a certain job? What happened if the work took longer than the time allotted for it? What were peasants' conceptions of the nature of the work they undertook? Did they appreciate the opportunity to work and sometimes to earn extra income? Did they conceive of their labor as a part of the state's maintenance administration? Despite the

did not differentiate between human and animal workers. They both belonged to the same bureaucratic category of worker, the result of a process of abstraction that turned both these living things into literal numbers on a worksheet page. As numbers on a page, the Ottoman bureaucracy of Egypt was thus able to enumerate them, to move them around, and to configure them as it deemed most fit. DWQ, al-Jusūr al-Sulṭāniyya 784, p. 129, no case no. (n.d.). On the village of Shūbar, see: *QJBM*, pt. 2, 2:101.

18 DWQ, al-Jusūr al-Sulṭāniyya 784, p. 131, no case no. (n.d.).

19 DWQ, al-Jusūr al-Sulṭāniyya 784, p. 134, no page no. (n.d.).

20 DWQ, al-Jusūr al-Sulṭāniyya 784, p. 18, no page no. (n.d.).

difficulty in answering these and other questions, one thing is clear: the vast repetitive data contained in the many cases similar to this one represent a mapping of the bureaucratic organization of labor in Egypt and of the size and character of the administrative network charged with managing that labor. Moreover, even in cases such as these that document the expansion of the Ottoman bureaucracy of Egypt's labor regime, projects still operated at the level of the collective communities of water described in Chapter 1. These ninety-six men were still working in the framework of their local ecosystem of irrigation in which their labor served their own village and that of their neighbors.

The major conceptual shift in the use and representation of labor in the bureaucratic record of the eighteenth-century Ottoman state in Egypt was its move toward the enumeration of laborers, canal lengths, wages, amounts of building materials, and eventually much more as the primary means of organizing public works projects. Building on earlier models, like the construction of the Süleymaniye Mosque complex and the survey of al-Jusūr al-Sulṭāniyya discussed previously, this administrative and centralizing mentality of counting, listing, and enumeration would not fully develop until the end of the long eighteenth century. There were, however, earlier echoes that prefigured the later processes.

For instance, a case from the late seventeenth century about the cleaning and dredging of a canal in al-Manṣūra known as Baḥr al-Fuḍālī serves in many ways as an example of a transitional kind of case.[21] The canal served as the main source of water and irrigation for eleven villages in the subprovince of al-Daqahliyya.[22] In response to the initiation of this case by the *multazim* of the village of Ṭunāmil, Muḥammad Aghā, the court sent its representatives to inspect the canal along with the engineer of al-Manṣūra, al-Muʿallim Ḥasan al-Bannā.[23] The officials reported back to the court that the canal's length from its beginning at the Nile to its end was eighty *zirāʿ* (sixty-one meters) and that its width was twenty *zirāʿ* (fifteen meters).[24]

[21] DWQ, Maḥkamat al-Manṣūra 7, p. 134, case 340 (7 Za 1091/29 Nov. 1680).

[22] The eleven villages were Dammās, Kafr al-Rūla, Minyyat Gharb, Durra, Tanbūl, Tūḥ, Nūr Ṭīq, al-Sandalāwī, Barhamnus, Shubrahūr, and Ṭunāmil.

[23] On Ṭunāmil, see: *QJBM*, pt. 2, 1:174 and 179. Central to the *multazim*'s assertion of authority was the fact that he had in his possession and presented to the court two *buyuruldus* previously issued by the divan of Cairo related to the repair of the canal. This serves as important evidence of the fact that legal orders sent from Cairo to the subprovinces were not only kept in registers of the court but also either were given to litigants and officials or were copied and then given to them. On this point, see: Peirce, *Morality Tales*, 282–85.

[24] Here I am using the conversion that 1 *zirāʿ* equals 0.758 meters. Ágoston, *Guns for the Sultan*, 247.

Moreover, the men also measured the distance between one of the canal's embankments and a large orchard in Ṭunāmil and found that there was not enough room between the two for people to pass on the narrow canal bank. This impassable section was, however, made passable by the presence of two bridges that spanned the canal on each of the two sides of the orchard. Each bridge was five *zirā*ʿ (3.8 meters) wide, twenty *zirā*ʿ (15.1 meters) long, and ten *zirā*ʿ (7.6 meters) high, and both were in need of repair. According to the engineer's report, this construction would require one hundred thousand mud bricks (*ṭūba*) and a large amount of stone. Work on the canal would last for thirty days, and on each day, forty workers and builders would be required. The men were to be paid the going rate for this kind of work and were to be provided with provisions of food during the period of their labor. All this information was presented to the court, which quickly approved the work and ordered the commencement of the repairs.

Although this case represented a rather large repair project for rural Egypt at the end of the seventeenth century, and although it shared with later projects the specific mention of the kinds and amounts of labor and materials used in the repair, the principal that local labor was to repair local irrigation works that fed water directly to the workers' own fields maintained in this case. The numbers in this repair job are indeed impressive for this earlier period. Forty men were needed to work on each of thirty days – 1,200 laborers in total. The total number of workers used in the project was surely much less because many men likely worked on more than one day. Moreover, the laborers were culled from the eleven villages irrigated by the canal in need of repair, which further suggests the importance of the locality of labor in this project. Unlike previous cases, each of the men in this repair job was given a wage for his work and food and other provisions during the period of his labor.[25] Because

[25] The payment of wages in cash or kind to peasant laborers was another aspect of the Ottoman state's early enumerating and accounting practices vis-à-vis irrigation repair projects in Egypt. In the first part of the long eighteenth century, wages were often paid to laborers on irrigation repair projects, especially as the repair works became more and more complicated. In 1646, for instance, there was a series of repairs carried out on a canal and its embankments in the city of al-Manṣūra. Although the numbers of workers employed in this job were not mentioned in the case, the amir Lāshīn, *kāshif* of the area, swore in court that he had provided each of the workers with a wage and that he had also given them proper food and provisions to ensure that they had all they needed to complete the construction work. This case does not give a breakdown of expenses but only states that the sum of all expenses related to the repair work totaled the significant amount of 18,120 *niṣf fiḍḍa* (or *para*). DWQ, Maḥkamat al-Manṣūra 1, p. 84, case 197 (20 Z 1055/6 Feb. 1646).

the men were from villages near the canal, they could sleep in their own homes at night and be with their families when their day's work was done. Indeed, the arrangement was likely quite welcome by many peasants, as they could make a significant amount of money and receive extra foodstuffs for their families while not being separated from them for an extended period.

Above all, this case serves as an early example of the importance of expertise and measurement in the repair of irrigation works and in the court's management of this work. In Chapter 1, I discussed how the state used local experts – referred to as *ahl al-khibra* or *erbab-ı vukuf* – to inform its repair of Egypt's irrigation network. This case, however, represents a deeper involvement of the Ottoman bureaucracy in the management of irrigation in rural Egypt and a deeper concern by the administration with detail and measure. The dimensions of the canal and its bridges were quoted in court, and numbers of workers and amounts of materials needed for the job were also enumerated in this case. The state's resort to precise measure was an effort to allow the court and the Ottoman administration of which it was an integral part to monitor and control, to some degree, the course of the irrigation works' repairs. As a kind of early dress rehearsal for what would come later, the state's insistence on precise metrics and the role of the subprovincial engineer's expertise in achieving the measurements was an imperial exercise in distancing the authority of local villagers from the repairs. Nevertheless, in cases such as this from the early period, the Ottoman bureaucracy's expertise was again still built on the extremely local – and, if you like, "unofficial" – knowledge of Egyptian peasants, who had been cultivating fields and using irrigation works for many years. As discussed in Chapter 1, here, as well, only by making that knowledge imperial was the state able to harness

Similarly, in a later case from 1701, concerning the repair of a broken dike, workers were also given a wage. Unlike the previous case, though, each individual expense was in fact listed in this case, giving us a sense of how much some of the workers involved in the project were actually paid. With this listing of individual expenses, we thus already see in this early case the beginnings of an enumerating logic in the Ottoman bureaucracy. Those who rode on the backs of animals to transport goods to and from the work site along with those fishermen and hunters who were to provide food for workers were together paid 546 *nisf fiḍḍa*. The only other class of laborer listed here are drummers (*al-ṭabbālīn*), who were given thirty-three *nisf fiḍḍa* and whose job was most likely to keep a cadence so as to regulate and synchronize workers' movements. DWQ, Maḥkamat al-Manṣūra 11, p. 8, case 16 (3 Ra 1113/8 Aug. 1701). For a comparative study of changes to workers' wages in seventeenth-century Foça and Sayda, see: Suraiya Faroqhi, "Long-Term Change and the Ottoman Construction Site: A Study of Builders' Wages and Iron Prices (with Special Reference to Seventeenth-Century Foça and Sayda)," *JTS* 10 (1986): 111–34.

peasant labor more effectively in the maintenance of Egypt's irrigation network.

Both the Ottoman imperialization of local peasant knowledge and experience and the maintenance of the use of local labor to repair local irrigation features serve as key pieces of evidence in explaining why the Ottoman bureaucracy in the early eighteenth century attempted to prevent the use of corvée labor (*al-sukhra*) in the repair of irrigation works. In addition to supplying peasant laborers with provisions, often paying them, limiting their work to local irrigation features, and specifying short periods of work, the Ottoman bureaucracy of Egypt in the early eighteenth century sent many orders to rural Egyptian courts explicitly instructing local officials to avoid the use of corvée labor in the repair of rural irrigation features. One such order from the court of al-Manṣūra from the year 1706 recorded that corvée labor had indeed been used previously during the cleaning of the canal of Baḥr al-Ṣaghīr in a village named Taḥa al-Marj.[26] The imperial decree, however, instructed local officials to forbid any of their own from again employing forced labor in the repair of the canal in this village because it visited oppression (*mazleme*) on the people of that area. This case seems to have fallen on deaf ears, however, as a nearly identical order attempting to outlaw the same practice of corvée was again sent to the court a few years later.[27]

As seen in these cases, the use of corvée in the repair of rural irrigation works was clearly not an unknown practice at the time.[28] Although it is difficult to speculate as to the relative numbers of projects that employed corvée labor and noncorvée labor, it is nevertheless clear that, at the beginning of the eighteenth century, there were more of the latter than the former. Certainly, as the century moved on, and unquestionably at the beginning of the nineteenth century, corvée became more and more common as a labor practice because repair works generally became larger and more complex. As seen in this chapter so far, however, repair works in the early years of the eighteenth century were clearly much smaller and

[26] DWQ, Maḥkamat al-Manṣūra 17, p. 391, no case no. (27 S 1118/9 Jun. 1706). On Taḥa al-Marj, see: *QJBM*, pt. 2, 1:192.

[27] DWQ, Maḥkamat al-Manṣūra 18, p. 252 or p. 253, no case no. (26 M 1121/7 Apr. 1709).

[28] For other examples of the use of corvée in the seventeenth-century countryside, see: Yūsuf Ibn Muḥammad al-Shirbīnī, *Kitāb Hazz al-Quḥūf bi-Sharḥ Qaṣīd Abī Shādūf*, ed. and trans. Humphrey Davies, 2 vols. (Leuven: Peeters, 2005–2007), 2:327–31. For a general discussion of the use of corvée in the seventeenth and eighteenth centuries, see: ʿAbd al-Ḥamīd Sulaymān, "al-Sukhra fī Miṣr fī al-Qarnayn al-Sābiʿ ʿAshar wa al-Thāmin ʿAshar, Dirāsa fī al-Asbāb wa al-Natāʾij," in *al-Rafḍ wa al-Iḥtijāj*, 89–126.

more localized. Indeed, there was a direct correlation between the size of repair projects and the amount of labor (forced or otherwise) employed in the repair jobs. Workers in the early eighteenth century had an incentive to repair irrigation works that fed water to their villages because their labor directly benefited themselves, their families, and their fields. The foregoing cases, however, are important reminders that corvée existed – however frowned upon – at the beginning of the eighteenth century and that it was not simply the invention of a modernizing nineteenth-century state.

In summary, then, the cases discussed in this section involving labor on irrigation works from the end of the seventeenth century and the beginning of the eighteenth show that labor during this period was generally of two kinds. The majority of repair projects were of a very local nature, involving peasants repairing dams and embankments that directly affected the flow of water to their own fields. Such projects were rather small-scale, involving dozens of peasants who were sometimes paid but were more likely only given provisions during the period of their work. Repairs usually lasted a few days, and workers were able to stay with their families as they worked. The returns on these peasants' labor were a functioning irrigation network that would benefit their fields and that would also eventually benefit them financially as their harvests grew. The other less common kind of labor during the period was labor on larger, more complex projects that were often set at a distance from any one village and that generally served a large number of villages. Such repair jobs employed perhaps one to a few hundred men who were more likely to be paid than those employed in the first kind of repair work. In addition, supplies for these repairs were often brought from elsewhere to the work site, and their transport most usually involved animals. Because this kind of maintenance work was carried out on significant irrigation features that had wide impact on a large number of villages, they were key to the overall health of the irrigation system of entire regions of rural Ottoman Egypt.

Masses of Men: An Expanding Order

Toward the middle and latter half of the eighteenth century, labor and the general type and scale of construction projects undertaken in Egypt began to change to meet the demands of the ever-expanding central provincial bureaucracy. Larger and more complicated structures were built that required many more hands (and hooves) and more building materials. Because of the ever-increasing scale of projects, the organization of the labor expended on the repairs became more structured and orderly. It was during the middle decades of the eighteenth century that the Ottoman bureaucracy began to more regularly compile increasingly detailed charts and lists of workers, materials, wages, and prices. Workers soon came to be enumerated as part of a category called individuals or men (*anfār*), a category used in reference to laborers since the sixteenth century but one that became especially important to Ottoman administrative practice in the eighteenth century. Wages were a regular feature of construction projects during this period, and there were set phases of work during which laborers were usually given food and shelter. Repairs in this period lasted months instead of days and employed hundreds or thousands of workers instead of dozens. As I explain in more detail later, this working out of a means of efficiently and effectively organizing workers on irrigation repair projects was the beginning of the Ottoman bureaucracy's conceptualization of population as a political and social problem in Egypt that had to be managed, enumerated, employed, acted upon, and instrumentalized.

A particularly good example of this increasingly larger and more complex kind of repair work in the middle of the eighteenth century was the repair of a *wakāla* in Rashīd in 1747 that formed part of the *waqf* of a man named Ibrāhīm Aghā.[29] The repair of the badly ruined structure required a few hundred workers that were organized and enumerated in a very orderly manner in the registers recording this work.[30] The first features to be repaired in the structure were the vaulted arches of some of the storage facilities located on the south side of the *wakāla*. Part of the south wall of the *wakāla* had also collapsed, so it, too, needed repair. Also in need of reinforcement were the northern and western warehouses of the *wakāla*. The walls, roofs, and long wooden roof supports of some of the storied levels of the *wakāla* were also in want of repair. Similarly, other storage areas, a coffeehouse, and a group of taverns – all of which served the *wakāla* and its patrons – were also in disrepair and were to be fixed. All the repairs were to be completed in a period of eighty-four days.

29 DWQ, Maḥkamat Rashīd 151, pp. 366–69, case 413 (25 Ra 1160/6 Apr. 1747).

30 On the construction and repair of *wakāla*s, see: Nelly Hanna, *Construction Work in Ottoman Cairo (1517–1798)* (Cairo: Institut français d'archéologie orientale, 1984), 46; Hanna, *Making Big Money*, 125–33. On the function of *wakāla*s in Ottoman Egypt generally, see: Raymond, *Artisans et commerçants*, 1:254–60. For the study of a particularly prominent Mamlūk and Ottoman *wakāla*, see: Muḥammad Ḥusām al-Dīn Ismāʿīl ʿAbd al-Fattāḥ and Suhayr Ṣāliḥ, "A Wikāla of Sulṭān Muʾayyid: Wikālat ʾŪda Pasha," *AI* 28 (1994): 71–96.

These many complex and labor-intensive repairs were to be carried out by a large number of workers using a wide variety of materials. Both the men and the materials they employed were carefully counted, organized, and assigned to various sections of the project. Thus, after an introductory paragraph explaining the necessary repairs, setting the length of the period of work, and naming those responsible for overseeing the repair work, this very long case goes on to enumerate in list form (as in an expense sheet) all the materials to be used in the repair work and their prices.

This list includes plaster (*jibs*), tiles (*balaṭ*), lime (*jīr*), nails (*masāmīr*), red brick (*ṭūb aḥmar*), stones (*aḥjār*), the cost of the ships required to bring these items from Cairo to Rashīd, and the cost of the heavy lifters (*shayyālīn*) hired in Cairo both to move the supplies from the market to the boats that would then carry them to Rashīd and to unload them once they reached their destination. Wood was an especially important material in this repair, and there were fourteen different varieties of wood listed as necessary for this work. This supply of lumber required its own group of laborers to serve as heavy lifters to transport and carry it. Thus, preparations to move building materials to Rashīd – even before the repair of the *wakāla* had actually begun in earnest – required a significant amount of intensive labor.

The written form of this case as captured on the pages of the register underlies the bureaucratic logic conceptualizing the workforce needed in the repair job (see Figure 4.1). The case consists of a daily entry for each of the eighty-four days of labor allotted for the construction project. Each of the eighty-four entries is first labeled with the date and the day of the week. Underneath that top row of information, there is a list of the kinds of laborers employed for that day along with the number of each kind of worker used. Underneath each kind of laborer and their number is the total amount spent on that type of laborer for that day. For instance, on Saturday, December 31, 1746, one engineer (*muhandis*), seven masons (*bannāʾ*), sixteen workers (*fāʿil*), one carpenter (*najjār*), three water carriers (*saqqāʾ*), and three other individuals (*anfār*) were employed in the construction work required on this *wakāla*. In addition, each entry records the amount of coffee allotted for that day's work. Coffee and water were the main forms of sustenance provided to the men. The last bit of information in the three rows of each of the daily entries was the total cost of men and materials for that day's work. On the same day mentioned earlier, December 31, 1746, the one engineer cost 17 *niṣf faḍḍa* (*para*); the seven masons, 98 *niṣf faḍḍa*; the sixteen workers,

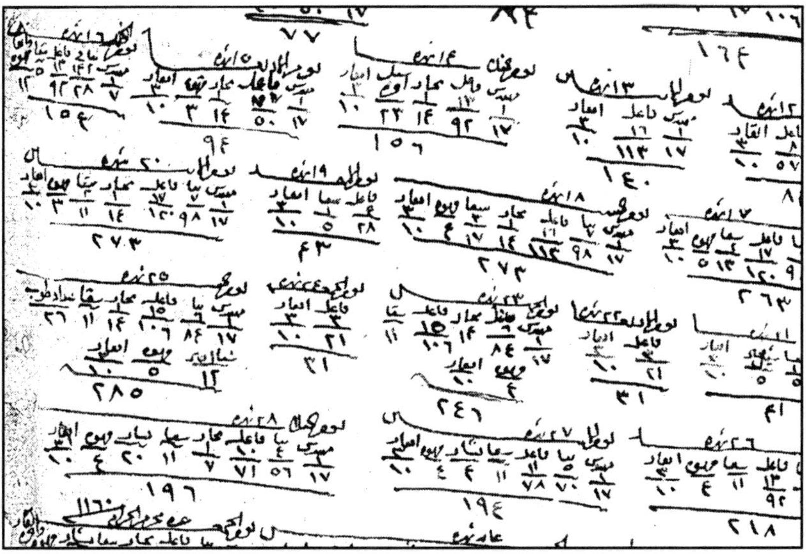

Figure 4.1. Case of the repair of a *wakāla* in Rashīd, 1747. DWQ, Maḥkamat Rashīd 151, p. 367, case 413 (25 Ra 1160/6 Apr. 1747). Used by permission of the Egyptian National Archives.

113 *niṣf faḍḍa*; the carpenter, 14 *niṣf faḍḍa*; the three water carriers, 17 *niṣf faḍḍa*; and the three other individuals, 10 *niṣf faḍḍa*. The coffee for that day cost 4 *niṣf faḍḍa*. The total cost of that day's work was thus 273 *niṣf faḍḍa*. The price of each of these kinds of labor remained fairly consistent throughout the eighty-four-day period of work.

Many, if not most, of the workers employed in the reconstruction were brought to the work site from elsewhere.[31] Those men used to carry materials to and from the boats transporting materials from Cairo came along with the materials – as if themselves cargo – from the city. Those used in the transport of lumber likely also came to Rashīd with their cargo. For the rest of the workers, we do not have an explicit statement of their origins, but the majority of them were most likely acquired from villages near Rashīd. Likewise, although no explicit mention is made of lodgings for the workers, temporary accommodations were probably constructed. Or, alternatively, perhaps the workers slept in their homes and were required to report for work at a certain hour every morning. The

[31] This was also the case in the construction of the Süleymaniye complex in the middle of the sixteenth century. Barkan, *Süleymaniye Cami.*

total cost of labor on this project was 16,278 *nisf fadda*, which represented nearly 29 percent of the total 56,290 *nisf fadda* associated with the repairs.

As in other cases I discuss later, one of the most striking aspects of this case is its casting of peasant labor on the pages of this court register from Rashīd. Workers were very carefully counted, organized, and assigned to work on various days. Their provisions were allotted in precise quantities, and the costs of all the expenses were dutifully calculated. This case and others like it thus represented the beginnings of a new conceptualization of labor and of bureaucracy in the middle of the eighteenth century. Laborers were plugged into an emerging bureaucratic structure in which they existed as parts of categories of workers – groups whose actions were now scheduled, arranged, and organized by the type of administrative logic summarized in this case.

Numerous other cases from the courts of rural Ottoman Egypt attest to the extent to which this new kind of bureaucratic organization of labor was put toward the management of larger and larger numbers of workers employed in ever more complex and expensive projects over the course of the middle of the eighteenth century. As laborers were more frequently seized by a bureaucratic mentality of charts and metrics that cast them as an abstract population of men to be managed by the state, they were in this period increasingly listed as numbers on a page to be moved around, counted, and organized in the most efficient way possible. Thus, in a case similar to the previous one, an individual of presumably Greek extraction named al-Khawāja Yūrghakī spent 14,314 *nisf fidda* (or *para*) of his own money to fix the north side of another *wakāla* in Rashīd.[32] The layout of this case on the pages of the court register is similar to that of the previous case, in that both contained a very detailed and precise accounting of the kinds and amounts of labor and materials used in the repair of a *wakāla*.

After an opening paragraph explaining the situation of the *wakāla* and introducing the interested parties, we read of the labor used during work on this building project. The repair of the *wakāla* was carried out over a

[32] DWQ, Maḥkamat Rashīd 142, p. 64, case 58 (14 Za 1149/16 Mar. 1737). The fact that a "foreigner" (*khawāja*) spent a large sum of money to repair this *wakāla* in Rashīd points to the importance of this institution as a site of capital accumulation in which vital foodstuffs were stored, traded, and transferred. On the foreign communities of Ottoman Alexandria, see: Reimer, "Ottoman Alexandria." On the influence of various Syrian communities in Ottoman Egypt, see: ʿAbd Allāh Muḥammad ʿAzabāwī, "al-Shawām fī Miṣr fī al-Qarn al-Thāmin ʿAshar," *EHR* 28–29 (1981–1982): 269–329. On connections between Rashīd's sister Mediterranean port city Damietta and French commerce, see: Crecelius and ʿAbd al-ʿAziz Badr, "French Ships between Damiette and Ottoman Ports."

period of sixty-five days divided into three separate stages: one of six days, one of twenty-five days, and then one of thirty-four days. In each period, a different group of workers, masons, water carriers, dirt movers, and others were hired at different wage levels. In addition, tiles, red brick, plaster, lime, lumber, and ash were also enumerated as necessary for the construction work. The total cost of the materials and of the labor required was 7,486 *niṣf fiḍḍa*. As before, coffee and water were again provided to the workers, at a total cost of 3,981 *niṣf fiḍḍa*. And al-Khawāja Yūrghakī spent an additional 2,847 *niṣf fiḍḍa* on the drainage (*nazḥ*) of water from some of the rooms and other areas of the *wakāla*.

It was, of course, not just *wakālas* that fell under this intense bureaucratic scrutiny of organization, counting, and ordering. In another case, for example, workers undertook repairs to the bath and mosque of a certain *waqf* and also repainted the walls of each.[33] The total given to the workers, masons, carpenters, and water carriers who worked on the project was 5,980 *niṣf fiḍḍa*. Plumbers, a specialist in working with marble, a weigher who measured lead, a donkey to remove dirt from the work area, a porter, lifters to carry lime and plaster, a group of sailors who moved sand and mud to and from the work site, and other workers all contributed to the rather complex repair project.[34] Likewise,

33 DWQ, Maḥkamat Rashīd 145, p. 126, case 101 (30 Z 1151/9 Apr. 1739).

34 The Ottoman bureaucracy of Egypt often used the expert knowledge of craftsmen like masons and plumbers in various kinds of repair work. For example, in 1743, a group of three specialists in water-pump usage (*tulumbacılar*) were sent to Egypt from Istanbul to work on the building and repair of dams, wells, and canals in several locations throughout the province. BOA, MM, 6:77 (Evasit C 1156/2-11 Aug. 1743). The word *tulumbacılar* would come to be used later to refer to those who worked to put out fires, which indicates that the operative referent here was to those who were expert in elevating water. Sertoğlu, *Osmanlı Tarih Lûgatı*, 345–46. The exact nature of their work was not specified in this case, but because most well water in rural Egypt was earmarked for human consumption, the men were likely sent to make available larger supplies of drinking water for rural populations or to move water from a lower canal to a higher one.

Although the workers whose wages are the subject of this imperial decree were not themselves Egyptian peasant laborers, this case clearly shows us that the organization of labor and its financial compensation were issues of great concern for the Ottoman administration of Egypt, no matter who was involved. Indeed, part of the justification for the vast system of enumeration and organization outlined in the cases discussed in this chapter was the need to manage the financial expenditures of the state with more responsibility, care, and control. The three men in the previous case were to be paid their daily wages starting from the first day they worked from monies under the control of the Bina Emîni of Egypt. Moreover, because they were to travel to different parts of Egypt during their residence in the province, the men were also to be given money to cover their toll expenses (*harc rahları*).

carpenters, masons, and other unspecified workers were employed for twenty-six days to repair a mosque and *maqam* in a *waqf* in the city of

The three men in this case were sent from Istanbul to Egypt to apply very technical and specific knowledge in the service of maintaining irrigation works and attending to other local concerns. Although the precise nature of their work was not specified in this case, they surely interacted with local Egyptian peasant populations in the various villages they visited in rural Egypt. Indeed, we see in this case the very opposite phenomenon of the one discussed in Chapter 1. Instead of local peasant knowledge and experience affecting the imperial management of irrigation works in rural Egypt, in this case it was the imperial expertise of men sent from the Ottoman capital that was put toward repairing Egypt's irrigation network. Although not stated in this case, it would be useful to know something of the interaction between the imperial functionaries and local Egyptian men of knowledge (*erbab-ı vukuf*). How exactly did the imperial officials interact with local "experts"? Did some sort of animosity develop between the "outsiders" and those accustomed to being the authorities in matters of local irrigation practice? In short, the case of these three technicians sent from Istanbul to Egypt shows us how the Empire sought to manage the province's rural irrigation network and how it organized the compensation of those who worked on it. Although the men were not part of the masses of Egyptian peasant laborers brought to work on the irrigation system throughout the long eighteenth century, they were part of the Ottoman bureaucratic conceptualization of how labor on irrigation works in Egypt was to be organized.

In a similar case, from the early spring of 1802, we learn of how a different class of imperial functionaries was compensated for its work and how it was generally treated by the Ottoman administration of Egypt. BOA, Cevdet Sıhhiye, 864 (3 Za 1216/8 Mar. 1802). This case concerns the payment of wages to doctors employed by the state to treat soldiers and others during the wars that followed the French departure from Egypt in 1801. More specifically, the case orders that the medical workers immediately be paid the amounts they were owed from the state's funds, as their compensation was long delayed. Table 4.1 outlines the wages of each doctor employed by the state.

Table 4.1. *Medical Workers Employed by the Ottoman Administration of Egypt, 1802*

Kind of Medical Worker	Wage (*Guruş*)
Kehhal Başı Effendi (a senior eye doctor with training in the use of antimony or *kühl*)	500
Kehhal Sani Effendi (a secondary rank of the above)	80
Tophâne'ye Memur Cerrah (a surgeon of the arsenal)	100
Tımar iden Hekim ve Cerrah (attendant doctor and surgeon)	67.5
Çıkıkçı (a bonesetter)	40
Total	787.5

These wages were to be paid to the doctors, officials of the royal navy, and others from the funds of the Imperial Treasury. To release the funds, a firman was issued outlining the wages and the work to be done. This case was, thus, a request to release funds and included the proper imperial signatures to authorize the payments.

al-Damanhūr using wood, brick, and a mixture of straw and mud.[35] And as we have already seen, there are many records of repairs to homes that surface in the courts of Ottoman Egypt. For example, numerous carpenters and masons were hired to carry out repairs to a home in Rashīd in 1720 using mud, brick, plaster, and wood.[36] I could very easily go on citing examples of large, complex, expensive, and labor-intensive projects undertaken during the period.[37]

One final case about a series of repairs to a *wakāla* in Rashīd in 1720 represents a further development of the bureaucratic logic of the Ottoman state vis-à-vis peasant laborers on large-scale construction

This case is one of the few in the archival record of Ottoman Egypt that deals with matters of medicine and public health, and yet even as it does this, it relates little about the actual practice of medicine in Ottoman Egypt. It does, however, suggest the relative values placed on different kinds of medical work and knowledge. As the wages outlined in this case show, the *kehhal* was by far the most handsomely compensated medical worker of the group. The salaries of the two *kehhal*s in this case make up more than 73 percent of the wages allocated for the five medical workers. Diseases of the eye – mostly notably trachoma – were quite common in Egypt throughout its history, given that the parasites that caused many such diseases lived in and were contracted through water. Perhaps Ottoman armies stationed in Egypt during this period were hit particularly hard by an outbreak of one of these diseases – a reasonable assumption given the high probability that soldiers shared a common source of water or relied on the Nile for their drinking supplies. As such, eye doctors would have been extremely busy treating soldiers and, thus, deserved the high wages specified here.

35 DWQ, Maḥkamat al-Baḥayra 30, p. 18, case 23 (Evail L 1219/2–11 Jan. 1805); DWQ, Maḥkamat al-Baḥayra 30, p. 18, case 24 (Evail L 1219/2–11 Jan. 1805). These two cases are individually numbered in the court register; however, this is a mistake. The second (case 24) can be read only as a continuation of the first (case 23), and the first makes no sense without the second. Together, they constitute one complete case and should be read as such.

36 DWQ, Maḥkamat Rashīd 124, p. 254, case 354 (26 Ra 1132/5 Feb. 1720).

37 In Rashīd in 1720, for example, during the thirteen days required for the repair of the roofs of a *waqf* complex, its bath, and waterwheel, as well as the repainting of the *waqf*'s walls, 220 workers were used at a total price of 1,885 *niṣf fiḍḍa*. This sum represented more than 25 percent of the total cost of the repair project. DWQ, Maḥkamat Rashīd 125, p. 179, case 300 (1 M 1133/2 Nov. 1720). In 1727, 5,967 *riyāl* (537,030 *para*), more than 20 percent of the total of 29,774 *riyāl* (2,679,660 *para*) spent on the repair of a *wakāla* in Rashīd, was given as compensation to masons, workers, and water carriers used in the project, which lasted for forty days between September 7 and October 15, 1727. DWQ, Maḥkamat Rashīd 134, p. 167, case 204 (30 S 1140/16 Oct. 1727). In 1746, repair work was done on the long wooden roof supports of the small prayer room (*zāwiya*) of a *wakāla* in Rashīd known as the *wakāla* of Muḥammad Bāshā. The work lasted for twelve days and required more than eighty masons, carpenters, and other unspecified workers. A blacksmith was also hired to reshape old metalwork in the *wakāla*. The cost of this labor was 1,026 *niṣf fiḍḍa* of a total of 5,821 *niṣf fiḍḍa* needed for the entire construction project. DWQ, Maḥkamat Rashīd 151, pp. 38–39, case 49 (28 Z 1158/20 Jan. 1746).

projects in the middle of the eighteenth century.[38] The number of workers in such cases grew so large that individuals completely disappeared. The state was concerned first and foremost with the overall cost of this labor project. Although this case, like others, lists the materials used throughout the repair job, and although it includes a very organized chart (clearer than most) with details about each day of work, it gives us no information about either the numbers or the kinds of workers used in this project.[39] Indeed, all we know about the work done in this case is the total amount spent on labor and materials for each day of the project. This case represents, then, the most basic expression of the interests of a state attempting to manage labor – cost. Details faded away into the dust of the *wakāla* work site leaving only that which was most important to the state – the distillation of an interest in the bottom line of how much was spent on each day of labor. This represents an even further step of abstraction beyond the enumeration of peasant laborers. Whereas in other cases workers were cast as numbers on a page, in this case, there were no workers at all. The costs of their labor were simply lumped together with the costs of brick and lime as entries on an expense sheet.

By collapsing humans, animals, natural resources, and material objects into lists of numbers, the Ottoman bureaucratic mentality of organization achieved the abstraction of actual living things into administrative categories and statistical figures. This emergent conceptualization of peasant labor over the course of the eighteenth century created a nameless collective category of interchangeable workers to be put toward the reconstruction and maintenance of irrigation works in rural Egypt. Human and animal workers who labored together on irrigation repair projects were thus entered into a regime of almost actuarial management that organized them into a mass of laborers. The seizure of these living beings by a bureaucratic mentality of charts and metrics that enumerated them by the thousands made them into a literal population of workers whose labor was meant to provide the necessary means to sustain populations throughout the Ottoman Empire.[40] This abstraction of labor from the living human, the living animal, and the living tree to the hollow casting of a number on the page of an administrative register is thus what I mean by an Ottoman attempt to deal with population as a political

38 DWQ, Maḥkamat Rashīd 125, pp. 92–93, case 159 (20 L 1132/25 Aug. 1720).

39 For a nearly identical case also involving repairs to a *wakāla*, see: DWQ, Maḥkamat Rashīd 123, pp. 97–98, case 170 (28 Z 1131/11 Nov. 1719).

40 On these points, see: Hacking, "Biopower and Printed Numbers"; William Coleman, *Death Is a Social Disease: Public Health and Political Economy in Early Industrial France* (Madison: University of Wisconsin Press, 1982), 124–48.

problem. How best was the Empire to sustain a large population over a wide expanse of territory that required the production of enormous quantities of food?

Thus, it was no mere coincidence that the largest and most detailed labor projects in the period concerned the maintenance of Egypt's irrigation infrastructure and the repair of *wakālas*. Egypt's irrigation network was, of course, the driving force behind the province's production of food that fed not only Egypt but also vast areas elsewhere in the Ottoman Empire, including Istanbul, Mecca and Medina, and other locales. And the *wakāla* was the most crucial institution for the movement of this food, because it served as a kind of crossroads where peasants, merchants, and state officials from various areas of Egypt and the Empire came to store, buy, and sell grains and other foodstuffs. Economic and political change in Egypt was thus always accompanied by changes in both the province's food supplies and the irrigation system that sustained those supplies. To this point, the enormous amount of bureaucratic energy and managerial acumen put toward organizing the massive expenditures of labor and materials needed to fix institutions like *wakālas* and to maintain Egypt's irrigation network expressed a concern for the economic well-being of the Empire as a whole and, more important, for the sustenance of its populations. The detailed accounts of labor seen here were therefore integral to a system that privileged the general over the specific, the population as a whole over the individual, the Empire over Egypt. Food production in Egypt and elsewhere served large swaths of the Ottoman population all over the Empire, and labor was the crucial caloric motor force constantly working to keep the system operational.

Listing individuals as was done in the labor charts discussed so far in this chapter was not meant to single out any one individual as an object of power but, rather, to highlight how individuals were of little concern from the perspective of the Ottoman state. Laborers could always be found and were interchangeable and erasable numbers on an accounting sheet. Indeed, the countryside, throughout most of Egyptian history (and even until today), has been seen as an endless supply of peasant laborers. Whether a project required one, seventeen, or ninety-eight heavy lifters was of no concern to the state.[41] From the perspective of the Ottoman

[41] This was a kind of power that Michel Foucault describes as "power that is not individualizing but, if you like, massifying, that is directed not at man-as-body but at man-as-species." Foucault, *"Society Must Be Defended": Lectures at the Collège de France, 1975–76*, ed. Mauro Bertani and Alessandro Fontana, trans. David Macey (New York: Picador, 2003), 243. Foucault's March 17, 1976, lecture to the Collège de France was partly concerned with his development of the concept of biopower, which would be a key feature of his thought

state, it was thus the maintenance of the imperial population, of the human species, if you will, not the individual laborer or peasant that was of the utmost concern. The expenditure of labor in Egypt – and eventually of human lives, as we will see in the case of the repair of the Maḥmūdiyya Canal in Chapter 6 – was of ancillary importance to guaranteeing the timely and efficient maintenance of the institutions that made possible a steady supply of grains to the Empire's population.

Labors of Life and Death

By the start of the nineteenth century, this biopolitical logic of power had fully crystallized in Egypt in the management and use of labor on irrigation repair projects meant to ensure the reliable flow of grains from the province to the rest of the Empire. Whereas at the beginning of the long eighteenth century, repair work on local dams or embankments employed a few or a dozen peasants laboring near their home village for several days at a time, by the beginning of the nineteenth century, the scale of repair projects had vastly increased, demanding the use of thousands or tens of thousands of peasants. Labor was no longer local, and workers were generally not paid for their labor. With the increase in scale demanded by a centralizing Egyptian bureaucracy came a proportional increase in the hardship and suffering experienced by laborers during the period of their work. The culmination of this march toward ever-expanding and deadly public works projects was the construction of the Maḥmūdiyya Canal. Before the Maḥmūdiyya, though, there were several other large-scale irrigation projects at the start of the nineteenth century that prefigured what was to come, that were in many ways dress rehearsals for the Maḥmūdiyya Canal project. Those projects were crucial steps in the transformation of the organization of Egyptian labor from the intimate locality that so characterized it at the end of the seventeenth century to the violence that overwhelmed it at the beginning of the nineteenth century.

One of the most important of these projects was the repair of the canal of Banī Kalb in the southern subprovince of Manfalūṭ in

over the course of the late 1970s. Foucault indeed devoted subsequent years' lectures at the Collège de France to the topics of biopolitics, population, and related concepts. For these lectures, see: Foucault, *Security, Territory, Population: Lectures at the Collège de France, 1977–78*, ed. Michel Senellart, trans. Graham Burchell (New York: Palgrave Macmillan, 2007); Foucault, *Naissance de la biopolitique: Cours au Collège de France (1978–1979)*, ed. Michel Senellart (Paris: Seuil/Gallimard, 2004). On biopower, see also: Foucault, *The History of Sexuality, Volume 1: An Introduction*, trans. Robert Hurley (New York: Vintage Books, 1978), 140–45; Paul Rabinow, *French DNA: Trouble in Purgatory* (Chicago: University of Chicago Press, 1999), 13–17.

1808.[42] Work on the canal lasted for seventy-nine days (more than two and a half months) from Thursday, May 5, 1808, to Friday, July 21, 1808, and required the labor of 33,412 men. On any given day, between 260 and 560 men were put to work; the average number of workers on each day of this seventy-nine-day period was 424 men. The sheer enormity of these numbers already suggests that this repair work was clearly of a very different order than those before it. Not only did the numbers dwarf the smaller projects of the early eighteenth century; but they were also much larger than those repairs undertaken on canals and *wakālas* in the middle of the eighteenth century. A crucial aspect in understanding this case is that the massive numbers of workers here were very precisely organized, measured, and enumerated. Every individual peasant laborer was counted to make up the large collective numbers used each day. Moreover, in contrast to many of the cases discussed previously in this chapter, the 33,412 laborers were not paid for their work. Indeed, given the large number of workers involved, it is not surprising that the state would not want to pay each man. They were, however, provided with barley and grain to sustain them as they toiled.

Pointing to the intensity of this repair job, there were no breaks during the seventy-nine days of work on the project. This stands in stark contrast to those similarly long construction projects on *wakālas* earlier in the eighteenth century during which time work customarily stopped on Fridays.[43] The location and timing of this labor is also noteworthy. The seventy-nine days required for the work were spread over the months of May, June, and July in Manfalūṭ in the south of Egypt, where temperatures in the summer regularly surpass one hundred degrees Fahrenheit (thirty-eight degrees Celsius).[44] Taking place in one of the hottest locations in Egypt during the hottest season of the year, work on the project was no doubt grueling, and although there is no specific mention in this case of any worker deaths or injuries, we can assume with near certainty (on the basis of similar cases) that some of the more than thirty-three thousand men in this case sustained injuries or died during the work.[45] Likewise, this case gives us no information as to how all the workers were

[42] DWQ, Maḥkamat Manfalūṭ 3, pp. 264–65, case 557 (24 Ş 1223/15 Oct. 1808). On Banī Kalb, see: *QJBM*, pt. 2, 4:77.

[43] See, e.g.: DWQ, Maḥkamat Rashīd 125, pp. 92–93, case 159 (20 L 1132/25 Aug. 1720).

[44] Said, *Geology of Egypt*, 8.

[45] Some cases of repairs to the irrigation network of Manfalūṭ made specific reference to the fact that the repairs should be carried out in winter when temperatures were cooler and demands for water not as high as during summer. See, e.g.: DWQ, Maḥkamat Manfalūṭ 2, p. 183, case 619 (16 Ca 1179/31 Oct. 1765).

brought to the canal. Some surely came without resistance, but certainly others did not come easily and had to be brought by force to the work site. In other words, the laborers in this case clearly experienced hardships during the period of their work.

As in earlier cases concerning repairs of *wakālas*, the bureaucratic positioning and casting of workers in this case took the form of a chart enumerating the daily amount of labor used in the repair (see Figure 4.2).

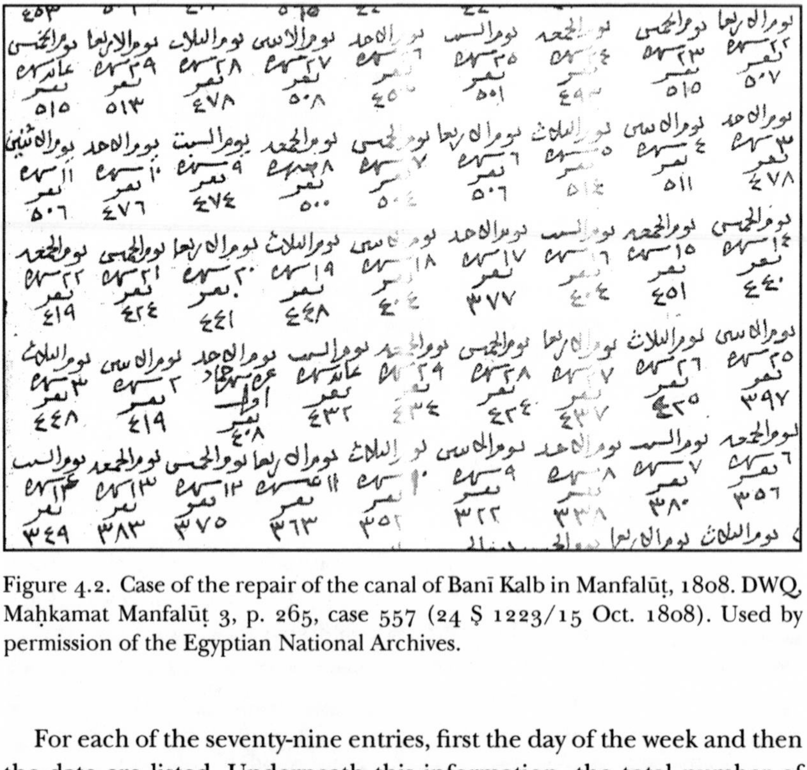

Figure 4.2. Case of the repair of the canal of Banī Kalb in Manfalūṭ, 1808. DWQ, Maḥkamat Manfalūṭ 3, p. 265, case 557 (24 Ş 1223/15 Oct. 1808). Used by permission of the Egyptian National Archives.

For each of the seventy-nine entries, first the day of the week and then the date are listed. Underneath this information, the total number of workers for that day is specified. There is no other information given. The 33,412 men were not further broken down into classes of workers as we saw earlier. All were simply referred to as *nafar* (an individual man). This mass of humanity that toiled, sweat, and was injured during the project became an empty set of numbers on a page – large numbers, to say the least, but numbers nonetheless.

Furthermore, this very matter-of-fact representation of workers used in the repair project suggests two things. First, the men had no identity other than being one in a group of individual men (*anfār*).[46] We are given no specific information about the origins or lives of the many individuals who came to work on this project. Where were their home villages? How were they brought to work on the project? What did they do after finishing a day's work? How and where did they live while working? As literal numbers on a page, the workers were first stripped of their subjective identity and then recast as parts of a different category – that of "laborer." As a bureaucratic abstraction, this grouping of peasants became a part of the state's administrative logic and order – objects (toy blocks, if you like) to be moved around, stacked in different formations, and arranged to optimize productivity. The numbers representing peasants were not then living things but rather hollow castings of peasants with no subjectivity or stake in their own fate. This abstraction from people to numbers achieved the move from reality to the theoretical possibilities of what workers could do. The irony and tragedy of the situation was the fact that these lifeless peasant forms were the very entities that provided and sustained the lives of others across Egypt and the Ottoman Empire. The commodification and instrumentalization of peasant life embodied in the bureaucratic abstraction of numbers of workers on a page thus allowed for the creation of human laborers who cultivated life-sustaining food and who at the very same time were not considered to have valuable lives of their own.[47]

This process of turning workers into numbers is part and parcel of the political technology James C. Scott terms *legibility*. And, as in Scott's discussion, the Egyptian case also involved great amounts of force, social

[46] The word *anfār* is one with a curious history. From at least as early as the sixteenth century to, as we see here, the early nineteenth century, it was used to refer to groups of male workers brought to work as faceless units of labor on irrigation repair projects and other construction ventures. Subsequently, it would be used to refer to the lowest orders of soldiers in the Egyptian army. Because of this military meaning and its similarity to the use of the word subaltern to refer to similar classes in Western armies, Egyptian historians have used the word *anfār* in the Arabic translation for the historiographical movement known as subaltern studies. Thus, we see that the move from worker to solider to subaltern is a very fluid one in Arabic. For a discussion of some of the meanings of the word *anfār* and of the choice to use *dirāsāt al-anfār* rather than *dirāsāt al-tābiʿ* as the Arabic translation of subaltern studies, see: Khālid Fahmī, *al-Jasad wa al-Ḥadātha: al-Ṭibb wa al-Qānūn fī Miṣr al-Ḥadītha*, trans. Sharīf Yūnis (Cairo: Dār al-Kutub wa al-Wathā'iq al-Qawmiyya, 2004), 33n10; Ālan Mīkhā'īl, "Tārīkh Dirāsāt al-Tābiʿ wa Naẓariyyatayn ʿan al-Sulṭa," in *Thaqāfat al-Nukhba wa Thaqāfat al-ʿĀmma fī Miṣr fī al-ʿAṣr al-ʿUthmānī*, ed. Nāṣir Aḥmad Ibrāhīm (Cairo: Markaz al-Buḥūth wa al-Dirāsāt al-Ijtimāʿiyya, 2008), 349–60.

[47] I revisit this issue in the final chapter with my discussion of the reconstruction of the Maḥmūdiyya Canal.

rupture, and violence. In his words, "The economic plan, survey map, record of ownership, forest management plan, classification of ethnicity, passbook, arrest record, and map of political boundaries acquire their force from the fact that these synoptic data are the points of departure for reality as state officials apprehend and shape it. . . . Where there is no effective way to assert another reality, fictitious facts-on-paper can often be made eventually to prevail on the ground, because it is on behalf of such pieces of paper that police and army are deployed."[48]

We can go a step further here. The chart used to position and cast Egyptian peasants on the pages of the registers of the court of Manfalūṭ evokes the administrative presentation of the feeding of humans and animals during repair work. Because clearly both humans and animals needed sustenance and energy while they worked, from the state's point of view, as stated previously, animals and humans were thus two kinds of living laborer to be fed, counted, organized, and manipulated as roughly commensurate numbers on a page. Oxen were best suited for certain kinds of work, whereas humans excelled at others. The Ottoman bureaucracy of Egypt thus had to match the correct kind of life and labor to the given project. Moreover, the food provided for both men and animals during their period of labor reminds us of the ultimate goal of the construction projects themselves – the growth of food to sustain life and income throughout the Ottoman Empire. To produce food, Egypt's irrigation network had to be in working order, and to achieve necessary levels of productivity, massive amounts of laborers (both human and nonhuman) had to be fed while they repaired dams, canals, embankments, and *wakālas*.

As further evidence of the centrality of food to the Ottoman conceptualization of population in Egypt, this case about repairs in Manfalūṭ also outlines how provisions of grain were given to villages along the length of the canal for a period of fifty-two days after the completion of the repair work (from August 13 to October 3, 1808). Though partly advance payment for the protection of the newly repaired canal, the grains were also given as compensation to the villages for the losses they incurred as a result of the canal's repair. The reason for giving grains to the villages was the same as the logic behind giving food to workers: the maintenance of a system of agricultural cultivation in Egypt that relied on the proper function of both peasant labor and the irrigation system. A village's complete loss of a summer's worth of grain because of repairs being carried out on a canal that fed water to its fields would mean a

48 Scott, *Seeing Like a State*, 83.

weak planting season in the fall and a weak harvest the following year. This interruption in planting and harvesting would result both in losses to the overall agricultural production of Egypt for that year and possibly widespread discontent among a large group of peasants. In the calculus of the Ottoman bureaucracy, therefore, staving off those possible outcomes was well worth the comparatively small cost of providing grains to the villages.

The Ottoman bureaucratic mentality of charts and metrics that enumerated workers in Manfalūṭ in 1808 by the thousands – that transformed them into a literal population of laborers acting to provide the necessary means to sustain other populations throughout the Ottoman Empire – was an attempt to deal with population as a political and social problem. How was the Ottoman Empire best to harness a particular environment and its natural resources to sustain a population that required large quantities of food? More specifically, how was the growing provincial administration of Egypt to use its laboring population in its efforts to pull away from the central Ottoman administration in Istanbul? Shifts in the organization of labor over the course of the eighteenth century that culminated in projects like the one in Manfalūṭ in 1808 were thus really about the emergence of population as a unit of sultanic power in Ottoman Egypt to be used, cultivated, enumerated, organized, and protected. Massive irrigation repair projects like the one in Manfalūṭ were thus part and parcel of the working out and formation of this idea of population in Egypt and the wider Ottoman world. Simultaneously managing large numbers of people, huge amounts of food traveling across vast distances, and thousands of laborers working for long periods of time was an endeavor that derived from and, at the same time, constituted ideas of how the Ottoman administration of Egypt was to rule the population both of that province and of other areas in the Empire.

The contributions of labor to the constitution and construction of this social body in Egypt at the end of the eighteenth century and beginning of the nineteenth was thus in the realm of social statistics and the actuarial. The detailed observation, enumeration, and documentation of more than thirty-three thousand male workers in Manfalūṭ in 1808 were enormously complicated bureaucratic procedures that required a new imagination of society and of the state's role in using and managing it.[49] Enumeration, as Ian Hacking observes, "demands *kinds* of things

49 This was an example, then, of "the power of arithmetical and mathematical techniques to render the political and social world more intelligible, and therefore more open to

or people to count. Counting is hungry for categories."[50] The often-violent apparatuses born of this new bureaucratic hunger for counting and categories were formed largely around the management of labor on irrigation repair projects and other construction works in rural Egypt. Enumeration defined a population in Egypt as a statement of the human potentials available in a given ecosystem. Those notions of an Egyptian social and environmental body and of the imperial state's role in counting its pieces and managing its whole would soon play out in other social realms besides labor – the management of disease, the organization of armies, welfare regimes, education, the law, and so forth. Indeed, most of the modern institutions upheld as formative of the Egyptian nation in the nineteenth century – the army, the public works administration, the census bureau, the medical establishment, and so on – relied on the strict management of the Egyptian social body through modes of counting, organizing, and general care developed much earlier.[51]

Having outlined how shifts in labor over the course of the long eighteenth century created the mechanisms necessary for the observation and organization of the Egyptian social body, I now turn to the definition of the borders of this social body and to the definition of this society as distinct from the natural world. To do this, I focus in the next chapter on the history of plague in Ottoman Egypt. During and before the long eighteenth century, plague was considered part and parcel of the Egyptian environment. It functioned as a regular environmental phenomenon like drought or flood and was constitutive of and integrated into society and social notions of the environment through various practices and institutions. Toward the end of the eighteenth century and at the beginning of the nineteenth, however, plague was reconceptualized as something foreign and external to the Egyptian social and environmental body and to the individual human body, as well. A series of very severe plague outbreaks led to the creation of regimes of quarantine that divided what was considered the healthy from the sickly, the social from the natural, and the human from the nonhuman. Thus, instead of plague being a regular part of Egyptians' lives, it became an offset force to be avoided, enclosed, buried, and purged. It moved, in other words, from being a normal and expected social and environmental phenomenon to being a disease.

control." John Brewer, *The Sinews of Power: War, Money and the English State, 1688–1783* (Cambridge, MA: Harvard University Press, 1988), 223.

50 Hacking, "Biopower and Printed Numbers," 280. Emphasis in original.

51 For example, on the importance of counting soldiers in Mehmet 'Ali's early-nineteenth-century army, see: Fahmy, *All the Pasha's Men*, 142–46.

5

FROM NATURE TO DISEASE

If labor contributed to the transformation of Egyptian peasants into a working population and helped define the contours, size, and shape of the population, then plague delineated the spaces and borders of that social body, with the disease becoming a target of new social, epidemiological, and environmental forms of knowledge at the end of the eighteenth century. At the outset, we must first understand that plague was considered "natural" in Ottoman Egypt. Throughout the Ottoman period (and long before), plague functioned as a regular part of society and the environment, like the annual flood, drought, or rain; it was something Egyptians expected and to which they had adapted their lives.[1] Plague was indeed a necessary and vital part of Egyptian culture, as it enabled the exercise and creation of sets of social practices and institutions. Thus, as I show in the first three sections of this chapter, plague existed and was thought of by eighteenth-century Egyptians as a regular part of their natural world – indeed, as an environmental force like any other.

By the end of the eighteenth century, however, and into the nineteenth, plague came to be set apart from society. Mainly through the implementation of the European technology of quarantine, Egyptian society was in this period cut into two: spaces of the living in which society and culture existed and quarantined spaces in which the infected went to die. Never before in Egypt had the sick and the dead been taken away from the living in so systematic and powerful a way. Perhaps the most significant consequence of this separation, as we will see at the end of this chapter, was the definition of spaces in which society (literally)

[1] For an excellent recent study of California's Central Valley that takes seriously the place of disease in environment and of environment in disease, see: Linda Nash, *Inescapable Ecologies: A History of Environment, Disease, and Knowledge* (Berkeley: University of California Press, 2006).

lived and in which what was external to it – disease and death – remained surrounded and enclosed. A growing emphasis on the productivity and health of individual human bodies was thus another result of Egypt's transition from being an imperial province to an increasingly independent polity.

Like the conceptual shifts that made possible the transformations of plants into caloric units of energy, of trees into lumber, and of peasants into abstract numbers on a worksheet, quarantine marked a similar conceptual shift by its designation of certain portions of the Egyptian population as diseased bodies that served no function in the healthy world of the productive and able-bodied living. Likewise, in the same way that Mehmet ʿAli's invasion of Greater Syria separated Egypt from the Ottoman imperial system in which it had existed for more than three centuries, so, too, did quarantine further cut off Egyptians from wider social, environmental, cultural, and political structures. Thus, quarantine worked to remove plague from Egyptian understandings of the environment and to separate death and sickness from Egyptian society. This redefinition of a cleansed and antisepticised social body imposed new expectations and demands on Egyptian society as it worked to adapt to a changed social, familial, environmental, epidemiological, and cultural landscape. This chapter, therefore, further extends my argument that the autonomy of Egyptian peasants over land, water, natural resources, their labor, and even their biological lives was slowly eroded at the end of the long eighteenth century through systemic changes in Egyptian society, environment, and politics.

The Body Environmental

Plague in Egypt was historically considered a regular part of the environment, to be dealt with as "normally" as Egyptians learned to interact with flood, famine, wind, rain, and other natural phenomena. Such ideas about disease emerged from an understanding of the place of the human body in the environment – ideas that had developed over the course of a long history of medical thought and writing in the Middle East that was still dominant well into the nineteenth century. The consensus of this work was that the human body was always in its environment and that what surrounded it, entered it, and left it determined its health.[2]

[2] In nineteenth-century California, bodies were similarly considered "malleable and porous entities that were in constant interaction with the surrounding environment, an environment that retained a complex agency of its own." Ibid., 18.

In Michael Dols's words, life was "a constant interplay between the body and the environment."[3] Indeed, the dominant miasmatic theory of disease causation, which posited that the body was made up of a series of four substances, each with its own specific properties, contained in it an understanding that the environmental world around a person could throw the balance of these substances out of order or, alternatively, could restore health. Vapors, ethers, heats, herbs, moisture, earth, food, plants, and all other sorts of "natural" forces were thus at play in the balance of human health. Water was perhaps the key factor in the health of the body. Water created moisture and its absence dryness, it washed and cleansed, and it flooded and rained. Unlike modern conceptions of the body as somehow set apart from nature, early modern ideas of the interaction between health and the environment understood humans to be very much a part of the environment. They were *in* it at the most basic level like all other living things. Thus, the health of the human body was understood as primarily a function of the environment around it.

One of the fullest treatments of these ideas as they relate to health, the body, and environment in Egypt is the treatise of the eleventh-century physician ʿAlī Ibn Riḍwān titled *On the Prevention of Bodily Ills in Egypt*. In the very first lines of this work, Ibn Riḍwān makes clear the intimate connections between place and health in Egypt. He writes that his work is for the benefit of all those who live in Egypt and for those many foreigners who regularly came to the country. He continues on to say that doctors will not be able to treat people without first having a thorough knowledge of the temperament of the country (*mizāj al-balad*) and the function of its environment.[4] These observations at the outset of the treatise set the tone for the rest of the work.

Disease, for Ibn Riḍwān and for the Egyptian population at large, was a function of place. Thus, this work was intended both for travelers to Egypt and for its residents, because what was most important to health was not the state of the body as it entered Egypt but the effects of the environment on that body once in Egypt. As such, the first chapter of this work specifically addresses the natural characteristics of Egypt. According to Ibn Riḍwān, Egypt, at its most basic level, is the land that the Nile inundates.[5] He goes on to describe the borders of the country, its climate,

[3] Adil S. Gamal, ed., *Medieval Islamic Medicine: Ibn Riḍwān's Treatise "On the Prevention of Bodily Ills in Egypt,"* trans. Michael W. Dols (Berkeley: University of California Press, 1984), 18. This volume contains both the Arabic text of the treatise and an English translation. Page numbers refer to the English translation.

[4] Ibid., 77–78.

[5] Ibid., 79.

the season of the annual flood, and the plant and animal life found in Egypt. He ends this section of the book with the statement "that the dominant temperament in Egypt is the excessive heat and moisture; that the country consists of many distinct parts; and that its air and water are bad."[6]

Given Ibn Riḍwān's descriptions of the land of Egypt itself, how are we to understand the relationships of the people of Egypt to this land? As noted earlier, this relationship was essentially "a direct one": the character of land, air, and water affected people's bodies and health. In Ibn Riḍwān's words:

> All the plants and animals resemble the temperament of Egypt in the weakness and lack of endurance of their bodies, in the abundance of change, in the swiftness of illness, and in the brevity of life – as wheat in Egypt is doomed to early ruin and is quick to decay. We do not think that the bodies of the people and animals are different from the wheat in its rapid transformation. How could the matter be otherwise, for their bodies are built from these things. Consequently, the weakness, the abundant surplus, the putrefaction, and the frequent disease of plants and animals in Egypt are parallel to the poor quality of the land, its putridity, its surplus, and its rapid change because *the relationship is a direct one.*[7]

Here, we see how animals, food, humans, plants, land, water, and disease are conceived of as different parts of the same functioning system of natural life in Egypt. Changes in any one part of this system affected the rest. A lack or excess of water, disease, or humans meant that the other constituent parts of this system had to change and adapt. Indeed, the likening of plant, animal, and human life to the decay of wheat in Ibn Riḍwān's treatise is a telling example of how disease and both the human and the animal body were thought to relate to food, cultivation, and earth in Egypt.

Lest we forget the paramount role of water in this story, Ibn Riḍwān goes on to describe how changes in the quality and quantity of water affected rates of epidemic disease (*al-wabāʾ*) in Egypt.

> The water may create epidemic illness if the water is excessive in its increase or decrease, or if a corrupt substance mixes with it. The people are forced to drink it, and the air surrounding their bodies is corrupted by the water as well. This corrupt substance may mix with the water, either in a nearby or distant place, when the water's course passes by a

6 Ibid., 85.
7 Ibid., 87–88. Emphasis added.

> battlefield where many dead bodies are found. Or the river passes by polluted swamps, and it carries and mixes with this stagnant water.[8]

These medical notions of the effects of water on disease causation remind us once again of how water and the reliance of all Egyptians on the Nile for the precious substance tied populations together into communities of cooperation and the shared usage of natural resources. Similar to dynamics discussed in Chapter 1, Ibn Riḍwān here warns that war or pollution very far upstream had the potential to affect the quality of the river's waters and, in turn, the health of those downstream. These medical ideas were thus essentially the same as those that came to govern the management of irrigation works and water in rural Egypt – namely, that what was done to the river or a canal at one point in the vast irrigation network affected people in very different and distant places. The river and its waters thus bound the economic and medical fates of people in Egypt together into a single working collective system.

Given the direct role of the environment on the health of Egyptians, what were the most effective treatments doctors could employ to heal their patients? Following from Hippocrates and Galen, Ibn Riḍwān states simply that, in treating their patients, doctors must "imitate nature in what it does to the body."[9] When dealing with patients, doctors must take note of the season, the temperament of the place in which the sick live, and the characteristics of the natural world around them. Ibn Riḍwān gives the specific example of the consumption and elimination of food to make his point that a doctor's treatment of patients must follow the lead of nature.

> Nature (*al-ṭabīʿa*) ... preserves the health of the body by the foods that it supplies and by the superfluities that it eliminates every day. The superfluities are eliminated by respiration, perspiration, urination, vomiting, spitting, nosebleed, menstruation, and by hemorrhoids; the elimination is according to the appropriate organ, the temperament of one's body, the current season of the year, the country, one's age, external appearance, and habits.... In every season give those foods and remedies that are agreeable to the temperament of the season and to what is produced in that season in the bodies.[10]

Thus, in the same way that environmental change was the primary determining factor in the health and sickness of Egyptians, nature also held

8 Ibid., 113.
9 Ibid., 119.
10 Ibid., 120 and 127.

solutions for curing diseases of those resident in Egypt. In other words, understanding that the body was always in nature was a prerequisite for using nature to cure disease.

Ibn Riḍwān then goes on to discuss various *materia medica* to be used in the treatment of different ailments. He addresses as well how, like the bodies they were meant to treat, those substances too were subject to the effects of environment, as the air of Egypt made the remedies weaker in strength than they would otherwise be elsewhere.[11] He then turns to what we might call issues of public health, such as the arrangement of neighborhoods, the interiors of homes, clothing, the use of fans, drinking water, perfumes, wells, food, and public markets. He suggests strategies for cooling environments in hot seasons and for heating interiors during the winter, outlines a system for purifying drinking water, and describes numerous kinds of foods useful in preventing and treating different ailments. The treatise ends with a chapter titled "On the Desirability of Choosing to Live in Egypt Although It Would Have a Bad Effect on the Body." Egypt, according to Ibn Riḍwān, offers the benefits of "many buildings and people" and "little discord and war," and, thus, despite the many adverse effects of the Egyptian environment on one's health, there were many reasons to live in Egypt – political stability and the cultural and economic resources of a large population and of one of the medieval and early modern world's biggest cities.[12]

The role of the environment and, specifically in the case of Egypt, of the Nile in the health of human bodies is a subject that arises over and over again in texts related to Egypt and medicine throughout the classical Islamic period. For example, in another classical text about the history of the Nile in Egypt, titled *Principles of the Rising Nile*, we find several chapters devoted to the subjects of epidemic diseases and their treatments.[13] The author of this text, Shihāb al-Dīn Aḥmad Ibn Muḥammad ʿAlī al-Anṣārī al-Ḥijāzī, was clearly influenced by classical Greek writers and by the works of medical practitioners like Ibn Riḍwān and Ibn al-Jazzār.[14] In

[11] Ibid., 127.

[12] Ibid., 148.

[13] Shihāb al-Dīn Aḥmad Ibn Muḥammad ʿAlī al-Anṣārī al-Ḥijāzī, *al-Nīl al-Rāʾid fī al-Nīl al-Zāʾid*, SK, Ayasofya 3528. For another version of this text, see: Badr al-Dīn ʿAlī Ibn Aḥmad Ibn Muḥammad al-Bulqīnī, *Kitāb al-Nīl al-Rāʾid fī al-Nīl al-Zāʾid*, SK, Fatih 4181.

[14] For similar narrative accounts of the Nile and of the topography and geography of the Nile Valley, see: Muḥammad Ibn ʿAbd al-Mu'min Ibn Muḥammad al-Jauharī, *Mūjaz fī Mabdāʾ al-Nīl wa Muntahāhu*, SK, Lâleli 3752; Jalāl al-Dīn al-Maḥallī, *Muqaddima fī Nīl Miṣr al-Mubārak*, SK, Ayasofya 3446; Muḥammad Ibn Shuʿayyib, *Zahr al-Basātīn fī Faḍl al-Nīl wa Faḍl Miṣr wa al-Qāhira wa al-Qarāfa*, DKM, Buldān Taymūr 60; Ibn al-ʿImād,

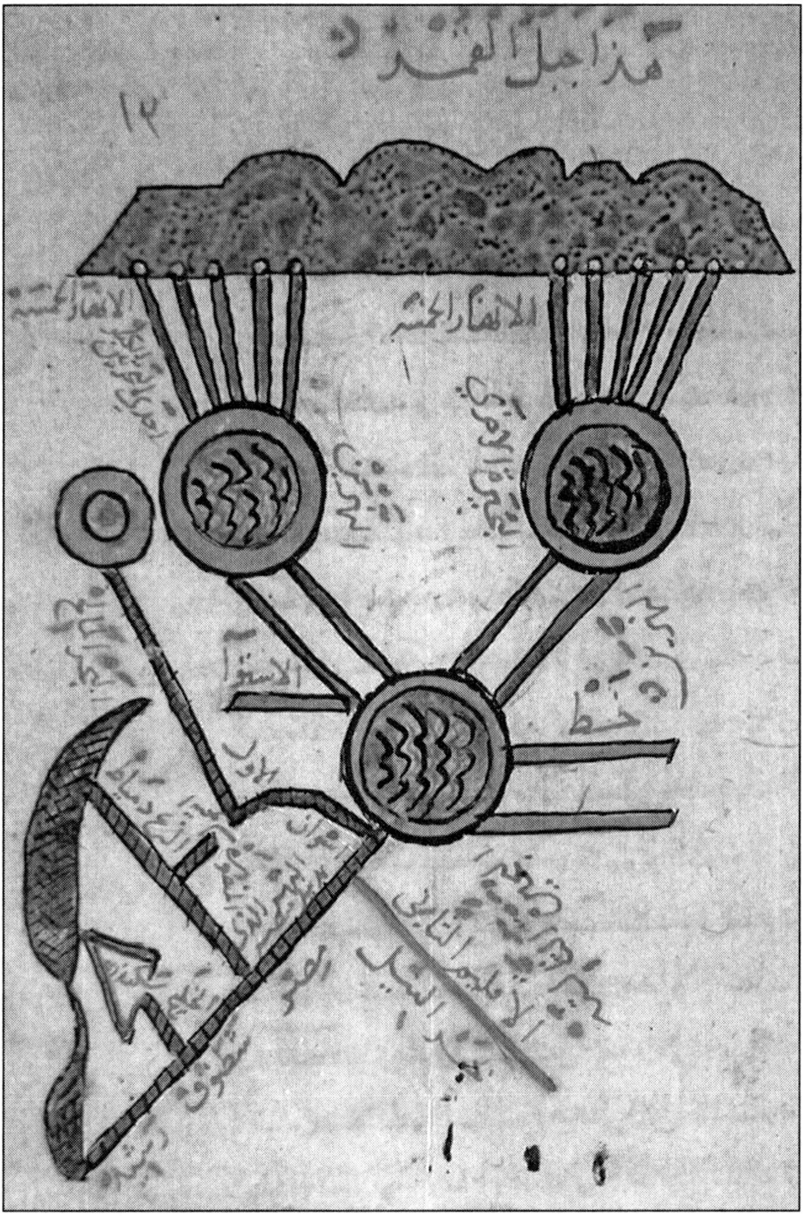

Figure 5.1. Moon Mountain, purported by some writers to be the source of the Nile. Al-Ḥijāzī, Shihāb al-Dīn Aḥmad Ibn Muḥammad ʿAlī al-Anṣārī, *al-Nīl al-Rāʾid fī al-Nīl al-Zāʾid*, SK, Ayasofya 3528, 13r. Used by permission of the Süleymaniye Library.

synthesizing these writings and addressing the role of the Nile in the health of Egyptians and in the onset of epidemic disease in Egypt, al-Ḥijāzī begins with a discussion of the origins of the river itself. The problematic specifically in question was how the waters of the Nile that flowed from an origin so far away came to Egypt with such a highly fertile and rich character. Some writers explained this phenomenon by saying that the lands through which the Nile flowed to Egypt were so redolent and cleansing (*dhakiyya wa ʿadhaba*) that they added nutrients to the water as it flowed through them, making it rich and fertile.[15] Others claimed that it was the character of the source of the Nile itself. Because this source was so pure, water springing from it remained clean and unspoiled even after traveling thousands of kilometers to Egypt. There was little consistency in ideas of where or what this source was. Galen, for his part, wrote that it came from some unspecified place in the east.[16] Most writers, though, thought the Nile sprung from a place called Moon Mountain (Jabal al-Qamar), so named because of the brightness of the moon's light in that location.[17]

Whatever the source of the Nile, most writers agreed that its waters were of a special character – the water of the Nile was superior to any other water in the world (*faḍl māʾ Nīl Miṣr ʿalā sāʾir al-miyāh*).[18] No less an authority than Galen himself agreed that the Nile's water was good for all bodies (*ṣalāḥiyya li-abdān al-jamīʿ*) and that it was preferred to all other water.[19] Ibn Sina also sang the praises of the Nile in his *Qānūn.*[20] The Ottoman intellectual Muṣṭafā ʿĀlī writing in the sixteenth century noted that the Nile "is an extremely good-tasting water and, although being of muddy appearance, in its utmost pleasantness more beneficial to digestion, purer and sweeter."[21]

Kitāb al-Nīl al-Saʿīd al-Mubārak, DKM, Jughrāfiyā Ḥalīm 5; Ibn Riḍwān, *Risāla fī Ziyādat al-Nīl wa Naqṣihi ʿalā al-Dawām*, DKM, Majāmīʿ Mīm 213.

15 Al-Ḥijāzī, *al-Nīl al-Rāʾid*, 85r.

16 Ibid.

17 Jalāl al-Dīn al-Maḥallī, *Muqaddima fī Mabdāʾ al-Nīl wa Muntahāhu*, SK, Serez 3838/11, 91v. For other versions of this text, see: al-Maḥallī, *Risāla fī Mabdāʾ al-Nīl*, DKM, Majāmīʿ Ṭalʿat 972; al-Maḥallī, *Kitāb Mabdāʾ al-Nīl*, DKM, Jughrāfiyā 381. Other accounts that mention Moon Mountain as the source of the Nile include the following: al-Jauharī, *Mūjaz fī Mabdāʾ al-Nīl wa Muntahāhu*, 37v; al-Bulqīnī, *Kitāb al-Nīl al-Rāʾid*, 12v–13r.

18 Al-Ḥijāzī, *al-Nīl al-Rāʾid*, 84v.

19 Ibid., 85r.

20 Ibid.

21 Tietze, *Muṣṭafā ʿĀlī's Description of Cairo*, 29.

After a discussion of the richness of the Nile and its possible sources, al-Ḥijāzī's text *Principles of the Rising Nile* goes on to the specific reasons plague was so consistent a presence in Egypt, and it is in this section of the work that al-Ḥijāzī relies most heavily on the writings of Ibn Riḍwān and Ibn al-Jazzār, both of whom rejected that the Nile's waters were pure, clean, and life giving.[22] The persistence of pestilence (*al-ʿafan*) in Egypt was a function of the climate's consistently high temperatures and the great amount of moisture in the air. Fall was the season in which Egypt was most susceptible to plague because of the mixing of changing air (*ikhtilāf taghayyur al-hawāʾ*) and, more important, because it was the season directly after the onset of the flood.[23]

Al-Ḥijāzī writes that both Egypt and the Ṣaʿīd (southern Egypt) lie in a valley between two mountains. When the Nile floods in the full heat of summer (*zaman al-qaiẓ*), it covers the earth between the two mountains like a bowl being filled with water. The speed, quantity, and suddenness of the river's inundation mean that all sorts of animals and venomous insects die in the rushing waters. Those animals that are lucky enough to escape the deluge perch themselves in trees above the water. Because of a lack of food and the intense heat of the sun, however, those animals eventually die as well and their carcasses fall into the water. All this dead animal matter – in addition, of course, to the dead plants rotting below the surface of the water – releases massive amounts of rotten vapors (*abkhira*) into the air. When all that air mixes in the early fall, it creates a situation ripe for the development of pestilence in Egypt during subsequent months.[24]

Moreover, according to Hippocrates, Egypt was more susceptible to the outbreak of plague than other places because cold and warm winds from the east and the west met and mixed together in the space between the two mountains that lined the Nile Valley. The mixing of temperatures and airs meant that those in Egypt's atmosphere were under constant threat of the outbreak of disease.[25] Following from a similar sort of logic, al-Ḥijāzī explains that, contrary to some opinions, the Nile's waters were not at all pure, because strong winds that blew at dawn mixed up the water to a great extent, thus making it impure. Moreover, the mixture of very strong sunlight hitting the water and very cold winds blowing over it

[22] Al-Ḥijāzī, *al-Nīl al-Rāʾid*, 85v.
[23] Ibid., 86r.
[24] Ibid., 86r–86v.
[25] Ibid., 86v.

also led to the water becoming impure. Hippocrates added that the sun's warm temperatures combined with cool winds to keep most Egyptians indoors during the daytime. It was only at dusk that they came out to cook their evening meals. This fact caused Egyptians to be pallid (*ḥāʾilay al-alwān*) and sickly (*ḍuʿafāʾ al-abdān*) and, thus, made them more likely to fall ill.[26] In summary, then, because of the variation of temperature during the fall and the coterminous presence of cool winds and strong sunlight, the season was an especially ripe time for the outbreak of plague and other diseases in Egypt.

A favorite topic of writers on the salubrious properties of Egypt, its land, and its water was the appropriateness of the Nile as a source of drinking water for humans and animals alike. We have already addressed the ways in which Ibn Riḍwān described how the Nile flood affected the etiology of plague and other epidemic diseases. Ibn Riḍwān, though, also dealt with the relative advantages and disadvantages of drinking the Nile's waters. As he explains, "the majority of Egyptians drink from the Nile . . . [,] some people drink spring water . . . [,] and fewer people drink stored water and rainwater."[27] Commenting on Ibn al-Jazzār's statement that "the water of the Nile is noticeably harmful for everyone who inhabits Egypt," Ibn Riḍwān states that he finds no evidence to support this claim. Indeed, he thinks that "the Nile is the greatest cause for the habitation of this land, and [that] the bodies of the Egyptians have become accustomed to it."[28]

A crucial exception to this observation, however, is the state of drinking water in the capital Cairo. As elsewhere in Egypt, Cairo's residents drew the majority of their drinking water from the Nile itself. In the city, though, Cairenes regularly threw into the Nile the droppings and carrion of their animals and also emptied the sewers of their latrines into the river.[29] Such water had to be purified according to Ibn Riḍwān through a series of clay and ceramic vessels. He adds that it is also advantageous to skim the surface of purified water to remove any undesirable excess elements. Water that seemed highly questionable as to its purity and safety for consumption was also to be boiled and then covered in sealed containers to prevent any mixing with corrupt air. The purest and best water for consumption, though, remained that taken from places in the

[26] Ibid., 86v–87r.
[27] Gamal, *Ibn Riḍwān's Treatise "On the Prevention of Bodily Ills,"* 91.
[28] Ibid., 102.
[29] Ibid., 106.

Nile where the current was strong and where there was no waste released into the water.[30]

Al-Ḥijāzī agrees with Ibn Riḍwān both that the waters of the Nile are suitable for human and animal consumption and that disease comes not from the water of the Nile itself but from what is in the water. Indeed, al-Ḥijāzī goes out of his way to praise the healthy taste and purity of the Nile's waters (*ladhīdh al-ṭaʿm khāliṣ al-khāliṣ al-jauhar*).[31] The dangers of disease arose when that water was infiltrated with foreign particles, dirt, and other substances that, when mixed inside the body with its own forces, could lead to the onset of plague. For the purest, best-tasting, and cleanest-possible Nile water free from any foreign agents, al-Ḥijāzī suggests that individuals be ready to collect Nile water during the one hundred days between the start of the rise of the river, its cresting, and its eventual recession.[32] This water was to be stored in tanks or cisterns made of lead or some other substance that was extremely strong and resistant to deterioration.[33] Drinking-water storage tanks were to be built in such a way as to allow the surface of the water to be exposed to open air so that water inside the vessels was given an amount of movement and sunlight. Owners of the tanks, though, should take care not to allow any fish or other living creatures to get into the water inside the tank. Should such an animal die in the water, then the entire project of storage and purification would be ruined by the corrupting flesh. The upper part of the tank exposed to the open air should also be outfitted with a removable top that could be closed should air around the tank become corrupt or in times of plague.

In addition to storing Nile water in tanks for human consumption, al-Ḥijāzī also mentions that Egyptians often drank from wells (*al-ābār*), especially when the waters of the Nile were dirty or thought to be corrupted.[34] He warns against drinking such water, though, because of its lack of movement and its possible contamination in the well. For some unexplained reason, however, well water mixed with corrupt Nile water (*māʾ al-Nīl al-fāsid*) was considered more suitable for consumption than unmixed well water.

Among the crucial aspects in the determination of the suitability of consuming water from different parts of the Nile were its color, smell,

30 Ibid., 135–36, 138, and 141.
31 Al-Ḥijāzī, *al-Nīl al-Rāʾid*, 88v.
32 Ibid., 88v–89r.
33 Ibid., 89r.
34 Ibid.

and taste.[35] Both Ibn Riḍwān and al-Ḥijāzī give similar accounts of the geographic course of the Nile and the effects of that passage on the color of the river. According to Ibn Riḍwān, along the course of the Nile through the Sudan, the river's waters accumulate a great deal of "putrid substances and filth" from the surrounding lands. As it enters Egypt, the Nile also collects animal cadavers, refuse, plant materials, clay, soil, and a large amount of various kinds of fish eggs. Those materials along with a great quantity of duckweed and water moss gave the river its distinctive green color at the beginning of the flood season.[36] Al-Ḥijāzī follows this general schema, although he begins his version of the Nile's course to Egypt by stating that the river begins fifteen degrees south of the equator. Rains in this southern region between early spring and late winter were the source of the Nile's flood that eventually reached Egypt in the middle of the summer during the warmest time of the year. On its way to Egypt, the river passed through al-Nuba, collecting in its waters all sorts of filth (*awsākh*) and dirt (*baqā'ī'*), along with rotting animal and plant materials. As in Ibn Riḍwān's account, the combination of all those elements was said to endow the river with its distinctive green color at the start of the flood season.[37] Both authors add, though, that with the accumulation of sand and dirt in the river as it moved down Egypt toward the Mediterranean, the color of the Nile during the flood season soon changed to a turbid yellow.[38]

Al-Ḥijāzī continues to account for how all of the organic matter collected in the Nile – reflected in the river's changing color – affected the quality of the water for human consumption as it reached populations in Egypt. He writes that all the dirt, plant and animal matter, and other particles found in the Nile mix together inside the body of the person drinking this water, thus leading to a variety of symptoms of epidemic disease (*ḍarūb al-asbāb al-waba'iyya*) and especially of plague. As the concoction of sediment-infused Nile water and bodily fluids ferments inside the drinker's body (*tatakhammar fī al-abdān*) in early fall, the person is highly susceptible to the contraction of diseases as the climate begins to change later in the season. The climate's change of temperature outside the body interacted with the matter from the Nile present inside the

35 For a discussion of how the release of trapped water in Fayyoum affected the color, quality, and taste of that region's drinking water, see: Gamal, *Ibn Riḍwān's Treatise "On the Prevention of Bodily Ills,"* 110.

36 Ibid., 84–85.

37 Al-Ḥijāzī, *al-Nīl al-Rā'id*, 87r–87v.

38 Gamal, *Ibn Riḍwān's Treatise "On the Prevention of Bodily Ills,"* 85; al-Ḥijāzī, *al-Nīl al-Rā'id*, 87r.

body and the body's own substances to create a mixing of humors that weakened the body as a whole and exposed it to the onset of disease.[39] Again, as we saw earlier, this is clearly a statement that the body existed in nature – the environment around the body affected the health inside it.

In addition to the importance of changes in the color and taste of water for the health of Egyptians, food – as another object of human and animal consumption – also played a central role in physicians' texts when discussing the well-being of Egyptians and others. Again, as with water, the concern with food revolved around the mixing together of various elements inside the human body. Al-Ḥijāzī notes that Egyptians were quite fond of mixing various foods together. Milky foods, fish, citrus fruits, cheeses, salt, and other foods mixed together in the blood of humans to the point of decay (*al-ʿafan*), thus making people all the more susceptible to epidemic diseases. According to al-Ḥijāzī, Egyptians consumed a great amount of citrus fruits because their stomachs craved them. The fruits caused the body to produce a great deal of phlegm (*al-balāghim*) that then needed to be counterbalanced by something sweet (*ḥalāwah*). This constant back-and-forth of foods in the interests of balancing the body's humors meant that many Egyptians had visible scabs (*al-jarab*) and hemorrhoids (*al-bawāsīr*) because of an excess of black bile. This situation led as well to a high incidence of heartburn, to colic (*qaulanj*), and to additional problems of the bowels.

For his part, as well, Ibn Riḍwān also devoted much of his treatise to a discussion of different kinds of foods and their effects on the body, stating very directly that "foods produce epidemic illness."[40] His advice for the consumption of food was to choose foods that were new, fresh, firm, and solid. He recommended that people avoid overeating and overindulgence. Only the most recently caught fish should be eaten, and meat should come from young animals that had been allowed to graze freely on fresh grass.[41] Above all else, physicians in Egypt were to achieve the optimal balance of humors and consumed substances and foods to maintain the health of the individual body. In the words of Ibn Riḍwān, "[C]onsider the objective of balance in every case and improve the air, water, and food in accordance with what is suitable to the temperament of each man, his habits, and his ability."[42]

39 Al-Ḥijāzī, *al-Nīl al-Rā'id*, 87v.

40 Gamal, *Ibn Riḍwān's Treatise "On the Prevention of Bodily Ills,"* 113.

41 Ibid., 136–37.

42 Ibid., 130.

Plague in Ottoman Egypt

The notion that disease, particularly plague, existed in Egypt as a constituent part of the environment – its land, water, and air – is reflected not only in the writings of doctors in Egypt from the medieval period to the nineteenth century but also, and more important, in the actual history of the many plague epidemics that affected Egypt during the same period. Indeed, of all the nonhuman actors in the eighteenth-century Egyptian countryside, one of the most important and least studied is *Xenopsylla cheopis*, or the plague flea. From Pharaonic times until the twentieth century, this organism was responsible for far more death in Egypt than all the country's wars combined. Moreover, because plague was a constant feature of the Egyptian environment that was experienced by Egyptians as a regularly recurring part of their natural world, numerous social institutions and cultural practices developed around the disease that bound the multiple experiences of dying and death in Ottoman Egypt quite intimately to the course of most Egyptians' lives.

Thus, as it was narrated by the foregoing writers and as it was experienced by Egyptians throughout the long eighteenth century, plague was not a kind of "foreign" invader, coming to Egypt in the hulls of ships from faraway ports. Indeed, though feared, plague was not a force from which one was to flee.[43] Like the annual Nile flood, increases in the prices of grain, famine, drought, or other hardships, plague was an accepted environmental reality to be expected and with which to negotiate. This meant that death was everywhere in Ottoman Egypt – ingrained in the fabric of society – and that death from plague was just one of the many

43 Muslim writers on the subject of plague constantly comment on and analyze the following three tenets derived from the teachings of the Prophet Muhammad: plague is a mercy and a form of martyrdom from God for a pious Muslim (and a form of punishment for infidels), a Muslim should neither flee from nor enter a region affected by plague, and plague is not contagious because it comes directly from God. Although these principles, of course, did not necessarily influence the actions of all (or any) Muslims, they did inform much of the writing on the subject and contributed to the religio-medico-legal underpinnings of many ideas about plague. Michael W. Dols, *The Black Death in the Middle East* (Princeton, NJ: Princeton University Press, 1977), 23–25 and 109–21; Dols, "Ibn al-Wardī's *Risālah al-Naba' 'an al-Waba'*, A Translation of a Major Source for the History of the Black Death in the Middle East," in *Near Eastern Numismatics, Iconography, Epigraphy and History: Studies in Honor of George C. Miles*, ed. Dickran K. Kouymjian (Beirut: American University of Beirut, 1974), 444–45; Jacqueline Sublet, "La Peste prise aux rêts de la jurisprudence: Le Traité d'Ibn Ḥağar al-ʿAsqalānī sur la peste," *Studia Islamica* 33 (1971): 141–49.

ways Egyptians experienced this most important of social phenomena.[44] To examine various plague epidemics and their multivalent histories properly, we must therefore study the disease as a regular feature of the Egyptian environment that functioned as one part of a specific kind of pathology of that environment that was known and understood by Egyptians in the eighteenth century to include floods, wind, drought, animals, and famine.

A new plague epidemic visited Egypt an average of once every nine years for the entire period from 1347 to 1894.[45] Thus, although Egypt was conquered by Ottoman armies and made an administrative unit of the Empire in 1517, pegging that year as the starting point for a discussion of plague in Egypt is somewhat misleading.[46] Indeed, all the evidence for a chronology and periodicity of plague points to the fact that 1517 did not represent a significant turning point in the frequency, severity, or treatment of plague in Egypt.[47] Given that fact, it is therefore curious that Michael Dols – the foremost recent historian of plague in the Middle East – divides his study of plague during this period between the years before and after 1517.[48] Taking the period as a whole, we note that plague was reported in Egypt in 193 of a total of

44 On plague in Ottoman Egypt, see: Nāṣir Aḥmad Ibrāhīm, *al-Azamāt al-Ijtimāʿiyya fī Miṣr fī al-Qarn al-Sābiʿ ʿAshar* (Cairo: Dār al-Āfāq al-ʿArabiyya, 1998); André Raymond, "Les Grandes Épidémies de peste au Caire aux XVIIe et XVIIIe siècles," *Bulletin d'Études Orientales* 25 (1973): 203–10; Alan Mikhail, "The Nature of Plague in Late Eighteenth-Century Egypt"; Michael W. Dols, "The Second Plague Pandemic and Its Recurrences in the Middle East: 1347–1894," *JESHO* 22 (1979): 162–89; Antoine Barthélemy Clot-Bey, *De le peste observée en Égypte: Recherches et considerations sur cette maladie* (Paris: Fortin, Masson, 1840). For a more general discussion of European debates about plague in Egypt, see: LaVerne Kuhnke, *Lives at Risk: Public Health in Nineteenth-Century Egypt* (Berkeley: University of California Press, 1990). See also the relevant sections of the following: Panzac, *Peste*; Panzac, *Quarantaines et lazarets: L'Europe et la peste d'Orient (XVIIe-XXe siècles)* (Aix-en-Provence, France: Édisud, 1986).

45 Dols, "Second Plauge," 169 and 176. For the period from 1416 to 1514, David Neustadt (Ayalon), reports that an outbreak of plague struck Egypt an average of once every seven years. David Neustadt (Ayalon), "The Plague and Its Effects upon the Mamlûk Army," *Journal of the Royal Asiatic Society of Great Britain and Ireland* (1946): 68. See also: Dols, *Black Death*, 223–24; Panzac, *Peste*, 197–207.

46 One could rightly make the point that the arbitrary geographic and political division of Egypt is just as misleading in a discussion of plague as is the identification of the year 1517 as a chronological divide.

47 For a discussion of some of the difficulties involved in establishing a chronology of plague in the Ottoman Middle East, see: Dols, "Second Plague," 167–68.

48 He cites a "dearth of oriental sources" as the reasons for his chosen periodization. Ibid., 166.

547 years.[49] Evidencing an even higher rate of incidence, Alexandria was subject to no less than fifty-nine separate plague epidemics between 1701 and 1844.[50] The extremely high incidence of plague suggests that the disease and its epidemics were regular and expected occurrences in the lives of most Egyptians. Indeed, commenting on the medieval period, William Tucker notes "that virtually every generation of Egyptians in the Mamlūk period experienced some untoward event in the course of their lives."[51] This high incidence of plague also suggests that historians should pay closer attention to the role of the disease in the shaping of Egyptian history, be it before or after 1517.

The numerous outbreaks of plague during the period of Ottoman rule in Egypt exemplify the ways in which the disease functioned and was considered an integral part of regular environmental cycles in Egypt. For example, in the summer of 1694 – at the very beginning of the long eighteenth century – the Nile did not rise a significant amount and receded quickly, leaving agricultural lands parched.[52] This meant that the year's agricultural yields were low, causing the prices of foodstuffs to rise and leading quickly to widespread famine throughout Egypt. As an indication of the severity of the situation, the Ottoman bureaucracy, citing "poor irrigation and drought," even lowered the amount of taxes owed to the state in that year.[53] The Ottoman bureaucracy of Egypt, moreover, created a rationing system in which vouchers were distributed to peasants allowing them to claim an amount of food for themselves and their families. The vouchers could be bought and sold as currency, and many tax farmers took advantage of the situation by buying vouchers from peasants at the price of 150 *niṣf fiḍḍa* (or *para*) for each ration.

49 Ibid., 168–69 and 175–76; Raymond, "Grandes Épidémies." The epidemics of plague included in Raymond's study represent a subset of those cited by Dols.

50 Daniel Panzac, "Alexandrie: Peste et croissance urbaine (XVIIe-XIXe siècles)," in *Population et santé dans l'Empire ottoman (XVIIIe-XXe siècles)* (Istanbul: Isis, 1996), 51.

51 William F. Tucker, "Natural Disasters and the Peasantry in Mamlūk Egypt," *JESHO* 24 (1981): 222. He further estimates that, on average, natural or social disasters (severe hardship stemming from extreme political injustice or from Bedouin raids) occurred once every two years during the period of Mamlūk rule from 1250 to 1517. Ibid., 222n53.

52 The account of this plague is taken from the following: al-Jabartī, *ʿAjāʾib al-Āthār*, 1:41–43.

53 Although rural areas hardest hit by the drought were allowed to pay their taxes the following year, agricultural regions receiving water as normal were still required to pay their taxes in that year.

By the late summer of the next year, 1695, the drought had yet to abate, and many Egyptians were dying of hunger. A group of angry men, women, and children thus stormed the Citadel of Cairo, throwing stones and demanding that the state make food rations available to them. When the vali of Egypt met the crowd with force, they resorted to looting the granaries and wheat and barley storehouses in Rumayla Square at the foot of the Citadel. August 1695 was the breaking point in this dire situation. Thousands of peasants had come to Cairo in search of food; villages were left empty; the poor stole food wherever they found it; people died in the streets of Cairo; some resorted to eating corpses (both human and feline).[54] Seeing no solution to this situation, the Ottoman sultan dismissed ʿAlī Paşa as the vali of Egypt and replaced him with a man named Ismāʿīl Paşa. As his first official order of business, Ismāʿīl Paşa gathered the poor and hungry of Egypt in the square near the Citadel, and once assembled, he assigned each person to a group to be looked after by an individual amir or some other notable who was to provide the destitute individuals with bread and food. The vali himself even took a group under his care.

The disasters the famine created were augmented by an extremely strong plague epidemic that visited Egypt in the late spring of 1695, during the time of that year's *khamāsīn* winds.[55] Thus, next to those dying of famine in the streets of Cairo, others fell from the pestilence. In the lanes and alleyways of Cairo, a fresh batch of corpses was found every morning.[56] So many died from the plague that the Ottoman state treasury was forced to underwrite the making of shrouds to wrap and bury plague victims, found not only in Cairo but throughout Egypt.[57] Not until the next summer – in May 1696, al-Jabartī tells us – did the plague begin to subside.[58] Thus, in the two years between the summers of 1694 and 1696, the full series of events in the cyclical pathology of

[54] Al-Damurdāshī, *al-Durra al-Muṣāna*, 29.

[55] Ibid.

[56] Ibid.

[57] For reference to the death of a notable scholar from this plague, see: al-Jabartī, *ʿAjāʾib al-Āthār*, 1:110.

[58] After the plague of 1695–1696 ended, the vali of Egypt gained a great deal of money from the *ḥulwān* of vacant lands and from payments by individuals seeking to overtake others' lands. He used part of the funds to celebrate the circumcision of his sons (and no doubt the end of the plague as well), and he also funded the circumcision of two hundred boys from among Egypt's poor. Ibid., 1:163. For other examples of the payment of *ḥulwān* funds, see: DWQ, Isqāṭāt al-Qurā 1, p. 14, case 13 (25 Ra 1141/29 Oct. 1728); DWQ, Isqāṭāt al-Qurā 2, p. 266, case 828 (15 Za 1144/10 May 1732).

which plague was an inextricable part played themselves out in Egypt: a low flood, drought, price inflation, famine, protest, revolt, and finally plague.[59] As we see in this case from the late seventeenth century, plague was one part of this environmental cycle of forces that came to be taken as normal in Egypt over the course of its long history with the disease.

This pathology of plague in Egypt continued throughout the long eighteenth century.[60] On average, as noted earlier, a major new plague outbreak was experienced in Egypt every nine years. Despite only the most fleeting of references to the majority of outbreaks, enough historical detail nevertheless remains for many of the epidemics to enable us to reconstruct part of the pathology of plague in Egypt.[61] In 1757–1758, for example, a great amount of rain fell, flooding Cairo and causing wanton destruction. The storms wrecked agricultural lands and food supplies and were followed by an outbreak of plague.[62] A few decades later, in the summer of 1784, there was another major outbreak of plague in southern Egypt.[63] And in the fall of that year, a low Nile flood led to great scarcity and dearth (*kaht ü galâ*) throughout the Egyptian countryside, as fields could not be cultivated.[64] Thus, by the following spring of 1785, much agricultural land throughout Egypt was in a wasteful state and many peasants had died from hunger and plague.[65] This lack of food led to increases in the prices of grains and other foodstuffs and soon plague and "fevers" began to spread throughout all of Egypt.[66] Hunger, disease, and death continued throughout Egypt into the summer of that year and led to food riots across Cairo. On July 8, 1785, for example, a group of poor students from al-Azhar locked the gates of the mosque and blocked Friday prayers in protest of their lack of food.

59 This series of events in 1694–1696 related to the pathology of plague in Egypt are also referenced in the following: al-Damurdāshī, *al-Durra al-Muṣāna*, 31.

60 For an example of a similar confluence of plague, famine, and inflation in Syria during the period, see: al-Jabartī, *ʿAjāʾib al-Āthār*, 2:179.

61 For references to the plague of 1717–1718, see: ibid., 1:153, 173, 580; al-Damurdāshī, *al-Durra al-Muṣāna*, 125. For the plague of 1733–1734, see: Crecelius and Bakr, *al-Damurdashi's Chronicle of Egypt: al-Durra al-Musana*, 319. For that of 1735–1736, see: al-Jabartī, *ʿAjāʾib al-Āthār*, 1:273–74; al-Damurdāshī, *al-Durra al-Muṣāna*, 202. For the plague of 1742, see: al-Jabartī, *ʿAjāʾib al-Āthār*, 2:403. For references to those who died in the plague of 1771–1772, see: ibid., 1:623, 629.

62 Al-Jabartī, *ʿAjāʾib al-Āthār*, 1:415.

63 BOA, HAT 29/1361 (13 Ş 1198/1 Jul. 1784).

64 BOA, HAT 28/1354 (7 Za 1198/22 Sep. 1784). There is no internal evidence for the date of this case. The date given is the one assigned by the BOA.

65 Al-Jabartī, *ʿAjāʾib al-Āthār*, 2:156–57.

66 For references to some of those who died from this plague, see: ibid., 2:210; 3:100.

Several years later, in the early summer of 1787, plague gripped the Egyptian countryside yet again, affecting both humans and cattle.[67] As in so many previous years, the outbreak again followed on the heels of drought, food losses, inflation, and massive rat incursions on grain and vegetable fields. Because the plague killed both humans and other animals, peasants were forced to work in place of their dead cattle, turning waterwheels themselves and laboring on other irrigation features as well. The cattle plague was most virulent in the Delta and in Cairo, where cattle collapsed in city streets and in fields. So many cattle died, in fact, that al-Jabartī reports that "the land was full of the stench of decaying carcasses."[68] Given the excess of cattle carcasses and the increased supply of meat they provided, the price of beef plummeted in Egypt during the period, though some were afraid to eat the meat of diseased animals. At the same time, the prices of cooking butter, milk, and cheese all increased because of their reduced supplies. In the following year (1788), plague and "various other troubles" also visited Egypt in a similar succession of natural phenomena.[69]

The consistent discursive trope of likening plague to wind further suggests to us the notion that plague was considered an environmental force in Ottoman Egypt.[70] For instance, al-Jabartī writes that the amir Riḍwān Bey's candle was extinguished by a plague that came like "the icy gale of death" (*ṣarṣar al-mawt*).[71] Plague is elsewhere described as something that scatters the lives and possessions of its victims.[72] In the only eyewitness account of the Black Death in the Middle East, Ibn al-Wardī (who died of plague in Aleppo in 1349) likened plague to a cloud: "it eclipsed totally the sun of Shemsin and sprinkled its rain upon al-Jubbah. In al-Zababani the city foamed with coffins."[73] Later, Ibn al-Wardī writes that "the air's corruption kills," an obvious reference to

67 Ibid., 2:232.

68 Ibid., 2:229.

69 Ibid., 2:260, 263. For references to some of those who died of this plague, see: ibid., 2:275, 280, 282.

70 The following paragraphs on wind, temperature, and plague and much of the subsequent section have been adapted from the following: Mikhail, "Nature of Plague in Late Eighteenth-Century Egypt." I have included only the most relevant parts here, but please see the article for more on the issues covered in these sections and on related topics.

71 Al-Jabartī, *ʿAjāʾib al-Āthār*, 2:364.

72 Ibid., 2:369.

73 Dols, "Ibn al-Wardī," 450–51. Ibn al-Wardī's account is written in rhymed prose (*sajʿ*). Its content, therefore, is to a large extent dictated by the need to conform to that literary form.

the then-still-dominant miasmatic theory of disease causation.[74] Shaykh Ḥasan al-ʿAṭṭār, an associate of al-Jabartī's who was present in Asyūṭ during a plague epidemic in 1801, compared the disease to winds that came and scattered the dried foods of the fields of southern Egypt.[75]

Perhaps the most important reason for the association of plague with wind is that, as in the example of the 1694–1696 epidemic, plague usually afflicted Egypt contemporaneously with the *khamāsīn* – the warm southerly winds that blew into Cairo every year in late spring and early summer.[76] The winds carry dust from the deserts south of Cairo and cover the city with sand, dust, and dirt. As one observer of the *khamāsīn* noted: "In spring it [the wind] often changes to south-east, and then it is of a whirling nature, filling the atmosphere with such quantities of sand and dust as to make it almost totally dark. I once remember being obliged to light a candle at noon on such a day, as the sky was at the same time covered with thick clouds."[77] The regular coincidence of the *khamāsīn* and plague caused many to think that plague, like dust and sand, was brought to Egypt in the annual winds. Al-Jabartī notes that, in 1735, plague arrived on the heels of a very ominous wind from the west that blocked the light of the sun and plunged all of Egypt into darkness.[78] The wind sank boats, blew over trees, and destroyed homes and various other structures. Elsewhere, Aḥmad al-Damurdāshī Katkhudā ʿAzabān draws a connection between the plague of 1690–1691 and the *khamāsīn* that occurred at the same time. Like the winds of the *khamāsīn*, he writes that plague swept into Cairo, filling the city's quarters and lanes with dead bodies.[79] Elsewhere, we are told that plague diffused itself into Cairo and its surroundings, spreading all around the region during a period when the markets were covered with dust (*muʿaffara*).[80]

The so-called season of plague in Egypt – the period of greatest regular recurrence of plague in Egypt in any given yearly cycle – also usually coincided with the winds of the yearly *khamāsīn*, which makes the point once again that plague was part of a regular cycle of environmental

74 Ibid., 454.
75 Al-Jabartī, *ʿAjāʾib al-Āthār*, 3:255.
76 Ibrāhīm, *al-Azamāt al-Ijtimāʿiyya*, 72–75; Dols, "Second Plague," 181.
77 Antes, *Observations*, 94. On wind in Egypt more generally, see: ibid., 93–99.
78 Al-Jabartī, *ʿAjāʾib al-Āthār*, 1:242–43.
79 Al-Damurdāshī, *al-Durra al-Muṣāna*, 29. Al-Damurdāshī, moreover, goes on to write that, during this plague, one would wake to find ten new victims every morning. As during other plagues, there was a shortage of corpse washers, and given the great number of dead bodies, gravediggers were forced to work long into the night.
80 Al-Jabartī, *ʿAjāʾib al-Āthār*, 3:171.

phenomena that included famine, flood, drought, and so on.[81] Plague epidemics usually began in late winter, seem to have been most deadly in the spring, and waned toward the middle of the summer. This pattern is the one most commonly observed for the course of plague in Cairo, which Daniel Panzac identifies as beginning in February, peaking in May, and dissipating toward its eventual end in July or August.[82] Examining the season of plague in Egypt more closely reveals a gradual movement of the disease from the south toward the Mediterranean.[83]

The reasons for this slow move of plague from south to north are climatic, as rising temperatures come first to the south and then move north as the country warms through spring into summer.[84] The ideal meteorological conditions for plague are temperatures between twenty and twenty-five degrees Celsius with mild humidity, precisely the conditions that move up the Nile Valley from spring into summer, taking mild temperatures – along with plague – up the country. Moreover, fleas – the primary agents of plague transmission – are most active during the warm months of spring and early summer.[85] The dry heat of the summer eventually makes conditions in Egypt unfavorable for the maintenance of plague and fleas, with temperatures well above twenty-seven degrees Celsius and humidity less than 40 percent.[86]

1791: A Pathology of Plague

One of the harshest and most well-documented plague epidemics in eighteenth-century Egypt was the outbreak of February 1791.[87] One eyewitness reported that at the start of the awful plague, a thousand people died every day. It was not long, however, before the number of dead

[81] For a general discussion of the periodicity, timing, and seasonal incidence of plague in the Middle East, see: Panzac, *Peste*, 195–227; Conrad, "Plague in the Early Medieval Near East," 323–27; Kuhnke, *Lives at Risk*, 72–78. For a more general treatment of these subjects, see: L. Fabian Hirst, *The Conquest of Plague: A Study of the Evolution of Epidemiology* (Oxford: Clarendon Press, 1953), 254–82.

[82] Panzac, *Peste*, 223.

[83] Kuhnke, *Lives at Risk*, 201n18.

[84] In Upper Egypt (as the south is known), plague began in March and ended in May. In the middle of the country, it began in April and ended in June. In the Egyptian Delta above Cairo, plague began in April and ended in July. And in Egypt's Mediterranean ports, the disease began in May and ended in October.

[85] Conrad, "Plague in the Early Medieval Near East," 326.

[86] Panzac, *Peste*, 225.

[87] Al-Jabartī, *ʿAjāʾib al-Āthār*, 2:314–15.

per day rose to 1,500.[88] Elsewhere, the same chronicler estimates that the plague killed two thousand people every day.[89] During this outbreak of plague, which coincided with that year's *khamāsīn*, the leader Ismāʿīl Bey died, along with many of his followers, before an attempted escape to Istanbul.[90] The plague indeed caused quite a crisis of leadership in Ottoman Egypt, as no appointed leader could stay alive long enough to rule effectively.[91] An Ottoman firman sent to Egypt from Istanbul about the plague of 1791 implores the surviving leadership of the province to do all it can to defend against the state of disorder (*perişanlık*) that had gripped Egypt because of the death of eight or nine of the province's most important beys. The decree further orders the leadership to inform Istanbul of the names, physical characteristics, and notable attributes of the important men who died and of those who replaced them.[92]

As plague intensified over the course of the spring of 1791, the apparatuses charged with the management of death were stretched to their limits as the demand for undertakers (*al-ḥawānīt*) and corpse washers (*al-mughassilīn*) far exceeded their available numbers. Most economic and social functions unrelated to the present grim circumstances ceased during the plague, as "there was not any work left for people except death and its attendant matters." Those worthy of note in Egypt during the spring of 1791 were the sick (*al-marīḍ*), the dead (*al-mayyit*), the visitor of the sick (*al-ʿāʾid*), the condoler (*al-muʿazzī*), the funeral goer (*al-mushayyiʿ*), the one returning from funeral or burial prayers, the one busy with preparing the dead, and the one weeping in anticipation of his own death.[93]

From the imperial perspective in Istanbul, the outbreak of plague in Egypt created a threatening opportunity for enemies of the state and

88 Ismāʿīl Ibn Saʿd al-Khashshāb, *Akhbār Ahl al-Qarn al-Thānī ʿAshar: Tārīkh al-Mamālīk fī al-Qāhira*, ed. ʿAbd al-ʿAzīz Jamāl al-Dīn and ʿImād Abū Ghāzī (Cairo: al-ʿArabī lil-Nashr wa al-Tawzīʿ, 1990), 58.

89 Ismāʿīl Ibn Saʿd al-Khashshāb, *Khulāṣat mā Yurād min Akhbār al-Amīr Murād*, ed. and trans. Hamza ʿAbd al-ʿAzīz Badr and Daniel Crecelius (Cairo: al-ʿArabī lil-Nashr wa al-Tawzīʿ, 1992), 40.

90 Al-Jabartī, *ʿAjāʾib al-Āthār*, 2:315, 318; al-Khashshāb, *Akhbār al-Amīr Murād*, 40; al-Khashshāb, *Akhbār Ahl al-Qarn al-Thānī ʿAshar*, 58.

91 For a discussion of the lives of various notables who died from the plague of 1791, see: al-Jabartī, *ʿAjāʾib al-Āthār*, 2:322–52, 359–72.

92 BOA, Cevdet Dahiliye, 1722 (Evasıt N 1205/15–24 May 1791). Al-Jabartī seems to be making reference to this Ottoman firman when he writes that "a messenger arrived from Turkey who was an agha appointed to seek out the legacy of Ismāʿīl Bey and of the other amīrs who perished in the plague." Al-Jabartī, *ʿAjāʾib al-Āthār*, 2:318.

93 Al-Jabartī, *ʿAjāʾib al-Āthār*, 2:315.

rebellious bureaucrats to escape to Egypt undetected amid the mayhem and general disarray brought on by the plague. Indeed, in very strong language, Ottoman authorities ordered leaders still present in Egypt to prevent any fugitives from the state from entering the province to hide.[94]

In another imperial firman from Istanbul, we read of the bureaucratic confusion and crisis brought on by the outbreak of plague in Egypt in 1791.[95] The order from the sultan came in response to a letter from the previous vali of Egypt, Ismail Paşa, reporting that more than three hundred thousand men, women, and children had died that year from plague in Egypt.[96] From among the vali's inner circle (*daire*) alone, one hundred people had died. As if this situation were not dire enough, the *şeyh ül-beled* himself, Ismail Bey, had also died that year.[97] After his death, the remaining amirs in the province, the defterdar, and other important men came to the vali's divan to appoint a replacement for Ismail Bey. After their deliberations, they settled on the apprentice (*çırak*) of the former *şeyh ül-beled*, a man named ʿUthmān Bey, who had formerly held the rank of *emir ül-hac*. Clearly, his previous position as *emir ül-hac* was an important factor in his selection, as the experience would aid him in his new position as *şeyh ül-beled*.[98]

Thus, the outbreak of plague in Egypt and officials' deaths from it forced the Ottoman administration of Egypt to deal with the confusion the disease caused in the province. Plague also threatened the normal imperial role of Egypt as a provider of money, food, and protection both to pilgrims and residents in the Hijaz and to the Empire as a whole. As did irrigation and food production in the Nile Valley, so too did plague hold important imperial consequences far beyond Egypt's borders. This fact points once again both to the central importance of Egypt to the whole of the Ottoman Empire and to the connections that the Ottoman order maintained and fostered between Egypt and various other parts of the eastern Mediterranean and beyond.

94 BOA, Cevdet Dahiliye, 1722 (Evasıt N 1205/15–24 May 1791).

95 BOA, HAT, 1399/56283 (29 Z 1205/29 Aug. 1791). There is no internal evidence for the date of this case. The date given is the one assigned by the BOA.

96 For another reference to Ismail Paşa's rule during this plague epidemic, see: al-Jabartī, *ʿAjāʾib al-Āthār*, 4:327.

97 The personality of Ismail Bey was often associated with the plague of 1791. See, e.g.: ibid., 4:39.

98 The *şeyh ül-beled* (*shaykh al-balad* in Arabic) was responsible – among other things – for collecting, organizing, and sending the yearly *irsāliyye-i ḫazīne* to Istanbul; for affairs connected to the organization of the pilgrimage and the welfare of pilgrims; for sending grains to the people of the Ḥaramayn; and for the payment of officials' salaries.

The economic implications of the 1791 plague were many. For example, in response to a letter (*kâğıt*) dated April 24, 1791, sent from an unnamed merchant in Alexandria to Istanbul informing the central bureaucracy of the names of those amirs who had died in Egypt that year, the sultan wrote that, because of the human and capital devastation wrought by plague, and because, in turn, a great state of confusion (*perişanlık*) had gripped Egypt, many rebellious beys (*bagi beyler*) would try to enter the province to take advantage of the situation and to grab hold of power and money.[99] To prevent such a scenario, the sultan ordered a firman to be sent immediately to the vali of Egypt and to any other important functionaries still in the province to make sure they took control of the chaotic situation by determining which beys had left Egypt and which remained in the province. This information was needed so that the state could seize the properties and monies of those beys who had abandoned Egypt.[100] During this plague epidemic, then, the Ottoman state was able to gain a great amount of property and capital by seizing the possessions of those who either had fled from Egypt or had died from the pest.[101] The disease was thus the death of some and an opportunity for others.[102]

99 BOA, HAT, 1412/57500 (29 Z 1205/29 Aug. 1791). There is no internal evidence for the date of this case. The date given is the one assigned by the BOA. In the sultan's order, we read that in April and May of 1791, the plague gripped Egypt and led to the passing (*kantara-i dar-ı fenadan dar-ı bekaya güzar etmiş oldukları*; literally "they passed over the bridge from this world to the next") of the same *şeyh ül-beled* mentioned above, Ismail Bey, and also to the death of eight or nine Egyptian Beys (*Mısır Beyi*).

100 For other examples of the state's seizure of properties belonging to those who recently died of plague, see: al-Jabartī, *ʿAjāʾib al-Āthār*, 3:295; 4:44–45.

101 For a petition to the sultan from a woman named Fatme attempting to gain her deceased father's assets from the state, see: BOA, Cevdet Maliye, 14383 (20 S 1197/24 Jan. 1783).

102 The timely payment of imperial officials was another victim of plague in Egypt. In an Ottoman imperial firman promulgated in 1792, we find an order to pay officials of the Egyptian mint (*Darbhane-ı Mısır*) the daily salary of one hundred *para* they had been accustomed to receiving before the plague outbreak under the rule of the former vali of Egypt Ismail Paşa. Since the time of the vali's death, however, the officials, who were among the learned men of al-Azhar (four of them were sons of the mufti of al-Azhar Aḥmad al-ʿArūs, and another named ʿAbd al-Wahhāb was a student of the prominent Shaykh Badāwī), had not received their salaries because of the general chaos that had gripped Egypt since the outbreak of plague the year earlier. Although an order in this regard had been previously issued from the divan of Egypt, the present order – a berat – was sent from Istanbul to reiterate and strengthen the Ottoman state's imperial demands. For those lucky enough to have personal connections (like the sons of the mufti of al-Azhar), there was some recourse to regaining funds, but for the majority of Egyptians, without such connections, the situation was surely more complicated. BOA, HAT, 209/11213 (29 Z 1206/18

What explains the outbreak and severity of plague in Egypt in 1791? To begin to answer this question, we would do well to remember that, even though plague was observably and historically endemic to Egypt, in strictly epidemiological terms, it was not. In other words, although Egypt regularly experienced plague, it did not house an endemic focus of the disease. Indeed, plague almost always came to Egypt from elsewhere through the movement of goods, rats, fleas, and people.[103] This was accomplished primarily through the arrival of hundreds of ships and caravans every week from places like Istanbul, India, Yemen, the Sudan, China, Central Africa, and Iraq, which ensured a consistent flow and constantly replenishing supply of goods, people, and vermin in Egypt. The two main entry points of the disease were through the major trading areas of Egypt: its Mediterranean ports and the southern route from the Sudan.[104]

An essential point to note about the history of plague in Egypt is that those living in the seventeenth and eighteenth centuries did not concern themselves with the question of whether plague was endemic to Egypt.[105] What mattered most was that plague functioned as though it

Aug. 1792). As in previous cases, the date given here is that assigned by the BOA. There is no internal evidence for the date of this case. The document begins by noting, as we saw in previous firmans, that after the deaths from plague of the *şeyh ül-beled* Ismail Bey, ten Egyptian amirs, and other noted officials, the former *emir ül-hac* ʿUthmān Bey was appointed as the new *şeyh ül-beled* of Egypt. We are told that, since the beginning of his appointment on the first of Ramadan, there had been renewed effort to collect state monies, to protect pilgrims going to the Hijaz, and generally to defend Egypt from all sorts of harm.

103 Michael W. Dols, "Plague in Early Islamic History," *Journal of the American Oriental Society* 94 (1974): 381; Raymond, "Grandes Épidémies," 208–9. My discussion of the relationships between the movements of peoples and goods and the spread of plague is informed by the following: William H. McNeill, *Plagues and Peoples* (Garden City, NY: Anchor Press/Doubleday, 1976); Janet L. Abu-Lughod, *Before European Hegemony: The World System A.D. 1250–1350* (New York: Oxford University Press, 1989).

104 Raymond, "Grandes Épidémies," 208–9; Dols, "Second Plague," 179–80. On the basis of the following, Dols compiles a list of plagues that came to Egypt and North Africa from the Sudan and Central Africa: Georg Sticker, *Abhandlungen aus der Seuchengeschichte und Seuchenlehre* (Giessen, Germany: A. Töpelmann, 1908–1912). For more on plague in the Sudan, see: Terence Walz, *Trade between Egypt and Bilād as-Sūdān, 1700–1820* (Cairo: Institut français d'archéologie orientale du Caire, 1978), 200–1.

105 Interesting to note on this point are the nineteenth-century discussions among European physicians about the endemic nature of plague in Egypt. The main antagonists in this debate were Étienne Pariset, permanent secretary to the French Academy of Medicine, who came to Egypt in 1827 to study plague, and Clot-Bey, a French surgeon and physician who was brought to Egypt by Mehmet ʿAli to organize the Egyptian army's medical division and who helped establish the Egyptian School of Medicine in

were endemic. In other words, though epidemiologically not endemic to Egypt, plague was a historically endemic disease because of the consistency of its incidence and, more important, because it operated as a regular force in the Egyptian environment, similar to famine, flood, and drought.[106] It came to Egypt on a regular basis and was a constant and basic feature of the Egyptian environment.

Another point to note about plague in late-eighteenth-century Egypt is that, despite descriptions of plague casualties similar to those discussed earlier, determining the demographic effects of plagues like the one of 1791 is a difficult task.[107] A corollary of the noted preference for the study of plague during both the medieval period and the nineteenth century

1827. Pariset ascribed to the cadaveric virus theory and postulated that Egypt did not suffer from plague during the ancient period because of Pharaonic embalming practices and the fact that corpses were entombed outside of the Nile's floodplain. Plague came to Egypt, he claimed, in the Christian era, when embalming was replaced with burial. Moreover, he described the Egyptian Delta as the world's largest area of warm and humid land filed with decaying animal matter. For his part, Clot-Bey believed that plague was endemic to Egypt. This belief contributed to his anticontagionist stance against plague, dramatically demonstrated when he publicly inoculated himself several times with the blood of plague victims without himself falling ill. For more on Clot-Bey's views on plague in Egypt, see: Clot-Bey, *De le peste.* For a more general discussion of European debates about plague in Egypt, see: Kuhnke, *Lives at Risk*, 70–71 and 87–88.

106 For their part, many European observers considered Egypt the so-called cradle of plague. Kuhnke, *Lives at Risk*, 70; J. Worth Estes and LaVerne Kuhnke, "French Observations of Disease and Drug Use in Late Eighteenth-Century Cairo," *Journal of the History of Medicine and Allied Sciences* 39 (1984): 123. There were, of course, different opinions on this point. John Antes writes, "I think Egypt cannot, with any truth, be called the mother of the plague." Antes, *Observations*, 41; see also: ibid., 36–37. Ibn al-Wardī writes of plague beginning "in the land of darkness," which Dols (citing Alfred von Kremer) identifies as "northern Asia." Dols, "Ibn al-Wardī," 448. Ibn al-Wardī then goes on to trace the disease's course from China and India, through Sind and the land of the Uzbeks, to Persia and the Crimea, and finally into Rūm, Egypt, Syria, and Palestine. Ibid., 448–53. The Mamlūk Egyptian chronicler al-Maqrīzī and others also place the origins of plague in a vague East or in parts of Mongolia. For more on these accounts, see: Borsch, *Egypt and England*, 4–5; Dols, *Black Death*, 35–42.

107 In Dols's words, "What we cannot judge accurately is the severity of the major plague epidemics from the late fifteenth to the late eighteenth centuries in the Middle East.... Therefore, we cannot propose, as we have done in the earlier period, a significant demographic effect of these epidemics." Dols, "Second Plague," 176–77. The Egyptian chronicler reports cited earlier claiming that 1,000, 1,500, or 2,000 people died every day of plague are difficult to interpret and likely inaccurate. Indeed, the descriptions seem to raise more questions than they answer. How were the figures determined? For how many days did those same numbers of people die? What were the relative mortality rates in cities and the countryside? Were the figures purposefully symbolic rather than precise statistical numbers meant to express the severity of a given outbreak?

is the fact that we have very few studies of the Egyptian population at the end of the eighteenth century and during the period of Ottoman rule more generally.[108] Although the exact demographic effects of the 1791 plague are not known and given that plague was not epidemiologically endemic to Egypt, we can propose several viable causes of the 1791 plague. To these ends, we must begin by examining the events of the fall preceding the spring of 1791, the season of the plague's attack on Egypt.

During the fall of 1790, there was an unusually large amount of rainfall in Egypt that resulted in the flooding of many parts of Cairo and significant destruction of the city and its resources.[109] There were two important results of this flood that will help us move toward a better understanding of the 1791 plague and of the pathology of the late-eighteenth-century Egyptian environment. First is the fact of the destruction itself. Similar to years in which the Nile flooded far beyond its banks, the waters of 1790 likely destroyed vast areas of agricultural land in and around Cairo and its hinterland.[110] This meant a significantly lower amount of food production for the coming harvest season. And more destructive than even an excessive flood season, the torrential rains of 1790 destroyed supplies of stored grain in the markets and *wakālas* of Cairo. This doubly magnified the danger for the coming year in and around Cairo, as both fields and grain supplies were destroyed. The population thus likely experienced food shortages and even famine, which weakened its resistance to and resolve against disease. That plague is preceded by famine is a common occurrence observed throughout the history of plague epidemics in the Middle East and elsewhere.[111]

[108] For statistics on and discussions of the demographic effects of the Black Death in Egypt, see: Dols, *Black Death*, 143–235; Dols, "The General Mortality of the Black Death in the Mamluk Empire," in *The Islamic Middle East, 700–1900: Studies in Social and Economic History*, ed. Abraham L. Udovitch (Princeton, NJ: Darwin Press, 1981), 397–428; Borsch, *Egypt and England*, 40–54. Studies of the demographic effects of plague in nineteenth-century Egypt include the following: Panzac, *Peste*, 231–78 and 339–80; Kuhnke, *Lives at Risk*, 84–86. For a critical discussion of plague mortality statistics, see: Lawrence I. Conrad, "The Plague in the Early Medieval Near East" (Ph.D. diss., Princeton University, 1981), 415–47.

[109] Al-Jabartī, *ʿAjāʾib al-Āthār*, 2:312.

[110] On this point, Antes writes, "Sometimes the river rises so rapidly, and to such a height, that all their [peasants'] endeavours are in vain, and all such vegetables are destroyed." Antes, *Observations*, 72.

[111] For instance, in 638 or 639, the plague struck Syria, killing at least twenty-five thousand soldiers and countless others. Important for our purposes here is the observation that this instance of plague was preceded by a severe famine, which likely, as in the plague

The second result of the floods in Cairo in 1790 was the movement of thousands of rats seeking refuge. Although most species of rat do swim, the animal generally prefers a dry habitat, and, in the case of flooding, the rodent will avoid rushing water at all costs for fear of death. Thus, rats – much like humans – seek out dry areas to escape rushing water.[112] This meant that, in the fall of 1790, rats and humans were competing for space in areas of Cairo not damaged by the floodwaters drenching the city.[113] Thus, the flood caused rats, fleas, and humans to come into much closer proximity than they normally would have.[114] This is a key factor in the etiology of plague, as the primary vectors of plague transmission in humans are rats and the fleas associated with them.[115] As long as the rat population in a particular area is large enough to support a sizable flea population, the plague epizootic will survive.

If the causes of the 1791 plague are to be found in an excess of water, then its effects and the continuing hardships experienced by Egyptians at the end of the eighteenth century are to be found in a dearth of water. On August 21, 1791, the Nile crested at an extremely low level.[116] Similar to instances of excessive flooding (like that seen in 1790), a poor inundation meant food shortages, famine, and death. These effects were even more acute in the late summer and fall of 1791 because of the ravages of plague earlier that year. The populations of Cairo and other parts of Egypt were already suffering from lowered resistance to

of 1791 in Egypt, weakened the population, thus making them all the more vulnerable to infection. Dols, "Plague in Early Islamic History," 376. See also: Tucker, "Natural Disasters," 217–19.

112 For more on the physical attributes and abilities of rats, see the following classic study of typhus: Hans Zinsser, *Rats, Lice and History, Being a Study in Biography, Which, after Twelve Preliminary Chapters Indispensable for the Preparation of the Lay Reader, Deals with the Life History of Typhus Fever* (London: George Routledge and Sons: 1935), 197–204.

113 On the competing histories of man and rat, Zinsser writes, "Like man – the rat is individualistic until it needs help. That is, it fights bravely alone against weaker rivals, for food or for love.... The natural history of the rat is tragically similar to that of man." Ibid., 196 and 207.

114 Dols makes a similar point about the proximity of humans and rats during the plague epidemic of 638 or 639 in Syria. Dols, "Plague in Early Islamic History," 376.

115 For more on the epidemiology, pathology, and etiology of plague, see: Conrad, "Plague in the Early Medieval Near East," 4–38; Dols, *Black Death*, 68–83; Borsch, *Egypt and England*, 2–8. For recent works in this regard, see: Hugo Kupferschmidt, *Die Epidemiologie der Pest: Der Konzeptwandel in der Erforschung der Infektionsketten seit der Entdeckung des Pesterregers im Jahre 1894* (Aarau, Switzerland: Sauerländer, 1993); Graham Twigg, *The Black Death: A Biological Reappraisal* (London: Batsford, 1984). The standard works nevertheless remain: Robert Pollitzer, *Plague* (Geneva: World Health Organization, 1954); Hirst, *The Conquest of Plague*.

116 Al-Jabartī, *ʿAjāʾib al-Āthār*, 2:322.

plague because of the floods of 1790. When plague hit Egypt in 1791, the stage was thus set for a very bad epidemic. By the end of 1791, then, we learn of a subsequent stage in the cycle of Egypt's plague pathology – namely that after floods and plague come drought and famine.[117] The flood of the fall of 1790, therefore, contributed to the ravages of plague in the spring of 1791. The combination of these forces with drought in the fall of 1791 resulted in widespread famine, severe price inflations, and massive death.

Indeed, as al-Jabartī tells us, later that year, irrigation canals dried up because of a lack of water, and fields, too, became parched because they did not receive adequate amounts of water.[118] As fields dried out, crops began to wither and die. Peasants worried and prepared for the onset of famine. The poor harvest meant an increase in grain prices for that year and the corollary of revolts and agitations by peasants and the poor against increased prices for basic foodstuffs and against their rulers. In November and December 1791, Egyptian authorities began to seize the properties and lands of merchants and peasants, ostensibly to relieve the economic pressures brought about by the plague and by famine.[119] Drought continued through those months and into January 1792. Al-Jabartī writes that "not one drop of water fell from heaven." Some peasants did their best to farm lands that seemed salvageable, but when they plowed, they found only worms and rats. The vermin competed among themselves and with their human rivals for fruits and the precious few crops that were grown in fields that year. Many people had to make do with weeds, and cattle had no spring feed.

The cycle of flood, plague, drought, famine, price inflation, and death in Egypt suggests that there was a kind of cyclical pathology to the economy that functioned alongside the ecological pathology of plague in Egypt.[120] As the amounts of available foodstuffs decreased, prices and the severity of official measures to secure adequate supplies for the powerful and for the military increased.[121] In response, one notices numerous

[117] For a discussion of the relationship between famine and plague in Mamlūk Egypt, see: Tucker, "Natural Disasters," 217–19. Also instructive on this point is the following: Elisabeth Carpentier, "Autour de la peste noire: Famines et épidémies dans l'histoire du XIVe siècle," *Annales* 17 (1962): 1062–92.

[118] Al-Jabartī, *ʿAjāʾib al-Āthār*, 2:373.

[119] Ibid., 2:374.

[120] Suggestive of a similar concept is Ira M. Lapidus's use of the phrase an "economic geography of Egypt." Lapidus, "The Grain Economy of Mamluk Egypt," *JESHO* 12 (1969): 13.

[121] For another example of the relationship between food shortages and price increases during plague epidemics, see: Michael W. Dols, "al-Manbijī's 'Report of the Plague:'

instances of agitations, complaints, and small-scale revolts on the part of peasants and merchants against those official actions. For example, when Mūrad Bey and his amirs entered Cairo in July 1791, grain prices began to soar.[122] Because of the low Nile and the weakness of the population (*ḍaʿf al-nās*) from plague and other hardships, the amirs began to seize grains for themselves and their entourage. Their cruelty was proved when one of them attempted to extract an unjustly large sum from a village outside of Cairo. A revolt broke out in Cairo and in the village itself in response to the draconian move on the part of one of Mūrad Bey's amirs. The villagers refused to pay, and the *ʿulamāʾ* denounced the amir's illegal actions. A violent struggle between the amir and the villagers soon ensued but was brought to an end when Mūrad Bey, fearful that unrest might spread, reined in his amir and apologized to the *ʿulamāʾ* and the villagers.

Quarantine: Defining the Social

The first instance of the systematic use of quarantine in Egypt as a defense against plague came a few years after the plague of 1791, during the French expedition to Egypt lasting from 1798 to 1801.[123] On Sunday, March 24, 1799, French forces printed and posted around Cairo an order concerning plague and its treatment through the new mechanism of quarantine.[124] I quote the order in full here:

> An address to the people of Cairo, Būlāq, Old Cairo and vicinity. You shall obey, uphold and observe, without opposition, the orders.

A Treatise on the Plague of 764–765/1362–1364 in the Middle East," in *The Black Death: The Impact of the Fourteenth-Century Plague*, ed. Daniel Williman, Papers of the Eleventh Annual Conference of the Center for Medieval and Early Renaissance Studies (Binghamton, NY: Center for Medieval and Early Renaissance Studies, 1982), 71.

122 This account is related in al-Khashshāb, *Akhbār al-Amīr Murād*, 33–34.

123 As mentioned previously, there were important precedents to quarantine in the Muslim world before the end of the eighteenth century, although none was applied with such rigor and on such a scale as that seen here. On the general history and application of quarantine in Ottoman Egypt, see: Kuhnke, *Lives at Risk*, 92–110; Panzac, *Peste*, 446–514. More generally, see: Panzac, *Quarantaines et lazarets*; Gülden Sarıyıldız, *Hicaz Karantina Teşkilâtı (1865–1914)* (Ankara: Türk Tarih Kurumu, 1996). On the French in Egypt, see: Cole, *Napoleon's Egypt*; Raymond, *Égyptiens et français*.

124 On the plague of 1799 and the issuance of the French quarantine order, see: BOA, HAT 245/13801A (3 Za 1213/9 Apr. 1799). On the quarantine of Russian and French ships on Egypt's Mediterranean coast during the plague outbreak of the winter of 1799 and the early spring of 1800, see: BOA, HAT 240/13451 (29 N 1214/24 Feb. 1800).

Anybody opposing them will encounter abundant vengeance, painful punishment, and severe retribution. They are precautions against the disease of the plague. In the case of anybody whom you know certainly, or believe, imagine, or suspect to be suffering from this illness in any place, house, caravansary or building, it is your duty and obligation to establish a quarantine, and the place must be closed off. The elder of the quarter or street in which this occurs must immediately inform the French officer who is the district supervisor. He, in turn, will report it to the *shaykh al-balad*, the commandant of Cairo and its districts. This must be done promptly. The same holds true for every community of Egypt, her provinces, and districts. If any physicians examine and verify an incident of this disease, each of them must go to the local commandant and report it to him, so that the latter can give appropriate orders to protect and safeguard from this illness. Any of the chiefs of sections, elders of quarters, and police of districts who has information concerning this disease and does not record it will be punished as the commandant sees fit. Neighborhood elders will be punished with 100 lashes for failure to report. It is also decreed that anyone who is infected, or in whose house a case has occurred among his family or relatives, and who moves from his house to somewhere else, shall suffer capital punishment. He will bring injury on himself because of his movement. Any head of a community in a district who does not immediately report incidents of the plague in his district or cases of death resulting from it, will be punished with death. If the washer of a corpse – be it a man or a woman – sees that the deceased died of the plague, or if he or she has suspicions about the death but fails to report it within 24 hours, the washer will be executed. These necessary ordinances are incumbent upon the agha of the Janissaries, and the French and Muslim authorities of the land are advised to alert the people concerning them. Indeed, these are fearful matters. Anybody disobeying will suffer severe punishment from the commandant. It is the duty of the police guard to search out and inspect for this virulent disease in order to protect and guard the people of the country and to alert them to violations. Peace.[125]

The quarantine orders by French forces stationed in Egypt were an extremely direct and powerful statement of the severity of the danger they believed existed in Egypt because of plague.[126] On the threat of execution, they warned Egyptians that plague was to be reported and corralled as quickly as possible so as to check the spread of the disease. Ironically, the French were ready to kill to prevent widespread death from

[125] Al-Jabartī, *ʿAjāʾib al-Āthār*, 3:81–82.

[126] For examples of the effects of plague and quarantine on the French military in Egypt and Palestine, see: ibid., 3:107, 135, 240, 251.

plague.[127] Although dire in its predictions and firm in its authority, the public statement by French authorities did not reveal to Egyptians the harsh severity of the quarantine that was about to envelop their society.[128] According to al-Jabartī:

> Quarantine... increased the people's anxiety and fear of the plague. Rumors spread that whoever was struck by the disease in a place discovered by the French, would be taken to a French quarantine, his family getting no news from him, unless he recuperates and returns home in good health. Otherwise his family will never see him again nor learn anything about him. For if he dies, the quarantine attendants seize him and bury him in a hole, in the clothes he is wearing. Nobody can enter his home or leave it for four days. All his clothes will be burnt, a guard will stand at the gate, and if anybody passes by, and merely touches the gate or crosses the line drawn there, he will be detained, taken into the house, and kept in quarantine. If one dies at home, and proves to have been struck by the plague, his clothes and bedding are assembled and burned. The deceased is washed and carried by special attendants, and is buried without a funeral. In front of the bier are people preventing passers-by from getting close. If anybody does get close, he is quarantined immediately; and after the burial, they will quarantine anybody who touched him while washing or carrying or burying him. The attendant will go out only for another such service, and on condition that he touch nothing else. This horrified the people, and filled them with repugnance; they started fleeing from Cairo to the countryside for this reason.[129]

Thus, as we see here, quarantine created a divided world whose borders were defended by force. No one, except the quarantine attendant,

[127] This same point was made in another French order posted throughout Cairo on May 2, 1799, a few short weeks after the foregoing decree. Perhaps confusing syphilis for plague, the French write:

> After due consideration, we have discerned that the readiest and most reliable means to alleviate or prevent the danger of plague is avoidance of contact with women of ill repute, since they are the foremost carriers of this disease. Therefore we have decreed and ordered a prohibition for a period of thirty days, starting from the above date, for all people, be they French, Muslims, Greeks, Christians, or Jews (from whatever community they may be) and that anyone who introduces to Cairo, Būlāq, or Old Cairo women of ill-repute, be it in the living quarters of the soldiers or any other place inside the city, will be punished with death.

Ibid., 3:90. Tellingly, it was the pimps who made their business from these women who were to be killed, not the infected women themselves.

[128] The French military's enforcement of quarantine during the 1720 plague in Marseille was similarly brutal in its application and likely served as a model for later quarantines. Charles Carrière, Marcel Courdurié, and Ferréol Rebuffat, *Marseille ville morte: La peste de 1720* (Marseille: M. Garçon, 1968).

[129] Al-Jabartī, *ʿAjāʾib al-Āthār*, 3:235–36.

was allowed to cross between the two worlds. If one had any exposure to anyone or anything from inside the quarantine, he or she, too, would become a part of that world until death or his or her unlikely recuperation from plague. Like death itself, quarantine did not discriminate between rich and poor, privileged and not. For example, even a high official like the agha of the Mustahfizan military bloc died in quarantine on March 21, 1801.[130] "He became sick on Saturday, and died by nightfall. They put him in a coffin, and only the carriers went with the bier, preceded by men chasing away passers-by. No funeral, no public. His home was under quarantine, with all the household locked within."[131]

Quarantine also served to increase Egyptians' fears of plague and its consequences, causing widespread discontent, rebellion, and escape from the quarantine regimes of Cairo.[132] The fear brought on by quarantine was not only the fear of biological death, but – and perhaps more important – the social fear of the separation of families from the sick, from the cultural institutions surrounding death, and from the bodies of plague victims. Because those taken to quarantine were usually never heard from again, force was often needed to move plague victims to quarantine.[133] Families received no news about their sick relatives whose homes could have been seized and their possessions burned. By dividing the sick and the dying from their families, quarantine not only affected the separation of plague from the regular environmental pathology in which it had existed for centuries in Egypt but also prevented Egyptians from engaging in the multiple institutions and practices associated with sickness, dying, healing, and death that had likewise developed over the course of centuries in Egypt.

The frustrations caused by this separation of families from their loved ones and sick relatives as a result of the establishment of quarantine were expressed in a letter sent to al-Jabartī from his friend Ḥasan al-ʿAṭṭār, who complained about the fact that quarantine prevented his travel from the southern city of Asyūṭ to Cairo to visit his family in a time of plague:

> When I decided definitely to travel, equipped myself, and made preparations, hurdles and obstacles built up on the way, but there is no refuge from what God has ordained. The difficulties arose from the quarantine, which was an affliction and trouble. It was established like a gag on

[130] The plague of 1801 and 1802 was most virulent in the central Egyptian city of Jirja, and all told, it claimed the lives of more than three hundred *kāshifs* and Circassian Mamlūks. BOA, HAT 86/3520 (29 N 1216/3 Feb. 1802).

[131] Al-Jabartī, *ʿAjāʾib al-Āthār*, 3:238.

[132] For an example of Egyptian resistance to French quarantine measures, see: ibid., 3:273.

[133] See, e.g., the case of Muṣṭafā Aghā Abṭāl in the following: ibid., 3:245.

> the mouth of land and sea in order to prevent the spread of the plague, an epidemic which broke out among us in accordance with the predictions of the sura of the Rending and the sura of the Dawn. It descended upon Cairo and its surroundings, and spread into all regions and areas. *All this is insignificant compared to what occurred and is heartrending: the separation from my home away from my kith and kin.* At that point I realized that there is not deliverance from this town and this is no time for escape.[134]

Despite the dissatisfaction of most Egyptians with quarantine as a method of defending against plague, and despite their numerous attempts, both large and small, to resist the measures, the government of Mehmet ʿAli nevertheless continued the use of quarantine once it had solidified its power in 1805 after the end of the French occupation. Like so much of his rule – whether in the realms of education, bureaucracy, medicine, construction, or the military – Mehmet ʿAli's use of quarantine was virtually a direct copy of French models. Thus, in January 1813, in one of his first acts of quarantine, Mehmet ʿAli established a quarantine in Alexandria "as the Europeans do in their country" to defend Egypt from a virulent plague epidemic reported in Istanbul.[135] Any person arriving from Istanbul, Anatolia, or the Ottoman Balkans would be forced to wait on ship in the port of Alexandria for forty days before being allowed to enter Egypt. Moreover, if someone died onboard the ship during the waiting period, the forty-day clock would begin anew.

As rumors of death from plague and the actual number of dead increased in Istanbul and Alexandria in early 1813, Mehmet ʿAli attempted to tighten his quarantine regime on Egypt's Mediterranean coast. The fact that plague moved so easily between Istanbul and Egypt was, of course, a function of the very intimate ties between the two places and the great amount of boat traffic between them that ensured a constant circulation of goods, peoples, and rats. Thus, in early 1813, Mehmet ʿAli ordered quarantines in the ports of Rashīd, Damietta, Burullus, and Shubra and directed the *kāshif* of the subprovince of al-Baḥayra to prevent any overland travelers from entering the area.[136] He further instructed that prayers be recited in al-Azhar for the end of the plague. These efforts notwithstanding, it soon became clear that the quarantine of Egypt's Mediterranean coast in early 1813 was not preventing plague from entering the province. Indeed, by the spring of 1813, plague had fully gripped Alexandria, killing many of the city's civilians and military

[134] Ibid., 3:171. Emphasis added.
[135] Ibid., 4:210.
[136] Ibid., 4:238.

troops.[137] Fearing the disease's penetration into the rest of Egypt, Mehmet ʿAli ordered the quarantine of Giza on April 12, 1813.[138] This order came on the heels of the pasha's decision to move his family and retinue to Giza to protect them during the period of plague. Giza was on the opposite bank of the Nile from the Citadel, Fustat, Bulaq, and the main population centers of Cairo and its environs. Mehmet ʿAli thought he would be more protected in Giza, especially given the recent news that several Europeans and an Egyptian legal clerk had died of plague in Fustat.

Mehmet ʿAli was clearly very worried about the outbreak of plague in Egypt. He feared for his own life and truly believed that quarantine was the best defense against the pest in Egypt. He and his functionaries "believed that the quarantine would be efficacious and would prevent the plague."[139] Given his paranoia about plague, Mehmet ʿAli sought to defend and to cleanse himself from any traces of contact with those who might have been exposed to the disease. For example, when he received mail or other correspondence, the letters had to be put through a rigorous fumigation and purification process. Before even arriving in Giza on the left bank of the Nile, where the pasha was stationed in his own self-imposed quarantine, letters were first to be fumigated using wormwood, olibanum, and sulfur. The letters were then attached to the end of a very long stick carried by a messenger on a boat. The messenger would sail near the shores of Giza to transfer the letters to the end of another very long stick carried by one of Mehmet ʿAli's own men stationed in his own boat off the Giza shore. Only after the transfer from stick to stick was completed, without any human contact, could a letter then be sailed to the shore where Mehmet ʿAli was residing. Taking care not to touch the letter with their own hands, Mehmet ʿAli's men would then dip it – still on the end of a stick – into vinegar and fumigate it with incense. It was then, and only then, that the letter could be delivered to the pasha. Thus, from the time of a letter's departure from the eastern shores of the Nile until it reached Mehmet ʿAli's hands, its paper was fumigated and cleansed several times and never touched by a human hand.

As during the French occupation, Mehmet ʿAli's complicated maneuvers to protect himself and his province from plague through quarantine imposed untold hardships on the population of Egypt. For example, when he first decided to reside in Giza during the plague outbreak of

137 Ibid., 4:243.
138 Ibid., 4:244.
139 Ibid.

1813, Mehmet ʿAli attempted to remove as many people as possible from the area. Families with their own food supplies, who could support themselves for at least sixty days, were allowed to stay in Giza, but everyone else had to leave immediately. This understandably created a state of panic among the people of Giza as the vast majority of them readied themselves to flee. As it was spring when fields were to be prepared for harvest, there were, under normal circumstances, many agricultural responsibilities to undertake. There was no time, however, for peasants in Giza to attend to such matters. Mehmet ʿAli pushed out of Giza as many people as possible in an effort to protect himself from plague.

This quarantined lockdown on Giza continued into the summer of 1813.[140] Throughout the entire period, people were steadily forced to leave the area and pushed into a life of roaming the countryside in search of shelter and sustenance. In short, "the people of Giza suffered immeasurably by being evacuated from their homes."[141] According to al-Jabartī:

> The whole population left the town except for a very small number. They scattered throughout the countryside, though many remained in the environs of the town and in the fields around the threshing floors and basins. They made shelters to shade themselves from the sun and the blast of the midday heat. Those who had had to stay in the town would call from atop the walls to friends and comrades outside; the answers to these persons would be passed on from afar. But those within the town were not permitted to receive anything from those without.[142]

Thus, the quarantine of Giza again clearly shows how measures to defend against plague created a kind of dual society: those in the quarantine and those outside it.[143] There were two worlds, divided between the diseased and the healthy, the living and the dying – between families and their sick relatives, between a society and those deemed a threat to its well-being, between a plagued landscape and the rest of the salubrious Egyptian environment.

Plague would continue to strike Egypt for decades to come.[144] And Egyptians would continue to suffer not only from the disease itself

[140] Ibid., 4:246–47.

[141] Ibid., 4:287.

[142] Ibid., 4:246.

[143] Later quarantines were also established in Giza. For a discussion of the plague quarantine in Giza in 1815, see: ibid., 4:307.

[144] For example, plague broke out in Cairo in 1804–1805 (ibid., 3:497) and in Alexandria in early 1813 (ibid., 4:241–42). On the plague of the spring of 1814, see: ibid., 4:287. On plague in the following year (1815), see: ibid., 4:307–8. For a general discussion of

but also from the quarantine measures imposed on them by various governments.[145] Indeed, the continuous use of quarantine in Egypt from the period of the French invasion through the rule of Mehmet ʿAli and later suggests the highly derivative nature of Mehmet ʿAli's state in Egypt. Not only in the realm of quarantine but in other domains of knowledge and practice as well, Mehmet ʿAli's Ottoman regime largely copied European techniques of rule and bureaucracy in its own administration. He was advised to do so by European consultants, who had been hired precisely to aid him in the application of European models of rule in Egypt. The wholesale borrowing of European regimes of power by what is considered by most Egyptian nationalist historians the beginnings of the modern Egyptian state, led by the figure many consider the "founder of modern Egypt," suggests to us the continuation – rather than the end – of European colonial notions of rule and authority in Egypt long after the French invasion.[146]

Mehmet ʿAli's government, in other words, upheld colonial policies and ideas as pillars of its own rule. Scholars of postcolonial nationalism have long observed and critiqued the derivative nature of postcolonial nationalist discourse as a problematic copy of a tragically violent original.[147] Mehmet ʿAli was thus not – as some would have it – a liberatory figure who came to Egypt after the French expedition to work toward the creation of an independent modern Egyptian state. Quite to the contrary, his was a state still largely in the Ottoman fold and one that would increasingly come to be built on colonial European models.

plague in the first half of the nineteenth century in Egypt, see: Kuhnke, *Lives at Risk*, 69–91.

145 On quarantine after the period discussed here, see: Kuhnke, *Lives at Risk*, 92–110. On resistance to quarantine by Egyptian soldiers stationed in Syria during Mehmet ʿAli's invasion, see: Fahmy, *All the Pasha's Men*, 226.

146 The phrase "the founder of modern Egypt" is taken from the title of the following: Dodwell, *The Founder of Modern Egypt*. For what has become one of the standard Egyptian nationalist accounts of Mehmet ʿAli's rule in Egypt, see: al-Rāfʿī, *ʿAṣr Muḥammad ʿAlī*. For a critique of the Egyptian nationalist school of history, see: Fahmy, *All the Pasha's Men*, 1–37.

147 One of the most sustained and influential works in this regard is the following: Partha Chatterjee, *Nationalist Thought and the Colonial World: A Derivative Discourse* (Minneapolis: University of Minnesota Press, 1998). Tellingly, the subtitle of the earlier edition of this book published by Zed Books in 1986 ends with a question mark, suggesting to us perhaps the author's greater certainty on the question of the derivative nature of postcolonial nationalism almost a decade after his book's original publication.

The postcolonial predicament of emulation is, however, not the only explanation for the despotic nature of Mehmet ʿAli's rule in Egypt.[148] As discussed in the previous chapter with regard to labor, the Ottoman bureaucracy of Egypt became increasingly sophisticated and violent over the course of the long eighteenth century in its use and control of the Egyptian peasantry. Mehmet ʿAli was both the beneficiary and descendent of this authoritarian logic of rule. He saw the Egyptian peasantry as an endless mass of laborers, soldiers, and potential disease vectors. In the words of one Egyptian historian, Mehmet ʿAli "despised the Egyptians."[149] Mehmet ʿAli's regime was thus in many ways the culmination of processes set in motion much earlier in the eighteenth century. As the bureaucracy of Egypt became increasingly despotic and even colonial, its mechanisms of rule became more exacting and regimented. Labor charts and quarantine were two of the mechanisms of rule developed over the course of the long eighteenth century that Mehmet ʿAli adapted and expanded.

As embodied in the preceding story of quarantine, and like the French who first used the new technology in Egypt, Mehmet ʿAli's state bureaucracy functioned largely through violence, the seizure of property, the forced movement of peasant populations, and other forms of coercion and force. As in the example of quarantine, however, Mehmet ʿAli's rule also represented new kinds and forms of knowledge that came to hold sway in Egypt. As I have argued throughout much of this book, Egyptian peasant expertise, experience, and knowledge more often than not came to inform Ottoman imperial policy with regard to irrigation matters over the course of the long eighteenth century. The Ottoman imperial system was one that cultivated local actors both to inform the state of matters related to irrigation and agriculture and to take the initiative in prompting the repair of irrigation works and other infrastructure. The state thus subsumed local peasant knowledge, which came to shape how the imperial state functioned in Egypt.

Mehmet ʿAli's continuation of the application of European ideas of disease and its treatment in Egypt represented the end of the influence of local knowledge on imperial state policies. The fates of thousands of

[148] I borrow the phrase "postcolonial predicament" from the following: Carol A. Breckenridge and Peter van der Veer, eds., *Orientalism and the Postcolonial Predicament: Perspectives on South Asia* (Philadelphia: University of Pennsylvania Press, 1993).

[149] Afaf Lutfi al-Sayyid Marsot, *Egypt in the Reign of Muhammad Ali* (Cambridge: Cambridge University Press, 1984), 97.

Egyptian peasants were taken out of their own hands and given over to foreign experts and technocrats who advised the pasha on how best to deal with disease, irrigation, and myriad other issues of state. The replacement of local peasant expertise and experience with European ideas of how best to rule a society and an environment was the end of the use of local knowledge in Egypt. Since those early decades of the nineteenth century, the Egyptian state has continued to privilege European notions and ideas of how to manage and organize rural Egypt over local experience in and knowledge of the countryside. Thus, Mehmet ʿAli's regime functioned to take power and influence away from Egyptian peasants as it sought to reorganize and reimagine Egypt along what were clearly European rather than historically experienced and molded local Ottoman-Egyptian lines.

Quarantine, as one of those European recastings, served to remove plague from the Egyptian environment in which it had functioned as a regular and expected phenomenon like flood, drought, and wind for at least a millennium and probably longer. By taking plague out of Egyptian nature, quarantine made it into a "foreign" disease that was to exist outside of the Egyptian social body and that therefore was to be feared, defended against, and removed. The point is not that Egyptians before the end of the eighteenth century enjoyed plague or somehow wanted to die from it. Clearly, that was not the case, nor is it the argument I have been advancing in this chapter. The point, rather, is that plague had come to be accepted as an environmental reality that affected Egypt on a regular basis. As an expected and accepted environmental reality, plague therefore became a social reality that both accrued to it and helped shape all sorts of social and cultural practices and institutions.

As we saw earlier, plague and death were indeed integral parts of life in Ottoman Egypt. Care for the sick, prayers on their behalf, rites of the dead, condolences, washing of the corpse, burial, funeral prayers, and all sorts of other social and cultural practices were attached to the presence of the sick and the dead in society and to its prerequisite, the presence of plague in the Egyptian environment. Once the sick and the dead were removed from society by their forced seizure to the space of quarantine, all those institutions, rites, and traditions were no longer afforded a space in which to occur. The practices and the people who carried them out were literally cut off from the bodies of the sick and the dead on which they relied. Families were thus no longer able to grieve in the ways they knew how, often did not even know when or if their loved ones had died, and were forced to accept that their sick relatives were no longer worthy of being considered a part of the living world.

Quarantine was thus one part of a new conception of Egyptian society at the end of the eighteenth century and the beginning of the nineteenth. Society and the social practices that made it up were no longer realms for disease, the sick, and the dead as they had been in previous centuries. Society was to be clean, sanitized, antisepticised, productive, healthy, and protected. Quarantine helped define the contours of this "healthy" Egyptian social body in which culture, thought, and politics could and would be practiced – one that was opposed to the space of quarantine in which the sick, the dead, and all those not fit for the exercise of the social were sent to be removed and forgotten. Thus, similar to the ways in which shifts in the organization of labor over the course of the eighteenth century worked to define a rough sketch of the human potentials of the Egyptian population in a particular environmental space, the application of quarantine to plague represented a new conception of the spaces and borders of Egyptian society, a kind of medical topography of disease and of the environment in which disease existed.

Both technologies of power – enumeration and quarantine – were integral but by no means the only pieces of a new – to use Paul Rabinow's term – social pathology that came to hold sway in Egypt at the end of the long eighteenth century. In reference to the 1832 outbreak of cholera in Paris, Rabinow writes, "Air, water, light, and circulation hardly disappeared as objects of inquiry and intervention; however, they were gradually assigned a subordinate role in a new conceptual order stressing social pathology. This emphasis opened up the possibility of postulating and elaborating norms for different milieux."[150] He continues: "The cholera epidemic catalyzed a new set of relationships, spurring a more precise and powerful analysis of the milieu focusing on *conditions de vie* that included local biological and social variables."[151] Thus, enumeration and quarantine were about the imagination and reality of how to manage the possibilities of new *conditions de vie* in late-eighteenth-century Egypt,

[150] Paul Rabinow, *French Modern: Norms and Forms of the Social Environment* (Chicago: University of Chicago Press, 1995), 32. The 1832 cholera outbreak has proved a fertile ground for social and cultural historians and theorists of public health and disease. See, e.g.: Catherine J. Kudlick, *Cholera in Post-Revolutionary France: A Cultural History* (Berkeley: University of California Press, 1996); Coleman, *Death Is a Social Disease*, 171–80; François Delaporte, *Disease and Civilization: The Cholera in Paris, 1832*, trans. Arthur Goldhammer (Cambridge: Massachusetts Institute of Technology Press, 1986).

[151] Rabinow, *French Modern*, 39.

and – crucially – the technologies were meant to be portable so as to be applicable to other social realms and environmental milieux.

Significantly, these newly emerging conceptions of Egypt and of how to govern it were not wholly a result of either the "enlightenment" of French rule in Egypt or the "modernity" of Mehmet ʿAli's regime; they were, rather, the latter stages of processes set into motion much earlier. As Egypt over the course of the long eighteenth century slowly pulled away from the Ottoman imperial system of natural resource management, it had to become more self-sufficient. Without the benefits of a system of import and export balance that provided Egypt with wood, grain markets, cash, labor, and other resources, the province had to ask more of its people and its environment. Thus, a growing population and the demands of an expanding economy weighed heavily on the environmental resources of Egypt. How was Egypt to meet those challenges with the resources it had? The environmental realities, excesses, and deficiencies of Egypt – an Egypt that was slowly disconnecting from the Ottoman Empire – largely determined the answer of Mehmet ʿAli's regime to this question. In the early nineteenth century, the answer was quarantine, corvée, conscription, and the seizure of natural and other kinds of resources from Egypt and elsewhere (as in the case of wood from Greater Syria, for instance). The regime's responses to the challenges posed by efforts to gain autonomy from the Empire thus took the form of numerous coercive and even colonial apparatuses of rule meant to order Egypt – the labor chart, quarantine, deforestation, forced labor, cadastral surveys, and maps. The potentialities of the new imagination and reality of society and of the environment embodied in these coercive technologies were to be tested in various ways with varying degrees of success throughout the first decades of the nineteenth century. We now turn to one of the most significant and least successful of the test cases: the reconstruction of the Maḥmūdiyya Canal.

6

ANOTHER NILE

As we have seen in the preceding two chapters, various sets of transformations over the course of the long eighteenth century served to shape the rough outlines of a new conception of society in Egypt as the province moved further and further away from its previous centrality in the Ottoman system of imperial natural resource management. Changes in the organization of labor formed the bases for ideas of an Egyptian population – its size, potentials, and resources. The advent of quarantine to address plague in Egypt not only represented a different conception of the place of disease in the environment but also served to define the physical realm of the social as opposed to that of the diseased and dying. This chapter returns us more squarely to irrigation works to examine how several of these new processes, ideas, and institutional formations came to bear on the development of a new imaginary of what Egypt was and into what it could be fashioned. The event around which these processes and ideas coalesced was the reconstruction of the Maḥmūdiyya Canal in the second decade of the nineteenth century.[1]

The project of rebuilding what would come to be known as the Maḥmūdiyya Canal was one meant to serve the society defined by technologies such as quarantine. It was a canal that would feed water to Alexandria,

[1] The most sustained study of the history of the canal from antiquity to its reconstruction in the nineteenth century is the following: ʿUmar Ṭūsūn, *Tārīkh Khalīj al-Iskandariyya al-Qadīm wa Turʿat al-Maḥmūdiyya* (Alexandria: Maṭbaʿat al-ʿAdl, 1942). It consists largely of selections from published accounts related to the canal, as well as some archival materials about its nineteenth-century history. As with most nationalist histories written in the first half of the twentieth century, Ṭūsūn's account completely jumps over the Ottoman period by moving directly from the writings of medieval scholars like al-Maqrīzī and Ibn Mammātī to the works of the savants of the French occupation – authors like M. A. Linant de Bellefonds and Felix Mengin. For a very general accounting of the various repairs undertaken on the canal from antiquity until the end of the nineteenth century based exclusively on published sources, see also: Isabelle Hairy and Oueded Sennoune, "Géographie historique du canal d'Alexandrie," *AI* 40 (2006): 247–78.

thus making the city a thriving economic and cultural metropolis to rival Cairo.[2] The canal was meant to serve the Egyptian social body while at the same time creating the requisite conditions for its development, growth, and longevity. To make this canal a reality, a veritable city of laborers was brought to work on the project. Employing more workers than the entire population of Cairo at the time (and killing one hundred thousand of them), the canal project harnessed the powers of the Egyptian working population that had been enumerated and organized in the previous decades, as we saw in Chapter 4. Projects like the 1808 canal repair in Manfalūṭ, a job that used more than thirty-three thousand workers, laid the groundwork for the Maḥmūdiyya project. Techniques of enumeration and bureaucratic organization similar to those discussed earlier made possible the use of the hundreds of thousands of workers who dug, dredged, and reinforced the Maḥmūdiyya. Moreover, this population of workers was specifically conceptualized as acting in the service of the population of Alexandria and, indeed, of the population of Egypt as a whole. Thus, the concepts of society and population that had emerged earlier in various forms and sizes were refashioned on a much grander scale in the reconstruction of the Maḥmūdiyya.

Before addressing changes wrought on the canal in the second decade of the nineteenth century, this chapter first outlines several of the most crucial and common themes in the history of the canal and also places the waterway in the context of other Egyptian irrigation works.[3] Perhaps the most important of those works was a series of dams along the Mediterranean coast constructed to protect the canal and the lands near it from the infiltration of the sea's salty waters. The dams and their maintenance embody many of the ideas I have already developed: the influence of local knowledge and expertise in the repair and maintenance of Egypt's irrigation network, the contingencies of the entire network on the proper function of all its parts, and the increasing emphasis placed on the role of measure and enumeration in labor projects. The dams were in many ways the last major irrigation works in Egypt to be managed along the lines described in this book. Because of their importance to the function of the Ashrafiyya Canal (as the Maḥmūdiyya was known until the nineteenth

[2] On the population and demography of eighteenth-century Alexandria, see: Reimer, "Ottoman Alexandria," 107–46.

[3] For a very useful comparative study of canal construction in seventeenth-century France, see: Chandra Mukerji, *Impossible Engineering: Technology and Territoriality on the Canal du Midi* (Princeton, NJ: Princeton University Press, 2009).

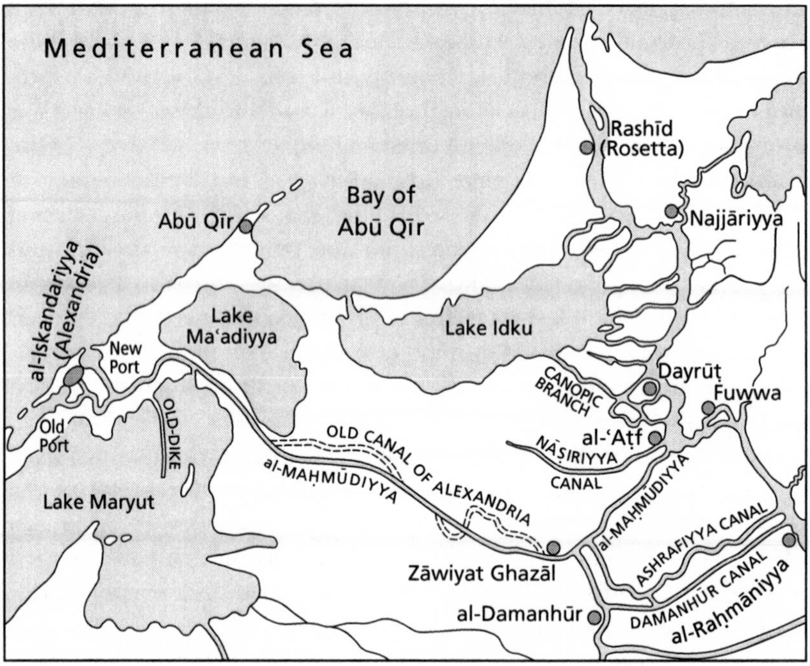

Map 6. The Maḥmūdiyya Canal, early nineteenth century.

century), their histories were intertwined with that of the waterway for centuries, but, as we will see in this chapter, they would soon fall away in importance as Mehmet ʿAli attempted to make the Ashrafiyya into a veritable second Nile.[4]

4 The nomenclature associated with the canal is rather problematic. As already mentioned, the canal would not come to be known as the Maḥmūdiyya until the third decade of the nineteenth century. The most general name for the canal for the majority of its history was simply the Alexandria Canal. However, since the period of the reign of Ashraf Qaitbay at the end of the fifteenth century, during which time major repairs were undertaken on the canal, the entire length of the waterway came to be known as the Ashrafiyya Canal. Technically, however, the Ashrafiyya refers only to the portion of the canal that begins in the village of al-Raḥmāniyya on the Rashīd branch of the Nile. The canal that begins in Fuwwa or al-ʿAṭf is usually referred to as the Nāṣiriyya Canal. On these names, see: Wizārat al-Ashghāl, *al-Nīl wa Tārīkh al-Riyy*, 152–54; Hairy and Sennoune, "Géographie historique," 276. In practice, however, the names were most often used interchangeably, especially as the mouth of the canal was moved several times. Nevertheless, Ashrafiyya remained the most common name for all parts of the canal until the nineteenth century. Unless otherwise noted, I use the name given in the original sources. On the various names of the canal from antiquity, see: Hairy and Sennoune, "Géographie historique," 269–71.

Irrigating Alexandria

Long before the exigencies of the second decade of the nineteenth century, various governments in Egypt recognized the need and benefit of connecting Egypt's second city to the Nile Valley via some sort of conduit of water. The main reason behind the construction of a canal from the Nile to Alexandria was the desire to create a consistent source of sweet drinking water for the people of Alexandria. Alexandria itself had no source of fresh water, and the lands in and around the city were dirty, rocky, and sandy. It was said that water near the city was so bad that it was not even suitable for washing clothes (*şöyle dursun esvap gaslına dahi salih değildir*)![5] Historically, there were three ways to supply Alexandria with drinking water: rain, transport overland by animal or via the Mediterranean by ship, and the various manifestations of the Ashrafiyya Canal.[6] Clearly, the construction and maintenance of a properly functioning canal was the most effective and reliable solution to the problem. Like many polities before it, the Ottoman government of Egypt thus sought to address the problem of water in Alexandria with the building of a canal.

Beginning at the end of the eighteenth century, Alexandria increasingly became a center of commerce and merchant traffic from all over the Mediterranean world – from Anatolia, the Arab world, Persia, and Europe (*Rum ve Arab ve Acem diyarından ve Frengistandan*).[7] And as Alexandria became a city in which a great deal of merchant capital came to be exchanged, in favor of other port cities like Rashīd, which had formerly held the role, it came to serve as a source for the spread of Egyptian goods like henna, flax, sugar, and rice to many parts of the Mediterranean littoral.[8] According to an Ottoman decree from late 1817, the human

5 BOA, HAT, 130/5404 (29 Z 1232/9 Nov. 1817).

6 There was indeed a thriving water import business in Alexandria. Much of the water was brought by boat from the Nile via Rashīd. In addition, in an area two or three hours away from Alexandria that foreigners called Süleyman Harbor, one could find some fresh water if he or she dug in certain sandy areas. Merchants who sold imported water, not surprisingly, charged very high prices for this rather rare commodity. For their part, wealthy residents of Alexandria built their own private cisterns to provide sweet water directly to their homes and properties.

7 For an account of the suitability of the port of Alexandria for maritime commerce, see: Ḥasan Sayyid Ḥasan, "Mīnā' al-Iskandariyya: Dirāsa fī Jughrāfiyyat al-Naql al-Baḥrī" (Ph.D. diss., ʿAyn Shams University, 1982).

8 On the hereditary nature of various positions connected with the management of the port of Alexandria during the Ottoman period, see: BOA, Cevdet Bahriye, 866 (9 S 1144/12 Aug. 1731).

population (*nüfus-i insaniyye*) of locals and foreigners (*yerli ve yabancı*) resident in Alexandria was more than twenty or thirty thousand.[9] For their own sake and, in turn, for the sake of the prosperity of the city, these people needed sweet water (*tatlı su*) to drink and to use for various other purposes. This was the function of the large series of cisterns in and around the city that stored water coming from the Ashrafiyya Canal. When the flood was low in a certain year or when the canal was in a state of disrepair, great hardship was visited on the people of Alexandria, which caused many of them to flee the city.

A lack of water also led to famine (*kaht ü galâ*) for the people of Alexandria and for those peasants living in villages around the city. Equally calamitous, if not more so, from the perspective of the Ottoman state was the prospect that a lack of water (*susuzluk*) would lead to commercial ruin for the city. If word spread that there were water and food shortages in Alexandria, it was feared that merchants from Anatolia, Rum, the Arab world, and Europe would stop coming to the city altogether, finding other more desirable destinations for their business and goods. Should this situation of a virtual boycott of commerce last for any extended period of time, the city and Egypt as a whole would very quickly become economically moribund (*kâr kalmadı*).

Thus, it was the Ottoman state's desire to create a situation in which water permanently flowed to Alexandria that drove its efforts to reconstruct the Ashrafiyya Canal. The Ottoman state indeed never wanted there to occur a dearth of water in Alexandria again (*İskenderiye'de su kıtlığı çıkılmıyıp*). When the city was well irrigated and tranquil (*asayiş*), commerce would gravitate toward it, making it larger and larger, and, eventually, it would come to seem "natural" (*tabiati*) for so many merchants to reside in Alexandria and for the city to be so big.[10] The Ottoman bureaucracy estimated that, at the very minimum, seventy or eighty thousand people would come to live in Alexandria.[11] There is no indication

9 These population numbers seem rather high in comparison to Daniel Panzac's estimate that the population of Alexandria in 1821 was 12,528. Panzac, "Alexandrie: Évolution d'une ville cosmopolite au XIXe siècle," in *Population et santé dans l'Empire ottoman (XVIIIe-XXe siècles)* (Istanbul: Isis, 1996), 147.

10 The word *natural* is used here idiomatically to suggest a preexisting state of affairs that was taken as given in the context of the current situation. It is curious that this word appears in documents from the early nineteenth century to refer only to the social, political, or economic condition of Alexandria and not to a canal or some other feature of the environment or Egypt's irrigation network.

11 The population of Alexandria in 1830 was one hundred thousand. Panzac, "Évolution d'une ville cosmopolite," 147.

as to how these numbers were determined or as to how much time was required for those people to move to the city. Not only would a larger population in Alexandria aid in the commercial and economic life of the city, but the high concentration of people in Egypt's second city would also make any attempts at foreign invasion much more difficult. Alexandria's demographic and economic well-being were, therefore, very clearly dependent on the availability of reliable amounts of water in the city – a common theme invoked throughout the record of correspondence between Istanbul and Egypt about the canal.

Thus, to maintain sufficient water levels in Alexandria's 210 large and small ancient (*eser-i kadim*) cisterns, the Ashrafiyya Canal had to be properly maintained and dredged so as to maximize the amount of water flowing to Alexandria during the season of the flood.[12] In 1738, for example, the canal was in such a poor state of repair that even with that year's exceptionally high flood of twenty-two cubits (the historical average was sixteen cubits), the canal could not bring enough drinking water to Alexandria.[13] During periods of water shortage in Alexandria, residents and merchants in the city resorted to seeking out alternative sources of water for themselves. Those with sufficient means paid to have

[12] For examples of the use of cisterns (*ṣihrīj*, pl. *ṣahārīj*) throughout Ottoman Egypt, see: DWQ, Maḥkamat al-Baḥayra 23, p. 28, case 46 (8 S 1208/14 Sep. 1793); DWQ, Maḥkamat Rashīd 6, p. 50, case 238 (10 Ca 981/7 Sep. 1573); DWQ, Maḥkamat Rashīd 155, pp. 8–9, case 9 (24 Ş 1163/28 Jul. 1750); DWQ, Maḥkamat Rashīd 125, p. 124, case 215 (17 Za 1132/20 Sep. 1720); DWQ, Maḥkamat Rashīd 134, pp. 257–58, case 335 (16 Ca 1140/29 Dec. 1727); DWQ, Maḥkamat Rashīd 146, pp. 247–50, case 237 (1 Za 1153/19 Jan. 1741); DWQ, Maḥkamat Rashīd 157, pp. 157–58, case 163 (23 Z 1165/31 Oct. 1752); DWQ, Maḥkamat Manfalūṭ 2, p. 150, case 522 (20 L 1180/21 Mar. 1767). The following case clearly states that the utility of cisterns lay in their ability to store the Nile's sweet water (*li-awfār al-māʾ al-ʿadhb min al-Nīl al-Mubārak*): DWQ, Maḥkamat Rashīd 155, pp. 271–272, case 288 (20 M 1164/19 Dec. 1750). For examples of cases involving underground cisterns, see: DWQ, Maḥkamat Rashīd 157, pp. 85–87, case 97 (4 C 1165/19 Apr. 1752); DWQ, Maḥkamat Rashīd 125, pp. 189–90, case 320 (26 S 1133/26 Dec. 1720); DWQ, Maḥkamat Rashīd 154, p. 290, case 320 (3 C 1163/9 May 1750); DWQ, Maḥkamat Rashīd 146, pp. 14–15, case 15 (12 Ra 1153/7 Jun. 1740); DWQ, Maḥkamat Rashīd 134, pp. 297–98, case 405 (14 Za 1138/14 Jul. 1726). On the use and maintenance of cisterns in *waqf* complexes, see: DWQ, Maḥkamat Rashīd 146, pp. 242–44, case 233 (27 L 1153/15 Jan. 1741); DWQ, Maḥkamat Rashīd 137, p. 100, case 174 (12 L 1144/8 Apr. 1732); DWQ, Maḥkamat Rashīd 146, pp. 242–44, case 233 (27 L 1153/15 Jan. 1741); DWQ, Maḥkamat al-Baḥayra 15, pp. 179–80, case 389 (20 Ca 1199/31 Mar. 1785); DWQ, Maḥkamat al-Baḥayra 16, p. 73, case 124 (10 Ş 1200/7 Jun. 1786). For a discussion of the uses and types of cisterns employed in fountains (*asbila*) in Ottoman Cairo, see: Maḥmūd Ḥāmid al-Ḥusaynī, *al-Asbila al-ʿUthmāniyya bi-Madīnat al-Qāhira, 1517–1798* (Cairo: Maktabat Madbūlī, 1988), 42–52.

[13] BOA, MM, 5:393 (Evahir L 1150/11–20 Feb. 1738).

jarīm ships from Rashīd transport fresh water to them in Alexandria. The poor and powerless (*fukara ve aceze*), however, most often dealt with the situation by fleeing to Cairo in search of secure supplies of drinking water.

The work most needed to sustain the waterway as a consistent supplier of sweet water to Alexandria was the dredging of the bottom of the canal and the clearing away of debris that collected in it.[14] Because of a lack of incline from the mouth of the canal toward Alexandria, the Ashrafiyya's current was very weak, and its waters did not flow fast enough to prevent large amounts of silt from collecting on the bottom of the canal. This buildup on the bed of the canal made it progressively more shallow and created large islands of mud in parts of the waterway where the current was especially weak. These factors made any sort of navigation of the canal extremely difficult. Moreover, the large amounts of sand and mud meant that water was often quite dirty when it reached Alexandria and had to be cleaned through a system of filters and storage tanks before human consumption.

The people who actually carried out the dredging and cleaning of the Ashrafiyya Canal were most usually those peasants who lived along its banks. In 1751, for instance, villagers from Minyyat Maṭṭiyya were charged with dredging the canal and reinforcing the embankments along its shores.[15] This work was overseen by elders in the community who had had experience with that sort of work in the past. As the ultimate bearers of responsibility in this regard, such men of knowledge and experience (*arbāb al-wuqūf* and *arbāb al-idrāk*), whom we met previously, were charged by the local court with inspecting this maintenance work while it was being done and after its completion.[16]

A common problem in the history of the Ashrafiyya Canal was the need to prevent peasants along its length from breaking the canal's embankments to siphon off water to their own fields. Because of the canal's weak current and shallowness, certain of its sections were extremely susceptible to drying up completely after peasants had drained water out of the main artery to their fields. From the perspective of the Ottoman administration of Egypt, the largest and most important community on the

[14] For a petition to the Ottoman administration of Egypt complaining about the obstruction of the canal's flow as a result of the collection of thorny branches and garbage (*har ü hâşâk*), see: BOA, MM, 8:139 (Evasıt L 1176/25 Apr.–4 May 1763).

[15] DWQ, Maḥkamat al-Baḥayra 5, pp. 9–10, case 15 (12 Ş 1164/6 Jul. 1751).

[16] For a similar case of repair involving the influence of local knowledge, see: DWQ, Maḥkamat al-Baḥayra 5, pp. 172–73, case 302 (10 Ş 1165/22 Jun. 1752).

Ashrafiyya Canal was the city of Alexandria at the canal's end. Because the waterway finished in Alexandria, it was deemed especially important to protect against the siphoning of water out of the canal as it ran through villages to the coastal city. Indeed, the waters of the Ashrafiyya were so precious and Alexandria was of such importance that every drop of the canal's waters was to be used by the residents of that city.

Much of the labor of peasants on the canal was thus devoted to damming any openings made on it and to fixing areas where peasants had attempted to siphon water out of the canal. Moreover, village leaders were often charged with protecting the Ashrafiyya's embankments by preventing their village's peasants from tapping into the canal's waters. Indeed, heads of villages (*ḥukkām*) along the canal seemed to use all kinds of force and oppression (*kāmil anwāʿ al-maẓālim*) to prevent villagers from filling their own smaller canals with water from the Ashrafiyya.[17] For their parts, in an effort to thwart village elders from preventing them from irrigating their land, peasants often came to courts to register hardships against them. Because of the common interests of the state and village heads in preventing peasants from taking water from the canal destined for Alexandria, peasant complaints did not do much to address concerns over access to water and the force used to prevent the taking of this water from the canal. Indeed, as the Ashrafiyya was considered a part – perhaps one of the most essential parts – of the imperial dikes system (*al-jusūr al-sulṭāniyya*) of the Ottoman bureaucracy of Egypt, local peasant leaders had to swear (*al-ishhād*) in court that they would remain responsible for the preservation and protection of the canal.[18]

Against the Sea

Because of the interconnected nature of irrigation in Egypt, one of the main factors in the proper function of the Ashrafiyya Canal and, hence, in ensuring that Alexandria received an adequate and consistent supply of sweet water was the maintenance of a series of dams on Egypt's Mediterranean coastline. Thus, in a stroke of irony, one of the greatest

[17] DWQ, Maḥkamat al-Baḥayra 7, p. 56, case 112 (2 Ra 1171/14 Nov. 1757).

[18] The full phrase is "al-ishhād ʿalayhim bi-ḥifẓihi wa ḥarāsatihi li-bilādihi." DWQ, Maḥkamat al-Baḥayra 5, p. 9, case 15 (12 Ş 1164/6 Jul. 1751). A variation on this phrase was "al-ishhād ʿalayhim bi-ḥifẓihi wa ḥarāsatihi leylan wa nahāran ṣabāḥan wa masā'an . . . ilā tamām al-riyy wa kāmil al-manfaʿa." DWQ, Maḥkamat al-Baḥayra 9, pp. 56–57, case 116 (14 R 1185/27 Jul. 1771).

threats to Alexandria's water supply was the overabundance of a different kind of water – the Mediterranean's. Indeed, it was very common for the sea to spill over the shore of the Egyptian coast and to flow all the way down to the canal itself (a distance of nearly forty kilometers in places). Not only did this infiltration of salt water render essentially unusable all agricultural land with which it came into contact; but when the water reached the Ashrafiyya Canal, it would quickly mix with the canal's sweet water making it impotable for the people of Alexandria. Thus, to defend against the sea's salty waters, a series of dikes was built along Egypt's Mediterranean coastline, especially on the stretch of more than seventy kilometers between Alexandria and Rashīd. Like the idea of the Ashrafiyya Canal itself, many of the dikes along the Mediterranean coast had ancient precedent, as it was obvious that the infiltration of salt water into the countryside near the coast greatly damaged those areas' agricultural potential.

Therefore, to understand fully the history of the Ashrafiyya Canal over the course of the long eighteenth century, we must first account for the role of the dams in the function of the canal. The dikes along the coast were in constant need of repair because of the sea's incessant pounding against them and because the costs of their failure were extremely high in terms of both food production and the hardships their breaching visited on the residents of Alexandria. The two most important dikes built along the Mediterranean coast were the Alexandria dike and the dam at Abū Qīr. The former most directly protected Alexandria from the waves of the sea and from its salty water infiltrating the city's drinking water supply and the villages in its hinterland in the subprovince of al-Baḥayra. The dike at Abū Qīr was built between the cities of Alexandria and Rashīd, and like the Alexandria Dam, it was also meant to protect both the hundreds of villages in the subprovince of al-Baḥayra just south of the Mediterranean coast and, perhaps more important, the sweet waters of the Ashrafiyya and Nāṣiriyya canals from the saltiness of the Mediterranean.[19]

As the primary defense of Egypt's second city against the dangers posed by the constant force of the Mediterranean's waters to the residents, infrastructure, and water supply of Alexandria, the Alexandria Dam was of particular importance to the overall irrigation infrastructure of Egypt. As such, numerous repairs were undertaken on this dam throughout the eighteenth century – in 1701–1702, 1715–1716, 1719–1720,

[19] On the village of Abū Qīr and the region around it, see: *QJBM*, pt. 2, 2:317.

1727–1728, 1741–1742, 1745–1746, 1746–1747, 1747–1748, 1748–1749, 1753–1754, 1754–1755, and 1762–1763.[20] The single Ottoman Turkish document listing these repairs covers only the period before 1768 and most likely does not include smaller repair projects undertaken on the dam, so there were clearly many more instances of the dam's repair over the course of the long eighteenth century. Indeed, on the basis of other archival evidence, we know that significant additional repairs to the dams on the northern coast of Egypt were undertaken in each of the following years: 1762,[21] 1763,[22] 1768,[23] 1774,[24] 1776,[25] 1784,[26] 1784,[27] 1785/1786,[28] 1802,[29] 1803,[30] 1803–1804,[31] 1804–1805,[32]

[20] BOA, Cevdet Nafia, 337 (Evasıt N 1181/31 Jan.–9 Feb. 1768). On the repairs carried out in 1753, see: BOA, MM, 7:151 (Evahir M 1167/17–26 Nov. 1753).

[21] BOA, Cevdet Nafia, 2386 (Evasıt N 1175/6–15 Apr. 1762).

[22] BOA, MM, 8:148 (Evail S 1177/11–20 Aug. 1763).

[23] BOA, Cevdet Nafia, 337 (Evasıt N 1181/31 Jan.–9 Feb. 1768).

[24] DWQ, Maḥkamat al-Baḥayra 10, pp. 35–36, case 70 (11 R 1188/21 Jun. 1774).

[25] BOA, Cevdet Nafia, 644 (28 R 1190/15 Jun. 1776).

[26] The full firman ordering the repair of the Abū Qīr dam is the following: BOA, HAT, 29/1360 (13 Ş 1198/1 Jul. 1784). This case is also recounted in a list of several letters to the sultan from the vali of Egypt, Muḥammad Paşa, which are summarized in the following: BOA, HAT, 29/1364 (28 N 1198/15 Aug. 1784). This document was a sort of quick checklist of the correspondence from the vali of Egypt to the sultan in Istanbul from the period around the year 1784. The sultan's directives with regard to each case are written at the top of each of the letters' summaries.

[27] BOA, Cevdet Nafia, 1640 (Evasıt M 1199/24 Nov.–3 Dec. 1784).

[28] The firman ordering the repairs and containing other directives is the following: BOA, HAT, 26/1256 (10 Za 1200/3 Sep. 1786). A summary of numerous memoranda from the vali of Egypt at that time, Muḥammad Paşa, to the sultan that includes information about the repair of this dam in 1200 (1785–1786) is the following: BOA, HAT, 26/1256B (10 Za 1200/3 Sep. 1786). The heading of this document and those similar to it is the following: "this is the summary of letters that arrived from the honored Mehmet Paşa, the present Vali of Egypt" (*hâlen Mısır Valisi Saadatlû Mehmet Paşa Hazretleri tarafından varid olan tahrirâtin hulâsasıdır*).

[29] BOA, Cevdet Nafia, 302 (23 Za 1216/28 Mar. 1802).

[30] BOA, HAT, 85/3474S (7 L 1217/31 Jan. 1803).

[31] BOA, HAT, 86/3509B (25 S 1218/15 Jun. 1803); BOA, HAT, 86/3536 (9 Ca 1218/27 Aug. 1803); BOA, HAT, 88/3591 (21 Ra 1218/11 Jul. 1803); BOA, HAT, 88/3601 (30 Za 1218/13 Mar. 1804); BOA, HAT, 254/14478A (16 L 1218/29 Jan. 1804). There is no internal evidence for the date of this final case. The date given is the one assigned by the BOA.

[32] BOA, MM, 11:498 (Evahir N 1219/24 Dec. 1804–2 Jan. 1805). According to al-Jabartī's account of Ṣāliḥ Effendi's repair of the Abū Qīr dike and the Ashrafiyya Canal, Ṣāliḥ spent more than a year and a half fixing the dike and the canal. Al-Jabartī also makes special mention of the numerous boats that came to Egypt with supplies and tools for the repair, presumably the same boats outlined in the previous Ottoman decree. Al-Jabartī, *ʿAjāʾib al-Āthār*, 2:400–1. See also: BOA, HAT, 86/3516A (6 Ra 1219/14 Jun. 1804); BOA, HAT, 86/3515 (7 B 1219/11 Oct. 1804); BOA, HAT, 86/3533 (7 B 1219/11

1805,[33] and 1807.[34] The point of this listing of dates is to show that the maintenance of the Alexandria Dam was a matter of constant concern over the course of the eighteenth century for the Ottoman administration of Egypt as it sought to protect the Ashrafiyya Canal for the people of Alexandria.[35]

As just one example of these cases, consider work carried out on the Alexandria Dam in 1743 to fix sections that had been damaged by the constant pounding of the waves of the Mediterranean and the strength of winds coming off the sea. This destruction was in spite of the fact that the dam had recently been reinforced with numerous massive wood supports. As the dam gave way, "the straits opened" (*boğazlar küşade*), turning the villages of al-Baḥayra into one "great sea" (*derya-i azîme*).[36] This description of the Mediterranean's waters covering the villages of al-Baḥayra paints a scene of vast destruction to agricultural lands and properties and to human and animal lives. The sea's flooding salt water not only covered many villages but also cut the main road leading from Alexandria to Rashīd and reached all the way to the canal. Although weakened by the deluge, the canal and its embankments held up against the Mediterranean's infiltrating waters, preserving this single lifeline of sweet water for the city of Alexandria. A few weeks after the breach of the Alexandria Dam, the sultan issued a decree to release funds needed to repair this and other irrigation features damaged by the flood.[37]

Oct. 1804); BOA, HAT, 130/5381 (29 Z 1219/31 Mar. 1805). There is no internal evidence for the date of this final case. The date given is the one assigned by the BOA.

33 BOA, HAT, 85/3478 (13 Ş 1220/5 Nov. 1805).

34 BOA, HAT, 1176/46442K (27 B 1222/30 Sep. 1807).

35 This archival evidence contradicts Michael Reimer's assertion – based solely on published Arabic- and European-language narrative sources – that the Ottoman administration of Egypt in the eighteenth century took little interest in the Ashrafiyya, thus allowing it to deteriorate because of imperial corruption, "marauding Bedouin tribes," and general official disinterestedness in the long-term well-being of the province. Reimer, "Ottoman Alexandria," 111–13. For a comparative example of the expenditure of funds by Ottoman officials to repair irrigation works in Ottoman Iraq, see: Murphey, "Mesopotamian Hydrology and Ottoman Irrigation Projects," 19.

36 BOA, MM, 6:2 (Evahir S 1156/16–25 Apr. 1743).

37 BOA, MM, 6:37 (Evasıt Ra 1156/6–15 May 1743). Totaling 279 *kise akçe* and 6,349 *para* (6,981,349 *para*), the funds were to be taken from the *irsāliyye-i ḫazīne* of the year 1741–1742 (1154). A subsequent decree further clarified the breakdown of the funds: 174 *kise akçe* and 20,424 *para* (4,370,424 *para*) for the dam and 50 *kise akçe* and 6,465 *para* (1,256,465 *para*) for the canal. BOA, MM, 6:69 (Evahir Ca 1156/13–22 Jul. 1743). The letter goes on to state, however, that, according to the inspection report submitted by the state functionary Yaḥyā Paşa, the repair of the damaged dam could wait if the embankments of the canal were repaired in an extremely strong and resilient manner.

Late-Eighteenth-Century Changes

As discussed in Chapter 4, the utilization of peasant labor in Ottoman Egypt became increasingly oppressive and calculated over the course of the long eighteenth century. This trend was particularly striking in the history of the Ashrafiyya Canal and the dams in its orbit and would ultimately culminate in the early nineteenth century, when more than three hundred thousand peasants were brought to work on the canal by the Egyptian provincial administration. Whereas during most of the eighteenth century the cleaning and maintenance of the Ashrafiyya Canal were carried out largely by those peasants who lived in its vicinity, things began to change late in the eighteenth century as peasants started being transported from various parts of the Egyptian countryside to work on ever larger projects in different parts of the province. As the projects grew in size and came to require greater amounts of labor and building materials, they also resulted in the movement of massive numbers of people, a process with profound implications for the human and ecological landscapes of Egypt. The dangers for those working on the repairs also grew in proportion to the ever-expanding size of the projects.

A representative example of this change in the organization of labor as it related to the Ashrafiyya was the repair of the dam of Abū Qīr in late 1784.[38] When the Ottoman administration of Egypt discovered in that year that the strength of the Mediterranean's inundation had completely destroyed this dam of ancient foundation (*kadim ül-esas*), the sultan directed that Arabic letters be dispatched and read to the people of Alexandria and to the residents of nearly two hundred villages in the subprovince of al-Baḥayra near Alexandria and near the subprovincial seat of al-Damanhūr.

In these letters to imperial subjects in al-Baḥayra, the sultan essentially charts out how the Ottoman state in Egypt was actively undertaking the kinds of transformations in labor discussed in Chapter 4. He wrote that, for many years, the dam of Abū Qīr had been maintained by the people

In other words, the Ottoman administration was confident that the canal would be able to withstand the force of the sea's waters on its own should the coastal dams give way again. Thus, the sultan issued another Hatt-ı Hümayun freezing the funds earmarked for the repair of the dam, because its repair was deemed no longer pressing. Although the order might well have ended this instance of repair, the issue of the dam and the financing of its repairs remained unresolved for several years. For details of the later repairs and of the fiscal machinations of those responsible for them, see: BOA, MM, 6:197 (Evahir S 1158/25 Mar.–3 Apr. 1745).

[38] BOA, Cevdet Nafia, 1640 (Evasıt M 1199/24 Nov.–3 Dec. 1784).

of that area, who benefited from its existence and enjoyed the protection it provided. The peasants would reinforce the dam from time to time with stones and dirt they moved themselves to the area of the dam, and in that way, the dam remained functional for quite a long time without any major problems. However, for whatever reason, these peasants eventually stopped reinforcing the dam, and it gradually became weaker and weaker, resulting in its total destruction by 1784.

To secure the labor and building materials needed for the massive repair work required in 1784, the sultan again turned to the people of al-Baḥayra, who had maintained the dam for so long. However, unlike earlier repairs that employed very local labor, in this case, the sultan was extremely specific that peasants were to be brought to the site of the broken dam from villages throughout the subprovince of al-Baḥayra. This important shift marks one of the earliest instances in which Egyptian peasants were forced to move significant distances to carry out repairs on an irrigation feature. As long as there was need for labor on the dam – the sultan writes – peasants were to be brought from all over the subprovince of al-Baḥayra. Moreover, in another indication that this was a very different kind of project from those we saw earlier in the eighteenth century, the workers were required to bring with them building materials to the work site – sand, stone, lime, and a kind of brick dust used to make cement (*kharasān*) – seemingly at their own expense. During this period of work, no tardiness (*te'hir*), sluggishness (*terahi*), or turning of a blind eye (*iğmaz*) was to be tolerated. Significant, as well, the funds for the repair were to come not from the Egyptian *irsāliyye-i ḫazīne*, as was customarily the case, but from the interest earned on lands managed by various mutassarifs in the subprovince.

Thus, in line with my discussion in Chapter 4, this case was part of a series of repair works at the end of the eighteenth century and the beginning of the nineteenth that broke with earlier labor practices.[39] To repair the Abū Qīr Dam, laborers were brought from areas not immediately adjacent to the dam itself; they were directed to bring building materials at a personal loss; they were forced to work largely against their

[39] For much of the period between the fall of 1801 and the spring of 1806, repairs to the Ashrafiyya Canal and its supporting irrigation works were overseen by the Ottoman functionary Ṣāliḥ Effendi. For more on his career with irrigation in Egypt, see: BOA, HAT 37/1871 (7 R 1219/15 Jul. 1804); BOA, HAT 39/1961 (13 Ş 1219/16 Nov. 1804); BOA, HAT 85/3474C (19 C 1220/13 Sep. 1805); BOA, HAT 85/3474D (1 B 1220/24 Sep. 1805); BOA, HAT 86/3516 (3 Ra 1219/11 Jun. 1804); BOA, HAT 88/3628 (29 Z 1220/20 Mar. 1806); BOA, HAT 93/3804 (7 Ra 1218/27 Jun. 1803).

will; and they were disconnected from their villages and communities. These changes in the character of rural labor were of the utmost importance because they altered the entire interaction between the Ottoman state and Egyptian peasants and between Egyptian peasants and their historical village communities and lands. These and other peasants were forcibly made into workers – into a productive force to be harnessed to expend the caloric energy stored in their muscles and bodies. They were no longer villagers of a certain area fulfilling a repair function directly beneficial to themselves and to the irrigation network of Egypt as a whole. They were stripped of this local identity and made part of a massive faceless pool of labor brought to work on projects throughout the countryside. The fact of the mobility of this labor meant that peasants' connections to specific places and to the waters, plants, and soils of those places were rent asunder through the movement of populations.

As with the more than thirty-three thousand workers brought to labor on a canal in Manfalūṭ in the early nineteenth century, projects like the repair of the Abū Qīr Dam discussed here began an oppressive and eventually unsustainable process of labor utilization in the Egyptian countryside that had an enormous impact on the lives of peasants throughout Egypt and that culminated in a massive number of dead peasants in the Maḥmūdiyya's reconstruction in the first quarter of the nineteenth century. Thus, not only did the rebuilding of the Maḥmūdiyya Canal in the second decade of the nineteenth century represent a qualitative shift in the scale and intensity of public works projects in Egypt; it also ushered in a new era of irrigation in Egypt in which peasants were disconnected from their homes and in which knowledge of the natural environment and relations to it were taken over as never before by the domains of the state. The Maḥmūdiyya was in many ways then Egypt's first grand state-development project. And thus it is not surprising that the rhetoric surrounding the project in Ottoman governmental correspondence posited its goals as the creation of life both in Alexandria and along the length of the canal itself. This attempt to create life in Alexandria was, however, a very deadly enterprise indeed.

Preparation

Work to repair permanently the Ashrafiyya Canal began in earnest in the fall of 1816, when Vali Mehmet ʿAli first sent a group of clerks, engineers, masons, carpenters, and workers to inspect the troublesome dam at Abū Qīr, whose destruction, as I have already discussed, was the cause of so much damage to the villages of al-Baḥayra and to the Ashrafiyya Canal.[40] These efforts by Mehmet ʿAli in 1816 were part of a larger strategy in the first quarter of the nineteenth century to improve the overall urban landscape of Alexandria and to increase its population and commerce. The goal of the reconstruction of the Ashrafiyya Canal was, in other words, to create the material and demographic means necessary for the increase of life in Alexandria and along the length of the canal itself. Quite tellingly, then, rather than simply using dirt and mud to fix the dam of Abū Qīr, as had usually been the case, Mehmet ʿAli sought to reinforce the dike in as permanent a way as possible with stone, steel, and timber.[41] He understood that, to deal effectively with the reconstruction of the canal between Alexandria and the Rashīd branch of the Nile, one first had to protect the canal from the sea by repairing the series of dams along the Mediterranean coast addressed in the previous section.

In May 1817, Mehmet ʿAli took further steps toward achieving his goals for the new canal. He wanted the Ashrafiyya to be a very deep canal. Its depth was necessary to accommodate the many large ships of grain, foodstuffs, and other commodities that would regularly use it. He estimated that the canal would be ten *qaṣabas* wide (approximately forty meters) and four *qaṣabas* deep (sixteen meters).[42] Initially, the newly constructed canal was to begin in the village of al-Raḥmāniyya at the same point on the Rashīd branch of the Nile as the old Ashrafiyya Canal and to end in a deep lake to be excavated near Pompey's Pillar in Alexandria.[43] Those plans, though, were soon scrapped, as it was determined that a shorter and equally effective canal could be constructed if the mouth of the canal were moved elsewhere on the Rashīd branch of the Nile. The distance from the historical mouth of the Ashrafiyya Canal at al-Raḥmāniyya to its end point in Alexandria was 26,000 *qaṣabas* (104 kilometers). The canal, however, could be made at least 5,000 *qaṣabas* (20 kilometers) shorter if it was begun instead at the village of al-ʿAṭf northwest of al-Raḥmāniyya near the town of Fuwwa, approximately 20,000 *bāʿ* (40 kilometers) to the

40 Al-Jabartī, *ʿAjāʾib al-Āthār*, 4:362–63. For accounts of Mehmet ʿAli's efforts to improve irrigation and agricultural output in Egypt, see: Rivlin, *Agricultural Policy of Muḥammad ʿAlī*; Cuno, *The Pasha's Peasants*; Marsot, *Egypt in the Reign of Muhammad Ali*, 137–61; ʿAbd al-ʿAẓīm Muḥammad Saʿūdī, *Tārīkh Taṭawwur al-Riyy fī Miṣr (1882–1914)* (Cairo: al-Hayʾa al-Miṣriyya al-ʿĀmma lil-Kitāb, 2001), 15–76.

41 In reference to earlier attempts to fix the dam, al-Jabartī writes that "previous governments had been unable to cope" with the dam, and thus salt water was allowed to flow freely into al-Baḥayra and into the Ashrafiyya Canal. Al-Jabartī, *ʿAjāʾib al-Āthār*, 4:362.

42 Ibid., 4:389; Rivlin, *Agricultural Policy of Muḥammad ʿAlī*, 218.

43 On the village of al-Raḥmāniyya, see: *QJBM*, pt. 2, 2:305.

south of Rashīd.[44] The total length of the new canal was to be 37,500 *bāʿ* (75 kilometers), and the portions of the canal that needed to be dredged totaled 30,000 *bāʿ* (60 kilometers) of this length.

Another factor that contributed to the decision to move the mouth of the canal was the presence of an island obstructing the old mouth at al-Raḥmāniyya, which weakened water flow and, hence, hindered the canal's effectiveness. The new mouth at al-ʿAṭf was to be nine *zirāʿ* (6.8 meters) wide, and both the mouth and the canal itself were to be made wide and deep enough to allow ships (*kayıklar*) to sail on them during the time of the flood.[45] The position of this new beginning section of the canal was also chosen very strategically in an attempt to take advantage of naturally strong winds in the area that would allow ships to sail more easily along the waterway. It was thought that harnessing the natural energy of wind to make the movement of commercial ships quicker and easier along this snakelike (*suʿbanvari*) waterway would in part justify the enormous amount of labor and money needed to build the new canal. There were, however, several potential problems with this planned new section of the canal. First, a series of bends in the canal

44 Al-Jabartī, *ʿAjāʾib al-Āthār*, 4:390. On the village of al-ʿAṭf, see: *QJBM*, pt. 2, 2:268. On Fuwwa, see: *QJBM*, pt. 2, 2:113–15. One *bāʿ* equals two meters. Hinz, *Islamische Masse und Gewichte*, 54.

45 Problems associated with the navigation of the canal were illustrated in the very same year as its repair. From June 20, 1817, until the end of the month, the Nile's floodwaters rose in the village of al-Raḥmāniyya only a small amount. The Nile's flood that year was measured by the Nilometer on the island of al-Rauḍa in Cairo to be only seven cubits and fifteen fingers – an extremely miniscule amount considering that the minimum height needed for purposes of taxation was slightly more than sixteen cubits. When that year's floodwaters finally reached the Ashrafiyya, they added only three cubits and twenty fingers to the canal's overall water level as measured at al-Raḥmāniyya, resulting in the total water level of the canal at al-Raḥmāniyya reaching the unimpressive height of merely five cubits and twelve fingers. As if this were not bad enough, it was further determined that the buildup of sand and dirt in the canal elevated the bed of the waterway's mouth by one *arshun* and twenty fingers (1.4 meters), which caused many ships to run aground as they attempted to enter the Ashrafiyya from the Nile. Because there was very little incline (*meyl*) in the canal's bed, it remained elevated to roughly this height for a third of its entire length until the village of Aflaqa. Moreover, the bed of the Rashīd branch of the Nile inclined as it flowed from al-Raḥmāniyya down to the Mediterranean. This fact also contributed to the buildup of sand and dirt at the mouth of the canal in al-Raḥmāniyya. According to the measurements of a group of engineers, the level of the flood for that year in both the harbor of Alexandria and the port of Rashīd was seven cubits and twenty fingers. The same engineers measured the overall level of the flood to be seventeen *arshun* (12.9 meters). For Amīn Sāmī's descriptions of the course of the canal's repairs from the summer of 1817 to the summer of 1819 – based almost entirely on al-Jabartī's account – see: Sāmī, *Taqwīm al-Nīl*, pt. 2, 261–65 and 276–80.

made water flow in these areas very weak. Second, at certain points along the banks of the new section of the canal, the soil was very loose and weak, and there were piles of sand along the canal. Both these factors made the possibility of siltation quite high. To protect against the potentially catastrophic silting of the canal, a series of protective embankments of stone and wood were proposed to reinforce the banks of the canal.

Having thus decided that the new course of the canal would begin at al-ʿAṭf, Mehmet ʿAli set about to collect and organize the labor and tools needed for the project. He ordered fifty thousand hoes and shovels to be made in the ironworks of cities in the Nile Delta.[46] He also instructed that one hundred thousand peasants were to be brought to the site of the dig. This initial collection of laborers for the project represented the largest number of workers used in any single irrigation project to date in Egypt. As we saw previously, the repair of a canal in Manfalūṭ in 1808 used more than thirty-thousand peasants, a mere third of the massive number required on the Ashrafiyya in 1817. The relative enormity of this initial number of peasant workers needed to labor on the canal is put in stark perspective when one considers that just a few years earlier, in 1800, the population of Cairo was 260,000. Thus, the equivalent of nearly 40 percent of the population of Egypt's largest city was brought from the countryside to work on the digging of the Ashrafiyya Canal.

The collection of workers commenced in the summer of 1817 and was organized as follows. Each provincial *kāshif* was instructed to enlist one full-grown man for every ten people in a village. Each man was given fifteen piasters to cover his travel expenses to and from the work site and thirty *para* for each day of work. As it was summer, most peasants were busy preparing their lands for the onset of the flood at the end of the summer, but once enlisted for work on the canal, the men took to readying themselves for their new charge of labor. The most important provision the men had to worry about was, not surprisingly, water. Like the city of Alexandria itself, the workers had to take special care to ensure that they had a ready and steady supply of the precious commodity. There were a few wells dug in the desert near the work site, but their water was extremely salty owing to centuries of the Mediterranean's infiltration of this area's soils. As such, most of the peasant men bought waterskins to bring with them to the work site to support them as they toiled. Although work on the canal was set to begin in the summer of 1817, plans were prematurely put on hold because of the early rise of the Nile that summer.

[46] Al-Jabartī, *ʿAjāʾib al-Āthār*, 4:388; Rivlin, *Agricultural Policy of Muḥammad ʿAlī*, 218.

The Egyptian chronicler al-Jabartī makes special note of peasants' delight at this delay in work, this despite the fact that Mehmet ʿAli took back from them the money he had provided to cover their travel expenses.

Beginning in the fall of 1817, we find numerous cases of correspondence between Mehmet ʿAli and Istanbul about the work needed to repair the Ashrafiyya Canal during this period. A letter dated November 7, 1817, from Mehmet ʿAli to Istanbul outlines many of the details of the project.[47] Before addressing the canal itself, however, Mehmet ʿAli informed the sultan of the difficulties ships faced when entering and exiting the Rashīd branch of the Nile because of strong seasonal winds. For one or two months every year (and occasionally longer), the Rashīd mouth of the Nile was made completely impassable by strong winds that blew across the city. The winds not only helped blow dirt and debris into the Rashīd branch of the Nile but also caused numerous shipwrecks (*kazazede*) near the coast, which led to great losses in money and cargo. The previous year (1816) was especially trying because, for four months after the receding of the Nile's water, the mouth of the Rashīd branch of the river was made completely impassable by strong wind. This meant that provisions (*erzak*) destined for Istanbul from Rashīd had to wait in the Egyptian port until the winds died down or changed direction to allow ships to leave Egypt. Likewise, ships destined for Egypt had to find another port besides Rashīd to dock and unload their goods. The mouth of the Rashīd branch of the Nile was, moreover, also very susceptible to the buildup of dirt and sand on its bed because its banks were made up of very loose soil (in part because of its relatively recent geological formation). Thus, earlier that summer, Mehmet ʿAli ordered the construction of a new set of protective walls along the banks of this branch of the Nile at the village of al-Ṭīna in an effort to prevent sand from falling into the waterway and collecting on its bed.[48]

Another critical consequence of the impassability of the port of Rashīd was the impossibility of moving ships, goods, and people between Alexandria and Rashīd. Although both were in Egypt, the majority of traffic between the two cities ran along the Mediterranean coast, as it was clearly much more expedient and efficient to travel between them by ship rather than overland. Thus, Mehmet ʿAli makes the point very strongly to the

47 BOA, HAT, 656/32064 (27 Z 1232/7 Nov. 1817).

48 Al-Jabartī, *ʿAjāʾib al-Āthār*, 4:390. A group of two hundred "building-craftsmen, carpenters, blacksmiths, and construction workers" sent to Egypt from Turkey around the time of the construction of these protective walls likely aided in their building and design. Ibid.

sultan that another path of water had to be found between the two cities. This need for an alternative route between Rashīd and Alexandria, one that bypassed the dangers and difficulties of the Mediterranean altogether, was therefore another justification for the reconstruction of the Ashrafiyya Canal.

The early stages of the canal's reconstruction in late 1817 commenced as follows. The first order of business was to ensure that the entire length of the old canal from the Nile to Alexandria was deepened and widened, making it as deep and wide as it had been in times of old (*kamā fī al-qadīm*). Next, at the point where the canal entered Alexandria, there had to be built a large lake that could easily accommodate the docking of many boats. Like the canal itself, there was precedent for this lake, though its remnants were barely visible and badly in need of repair. Moreover, protective walls were to surround the entire perimeter of the lake both to prevent its banks from collapsing and to fight against seepage. Besides the construction of this wall, several other areas of the lake needed dredging. In addition to serving as a conduit of goods among Alexandria, Rashīd, and the rest of Egypt, the reconstruction of the canal was also to aid in the movement of pilgrims between the Mediterranean and the Hijaz during the annual pilgrimage season.[49]

An engineer named Rohidin was assigned to oversee the canal's repairs. Rohidin was an Ottoman functionary sent from Istanbul to Cairo who proved instrumental in the creation and development of the Egyptian School of Engineering, founded in October 1816.[50] He continued to serve as a teacher in the school until the summer of 1817, when work on the reconstruction of the Ashrafiyya demanded his full attention. He was especially gifted in the instruction of mathematics and geometry and

49 According to Mehmet ʿAli, this service provided to those going on the pilgrimage each year would surely bring to the state many entreats of goodness (*daʿvat-ı hayırıyya*) from pilgrims.

50 Al-Jabartī gives the following description of the founding of this school:

> He [Mehmet ʿAli] ordered that a school be built in the courtyard of his palace in which a group of natives and the pasha's mamluks were enrolled under the teacher Hasan Efendi, known as al-Darwish al-Mawsili. With the collaboration of a Turk named Ruh al-Din [Arabic for the Turkish Rohidin] Efendi and several Europeans the principles of accounting and engineering were taught, as well as arithmetic, geometry, and trigonometry, and algebra. Various technical instruments of English manufacture were provided, with which the students could measure distance, elevation, and area. Provided monthly stipends and yearly clothing allowances, they met regularly in this school, which was called the School of Engineering, every morning of the week until shortly past noon, when they returned to their homes. Some days they made field trips to the open

was responsible for teaching those students who knew no Arabic.[51] It was, of course, no coincidence either that Mehmet ʿAli opened the school of engineering only months before the Ashrafiyya's repairs were to begin in earnest or that his main goal in opening the school was to teach land surveying. Whereas previously in the eighteenth century it was local peasant men of knowledge who served as the primary advisers on matters of construction, here we see that the "experts" used in the repair of the Ashrafiyya were to be those with knowledge of the engineering sciences (*eshab-i ulûm-i hendese*), most of whom were trained in the new Egyptian School of Engineering. The opening of the first school of engineering in Egypt was thus intimately intertwined with the project of reconstructing the Ashrafiyya Canal.[52]

Given his technical expertise, Rohidin was instructed to undertake several kinds of inspections before beginning the actual rebuilding of the canal. First, he was to measure the length, depth, width, and incline of the canal from its historical mouth in the village of al-Raḥmāniyya to its end in the lake of Alexandria. He was to determine, as well, the dimensions of the areas of the final lake that needed dredging and repair.[53] He was, in short, to report to the state on the current condition (*şimdikihalda*) of the canal and its ending lake.[54] In addition, and perhaps

country to study surveying. In fact, knowledge of surveying was the pasha's main goal.

Al-Jabartī, *ʿAjāʾib al-Āthār*, 4:359. On the founding and function of the school of engineering, see also: Aḥmad ʿIzzat ʿAbd al-Karīm, *Tārīkh al-Taʿlīm fī ʿAṣr Muḥammad ʿAlī* (Cairo: Maktabat al-Nahḍa al-Miṣriyya, 1938), 359–75.

51 Al-Jabartī, *ʿAjāʾib al-Āthār*, 4:368.

52 On the participation of many of the school's teachers and students in the reconstruction of the Maḥmūdiyya and in the repair and upkeep of other irrigation works, see: ʿAbd al-Karīm, *Tārīkh al-Taʿlīm*, 360–63.

53 To measure the overall slope of the canal, Ottoman officials had to determine the difference in the height of embankments at the start of the canal and at its end. According to their measurements and calculations, the two embankments around the canal's final lake were at an elevation of 3.5 *arshun* (2.7 meters) below that of the embankments at the start of the canal in al-Raḥmāniyya. The total height of the lake's supporting walls, as measured from its bed, was six *arshun* (4.6 meters), with two *arshun* and fourteen fingers (1.95 meters) of that height below ground level. In other words, to aid in the lake's flow, it was positioned both below ground level and at a lower elevation than the start of the canal. Thus, the walls constructed around the lake were sufficient to prevent water from overflowing its banks. The average depth of the lake was five *arshun* and four fingers (3.9 meters), and in times of low water, the lake's depth was around four *arshun* and nine fingers (3.3 meters). In quite telling language, this case describes the lake as a kind of large reserve receptacle of water (*yedek-i su*).

54 Previously, the lake at the canal's end had a total of six large embankments around it. At present, however, only two were functional, whereas the other four were badly in

most important, he was to give the state an estimate of the total cost of repairs. To avoid burdening those peasants who lived near the canal, Rohidin was instructed to inform them personally that the repair of the waterway was to take place gradually over the course of three years, in such a way as to cause as little disturbance as possible to their affairs. Having done all of this, Rohidin was then to see to the acquisition of pickaxes (*kazma*), shovels (*kürek*), and other essentials for the repair work.

Rohidin's final directives to care for the welfare of peasants near the canal marked a new conception of Egyptian peasants as *reaya* of the Ottoman state in the early nineteenth century rather than as the *ahali* of a certain village or town – as imperial subjects rather than residents of a specific place. Instead of being from the *ahali* of a certain village – a specific community identifiable as distinct from others – people were now entered into the larger universal category of *reaya* that, theoretically, included all subjects of the Ottoman Empire, regardless of location, language, religion, or allegiance. This represents not simply a semantic shift – I want to argue – but rather one facet of the changing conceptions of Egyptian society forged in this period through mechanisms like labor and quarantine discussed previously. This difference in terminology, in other words, marked a new Ottoman conception of those living in Egypt, a conception of them as a population to be organized, protected, cared for, managed, and ultimately – as we shall soon see – harnessed and killed. As in the case of the ever-expanding bureaucracy of labor that turned peasants into replaceable and indistinguishable masses of workers on a worksheet, in this instance all Egyptians were conceptualized not as locals from a particular village or town but as units in an abstract category of *reaya*. The imperial preference for a category like *reaya* served yet again to disconnect Egyptian peasants from their immediate rural surroundings and historical experiences.[55]

By this point in the early nineteenth century, the importance of enumeration and measurement to the building of a major canal like the

need of repair. It was further determined in this regard that two embankments and two gated *havzs* (basins) were to be constructed on either side of the canal as it entered the final lake. Moreover, three additional arched embankments were to be built along the length of the canal: one at the canal's mouth in al-Raḥmāniyya, another in the village of Mutaḥawwar, and a third in the village of Qabīl. Two of these embankments had two arches each, whereas the third was built with a bridge to allow boats to pass underneath it. At the canal's final lake near one of the *havzs*, a small fort to be used for storage and other purposes was also to be built.

55 For another example of this shift from *ahali* to *reaya*, see: BOA, HAT, 631/31183 (23 Z 1230/25 Nov. 1815).

Ashrafiyya had been fully ensconced in the bureaucratic mechanisms and mentalities of the Ottoman state in Egypt. Even before work on the canal was to commence, the head engineer, Rohidin, was to send the state an estimate of costs, an outline of the measures of the project, a list of needed supplies, and a report on all the dimensions of the canal's and lake's different parts. This measuring of the remnants of the old canal was surely a massive task in and of itself, yet the case unfortunately does not give us further details as to how it was accomplished. Nevertheless, the fact remains that the emphasis on numbers, enumeration, and measure that had emerged in the latter part of the eighteenth century as a means of managing ever-larger construction projects was here fully articulated as part of a new regime of rule that, by the second decade of the nineteenth century, had been fully mobilized in Ottoman Egypt and was here put to the task of the reconstruction of the Ashrafiyya Canal.

Narrative, Imagination, Expectation

The Ottoman administration of Egypt sincerely hoped that this new regime of order, its own gargantuan imperial efforts, and a massive expenditure of resources would ensure the greatness of Alexandria as a commercial city; would provide adequate supplies of irrigation and drinking water to all villages in al-Baḥayra near the canal; and would allow all the fields, villages, gardens, and orchards along the length of the canal to thrive. Egypt as a whole would be strengthened, and Alexandria in particular would be supported and built up by all the merchants and people who would flock to the city, making it one of the Empire's key metropoles. It was hoped, moreover, that newly prosperous villages along the length of the canal would serve as ready sources of soldiers for the imperial army. The enormous amount of work needed to transform the canal into a literal river (*nehir*) flowing to Alexandria – elsewhere, the reconstructed canal was referred to as a new thoroughfare (*cadde-i cedide*) – was estimated to require four or five months of continuous labor. Whether described as a new river or a new thoroughfare, clearly the canal was conceptualized and was indeed actually meant to function as the lifeline of Alexandria. This was also part of the economic justification for the canal's reconstruction, as it was estimated that the customs collected on increased commercial traffic into Alexandria would easily repay the costs of the canal in four or five years.

An extremely long report, most likely compiled by the engineer Rohidin, complete with a map, many figures, estimates, measurements, directives, and descriptions of the proposed improvements to the canal, was meant to serve both as a record of the canal's repairs and as a persuasive argument for its reconstruction and for the expenses this work would incur.[56] One of the most striking aspects of this case – a feature that indeed makes it quite unique in the archival record of Ottoman Egypt – was that it began with a rather long section outlining the history of repair work on the canal. Although we have encountered some cases that reviewed recent reconstructions carried out on a canal or some other irrigation work over the course of the previous few decades or perhaps even a century, what we find here is an altogether different sort of narration. It was a history of repairs on the canal that went back nearly a millennium and that was culled not from documents of the Ottoman bureaucracy but from narrative histories and chronicles of Egypt.[57]

[56] BOA, HAT, 130/5404 (29 Z 1232/9 Nov. 1817). There is no internal evidence for the date of this case. The date given is the one assigned by the BOA. This document is one of the most important sources for the history of the canal's repair and, as I will discuss later, is truly unique in the archival record of Ottoman Egypt. Not only does it include a narrated a history of the canal and a map, but more important, it also puts forth a vision of the future of this waterway and of the entire idea of what Egypt was and of what it was to become after the canal's reconstruction. On the interplay between the textual (*tahrir*) and the graphic (*resm*) in Ottoman maps, see the following very important discussion of an Ottoman map of Eurasia compiled between 1727 and 1728: Ariel Salzmann, *Tocqueville in the Ottoman Empire: Rival Paths to the Modern State* (Leiden: E. J. Brill, 1994), 31–74.

[57] This history of the canal was compiled from the works of several major Egyptian historians. For example, citing the historian al-Maqrīzī, we are told that in 859 or 860, the ruler of Egypt, Ḥārij Ibn Miskīn, undertook a major project aimed at repairing the Ashrafiyya Canal. Aḥmad Ibn Ṭūlūn also dredged the canal and repaired various problems with it in 872 or 873. In 943 or 944, the Nile's flood was so weak that the river's waters stopped short in the canal at a distance of one hour's walk from Alexandria. Boats trying to navigate the canal were left stuck in its mud, and the people of Alexandria were forced to drink water stored in the city's cisterns. Later, in the year 1013 or 1014, al-Ḥākim bi-Amr Allah – who we are told in this text was known for his cruelty and injustice (*gadr ve zulm*) – undertook a complete reconstruction of the canal costing fifteen thousand dinars. A government official named Amīr ʿAlī also repaired the canal in 1263 or 1264. As part of the repairs, a masonry structure complete with several large wooden supports (*sandıklar*) was built in the village of Umm Dinār on the banks of the canal to aid in controlling its flow. When the flood came, however, the structure failed to serve its intended purpose, and water flowed in the canal for only two months. As earlier, the people of Alexandria were thus forced to resort to their supply of stored cistern water to survive.

In the year 1310 or 1311, in the reign of Sultan al-Nāṣir Muḥammad Ibn Qalāwūn, a rather large reconstruction effort was carried out on the canal. On this repair, see: Sato, *State and Rural Society*, 229; Hairy and Sennoune, "Géographie historique," 267–69. So that the canal could be dredged in this year as efficiently and quickly as possible, forty thousand peasants from villages around the length of the canal were brought to work on

Indicating the amount of research undertaken to compile the list of repairs, its author cited the writings of famous Egyptian historians like al-Maqrīzī and Şems ül-Din, who wrote about different repair efforts on the canal over the centuries. Why would a bureaucrat of the Ottoman state take the time to read through those historical sources for the purposes of writing an administrative governmental document? This is akin to a lawyer writing a brief about a contract dispute in which she reviewed the history of contract disputes over the past millennium. What purpose, in other words, did this history of repairs on the canal serve with respect to the proposed repairs in 1817? Why include such information in a document of state?

Above all, this report made a case for the necessity of the reconstruction of the canal in 1817 and suggested why and how the state should

its maintenance for a period of twenty days. The total length of this canal from its mouth to its end was sixteen thousand *qaṣaba* (sixty-four kilometers). Seventy-five thousand *zirāʿ* (fifty-seven kilometers) of that length were in need of dredging and cleaning so that the waters of the annual flood could flow freely through the waterway to Alexandria. This work in 1310 or 1311 was made all the more pressing by several factors.

First, the people of Alexandria did not have enough water in their cisterns to last them until the end of the year. Second, because of a lack of irrigation water, more than one hundred thousand feddans (or, as this case mentions, approximately five hundred thousand dunams) of agricultural land along the length of the canal were rotten and barren (*müteaffin ve bihasıl*). Moreover, more than one thousand orchards and gardens around the city of Alexandria were also under threat because of the lack of water. Although the total cost of the repairs of the canal, its old protective walls, and all other related features came to the hefty sum of sixty thousand Egyptian dinars, once repaired, the waterway would feed fields, orchards, and gardens in areas around the canal and around Alexandria and would make the land fertile once again.

Nevertheless, despite those efforts, the document goes on to tell us that in 1368 or 1369, the fertile (*münbit*) grounds around the canal had once again fallen into ruin. And in the year 1422 or 1423, 875 workers were brought to work on the canal for a total of ninety days to dredge and level parts of the waterway that had silted over with mud and sand. After the workers had finished cleaning the canal, it did not take long for the waterway to once again gradually fill with the sand and silt that steadily collected on its bottom. Likewise, in 1499 or 1500, the water level in the canal was quite low, and ships could navigate the waterway only during the time of the flood. In 1550 or 1551, the canal was again repaired before quickly falling back into ruin. The last of the historical repairs of the canal recorded in this document were those undertaken in 1572 or 1573, during the reign of the Ottoman Sultan Selim II. As reported by the historian Şems ül-Din, the sultan's grand vizier Sinan Paşa not only built a market, mosque, and *ḥammām* in Egypt but also dredged, cleaned, and repaired the Ashrafiyya Canal. The dates of the repairs related in this document are corroborated by the following: Hairy and Sennoune, "Géographie historique," 267–69. The spelling of names in this source is often slightly different from those given in the archival document. I have preserved the spelling of the original document. Some of this history of repairs is also recounted in the following: Ṭūsūn, *Tārīkh Khalīj al-Iskandariyya*, 14–33 and 98–99.

undertake the repairs. As such, the rather long introductory history of repair work on the canal served several purposes. First, it made the simple point that the goal of connecting Alexandria to the Nile was one of ancient provenance, recognized to be of crucial importance by leaders throughout Egypt's history. Furthermore, it was a feat many of Egypt's greatest rulers had attempted and, ultimately, failed to accomplish to any lasting degree. Thus, the recounted history served to mark both a continuity and a break with the past. Unlike Egypt's previous rulers who had tried and failed to build the canal, the present Ottoman leadership of the province in 1817, through its unwavering effort and unprecedented reliance on precision and measurement, would succeed in building the canal where others before it could not. The narrative history of canal repairs served, in other words, as a backdrop to Ottoman efforts in 1817, suggesting both how the Ottomans conceived of Egypt's past and how they saw their own place in that history.

This was nothing short of the Ottoman administration of Egypt consciously constructing and actively refining its own self-image against that of past empires that had attempted to connect Alexandria to the Nile. As I show later in this chapter, the canal was meant to change the course not only of the Nile but of the history of Alexandria and of Egypt as a whole as well. The canal's reconstruction was thus part of changing conceptions of history and of Egypt in the early nineteenth century that posited biological life – usually in the form of male peasant laborers – and even history itself as entities to be forged, manipulated, and shaped through massive governmental projects of construction, education, and military conquest. Big things like the Ashrafiyya literally changed life and history. And as the nineteenth century wore on, changing history became more and more the concern and the work of the Egyptian state.

An integral facet of this new imperial conception of Egypt was the Ottoman bureaucracy's intense reliance on the perceived precision and utility of measurement, science, and numbers. Though unique in its recounting of the canal's history, the written record of this case is perhaps most distinctive because of the map that accompanied it (see Maps 7 to 9).

Very rarely before or during this period do we find maps as part of the archival record of Ottoman Egypt.[58] As with the narrative of the

[58] The earlier map analyzed by Ariel Salzmann did include Egypt. For her discussions of Egypt's place on the map, see: Salzmann, *Tocqueville in the Ottoman Empire*, 34, 49, 53, 55, 74.

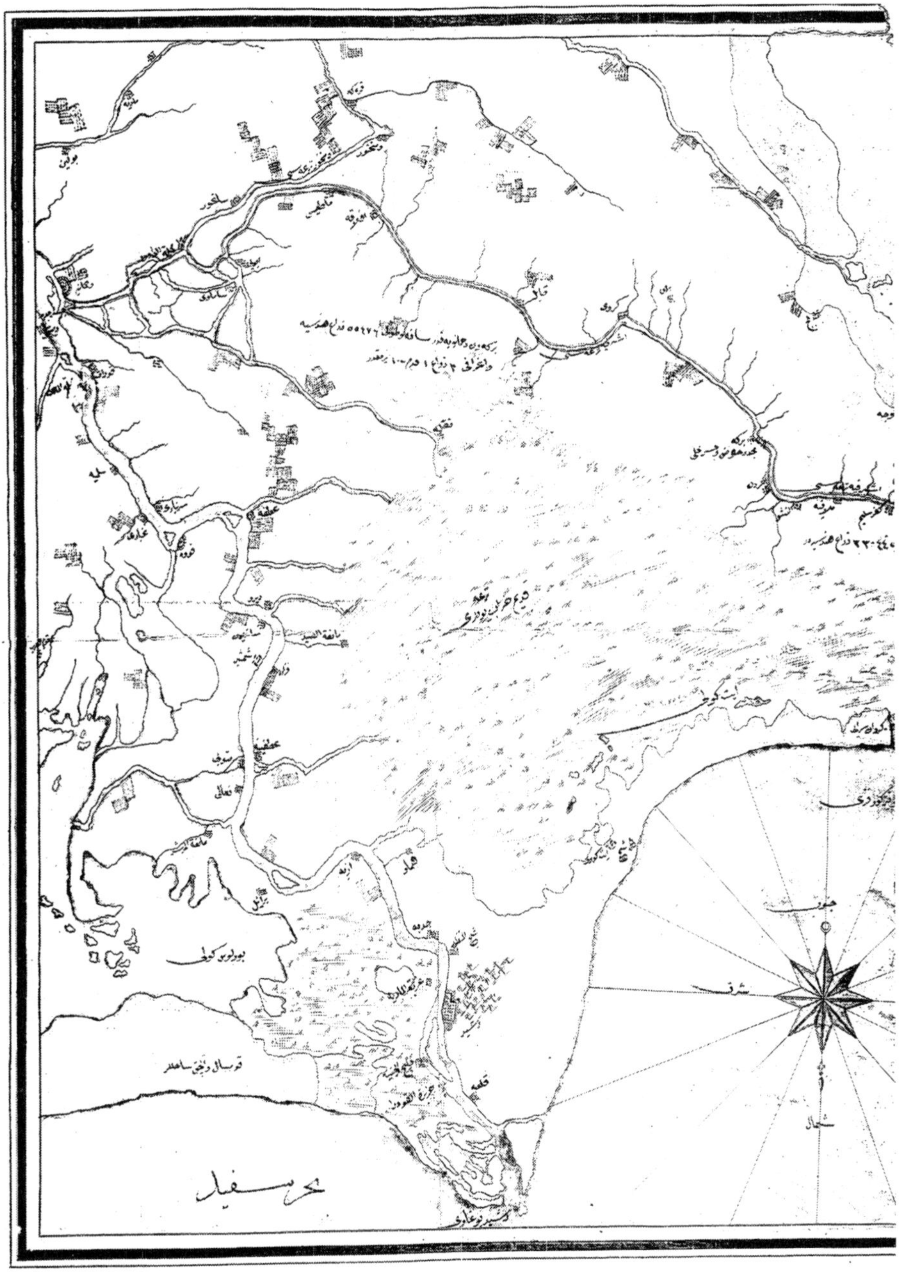

Map 7. First section of Ashrafiyya reconstruction map. This map and the two that follow are three sections of the same map. BOA, HAT, 130/5404A (29 Z 1232/9 Nov. 1817). All are used by permission of the Prime Ministry's Ottoman Archive.

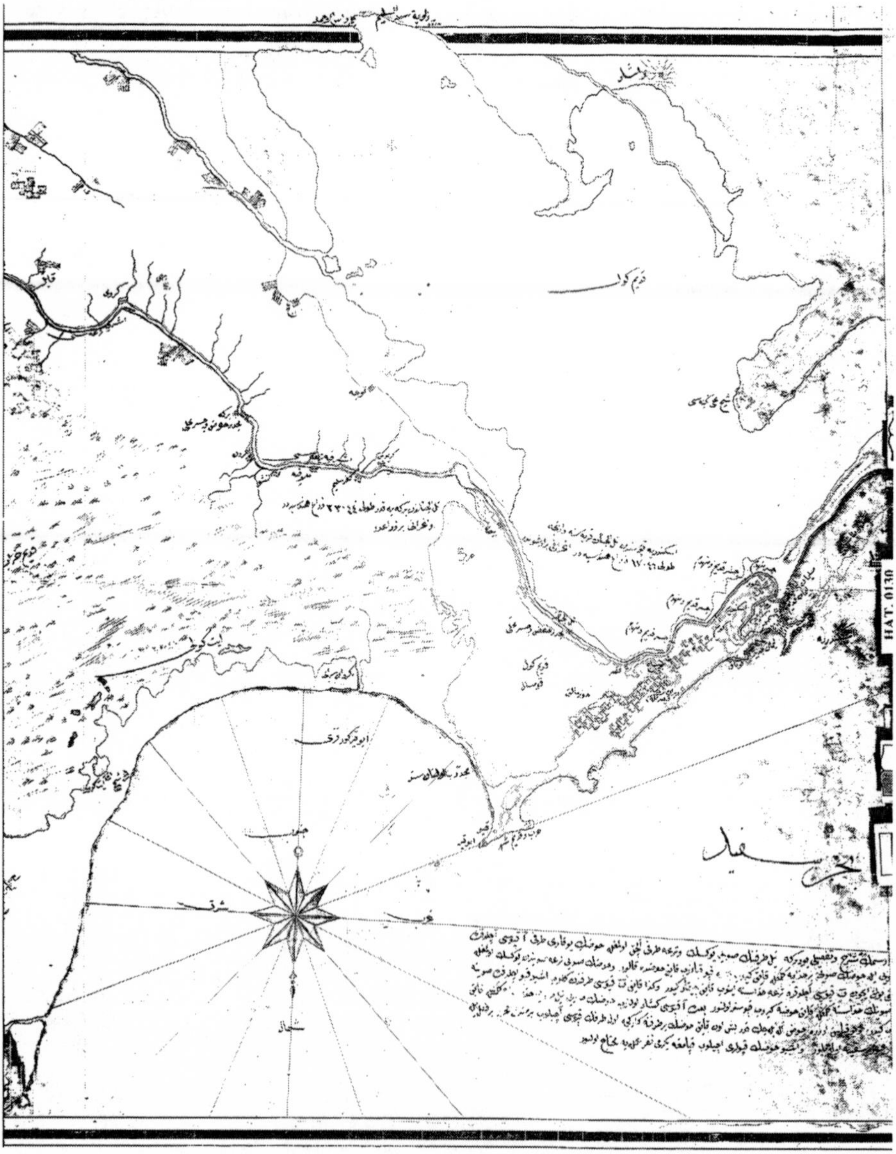

Map 8. Second section of Ashrafiyya reconstruction map.

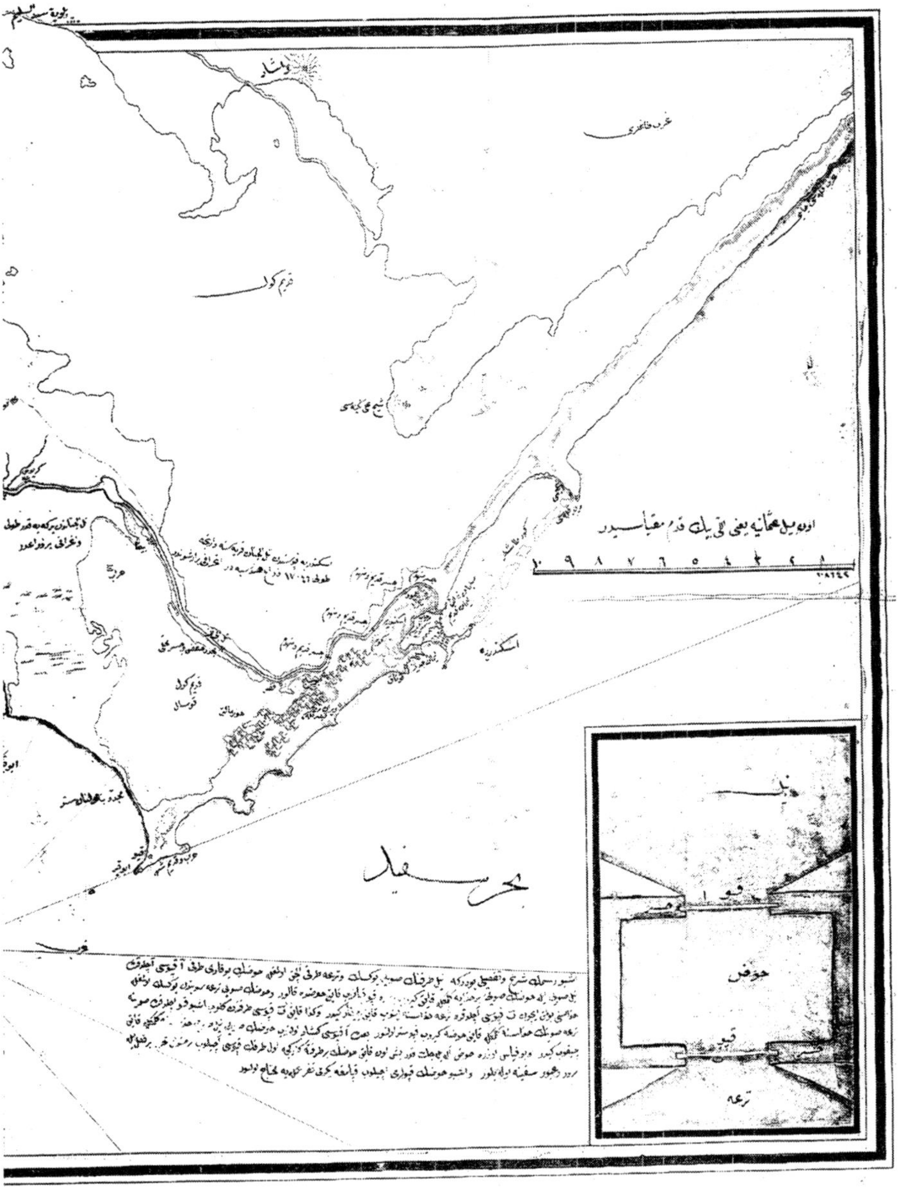

Map 9. Third section of Ashrafiyya reconstruction map.

canal's history, one wonders why these maps were included in this particular project and not with hundreds of others before or after it. At various points throughout this case, reference is made to the map, which – the text of this document emphasized consistently – was drawn in precise accord with principles of engineering and proper measure. It was a technical map, a tool of the utmost precision that was the key to the entire project. Certain sections and figures on the map were written in red ink to emphasize their importance. The map sketches out the construction of three gated basins (*kapılı havz*) in areas along the canal that were needed to help regulate the channel's water flow. And the map shows the relative lengths of various sections of the canal, the course of the canal itself and many of its branches, villages in the vicinity of the canal, parts of the canal that needed to be dredged and widened, and the locations of various irrigation features connected to the canal complex.

The technical details of all these irrigation features are given on the right side of the map, complete with full figures and enumeration (*tersim ve terkim*). Above all, the map was clear and precise and laid bare the separate parts of the needed repair work. The overall goal of the detailed engineering principles and metrics made to bear on the canal was to ensure that its waters flowed cleanly and refreshingly like the waters of heaven (*gök suyu gibi*). In times of drought (*kuraklık*), moreover, it was hoped that the canal would serve as a sufficient source of pure water to sustain both lands and populations, and it was also, of course, to be wide and deep enough to allow for the passage of large ships. In the words of this case, the canal was in short to be the size of a large river (*nehr-i kebir gibi büyücük-i ırmak olup*) – another Nile.

This case about the mapping of the canal is full of numbers: various lengths and depths of the canal, numbers of workers, canal slope inclines, prices, flood levels, populations, land area, and so forth. The emphasis on enumerating various facets of the project was a key aspect in its technical nature and reminds us conceptually of the enumeration of peasant laborers seen in Chapter 4. As with the case of those peasant laborers, in the Ashrafiyya reconstruction, there was a sense that technical precision and bureaucratic rigor could overcome the enormous scale of this project. Hence, to manage this project more precisely, the entire length of the canal from its historical mouth at al-Raḥmāniyya was split into three sections. This segmentation of the waterway allowed for further magnification of its many parts and, in turn, focus on their details. The length and depth of each section was measured, and its attendant and notable irrigation features were described: certain areas in each section needed embankments; others were badly in need of dredging; in other areas, gated dams were to be constructed; and so forth.[59] Like the

59 The details of the process of segmenting the canal to make its repair more manageable were as follows. The first of the three sections (with a total length of 55,476 engineering *zirā*ʿ, or 36.4 kilometers) branched off from the Nile at al-Raḥmāniyya and passed the villages of Semtahur, Yakhis, Aflaqa, Qabīl, al-Kurwi, and Birkat al-Jidda. On the village of Qabīl, see: *QJBM*, pt. 2, 2:288. The depth of the water in this section of the canal was 3 *zirā*ʿ, 1 foot, and 10.5 fingers (approximately 2.6 meters). It was also decided that the mouth of the canal in al-Raḥmāniyya needed to be reinforced with a series of embankments that would serve both to keep soil and debris from falling into the canal and to channel water more efficiently from the Nile into the narrow waterway. At the same time, two sluice gates were built on either side of the mouth of the canal to relieve excess floodwaters and to prevent the entire canal from overflowing.

In the second section of the canal, there was a constant struggle to clean and dredge the waterway of the sand and earth that regularly clogged it. This section was also the one most directly affected by the conditions of the Abū Qīr Dam on the Mediterranean. When that dam gave way and the sea's salty waters were allowed to flow south, they reached this section of the canal first. This contributed to the already-high salt content of the soil in that area – built up by centuries of the sea's infiltration of that land – and to the fact that water in that part of the canal was historically very laden with sand (*kumsal*). The length of this section of the canal was 33,044 arshuns (twenty-five kilometers), and the villages it flowed past included al-Karyūn, al-Nishū, Kafr Silīm, and Bīḍā. On Kafr Silīm, see: *QJBM*, pt. 2, 2:320. On Bīḍā, see: *QJBM*, pt. 2, 2:318. On al-Nishū, see: *QJBM*, pt. 2, 2:319. On al-Karyūn, see: *QJBM*, pt. 2, 2:318–19. A portion of this section of the canal measuring 1,377 *arshun* and 1 finger (1,044 meters) was covered with 1 *arshun* of water (75.8 centimeters). This section of the canal ended at a gated reservoir (*kapılı bend*; later referred to as a *havz*) built to aid in increasing the water flow over parts of the canal bed that regularly suffered from the buildup of sand. This reservoir, the sandy areas it served, and the embankments of the canal near it were all 3.5 *zirā*ʿ (2.7 meters) below the elevation of Tall al-Jannāb at the canal's end.

The third section of the canal was also very shallow and could not accommodate any boats on its surface because of the low water level. As with the middle section of the canal, a *havz* was built near sandy areas of this portion to increase the force of the canal's overall water flow. This section was 17,046 *zirā*ʿ (12.9 kilometers) long, and it ended in Alexandria after passing the villages of Tall al-Jannāb and Abū Sāj. As before, a length of 710 *arshun* and 1 finger (538 meters) of this portion of the canal was submerged in 1 *arshun* (75.8 centimeters) of water. To prevent this section of the canal from overflowing its banks into agricultural areas near the waterway, a dam with gates that could be opened and closed as needed and a reservoir with two gates were built at the mouth of this final section of the canal, parallel (*muhazi*) to the coastline.

The work of cleaning and dredging the entire length of the canal from its mouth in al-Raḥmāniyya to its end in Alexandria was also divided into three sections. In the first two sections, there were a number of either sunken, crashed, or stuck *qayiq*s in the bed of the canal, and the remaining third was very shallow (*sığ*) and was, we are told, hardly a waterway at all. The area of dirt to be dredged in the first section from al-Raḥmāniyya to the village of Birka was 848,730 square *zirā*ʿ (487,650 square meters). Between the villages of Birka and Tall al-Jannāb, the area of dirt to be dredged was 4,752,886 square *zirā*ʿ (2,730,837 square meters). The area of the third portion of the canal to be cleaned

process of collectivizing Egyptian peasants into masses of laborers (*anfār*), compartmentalizing the canal made it easier to measure, control, and repair.[60]

Indeed, reconstructing the canal was clearly an enormous undertaking that required months of work, thousands of *akçe* and workers, and tons of dirt. The scale of the repair, though, never seemed to be a cause of concern. It was as if a project of any scale could be accomplished with the proper amount of organization, enumeration, measure, and numbers. This bureaucratic confidence in the utility and efficacy of numbers was the result of multiple apparatuses of rule and governance developed over the course of the long eighteenth century to manage Egypt's irrigation network and environment. As I have already discussed, one of these new conceptions of rule in Egypt at the end of the eighteenth century was population, and as evidenced in this repair, numbers were clearly significant for the delineation of population – of how many people would be drawn to Alexandria, of how many peasants would come to live along the length of the canal, and of how many merchants were avoiding the city because of its problems with water and food. Because at its base the ultimate goal of the canal reconstruction project was to increase the overall population of Alexandria, counting the number of people in the city had to be an easily available and viable mechanism of administration. Counting things – whether people, canal lengths, villages, or money – was a way to control them. Thus, the canal's repair again points to how this logic of counting, and the attendant process of enumeration in irrigation works, evolved over the course of the long eighteenth century.

and dredged ran from Tall al-Jannāb to Alexandria and measured 339,492 square *zirā*ʿ (195,060 square meters). Thus, the total area of dirt to be dredged was the enormous amount of 5,941,108 square *zirā*ʿ (3,413,547 square meters).

The expenses for the workers who were to carry out the digging and dredging, for the necessary equipment and tools, and for all other related matters was ten *kise akçe* and two *guruş* (250,070 *para*) per *arshun* of dirt. The initial total for the work was thus 23,764 *kise akçe* and 216 *guruş* (594,107,560 *para*). There were also other additional expenses associated with the building of embankments, dams, and other irrigation works along the canal. In al-Raḥmāniyya, one *havz* and three embankments were to be built; in and around the lake at the canal's end, one *havz*, two embankments, two dams, and a few other structures were needed; in the village of Tall al-Jannāb, a series of dams, a *havz*, and many walls were to be constructed. The total estimated for the building of the additional irrigation works was 14,300 *kise akçe* (357,500,000 *para*). Thus, the total amount needed for the building of these irrigation works and for the dredging of the canal itself was 38,064 *kise akçe* and 216 *guruş* (951,607,560 *para*). Moreover, this case quotes that the minimum required to begin this work was 26 *Rumi kise akçe* (1,300,000 *akçe*).

60 For another archival example of the use of the word *anfār* to describe the collection of workers used on the canal, see: Ṭūsūn, *Tārīkh Khalīj al-Iskandariyya*, 105.

This case also illustrates the crucial role of water in the creation and maintenance both of life and of urban landscape in Alexandria. The case begins by emphasizing the empirewide trade and commercial connections that Alexandria maintained with parts of the Empire in Anatolia, the Arab world, and Europe, and with other regions outside the Ottoman realm, whether in Iran or non-Ottoman parts of Europe. Reviving the Ashrafiyya Canal would clearly allow the Ottoman bureaucracy to take advantage of Alexandria's place as a center of trade with those and other locales. This case also explains how water was acquired in Alexandria in times of low flood or when the city's cisterns were not sufficiently full. One of the city's alternative sources of sweet water was an area near Alexandria known as Süleyman Harbor and another was the Rashīd branch of the Nile. Fresh water merchants brought water from those areas to Alexandria to sell it at very high prices to the city's residents.[61] Overcoming the natural dearth of fresh water in Alexandria was thus the most important of the many reasons to build the Ashrafiyya. Because the natural well water around Alexandria was – in the words of the Ottoman bureaucracy – not even suitable for washing clothes, the canal was needed to serve as a consistent and steady supply of clean and free water for Alexandrians.

Not only was the canal meant to serve as a conduit of fresh water; it was to be a purveyor of food and other goods as well. Thus, because the Ashrafiyya was to be a lifeline of commerce between Alexandria and the rest of Egypt, it had to be able to accommodate large amounts of ship traffic. There were, however, two main problems boats faced on the canal. The first and most important was that the canal was simply too shallow to allow large ships to navigate its waters without running aground on the canal's bed, hence the fact that much of the Ottoman bureaucracy's efforts concentrated on dredging the canal. Even after its dredging, though, the canal was quick to become shallow again because its extremely weak current allowed sand, silt, dirt, rocks, and other debris to settle easily on its bottom. In addition to the fact that the canal's weak current allowed particles and debris to accumulate on its bed and that it was not powerful enough to move them along once there, another reason for the waterway's shallowness was that all its waters came from the flooding of the Nile. Thus, if the Nile's flood was low in a particular year, then the canal would not be filled with large amounts of water and would, thus, be left quite shallow. Add to this the facts of evaporation, the

[61] On the freshwater resources of Rashīd, see: Wizārat al-Ashghāl, *al-Nīl wa Tārīkh al-Riyy*, 152–53.

siphoning off of the canal's waters by peasants along its length, and the fact that soil and earth from the loose banks of the canal regularly fell into it, and it becomes clear why it was indeed quite difficult to maintain a sufficiently high and consistent level of water in the canal for ship navigation.

The problem of siltation was especially pronounced at the mouth of the canal, where a great amount of sand and dirt accumulated as the waters of the Nile flowed into the canal. The diversion of water into the canal greatly slowed the Nile's current, allowing the rich sediment and debris in the water to fall more easily to the canal bed and, hence, to collect at its mouth. The underwater ridge formed by the buildup at the mouth of the canal was the cause of many ships running aground as they tried to enter the canal from the Nile. This fact alone goes a long way in explaining motivations to move the mouth of the canal from its older location in the village of al-Raḥmāniyya to the village of Fuwwa further north on the Nile. Moreover, Fuwwa was also considered more advantageous as a starting point for the canal than al-Raḥmāniyya because the length of the new waterway from Fuwwa to the point at which it would join the existing canal was very windy and would thus be highly supportive of the navigation of ships. Also, the land through which the new section of the canal would be cut was such that it would allow the new channel to be made very straight. Thus, ships sailing from Fuwwa along the canal to Alexandria would have plenty of wind to move them along quickly and could sail straight without having to waste the wind's or sailors' energies by maneuvering around curves and bends in the waterway. Needless to say, the new mouth of the canal was also to be made extremely wide to allow rapid water flow and to facilitate large ships entering and exiting the canal.

Worries about the ability of ships to navigate the canal and about the strength of the canal's current led to concerns about the canal's overall incline and course as well. Clearly, the greater the canal's incline from beginning to end, the faster the canal's waters would flow. Many bends and corners in the course of the canal would slow its waters and so were also to be avoided. Thus, great efforts were put toward organizing the dredging of the canal's bed to increase its overall incline. Moreover, using embankments and excess dirt, the course of the canal was also to be manipulated by straightening the waterway's larger bends. Not only would this allow the canal's water to flow more quickly, but also a straighter canal would facilitate the movement of ships on the waterway, because they could sail with the wind more quickly in a straight line than if they had to tack continually. This case uses the term *snakelike* – long and fluid with easy undulating curves – to describe the desired course of the canal.

At various points in the repairs' documents, there were expressions about the goal of making the canal into a large river – one that was wide, fast moving, could accommodate many ships, and never dried. This very clear statement of the desire to make a new river – literally to make what nature did not through the use of engineering expertise, maps, shovels, workers, numbers, and embankments – expressed a confidence that nature could be emulated, constructed, recast, and harnessed productively through human knowledge, experience, and precision. Making the canal into a river was a process that meant turning human energy and knowledge into a synthetic entity that mimicked a natural one and that could function productively in the Egyptian environment. It was an attempt to overcome nature through human expertise and labor to create a lasting feature of the natural environment that would, over time, come to function as a regular and permanent (dare I say "natural") part of that environment.[62]

Those humans who were actually to work on the canal make only occasional and very fleeting appearances in the bureaucratic record of the repairs. There are references to the 40,000 workers employed by Sultan al-Nāṣir Muḥammad Ibn Qalāwūn in 1310 or 1311 in his repair efforts and to 875 workers brought to work on the canal for a total of ninety days in 1422 or 1423. With respect to the repairs proposed in 1817, there was only one mention in this early case of the workers who were to carry them out. They appear as an entry in a list of expenses related to the canal, which also included tools, digging equipment, and other essentials for the work. Although it would be made clearer in subsequent cases, here there was no mention of the number of workers to be used on the project, their wages, or from whence they were to be acquired. Nevertheless, we do have some details of others who were to be employed during work on the canal. The sultan recommended that the vali of Egypt, Mehmet ʿAli, appoint a responsible individual from the village of Birka to be in charge of the yearly maintenance of the canal once the waterway was "corrected." This person was to be given the proper bureaucratic and financial support needed to carry out the necessary dredging and cleaning of the canal before the onset of the annual flood. It was imperative that the work be carried out every year

62 For a comparative example of the creation of artificial "rivers" in California, see: Worster, *Rivers of Empire*.

before the flood season so as to maximize the amount of floodwater the canal could receive.

This individual Egyptian peasant was to serve as a kind of local representative of the Ottoman state along the canal invested with the power and responsibility to monitor its status on a regular basis. This is yet another example of how the Ottoman bureaucracy in Egypt used the knowledge and experience of local individuals to carry out its own work in the countryside. With the authority and control to harness various powers of the state to complete repair works in his own local area, the appointed peasant entered the Ottoman state's bureaucratic framework by essentially becoming one of its imperial functionaries. In contrast to earlier uses of local knowledge and experience in the long eighteenth century, in this instance, repairs were meant to serve a place – Alexandria – quite far away from this individual peasant's local community and village. Like those many laborers brought from various parts of Egypt to work on a distant irrigation project, this individual put his labor toward improving the situation of a place that was not his own. Neither he nor his immediate community, in other words, benefited from his labor. Thus, by entering the Ottoman administration of Egypt through his labor, this Egyptian peasant from Birka became just one more Ottoman bureaucrat in the imperial machine.

The enormity of the Ashrafiyya's reconstruction was also evidenced by the fact that a whole series of irrigation works connected to the proper function of the canal was to be built or repaired at this same time. Many basins were to be constructed at various points in the canal; there were numerous areas that needed to be reinforced with strong embankments; the lake at the canal's end was to have three new embankments built around it to go along with the six already there; a group of dams and bridges were also to be built in connection to the canal. The Ashrafiyya's repair was, in short, a huge project that required the presence of various other kinds of irrigation works to support the canal's function. As we see here and as we saw in Chapter 1, irrigation in Egypt was a process that relied on the coordination of thousands of moving parts spread over a wide geographic area. Thus, in addition to these many auxiliary irrigation works, the dam at Abū Qīr also received special mention in this case, because, like the other irrigation works, it too had to function properly for the canal to be operational. Transforming the Ashrafiyya Canal into a river of relatively uniform depth throughout with water present all year round and dimensions wide enough for ships was thus no simple affair. Indeed, the more "natural" its function was to be, the more complicated the reconstruction work required. For the canal to act like a river, it needed an entire supporting cast of embankments, peasants, dams, wind, and basins to sustain its operation. Creating and maintaining a river, as it turned out, was a very complex matter indeed.

Implementation

With a highly detailed vision for the canal in place, its reconstruction was in full swing by November 1817. An exchange of letters from this period between Mehmet ʿAli and the sultan in Istanbul makes clear that work to repair the course of the canal had commenced with great speed and an enormous expenditure of energy and materials.[63] Mehmet ʿAli wrote to the sultan informing him that the entire length of the canal (*başdan başa*) was currently being cleaned, dredged, and widened and that the canal's many shallow places were soon to be thoroughly dredged of the silt and mud that had settled on them. Moreover, walls and embankments along the length of the canal were also being rebuilt and strengthened. In terms of the labor required for the project, Mehmet ʿAli estimated that it would take three to four years and 30,000 or 40,000 *kise akçe* (750,000,000 to 1,000,000,000 *para*) to organize the necessary labor. This was, of course, in addition to the hundred thousand peasants already brought to work on the canal. Mehmet ʿAli also wrote to the sultan of the meaning of the canal for the life of Alexandria. If the repair work was carried out effectively and if any problems that arose with it were dealt with quickly and efficiently, then the built environment of Alexandria would greatly expand to accommodate all the new commerce that would move through the city. Mehmet ʿAli added that the city's growth in both geographic size and population would make Alexandria so beautiful that people would praise the sultan until the day of judgment.

The sultan's response to his Egyptian vali's letter makes the point – in terms even stronger than Mehmet ʿAli's – that Alexandria must be made into a thriving city through the canal's reconstruction. The goal in repairing the canal was clearly to allow water to flow along its entire length at all times (*ʿalā ül-devam*) so as to end forever Alexandria's problems in securing adequate amounts of drinking water. The sultan added that a properly dredged and widened canal would allow ships to travel between Alexandria, Cairo, and many other places throughout Egypt and the Empire so that there would never again be any shortages of food in the

[63] BOA, HAT, 131/5411 (29 Z 1232/9 Nov. 1817).

city. The city would thus gradually expand more and more attracting to it merchants and others from all around the Mediterranean and Red seas.

The sultan then waxed rather poetic in a very significant statement about what such changes to Alexandria would imply about the very meaning of the city itself. If Alexandria was never again exposed to threats of food and water shortages, then the Ottoman provincial vali himself would make the city his seat of power, owing to its pleasant climate, favorable markets, and general agreeability. The sultan went on to say that the Ashrafiyya Canal would forever change the entire meaning of Egypt itself. Instead of the word *Mısır* (the proper name of Egypt in Turkish) standing in reference to the city of Cairo, a common convention, it would come to mean Alexandria, because after the Ashrafiyya, the city would surely surpass Cairo as the province's first city and capital. At the most basic level, this was thus a statement of the power of public works to change the entire imagination and reality of what Egypt was. Egypt after the Ashrafiyya would never again be the same.

In addition to these semantic shifts, according to the sultan, the rebuilding of the canal was to have two immediate benefits for the state. First, as noted previously, with a consistent and reliable supply of water and food, Alexandria would rapidly grow and become a massive center of commerce and trade. Second, if the canal was built properly, many thousands of peasants would move to live along its banks. The new villages would offer the state a fresh source of conscripts for the imperial army, and the sultan estimated that the army would be able to secure thirty to forty thousand new soldiers from the young men who came to settle along the canal. Thus, the canal would serve to create life both in Alexandria and along its entire length. Moreover, a powerful city like Alexandria on the Mediterranean coast of Egypt would make any invasion of the province much more difficult.[64] Given these potential advantages, the sultan instructed his vali to expend all he could in attempting to complete this huge project successfully. The sultan also specifically acknowledged that securing the necessary labor for this project would be very difficult, but he entreated Mehmet ʿAli to complete the project no matter the costs. To start a project of this sort and then leave it unfinished would reflect very poorly on the Ottoman state in Egypt, and so it had to be done as quickly as possible to make Alexandria into a thriving city.

About five months later, in April 1818, Mehmet ʿAli reported that several sections of the canal had been successfully rebuilt, thus allowing

[64] For more on the utility of the Ashrafiyya Canal for military purposes, see: TSMA, E. 9213 (n.d.).

water to flow in both summer and winter.[65] Food and water were thankfully moving smoothly to Alexandria with little obstacle, ensuring that the city was in a generally good state. By the spring of 1818, Mehmet ʿAli had also made significant headway in the organization of workers for the canal's reconstruction.

This positive news aside, major problems remained with the construction and repair of the large lake that was to serve as the end of the canal in Alexandria.[66] This was a crucial part of the construction work because this final node was to function as a docking point for ships coming to Alexandria from other parts of Egypt. Faced with many difficulties in the construction of this artificial basin, Mehmet ʿAli did as most of his predecessors had when confronted with such a problem in the construction of irrigation works – he sought the advice of local elders (*meşayih-i kura*) who had experience with digging and irrigation in that area and who understood the local topography and geography of the land in which the construction was taking place.[67] Those men were evidently much more useful in the reconstruction of the canal and its lake than those trained at the recently founded Egyptian School of Engineering, as the former come through in the archival record (even in this later period) much more than the latter.[68] Mehmet ʿAli also enlisted the aid of the director of tariffs (*gümrük emini*) in Alexandria to advise him on the lake's construction.[69] After those men's inspections, Mehmet ʿAli heard their recommendations; implemented many of them; and was, in turn, happy to report that work on this lake had recommenced and was on its way to completion. The men were furthermore also instructed to measure certain parts of the canal at its beginning, middle, and end: at the beginning of the canal in the village of al-ʿAṭf; in its middle, near the village of Birka; and near Alexandria, in the village of Kafr Silīm.[70]

65 BOA, HAT, 342/19546 (17 C 1233/23 Apr. 1818).

66 Siltation as well remained a constant problem for the canal throughout the spring and summer of 1818. Ṭūsūn, *Tārīkh Khalīj al-Iskandariyya*, 95.

67 He writes that the men had worked for a long time (*müddet-i medid*) in the business of digging canals (*hafr-ı türʿa şuglu*) and, through experience (*bil-tecrübe*), had learned all the details of such work (*her bir dakaik ameliyesi*).

68 As noted earlier, however, graduates of and teachers in the school did participate in the reconstruction effort, and there is mention in this case of a single expert engineer who may or may not have attended the school. For other examples of archival documents that cite the participation of engineering school graduates in the canal's repair, see: Ṭūsūn, *Tārīkh Khalīj al-Iskandariyya*, 104 and 126.

69 This man's name was Osman Ağa. Ibid., 96 and 103.

70 In each area, the canal was found to be five *qaṣabas* (twenty meters) deep and ten *qaṣabas* (forty meters) wide, and the canal's protective embankments in each of the

The labor costs of the project to this point were as follows. Peasant diggers (no specific number is cited) received an average wage of 25 *para* a day to dig the approximately 20,000 *qaṣabas* (80 kilometers) of the canal. According to Mehmet ʿAli, most of the workers were to be secured from villages in al-Baḥayra, whose peasants would be happy to have paid work after the completion of the grain harvest season. An additional 520 *kise akçe* (1,300,000 *para*) were needed for pickaxes and palm-leaf baskets (*kazma ve zenbil*), and 1,000 *kise akçe* (25,000,000 *para*) were required for stone masonry work (*kârgir*) to build strong walls in particularly weak places in the canal.[71] Mehmet ʿAli estimated that the entire job could be accomplished with a total of 6,000 *kise akçe* (150,000,000 *para*).

Work on the vast basin in Alexandria continued well into February 1819, largely in consultation with the newly appointed French architect Pascal Coste.[72] This part of the project continued to be the most difficult. Many carpenters, blacksmiths, engineers, and workers were employed in the construction of the stone wall that was to encircle the lake so that boats could easily dock in the city.[73] Provincial *kāshifs* were charged with organizing groups of peasants to work on the lake.[74] These peasants were paid a piaster a day for their work, which enticed many to join the project. Villages that had many date trees were required to contribute baskets, panniers, dates, and rope to the lake's construction effort. Larger cities were to provide pickaxes, shovels, and pumps. Mehmet ʿAli even employed divers to aid him in the digging of the lake in this period.

The spring of 1819 represented the pinnacle of labor, resources, and effort put toward the building of the canal. Indeed, by March there were more than three hundred thousand peasants working on the project, and peasants were being brought from all parts of Egypt to labor on the

areas extended two *qaṣabas* (eight meters) above the present level of the surface of the water to be able to accommodate even higher future levels in the canal. For comparative details about the process of measuring the canal, see the following example from March 1819: Ibid., 100–2.

71 On the bricks used in this period of repair work and the oxen used to move them, see: Ibid., 102–3.

72 Rivlin, *Agricultural Policy of Muḥammad ʿAlī*, 219. On Coste and his involvement with the canal reconstruction project, see: Ṭūsūn, *Tārīkh Khalīj al-Iskandariyya*, 59–77, 121, 123, 126.

73 Al-Jabartī, *ʿAjāʾib al-Āthār*, 4:423–24.

74 Each *kāshif* was required to enlist a number of peasant workers proportional to the amount of cultivated acreage under his control. For a series of letters tracing negotiations over the organization of peasant labor in November 1819, see: Ṭūsūn, *Tārīkh Khalīj al-Iskandariyya*, 112–18.

canal. Village shaykhs were to assemble peasants from their villages to meet at a location designated by the Ottoman bureaucracy. From there, they would march to the cadence of drums and horns to the work site. Work was divided on the basis of one's village of origin, so that villagers from a certain region were working alongside their fellow villagers on a particular section of the canal.[75] If they completed their assigned task, they were quickly reshuffled to work elsewhere.[76]

At the end of April 1819, many peasants left the Ashrafiyya work site to return to their villages. Many less fortunate peasants who had come to work on the canal, however, had died during the previous months from fatigue, cold, and harsh and unsafe working conditions.[77] As if these circumstances were not bad enough, a plague epidemic broke out in the late spring of 1819, killing many of the workers and others as well. It was in the period from February to August 1819 that the canal's construction was completed. This was the most deadly period of work on the canal, as imperial authorities strove to finish the job as quickly as possible. Indeed, tens of thousands of peasants died on the canal in the spring and summer of 1819. By the end of August 1819, the total number of peasants who had been brought to work on the canal was approximately 315,000.[78] Some historians have put the number as high as 360,000.[79] By way of comparison, the population of Cairo in 1821 was measured to be 218,560 (260,000 in 1800), and that of all of Egypt was around 4.5 million in 1800 and 5 million in 1830.[80] In other words, a number of peasants larger than the population of Cairo and equal to approximately 8 percent of the total population of Egypt was brought to work on the canal's reconstruction.

75 Al-Jabartī, *ʿAjāʾib al-Āthār*, 4:424.

76 During this stage of digging, it was quite common for workers to stumble on ancient ruins in the soil. Al-Jabartī writes that an entire bathhouse was unearthed, complete with tubs, arches, and basins. Many chests and storage receptacles – some filled with ancient coins – were also found and taken promptly to Mehmet ʿAli.

77 Al-Jabartī, *ʿAjāʾib al-Āthār*, 4:425.

78 Rivlin, *Agricultural Policy of Muḥammad ʿAlī*, 219–20 and 353n15. Without citation, Marsot writes that a quarter of a million peasants were brought to work on the canal. Marsot, *Egypt in the Reign of Muhammad Ali*, 151.

79 M. A. Linant de Bellefonds, *Mémoires sur les principaux travaux d'utilité publiqué exécutés en Egypte depuis la plus haute antiquité jusqu'à nos jours: accompagné d'un atlas renfermant neuf planches grand in-folio imprimées en couleur* (Paris: Arthus Bertrand, 1872–1873), 351, cited in Rivlin, *Agricultural Policy of Muḥammad ʿAlī*, 353n15.

80 On the population of Cairo, see: Panzac, "Évolution d'une ville cosmopolite," 147. On the population of Egypt as a whole, see: Panzac, *Peste*, 271; Raymond, "La population du Caire et de l'Égypte."

Even more shocking than the scale of these numbers was the fact that approximately a third of the workers – or one hundred thousand men – died during the construction of the canal from exhaustion, starvation, disease, dehydration, accident, or extreme temperatures.[81] Again, this outstanding quantity of dead men was the equivalent of more than 45 percent of the population of Cairo dying in a two-year period. Peasant laborers worked under very harsh conditions, often from sunrise to sunset, with few breaks in between.[82] The following passage about events in August 1819 gives a good sense of the severity of these working conditions:

> He [Mehmet ʿAli] ordered the governors of the rural districts to assemble the peasants for work, and this command was executed. They were roped together and delivered by boats, thus missing the cultivation of sorghum, which is their sustenance. This time they suffered hardship over and above what they had originally suffered. Many died from cold and fatigue. Dirt from the excavation was dumped on every peasant who fell, even if he were still alive. When the peasants had been sent back to their villages for the harvest, money was demanded from them plus a camel-load of straw for every *faddān*, and a *kayl* each of wheat and beans. They had to sell their grain at a low price but at a full measure. No sooner had they done this than they were called back to work on the canal in order to drain the extremely saline water which continued to spring from the ground. The first time they had suffered from extreme cold; now, from extreme heat and scarcity of potable water.[83]

Getting water to Alexandria to increase the amount and quality of life in that city was thus clearly a very deadly affair for the hundreds of thousands of peasants who made the Ashrafiyya a reality.

[81] Rivlin, *Agricultural Policy of Muḥammad ʿAlī*, 221. As Rivlin notes, causality estimates range quite considerably from twelve thousand to one hundred thousand dead men. With reference to the Maḥmūdiyya project, though, she writes, "So vivid was the recollection of the horrors of those months that when years later the necessity for dredging the canal became vital the government hesitated to call out the *corvée* for that purpose." Ibid. Although Cuno expresses skepticism at these high casualty rates because "al-Jabartī's account may have been exaggerated out of animosity toward Muhammad Ali" (Cuno, *The Pasha's Peasants*, 122), he nevertheless cites Linant's estimates that more than four hundred thousand peasants were needed annually during the 1820s to clean various canals across Egypt. Ibid., 121–22. See also: Fahmy, *All the Pasha's Men*, 10; Fahmy, "The Era of Muhammad ʿAli Pasha, 1805–1848," in *Modern Egypt, from 1517 to the End of the Twentieth Century*, vol. 2 of *The Cambridge History of Egypt*, ed. M. W. Daly (Cambridge: Cambridge University Press, 1998), 152–53.

[82] On the general mistreatment of peasants during the period of Mehmet ʿAli's rule, see: Najm, "Tasaḥḥub al-Fallāḥīn," 259–82.

[83] Al-Jabartī, *ʿAjāʾib al-Āthār*, 4:427.

In late 1819, after the completion of this intense amount of work on the canal, Alexandria was – at least temporarily – connected to the Nile.[84] As anticipated, this integration of Alexandria into the network of waterways centered around the Nile meant that Egypt's second city was much easier to reach and that ships carrying food, water, and people could move much more seamlessly between Alexandria and other parts of Egypt, thus avoiding the dangers of the Mediterranean coastline. It took only a few months, however, before some of the same problems of old resurfaced. In January 1820, for example, the very month in which all reconstruction on the canal officially ended, it became clear that there were several major problems with the canal.[85] Its water was found to be extremely salty because of the large amount of salt water that continually sprung from the bed of the canal. Moreover, the canal's water often overflowed its banks, flooding fertilized areas with salty water and thereby ruining those lands' agricultural capacities. As if this were not troublesome enough, the dike at Abū Qīr was also overwhelmed with a storm that January, which meant that the canal was inundated with seawater from the Mediterranean as well.[86] Rumors soon circulated among Egyptians that the newly completed canal had been thoroughly destroyed and that salt water had flooded all of Alexandria. Peasants fled from villages around the canal, returning later to find them completely decimated.

Failure

In September 1820, the canal's waters were still hopelessly salty.[87] Thus, less than a year after the Ashrafiyya's massive reconstruction, the goal of building a consistent and reliable source of sweet water for Alexandria remained unfulfilled. Alexandrians still had no adequate source of potable water and were forced to pay the hefty sum of two piasters for a single bag of drinking water. Earlier that summer in July 1820, the canal was officially renamed the Maḥmūdiyya Canal after Ottoman Sultan Mahmud II, who ruled from 1808 to 1839.[88]

In October 1820 – only about a year after the major repairs of 1817 to 1819 – further work was undertaken on the waterway.[89] As before,

84 Official ceremonies marking the opening of the canal were observed in December 1819. Ṭūsūn, *Tārīkh Khalīj al-Iskandariyya*, 118–21.

85 Al-Jabartī, *'Ajā'ib al-Āthār*, 4:431.

86 Ṭūsūn, *Tārīkh Khalīj al-Iskandariyya*, 122.

87 Al-Jabartī, *'Ajā'ib al-Āthār*, 4:438.

88 Ibid.; Ṭūsūn, *Tārīkh Khalīj al-Iskandariyya*, 127.

89 BOA, HAT, 593/29055 (29 Z 1235/7 Oct. 1820).

the blowing of various winds (*hübub-i riyah-i muhtelife*) served to make the port of Rashīd impassable for ships attempting to enter and leave the city. As discussed previously, a major impetus behind the building of the Ashrafiyya Canal in the first place was to allow ships to bypass the port of Rashīd altogether so as to avoid the city's winds, which often made transport nearly impossible. Most worrisome about this situation from Istanbul's perspective was the fact that provisions (*erzak*) originating in Rashīd and destined for Istanbul could not leave Egypt. As a principal source of grains and foodstuffs for the imperial capital, this was clearly a major problem. In 1820, though, the Ottoman administration of Egypt could not use the Maḥmūdiyya to avoid Rashīd, because both the canal and its final lake near Alexandria were in a state of disrepair and needed to be dredged to allow ships to pass from the Nile. To undertake these repairs, Rohidin, the supervising engineer and instructor at the Egyptian School of Engineering whom we met earlier, was again dispatched to Egypt to oversee the work. The same map used in the previous repairs – the one, as this case says, marked with red (*sürh-i işaretile*) to redraw the fate of Alexandria – was again to be used as a guide in the present repairs.[90]

Thus, by late 1820, it had become clear that the Maḥmūdiyya Canal would continue to be a source of trouble and concern both immediately after the enormous repairs of only a year earlier and for many years to come. Indeed, given that the canal had to be repaired only a year after the massive repairs of the period between 1817 and 1819, it would be fair to say that the considerable bureaucratic effort put toward a permanent solution to the canal's problems, the enormous number of peasants who died on the canal's repair, and the great amount of money spent on this work did not amount to very much. Silt continued to collect in the

90 A subsequent case about the same repairs, also from October 1820, made many of the same points: the need for dredging and cleaning the canal and its lake, the importance of the map with red markings, the role of Rohidin in these repairs, and the vital nature of the Ashrafiyya for the well-being of Egypt and of the Ottoman Empire as a whole. BOA, HAT, 795/36893 (29 Z 1235/7 Oct. 1820). As in other cases about the repair of the Ashrafiyya Canal, this one also stated that the canal was key to the prosperity and, indeed, to the very survival of Alexandria, because it was the only direct link of food and water between Alexandria and the rest of Egypt. With full water in the canal, Egypt's second city would grow by leaps and bounds as more and more people would come to reside there to benefit from its prosperity. Not only was the canal key to the growth of Alexandria, but its proper function also meant that those villages already present around the canal would grow even larger and that entirely new villages would form as more and more people came to settle along its length.

canal, and the water in it and the soil around it remained very salty. The canal did, of course, have moments in which it functioned properly and productively, but for the most part, its well-known historical problems remained unsolved after 1817.

Shipwreck

Although troubles with the canal remained well into the nineteenth century, in the first few years of the 1820s, boat traffic on the Maḥmūdiyya Canal to and from Alexandria did in fact increase as merchants and traders took advantage of the new waterway and of the city's growing population.[91] The larger number of boats sailing to and from Alexandria on the Maḥmūdiyya led to an increase in the number of cases of shipwreck and of the sinking of boats in the canal in those years.[92] For example, a merchant came to the court of al-Baḥayra to register that on Wednesday, October 4, 1820, he was sailing on the Maḥmūdiyya Canal to Alexandria with fifty *ardabbs* of *fūl*.[93] When he neared the village of Qabīl, a strong gust of wind blew across his vessel, flipping it over into the water.[94] He

91 For cases about the canal's later repairs, see: Ṭūsūn, *Tārīkh Khalīj al-Iskandariyya*, 127–31.

92 Most of these cases came to the court of al-Baḥayra. Why would ship captains go through the trouble of securing two witnesses (solid legal proof in Islamic courts) to go to the court of al-Baḥayra to register the sinking of their ships? One answer is that the captains were most likely using the institution of the court to protect themselves against liability for the losses of their ships' cargoes. Even if captains owned their own ships (which was often not the case), they did not own the cargo on them. These sailors were hired in Bulaq by grain and wheat merchants to carry a certain load to Alexandria and to deliver the goods to the merchants' customers or representatives in the city. They were hired simply as the transporters of those foodstuffs, and when their boats sank, they likely went to the court of al-Baḥayra to secure an official record of the fact that the ships' losses were not their fault. Whether because of wind, the ineptitude of another ship captain, or the breaking (or cutting) of a ship's ropes, the captains wanted at all costs to avoid any liability for the loss of Bulaqi merchants' goods. The court, in other words, served as an official venue that – with the testimony of two witnesses – offered the captains legal evidence they could use to convince the merchants who hired them that they did not lose the grains through any fault of their own. Whether or not the grain merchants actually accepted the liability of the losses themselves is not recorded in any of these cases.

93 DWQ, Maḥkamat al-Baḥayra 38, p. 336, case 789 (8 M 1236/16 Oct. 1820).

94 In the following case, another merchant was on his way to Alexandria via the canal with three hundred *ardabbs* of wheat: DWQ, Maḥkamat al-Baḥayra 38, p. 329, case 772 (8 Za 1237/27 Jul. 1822). During his trip down the Maḥmūdiyya to the port city, he transferred 108 *ardabbs* of his load to the boat of one Ibrāhīm Faraḥāt. With the load now split between the two ships, the men sailed together toward Alexandria. When the two ships reached the village of al-Naẓīriyya, a mighty gust of wind met them in the

lost his entire load of foodstuffs and brought to court two witnesses from the village of Qabīl who testified that they saw his boat upside down (*maqlūba*) in the canal between their village and that of Basṭara.[95]

Wind was not the only reason ships sank in the Maḥmūdiyya. On May 12, 1822, a man named ʿĀmir Ibn al-Marḥūm Sālim al-Sufayrāb came to the court of al-Baḥayra to report that on Tuesday, April 30 of that year, he brought his ship carrying one hundred *ardabbs* of sesame to moor for the night on the banks of the Maḥmūdiyya near the village of Salamun.[96] ʿĀmir was carrying his load from Bulaq to Alexandria – perhaps the most common route taken by ships sailing on the Maḥmūdiyya. The merchant tied his ship to the shore for the night and went to sleep. At some point during his slumber, the ropes securing his ship either came loose or were cut. While ʿĀmir was still asleep, his ship floated without a captain directionless along the canal, eventually crashing and overturning in the waterway. As in the previous case, the ship's entire load was lost, and ʿĀmir brought two witnesses with him to court to testify that his story about the ship was indeed an accurate, complete, and true recounting of events.

In another case, we learn that some shipwrecks on the Maḥmūdiyya were the result of ships colliding with one another along the narrow waterway. Such was the fate of a ship operated by a merchant named Ḥama Ibn al-Marḥūm ʿAbd al-Fattāḥ Abū Fāṭa. On Saturday, July 27, 1822, he was navigating his ship from Bulaq to Alexandria along the Maḥmūdiyya with one hundred *ardabbs* of *fūl*.[97] As he passed between the villages of al-Kawīyun and Birkat Ghiṭās early that Saturday afternoon, his ship collided with that of a man named al-Ḥājj ʿAbd al-Sūbanātī.[98] Ḥama's boat was badly damaged and started to take on a great amount of water. Unable to stop the water from flooding his ship, Ḥama lost his full load of *fūl* and was forced to abandon his vessel in the middle of the waterway, where it remained as he went to court. As did other unlucky

late afternoon and overturned Ibrāhīm Faraḥāt's ship containing the 108 *ardabbs* of wheat. Thus, as with numerous other cases, the merchants lost a load of foodstuffs to the waters of the Maḥmūdiyya as a result of a great gust of wind that overturned their ship. For another example of a ship overturning in the Maḥmūdiyya Canal as a result of powerful winds, see: DWQ, Maḥkamat al-Baḥayra 38, p. 336, case 791 (28 M 1236/5 Nov. 1820). In this case, a ship carrying two hundred *ardabbs* of wheat to Alexandria overturned between the villages of Kafr Silīm and Malqaṭ al-Bidfa and lost its entire load of foodstuffs.

95 On the village of Basṭara, see: *QJBM*, pt. 2, 2:284.

96 DWQ, Maḥkamat al-Baḥayra 38, p. 329, case 770 (20 Ş 1237/12 May 1822).

97 DWQ, Maḥkamat al-Baḥayra 38, p. 335, case 788 (16 Za 1237/4 Aug. 1822).

98 On Birkat Ghiṭās, see: *QJBM*, pt. 2, 2:239.

ship captains, Ḥama came to court with two witnesses who could verify his story to the judge.

As these and other cases like them show, the Maḥmūdiyya Canal after its massive repairs in 1819 did momentarily connect Alexandria to the Nile as a major thoroughfare for the transport of goods, foodstuffs, and people between the Mediterranean city and Cairo, Bulaq, and other areas of Egypt.[99] That the Maḥmūdiyya would aid in the revitalization of Egypt's second city by serving as a constant and reliable supply of food and water was, of course, one of the main justifications for building the canal. Although the cases here are about ships that never made it to Alexandria, they serve as evidence of the heavy boat traffic to and from the city. Indeed, that the vessels sometimes could not avoid crashing into one another is proof enough that the canal served as a major link of goods and people between the Nile and Alexandria for certain periods in the early nineteenth century.

Moreover, these cases shed light on the natural history of the canal after its major repair in 1819. As suggested by cases involving ships overturned by wind (and as we have seen throughout this chapter), the Maḥmūdiyya was historically – and indeed continued to be in the early nineteenth century – a very shallow waterway that was difficult for most ships to navigate. Not only did ships regularly run aground in the canal, but its inadequate depth also made ships very susceptible to overturning, because they were not submerged very deeply underwater. Thus, the many reasons for the canal's shallowness remained: a weak current, the siphoning off of its waters by those living along the canal, evaporation, and seepage.

The problems of the Maḥmūdiyya were not solved by its reconstruction in the first quarter of the nineteenth century. Indeed, the lives of one hundred thousand peasants and massive amounts of building materials, money, and labor were not enough to prevent natural forces like wind, siltation, salinization, and seepage from regularly rendering the canal nearly unusable. If the goals of the canal's reconstruction were to overcome the environmental forces of the nature of the Egyptian countryside, then this project was a clear failure. The canal continued to lose water, to collect silt and salt, and to be nearly impassable for ships sailing to and

99 For more examples of cases involving the sinking of ships in the Maḥmūdiyya, see: DWQ, Maḥkamat al-Baḥayra 38, p. 336, case 792 (22 S 1236/28 Nov. 1820); DWQ, Maḥkamat al-Baḥayra 38, p. 336, case 790 (n.d.).

from Alexandria. Furthermore, the many shipwrecked vessels left in the canal for long periods of time by their captains going to court made the canal even more difficult to pass.

In the reconstruction of the Ashrafiyya Canal and throughout correspondence about the canal between Mehmet ʿAli and the Sublime Porte, we notice many familiar features from work on irrigation projects done earlier in the long eighteenth century. Mehmet ʿAli's administration in the early nineteenth century clearly continued to rely on the knowledge and experience of local older Egyptian peasants with respect to matters of irrigation. As Mehmet ʿAli himself admitted, locals understood the digging of canals in various locations throughout Egypt better than anyone else because they had gained so much experience with this work over the years. They had a kind of knowledge found nowhere else – not even in the state's own school of engineering – and that could not be matched by any amount of wood or stone. Another familiar theme in this correspondence between Egypt and Istanbul was the emphasis on bringing drinking water for Alexandria. Throughout the eighteenth century and into the early nineteenth, the goals of providing drinking water for Alexandria and of creating a shipping lane between the city and the Nile remained the two main justifications for the repair and maintenance of the Ashrafiyya Canal.

What was most strikingly different about the repair work undertaken by Mehmet ʿAli in the second decade of the nineteenth century was the sheer size it proposed and the novel imagination it demanded. Although channeling drinking water to Alexandria had always been the primary reason for the canal, never before had constructing life in and around that city been made so specifically explicit a goal of the Ottoman state in Egypt. The Ashrafiyya Canal was made out to be a kind of cathartic entity with the ability to change the entire meaning of Egypt itself. Again, the Ashrafiyya was to change the literal meaning of the word *Mısır* from Cairo to Alexandria. The canal was to change Egypt forever; it was to bring Alexandria to life and life to Alexandria. Along with this new kind of imagination about the potential of irrigation works like the Ashrafiyya to change Egypt was the monumental size of the project itself and the enormous impact it had on the peasant communities it touched. Never before had so much energy, labor, material, effort, and death been put toward the maintenance of a canal in Egypt. As we saw in Chapter 4, the organization of labor on irrigation works in Egypt gradually transformed from its local and relatively small-scale character at the beginning of the long eighteenth century, to ever larger and more complex projects as the century wore on, and eventually to the magnitude of the Ashrafiyya at the beginning of the nineteenth century.

Fundamental to the canal construction project was the tension between the massive numbers of dead produced as a result of the canal's construction and the discourse of creating life both in Alexandria and along the length of the canal that we find repeated over and over again in the correspondence between Mehmet ʿAli and Istanbul and that served as the most common justification for the reconstruction of the canal. How are we to reconcile this seeming contradiction between a stated desire for life and the reality of one hundred thousand dead peasants put toward that goal? How could efforts at life result in so much death? The keys to understanding this inherent tension in the Ashrafiyya reconstruction project lie in the transformations outlined in the previous chapters that followed Egypt's move away from its primary position in an early modern Ottoman system of natural resource management toward a more centrally controlled Egyptian bureaucracy. As shown in Chapter 4, Egyptian peasants were turned into laborers through the bureaucratic abstraction of the labor chart and through various mechanisms of enumeration. They became literal numbers on a page to be maximized and harnessed by the bureaucracy managing them. As such, they were lifeless forms with no identity other than the one given to them by an administration that had made them into laborers. Thus, it was quite easy on the balance sheet of the state to move around massive numbers of peasants to do the work it deemed useful. As we saw previously, however, with the Ashrafiyya's repairs, the process was never as seamless, clean, and unproblematic as that envisaged on the page. Peasants tired, had to be transported, were injured, and died; dirt fell into the canal; soil was saline; wind blew ships over; and water did not flow through the canal fast enough. The Ottoman bureaucracy attempted to overcome this disconnect between the idea of the reconstruction on paper and the reality of the challenges facing the work through the hundreds of thousands of peasants it brought to the canal, a solution which reflected a cruel belief that anything could be accomplished given enough labor, resources, and administration.

Also clear in this project was for whom peasants were working and dying. The living social space of Egypt had already been defined through the mechanisms of quarantine and through other projects aimed at caring for, organizing, cleaning, and delineating society. Opposite the realms of the living were other spaces in Egypt where the sick, the dying, the insane, the poor, and others deemed undesirable were sent to wallow until their deaths. Those people were not to benefit from the reconstruction of the canal; rather, the Ashrafiyya was a project meant to improve the lives of those deemed active and constructive members of Egyptian society: merchants, ruling and religious elites, the educated, and so on. These were the social subjects created through quarantine who inhabited a realm of society to be managed and cared for through projects like the Ashrafiyya's reconstruction.

Ideas informing the transformations of Egypt at the end of the eighteenth century and the beginning of the nineteenth and the apparatuses of rule created by and for them were put to affect most spectacularly and tragically in the rebuilding of the Ashrafiyya. The project thus represented the pinnacle of these ideas of society and of the government's role in the use and management of this society and of the environment that sustained it. By combining both the bureaucratic abstraction of peasant life accomplished through enumeration and quarantine's delineation of the social, the Ottoman administration of Egypt in the reconstruction of the Ashrafiyya served to make life an expense like any other. This was the ultimate significance of the canal project. It made Egyptian peasant life into a commodity to be traded, organized, harnessed, cared for, used, and disposed of at the state's discretion.

CONCLUSION

THE IMAGINATION AND REALITY OF PUBLIC WORKS

After the completion of the Maḥmūdiyya's reconstruction in 1819, a stone tablet was placed at the canal's mouth and another at its end in Alexandria to commemorate the project.[1] The tablet at the canal's start claimed that "the glories of the Sultan had brought life to dead lands" near the waterway and had "reanimated" them through a return to cultivation. The tablet at the end of the canal continued this theme by asserting that the Ottoman dynasty had caused the Nile "to flow once more." These triumphalist declarations by the Ottoman bureaucracy that described the Empire as the source of agriculture's rebirth and of the return of water to Egypt contributed to the notion that an irrigation work like the Maḥmūdiyya could serve as the single necessary magic solution to the very complex ecological problems of water scarcity, siltation, seepage, and salinization. The idea of the renewal of land and water through public works in Egypt began with the Maḥmūdiyya and would prove a fundamental conceptual cornerstone of similar projects throughout the nineteenth and twentieth centuries.

Renewal, rebirth, and revitalization of course all mark both an end and a beginning. In the case of the Maḥmūdiyya, its reconstruction represented the end of an early modern system of Ottoman imperial natural resource management that served to move food, wood, and other items around the entirety of the Empire. The canal was also the end of an imperially coordinated system of hyperlocalism in which Egyptian peasants controlled the Empire's management of irrigation and water usage through their knowledge of and experience in local environments. More tragically, the canal's reconstruction was also the end of one hundred thousand of the three hundred thousand peasants who were forcibly brought to work on it. As silt and salt continued to collect in the canal, making it unnavigable, rendering soil around it too saline, and

[1] Ṭūsūn, *Tārīkh Khalīj al-Iskandariyya*, 108–13.

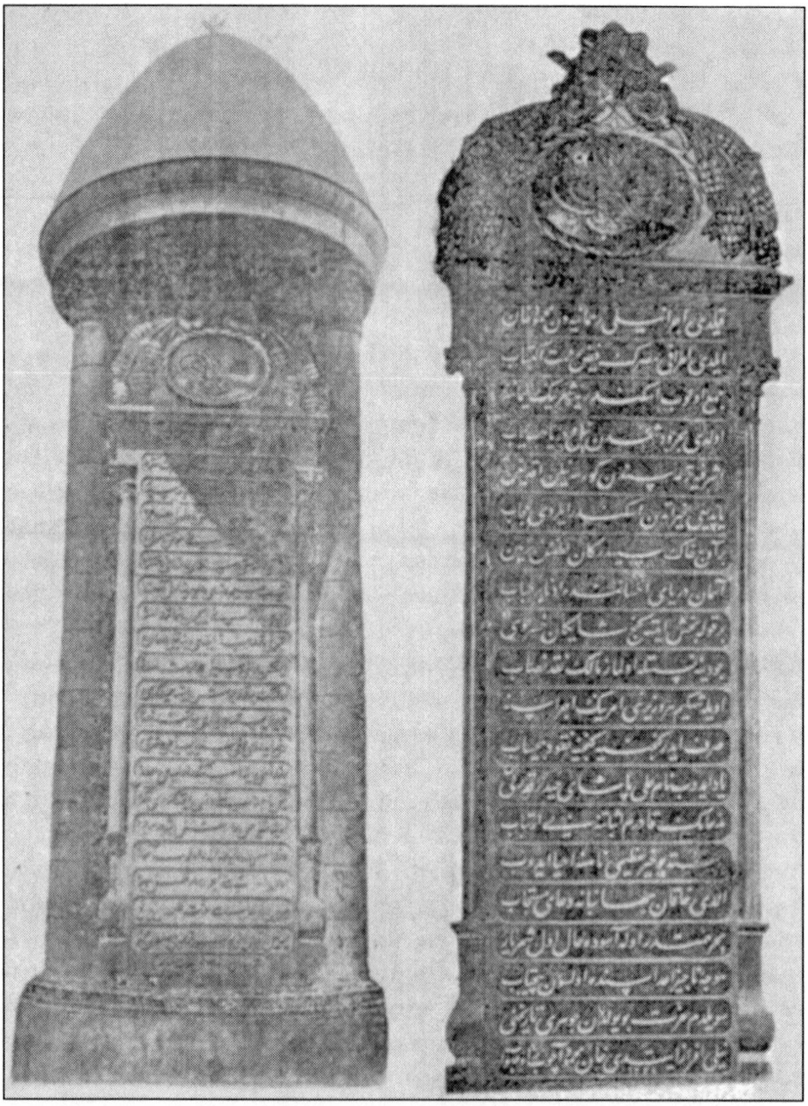

Figure C.1. Stone tablets placed at the beginning (*right*) and end (*left*) of the Maḥmūdiyya Canal. ʿUmar Ṭūsūn, *Tārīkh Khalīj al-Iskandariyya al-Qadīm wa Turʿat al-Maḥmūdiyya* (Alexandria: Maṭbaʿat al-ʿAdl, 1942), after pp. 108 and 112, respectively.

preventing water from flowing to the people of Alexandria, the Maḥmūdiyya soon came to symbolize the end of Egypt's place as the most lucrative province in the Ottoman system.

As we have seen in this book, the environmental history of Ottoman Egypt that ended with the Maḥmūdiyya was at its heart a history of struggle between Egyptian peasants and various forms of Ottoman administration over the control of natural resources. It was a struggle over what kind of empire by nature Ottoman Egypt was to be. In the first two centuries of Ottoman rule in Egypt, the province functioned as one of the most integral parts of an early modern system of natural resource management. The Empire in this period was sustained in large part by its abilities to move wood and food, to use peasants' knowledge and labor constructively and collectively, to harness the productive capacities of various environments around the Mediterranean, and to keep irrigation networks functioning. It was, in short, largely by nature that the Empire maintained its rule.

At the end of the eighteenth century, Ottoman provincial administration in Egypt began to change into a very different kind of empire by nature as it increasingly pulled away from Ottoman central control. As I have shown in the preceding chapters, no longer were peasants the experts who controlled irrigation and rural agricultural production; no longer did Egypt have access to forests in Anatolia and the Levant; no longer was plague a constructive part of social relationships; and, most significantly, no longer was the irrigated environment of Egypt managed sustainably and productively. As the bureaucracy of Egypt expanded its control, it placed much more pressure on the Egyptian environment and on peasant populations who worked in that environment. They had to irrigate more land, work longer days, and produce more food. It was in this and in innumerable other ways that Egyptian peasants were made into new kinds of imperial subjects by a new kind of empire. Thus, this book can be read as telling part of the story of how Egypt came to colonize itself, or, more precisely, of how the Egyptian state came to colonize the Egyptian peasantry and countryside.[2]

[2] For a comparative analysis of a similar process of "colonization" in France, see: Eugen Weber, *Peasants into Frenchmen: The Modernization of Rural France, 1870–1914* (Stanford, CA: Stanford University Press, 1976). For Weber's use of the word *colonization* specifically, see esp. pp. 241, 486, 492–93. James C. Scott also usefully writes that "modern statecraft is largely a project of internal colonization, often glossed, as it is in imperial rhetoric, as a 'civilizing mission.' The builders of the modern nation-state do not merely describe, observe, and map; they strive to shape a people and landscape that will fit their techniques of observation." Scott, *Seeing Like a State*, 82.

As part of this process of administrative centralization and expansion in Ottoman Egypt, Mehmet ʿAli's government amplified its imperial ambitions; founded lasting institutions; and built canals, roads, schools, and an immense bureaucracy.[3] Projects like the Maḥmūdiyya contained in them the imaginatory potential of all of this. And this was the canal's significance as a beginning. The Maḥmūdiyya was the first large-scale public works project in Egypt imagined to have the potential to change the entire meaning of what Egypt was and of what it could be. The canal was, as we have seen, indeed meant to change the very meaning of the word *Mısır* from Cairo to Alexandria. The decades after the Maḥmūdiyya saw a string of similar enormous public works projects: the construction of the Suez Canal in the 1850s and 1860s;[4] the building of the first Aswan Dam in the 1890s;[5] the construction of the Aswan High Dam in the 1950s and 1960s;[6] and the current project known as Toshka, whose goal is to irrigate an entirely new Nile Valley parallel to the current one.[7] In other words, every forty to fifty years since the beginning of the nineteenth century, governments in Egypt have undertaken a massive public works project with the goal of remaking Egypt anew as an economically and politically independent entity.

The commonalities in each of these projects are striking. Each embodied the imagined potential of public works – and usually of water – to change both the environmental and the political landscape of Egypt. In each case, Egypt was to become something radically different after the completion of a canal or a dam.[8] Another common feature of each of

3 Much of this is recounted in the following: Marsot, *Egypt in the Reign of Muhammad Ali*.

4 On the construction of the Suez Canal, see: D. A. Farnie, *East and West of Suez: The Suez Canal in History, 1854–1956* (Oxford, UK: Clarendon Press, 1969), 55–80; John Marlowe, *World Ditch: The Making of the Suez Canal* (New York: Macmillan, 1964).

5 Robert O. Collins, *The Nile* (New Haven, CT: Yale University Press, 2002), 142-46. For an extremely useful analysis of the first Aswan Dam, see: Timothy Mitchell, "Can the Mosquito Speak?" in *Rule of Experts*, 19–53.

6 On the politics and construction of the Aswan High Dam, see: Collins, *Nile*, 177-94; Yusuf A. Shibl, *The Aswan High Dam* (Beirut: Arab Institute for Research and Publishing, 1971); Hussein M. Fahim, *Dams, People and Development: The Aswan High Dam Case* (New York: Pergamon Press, 1981). See also the relevant sections of John Waterbury, *Hydropolitics of the Nile Valley* (Syracuse, NY: Syracuse University Press, 1979).

7 On Toshka, see: Timothy Mitchell, "Dreamland," in *Rule of Experts*, 272–303.

8 Bruno Latour's concept of *quasi-objects* is very useful in thinking about the significance of these public works projects. About these quasi-objects, he writes, "Boyle's air pump, Pasteur's microbes, Archimedes' pulleys, are such objects. These new nonhumans possess miraculous properties because they are at one and the same time both social and asocial, producers of natures and constructors of subjects." Latour, *We Have Never Been Modern*, trans. Catherine Porter (Cambridge, MA: Harvard University Press, 1993), 112.

these projects is their failure. Although the projects did in some ways meet the original intentions behind them, their huge human, economic, and ecological costs usually far outweighed their returns. We have already discussed the problems with the Maḥmūdiyya project. Suez exploded Egypt's foreign economic debt and was a contributing factor to its colonization at the end of the nineteenth century.[9] The political, economic, human, and environmental price tag of the Aswan High Dam was likewise enormous: the destruction of much of historical Nubia, increased reliance on chemical fertilizers to overcome salinization, shrinkage of the Nile Delta, and massive water losses as a result of evaporation from Lake Nasser (to name only the most obvious).[10] And we can only guess that Toshka will be similarly troublesome. What is more – and this is perhaps the most nefarious result of these projects – all of these canals and dams further alienated Egyptian peasants from their lands and the environments their families had been cultivating for generations. As projects grew exponentially in size and complexity, from the Maḥmūdiyya to Toshka, bulldozers came to replace pickaxes and shovels; multinational companies replaced local village leaders; foreign laborers replaced Egyptian ones; and peasants' knowledge and experience of canals, embankments, and soils became deemed increasingly less important.

As I have shown in this book, as bureaucracies expand and become more sophisticated, they come to separate people from their environments, accustomed means of work, and social forms and norms. Put differently, as the distance between those making decisions and the impacts of those decisions increases, so, too, do the deleterious, unforeseen, and costly effects of those decisions. Though surely an enormous bureaucratic

[9] Farnie, *East and West*; Marlowe, *World Ditch*. The British formally colonized Egypt in 1882, beginning a period at the end of the nineteenth century in which numerous British engineers, hydrologists, geologists, and others with interests in the Nile came to Egypt to study various aspects of the river. The concerns of these men in Egypt were, of course, much more than merely scientific. Exploring the sources of the Nile, irrigating more land in Egypt and the Sudan, building various dams and other irrigation works, and regulating water distribution were all parts of British efforts to manage the entire Nile system – an integral aspect of imperial attempts to control and protect the Suez Canal and British trade routes to India. One of the most important works on irrigation to be authored by British imperial officials in this period was the following: Willcocks and Craig, *Egyptian Irrigation*. On British imperial designs for the Nile, see: Terje Tvedt, *The River Nile in the Age of the British: Political Ecology and the Quest for Economic Power* (London: I. B. Tauris, 2004).

[10] McNeill, *Something New under the Sun*, 166–73; Collins, *Nile*, 177-94. See also: Shibl, *Aswan High Dam*, 73–123; Fahim, *Dams, People and Development*; Waterbury, *Hydropolitics*, 154–73 and 210–41.

system in its own right, the Ottoman imperial structure of managing irrigation in Egypt afforded Egyptian peasants the autonomy and space to control irrigation and ecology in their own local environments. The system was not a function of the largesse of the imperial state but rather the reflection of an understanding of the most efficient and effective means to govern natural resources and landscapes in Egypt. Toward the end of the eighteenth century, as irrigation repair projects became larger and larger, so, too, expanded their bureaucratic demands. Since that period, bureaucracy in Egypt – not only in the realms of irrigation and the environment but in others as well – has continued to refine and expand. As a result of these processes, Egyptian peasants have been pushed further and further away from the control of their lands and of those lands' inputs and outputs.

The Egyptian experience is therefore instructive of how the transition from early modern political rule to nineteenth-century state bureaucracy affected the management of natural resources, irrigation, rural labor, disease, and public works. Much, as I have argued in this book, was lost in this transition. Perhaps the most significant of these losses was the knowledge of the historical reality of how the environment functioned and of how it was managed for millennia. Thus, in contrast to the delusional imagination that a single canal or dam could solve all of Egypt's ecological, economic, political, and social problems in one fell swoop, I hope I have shown in this book that the potential solutions to those problems lie in the realm of reality rather than imagination – the reality of centuries of peasant interaction with water and soil; the reality of local knowledge of how best to manage the environment; and the reality that equitable, sustainable, and cooperative management of natural resources is the only way to preserve and harness the productivity of a land like Egypt.

APPENDIX

CITATIONS FOR CASES INCLUDED IN TABLES 2.1–2.4

1718–1719 (1131)

DWQ, Maḥkamat Rashīd 122, p. 67, case 113 (21 Ca 1131); DWQ, Maḥkamat Rashīd 123, p. 133, case 224 (10 Ş 1131); DWQ, Maḥkamat Rashīd 123, p. 132, case 221 (6 L 1131); DWQ, Maḥkamat Rashīd 123, p. 132, case 220 (17 N 1131); DWQ, Maḥkamat Rashīd 123, p. 142, case 241 (25 B 1131); DWQ, Maḥkamat Rashīd 123, p. 134, case 225 (10 Ş 1131); DWQ, Maḥkamat Rashīd 123, p. 134, case 226 (10 Ş 1131); DWQ, Maḥkamat Rashīd 123, p. 134, case 227 (10 Ş 1131); DWQ, Maḥkamat Rashīd 123, p. 140, case 233 (8 N 1131); DWQ, Maḥkamat Rashīd 123, p. 140, case 234 (7 L 1131); DWQ, Maḥkamat Rashīd 123, p. 140, case 235 (20 Ş 1131).

1727–1728 (1140)

DWQ, Maḥkamat Rashīd 134, p. 344, case 462 (28 Ş 1140); DWQ, Maḥkamat Rashīd 134, p. 344, case 463 (23 Ş 1140); DWQ, Maḥkamat Rashīd 134, p. 345, case 464 (23 Ş 1140); DWQ, Maḥkamat Rashīd 134, p. 345, case 465 (23 Ş 1140).

1740–1741 (1153)

DWQ, Maḥkamat Rashīd 146, p. 138, case 115 (1 C 1153); DWQ, Maḥkamat Rashīd 146, p. 139, case 116 (1 C 1153); DWQ, Maḥkamat Rashīd 146, p. 158, case 143 (10 B 1153); DWQ, Maḥkamat Rashīd 146, p. 158, case 144 (10 B 1153); DWQ, Maḥkamat Rashīd 146, p. 205, case 187 (26 Ş 1153); DWQ, Maḥkamat Rashīd 146, p. 205, case 188 (26 Ş 1153); DWQ, Maḥkamat Rashīd 146, p. 205, case 189 (26 Ş 1153); DWQ, Maḥkamat Rashīd 146, p. 205, case 190 (26 Ş 1153).

1741–1742 (1154)

DWQ, Maḥkamat Rashīd 148, p. 5, case 6 (13 Ş 1154); DWQ, Maḥkamat Rashīd 148, p. 176, case 217 (21 Z 1154); DWQ, Maḥkamat Rashīd 148, p. 176, case 218 (21 Z 1154); DWQ, Maḥkamat Rashīd

148, p. 176, case 219 (21 Z 1154); DWQ, Maḥkamat Rashīd 148, p. 177, case 220 (21 Z 1154); DWQ, Maḥkamat Rashīd 148, p. 177, case 221 (21 Z 1154); DWQ, Maḥkamat Rashīd 148, p. 177, case 222 (21 Z 1154).

1747–1748 (1160)

DWQ, Maḥkamat Rashīd 151, p. 315, case 356 (12 M 1160); DWQ, Maḥkamat Rashīd 151, p. 315, case 357 (12 M 1160); DWQ, Maḥkamat Rashīd 151, p. 321, case 364 (14 S 1160); DWQ, Maḥkamat Rashīd 151, p. 321, case 365 (14 S 1160); DWQ, Maḥkamat Rashīd 151, p. 321, case 366 (14 S 1160).

1748–1749 (1162)

DWQ, Maḥkamat Rashīd 154, p. 181, case 201 (25 Z 1162); DWQ, Maḥkamat Rashīd 154, p. 182, case 202 (25 Z 1162); DWQ, Maḥkamat Rashīd 154, p. 182, case 203 (25 Z 1162); DWQ, Maḥkamat Rashīd 154, p. 182, case 204 (25 Z 1162); DWQ, Maḥkamat Rashīd 154, p. 182, case 205 (25 Z 1162); DWQ, Maḥkamat Rashīd 154, p. 183, case 206 (30 Z 1162); DWQ, Maḥkamat Rashīd 154, p. 13, case 3 (21 Ca 1162); DWQ, Maḥkamat Rashīd 154, p. 13, case 4 (15 R 1162); DWQ, Maḥkamat Rashīd 154, p. 13, case 5 (15 R 1162); DWQ, Maḥkamat Rashīd 154, p. 13, case 6 (15 R 1162); DWQ, Maḥkamat Rashīd 154, p. 13, case 7 (15 R 1162); DWQ, Maḥkamat Rashīd 154, p. 14, case 8 (25 R 1162); DWQ, Maḥkamat Rashīd 154, p. 14, case 9 (13 R 1162); DWQ, Maḥkamat Rashīd 154, p. 14, case 10 (13 R 1162); DWQ, Maḥkamat Rashīd 154, p. 14, case 11 (13 R 1162); DWQ, Maḥkamat Rashīd 154, p. 14, case 12 (14 R 1162); DWQ, Maḥkamat Rashīd 154, p. 14, case 13 (13 R 1162); DWQ, Maḥkamat Rashīd 154, p. 149, no case no. (3 Ra 1162); DWQ, Maḥkamat Rashīd 154, p. 2, no case no. (15 R 1162); DWQ, Maḥkamat Rashīd 154, p. 3, case 4 (12 M 1162); DWQ, Maḥkamat Rashīd 154, p. 3, case 6 (8 R 1162); DWQ, Maḥkamat Rashīd 154, p. 4, no case no. (25 S 1162); DWQ, Maḥkamat Rashīd 154, p. 4, case 7 (12 M 1162); DWQ, Maḥkamat Rashīd 154, p. 4, case 8 (12 M 1162); DWQ, Maḥkamat Rashīd 154, p. 5, case 10 (23 M 1162); DWQ, Maḥkamat Rashīd 154, p. 5, case 11 (20 Ra 1162); DWQ, Maḥkamat Rashīd 154, p. 5, case 12 (12 M 1162); DWQ, Maḥkamat Rashīd 154, p. 8, no case no. (A) (12 M 1162); DWQ, Maḥkamat Rashīd 154, p. 8, no case no. (B) (24 S 1162); DWQ, Maḥkamat Rashīd 155, p. 297, case 323 (12 M 1162); DWQ, Maḥkamat Rashīd 155, p. 320, case 403 (4 N 1162).

1749–1750 (1163)

DWQ, Maḥkamat Rashīd 154, p. 341, no case no. (A) (4 Ra 1163); DWQ, Maḥkamat Rashīd 154, p. 341, no case no. (B) (8 S 1163); DWQ, Maḥkamat Rashīd 154, p. 341, no case no. (C) (22 M 1163); DWQ, Maḥkamat Rashīd 154, p. 341, no case no. (D) (6 R 1163); DWQ, Maḥkamat Rashīd 155, p. 17, case 17 (15 Ş 1163); DWQ, Maḥkamat Rashīd 155, p. 17, case 18 (15 Ş 1163); DWQ, Maḥkamat Rashīd 155, p. 17, case 19 (22 N 1163); DWQ, Maḥkamat Rashīd 155, p. 17, case 20 (22 N 1163); DWQ, Maḥkamat Rashīd 155, p. 24, case 29 (3 L 1163); DWQ, Maḥkamat Rashīd 155, p. 42, case 51 (7 L 1163); DWQ, Maḥkamat Rashīd 155, p. 99, case 105 (1 Za 1163); DWQ, Maḥkamat Rashīd 155, p. 100, case 106 (15 L 1163); DWQ, Maḥkamat Rashīd 155, p. 100, case 107 (14 Z 1163); DWQ, Maḥkamat Rashīd 155, p. 100, case 108 (14 Z 1163); DWQ, Maḥkamat Rashīd 155, p. 100, case 109 (15 L 1163); DWQ, Maḥkamat Rashīd 155, p. 101, case 110 (15 L 1163); DWQ, Maḥkamat Rashīd 155, p. 101, case 111 (15 Z 1163); DWQ, Maḥkamat Rashīd 155, p. 292, case 308 (7 R 1163); DWQ, Maḥkamat Rashīd 155, p. 298, case 328 (22 L 1163); DWQ, Maḥkamat Rashīd 155, p. 298, case 330 (7 Z 1163); DWQ, Maḥkamat Rashīd 155, p. 299, case 332 (7 Z 1163); DWQ, Maḥkamat Rashīd 155, p. 299, case 333 (7 Z 1163); DWQ, Maḥkamat Rashīd 155, p. 300, case 334 (19 Z 1163); DWQ, Maḥkamat Rashīd 155, p. 300, case 336 (6 Za 1163); DWQ, Maḥkamat Rashīd 155, p. 301, case 339 (6 Za 1163); DWQ, Maḥkamat Rashīd 155, p. 302, case 340 (21 Z 1163); DWQ, Maḥkamat Rashīd 155, p. 302, case 342 (7 Z 1163); DWQ, Maḥkamat Rashīd 155, p. 303, case 343 (7 Z 1163); DWQ, Maḥkamat Rashīd 155, p. 305, case 348 (7 Z 1163); DWQ, Maḥkamat Rashīd 155, p. 306, case 352 (6 Za 1163); DWQ, Maḥkamat Rashīd 155, p. 308, case 355 (1 C 1163); DWQ, Maḥkamat Rashīd 155, p. 308, case 356 (8 Ra 1163); DWQ, Maḥkamat Rashīd 155, p. 310, case 362 (8 R 1163); DWQ, Maḥkamat Rashīd 155, p. 311, case 364 (4 Ra 1163); DWQ, Maḥkamat Rashīd 155, p. 311, case 365 (6 Ş 1163); DWQ, Maḥkamat Rashīd 155, p. 311, case 366 (23 S 1163); DWQ, Maḥkamat Rashīd 155, p. 311, case 367 (12 Ra 1163); DWQ, Maḥkamat Rashīd 155, p. 312, case 368 (6 Za 1163); DWQ, Maḥkamat Rashīd 155, p. 312, case 369 (7 L 1163); DWQ, Maḥkamat Rashīd 155, p. 318, case 393 (6 Za 1163); DWQ, Maḥkamat Rashīd 157, p. 16, case 24 (19 Za 1163). For the period from 1161 to 1163 (1748 to 1750), note that between pages 342 and 356 of register 154 of the court of Rashīd, there are an additional thirty-nine cases, very similar to the foregoing ones, about the shipment of food from Rashīd to Istanbul, Crete, and various areas of Anatolia.

1750–1751 (1164)

DWQ, Maḥkamat Rashīd 155, p. 229, case 239 (1 Ra 1164); DWQ, Maḥkamat Rashīd 155, p. 230, case 240 (1 Ra 1164); DWQ, Maḥkamat Rashīd 155, p. 230, case 241 (15 S 1164); DWQ, Maḥkamat Rashīd 155, p. 230, case 242 (3 Ra 1164); DWQ, Maḥkamat Rashīd 155, p. 230, case 243 (15 S 1164); DWQ, Maḥkamat Rashīd 155, p. 290, case 304 (28 R 1164); DWQ, Maḥkamat Rashīd 155, p. 291, case 305 (22 R 1164); DWQ, Maḥkamat Rashīd 155, p. 291, case 306 (21 R 1164); DWQ, Maḥkamat Rashīd 155, p. 291, case 307 (22 Ca 1164); DWQ, Maḥkamat Rashīd 155, p. 292, case 309 (21 R 1164); DWQ, Maḥkamat Rashīd 155, p. 292, case 310 (7 S 1164); DWQ, Maḥkamat Rashīd 155, p. 293, case 311 (11 R 1164); DWQ, Maḥkamat Rashīd 155, p. 293, case 312 (9 Ca 1164); DWQ, Maḥkamat Rashīd 155, p. 293, case 313 (25 R 1164); DWQ, Maḥkamat Rashīd 155, p. 294, case 314 (5 S 1164); DWQ, Maḥkamat Rashīd 155, p. 294, case 315 (5 S 1164); DWQ, Maḥkamat Rashīd 155, p. 294, case 316 (21 R 1164); DWQ, Maḥkamat Rashīd 155, p. 295, case 318 (10 R 1164); DWQ, Maḥkamat Rashīd 155, p. 295, case 319 (4 R 1164); DWQ, Maḥkamat Rashīd 155, p. 296, case 322 (28 S 1164); DWQ, Maḥkamat Rashīd 155, p. 297, case 324 (5 S 1164); DWQ, Maḥkamat Rashīd 155, p. 297, case 325 (5 S 1164); DWQ, Maḥkamat Rashīd 155, p. 297, case 326 (17 Ra 1164); DWQ, Maḥkamat Rashīd 155, p. 298, case 327 (8 Ra 1164); DWQ, Maḥkamat Rashīd 155, p. 298, case 329 (8 Ra 1164); DWQ, Maḥkamat Rashīd 155, p. 299, case 331 (27 M 1164); DWQ, Maḥkamat Rashīd 155, p. 301, case 337 (20 M 1164); DWQ, Maḥkamat Rashīd 155, p. 313, case 372 (2 Za 1164); DWQ, Maḥkamat Rashīd 155, p. 314, case 377 (1 Z 1164); DWQ, Maḥkamat Rashīd 155, p. 315, case 380 (15 Za 1164); DWQ, Maḥkamat Rashīd 155, p. 316, case 381 (15 Za 1164); DWQ, Maḥkamat Rashīd 155, p. 316, case 382 (9 Ra 1164); DWQ, Maḥkamat Rashīd 155, p. 316, case 384 (1 C 1164); DWQ, Maḥkamat Rashīd 155, p. 317, case 385 (2 Z 1164); DWQ, Maḥkamat Rashīd 155, p. 317, case 386 (9 Ra 1164); DWQ, Maḥkamat Rashīd 155, p. 317, case 387 (8 Z 1164); DWQ, Maḥkamat Rashīd 155, p. 317, case 388 (15 Za 1164); DWQ, Maḥkamat Rashīd 155, p. 318, case 389 (20 C 1164); DWQ, Maḥkamat Rashīd 155, p. 318, case 390 (1 Z 1164); DWQ, Maḥkamat Rashīd 155, p. 318, case

391 (12 Za 1164); DWQ, Maḥkamat Rashīd 155, p. 318, case 392 (22 B 1164); DWQ, Maḥkamat Rashīd 155, p. 319, case 394 (9 B 1164); DWQ, Maḥkamat Rashīd 155, p. 319, case 395 (12 Za 1164); DWQ, Maḥkamat Rashīd 155, p. 319, case 396 (21 Za 1164); DWQ, Maḥkamat Rashīd 155, p. 319, case 397 (2 Z 1164); DWQ, Maḥkamat Rashīd 155, p. 319, case 398 (1 R 1164); DWQ, Maḥkamat Rashīd 155, p. 320, case 399 (12 Za 1164); DWQ, Maḥkamat Rashīd 155, p. 320, case 400 (7 Za 1164); DWQ, Maḥkamat Rashīd 155, p. 320, case 401 (10 C 1164); DWQ, Maḥkamat Rashīd 155, p. 320, case 402 (22 C 1164); DWQ, Maḥkamat Rashīd 155, p. 321, case 405 (24 Ş 1164); DWQ, Maḥkamat Rashīd 155, p. 321, case 406 (24 Ş 1164); DWQ, Maḥkamat Rashīd 155, p. 321, case 407 (14 Ş 1164); DWQ, Maḥkamat Rashīd 155, p. 322, case 408 (25 N 1164); DWQ, Maḥkamat Rashīd 155, p. 322, case 409 (24 C 1164); DWQ, Maḥkamat Rashīd 155, p. 322, case 410 (16 L 1164); DWQ, Maḥkamat Rashīd 155, p. 323, case 412 (17 B 1164); DWQ, Maḥkamat Rashīd 155, p. 323, case 413 (28 S 1164); DWQ, Maḥkamat Rashīd 155, p. 323, case 414 (22 B 1164); DWQ, Maḥkamat Rashīd 155, p. 323, case 415 (25 N 1164); DWQ, Maḥkamat Rashīd 155, p. 324, case 416 (14 Ş 1164); DWQ, Maḥkamat Rashīd 155, p. 324, case 417 (14 Ş 1164); DWQ, Maḥkamat Rashīd 155, p. 324, case 418 (21 R 1164); DWQ, Maḥkamat Rashīd 155, p. 325, case 419 (21 R 1164); DWQ, Maḥkamat Rashīd 155, p. 325, case 420 (24 M 1164); DWQ, Maḥkamat Rashīd 155, p. 325, case 421 (25 R 1164); DWQ, Maḥkamat Rashīd 155, p. 326, case 422 (16 C 1164); DWQ, Maḥkamat Rashīd 155, p. 326, case 423 (10 R 1164); DWQ, Maḥkamat Rashīd 155, p. 326, case 424 (21 R 1164); DWQ, Maḥkamat Rashīd 155, p. 327, case 425 (24 R 1164); DWQ, Maḥkamat Rashīd 155, p. 327, case 426 (21 R 1164); DWQ, Maḥkamat Rashīd 155, p. 327, case 427 (22 C 1164); DWQ, Maḥkamat Rashīd 155, p. 327, case 428 (25 Ra 1164); DWQ, Maḥkamat Rashīd 155, p. 328, case 430 (21 Ra 1164); DWQ, Maḥkamat Rashīd 155, p. 328, case 431 (28 Ca 1164); DWQ, Maḥkamat Rashīd 155, p. 328, case 432 (23 S 1164); DWQ, Maḥkamat Rashīd 155, p. 329, case 433 (22 R 1164); DWQ, Maḥkamat Rashīd 155, p. 329, case 434 (10 C 1164); DWQ, Maḥkamat Rashīd 155, p. 329, case 435 (11 R 1164); DWQ, Maḥkamat Rashīd 155, p. 330, case 436 (1 Ca 1164); DWQ, Maḥkamat Rashīd 155, p. 330, case 437 (1 C 1164); DWQ, Maḥkamat Rashīd 155, p. 330, case 438 (10 C 1164); DWQ, Maḥkamat Rashīd 155, p. 331, case 439 (28 S 1164); DWQ, Maḥkamat Rashīd 155, p. 331, case 440 (26 S 1164); DWQ, Maḥkamat Rashīd 155, p. 331, case 441 (22 C 1164);

DWQ, Maḥkamat Rashīd 155, p. 332, case 442 (28 R 1164); DWQ, Maḥkamat Rashīd 155, p. 332, case 443 (1 C 1164); DWQ, Maḥkamat Rashīd 155, p. 332, case 444 (24 R 1164); DWQ, Maḥkamat Rashīd 156, p. 265, case 213 (25 Z 1164); DWQ, Maḥkamat Rashīd 156, p. 265, case 214 (15 Z 1164); DWQ, Maḥkamat Rashīd 156, p. 266, case 215 (25 Z 1164); DWQ, Maḥkamat Rashīd 156, p. 266, case 216 (25 Z 1164); DWQ, Maḥkamat Rashīd 156, p. 266, case 217 (30 Z 1164); DWQ, Maḥkamat Rashīd 156, p. 266, case 218 (30 Z 1164); DWQ, Maḥkamat Rashīd 156, p. 266, case 219 (30 Z 1164); DWQ, Maḥkamat Rashīd 156, p. 267, case 220 (25 Z 1164); DWQ, Maḥkamat Rashīd 156, p. 267, case 222 (30 Z 1164); DWQ, Maḥkamat Rashīd 156, p. 267, case 223 (25 Z 1164); DWQ, Maḥkamat Rashīd 156, p. 288, case 250 (30 L 1164); DWQ, Maḥkamat Rashīd 156, p. 288, case 251 (30 Z 1164); DWQ, Maḥkamat Rashīd 156, p. 288, case 252 (10 Z 1164); DWQ, Maḥkamat Rashīd 156, p. 288, case 253 (15 Z 1164); DWQ, Maḥkamat Rashīd 156, p. 289, case 254 (15 Z 1164); DWQ, Maḥkamat Rashīd 156, p. 289, case 255 (15 Z 1164); DWQ, Maḥkamat Rashīd 156, p. 289, case 256 (15 Z 1164); DWQ, Maḥkamat Rashīd 156, p. 289, case 257 (15 Z 1164); DWQ, Maḥkamat Rashīd 157, p. 354, case 356 (1 R 1164); DWQ, Maḥkamat Rashīd 157, p. 355, case 359 (27 Ra 1164); DWQ, Maḥkamat Rashīd 157, p. 355, case 360 (1 R 1164); DWQ, Maḥkamat Rashīd 157, p. 358, case 368 (1 Z 1164); DWQ, Maḥkamat Rashīd 157, p. 358, case 369 (1 R 1164); DWQ, Maḥkamat Rashīd 157, p. 358, case 370 (22 B 1164); DWQ, Maḥkamat Rashīd 157, p. 359, case 371 (18 Ş 1164); DWQ, Maḥkamat Rashīd 157, p. 359, case 372 (1 R 1164); DWQ, Maḥkamat Rashīd 157, p. 359, case 373 (1 R 1164); DWQ, Maḥkamat Rashīd 157, p. 360, case 374 (1 R 1164); DWQ, Maḥkamat Rashīd 157, p. 366, case 398 (1 R 1164); DWQ, Maḥkamat Rashīd 157, p. 230, case 226 (1 Ra 1164); DWQ, Maḥkamat Rashīd 157, p. 13, case 15 (16 C 1164); DWQ, Maḥkamat Rashīd 157, p. 14, case 19 (1 R 1164); DWQ, Maḥkamat Rashīd 157, p. 15, case 20 (2 Za 1164); DWQ, Maḥkamat Rashīd 157, p. 15, case 22 (27 Z 1164); DWQ, Maḥkamat Rashīd 157, p. 16, case 25 (1 R 1164); DWQ, Maḥkamat Rashīd 157, p. 16, case 26 (13 L 1164); DWQ, Maḥkamat Rashīd 157, p. 16, case 27 (3 Z 1164).

1751–1752 (1165)

DWQ, Maḥkamat Rashīd 155, p. 314, case 374 (26 S 1165); DWQ, Maḥkamat Rashīd 155, p. 314, case 375 (1 Ra 1165); DWQ, Maḥkamat

Rashīd 155, p. 316, case 383 (26 S 1165); DWQ, Maḥkamat Rashīd 156, p. 297, case 265 (8 Ca 1165); DWQ, Maḥkamat Rashīd 156, p. 298, case 267 (8 Ca 1165); DWQ, Maḥkamat Rashīd 157, p. 354, case 354 (12 B 1165); DWQ, Maḥkamat Rashīd 157, p. 357, case 365 (14 L 1165); DWQ, Maḥkamat Rashīd 157, p. 357, case 366 (14 Ra 1165); DWQ, Maḥkamat Rashīd 157, p. 357, case 367 (7 B 1165); DWQ, Maḥkamat Rashīd 157, p. 360, case 376 (8 Ra 1165); DWQ, Maḥkamat Rashīd 157, p. 360, case 377 (12 Ra 1165); DWQ, Maḥkamat Rashīd 157, p. 365, case 394 (7 S 1165); DWQ, Maḥkamat Rashīd 157, p. 365, case 396 (8 Ra 1165); DWQ, Maḥkamat Rashīd 157, p. 366, case 397 (3 Ca 1165); DWQ, Maḥkamat Rashīd 157, p. 366, case 399 (3 C 1165); DWQ, Maḥkamat Rashīd 157, p. 13, case 16 (14 Ca 1165); DWQ, Maḥkamat Rashīd 157, p. 13, case 17 (8 Ca 1165); DWQ, Maḥkamat Rashīd 157, p. 14, case 18 (1 Za 1165); DWQ, Maḥkamat Rashīd 157, p. 15, case 21 (25 M 1165); DWQ, Maḥkamat Rashīd 157, p. 15, case 23 (25 Ca 1165).

1752–1753 (1166)

DWQ, Maḥkamat Rashīd 157, p. 352, case 349 (21 M 1166); DWQ, Maḥkamat Rashīd 157, p. 323, case 313 (3 Ra 1166); DWQ, Maḥkamat Rashīd 157, p. 323, case 314 (3 Ra 1166); DWQ, Maḥkamat Rashīd 157, p. 323, case 315 (3 Ra 1166); DWQ, Maḥkamat Rashīd 157, p. 323, case 316 (3 Ra 1166); DWQ, Maḥkamat Rashīd 157, p. 324, case 317 (13 R 1166); DWQ, Maḥkamat Rashīd 157, p. 324, case 318 (1 R 1166); DWQ, Maḥkamat Rashīd 157, p. 324, case 319 (15 R 1166); DWQ, Maḥkamat Rashīd 157, p. 270, case 264 (25 S 1166); DWQ, Maḥkamat Rashīd 157, p. 270, case 265 (25 S 1166); DWQ, Maḥkamat Rashīd 157, p. 270, case 266 (25 S 1166); DWQ, Maḥkamat Rashīd 157, p. 270, case 267 (25 S 1166); DWQ, Maḥkamat Rashīd 157, p. 270, case 268 (25 S 1166); DWQ, Maḥkamat Rashīd 157, p. 271, case 269 (25 S 1166); DWQ, Maḥkamat Rashīd 157, p. 271, case 270 (25 S 1166); DWQ, Maḥkamat Rashīd 157, p. 271, case 271 (25 S 1166); DWQ, Maḥkamat Rashīd 157, p. 271, case 272 (25 S 1166); DWQ, Maḥkamat Rashīd 157, p. 230, case 227 (12 C 1166); DWQ, Maḥkamat Rashīd 158, p. 241, case 209 (30 Za 1166); DWQ, Maḥkamat Rashīd 158, p. 242, case 210 (30 Za 1166); DWQ, Maḥkamat Rashīd 158, p. 242, case 211 (18 Za 1166); DWQ, Maḥkamat Rashīd 158, p. 242, case 212 (5 Z 1166); DWQ, Maḥkamat Rashīd 158, p. 242, case 213 (15 Za 1166).

1753–1754 (1167)

DWQ, Maḥkamat Rashīd 159, p. 162, case 109 (12 Z 1167); DWQ, Maḥkamat Rashīd 159, p. 162, case 110 (12 Z 1167); DWQ, Maḥkamat Rashīd 159, p. 162, case 111 (15 Za 1167); DWQ, Maḥkamat Rashīd 159, p. 163, case 112 (15 Za 1167); DWQ, Maḥkamat Rashīd 159, p. 163, case 113 (15 Za 1167). There are more cases about shipments of food from Rashīd in the year 1167 in subsequent registers of the court.

BIBLIOGRAPHY

Archival Sources

I. Dār al-Wathā'iq al-Qawmiyya (Egyptian National Archives, Cairo)

al-Dīwān al-ʿĀlī
Registers – 1, 2
Isqāṭāt al-Qurā
Registers – 1, 2
al-Jusūr al-Sulṭāniyya
Registers – 784, 785, 786, 787, 788
Maḍābiṭ al-Daqahliyya
Registers – 19, 20, 34
Maḥkamat Asyūṭ
Registers – 1, 2, 3, 4, 5, 6, 7, 8, 9
Maḥkamat al-Bāb al-ʿĀlī
Register – 120
Maḥkamat al-Baḥayra
Registers – 5, 6, 7, 8, 9, 10, 11, 12, 13, 14, 15, 16, 21, 22, 23, 24, 25, 26, 30, 31, 32, 37, 38, 39
Maḥkamat Isnā
Registers – 3, 5, 6, 7, 8
Maḥkamat Manfalūṭ
Registers – 1, 2, 3
Maḥkamat al-Manṣūra
Registers – 1, 2, 3, 4, 7, 9, 11, 12, 14, 15, 16, 17, 18, 19, 22, 24, 51
Maḥkamat Miṣr al-Qadīma
Register – 90
Maḥkamat Rashīd
Registers – 6, 8, 120, 122, 123, 124, 125, 130, 132, 134, 137, 139, 142, 144, 145, 146, 148, 151, 154, 155, 156, 157, 158, 159
al-Rizaq al-Iḥbāsī
Registers – 5, 24

al-Rūznāma, Daftar Irtifāʿ al-Miyāh bi-Baḥr Sayyidnā Yūsuf lihi al-Ṣalāh wa al-Salām ʿan al-Qabḍa al-Yūsufiyya Tābiʿ Wilāyat al-Fayyūm
Register – 4557 (Raqam al-Ḥifẓ al-Nauʿī 1, ʿAyn 59, Makhzin Turkī 1, Musalsal 4557)
Rūznāmja, Daftar Furūkh Muqāṭaʿāt
Register – 92 (Raqam al-Ḥifẓ al-Nauʿī 325, ʿAyn 5, Makhzin Turkī 1, Musalsal ʿUmūmī 325)
Taḥrīr Aṭyān al-Sharāqī wa al-Riyy
Registers – 3019, 3020, 3021, 3022, 3023, 3024, 3025, 3026, 3027, 3028
Taqārīr al-Naẓar
Register – 10

II. Başbakanlık Osmanlı Arşivi (Prime Ministry's Ottoman Archive, Istanbul)

Cevdet Bahriye
Documents – 208, 698, 769, 866, 1334, 1413, 1513, 1568, 5701, 6306, 7333
Cevdet Belediye
Document – 4804
Cevdet Dahiliye
Document – 1722
Cevdet Maliye
Documents – 14383, 15566, 27049
Cevdet Nafia
Documents – 120, 302, 337, 458, 644, 1605A, 1605B, 1640, 2386, 2570
Cevdet Sıhhiye
Documents – 518, 864
Evkaf
Register – 5401
Hatt-ı Hümayun
Documents – 16/716A, 26/1256, 26/1256B, 28/1354, 29/1358, 29/1360, 29/1361, 29/1364, 37/1871, 39/1961, 85/3474C, 85/3474D, 85/3474S, 85/3478, 86/3509B, 86/3515, 86/3516, 86/3516A, 86/3520, 86/3533, 86/3536, 88/3591, 88/3601, 88/3628, 93/3804, 95/3856A, 130/5381, 130/5404, 130/5404A, 131/5411, 177/4744, 209/11213, 228/12681, 240/13451, 245/13801A, 254/14478A, 266/15433, 342/19546, 547/26996, 593/29055, 631/31183, 656/32064, 795/36893, 1176/46442K, 1301/50670, 1399/56283, 1412/57500
Mühimme-i Mısır
Registers – 1, 3, 4, 5, 6, 7, 8, 9, 10, 11, 12, 15

III. Topkapı Sarayı Müzesi Arşivi (Topkapı Palace Museum Archive, Istanbul)

Documents
510, 664/4, 664/6, 664/10, 664/33, 664/40, 664/51, 664/52, 664/55, 664/59, 664/63, 664/64, 664/66, 840, 1173/75, 1605/114, 2229/3, 2380/25, 2444/107, 2445/124, 3218, 3522, 4070, 4675/2, 4830,

5204/11, 5207/49, 5207/57, 5207/58, 5207/62, 5211/22, 5225/9, 5225/12, 5419/16, 5581, 5657, 7008/12, 7016/95, 7019/251, 7544/2, 9213, 11901

Register

2886

Unpublished Primary Sources

I. Topkapı Sarayı Müzesi Kütüphanesi (Topkapı Palace Museum Library, Istanbul)

Ḳānūn-nāme-i Mıṣr, 1845 (E.H. 2063).
Niẓām-nāme-i Mıṣr, 1846 (B. 288).

II. Süleymaniye Kütüphanesi (Süleymaniye Library, Istanbul)

al-Bulqīnī, Badr al-Dīn ʿAlī Ibn Aḥmad Ibn Muḥammad. *Kitāb al-Nīl al-Rāʾid fī al-Nīl al-Zāʾid.* Fatih 4181.
al-Ḥijāzī, Shihāb al-Dīn Aḥmad Ibn Muḥammad ʿAlī al-Anṣārī. *al-Nīl al-Rāʾid fī al-Nīl al-Zāʾid.* Ayasofya 3528.
al-Jauharī, Muḥammad Ibn ʿAbd al-Muʾmin Ibn Muḥammad. *Mūjaz fī Mabdāʾ al-Nīl wa Muntahāhu.* Lâleli 3752.
al-Maḥallī, Jalāl al-Dīn. *Muqaddima fī Mabdāʾ al-Nīl wa Muntahāhu.* Serez 3838/11.
———. *Muqaddima fī Nīl Miṣr al-Mubārak.* Ayasofya 3446.
al-Nābulusī, Fakhr al-Dīn ʿUthmān. *Iẓhār Ṣanʿat al-Ḥayy al-Fayyūm fī Tartīb Bilād al-Fayyūm.* Ayasofya 2960.

III. İstanbul Üniversitesi Kütüphanesi (Istanbul University Library, Istanbul)

Piri Reis. *Kitâb-ı Bahriye.* Nadir Eserler, TY. 6605.

IV. Dār al-Kutub al-Miṣriyya (Egyptian National Library, Cairo)

ʿAwāʾid al-Miṣriyyīn ʿand Izdiyād al-Nīl. Zakiyya 584.
Ibn al-ʿImād. *Kitāb al-Nīl al-Saʿīd al-Mubārak.* Jughrāfiyā Ḥalīm 5.
al-Maḥallī, Jalāl al-Dīn. *Kitāb Mabdāʾ al-Nīl.* Jughrāfiyā 381.
———. *Risāla fī Mabdāʾ al-Nīl.* Majāmīʿ Ṭalʿat 972.
al-Nābulusī al-Ṣafadī, Abī ʿUthmān. *Tārīkh al-Fayyūm wa Bilādihi.* Tārīkh 1594.
Ibn Riḍwān. *Risāla fī Ziyādat al-Nīl wa Naqṣihi ʿalā al-Dawām.* Majāmīʿ Mīm 213.
Ibn Shuʿayyib, Muḥammad. *Zahr al-Basātīn fī Fal al-Nīl wa Faḍl Miṣr wa al- Qāhira wa al-Qarāfa.* Buldān Taymūr 60.

Published Primary and Secondary Sources

ʿAbd al-Fattāḥ, Muḥammad Ḥusām al-Dīn Ismāʿīl, and Suhayr Ṣāliḥ. "A Wikāla of Sulṭān Muʾayyid: Wikālat ʾŪda Pasha." *AI* 28 (1994): 71–96.

ʿAbd al-Karīm, Aḥmad ʿIzzat. *Tārīkh al-Taʿlīm fī ʿAṣr Muḥammad ʿAlī.* Cairo: Maktabat al-Nahḍa al-Miṣriyya, 1938.

ʿAbd al-Mutajallī, Naṣra. "al-Muqāwama bil-Tasaḥḥub fī Rīf Miṣr al-ʿUthmāniyya." In *al-Rafḍ wa al-Iḥtijāj fī al-Mujtamaʿ al-Miṣrī fī al-ʿAṣr al-ʿUthmānī,* edited by Nāṣir Ibrāhīm and Raʾūf ʿAbbās, 127–36. Cairo: Markaz al-Buḥūth wa al-Dirāsāt al-Ijtimāʿiyya, 2004.

ʿAbd al-Muʿṭī, Ḥusām Muḥammad. *al-ʿAlāqāt al-Miṣriyya al-Ḥijāziyya fī al-Qarn al-Thāmin ʿAshar.* Cairo: al-Hayʾa al-Miṣriyya al-ʿĀmma lil-Kitāb, 1999.

———. "al-Buyūt al-Tijāriyya al-Maghribiyya fī Miṣr fī al-ʿAṣr al-ʿUthmānī." Ph.D. diss., Manṣūra University, 2002.

———. "Riwāq al-Maghāriba fī al-Jāmiʿ al-Azhar fī al-ʿAṣr al-ʿUthmānī." *al-Rūznāma: al-Ḥauliyya al-Miṣriyya lil-Wathāʾiq* 3 (2005): 165–204.

ʿAbd al-Raḥīm, ʿAbd al-Raḥīm ʿAbd al-Raḥman. *al-Maghāriba fī Miṣr fī al-ʿAṣr al-ʿUthmānī (1517–1798): Dirāsa fī Taʾthīr al-Jāliya al-Maghāribiyya min Khilāl Wathāʾiq al-Maḥākim al-Sharʿiyya al-Miṣriyya.* Tunis: al-Majalla al-Tārīkhiyya al-Maghribiyya, 1982.

———. *al-Rīf al-Miṣrī fī al-Qarn al-Thāmin ʿAshar.* Cairo: Maktabat Madbūlī, 1986.

———. *Wathāʾiq al-Maḥākim al-Sharʿiyya al-Miṣriyya ʿan al-Jāliya al-Maghāribiyya ibbāna al-ʿAṣr al-ʿUthmānī,* edited and introduced by ʿAbd al-Jalīl al-Tamīmī. Zaghwan, Tunisia: Markaz al-Dirāsāt wa al-Buḥūth al-ʿUthmāniyya wa al-Mūrīskiyya wa al-Tawthīq wa al-Maʿlūmāt, 1992.

Abdul Muʿti, Husam Muhammad. "The Fez Merchants in Eighteenth-Century Cairo," translated by Sawsan al-Baqli. In *Society and Economy in Egypt and the Eastern Mediterranean, 1600–1900: Essays in Honor of André Raymond,* edited by Nelly Hanna and Raouf Abbas, 117–41. Cairo: American University in Cairo Press, 2005.

Abu-Lughod, Janet L. *Before European Hegemony: The World System* A.D. *1250–1350.* New York: Oxford University Press, 1989.

Abū Salīm, Aymān Muḥammad. "Wathāʾiq Waqf al-Wazīr Muḥammad Bāshā al-Silaḥdār fī Miṣr: Dirāsa wa Taḥqīq wa Nashr." M.A. thesis, Cairo University, 1987.

Adams, Robert McC. *Land behind Baghdad: A History of Settlement on the Diyala Plains.* Chicago: University of Chicago Press, 1965.

Adas, Michael. "From Avoidance to Confrontation: Peasant Protest in Precolonial and Colonial Southeast Asia." *Comparative Studies in Society and History* 23 (1981): 217–47.

ʿAfīfī, Muḥammad. "Asālīb al-Intifāʿ al-Iqtiṣādī bil-Awqāf fī Miṣr fī al-ʿAṣr al-ʿUthmānī." *AI* 24(1988): 103–38.

———. *al-Awqāf wa al-Ḥayāh al-Iqtiṣādiyya fī Miṣr fī al-ʿAṣr al-ʿUthmānī.* Cairo: al-Hayʾa al-Miṣriyya al-ʿĀmma lil-Kitāb, 1991.

Ágoston, Gábor. *Guns for the Sultan: Military Power and the Weapons Industry in the Ottoman Empire.* Cambridge: Cambridge University Press, 2005.

Aḥmad, Laylā ʿAbd al-Laṭīf. *al-Idāra fī Miṣr fī al-ʿAṣr al-ʿUthmānī.* Cairo: Maṭbaʿat Jāmiʿat ʿAyn Shams, 1978.

———. *al-Mujtamaʿ al-Miṣrī fī al-ʿAṣr al-ʿUthmānī.* Cairo: Dār al-Kitāb al-Jāmiʿī, 1987.

———. *al-Ṣaʿīd fī ʿAhd Shaykh al-ʿArab Hammām.* Cairo: al-Hayʾa al-Miṣriyya al-ʿĀmma lil-Kitāb, 1987.

———. *Tārīkh wa Muʾarrikhī Miṣr wa al-Shām ibbāna al-ʿAṣr al-ʿUthmānī.* Cairo: Maktabat al-Khānjī, 1980.

ʿAjīmī, Hishām Ibn Muḥammad ʿAlī. "al-Qilāʿ wa Manāhil al-Miyāh fī Ṭarīq al-Ḥājj al-Shāmī min Khilāl Wathīqa ʿUthmāniyya." *al-Rūznāma: al-Ḥauliyya al-Miṣriyya lil-Wathāʾiq* 3 (2005): 545–82.

Akādīmiyyat al-Baḥth al-ʿIlmī wa al-Tiknūlūjiyā. *Tārīkh al-ʿUlūm wa al-Tiknūlūjiyā al-Handasiyya fī Miṣr fī al-Qarnayn al-Tāsiʿ ʿAshar wa al-ʿAshrīn.* 2 vols. Cairo: Akādīmiyyat al-Baḥth al-ʿIlmī wa al-Tiknūlūjiyā, 1993.

Aksan, Virginia H. "Feeding the Ottoman Troops on the Danube, 1768–1774." *War and Society* 13 (1995): 1–14.

Albert, Jeff, Magnus Bernhardsson, and Roger Kenna, eds. *Transformations of Middle Eastern Natural Environments: Legacies and Lessons.* New Haven, CT: Yale School of Forestry and Environmental Sciences, 1998.

ʿAlī, Nāṣira ʿAbd al-Mutajallī Ibrāhīm. "al-Daqahliyya fī al-ʿAṣr al-ʿUthmānī." M.A. thesis, ʿAyn Shams University, 2005.

ʿAlī, Ṣalāḥ Aḥmad Harīdī. "al-Ḥayāh al-Iqtiṣādiyya wa al-Ijtimāʿiyya fī Madīnat Rashīd fī al-ʿAṣr al-ʿUthmānī, Dirāsa Wathāʾiqiyya." *EHR* 30–31 (1983–1984): 327–78.

Alleaume, Ghislaine. "Hygiène publique et travaux publics: Les ingénieurs et l'assainissement du Caire (1882–1907)." *AI* 20 (1984): 151–82.

———. "Les systemes hydrauliques de l'Égypte pré-moderne: Essai d'histoire du paysage." In *Itinéraires d'Égypte: Mélanges offerts au père Maurice Martin S.J.*, edited by Christian Décobert, 301–22. Cairo: Institut français d'archéologie orientale, 1992.

Altundağ, Şinasi. *Kavalalı Mehmet Ali Paşa Isyanı: Mısır Meselesi, 1831–1841.* Ankara: Türk Tarih Kurumu, 1988.

Amanat, Abbas, and Frank Griffel, eds. *Shariʿa: Islamic Law in the Contemporary Context.* Stanford, CA: Stanford University Press, 2007.

Ambraseys, N. N., and C. F. Finkel. *The Seismicity of Turkey and Adjacent Areas: A Historical Review, 1500–1800.* Istanbul: Eren, 1995.

ʿĀmir, Umniyya. "Niẓām al-Iltizām: al-Taḥawwul min al-Milkiyya al-Ḥukūmiyya ilā al-Milkiyya al-Khāṣṣa." *al-Rūznāma: al-Ḥauliyya al-Miṣriyya lil-Wathāʾiq* 1 (2003): 267–85.

Anastasopoulos, Antonis. "In Preparation for the Hajj: The Will of a *Serdengeçti* from Crete (1782)." *AO* 23 (2005–2006): 79–92.

Anīs, Muḥammad. "Ziyārat al-Muʾarrikh Arnūld Tawīnbī lil-Jumhūriyya al-ʿArabiyya al-Muttaḥida." *EHR* 9–10 (1960–1962): 267–68.

Antes, John. *Observations on the Manners and Customs of the Egyptians, the Overflowing of the Nile and Its Effects; with Remarks on the Plague and Other Subjects. Written during a Residence of Twelve Years in Cairo and Its Vicinity.* London: Printed for J. Stockdale, 1800.

Appadurai, Arjun. "Wells in Western India: Irrigation and Cooperation in an Agricultural Society." *Expedition* 26 (1984): 3–14.

Appuhn, Karl. *A Forest on the Sea: Environmental Expertise in Renaissance Venice.* Baltimore: Johns Hopkins University Press, 2009.

Artan, Tülay. "Aspects of the Ottoman Elite's Food Consumption: Looking for 'Staples,' 'Luxuries,' and 'Delicacies' in a Changing Century." In *Consumption Studies and the History of the Ottoman Empire, 1550–1922: An Introduction*, edited by Donald Quataert, 107–200. Albany: State University of New York Press, 2000.

ʿAzabāwī, ʿAbd Allāh Muḥammad. "al-ʿAlāqāt al-ʿUthmāniyya-al-Maghribiyya fī ʿAhd Kullin min Maulāya Muḥammad (1757–1790) wa Ibnihi Yazīd (1790–1792)." *EHR* 30–31 (1983–1984): 379–413.

———. "al-Shawām fī Miṣr fī al-Qarn al-Thāmin ʿAshar." *EHR* 28–29 (1981–1982): 269–329.

Badawi, El-Said, and Martin Hinds. *A Dictionary of Egyptian Arabic*. Beirut: Librairie du Liban, 1986.

Badr, Hamza ʿAbd al-ʿAziz, and Daniel Crecelius. "The Waqf of the Zawiyya of the Amir ʿIsa Agha Çerkis: A Circassian Legacy in XVIIth Century Jirje." *AI* 32 (1998): 65–85 and 239–47.

Bagnall, Roger S. *Egypt in Late Antiquity*. Princeton, NJ: Princeton University Press, 1993.

Bakr, ʿAbd al-Wahhāb. *al-Būlīs al-Miṣri, 1922–1952*. Cairo: Maktabat Madbūlī, 1988.

Balta, Evangelia. "The Bread in Greek Lands during the Ottoman Rule." *Tarih Araştırmaları Dergisi* 16 (1992–1994): 199–226.

Barkan, Ömer Lûtfi. *Kanunlar*. Vol. 1 of *XV ve XVIinci asırlarda Osmanlı İmparatorluğunda Ziraî Ekonominin Hukukî ve Malî Esasları*. İstanbul Üniversitesi Yayınlarından 256. Istanbul: Bürhaneddin Matbaası, 1943.

Barkan, Ömer Lütfi. *Süleymaniye Cami ve İmareti İnşaatı (1550–1557)*. 2 vols. Ankara: Türk Tarih Kurumu Basımevi, 1972–1979.

Barkey, Karen. *Bandits and Bureaucrats: The Ottoman Route to State Centralization*. Ithaca, NY: Cornell University Press, 1994.

———. *Empire of Difference: The Ottomans in Comparative Perspective*. Cambridge: Cambridge University Press, 2008.

Behrens-Abouseif, Doris. *Egypt's Adjustment to Ottoman Rule: Institutions, Waqf, and Architecture in Cairo, 16th and 17th Centuries*. Leiden: E. J. Brill, 1994.

Beldiceanu, N., and Irène Beldiceanu-Steinherr. "Riziculture dans l'Empire ottoman (XIVᵉ-XVᵉ siècle)." *Turcica* 9:2–10 (1978): 9–28.

Blackbourn, David. *The Conquest of Nature: Water, Landscape, and the Making of Modern Germany*. New York: W. W. Norton, 2006.

Borsch, Stuart J. *The Black Death in Egypt and England: A Comparative Study*. Austin: University of Texas Press, 2005.

———. "Environment and Population: The Collapse of Large Irrigation Systems Reconsidered." *Comparative Studies in Society and History* 46 (2004): 451–68.

———. "Nile Floods and the Irrigation System in Fifteenth-Century Egypt." *Mamlūk Studies Review* 4 (2000): 131–45.

Bostan, İdris. *Kürekli ve Yelkenli Osmanlı Gemileri*. Istanbul: Bilge, 2005.

———. *Osmanlı Bahriye Teşkilâtı: XVII. Yüzyılda Tersâne-i Âmire*. Ankara: Türk Tarih Kurumu Basımevi, 1992.

Braudel, Fernand. *The Wheels of Commerce*. Vol. 2 of *Civilization and Capitalism, 15th–18th Century*, translated by Siân Reynolds. London: Collins, 1982.

Breckenridge, Carol A., and Peter van der Veer, eds. *Orientalism and the Postcolonial Predicament: Perspectives on South Asia.* Philadelphia: University of Pennsylvania Press, 1993.

Brewer, John. *The Sinews of Power: War, Money and the English State, 1688–1783.* Cambridge, MA: Harvard University Press, 1988.

Brice, William C., ed. *The Environmental History of the Near and Middle East since the Last Ice Age.* London: Academic Press, 1978.

Brouwer, C. G. "Non-Western Shipping Movements in the Red Sea and Gulf of Aden during the 2nd and 3rd Decades of the 17th Century, According to the Records of the Dutch East India Company, Part 1." *Die Welt des Islams* 31 (1991): 105–67.

———. "Non-Western Shipping Movements in the Red Sea and Gulf of Aden during the 2nd and 3rd Decades of the 17th Century, According to the Records of the Dutch East India Company, Part 2." *Die Welt des Islams* 32 (1992): 6–40.

Brummett, Palmira. *Ottoman Seapower and Levantine Diplomacy in the Age of Discovery.* Albany: State University of New York Press, 1994.

———. "The River Crossing: Breaking Points (Metaphorical and 'Real') in Ottoman Mutiny." In *Mutiny and Rebellion in the Ottoman Empire,* edited by Jane Hathaway, 45–60. Madison: University of Wisconsin Press, 2002.

Bulliet, Richard W. *The Camel and the Wheel.* New York: Columbia University Press, 1990.

———. *Cotton, Climate, and Camels in Early Islamic Iran: A Moment in World History.* New York: Columbia University Press, 2009.

Burke, Edmund, III. "The Transformation of the Middle Eastern Environment, 1500 B.C.E.–2000 C.E." In *The Environment and World History,* edited by Edmund Burke III and Kenneth Pomeranz, 81–117. Berkeley: University of California Press, 2009.

Butzer, Karl W. *Early Hydraulic Civilization in Egypt: A Study in Cultural Ecology.* Chicago: University of Chicago Press, 1976.

Carpentier, Elisabeth. "Autour de la peste noire: Famines et épidémies dans l'histoire du XIVe siècle." *Annales* 17 (1962): 1062–92.

Carrière, Charles, Marcel Courdurié, and Ferréol Rebuffat. *Marseille ville morte: La peste de 1720.* Marseille: M. Garçon, 1968.

Casale, Giancarlo. "An Ottoman Intelligence Report from the Mid Sixteenth-Century Indian Ocean." *JTS* 31 (2007): 181–88.

Casale, Giancarlo L. "The Ottoman Age of Exploration: Spices, Maps and Conquest in the Sixteenth-Century Indian Ocean." Ph.D. diss., Harvard University, 2004.

Casanova, Paul. *Two Studies on the History and Topography of Cairo.* Frankfurt: Institute for the History of Arabic-Islamic Science at the Johann Wolfgang Goethe University, 1992.

Chatterjee, Partha. *Nationalist Thought and the Colonial World: A Derivative Discourse.* Minneapolis: University of Minnesota Press, 1998.

Christensen, Peter. *The Decline of Iranshahr: Irrigation and Environments in the History of the Middle East, 500 B.C. to A.D. 1500.* Copenhagen: Museum Tusculanum Press, 1993.

Clot-Bey, Antoine Barthélemy. *De le peste observée en Égypte: recherches et considerations sur cette maladie.* Paris: Fortin, Masson, 1840.

Cole, Juan. *Napoleon's Egypt: Invading the Middle East.* New York: Palgrave Macmillan, 2007.

Coleman, William. *Death Is a Social Disease: Public Health and Political Economy in Early Industrial France.* Madison: University of Wisconsin Press, 1982.

Collins, Robert O. *The Nile.* New Haven, CT: Yale University Press, 2002.

Commission des Sciences et Arts d'Egypte. *État moderne II.* Vol. 9 of *Description de l'Égypte, ou, recueil de observations et des recherches qui ont été faites en Égypte pendant l'éxpédition de l'armée française, publié par les ordres de Sa Majesté l'empereur Napoléon le Grand.* Paris: Imprimerie impériale, 1809–1828.

Conrad, Lawrence I. "The Plague in the Early Medieval Near East." Ph.D. diss., Princeton University, 1981.

Cordova, Carlos E. *Millennial Landscape Change in Jordan: Geoarchaeology and Cultural Ecology.* Tucson: University of Arizona Press, 2007.

Coşkun, Menderes. "Stations of the Pilgrimage Route from Istanbul to Mecca via Damascus on the Basis of the *Menazilü'l-Tarik İla Beyti'llahi'l-ʿAtik* by Kadri (17th Century)." *OA* 21 (2001): 307–22.

Crecelius, Daniel. "Incidences of *Waqf* Cases in Three Cairo Courts: 1640–1802." *JESHO* 29 (1986): 176–89.

———. "The Organization of *Waqf* Documents in Cairo." *IJMES* 2 (1971): 266–77.

———. *The Roots of Modern Egypt: A Study of the Regimes of ʿAli Bey al-Kabir and Muhammad Bey Abu al-Dhahab, 1760–1775.* Minneapolis, MN: Bibliotheca Islamica, 1981.

———. "The Waqf of Muhammad Bey Abu al-Dhahab in Historical Perspective." *IJMES* 23 (1991): 57–81.

Crecelius, Daniel, and Hamza ʿAbd al-ʿAziz Badr. "French Ships and Their Cargoes Sailing between Damiette and Ottoman Ports 1777–1781." *JESHO* 37 (1994): 251–86.

Crecelius, Daniel, and ʿAbd al-Wahhab Bakr, trans. *al-Damurdashi's Chronicle of Egypt, 1688-1755: al-Durra al-Musana fi Akhbar al-Kinana.* Leiden: E. J. Brill, 1991.

Cronon, William. *Changes in the Land: Indians, Colonists, and the Ecology of New England.* Rev. ed. New York: Hill and Wang, 2003.

———. *Nature's Metropolis: Chicago and the Great West.* New York: W. W. Norton, 1991.

———. "A Place for Stories: Nature, History, and Narrative." *Journal of American History* 78 (1992): 1347–76.

Crosby, Alfred W. "The Past and Present of Environmental History." *AHR* 100 (1995): 1177–89.

Cuno, Kenneth M. "Commercial Relations between Town and Village in Eighteenth and Early Nineteenth-Century Egypt." *AI* 24 (1988): 111–35.

———. *The Pasha's Peasants: Land, Society, and Economy in Lower Egypt, 1740–1858.* Cambridge: Cambridge University Press, 1992.

Çağlar, Yücel. *Türkiye Ormanları ve Ormancılık.* Istanbul: İletişim Yayınları, 1992.

Çevre ve Orman Bakanlığı. *Osmanlı Ormancılığı ile İlgili Belgeler.* 3 vols. Ankara: Çevre ve Orman Bakanlığı, 1999–2003.
Daly, M.W., ed. *Modern Egypt, from 1517 to the End of the Twentieth Century.* Vol. 2 of *The Cambridge History of Egypt.* Cambridge: Cambridge University Press, 1998.
al-Damurdāshī Katkhudā ʿAzabān, Aḥmad. *Kitāb al-Durra al-Muṣāna fī Akhbār al-Kināna,* edited by ʿAbd al-Raḥīm ʿAbd al-Raḥman ʿAbd al-Raḥīm. Cairo: Institut français d'archéologie orientale, 1989.
Dankoff, Robert. "The Languages of the World According to Evliya Çelebi." *JTS* 13 (1989): 23–32.
Davis, Diana K. *Resurrecting the Granary of Rome: Environmental History and French Colonial Expansion in North Africa.* Athens: Ohio University Press, 2007.
Delaporte, François. *Disease and Civilization: The Cholera in Paris, 1832,* translated by Arthur Goldhammer. Cambridge: Massachusetts Institute of Technology Press, 1986.
de Vries, Jan. *Barges and Capitalism: Passenger Transportation in the Dutch Economy, 1632–1839.* Utrecht: HES Publishers, 1981.
———. *The Dutch Rural Economy in the Golden Age, 1500–1700.* New Haven, CT: Yale University Press, 1974.
Di-Capua, Yoav. "The Thought and Practice of Modern Egyptian Historiography, 1890–1970." Ph.D. diss., Princeton University, 2004.
Dodge, Bayard. *Al-Azhar: A Millennium of Muslim Learning.* Washington, D.C.: Middle East Institute, 1961.
Dodwell, Henry. *The Founder of Modern Egypt: A Study of Muhammad ʿAli.* Cambridge: The University Press, 1931.
Dols, Michael W. *The Black Death in the Middle East.* Princeton, NJ: Princeton University Press, 1977.
———. "The General Mortality of the Black Death in the Mamluk Empire." In *The Islamic Middle East, 700–1900: Studies in Social and Economic History,* edited by Abraham L. Udovitch, 397–428. Princeton, NJ: Darwin Press, 1981.
———. "Ibn al-Wardī's *Risālah al-Nabaʾ ʿan al-Wabaʾ*, A Translation of a Major Source for the History of the Black Death in the Middle East." In *Near Eastern Numismatics, Iconography, Epigraphy and History: Studies in Honor of George C. Miles,* edited by Dickran K. Kouymjian, 443–55. Beirut: American University of Beirut, 1974.
———. "al-Manbijī's 'Report of the Plague:' A Treatise on the Plague of 764–765/1362–1364 in the Middle East." In *The Black Death: The Impact of the Fourteenth-Century Plague,* edited by Daniel Williman, 65–75. Papers of the Eleventh Annual Conference of the Center for Medieval and Early Renaissance Studies. Binghamton, NY: Center for Medieval and Early Renaissance Studies, 1982.
———. "Plague in Early Islamic History." *Journal of the American Oriental Society* 94 (1974): 371–83.
———. "The Second Plague Pandemic and Its Recurrences in the Middle East: 1347–1894." *JESHO* 22 (1979): 162–89.
Doumani, Beshara. "Endowing Family: *Waqf,* Property Devolution, and Gender in Greater Syria, 1800 to 1860." *Comparative Studies in Society and History* 40 (1998): 3–41.

———. *Rediscovering Palestine: Merchants and Peasants in Jabal Nablus, 1700–1900.* Berkeley: University of California Press, 1995.

Dunyā, Rasmī Dummar Muḥammad. "Madīnat Ṭanṭā: Dirāsa fī Jughrāfiyyat al-Mudun." Ph.D. diss., ʿAyn Shams University, 1982.

Dursun, Selçuk. "Forest and the State: History of Forestry and Forest Administration in the Ottoman Empire." Ph.D. diss., Sabancı University, 2007.

Elmusa, Sharif, ed. *Culture and the Natural Environment: Ancient and Modern Middle Eastern Texts.* Cairo: American University in Cairo Press, 2005.

Elvin, Mark. *The Retreat of the Elephants: An Environmental History of China.* New Haven, CT: Yale University Press, 2004.

Ergene, Boğaç. "Document Use in Ottoman Courts of Law: Observations from the *Sicils* of Çankırı and Kastamonu." *Turcica* 37 (2005): 83–111.

Ergene, Boğaç A. *Local Court, Provincial Society and Justice in the Ottoman Empire: Legal Practice and Dispute Resolution in Çankırı and Kastamonu (1652–1744).* Leiden: E. J. Brill, 2003.

Estes, J. Worth, and LaVerne Kuhnke. "French Observations of Disease and Drug Use in Late Eighteenth-Century Cairo." *Journal of the History of Medicine and Allied Sciences* 39 (1984): 121–52.

Fahd, T., M. J. L. Young, D. R. Hill, Hassanein Rabie, Cl. Cahen, A. K. S. Lambton, Halil İnalcık, I. H. Siddiqui, K. S. McLachlan, and J. Burton-Page. "Māʾ." *EI.*

Fahim, Hussein M. *Dams, People and Development: The Aswan High Dam Case.* New York: Pergamon Press, 1981.

Fahmī, Khālid. *al-Jasad wa al-Ḥadātha: al-Ṭibb wa al-Qānūn fī Miṣr al-Ḥadītha,* translated by Sharīf Yūnis. Cairo: Dār al-Kutub wa al-Wathāʾiq al-Qawmiyya, 2004.

Fahmy, Khaled. *All the Pasha's Men: Mehmed Ali, His Army and the Making of Modern Egypt.* Cambridge: Cambridge University Press, 1997.

———. "The Era of Muhammad ʿAli Pasha, 1805–1848." In *Modern Egypt, from 1517 to the End of the Twentieth Century.* Vol. 2 of *The Cambridge History of Egypt,* edited by M. W. Daly, 139–79. Cambridge: Cambridge University Press, 1998.

———. "Medical Conditions in Egyptian Prisons in the Nineteenth Century." In *Marginal Voices in Literature and Society: Individual and Society in the Mediterranean Muslim World,* edited by Robin Ostle, 135–55. Strasbourg: European Science Foundation, in collaboration with Maison méditerranéenne des sciences de l'homme d'Aix-en-Provence, 2000.

———. *Mehmed Ali: From Ottoman Governor to Ruler of Egypt.* Oxford: Oneworld, 2009.

———. "An Olfactory Tale of Two Cities: Cairo in the Nineteenth Century." In *Historians in Cairo: Essays in Honor of George Scanlon,* edited by Jill Edwards, 155–87. Cairo: American University in Cairo Press, 2002.

———. "The Police and the People in Nineteenth-Century Egypt." *Die Welt des Islams* 39 (1999): 340–77.

Farnie, D. A. *East and West of Suez: The Suez Canal in History, 1854–1956.* Oxford: Clarendon Press, 1969.

Faroqhi, Suraiya. "Agriculture and Rural Life in the Ottoman Empire (ca 1500–1878) (A Report on Scholarly Literature Published between 1970 and 1985)." *NPT* 1 (1987): 3–34.

———. *Approaching Ottoman History: An Introduction to the Sources.* Cambridge: Cambridge University Press, 1999.

———. "Camels, Wagons, and the Ottoman State in the Sixteenth and Seventeenth Centuries." *IJMES* 14 (1982): 523–39.

———. "Coffee and Spices: Official Ottoman Reactions to Egyptian Trade in the Later Sixteenth Century." *Wiener Zeitschrift für die Kunde des Morgenlandes* 76 (1986): 87–93.

———. "Crisis and Change, 1590–1699." In *An Economic and Social History of the Ottoman Empire: Volume 2, 1600–1914*, edited by Halil İnalcık, with Donald Quataert, 411–636. Cambridge: Cambridge University Press, 1994.

———. "Long-Term Change and the Ottoman Construction Site: A Study of Builders' Wages and Iron Prices (with Special Reference to Seventeenth-Century Foça and Sayda)." *JTS* 10 (1986): 111–34.

———. "Ottoman Peasants and Rural Life: The Historiography of the Twentieth Century." *AO* 18 (2000): 153–82.

———. "The Peasants of Saideli in the Late Sixteenth Century." *AO* 8 (1983): 215–50.

———. *Pilgrims and Sultans: The Hajj under the Ottomans.* London: I. B. Tauris, 1994.

———. "Red Sea Trade and Communications as Observed by Evliya Çelebi (1671–72)." *NPT* 5–6 (1991): 87–105.

———. "Rural Society in Anatolia and the Balkans during the Sixteenth Century, I." *Turcica* 9 (1977): 161–95.

———. "Rural Society in Anatolia and the Balkans during the Sixteenth Century, II." *Turcica* 11 (1979): 103–53.

———. "Trade Controls, Provisioning Policies, and Donations: The Egypt-Hijaz Connection during the Second Half of the Sixteenth Century." In *Süleymân the Second and His Time*, edited by Halil İnalcık and Cemal Kafadar, 131–43. Istanbul: Isis Press, 1993.

Faroqhi, Süreyya. "Water, Work and Money-Grabbing: Mobilizing Funds and Rural Labour in the Bursa Region around 1600." *AO* 23 (2005–2006): 143–54.

Finkel, Caroline. *Osman's Dream: The History of the Ottoman Empire, 1300–1923.* New York: Basic Books, 2006.

Fisher, Alan. "Sources and Perspectives for the Study of Ottoman-Russian Relations in the Black Sea Region." *IJTS* 1 (1980): 77–84.

Fleet, Kate. "Grain Exports from Western Anatolia at the End of the Fourteenth Century." *JESHO* 40 (1997): 283–93.

Foucault, Michel. *The History of Sexuality, Volume 1: An Introduction*, translated by Robert Hurley. New York: Vintage Books, 1978.

———. *Naissance de la biopolitique: Cours au Collège de France (1978–1979)*, edited by Michel Senellart. Paris: Seuil/Gallimard, 2004.

———. *Security, Territory, Population: Lectures at the Collège de France, 1977–78*, edited by Michel Senellart and translated by Graham Burchell. New York: Palgrave Macmillan, 2007.

———. *"Society Must be Defended:" Lectures at the Collège de France, 1975–76*, edited by Mauro Bertani and Alessandro Fontana and translated by David Macey. New York: Picador, 2003.

Frantz-Murphy, G. "Parallel Cyclical Patterns in Pre-Ottoman and Ottoman Land Tenure in Egypt." *AO* 9 (1988): 17–24.
Fu'ād, Nihād Muḥammad Kamāl al-Dīn. "Sijillāt Dīwān al-Ashghāl al-ʿUmūmiyya fī al-Fatra min 1277 ilā 1297 (1860–1880): Dirāsa Arshīfiyya wa Wathā'iqiyya wa Tārīkhiyya." Ph.D. diss., Cairo University, 1993.
Gamal, Adil S., ed. *Medieval Islamic Medicine: Ibn Riḍwān's Treatise "On the Prevention of Bodily Ills in Egypt,"* translated by Michael W. Dols. Berkeley: University of California Press, 1984.
Gazalé, Marie-Pascale. "Généalogies patrimoniales. La constitution des fortunes urbaines: Le Caire, 1780–1830." Ph.D. diss., École des hautes études en sciences sociales, 2004.
Geertz, Clifford. "The Wet and the Dry: Traditional Irrigation in Bali and Morocco." *Human Ecology* 1 (1972): 23–39.
Genç, Mehmed. "Osmanlı Maliyesinde Malikane Sistemi." In *Türkiye İktisat Tarihi Semineri Metinler/Tartışmalar,* edited by Osman Okyar, 231–96. Ankara: Hacıtepe Üniversitesi Yayınları, 1975.
Genç, Mehmet. "Contrôle et taxation du commerce du café dans l'Empire ottoman fin XVIIe – première moitié du XVIIIe siècle." In *Le commerce du café avant l'ère des plantations coloniales: espaces, réseaux, sociétés (XVe-XIXe siècle),* edited by Michel Tuchscherer, 161–79. Cairo: Institut français d'archéologie orientale, 2001.
Glick, Thomas F. *Irrigation and Hydraulic Technology: Medieval Spain and Its Legacy.* Brookfield, VT: Variorum, 1996.
———. *Irrigation and Society in Medieval Valencia.* Cambridge, MA: Harvard University Press, 1970.
Goubert, Jean-Pierre. *The Conquest of Water: The Advent of Health in the Industrial Age,* translated by Andrew Wilson. Princeton, NJ: Princeton University Press, 1989.
Gran, Peter. *Islamic Roots of Capitalism: Egypt, 1760–1840.* Austin: University of Texas Press, 1979.
———. "Late-Eighteenth–Early-Nineteenth-Century Egypt: Merchant Capitalism or Modern Capitalism?" In *The Ottoman Empire and the World-Economy,* edited by Huri İslamoğlu-İnan, 27–41. Cambridge: Cambridge University Press, 1987.
Greene, Molly. "The Ottomans in the Mediterranean." In *The Early Modern Ottomans: Remapping the Empire,* edited by Virginia Aksan and Daniel Goffman, 104–16. Cambridge: Cambridge University Press, 2007.
———. *A Shared World: Christians and Muslims in the Early Modern Mediterranean.* Princeton, NJ: Princeton University Press, 2000.
Greenwood, Antony. "Istanbul's Meat Provisioning: A Study of the *Celepkeşan* System." Ph.D. diss., University of Chicago, 1988.
Grist, D. H. *Rice.* 5th ed. London: Longman, 1975.
Griswold, William. "Climatic Change: A Possible Factor in the Social Unrest of Seventeenth Century Anatolia." In *Humanist and Scholar: Essays in Honor of Andreas Tietze,* edited by Heath W. Lowry and Donald Quataert, 37–57. Istanbul: Isis Press, 1993.
———. *The Great Anatolian Rebellion, 1000–1020/1591-1611.* Berlin: Klaus Schwarz Verlag, 1983.

Grove, A. T., and Oliver Rackham. *The Nature of Mediterranean Europe: An Ecological History.* New Haven, CT: Yale University Press, 2001.

Guillerme, André E. *The Age of Water: The Urban Environment in the North of France, A.D. 300–1800.* College Station: Texas A&M University Press, 1988.

Gupta, Akhil. *Postcolonial Developments: Agriculture in the Making of Modern India.* Durham, NC: Duke University Press, 1998.

Hacking, Ian. "Biopower and the Avalanche of Printed Numbers." *Humanities in Society* 5 (1982): 279–95.

Hairy, Isabelle, and Oueded Sennoune. "Géographie historique du canal d'Alexandrie." *AI* 40 (2006): 247–78.

Ḥamdān, Jamāl. *Shakhṣiyyat Miṣr: Dirāsa fī ʿAbqariyyat al-Makān.* 4 vols. Cairo: ʿĀlam al-Kutub,1981–1984.

Ḥāmid, Nawāl Fu'ād. "Muḥāfaẓat al-Sharqiyya: Dirāsa fī Jughrāfiyyat al-Rīf." Ph.D. diss., Zaqāzīq University, 1987.

Hanks, Lucien M. *Rice and Man: Agricultural Ecology in Southeast Asia.* Chicago: Aldine Atherton, 1972.

Hanna, Nelly. *Construction Work in Ottoman Cairo (1517–1798).* Cairo: Institut français d'archéologie orientale, 1984.

———. *Making Big Money in 1600: The Life and Times of Ismaʿil Abu Taqiyya, Egyptian Merchant.* Syracuse, NY: Syracuse University Press, 1998.

———. *In Praise of Books: A Cultural History of Cairo's Middle Class, Sixteenth to the Eighteenth Century.* Syracuse, NY: Syracuse University Press, 2003.

———. *An Urban History of Bulaq in the Mamluk and Ottoman Periods.* Cairo: Institut français d'archéologie orientale, 1983.

Hardin, Garrett. "The Tragedy of the Commons." *Science* 162 (1968): 1243–48.

Harms, J. C., and J. L. Wray. "Nile Delta." In *The Geology of Egypt,* edited by Rushdi Said, 329–43. Rotterdam: A. A. Balkema, 1990.

Ḥasan, Ḥasan Sayyid. "Mīnā' al-Iskandariyya: Dirāsa fī Jughrāfiyyat al-Naql al-Baḥrī." Ph.D. diss., ʿAyn Shams University, 1982.

Hathaway, Jane. *The Politics of Households in Ottoman Egypt: The Rise of the Qazdağlıs.* Cambridge: Cambridge University Press, 1997.

———. *A Tale of Two Factions: Myth, Memory, and Identity in Ottoman Egypt and Yemen.* Albany: State University of New York Press, 2003.

Hathaway, Jane, with contributions by Karl K. Barbir. *The Arab Lands under Ottoman Rule, 1516–1800.* Harlow, UK: Pearson Education, 2008.

Hattox, Ralph. *Coffee and Coffeehouses: The Origins of a Social Beverage in the Medieval Near East.* Seattle: University of Washington Press, 1985.

Herodotus. *The History,* translated by David Grene. Chicago: University of Chicago Press, 1987.

Hess, Andrew. "The Evolution of the Ottoman Seaborne Empire in the Age of Oceanic Discoveries, 1453–1525." *AHR* 75 (1970): 1892–1919.

Hewison, R. Neil. *The Fayoum: A Practical Guide.* Cairo: American University in Cairo Press, 1984.

Heywood, Colin. "A Red Sea Shipping Register of the 1670s for the Supply of Foodstuffs from Egyptian *Wakf* Sources to Mecca and Medina (Turkish Documents from the Archive of ʿAbdurrahman "ʿAbdi' Pasha of Buda, I)." *Anatolia Moderna* 6 (1996): 111–74.

Hinz, Walther. *Islamische Masse und Gewichte umgerechnet ins metrische System.* Leiden: E. J. Brill, 1955.

Hirst, L. Fabian. *The Conquest of Plague: A Study of the Evolution of Epidemiology.* Oxford: Clarendon Press, 1953.

Holt, P.M. *Egypt and the Fertile Crescent, 1516–1922: A Political History.* London: Longmans Green, 1966.

———. "al-Fayyūm." *EI.*

Holt, P.M., ed. *Political and Social Change in Modern Egypt: Historical Studies from the Ottoman Conquest to the United Arab Republic.* London: Oxford University Press, 1968.

Hughes, J. Donald. *The Mediterranean: An Environmental History.* Santa Barbara, CA: ABC-CLIO, 2005.

Hundley, Norris, Jr. *The Great Thirst: Californians and Water, A History.* Berkeley: University of California Press, 2001.

Hunt, Robert C., and Eva Hunt. "Canal Irrigation and Local Social Organization." *Current Anthropology* 17 (1976): 389–98.

al-Ḥusaynī, Maḥmūd Ḥāmid. *al-Asbila al-ʿUthmāniyya bi-Madīnat al-Qāhira, 1517–1798.* Cairo: Maktabat Madbūlī, 1988.

Hütteroth, Wolf-Dieter. "Ecology of the Ottoman Lands." In *The Cambridge History of Turkey, Volume 3: The Later Ottoman Empire, 1603–1839,* edited by Suraiya N. Faroqhi, 18–43. Cambridge: Cambridge University Press, 2006.

Ibrāhīm, Ihāb Aḥmad. "Muhandis Miqyās al-Nīl: Maʿlūmāt Jadīda fī Ḍauʾ al-Nuqūsh al-Kitābiyya lil-Miqyās." *AI* 39 (2005): 1–8.

Ibrāhīm, ʿĪsā ʿAlī. "Muḥāfaẓat Aswān: Dirāsa fī Jughrāfiyyat al-Tanmiyya al-Iqtiṣādiyya." Ph.D. diss., Alexandria University, 1984.

Ibrāhīm, Nāṣir. "al-Firinsiyūn wa Niẓām al-Iltizām." *AI* 37 (2003): 31–54.

Ibrāhīm, Nāṣir Aḥmad. *al-Azamāt al-Ijtimāʿiyya fī Miṣr fī al-Qarn al-Sābiʿ ʿAshar.* Cairo: Dār al-Āfāq al-ʿArabiyya, 1998.

Imber, Colin H. "The Costs of Naval Warfare, The Account of Hayreddin Barbarossa's Herceg Novi Campaign in 1539." *AO* 4 (1972): 203–16.

———. "The Navy of Süleiman the Magnificent." *AO* 6 (1980): 211–82.

———. *The Ottoman Empire, 1300–1650: The Structure of Power.* New York: Palgrave Macmillan, 2002.

Ismāʿil, Muhammad Husām al-Din. "Le café dans la ville de Rosette à l'époque ottomane XVIe-XVIIe siècle." In *Le commerce du café avant l'ère des plantations coloniales: espaces, réseaux, sociétés (XVe-XIXe siècle),* edited by Michel Tuchscherer, 103–9. Cairo: Institut français d'archéologie orientale, 2001.

İhsanoğlu, Ekmeleddin. *Mısır'da Türkler ve Kültürel Mirasları: Mehmed Ali Paşa'dan Günümüze Basılı Türk Kültürü Bibliyografyası ve Bir Değerlendirme.* Istanbul: İslam Tarih, Sanat, ve Kültür Araştırma Merkezi, 2006.

İnalcık, Halil. "'Arab' Camel Drivers in Western Anatolia in the Fifteenth Century." *Revue d'Histoire Maghrebine* 10 (1983): 256–70.

———. "Centralization and Decentralization in Ottoman Administration." In *Studies in Eighteenth Century Islamic History,* edited by Thomas Naff and Roger Owen, 27–52. Carbondale: Southern Illinois University Press, 1977.

———. "Introduction to Ottoman Metrology." *Turcica* 15 (1983): 311–48.

———. "Māʾ. 8. Irrigation in the Ottoman Empire." *EI.*

______. "The Ottoman State: Economy and Society, 1300–1600." In *An Economic and Social History of the Ottoman Empire: Volume 1, 1300–1600*, edited by Halil İnalcık, with Donald Quataert, 9–409. Cambridge: Cambridge University Press, 1994.

______. "Rice Cultivation and the Çeltükci-Re'âyâ System in the Ottoman Empire." *Turcica* 14 (1982): 69–141.

______. *Sources and Studies on the Ottoman Black Sea.* Cambridge, MA: Harvard University Press, 1996.

İslamoğlu-İnan, Huri. *State and Peasant in the Ottoman Empire: Agrarian Power Relations and Regional Economic Development in Ottoman Anatolia during the Sixteenth Century.* Leiden: E. J. Brill, 1994.

İslamoğlu-İnan, Huri, ed. *The Ottoman Empire and the World-Economy.* Cambridge: Cambridge University Press, 1987.

Issawi, Charles. *The Economic History of Turkey, 1800–1914.* Chicago: University of Chicago Press, 1980.

al-Jabartī, ʿAbd al-Raḥman. *ʿAbd al-Raḥman al-Jabartī's History of Egypt: ʿAjāʾib al-Āthār fī al-Tarājim wa al-Akhbār*, edited by Thomas Philipp and Moshe Perlmann. 4 vols. Stuttgart: Franz Steiner Verlag, 1994.

al-Jabartī, ʿAbd al-Raḥman Ibn Ḥasan. *ʿAjāʾib al-Āthār fī al-Tarājim wa al-Akhbār*, edited by ʿAbd al-Raḥīm ʿAbd al-Raḥman ʿAbd al-Raḥīm. 4 vols. Cairo: Maṭbaʿat Dār al-Kutub al-Miṣriyya, 1998.

Jahāwī, Muḥammad Ḥākim Jād. "al-Taʾthīrāt al-Tabāduliyya bayn al-Qarya wa al-Madīna: Taḥlīl Sūsiyūlūjī li-Namaṭ al-Taḥaḍḍur fī Miṣr fī al-Qarn al-Tāsiʿ ʿAshar." M.A. thesis, Cairo University, 1995.

Jennings, Ronald C. "The Locust Problem in Cyprus." In *Studies on Ottoman Social History in the Sixteenth and Seventeenth Centuries: Women, Zimmis and Sharia Courts in Kayseri, Cyprus and Trabzon*, 471–516. Istanbul: Isis Press, 1999.

al-Jirjāwī, Muḥammad Ibn Muḥammad Ḥāmid al-Marāghī. *Tārīkh Wilāyat al-Ṣaʿīd fī al-ʿAṣrayn al-Mamlūkī wa al-ʿUthmānī: al-Musammā bi-"Nūr al-ʿUyūn fī Dhikr Jirjā min ʿAhd Thalāthat Qurūn,"* edited by Aḥmad Ḥusayn al-Namakī. Cairo: Maktabat al-Nahḍa al-Miṣriyya, 1998.

Jirjis, Majdī. "Manhaj al-Dirāsāt al-Wathāʾiqiyya wa Wāqiʿ al-Baḥth fī Miṣr." *al-Rūznāma: al-Ḥauliyya al-Miṣriyya lil-Wathāʾiq* 2 (2004): 237–87.

Johansen, Baber. *The Islamic Law on Land Tax and Rent: The Peasants' Loss of Property Rights as Interpreted in the Hanafite Legal Literature of the Mamluk and Ottoman Periods.* London: Croom Helm, 1988.

Jumʿa, Mājida Muḥammad Aḥmad. "Madīnat al-Aqṣur: Dirāsa Jughrāfiyya." M.A. thesis, ʿAyn Shams University, 1983.

Kafadar, Cemal. "The Question of Ottoman Decline." *Harvard Middle Eastern and Islamic Review* 4 (1997–1998): 30–75.

Kasaba, Reşat. *A Moveable Empire: Ottoman Nomads, Migrants, and Refugees.* Seattle: University of Washington Press, 2009.

Keyder, Çağlar, and Faruk Tabak, eds. *Landholding and Commercial Agriculture in the Middle East.* Albany: State University of New York Press, 1991.

al-Khashshāb, Ismāʿīl Ibn Saʿd. *Akhbār Ahl al-Qarn al-Thānī ʿAshar: Tārīkh al-Mamālīk fī al-Qāhira*, edited by ʿAbd al-ʿAzīz Jamāl al-Dīn and ʿImād Abū Ghāzī. Cairo: al-ʿArabī lil-Nashr wa al-Tawzīʿ, 1990.

———. *Khulāṣat mā Yurād min Akhbār al-Amīr Murād*, edited and translated by Hamza ʿAbd al-ʿAzīz Badr and Daniel Crecelius. Cairo: al-ʿArabī lil-Nashr wa al-Tawzīʿ, 1992.

Khazeni, Arash. *Tribes and Empire on the Margins of Nineteenth-Century Iran*. Seattle: University of Washington Press, 2010.

Khoury, Dina Rizk. "The Ottoman Centre versus Provincial Power-Holders: An Analysis of the Historiography." In *The Cambridge History of Turkey, Volume 3: The Later Ottoman Empire, 1603–1839*, edited by Suraiya N. Faroqhi, 135–56. Cambridge: Cambridge University Press, 2006.

———. *State and Provincial Society in the Ottoman Empire: Mosul, 1540–1834*. Cambridge: Cambridge University Press, 1997.

Kırlı, Cengiz. "The Struggle over Space: Coffeehouses of Ottoman Istanbul, 1780–1845." Ph.D. diss., State University of New York, Binghamton, 2000.

King, Charles. *The Black Sea: A History*. Oxford: Oxford University Press, 2004.

Koç, Bekir. "Tanzimat Sonrası Hukuk Metinlerinde Çevre Bilincinin Arkaplanı Olarak 'Av Yasak ve Sınırlılıkları' Üzerine Bazı Düşünceler." *Ankara Üniversitesi Osmanlı Tarihi Araştırma ve Uygulama Merkezi Dergisi*, no. 19 (2006): 271–81.

Kondrashov, D., Y. Feliks, and M. Ghil. "Oscillatory Modes of Extended Nile River Records (A.D. 622–1922)." *Geophysical Research Letters* 32 (2005), L10702.

Krīsaliyūs, Dānyāl, ed. *Fihris Waqfiyyāt al-ʿAṣr al-ʿUthmānī al-Maḥfūẓa bi-Wizārat al-Awqāf wa Dār al-Wathāʾiq al-Tārīkhiyya al-Qawmiyya bil-Qāhira*. Cairo: Dār al-Nahḍa al-ʿArabiyya, 1992.

Kudlick, Catherine J. *Cholera in Post-Revolutionary France: A Cultural History*. Berkeley: University of California Press, 1996.

Kuhnke, LaVerne. *Lives at Risk: Public Health in Nineteenth-Century Egypt*. Berkeley: University of California Press, 1990.

Kupferschmidt, Hugo. *Die Epidemiologie der Pest: Der Konzeptwandel in der Erforschung der Infektionsketten seit der Entdeckung des Pesterregers im Jahre 1894*. Aarau, Switzerland: Sauerländer, 1993.

Kutluk, Halil, ed. *Türkiye Ormancılığı ile İlgili Tarihi Vesikalar, 893–1339 (1487–1923)*. Istanbul: Osmanbey Matbaası, 1948.

Kutluoğlu, Muhammad H. *The Egyptian Question (1831–1841): The Expansionist Policy of Mehmed Ali Paşa in Syria and Asia Minor and the Reaction of the Sublime Porte*. Istanbul: Eren, 1998.

Lancaster, William, and Fidelity Lancaster. *People, Land and Water in the Arab Middle East: Environments and Landscapes in the Bilâd ash-Shâm*. Amsterdam: Harwood Academic Publishers, 1999.

Lane, Edward William. *An Arabic-English Lexicon*. 8 vols. Beirut: Librairie du Liban, 1968.

Lapidus, Ira M. "The Grain Economy of Mamluk Egypt." *JESHO* 12 (1969): 1–15.

Laqueur, Thomas W. "Bodies, Details, and the Humanitarian Narrative." In *The New Cultural History*, edited by Lynn Hunt, 176–204. Berkeley: University of California Press, 1989.

Latour, Bruno. *We Have Never Been Modern*, translated by Catherine Porter. Cambridge, MA: Harvard University Press, 1993.

Lawson, Fred H. *The Social Origins of Egyptian Expansionism during the Muhammad ʿAli Period.* New York: Columbia University Press, 1992.
Lees, Susan H. "On Irrigation and the Conflict Myth." *Current Anthropology* 30 (1989): 343–44.
Le Roy Ladurie, Emmanuel. *Times of Feast, Times of Famine: A History of Climate since the Year 1000,* translated by Barbara Bray. Garden City, NY: Doubleday, 1971.
Lewis, Bernard. *The Emergence of Modern Turkey.* London: Oxford University Press, 1962.
______. *Istanbul and the Civilization of the Ottoman Empire.* Norman: University of Oklahoma Press, 1963.
______. "Some Reflections on the Decline of the Ottoman Empire." *Studia Islamica* 9 (1958): 111–27.
Lewis, Norman N. "Malaria, Irrigation and Soil Erosion in Central Syria." *Geographical Review* 39 (1949): 278–90.
Li, Lillian M. *Fighting Famine in North China: State, Market, and Environmental Decline, 1690s–1990s.* Stanford, CA: Stanford University Press, 2007.
Lisān al-ʿArab. 4 vols. Beirut: Dār Lisān al-ʿArab, 1970.
Lowi, Miriam R. *Water and Power: The Politics of a Scarce Resource in the Jordan River Basin.* Cambridge: Cambridge University Press, 1993.
Lutfi, Huda. "Coptic Festivals of the Nile: Aberrations of the Past?" In *The Mamluks in Egyptian Politics and Society,* edited by Thomas Philipp and Ulrich Haarmann, 254–82. Cambridge: Cambridge University Press, 1998.
Lybyer, Albert Howe. *The Government of the Ottoman Empire in the Time of Suleiman the Magnificent.* Cambridge, MA: Harvard University Press, 1913.
Maass, Arthur, and Raymond L. Anderson. *. . . And the Desert Shall Rejoice: Conflict, Growth, and Justice in Arid Environments.* Cambridge: Massachusetts Institute of Technology Press, 1978.
Magnusson, Roberta J. *Water Technology in the Middle Ages: Cities, Monasteries, and Waterworks after the Roman Empire.* Baltimore: Johns Hopkins University Press, 2001.
Maḥārīq, Yāsir ʿAbd al-Minʿam. *al-Minūfiyya fī al-Qarn al-Thāmin ʿAshar.* Cairo: al-Hayʾa al-Miṣriyya al-ʿĀmma lil-Kitāb, 2000.
Māhir, Suʿād. "Majrī Miyāh Famm al-Khalīj." *EHR* 7 (1958): 134–57.
Makovsky, A. "Sixteenth-Century Agricultural Production in the Liwā of Jerusalem: Insights from the *Tapu Defters* and an Attempt at Quantification." *AO* 9 (1984): 91–127.
Mallat, Chibli. "The Quest for Water Use Principles: Reflections on *Sharīʿa* and Custom in the Middle East." In *Water in the Middle East: Legal, Political and Commercial Implications,* edited by J. A. Allan and Chibli Mallat, with Shai Wade and Jonathan Wild, 127–37. London: I. B. Tauris Academic Studies, 1995.
Ibn Mammātī, al-Asʿad Ibn Muhadhdhab. *Kitāb Qawānīn al-Dawāwīn,* edited by Aziz Suryal Atiya. Cairo: Royal Agricultural Society, 1943.
Mardin, Şerif. "Center-Periphery Relations: A Key to Turkish Politics." *Daedalus* 102 (1973): 169–91.

Marlowe, John. *World Ditch: The Making of the Suez Canal.* New York: Macmillan, 1964.

Marsot, Afaf Lutfi al-Sayyid. *Egypt in the Reign of Muhammad Ali.* Cambridge: Cambridge University Press, 1984.

Matuz, Joseph E. "Contributions to the Ottoman Institution of the *Iltizâm.*" *OA* 11 (1991): 237–49.

McGowan, B. "Food Supply and Taxation on the Middle Danube (1568–1579)." *AO* 1 (1969): 139–96.

McNeill, J. R. *The Mountains of the Mediterranean World: An Environmental History.* Cambridge: Cambridge University Press, 1992.

———. "Observations on the Nature and Culture of Environmental History." *History and Theory* 42 (2003): 5–43.

———. *Something New under the Sun: An Environmental History of the Twentieth-Century World.* New York: W. W. Norton, 2000.

McNeill, William H. *Plagues and Peoples.* Garden City, NY: Anchor Press/Doubleday, 1976.

Meiggs, Russell. *Trees and Timber in the Ancient Mediterranean World.* Oxford: Clarendon Press, 1982.

Michel, Nicolas. "Les Dafātir al-ğusūr, source pour l'histoire du réseau hydraulique de l'Égypte ottoman." *AI* 29 (1995): 151–68.

———. "Migrations de paysans dans le Delta du Nil au début de l'époque ottoman." *AI* 35 (2001): 241–90.

———. "Les rizaq iḥbāsiyya, terres agricoles en mainmorte dans l'Égypte mamelouke et ottoman. Étude sur les Dafātir al-Aḥbās ottomans." *AI* 30 (1996): 105–98.

———. "Villages désertés, terres en friche et reconstruction rurale en Égypte au début de l'époque ottoman." *AI* 36 (2002): 197–251.

Mikhail, Alan. "Animals as Property in Early Modern Ottoman Egypt." *JESHO* 53 (2010): 621–52.

———. "The Heart's Desire: Gender, Urban Space and the Ottoman Coffee House." In *Ottoman Tulips, Ottoman Coffee: Leisure and Lifestyle in the Eighteenth Century,* edited by Dana Sajdi, 133–70. London: Tauris Academic Studies, 2007.

———. "An Irrigated Empire: The View from Ottoman Fayyum." *IJMES* 42 (2010): 569–90.

———. "The Nature of Plague in Late Eighteenth-Century Egypt." *Bulletin of the History of Medicine* 82 (2008): 249–75.

———. "Piles of History: The Nile, Dirt, and Humans in Ottoman Egypt." Forthcoming in *Environmental Imaginaries of the Middle East: History, Policy, Power, and Practice,* edited by Diana K. Davis and Edmund Burke III. Athens: Ohio University Press.

Mīkhā'īl, Ālan. "Tārīkh Dirāsāt al-Tābiʿ wa Naẓariyyatayn ʿan al-Sulṭa." In *Thaqāfat al-Nukhba wa Thaqāfat al-ʿĀmma fī Miṣr fī al-ʿAṣr al-ʿUthmānī,* edited by Nāṣir Aḥmad Ibrāhīm, 349–60. Cairo: Markaz al-Buḥūth wa al-Dirāsāt al-Ijtimāʿiyya, 2008.

Miles, M. "Signing in the Seraglio: Mutes, Dwarfs and Jestures at the Ottoman Court 1500–1700." *Disability and Society* 15 (2000): 115–34.

Millon, Rene, Clara Hall, and May Diaz. "Conflict in the Modern Teotihuacan Irrigation System." *Comparative Studies in Society and History* 4 (1962): 494–524.

Mink, Nicolaas, Robert N. Chester III, Jane Dusselier, and Nancy Shoemaker. "Having Our Cake and Eating It Too: Food's Place in Environmental History, a Forum." *Environmental History* 14 (2009): 309–44.

Mirzoeff, Nicholas. "Framed: The Deaf in the Harem." In *Deviant Bodies: Critical Perspectives on Difference in Science and Popular Culture*, edited by Jennifer Terry and Jacqueline Urla, 49–77. Bloomington: Indiana University Press, 1995.

Mitchell, Timothy. *Rule of Experts: Egypt, Techno-Politics, Modernity*. Berkeley: University of California Press, 2002.

el-Mouelhy, Ibrahım. *Organisation et fonctionnement des institutions ottomanes en Egypte (1517–1917): étude documentaire, d'après les sources archivistiques égyptiennes*. Ankara [?]: Imprimerie de la Société Turque d'Histoire, 1989.

Muḥammad, ʿIrāqī Yūsuf. *al-Wujūd al-ʿUthmānī al-Mamlūkī fī Miṣr fī al-Qarn al-Thāmin ʿAshar wa Awāʾil al-Qarn al-Tāsiʿ ʿAshar*. Cairo: Dār al-Maʿārif, 1985.

———. *al-Wujūd al-ʿUthmānī fī Miṣr fī al-Qarnayn al-Sādis ʿAshar wa al-Sābiʿ ʿAshar (Dirāsa Wathāʾiqiyya)*, Vol. 1. Cairo: Markaz Kliyūbātrā lil-Kumbiyūtar, 1996.

Mughayth, Kammāl Ḥāmid. *Miṣr fī al-ʿAṣr al-ʿUthmānī 1517–1798: al-Mujtamaʿ ... wa al-Taʿlīm*. Cairo: Markaz al-Dirāsāt wa al-Maʿlūmāt al-Qānūniyya li-Ḥuqūq al-Insān, 1997.

Mukerji, Chandra. *Impossible Engineering: Technology and Territoriality on the Canal du Midi*. Princeton, NJ: Princeton University Press, 2009.

Murphey, Rhoads. "The Ottoman Centuries in Iraq: Legacy or Aftermath? A Survey Study of Mesopotamian Hydrology and Ottoman Irrigation Projects." *JTS* 11 (1987): 17–29.

———. *Ottoman Warfare, 1500–1700*. New Brunswick, NJ: Rutgers University Press, 1999.

———. "Provisioning Istanbul: The State and Subsistence in the Early Modern Middle East." *Food and Foodways* 2 (1988): 217–63.

Mutawallī, Aḥmad Fuʾād. *al-Alfāẓ al-Turkiyya fī al-Lahjāt al-ʿArabiyya wa fī Lughat al-Kitāba*. Cairo: Dār al-Zahrāʾ lil-Nashr, 1991.

Mutawallī, Aḥmad Fuʾād, trans. and intro. *Qānūn Nāmah Miṣr, alladhī Aṣdarahu al-Sulṭān al-Qānūnī li-Ḥukm Miṣr*. Cairo: Maktabat al-Anjlū al-Miṣriyya, 1986.

El-Nahal, Galal H. *The Judicial Administration of Ottoman Egypt in the Seventeenth Century*. Minneapolis, MN: Bibliotheca Islamica, 1979.

Najm, Zayn al-ʿĀbidīn Shams al-Dīn. "Tasaḥḥub al-Fallāḥīn fī ʿAṣr Muḥammad ʿAlī, Asbābuhu wa Natāʾijuhu." *EHR* 36 (1989): 259–316.

Nash, Linda. *Inescapable Ecologies: A History of Environment, Disease, and Knowledge*. Berkeley: University of California Press, 2006.

Neustadt (Ayalon), David. "The Plague and Its Effects upon the Mamlûk Army." *Journal of the Royal Asiatic Society of Great Britain and Ireland* (1946): 67–73.

Ostapchuk, Victor. "Five Documents from the Topkapı Palace Archive on the Ottoman Defense of the Black Sea against the Cossacks (1639)." *JTS* 11 (1987): 49–104.

Ostrom, Elinor. *Governing the Commons: The Evolution of Institutions for Collective Action.* Cambridge: Cambridge University Press, 1990.

Ostrom, Elinor, and Roy Gardner. "Coping with Asymmetries in the Commons: Self-Governing Irrigation Systems Can Work." *Journal of Economic Perspectives* 7 (1993): 93–112.

Owen, E. R. J. *Cotton and the Egyptian Economy, 1820–1914.* Oxford: Clarendon Press, 1969.

Özbaran, Salih. "Bahrain in 1559: A Narrative of Turco-Portuguese Conflict in the Gulf." *OA* 3 (1982): 91–104.

Pandian, Anand Sankar. "Landscapes of Redemption: Cultivating Heart and Soil in South India." Ph.D. diss., University of California, Berkeley, 2004.

Panzac, Daniel. "Alexandrie: Peste et croissance urbaine (XVIIe-XIXe siècles)." In *Population et santé dans l'Empire ottoman (XVIIIe-XXe siècles),* 141–59. Istanbul: Isis, 1996.

———. "International and Domestic Maritime Trade in the Ottoman Empire during the 18th Century." *IJMES* 24 (1992): 189–206.

———. *La peste dans l'Empire Ottoman, 1700–1850.* Louvain: Association pour le développement des études turques, 1985.

———. *Quarantaines et lazarets: l'Europe et la peste d'Orient (XVIIe-XXe siècles).* Aix-en-Provence, France: Édisud, 1986.

Parveva, Stefka. "Agrarian Land and Harvest in South-West Peloponnese in the Early 18th Century." *Études Balkaniques* 1 (2003): 83–123.

Peirce, Leslie. *Morality Tales: Law and Gender in the Ottoman Court of Aintab.* Berkeley: University of California Press, 2003.

———. "'She is trouble . . . and I will divorce her': Orality, Honor, and Representation in the Ottoman Court of Aintab." In *Women in the Medieval Islamic World: Power, Patronage, Piety,* edited by Gavin R. G. Hambly, 267–300. New York: St. Martin's Press, 1998.

Peirce, Leslie P. *The Imperial Harem: Women and Sovereignty in the Ottoman Empire.* Oxford: Oxford University Press, 1993.

Perdue, Peter C. *China Marches West: The Qing Conquest of Central Eurasia.* Cambridge, MA: Harvard University Press, 2005.

Perlin, John. *A Forest Journey: The Story of Wood and Civilization.* Woodstock, VT: Countryman Press, 2005.

Peters, Rudolph. "Controlled Suffering: Mortality and Living Conditions in 19th-Century Egyptian Prisons." *IJMES* 36 (2004): 387–407.

———. "Egypt and the Age of the Triumphant Prison: Legal Punishment in Nineteenth Century Egypt." *AI* 36 (2002): 253–85.

———. "Prisons and Marginalisation in Nineteenth-century Egypt." In *Outside In: On the Margins of the Modern Middle East,* edited by Eugene Rogan, 31–52. London: I. B. Tauris, 2002.

Pienaru, Nagy. "The Black Sea and the Ottomans: The Pontic Policy of Bayezid the Thunderbolt." *IJTS* 9 (2003): 33–57.

Pollitzer, Robert, *Plague.* Geneva: World Health Organization, 1954.

Poonawala, I. K. "Āb ii. Water in Muslim Iranian Culture." *Encyclopaedia Iranica.*

Popper, William. *The Cairo Nilometer: Studies in Ibn Taghrî Birdî's Chronicles of Egypt, I.* Berkeley: University of California Press, 1951.

Quataert, Donald. *The Ottoman Empire, 1700–1922*. Cambridge: Cambridge University Press, 2000.

———. "Ottoman History Writing and Changing Attitudes Towards the Notion of 'Decline.'" *History Compass* 1 (2003): 1–9.

Rabbat, Nasser O. *The Citadel of Cairo: A New Interpretation of Royal Mamluk Architecture.* Leiden: E. J. Brill, 1995.

Rabinow, Paul. *French DNA: Trouble in Purgatory.* Chicago: University of Chicago Press, 1999.

———. *French Modern: Norms and Forms of the Social Environment.* Chicago: University of Chicago Press, 1995.

al-Rāfʿī, ʿAbd al-Raḥman. *ʿAṣr Muḥammad ʿAlī.* Cairo: Dār al-Maʿārif, 1989.

Ramaḍān, Muṣṭafā Muḥammad. *Dawr al-Azhar fī al-Ḥayah al-Miṣriyya ibbāna al-Ḥamlah al-Faransiyya wa Maṭlaʿ al-Qarn al-Tāsiʿ ʿAshar.* Cairo: Maṭbaʿat al-Jabalāwī, 1986.

Ramzī, Muḥammad. *al-Qāmūs al-Jughrāfī lil-Bilād al-Miṣriyya min ʿAhd Qudamāʾ al-Miṣriyyīn ilā Sanat 1945.* 6 vols. in 2 pts. Cairo: al-Hayʾa al-Miṣriyya al-ʿĀmma lil-Kitāb, 1994.

Rashwān, Mālik Muḥammad Aḥmad. "al-Shām Taḥt Ḥukm Muḥammad ʿAlī (1247–57)." Ph.D. diss., al-Azhar University, 1984.

Raymond, André. *Artisans et commerçants au Caire au XVIIIe siècle.* 2 vols. Damascus: Institut français de Damas, 1973.

———. "Les bains publics au Caire à la fin du XVIIIe siècle." *AI* 8 (1969): 129–50.

———. *Cairo: City of History,* translated by Willard Wood. Cairo: American University in Cairo Press, 2001.

———. "A Divided Sea: The Cairo Coffee Trade in the Red Sea Area during the Seventeenth and Eighteenth Centuries." In *Modernity and Culture: From the Mediterranean to the Indian Ocean,* edited by Leila Tarazi Fawaz and C. A. Bayly, 46–57. New York: Columbia University Press, 2002.

———. *Égyptiens et français au Caire (1798–1801).* Cairo: Institut français d'archéologie orientale, 2004.

———. "Une famille de grands négociants en café au Caire dans la première moitié du XVIIIe siècle: les Sharāybī." In *Le commerce du café avant l'ère des plantations coloniales: espaces, réseaux, sociétés (XVe-XIXe siècle),* edited by Michel Tuchscherer, 111–24. Cairo: Institut français d'archéologie orientale, 2001.

———. "Les Grandes Épidémies de peste au Caire aux XVIIe et XVIIIe siècles." *Bulletin d'Études Orientales* 25 (1973): 203–10.

———. "La localization des bains publics du Cairo au quinzième siècle d'aprés les Hitat de Makrizi." *Bulletin d'Études Orientales* 30 (1978): 347–60.

———. "La population du Caire et de l'Égypte à l'époque ottomane et sous Muḥammad ʿAlî." In *Mémorial Ömer Lûtfi Barkan,* 169–78. Paris: Librairie d'Amérique et d'Orient Adrien Maisonneuve, 1980.

Reimer, Michael J. "Ottoman Alexandria: The Paradox of Decline and the Reconfiguration of Power in Eighteenth-Century Arab Provinces." *JESHO* 37 (1994): 107–46.

Richards, Alan R. "Primitive Accumulation in Egypt, 1798–1882." In *The Ottoman Empire and the World-Economy,* edited by Huri İslamoğlu-İnan, 203–43. Cambridge: Cambridge University Press, 1987.

Richards, John F. *The Unending Frontier: An Environmental History of the Early Modern World.* Berkeley: University of California Press, 2003.

Risso, Patricia. "Cross-Cultural Perceptions of Piracy: Maritime Violence in the Western Indian Ocean and Persian Gulf Region during a Long Eighteenth Century." *Journal of World History* 12 (2001): 293–319.

———. "Muslim Identity in Maritime Trade: General Observations and Some Evidence from the 18th Century Persian Gulf/Indian Ocean Region." *IJMES* 21 (1989): 381–92.

Rivlin, Helen Anne B. *The Agricultural Policy of Muḥammad ʿAlī in Egypt.* Cambridge, MA: Harvard University Press 1961.

Rotberg, Robert I., and Theodore K. Rabb, eds. *Climate and History: Studies in Interdisciplinary History.* Princeton, NJ: Princeton University Press, 1981.

el-Rouayheb, Khaled. "Was There a Revival of Logical Studies in Eighteenth-Century Egypt?" *Die Welt des Islams* 45 (2005): 1–19.

al-Rūqī, ʿĀiḍ bin Khazzām. "Juhūd al-Dawla al-ʿUthmāniyya fī Taʾmīn al-Ṭarīq al-Baḥrī min ʿĀṣimat al-Dawla ilā al-Ḥaramayn al-Sharīfayn." *EHR* 42 (2004–2005): 541–72.

Rustom, Asad J. *The Royal Archives of Egypt and the Origins of the Egyptian Expedition to Syria, 1831–1841.* Beirut: American Press, 1936.

Said, Rushdi. *The Geology of Egypt.* New York: Elsevier Publishing, 1962.

Sajdi, Dana. "Decline, Its Discontents and Ottoman Cultural History: By Way of Introduction." In *Ottoman Tulips, Ottoman Coffee: Leisure and Lifestyle in the Eighteenth Century,* edited by Dana Sajdi, 1–40. London: Tauris Academic Studies, 2007.

Ṣāliḥ, Rushdī. *Miṣr wa al-Fallāḥ wa al-Nīl.* Cairo: al-Hayʾa al-Miṣriyya al-ʿĀmma lil-Kitāb, 1975.

Sallares, Robert. *The Ecology of the Ancient Greek World.* Ithaca, NY: Cornell University Press, 1991.

Salzmann, Ariel. *Tocqueville in the Ottoman Empire: Rival Paths to the Modern State.* Leiden: E. J. Brill, 1994.

Sāmī, Amīn. *Taqwīm al-Nīl.* 5 vols. in 3 pts. Cairo: Dār al-Kutub wa al-Wathāʾiq al-Qawmiyya, 2003.

Sanders, Paula. *Ritual, Politics, and the City in Fatimid Cairo.* Albany: State University of New York Press, 1994.

Sarıyıldız, Gülden. *Hicaz Karantina Teşkilâtı (1865–1914).* Ankara: Türk Tarih Kurumu, 1996.

Saʿūdī, ʿAbd al-ʿAẓīm Muḥammad. *Tārīkh Taṭawwur al-Riyy fī Miṣr (1882–1914).* Cairo: al-Hayʾa al-Miṣriyya al-ʿĀmma lil-Kitāb, 2001.

al-Ṣawāliḥī al-ʿUfī al-Ḥanbalī, Ibrāhīm Ibn Abī Bakr. *Tarājim al-Ṣawāʿiq fī Wāqiʿat al-Ṣanājiq,* edited by ʿAbd al-Raḥīm ʿAbd al-Raḥman ʿAbd al-Raḥīm. Cairo: Institut français d'archéologie orientale, 1986.

al-Sayūṭī, Jalāl al-Dīn. *Kawkab al-Rauḍa,* edited by Muḥammad al-Shashtāwī. Cairo: Dār al-Āfāq al-ʿArabiyya, 2002.

al-Sayyid, Mirfat Aḥmad. "Idārat al-Shurṭa fī Miṣr fī al-ʿAṣr al-ʿUthmānī." *AI* 40 (2006): 51–70.

Scalenghe, Sara. "Being Different: Intersexuality, Blindness, Deafness, and Madness in Ottoman Syria." Ph.D. diss., Georgetown University, 2006.

———. "The Deaf in Ottoman Syria, 16th–18th Centuries." *Arab Studies Journal* 12–13 (2004–2005): 10–25.

Scott, James C. *Seeing Like a State: How Certain Schemes to Improve the Human Condition Have Failed.* New Haven, CT: Yale University Press, 1998.

Sertoğlu, Midhat. *Osmanlı Tarih Lûgatı.* Istanbul: Enderun Kitabevi, 1986.

Sezgin, Fuat, Mazen Amawi, Carl Ehrig-Eggert, and Eckhard Neubauer, eds. *Studies of the Faiyūm Together with Tārīḫ al-Faiyūm wa-Bilādihī by Abū ʿUṯmān an-Nābulusī (d. 1261).* Vol. 54 of *Islamic Geography.* Frankfurt: Institute for the History of Arabic-Islamic Science at the Johann Wolfgang Goethe University, 1992.

Shafei Bey, Ali. "Fayoum Irrigation as Described by Nabulsi in 1245 A.D. with a Description of the Present System of Irrigation and a Note on Lake Moeris." In *Studies of the Faiyūm together with Tārīḫ al-Faiyūm wa-Bilādihī by Abū ʿUṯmān an-Nābulusī (d. 1261),* edited by Fuat Sezgin, Mazen Amawi, Carl Ehrig-Eggert, and Eckhard Neubauer, 103–55. Vol. 54 of *Islamic Geography.* Frankfurt: Institute for the History of Arabic-Islamic Science at the Johann Wolfgang Goethe University, 1992.

Shaw, Stanford J. *Between Old and New: The Ottoman Empire under Sultan Selim III, 1789–1807.* Cambridge, MA: Harvard University Press, 1971.

———. *The Budget of Ottoman Egypt, 1005–1006/1596–1597.* The Hague: Mouton, 1968.

———. "Cairo's Archives and the History of Ottoman Egypt." *Middle East Institute Report on Current Research* (1956): 59–72.

———. *The Financial and Administrative Organization and Development of Ottoman Egypt, 1517–1798.* Princeton, NJ: Princeton University Press, 1962.

———. "Landholding and Land-Tax Revenues in Ottoman Egypt." In *Political and Social Change in Modern Egypt: Historical Studies from the Ottoman Conquest to the United Arab Republic,* edited by P. M. Holt, 91–103. London: Oxford University Press, 1968.

———. "The Ottoman Archives as a Source for Egyptian History." *Journal of the American Oriental Society* 83 (1962): 447–52.

———. "The Population of Istanbul in the Nineteenth Century." *IJMES* 10 (1979): 265–77.

Shaw, Stanford J., ed. and trans. *Ottoman Egypt in the Eighteenth Century: The Niẓâmnâme-i Mıṣır of Cezzâr Aḥmed Pasha.* Cambridge, MA: Center for Middle Eastern Studies of Harvard University, 1964.

Shibl, Yusuf A. *The Aswan High Dam.* Beirut: Arab Institute for Research and Publishing, 1971.

al-Shirbīnī, Yūsuf Ibn Muḥammad. *Kitāb Hazz al-Quḥūf bi-Sharḥ Qaṣīd Abī Shādūf,* edited and translated by Humphrey Davies. 2 vols. Leuven: Peeters, 2005–2007.

Singer, Amy. *Palestinian Peasants and Ottoman Officials: Rural Administration around Sixteenth-Century Jerusalem.* Cambridge: Cambridge University Press, 1994.

———. "Peasant Migration: Law and Practice in Early Ottoman Palestine." *NPT* 8 (1992): 49–65.

al-Sirsī, Majdī ʿAbd al-Ḥamīd Muḥammad. "al-Riyy wa Mushkilāt al-Zirāʿa fī Daltā al-Nīl: Dirāsa Jughrāfiyya." Ph.D. diss., ʿAyn Shams University, 1985.

Siy, Robert Y., Jr. *Community Resource Management: Lessons from the Zanjera.* Quezon City: University of the Philippines Press, 1982.

Soucek, Svat. "Certain Types of Ships in Ottoman-Turkish Terminology." *Turcica* 7 (1975): 233–49.

Speiser, Philipp. "The Remodeling of the Cairo Citadel from the 16th to the 20th Century." *AI* 38 (2004): 79–93.

Squatriti, Paolo. *Water and Society in Early Medieval Italy,* A.D. *400–1000.* Cambridge: Cambridge University Press, 1998.

Sticker, Georg. *Abhandlungen aus der Seuchengeschichte und Seuchenlehre.* Giessen, Germany: A. Töpelmann, 1908–1912.

Sublet, Jacqueline. "La Peste prise aux rêts de la jurisprudence: Le Traité d'Ibn Ḥağar al-ʿAsqalānī sur la peste." *Studia Islamica* 33 (1971): 141–49.

Sulaymān, ʿAbd al-Ḥamīd. "al-Sukhra fī Miṣr fī al-Qarnayn al-Sābiʿ ʿAshar wa al-Thāmin ʿAshar, Dirāsa fī al-Asbāb wa al-Natāʾij." In *al-Rafḍ wa al-Iḥtijāj fī al-Mujtamaʿ al-Miṣrī fī al-ʿAṣr al-ʿUthmānī,* edited by Nāṣir Ibrāhīm and Raʾūf ʿAbbās, 89–126. Cairo: Markaz al-Buḥūth wa al-Dirāsāt al-Ijtimāʿiyya, 2004.

Sulaymān, ʿAbd al-Ḥamīd Ḥāmid. *al-Milāḥa al-Nīliyya fī Miṣr al-ʿUthmāniyya (1517–1798).* Cairo: al-Hayʾa al-Miṣriyya al-ʿĀmma lil-Kitāb, 2000.

Tabak, Faruk. *The Waning of the Mediterranean, 1550–1870: A Geohistorical Approach.* Baltimore: Johns Hopkins University Press, 2008.

Thirgood, J. V. *Man and the Mediterranean Forest: A History of Resource Depletion.* London: Academic Press, 1981.

Tietze, Andreas. *Muṣṭafā ʿĀlī's Description of Cairo of 1599: Text, Transliteration, Translation, Notes.* Vienna: Verlag Der Österreichischen Akademie Der Wissenschaften, 1975.

Toynbee, Arnold. "Review of *Oriental Despotism: A Comparative Study of Total Power* by Karl A. Wittfogel." *American Political Science Review* 52 (1958): 195–98.

Trawick, Paul. "The Moral Economy of Water: Equity and Antiquity in the Andean Commons." *American Anthropologist* 103 (2001): 361–79.

Trawick, Paul B. "Successfully Governing the Commons: Principles of Social Organization in an Andean Irrigation System." *Human Ecology* 29 (2001): 1–25.

Tsugitaka, Sato. *State and Rural Society in Medieval Islam: Sultans, Muqtaʿs and Fallahun.* Leiden: E. J. Brill, 1997.

Tuchscherer, Michel. "Commerce et production du café en mer Rouge au XVIe siècle." In *Le commerce du café avant l'ère des plantations coloniales: espaces, réseaux, sociétés (XVe-XIXe siècle),* edited by Michel Tuchscherer, 69–90. Cairo: Institut français d'archéologie orientale, 2001.

———. "La flotte impériale de Suez de 1694 à 1719." *Turcica* 29 (1997): 47–69.

Tucker, William F. "Natural Disasters and the Peasantry in Mamlūk Egypt." *JESHO* 24 (1981): 215–24.

Ṭūsūn, ʿUmar. *Tārīkh Khalīj al-Iskandariyya al-Qadīm wa Turʿat al-Maḥmūdiyya.* Alexandria: Maṭbaʿat al-ʿAdl, 1942.

Tvedt, Terje. *The River Nile in the Age of the British: Political Ecology and the Quest for Economic Power.* London: I. B. Tauris, 2004.

Tvedt, Terje, and Eva Jakobsson, eds. *Water Control and River Biographies.* Vol. 1 of *A History of Water.* London: I. B. Tauris, 2006.

Tvedt, Terje, and Richard Coopey, eds. *The Political Economy of Water.* Vol. 2 of *A History of Water.* London: I. B. Tauris, 2006.
Tvedt, Terje, and Terje Oestigaard, eds. *The World of Water.* Vol. 3 of *A History of Water.* London: I. B. Tauris, 2006.
Twigg, Graham. *The Black Death: A Biological Reappraisal.* London: Batsford, 1984.
Udovitch, Abraham L. "An Eleventh Century Islamic Treatise on the Law of the Sea." *AI* 27 (1993): 37–54.
ʿUmrān, Jīhān. "Wathīqat Kashf ʿalā al-Sawāqī wa al-Majrā al-Sulṭānī (Dirāsa Wathāʾqiyya)." *AI* 40 (2006): 1–23.
ʿUmrān, Jīhān Aḥmad. "Dirāsa Diblūmātiyya li-Wathāʾiq Wafāʾ al-Nīl bi-Sijillāt al-Dīwān al-ʿĀlī maʿ Nashr Namādhij minhā." *Waqāʾiʿ Tārīkhiyya: Dauriyya ʿIlmiyya Muḥakkama* (2004): 347–81.
ʿUthmān, Nāṣir. "Maḥkamat Rashīd ka-Maṣdar li-Dirāsat Tijārat al-Nasīj fī Madīnat al-Iskandariyya fī al-ʿAṣr al-ʿUthmānī." *al-Rūznāma: al-Ḥauliyya al-Miṣriyya lil-Wathāʾiq* 3 (2005): 355–85.
Uzunçarşılı, İsmail Hakkı. *Osmanlı Devletinin Merkez ve Bahriye Teşkilâtı.* Ankara: Türk Tarih Kurumu Basımevi, 1948.
Venzke, Margaret L. "The Ottoman Tahrir Defterleri and Agricultural Productivity: The Case for Northern Syria." *OA* 17 (1997): 1–61.
———. "The Question of Declining Cereals' Production in the Sixteenth Century: A Sounding on the Problem-Solving Capacity of the Ottoman Cadastres." *JTS* 8 (1984): 251–64.
Venzke, M. L. "Rice Cultivation in the Plain of Antioch in the 16th Century: The Ottoman Fiscal Practice." *AO* 12 (1987–1992): 175–276.
Wade, Robert. *Village Republics: Economic Conditions for Collective Action in South India.* Cambridge: Cambridge University Press, 1988.
Wagstaff, J. M. *The Evolution of Middle Eastern Landscapes: An Outline to* A.D. *1840.* London: Croon Helm, 1985.
Walz, Terence. *Trade between Egypt and Bilād as-Sūdān, 1700–1820.* Cairo: Institut français d'archéologie orientale, 1978.
Ward, Cheryl. "The Sadana Island Shipwreck: An Eighteenth-Century A.D. Merchantman off the Red Sea Coast of Egypt." *World Archaeology* 32 (2001): 368–82.
———. "The Sadana Island Shipwreck: A Mideighteenth-Century Treasure Trove." In *A Historical Archaeology of the Ottoman Empire: Breaking New Ground,* edited by Uzi Baram and Lynda Carroll, 185–202. New York: Kluwer Academic/Plenum, 2000.
Ward, Cheryl, and Uzi Baram. "Global Markets, Local Practice: Ottoman-Period Clay Pipes and Smoking Paraphernalia from the Red Sea Shipwreck at Sadana Island, Egypt." *International Journal of Historical Archaeology* 10 (2006): 135–58.
Warner, Nicholas. "Taking the Plunge: The Development and Use of the Cairene Bathhouse." In *Historians in Cairo: Essays in Honor of George Scanlon,* edited by Jill Edwards, 49–79. Cairo: American University in Cairo Press, 2002.
———. *The True Description of Cairo: A Sixteenth-Century Venetian View.* 3 vols. Oxford: Arcadian Library, in association with Oxford University Press, 2006.
Waterbury, John. *Hydropolitics of the Nile Valley.* Syracuse, NY: Syracuse University Press, 1979.

Watson, Andrew M. *Agricultural Innovation in the Early Islamic World: The Diffusion of Crops and Farming Techniques, 700–1100.* Cambridge: Cambridge University Press, 1983.

Weber, Eugen. *Peasants into Frenchmen: The Modernization of Rural France, 1870–1914.* Stanford, CA: Stanford University Press, 1976.

White, Richard. "Environmental History: The Development of a New Historical Field." *PHR* 54 (1985): 297–335.

———. *The Organic Machine: The Remaking of the Columbia River.* New York: Hill and Wang, 1995.

White, Sam. "Ecology, Climate, and Crisis in the Ottoman Near East." Ph.D. diss., Columbia University, 2008.

Wigley, T. M. L., M. J. Ingram, and G. Farmer. *Climate and History: Studies in Past Climates and Their Impact on Man.* Cambridge: Cambridge University Press, 1981.

Willcocks, W., and J. I. Craig. *Egyptian Irrigation.* 2 vols. London: E. & F. N. Spon, 1913.

Winter, Michael. *Egyptian Society under Ottoman Rule, 1517–1798.* London: Routledge, 1992.

Wittfogel, Karl A. "The Hydraulic Civilizations." In *Man's Role in Changing the Face of the Earth,* edited by William L. Thomas Jr., 152–64. Chicago: University of Chicago Press, 1956.

———. *Oriental Despotism: A Comparative Study of Total Power.* New Haven, CT: Yale University Press, 1957.

Wizārat al-Ashghāl al-ʿĀmma wa al-Mawād al-Māʾiyya. *al-Nīl wa Tārīkh al-Riyy fī Miṣr.* Cairo: al-Lajna al-Ahliyya al-Miṣriyya lil-Riyy wa al-Ṣarf, n.d.

Worster, Donald. "History as Natural History: An Essay on Theory and Method." *PHR* 53 (1984): 1–19.

———. "Hydraulic Society in California: An Ecological Interpretation." *Agricultural History* 56 (1982): 503–15.

———. *Rivers of Empire: Water, Aridity, and the Growth of the American West.* Oxford: Oxford University Press, 1992.

———. "Transformations of the Earth: Toward an Agroecological Perspective in History." *Journal of American History* 76 (1990): 1087–1106.

———. "World without Borders: The Internationalizing of Environmental History." *Environmental Review* 6 (1982): 8–13.

Yūsuf, ʿAbd al-Wudūd. "Sijillāt al-Maḥākim al-Sharʿiyya ka-Maṣdar Asāsī li-Tārīkh al-ʿArab fī al-ʿAṣr al-ʿUthmānī." *EHR* 19 (1972): 325–35.

Zachariadou, Elizabeth, ed. *Natural Disasters in the Ottoman Empire.* Rethymnon: Crete University Press, 1999.

Ze'evi, Dror. *An Ottoman Century: The District of Jerusalem in the 1600s.* Albany: State University of New York Press, 1996.

Zinsser, Hans. *Rats, Lice and History, Being a Study in Biography, which, after Twelve Preliminary Chapters Indispensable for the Preparation of the Lay Reader, Deals with the Life History of Typhus Fever.* London: George Routledge and Sons, 1935.

INDEX

Other Books in the Series (continued from page iii)

Adam Rome *The Bulldozer in the Countryside: Suburban Sprawl and the Rise of American Environmentalism*
Nancy J. Jacobs *Environment, Power, and Injustice: A South African History*
Matthew D. Evenden *Fish versus Power: An Environmental History of the Fraser River*
Myrna I. Santiago *The Ecology of Oil: Environment, Labor, and the Mexican Revolution, 1900–1938*
Frank Uekoetter *The Green and the Brown: A History of Conservation in Nazi Germany*
James L. A. Webb, Jr. *Humanity's Burden: A Global History of Malaria*
Richard W. Judd *The Untilled Garden: Natural History and the Spirit of Conservation in America, 1740–1840*
Edmund Russell *Evolutionary History: Uniting History and Biology to Understand Life on Earth*
Alan Mikhail *Nature and Empire in Ottoman Egypt: An Environmental History*
Gregory T. Cushman *Guano and the Opening of the Pacific World: A Global Ecological History*
Emmanuel Kreike *Environmental Infrastructure in African History: Examining the Myth of Natural Resource Management in Namibia*

CPSIA information can be obtained at www.ICGtesting.com
Printed in the USA
LVOW12s2156251013

358547LV00003B/4/P

9 781107 640184